THE PAPERS OF
JOSEPH SMITH

VOLUME 2
JOURNAL, 1832–1842

THE PAPERS OF
JOSEPH SMITH

VOLUME 2
JOURNAL, 1832–1842

EDITED BY
DEAN C. JESSEE

Deseret Book Company
Salt Lake City, Utah

Library of Congress Cataloging-in-Publication Data

(Revised for vol. 2)

Smith, Joseph, 1805–1844.
 The papers of Joseph Smith.

 Includes bibliographical references.
 Contents: v. 1–2. Autobiographical and historical writings.
  1. Smith, Joseph, 1805–1844. 2. Mormon Church — History — Sources.   3. Church of Jesus Christ of Latter-day Saints — History — Sources.
 I. Jessee, Dean C. II. Title.
BX8695.S6A3 1989a   289.3'092 [B]   89-11720
ISBN 0-87579-199-9 (v. 1 : alk. paper)
ISBN 0-87579-545-5 (v. 2)

Printed in the United States of America

10   9   8   7   6   5   4   3   2   1

+

CONTENTS

ILLUSTRATIONS

ACKNOWLEDGMENTS

This edition of the Papers of Joseph Smith is made possible by the help and cooperation of many people. I give special acknowledgment to officials of The Church of Jesus Christ of Latter-day Saints, who made available sources from the Church archives where the bulk of the Joseph Smith Papers are housed. I am indebted to administrators at Brigham Young University for resources provided by that institution, including research grants that have helped facilitate this work. I am grateful to Ronald K. Esplin, director of the Joseph Fielding Smith Institute for Church History at the university, who was instrumental in getting the project started and has given freely of his talents and knowledge as the work has progressed.

Further, I particularly acknowledge Richard L. Jensen, Richard L. Anderson, and James L. Kimball, Jr., who provided invaluable insight and suggestions, and the publishing staff at Deseret Book Company, especially Jack M. Lyon, Patricia J. Parkinson, Kent Ware, and Emily Watts. Many others shared information and talent in helpful ways. These include Leonard J. Arrington, Maureen Ursenbach Beecher, Jill Mulvay Derr, William G. Hartley, Carol Cornwall Madsen, Marilyn Rish Parks, and Ronald W. Walker, colleagues in the Smith Institute at Brigham Young University; Glen Rowe, William Slaughter, Steven Sorenson, Richard E. Turley, Jr., and Ronald Watt at the LDS Church Historical Department in Salt Lake City; Glen Leonard, LDS Museum of Church History and Art; Noel Barton, LDS Family History Library; Chad Flake, Keith Perkins, and David J. Whittaker, Brigham Young University; Ronald A. Millett, Deseret Book Company; Richard P. Howard and Ronald E. Romig, Reorganized Church of Jesus Christ of Latter Day Saints, Library and Archives, Independence, Missouri; Steven R. Thomas, University of Utah; and Mary Alma Kay, Keokuk, Iowa. I am grateful for the research assistance and technical help of many students at Brigham Young University, including Mark Davies, Craig Livingston, Drew Smith, Byron Ellenberg, David Brizee, Kurt Rowley, Quinn Haddock, Michael Mitchell, Elizabeth White, and Carlos Domingues.

In addition to the LDS Church archives, other repositories have provided valuable material and assistance, including Brigham Young University Library, Provo, Utah; Chicago Historical Society; Hancock County Historical Society, Carthage, Illinois; Illinois State Historical Library, Springfield, Illinois; RLDS Library and Archives, Independence, Missouri; Lake County Genealogical Society, Painesville, Ohio; Library of Congress, Washington, D.C.; the LDS Church Family History Library, Salt Lake City, Utah; Missouri Historical Society, St. Louis, Missouri; and the Utah Historical Society, Salt Lake City.

This edition of the Joseph Smith Papers has also benefited from the guidelines and experience developed during the renaissance in editing historical and literary works in America since 1950.

In acknowledging my indebtedness to many people for their help, I nevertheless remain solely responsible for the content and for any errors that may appear in the pages that follow.

GUIDE TO EDITORIAL PROCEDURES

The editorial rules governing this edition of the Papers of Joseph Smith are derived from the proposition that his personality is a reflection of the totality of his being, including his handwritten prose. For this reason, in the present edition, emphasis is placed on the integrity of the original sources. To accomplish this, an effort has been made to reproduce the original text as accurately as typography will allow.

Very little of the visual element of writing — the formation of letters and words and their placement on the page — can be portrayed in print short of a photographic facsimile. But the literary content — the message conveyed by the writing, including the spelling, punctuation, crossed-out words, insertions, and so on — can be fairly accurately transcribed.

Hence, the following guidelines govern the presentation of the text:

A uniform format has been employed for paragraph indentation; the placement of the date, salutation, and signature of letters; and the date of journal entries.

All Joseph Smith holograph writing is in this typeface.

Handwriting other than Joseph Smith's follows a slash mark and note identifying the writer: /[15].

With the exception of journal entry dates, all spelling, punctuation, and capitalization have been retained as they appear in the original manuscripts. Where the original is unclear, current usage is given.

Insertions in the text are enclosed in angle brackets at the place of insertion: ⟨heavy⟩.

Material that was crossed out is retained as in the original: ~~stone~~.

Missing or unreadable letters or words are indicated by dots and dashes within brackets, with dots [..] representing the approximate number of missing letters, and dashes [– –]the approximate number of missing words.

Editorial insertions that enlarge the text or supply missing or unintelligible words are enclosed in brackets: H[eber].

Editorial comments not part of the text are enclosed in brackets and italicized: [*page torn*].

Underlined words appear in italics: *several*.

Shorthand has been deciphered where possible and enclosed in braces: {married}.

Bracketed page numbers designate the end of each page of the original text: [p. 1].

Superscript letters are lowered: J^r to Jr.

People mentioned in the text are identified in the Biographical Register rather than in the footnotes.

JOSEPH SMITH CHRONOLOGY

1805	Dec 23	Born at Sharon, Windsor County, Vermont.
1811		Family moved to Lebanon, New Hampshire.
1813		Contracted typhus fever; leg operation.
1816		Family moved to Palmyra, New York.
1820	Spring	First Vision.
1823	Sep 21	First Moroni visitation.
	Nov 19	Death of brother Alvin.
1826	Mar	Tried and acquitted on charges of being disorderly.
1827	Jan 18	Married Emma Hale at Bainbridge, New York.
	Sep 22	Obtained Book of Mormon plates.
	Dec	Moved to Harmony, Pennsylvania.
1828		116 pages of Book of Mormon manuscript lost.
	Jun 15	Son born; died same day.
1829	May–Jun	Priesthood received.
		Moved to Fayette, New York.
	Jun	Finished Book of Mormon translation.
1830	Mar	Book of Mormon published.
	Apr 6	Church organized.
	Jun	Visions of Moses revealed.
		Commenced bible revision.
	Dec	Writings of Moses revealed.
1831	Jan	Moved to Kirtland, Ohio.
	Apr 30	Twins born; lived only three hours.
	May 9	Adopted Murdock twins (Joseph and Julia).
	Jun 19	Started for Jackson County, Missouri.
	Jul	Revelation designating site for city of Zion (D&C 57).
	Sep 12	Moved to Hiram, Ohio.
	Dec	Preached in area of Kirtland-Ravenna, Ohio, to counteract effects of anti-Mormon *Ohio Star* articles.

1832	Jan 25	Sustained president of High Priesthood at Amherst, Ohio, conference.
	Feb 16	Revelation of postmortal state of mankind (D&C 76).
	Mar 24	Tarred and feathered by mob at Hiram, Ohio.
	Mar 29	Adopted son, Joseph M., died.
	Apr	Traveled to Jackson County, Missouri.
	Jun	Arrived in Kirtland after delay at Greenville, Indiana.
	Oct	Traveled to Albany, New York City, and Boston, with Newel K. Whitney.
	Nov 6	Returned to Kirtland. Son, Joseph III, born.
	Dec 25	Revelation on war (D&C 87).
1833	Jan	Organized School of the Prophets.
	Feb 27	Revelation known as the Word of Wisdom (D&C 89).
	Mar 18	First Presidency organized.
	Jul 23	Cornerstone for Kirtland Temple laid.
	Oct 5	Left Kirtland on proselyting mission to Canada.
	Nov 4	Returned to Kirtland.
	Nov 22	News of expulsion of Saints from Jackson County, Missouri.
1834	Feb 17	High council organized at Kirtland.
	Feb 26	Left Kirtland to recruit volunteers for Zion's Camp.
	Mar 28	Returned to Kirtland.
	Apr 1–3	Attended court at Chardon in Hurlbut case.
	Apr 12	Fishing on Lake Erie.
	Apr 22	Conference at Norton, Ohio.
	May 5	Left Kirtland for Missouri at head of Zion's Camp.
	Jun 19	Arrived in Clay County, Missouri.
	Aug 1	Returned to Kirtland, Ohio.
	Oct	Visited Saints in Michigan.
	Nov	Organized School for the Elders at Kirtland.
1835	Feb 14	Organization of Quorum of Twelve.
	Feb 28	Organization of Quorum of Seventy.
	Mar 28	Revelation on priesthood (D&C 107).
	Jul	Egyptian mummies and papyrus purchased.
	Oct 8–11	Attended father during his illness.
1836	Mar 27	Dedicated Kirtland Temple. Studying Hebrew.
	Apr 3	Vision of Savior in Kirtland Temple.

	May 17	Met grandmother, Mary Duty, at Fairport and accompanied her to Kirtland.
	Jun 20	Son Frederick born.
	Jul 25	Left Kirtland for the East.
	Jul 30	Visited part of New York City burned in 1835 fire.
	Sep	Returned to Kirtland.
	Nov 2	Kirtland Safety Society Bank organized.
1837	Apr 6	Solemn assembly in Kirtland Temple.
	May	Denounced by dissenters at Kirtland.
	May 30	Acquitted in Grandison Newell case.
	Jun	Seriously ill; sent first missionaries to British Isles.
	Jul 23	Revelation to the Twelve (D&C 112).
	Aug	Visited saints in Canada.
	Sep 3	Conference in Kirtland; three of Twelve rejected.
	Sep 27	Left Kirtland for Missouri.
	Nov 7	Conference at Far West, Missouri.
	Dec	Returned to Kirtland, dissension in Church.
1838	Jan 12	Left Kirtland to escape mob violence.
	Mar 14	Arrived with family at Far West, Caldwell County, Missouri.
	Apr 30	Writing history.
	May 14	Plowed garden.
	May 19	Selected site for new settlement, Adam-ondi-Ahman.
	Jun 2	Son Alexander born.
	Aug 6	Election-day fight at Gallatin, Missouri.
	Oct	Led harrassed saints from DeWitt, Carroll County, Missouri to Far West, Caldwell County.
	Oct 27	Extermination order issued by Governor Boggs.
	Oct 30	Haun's Mill massacre.
	Oct 31	Surrendered to Missouri militia at Far West; imprisoned.
	Nov 1	Sentenced to death; opposition by General Doniphan prevented execution.
	Nov 4	Arrived under guard at Independence, Jackson County, Missouri.
	Nov	Court of inquiry at Richmond, Ray County.
	Dec 1	Imprisoned at Liberty, Clay County.
1839	Apr 6	Taken from Liberty jail to Gallatin, Daviess County, for trial.

	Apr 11	Indicted; granted change of venue to Boone County.
	Apr 15	En route to Boone County, allowed by guards to escape.
	Apr 22	Reunited with family at Quincy, Illinois.
	May 10	Moved to Commerce (later renamed Nauvoo), Hancock County, Illinois.
	Jun	Involved in resettlement of Saints at Nauvoo.
	Jul 21–22	Administered to sick.
	Oct 29	Left Nauvoo to present Mormon grievances to federal government.
	Nov 29	Visited President Martin Van Buren.
	Dec	Visited Saints in Philadelphia and New Jersey.
1840	Feb	Left Washington, D.C., for home.
	Mar 4	Arrived at Nauvoo.
	Sep 14	Death of father, Joseph Smith, Sr.
1841	Jan 30	Elected Trustee-in-trust.
	Feb 1	Elected to Nauvoo city council.
	Feb 4	Elected lieutenant general of Nauvoo Legion.
	Apr 5	Sealed to Louisa Beaman.
	Apr 6	Laid cornerstone for Nauvoo Temple.
	May 2	Entertained Stephen A. Douglas.
	Jun 4	Arrested on old Missouri charges.
	Jun 9–10	Trial before Judge Douglas at Monmouth, Illinois; acquitted.
	Jul 3	Patriotic address to Nauvoo Legion.
	Aug 7	Brother, Don Carlos, died at age twenty-six.
	Aug 12	Spoke to visiting Sac and Fox Indians at Nauvoo.
	Sep 14	Attended military parade at Montrose, Iowa.
	Nov 8	Dedicated baptismal font in Nauvoo temple.
1842	Jan 5	Commenced selling goods at his new store in Nauvoo.
	Jan 15	Correcting proof for new edition of Book of Mormon.
	Feb 7	Infant son born and died.
	Mar 1	Commenced publication of Book of Abraham.
	Mar 15	Officiated at installation of Nauvoo Masonic Lodge; received first degree of Masonry.
	Mar 15	Became editor of *Times and Seasons*.
	Mar 17	Organized Female Relief Society.
	Mar 27	Engaged in baptisms for dead in Mississippi River.
	Apr	Forced to apply for bankruptcy.

	May 4	Introduced temple endowment.
	May 7	Life endangered during review of Nauvoo Legion.
	May 14	Working in garden after city council meeting.
	May 19	Elected mayor of Nauvoo.
	Aug 8	Arrested for alleged complicity in Boggs assassination attempt; forced into hiding.
	Sep 16	Sitting for portrait.
	Dec 13	Chopped and hauled wood.
	Dec 26	Second arrest in Boggs case.
1843	Jan 5	Acquitted in Boggs case by Judge Nathaniel Pope.
	Jan 18	Fifteenth wedding anniversary; enjoyed day with invited guests at dinner.
	Feb 3	Studied German; read proof on Doctrine and Covenants.
	Feb 8	Went sliding on ice with son Frederick.
	Feb–Mar	Attended mother during her illness.
	Mar 4	Sealed to Emily Partridge.
	Mar 13	Wrestled William Wall; blessed twenty-seven children in evening.
	Apr 23	Took his children on pleasure ride in carriage.
	May 1	Sealed to Lucy Walker.
	May 16	Traveled to Ramus, Hancock County, Illinois.
	May 28	Sealed to Emma for time and eternity.
	Jun 3	Pleasure trip to Quincy, Illinois with family and friends on Mississippi River.
	Jun 13	Left Nauvoo to visit relatives at Dixon, Illinois.
	Jun 23	Arrested at Dixon by officers disguised as missionaries.
	Jun 30	Arrived at Nauvoo.
	Jul 1	Discharged by Nauvoo court.
	Jul 12	Revelation on marriage recorded (D&C 132).
	Aug 31	Moving into new residence, Nauvoo Mansion.
	Sep 4	Attended circus with family.
	Sep 16	Reviewed Nauvoo Legion.
	Sep 28	Introduced fulness of priesthood ordinances.
	Dec 25	Entertained fifty couples on Christmas Day.
1844	Feb 20	Instructed Twelve to select a location for Saints in California or Oregon.
	Mar 11	Organized Council of Fifty.
	Mar 18	Studying German.
		"Last Charge" to the Twelve.
	Apr 3	Presided at municipal court hearing.

Apr 5	Attended dedication of Nauvoo Masonic hall.
Apr 5–7	Delivered King Follett funeral discourse.
Apr 26	Life threatened by Nauvoo dissenters.
May 10	Prospectus of Nauvoo *Expositor* distributed by dissenters.
May 17	Nominated as U.S. presidential candidate at Nauvoo convention.
Jun 7	Nauvoo *Expositor* published.
Jun 10	Ordered destruction of Nauvoo *Expositor* press.
Jun 12	Arrested on charge of riot for destroying press.
Jun 18	Placed Nauvoo under martial law.
Jun 25	Surrendered at Carthage, Hancock County.
Jun 27	Shot to death by mob at Carthage jail.

JOSEPH SMITH'S FAMILY

Grandparents of Joseph Smith	Parents, Aunts, Uncles of Joseph Smith	Joseph Smith and His Brothers and Sisters (Spouses Listed in Italics)	Children of Joseph Smith

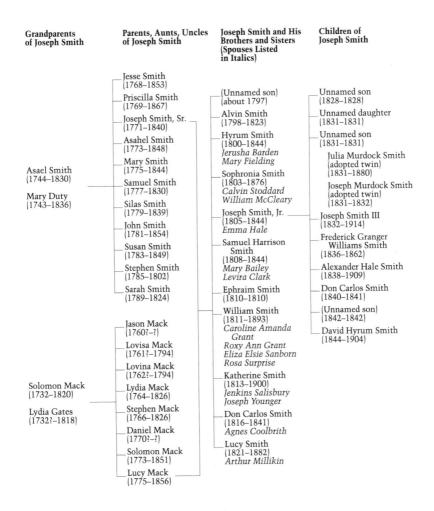

Grandparents of Joseph Smith

Asael Smith (1744–1830)

Mary Duty (1743–1836)

Solomon Mack (1732–1820)

Lydia Gates (1732?–1818)

Parents, Aunts, Uncles of Joseph Smith

Jesse Smith (1768–1853)

Priscilla Smith (1769–1867)

Joseph Smith, Sr. (1771–1840)

Asahel Smith (1773–1848)

Mary Smith (1775–1844)

Samuel Smith (1777–1830)

Silas Smith (1779–1839)

John Smith (1781–1854)

Susan Smith (1783–1849)

Stephen Smith (1785–1802)

Sarah Smith (1789–1824)

Jason Mack (1760?–?)

Lovisa Mack (1761?–1794)

Lovina Mack (1762?–1794)

Lydia Mack (1764–1826)

Stephen Mack (1766–1826)

Daniel Mack (1770?–?)

Solomon Mack (1773–1851)

Lucy Mack (1775–1856)

Joseph Smith and His Brothers and Sisters (Spouses Listed in Italics)

(Unnamed son) (about 1797)

Alvin Smith (1798–1823)

Hyrum Smith (1800–1844)
Jerusha Barden
Mary Fielding

Sophronia Smith (1803–1876)
Calvin Stoddard
William McCleary

Joseph Smith, Jr. (1805–1844)
Emma Hale

Samuel Harrison Smith (1808–1844)
Mary Bailey
Levira Clark

Ephraim Smith (1810–1810)

William Smith (1811–1893)
Caroline Amanda Grant
Roxy Ann Grant
Eliza Elsie Sanborn
Rosa Surprise

Katherine Smith (1813–1900)
Jenkins Salisbury
Joseph Younger

Don Carlos Smith (1816–1841)
Agnes Coolbrith

Lucy Smith (1821–1882)
Arthur Millikin

Children of Joseph Smith

Unnamed son (1828–1828)

Unnamed daughter (1831–1831)

Unnamed son (1831–1831)

Julia Murdock Smith (adopted twin) (1831–1880)

Joseph Murdock Smith (adopted twin) (1831–1832)

Joseph Smith III (1832–1914)

Frederick Granger Williams Smith (1836–1862)

Alexander Hale Smith (1838–1909)

Don Carlos Smith (1840–1841)

(Unnamed son) (1842–1842)

David Hyrum Smith (1844–1904)

INTRODUCTION TO
JOSEPH SMITH'S
JOURNAL

On 27 November 1832, in the twenty-sixth year of his life, Joseph Smith took pen in hand to begin writing a diary. His intention was "to keep a minute account of all things that come under my observation." He began his record with a supplication: "Oh may God grant that I may be directed in all my thoughts. Oh bless thy servent Amen." Less than twelve years later, on 27 June 1844, the Prophet's secretary, Willard Richards, who at that time was keeping his journal for him, hastily scribbled in broken phrases the rush of events that culminated in the murder of the Church leader and his brother Hyrum in the jail at Carthage, Illinois. The Prophet's journal, written exclusively during the years of his public ministry, when he finished laying the foundation of The Church of Jesus Christ of Latter-day Saints, is at the core of the sources that pertain to his life.

Once Joseph Smith's record-keeping consciousness had been awakened in the early 1830s, few subjects brought him more concern than that of preserving a record of his life. He rejoiced in 1844 that for the three previous years he had been able to produce an unbroken account of his acts and proceedings: "I have kept several good, faithful, and efficient clerks in constant employ: they have accompanied me everywhere . . . and they have written down what I have done, where

I have been, and what I have said."[1] Considering his lack of literary training, the heavy administrative burdens that demanded his time, and continual harrassment from those who opposed him and his work, it is remarkable that he kept a journal at all. Although his journal is the main chronological source for the study of his life, there are limitations in the record that restrict the clarity and completeness of the story it would preserve.

The Joseph Smith journal is a significant record for the years it covers, but it was started late in relation to his early religious experiences, leaving pivotal events of his life—his prophetic call, his early visions, the translation of the Book of Mormon, and the organization of the Church—to be dealt with only by occasional reminiscence. In addition, lengthy gaps in the journal prevent an unbroken chronicle of the time period it encompasses. These blanks in the record, plus the lack of contemporary sources to adequately fill them, make it difficult to reconstruct an unbroken narrative of Joseph Smith's life and labors.

A situation that tends to distort the view of the Prophet reflected in the pages of his journal stems from his dependence upon others to write for him. He stated his philosophy of journal-keeping when he observed that greatness requires that a man "must not dwell upon small things, though he may enjoy them," which he explained to mean that a prophet cannot be his own scribe.[2] This ideology transformed his journal from a record of personal observation and introspection to one filtered through the minds of other men. Of the 1,587 manuscript pages comprising the Smith journal, 31 contain holograph writing, where he is known to have put his own

---

1. *History of the Church of Jesus Christ of Latter-day Saints, Period I. History of Joseph Smith, the Prophet, by Himself,* edited by Brigham H. Roberts, 7 vols. (Salt Lake City: Deseret Press, 1964), 4:66, 409.

2. See Joseph Smith Journal, 4 March 1843, MS., LDS Church Archives.

thoughts on the paper. Another 250 were evidently dictated to scribes. The remaining pages were primarily the work of four men: William Clayton, James Mulholland, Willard Richards, and George W. Robinson. Robinson and Mulholland wrote all of the Prophet's journal for 1838. Richards wrote the remaining Smith journal, except for the small segment produced by Mulholland in 1839, and about six months of 1842 when William Clayton and two other scribes took his place. Hence, although the journal provides a valuable record of Joseph Smith's life, it is uneven in its reflection of his personality. The holograph and dictated entries preserve immediacy, color, and a range of emotions. The pages written by observers generally portray the Prophet as more formal, colorless, and insensitive than he was in reality.

The part of the journal written by clerks shows a detachment from the Prophet in another way, in that the writers were able to record only what they saw, and they were not always in a position to give a complete account of his day-to-day activities. There is the problem of reporting his domestic and private affairs when the main contact his clerks had with him was in his office or place of business.

Although he was a devoted husband, father, and friend, there is very little in the Prophet's journal that illuminates his domestic life. And yet what John Bernhisel saw in the Smith home while boarding there over an extended period of time persuaded him that it was in "the gentle charities of domestic life, as the tender and affectionate husband and parent, the warm and sympathising friend, that the prominent traits" of Joseph Smith's character were revealed.[1] And Orson Pratt, who also became well-acquainted with the Prophet while living for a time in his home, witnessed "his earnest and humble devotions both morning and evening in his family. I heard the

---

1. John Bernhisel to Thomas Ford, 14 June 1844, MS., Bernhisel Collection, LDS Church Archives.

words of eternal life flowing from his mouth, nourishing, sooth-
ing, and comforting his family, neighbours, and friends." And
although Orson attributed his conviction of the Prophet's calling to a divine source, he wrote, "I could form some kind of
an opinion about Joseph Smith as a natural man . . . from his
conversation, from his acts, from his dealings."[1]

While the clerks who kept a substantial part of the Prophet's journal for him did their best to preserve a full and accurate
report of what he did and said, human limitations, such as
the lack of shorthand skills, or failure to follow through to flesh
out hastily written and disconnected notes, tend to further
limit the reader's perceptions of him.[2]

To those already familiar with the documentary *History
of the Church*, the publication of Joseph Smith's journal does
not present a great amount of new information about his life
and times. This is because the journal was used as the basis
for much of the text of the *History* — a work that was published
serially in Church periodicals and newspapers in the nineteenth century, and, since the beginning of the twentieth century, has been available as a six-volume work. The significance
of the present edition lies in presenting the complete text of
the original journal as accurately as human limitations will
allow. The reader will also gain a clearer view of Joseph Smith
by being able to distinguish his personality from those who
wrote for him.

As one studies the Joseph Smith journal, there is a sense
of loss at not finding more that was produced directly by his
own mind. And yet, the 1,500 manuscript pages that were
written as the result of his effort to preserve a record give

---

1. Orson Pratt speech of 10 July 1859, *Journal of Discourses*, 26 vols. (Liverpool, England: Printed and published by Albert Carrington [and others]), 7:176–
77.

2. See Dean Jessee, "Return to Carthage: Writing the History of Joseph
Smith's Martyrdom," *Journal of Mormon History* 8 (1981):3–19.

penetrating insight into the life of one of the important religious figures of nineteenth-century America.

Volume 2 of *The Papers of Joseph Smith* contains the Prophet's journal during the years 1832–1842; volume 3, from 1843 to the end of his life in June 1844.

OHIO JOURNAL,
1832–1834

MS. Joseph Smith Papers, LDS Church Archives, Salt Lake City, Utah.

Editorial Note

Joseph Smith's first journal records events in his life between 27 November 1832 and 5 December 1834. Kirtland, Geauga County, Ohio, had become the gathering place for the Latter-day Saints after the Prophet arrived there from New York about 1 February 1831. Beside activities in Kirtland, the journal records two brief trips. The first was a proselyting mission to Canada with Sidney Rigdon in October 1833 — probably the only time a Latter-day Saint prophet was engaged in proselyting work after his appointment as church president. The two men traveled to the area of Brantford, Ontario, Canada. The second departure from Kirtland occurred in March 1834, when the Prophet went to New York to solicit volunteers for Zion's Camp. There are two long gaps in the journal, from 6 December 1832 to 4 October 1833, and 30 April 1834 to 21 August 1834. During the latter, Joseph was involved in the march of Zion's Camp to Missouri.

Although small, this first journal merits attention because it contains more of Joseph Smith's own handwriting than any of his other journals. It reveals personal feelings and a sensitivity not reflected in the journals recorded for him by his scribes.

This journal consists of 93 pages written in brown ink, measuring 5 7/8 × 3 3/4 inches. The front and back covers are stiff cardboard with marble-design paper pasted over them. A strip of black paper is wrapped around the spine. "Joseph Smith, 1832.34" is written in ink by Joseph Smith on the front cover; the back cover is blank. The book contains fifty-three leaves numbered to 105 pages. The paper has faint vertical lines as if intended for a ledger. The first page of the book is blank. Sideways near the outer edge, Joseph wrote his name on the second page. The text of the diary continues from page 3 to 93. Pages 94 to 105 are blank except for Joseph Smith's name in pencil at the top of page 98 and some miscellaneous notes on pages 103–5. The writing is in various shades of brown ink. The last page is pasted to the back cover along its front edge to hold two leather tabs in place.

~~Joseph Smith Jr—Record Book Baught for to note all the minute circumstances that comes under my observation~~

Joseph Smith Jrs Book for Record Baught on the 27th of November 1832 for the purpose to keep a minute acount of all things that come under my obse[r]vation &c—

Oh may God grant that I may be directed in all my thoughts Oh bless thy Servent Amen [p. 1]

28 November 1832 · Wednesday

this day I have [spent] in reading and writing this Evening my mind is calm and serene for which I thank the Lord—

29 November 1832 · Thursday

this day road from Kirtland¹ to Chardon² to see my Sister Sop[h]ronia and also ca[lled] to see my Sister Catherine³ [and fou]nd them [well]

---

1. First settled twenty years previous, Kirtland, Geauga County, became the Latter-day Saint gathering place in Ohio in 1831. When Joseph Smith arrived there from New York on 1 February 1831 the population of the town was about a thousand people. The Mormon experience in Ohio is treated in Allen and Leonard, *Story of the Latter-day Saints* (Salt Lake City: Deseret Book Company, 1976), 53–101; Backman, *The Heavens Resound: A History of the Latter-day Saints in Ohio, 1830–1838* (Salt Lake City: Deseret Book Company, 1983); and Parkin, "Conflict at Kirtland: A Study of the Nature and Causes of External and Internal Conflict of the Mormons in Ohio Between 1830 and 1838" (Salt Lake City: Max H. Parkin, 1966).

2. Chardon, first settled in 1812, was the county seat of Geauga County, Ohio.

3. Joseph Smith's sister consistently spelled her name, "Katherine." See, for example, "Testimony of Katherine Salisbury," *The True Latter Day Saints' Herald* 28 (1 June 1881):169.

Joseph Smith, Ohio Journal, 1832–1834, p. 1. LDS Church Archives.

this Evening Brother Frederic [G. Williams] Prophecyed that next spring I should go to the city of PittsBurg to establish a Bishopwrick and within one year I should go to the City of New York the Lord spare the life of thy servent Amen [p. 2]

30 November 1832 · Friday[1]

this day retu[r]ned home to Kirtland found all well to the Joy and satisfaction of my soul on my return home stopped at Mr Kings[2] bore testmony to him and Family &c-

1 December 1832 · Saturday[3]

⟨bore testimony to Mr Gilmore⟩[4] wrote and corrected revelations &c –

2 December 1832 · Sunday[5]

the sabath went ~~to went~~ to meeting &c

3 December 1832 · Monday

ordaind Brother Packherd [Noah Packard] with my own hand also Brother umfiry [Solomon Humphrey] came to see me from the East & braught news from Brother Lyman Johnson and Orson Pratt &c. also held a conference in the Evening Br Jese [Jesse Gause?] and Mogan [Morgan?] and William Mclelen [McLellin] was excommunicated from the church &c – [p. 3]

---

1. Date inadvertently written "1830" in MS.
2. A David King owned property in Chester township bordering Kirtland on the south.
3. MS. reads "December 1th."
4. No Gilmores are listed in the Kirtland census or tax lists. However, three Gilmores (Samuel, James, and Ashbel) owned property in Chester township bordering Kirtland on the south.
5. MS. reads "December 2th."

4 December 1832 · Tuesday

this day I been unwell done but litle been at home all day regulated some things this Evening feel better in my mind then I have for a few days back Oh Lord deliver ~~out~~ thy servent out of temtations and fill his heart with wisdom and understanding

5 December 1832 · Wednesday

this day ~~wrote leters~~ copying letters and translating and in evening held a council to advise with Brother Solomon Humphry it was ordered by the council that he should be a companion with Brother Noah packard in the work of the ministry — [1]

6 December 1832 · Thursday

translating and received a revelation explaining the Parable [of] the wheat and the tears[2] &c — [p. 4]

4 October 1833 · Friday

makeing preperation to go East with Freeman Nickerson[3] A request of Brother David Elliott to call on his Brother in Law Peter Warrin St. kathrine upper Cannada —

Coburg[4] Richard Lyman request of Uncle John [Smith] —

---

1. A council of high priests had met at the request of Solomon Humphrey to learn "the will of the Lord respecting him." The council advised Humphrey to "devote himself entirely." to the work of the ministry, commencing at Parkman, Ohio with Noah Packard. (Kirtland Council Minutes, 5 December 1832.)
2. D&C 86.
3. The Nickersons lived at South Dayton in the township of Perrysburg, Cattaraugus County, New York. Freeman Nickerson had been converted to the Church earlier in the year, had traveled to Kirtland, Ohio, and prevailed upon Joseph Smith and Sidney Rigdon to accompany him to Mt. Pleasant, Ontario, Canada to introduce the gospel to members of his family. (*Lydia Knight's History* [Salt Lake City: Juvenile Instructor Office, 1883], 16ff; information supplied by Wayne A. Mori, Dunkirk, New York.)
4. Possible reference to Colborne, Ontario, Canada.

5 October 1833 · Saturday

this day started and Journy[ed] to the East came to Ashtibuly [Ashtabula, Ohio] ⟨stayed⟩ [at] Lambs tavern

6 October 1833 · Sunday

arrived at Springfield [Erie County, Pennsylvania] ⟨on the Sabbath⟩ found the Brotheren in meeting Brother Sidney [Rigdon] spoke to the people &c — and in the [p. 5] ⟨Evening⟩ held a meeting at Brother Ruds [John Rudd] had a great congregation paid good attention Oh God Seal our te[s]timony — to their hearts Amen — /[1] Continued at springfield untill tuesday the 8th [October 1833] Journeyed that day to br. Roundays [Shadrach Roundy] at Elk creek [Erie County, Pennsylvania] taried there over night came the next day to a tavern the next day thursday the 10th [October 1833] we ar[i]ved at Br Job Lewises[2] at Westfield the breatheren by a previous appointment met there for meeting we spoke to them as the spirite gave [p. 6] utterence they were greatly gratifyed they appeared to be strong in the faith left there friday the 11 [October 1833] and came to the house of an infidel by the Name of Nash[3] reasond with him but to no effect came Saturday the 12th [October 1833 to] the house of[4] father Nicke[r]son[5] **I feel very well in my mind the Lord is with us but have much anxiety about my family &c; —**[6]

---

1. Handwriting of Sidney Rigdon.
2. The 1830 Federal Census lists Job Lewis (in his fifties), his wife, and nine others in his family at Westfield, Chautauqua, New York.
3. Census records identify Burl and Cotton Nash living in Portland, Chautauqua County, New York, a few miles east of Westfield.
4. "of" repeated in MS.
5. At Perrysburg, Cattaraugus County, New York.
6. Joseph Smith's concern for his family was the subject of a revelation this day at Perrysburg, New York. (See D&C 100.)

At this point in the diary, a later hand (possibly that of Willard Richards) wrote, "See forward 20 pages 12 baptized," erroneously keying this entry to the list of those baptized at Mount Pleasant, Canada, on 27 and 28 October. See note 3, p. 13 below.

13 October 1833 · Sunday

held a meeting at freeman Nickerson['s] had a large congregation Brother Sidney preached & I bear record to the people the Lord gave his spirit in [a] [p. 7] marvilous maner for which I am thankful to the God of Ab[r]aham Lord bless my family and preserve them

14 October 1833 · Monday

at the same place this day expect to start for Canada Lord be with us on our Journy Amen &c — /[1] Monday evening arived at Lodi [Cattaraugus County, New York] had an appointment preached to a small congregation made an appointment for tuesday at 10 oclock the 15th the meeting was appointed to be held in the Presbetarian meeting house [p. 8] but when the hour arived the man who kept the key of the house refused to open the door the meeting was thus prevented we came immedeately away and left the people in great confusion journeyed till ~~satturday~~ friday [18 October 1833][2] Arived at Freeman Nickerson's in upper Canada having after we came into Canada passed through a very fine Country and well cultivated and had many peculiar feelings in relation to both the country and people we were kindly received at freeman Nickersons [p. 9]

20 October 1833 · Sunday

held meeting at brantford[3] on Sunday at 10 o clock to a very attentive congregation at candle lighting the same evening

---

1. Handwriting of Sidney Rigdon.
2. In the MS. the entries of 18, 20, and 21 October were inadvertently written one day earlier than the actual calendar date.
3. Brantford, with an 1846 population of 2,000, was the predominant settlement in the Brantford Township, Gore District, Upper Canada. (Wm. H. Smith, *Smith's Canadian Gazetteer*, [Toronto, 1846] 18-19.)

held meeting at mount plesent[1] where freeman Nickerson lived to a very large congregation which gave good heed to the things which were spoken[2] what may be the result we cannot tell but the p[r]ospect is flattering this morning Monday the 21 [October 1833] enjoy pretty good [p. 10] health with good prospects of doing good calculate to stay in Canada till the Monday of next week then the Lord willing will start for home. left Mount plesent tuesday [22 October 1833] and arived at the village of Coulburn[3] held meeting at candle lighting the evening was very bad snowing vehemently we were publickly opposed by a Wesleyen Methodist he was very tumultious but destitute of reason or knowledge he would not [p. 11] give us an oppertunity to reply this was on the 22nd [October 1833] we find that conviction is resting on the minds of some we hope that great good may yet be done in Canada which O Lord grant for thy names sake during our stay at mount plesent we [had] an interview with a Mr Wilkeson of the methodist order being a leader in that sect he could not stand against our words whether he will receive the[4] truth the Lord only knows he seemed to [be] honest [p. 12] Written at Coulburn wednesday morning the 23 [October 1833] at the house of a Mr Bemer [Philip Beemer] left Mr Bemers on thursday 24 [October 1833]

---

1. Mt. Pleasant is a small village in the south of Brantford Township, five miles from the town of Brantford on the Simcoe Road. Mt. Pleasant had a population of about 130 in the 1840s. (Wm. H. Smith, *Smith's Canadian Gazetteer*, 119.)

2. Lydia Knight's recollection of this meeting is in *Lydia Knight's History*, 16–18. She recalled that "the Prophet commenced by relating the scenes of his early life. He told how the angel visited him, of his finding the plates, the translation of them, and gave a short account of the matter contained in the Book of Mormon." She added that he "bore a faithful testimony that the Priesthood was again restored to the earth, and that God and His Son had conferred upon him the keys of the Aaronic and Melchisedek Priesthoods."

3. Colborne is a small village in Norfolk District, Upper Canada, one mile from Simcoe. Colborne had an 1881 population of 80. (P. A. Crossby, ed., *Lovell's Gazetteer of British North America* [Montreal, 1881], 214.)

4. "the" repeated in MS.

came to watterford[1] held meeting at 1 o clock ~~to~~ spoke to a small congregation being a very wet day after meeting returned to mount plesent and held meeting ~~at~~ at candle lighting to a large congregation one man [Eleazer] Freeman Nickerson declared his full belief in the truth of the work is with his wife who is also convinced to be baptised on sunday great excitement [p. 13] prevailes in every place where we have been the result we leave in the hand of God. written at the house of Freeman Nickerson in mount plesent on friday morning the **[25th October 1833][2] this afternoon at Mr Pattricks[3] expect to hold a Meeting this Evening &c — people very superstitious Oh God esta[b]lish thy word among this people held a meeting this evening had an attentive conngregation the spirit gave utterance [p. 14]**

26 October 1833 · Saturday

held a meeting at Mount Plasant the people very tender

/[4] *27 October 1833 · Sunday*

held a meeting in Mount plesent to a large congregation twelve came forward and was baptized and many more were deeply impressed appointed a meeting for this day

28 October 1833 · Monday

at the request of some who desires to be baptized at candle lighting held a meeting for confirmation we broke bread laid

---

1. Waterford, Ontario, seven miles from Simcoe and eighteen from Brantford, is located in a valley surrounded by high hills and intersected by the Nanticoke creek. In 1846 the village had about 150 inhabitants, one Baptist church, a gristmill, a sawmill, and three stores. (Wm. H. Smith, *Smith's Canadian Gazetteer*, 205.)

2. In the MS. October 24 was inadvertently repeated. The error was not corrected until the 29th.

3. Possibly Jacob Patrick in Burford Township.

4. Handwriting of Sidney Rigdon.

on hands for the gift of the holy spirit had a good [p. 15] meeting the spirit was given in great ~~to~~ power to some and the rest had great ~~pease~~ peace may God carry on his work in this place till all shall know him Amen. Held meeting yesterday at 10 o clock after meeting two came forward and were baptized confirmed them at the watters edge held meeting last evening ordained br E[leazer]. F[reeman]. Nickerson to the office of Elder had a good meeting one of the sisters got the [p. 16] gift of toungues which made the saints rejoice may God increse the gifts among them for his sons sake this morning we bend our course for home may the Lord prosper our journey Amen

29 October 1833 · Tuesday

left Mountpleasant for home

30 October 1833 · Wednesday

continued on our Journy Wensday and on

31 October 1833 · Thursday

arrived at Buffalo

~~Friday 32th Started from Buffalo~~ **[p. 17]**

/¹ 1 November 1833 · Friday ⟨*Nove*⟩

Left Buffalo, N. Y. at 8 o'clock A.M. and arrived at home Monday, the 4th [November 1833] at 10, A.M. found my family all well according to the promise of the Lord, for which blessing I feel to thank his holy name; Amen.

13 November 1833 · Wednesday

nothing of note transpired from the 4th of Nove[m]ber u[n]til this day in the morning at 4 Oh clock I was awoke

---

1. Handwriting of Oliver Cowdery.

by Brother Davis[1] knocking at ⟨my⟩ door saying Brother Joseph [p. 18] come git ⟨up⟩ and see the signs in the heavens and I arrose and beheld to my great Joy the stars fall from heaven[2] yea they fell like hail stones a litteral fullfillment of the word of God as recorded in the holy scriptures[3] and a sure sign that the coming of Christ is clost at hand Oh how marvellous are thy works Oh Lord and I thank thee for thy me[r]cy u⟨n⟩to me thy servent Oh Lord save me in thy kingdom for Christ sake Amen [p. 19]

19 November 1833 · Tuesday

from the 13th u[n]till this date nothing of note has transpired since the great sign in the heavins this day my ⟨h[ea]rt⟩

---

1. Possibly Marvel C. Davis.

2. This phenomenon was widely observed. Exiled Latter-day Saints driven from Jackson County, Missouri, and encamped on the north bank of the Missouri River also reported the spectacular incident: "An unmeasurable shower of stars were dancing about in every direction, with the velocity of lightning," wrote one. Another noted, "I witnessed the beautiful scene of the falling of the stars and went from house to house waking up the people to have them see it." (See Max H. Parkin, "History of the Latter-day Saints in Clay County, Missouri, from 1833 to 1837" [Ph.D. diss., Brigham Young University, 1976], 44–47.)

Newspapers throughout the country reported the incident. It was described as "a constant succession of fire balls, resembling sky rockets, radiating in all directions from a point in the heavens near the zenith, and following the arch of the sky towards the horizon. They proceeded to various distances from the radiating point, leaving after them a vivid streak of light, and usually exploding before they disappeared. The balls were of various sizes, and degrees of splendour; some were mere points, but others were larger and brighter than Jupiter or Venus. . . . The flashes of light, though less intense than lightning, were so bright as to awaken people in their beds. One ball that shot in a northwest direction, and exploded near the star Capella, left, just behind the place of explosion, a phosphorescent train, of peculiar beauty." ("Atmospheric Phenomenon," *The Maryland Gazette* [Annapolis, Maryland], 21 November 1833.)

In the wake of a cholera epidemic that had killed millions, one observer saw the phenomenon as "the action of the Almighty . . . visibly restoring to our atmosphere some unknown principle of health which had been lost or injured." Another saw it as "a sure *forerunner* — a merciful SIGN of that great and dreadful Day which the inhabitants of the earth shall witness when the SIXTH SEAL SHALL BE OPENED." ("Meteoric Phenomenon," *The Oswego Palladium* [Oswego, New York], 27 November 1833.)

3. Revelation 6:13; D&C 29:14; 45:42.

is somewhat sorrowfull but feel to trust in the Lord the god of Jacob I have learned in my travels that man is treche[r]ous and selfish but few excepted Brother ⟨Sidney⟩ is a man whom I love but is not capa[b]le of that pure and stedfast love for those who are his benefactors as should ~~posess~~ p⟨o⟩sess the breast of ~~a man~~ ⟨a ~~Pred~~⟩ President of the Chu[r]ch of Christ [p. 20] this with some other little things such as a selfish and indipendance of mind which to often manifest distroys the confidence of those who would lay down their lives for him[1] but notwithstanding these things he is ⟨a⟩ very great and good man a man of great power of words and can ⟨gain⟩ the friendship of his hearrers very quick he is a man whom god will uphold if he will continue faithful to his calling O God grant that he may for the Lords sake Amen [p. 21] the man who willeth to do well we should extoll his virtues and speak not of his faults behind his back a man who willfuly turneth away from his friend without a cause is not ~~lightly to be forgiven~~ ⟨easily forgiven⟩ the kindness of a man ⟨should⟩ ~~is~~ never ~~to~~ be forgotten that person who never forsaketh his trust should ever have the highest place for regard in our hearts and our love should never fail but increase more and more and this [is] my disposition and sentiment &c Amen [p. 22] Brother Frederick [G. Williams] ~~is a man who~~ ⟨is one of those men⟩ in whom I place the greatest confidence and trust for I have found him ever full of love and Brotherly

---

1. Joseph Smith's sentiments regarding Sidney Rigdon may be rooted in events of the previous year in which Rigdon had declared to the Saints in Kirtland during Joseph's absence that "God had rejected them," and that "the keys of the kingdom" had been taken from the Church. The incident resulted in Rigdon losing his position as counselor to Joseph Smith in the Church presidency. A short time later, after sincere repentance, Rigdon was reinstated. (Leonard J. Arrington, *Charles C. Rich* [Provo, Utah: BYU Press, 1974], 20–21; Lucy Smith, *Biographical Sketches of Joseph Smith the Prophet* [Liverpool, 1853], 194–96; Joseph Smith to William W. Phelps, 31 July 1832, published in Jessee, *The Personal Writings of Joseph Smith* [Salt Lake City: Deseret Book Company, 1984], 246–47.)

kindness he is not a man of many words but is ever wining because of his constant mind he shall ever have place in my heart and is ever intitled to my confiden⟨ce⟩ /[1] He is perfectly honest and upright, and seeks with all his heart to magnify his presidency in the church of ch[r]ist, but fails in many instances, in consequence of a ~~lack~~ ⟨want⟩ of confidence in himself: God grant that he may [p. 23] overcome all evil: Blessed be brother Frederick, for he shall never want a friend; and his generation after him shall flourish. The Lord hath appointed him an inheritance upon the land of Zion. Yea, and his head shall blossom. ⟨And he shall be⟩ as an olive branch that is bowed down with fruit: even so; Amen.

And again, blessed be brother Sidney, also notwithstanding he shall be high and lifted up, yet he shall bow down under the yoke like unto an ass that [p. 24] coucheth beneath his burthen; that learneth his master's ⟨will⟩ by the stroke of the rod: thus saith the Lord. Yet the Lord will have mercy on him, and he shall bring forth much fruit; even as the ~~vun~~ ⟨vine⟩ of the choice grape when her clusters are ⟨is⟩ ripe, before the time of the gleaning of the vintage: and the Lord shall make his heart merry as with sweet wine because of him who putteth forth his hand and lifteth him up ~~from~~ ⟨out of⟩ [a] deep mire, and pointeth him out the way, and guideth his [p. 25] feet when he stumbles; and humbleth him in his pride. Blessed are his generations. Nevertheless, one shall hunt after them as a man hunteth after an ass that hath strayed in the wilderness, & straitway findeth him and bringeth him into the fold. Thus shall the Lord watch over his generation that they may be saved: even so; Amen.

/[2] on the 13th and 14th days of October [1833] I baptised the following person[s][3] in[4] Mount Pleasant viz [p. 26]

---

1. Handwriting of Oliver Cowdery.
2. Handwriting of Frederick G. Williams.
3. The date of these baptisms is evidently incorrect. On 13 and 14 October Joseph Smith was at Perrysburg, New York. The baptisms referred to here took place at Mt. Pleasant, Canada, on 27 and 28 October.
4. "in" repeated in MS.

Moses Chapman Nickerson
Eleser [Eleazer] Freeman Nickerson
Prechard [Richard] Ramon Strowbridge
Andrew Rose
Harvey John Cooper
Samuel Mc Alester [McAllister]
Eliza [McAllister] Nickerson
Mary Gates
Mary Birch [Burtch]
Lidia Baeley [Lydia Goldthwait Bailey Knight]
Elisabeth Gibbs
Phebe [Andrews] Cook
Margrett Birch [Burtch]
Esthe[r] Birch [Burtch]

25 November 1833 · Monday

Brother Orson Hyde & John Gould [p. 27] returned from Zion and brough[t] the melencholly intelegen[ce] of the riot in Zion with the inhabitants in pers[ec]uting the brethren.[1]

4 December 1833 · Wednesday

commenced distributing the type—and commenced setting on the 6 [December 1833] and being prepared to commence our Labours in the printing buisness I ask God in the

---

1. After a July 1831 revelation had designated the area of Jackson County, Missouri, as Zion, the gathering place of the Latter-day Saints, Church members began migrating to that place in anticipation of establishing a holy city and a temple. However, political, economic, social, and religious differences between the Mormon community and old settlers gave rise to antagonism and finally violence. In July 1833, a mob destroyed Church property at Independence and committed violence upon Church leaders there. By the end of the year the entire LDS population had been driven from the county. (See Allen and Leonard, *The Story of the Latter-day Saints*, 81–90; Warren Jennings, "The Expulsion of the Mormons from Jackson County, Missouri," *Missouri Historical Review*, 64 [October 1969]: 41–63; and Jennings, "Zion is Fled: The Expulsion of the Mormons from Jackson County, Missouri" [Ph.D. diss., University of Florida, 1962].)

[p. 28] name of Jesus to establish it for ever and cause that his word may speedily go for[th to] the Nations of the earth to the accomplishing of his great work in bringing about the restoration of the house of Israel[1]

22 November 1833 · Friday

my brother [Don] Carlos Smith came to live with me and also learn the printing art [p. 29] on the 9 of Dec[ember 1833] bro Phi[neas] Young came to board with me to board rent & lodge at one dollar & twenty five cents p[er] week

Bro [Solomon] Wilbor Denton came to board 11 Dec[ember 1833] at one Dollar and twenty five cents per week.

18 December 1833 · Wednesday

This day the Elders assembled togeth[er] in the printing office [p. 30] and then proceded to bow down before the Lord and dedicate the printing press and all that pertains thereunto to God by mine own hand and confirmed by bro Sidney Rigdon and Hyrum Smith and then proceded to take the first proof sheet of the star[2] edited by Bro Oliv[er] Cowd[er]y[3] blessed of the Lord is bro Oliver nevertheless there are[4] [p. 31] two evils in him that he must needs forsake or he cannot altogeth[er]

---

1. A council held in Kirtland on 11 September 1833, consisting of Frederick Williams, Sidney Rigdon, Newel Whitney, Joseph Smith, and Oliver Cowdery, resolved that a printing office be established there under the name of F. G. Williams & Co. to commence a new publication, the *Latter Day Saints' Messenger and Advocate*. The council also resolved to continue publication of *The Evening and the Morning Star*, printed at Independence, Missouri, prior to the destruction of the press there the previous July. The *Star* was to be published by Oliver Cowdery in Kirtland until it could be transferred to its former location in Missouri. The first Kirtland issue of the *Star* is dated December 1833. The *Messenger and Advocate* did not appear until the following October. (*History of the Church*, 1:409.)

2. *The Evening and the Morning Star* reprint.

3. Patriarchal Blessings, Book 1, 8–13, MS., contains a more complete account of the proceedings of this meeting written by Oliver Cowdery at the time.

4. "are" repeated in MS.

escape the buffitings of the adver[sar]y if he shall forsak[e]
these evils he shall be forgiven and shall be made like unto
the bow which the Lord hath set in the heavens he shall be a
sign and an ensign unto the nations. behold he is blessed of
the Lord for his constancy [p. 32] and steadfastness in the
work of the Lord wherefore he shall be blessed in his generation
and they shall never be cut off and he shall be helped out of
many troubles and if he keep the commandments and harken
unto the ⟨council of the⟩ Lord his and [and] his rest shall be
glorious and again blessed of the Lord is my father and also
my mother and my brothers and my sisters for they shall [p.
33] yet find redemption in the house of the Lord and their
ofsprings shall be a blessing a Joy and a comfort unto them
blessed is my mother for her soul is ever fill[ed] with benevolence and phylanthropy and notwithstanding her age yet she
shall receive strength and shall be comforted in the midst of
her house and she shall have eternal life and blessed is my
father for the hand of the Lord shall be [p. 34] over him for
he shall see the affliction ⟨of his children⟩ pass away and when
his head is fully ripe he shall behold himself as an olive tree
whose branches are bowed down with much fruit he shall also
possess a mansion on high blessed of the Lord is my brother
Hyrum for the integrity of his heart he shall be girt about with
truth and faithfulness shall be the strength of his loins [p. 35]
from generation to generation he shall be a shaft in the hand
of his God to exicute Judgment upon his enemies and he shall
be hid by the hand of the Lord that none of his secret parts
shall be discovered unto his hu[r]t his name shall be accounted
a blessing among men and when he is in trouble and great
tribulation hath come upon him [p. 36] he shall remember
the God of Jacob and he will shield him from the power of
satan and he shall receive counel ⟨councel⟩ in the house of the
most high that he may be streng[t]hened in hope that the going
⟨of his feet⟩ may be established for eve[r] blessed of the Lord is
bro Samuel [Harrison Smith] because the Lord shall say unto

him Sam[ue]l, Sam[ue]l, therefore he shall be made a teache[r] in [p. 37] the house of the Lord and the Lord shall mature his mind in Judgment and thereby he shall obtain the esteem and fellowship of his brethren and his soul shall be established and he shall benefit the house of the Lord because he shall obtain answer to prayer in his faithfulness — Bro William [Smith] is as the fi[e]rce Lion [p. 38] who devideth not the spoil because of his strength and in the pride of his heart he will neglect the more weighty[1] matters until his soul is bowed down in sorrow and then he shall return and call on the name of his God and shall find forgiveness and shall wax valient therefor he shall be saved unto the utter most and as the [p. 39] roaring Lion of the forest in the midst of his prey so shall the hand of his generation be lifted up against those who are set on high that fight against the God of Israel fearless and unda[u]nted shall they be in battle in avenging the [w]rongs of the innocent and relieving the oppressed ther[e]for the blessings of the God of Jacob [p. 40] shall be in the midst of his house notwithstanding his rebelious heart and ⟨now⟩ O God let the residue of my fathers house ever come up in remembrance before thee that thou mayest save them from the hand of the oppressor and establish their feet upon the rock of ages that they may have place in thy house and be saved in thy Kingdom [p. 41] and let all these things be even as I have said for Christs sake Amen

19 December 1833 · Thursday

This day Bro William Pratt and David Pattin [Patten] took their Journey to the Land of Zion for the purpose of bearing dispatches to the Brethren in that place from Kirtland O may God grant it a blessing for Zion as a kind Angel from heaven Amen [p. 42]

---

1. "weightier" changed to read "weighty" in MS.

16 January 1834

this night at Brother Jinkins [Wilkins Jenkins] Salis-bury['s][1] came from home Oh Lord keep us and my Family safe untill I can return to them again Oh my God have mercy on my Bretheren in Zion for Christ Sake Amen

/[2] 11 January 1834

This evening Joseph Smith Jr, Frederick G. Williams, Newel K. Whitney, John Johnson, Oliver Cowdery, and Orson Hyd[e] united in prayer and asked the Lord to grant the following petition: [p. 43] Firstly, That the Lord would grant that our lives might be precious in his sight, that he would watch over our persons and give his angels charge concerning us and our families that no evil nor unseen hand might be permitted to harm us.[3]

Secondly, That the Lord would also hold the lives of all the United Firm,[4] and not suffer that any of them shall be taken.

---

1. Salisbury, who had married Joseph Smith's sister Katherine, was evidently living in the area of Chardon, Geauga County, Ohio, at the time of this visit by Joseph Smith. (See journal entry of 29 November 1832.)
2. Handwriting of Oliver Cowdery.
3. As the social, religious, and political beliefs and practices of the Latter-day Saints came into contact with those not of their persuasion, the Saints were confronted with agitation, distrust, and finally persecution. Antagonism against the Church in Ohio grew to such proportions, according to one witness, that "our enemies were raging and threatening destruction upon us, and we had to guard ourselves night after night, and for weeks were not permitted to take off our clothes, and were obliged to lay with our fire locks in our arms." ("Extract from the Journal of Elder Heber C. Kimball," *Times and Seasons*, 6:771; see also Parkin, "Conflict at Kirtland," 248–63.)
4. To consolidate and strengthen the business affairs of the Church for the benefit of the poor, the "United Order" or "United Firm" was established in March 1832, consisting of prominent Latter-day Saint merchants and land-holders in Ohio and Missouri who united their holdings in a joint stewardship. The Firm, consisting of about a dozen Church leaders, was discontinued in April 1834. (D&C 78 and 104; Leonard J. Arrington, Feramorz Y. Fox, and Dean L. May, *Building the City of God* [Salt Lake City: Deseret Book Company, 1976],

Thirdly, That the Lord would grant that our brother Joseph might prevail over [p. 44] his enemy, even Docter P. Hurlbut, who has threatened his life, whom brother Joseph has ⟨caused to be⟩ taken with a precept; that the Lord would fill the heart of the court with a spirit to do justice, and cause that the law of the land may be magnified in bringing him to justice.[1]

Fourthly, That the Lord would provide, in the order of his Providence, the bishop of this Church with means sufficient to discharge every debt that the Firm owes, in due season, that [p. 45] the Church may not be braught into disrepute, and the saints be afflicted by the hands of their enemies.

Fifthly, That the Lord would protect our printing press from the hands of evil men, and give us means to send forth his word, even his gospel that the ey ears of all may hear it, and also that we may print his scriptures; and also that he would give those who were appointed to conduct the press, wisdom sufficient that the cause [p. 46] may not be hindered, but that men's eyes may thereby be opened to see the truth.

Sixthly, That the Lord would deliver Zion, and gather in his scattered people, to possess it in peace; and also, while in their dispersion, that he would provide for them that they perish not with hunger nor fam cold. And finally, that God in the name of Jesus would gather his elect speedily, and unveil his face that his saints [p. 47] might behold his glory and dwell with him; Amen.

31; Lyndon W. Cook, *The Revelations of the Prophet Joseph Smith* [Provo, Utah: Seventy's Book Store, 1981], 113–14, 167–68; Lyndon Cook, *Joseph Smith and The Law of Consecration* [Provo, Utah: Grandin Book Company, 1985], chapter 5.)

1. After Doctor Philastus Hurlbut joined the Latter-day Saints in 1833, he was excommunicated for immorality and threatened Joseph Smith's life. The Prophet filed a complaint against Hurlbut in the county court on 21 December 1833. The preliminary hearing was held 13–15 January 1834, and Hurlbut was bound over to appear at the next session of court. (Geauga County, Ohio, Court of Common Pleas, Book P, pp. 431–32; see also, Parkin, "Conflict at Kirtland," 120–28; Maria S. Hurlbut statement, 9 September 1883, MS., Chicago Historical Society; entry of 9 April on pp. 28–29.)

On the 13th of March A. D. 1833, Docter P. Hurlbut came to my house; I conversed with him considerably about the book of Mormon. He was ordained to the office of an elder in this Church under the hand of Sidney Rigdon on the **18th**[1] of March in the same year above written. According to my best recollection, I heard him say, in the [p. 48] course of conversing with him, that if he ever became convinced that the book of Mormon was false, he would be the cause of my destruction, &c.

He was tried before a counsel of high priests on the 21st day of June, 1833, and his license restored to him again, it ⟨he⟩ previously having been taken by the church at ⟨cut off from the⟩ Church by the bishop's court. He was finally cut off from the church [p. 49] a few days after having his license restored, on the 21st of June. /[2] and then saught the distruction of the saints in this place and more particularly myself and family and as the Lord has in his mercy Delivered me out of his hand till the present and also the church that he has not prevailed viz the 28 day of Jany [p. 50] 1834 for which I off[er] the gratitud[e] of my heart to Allmighty God for the same and on this night Bro Oliv[er] and bro Frederick and my self bowed before the Lord being agred and united in pray[er] that God would continue to deliver me and my brethren from ⟨him⟩ that he may not prevail again[st] us in the law suit that is pending [p. 51] and also that God would soften down the hearts of E[lijah] Smith J[osiah] Jones Lowd [Austin Loud] & [Azariah] Lyman and also [Andrew] Bardsly that they might obey the gospel or if they would not repent that the Lord would send faithful saints to purchase their farms that this stake may be strengthened and ⟨its⟩ the borders enlarged[3] **O Lord grant it for Christ Sake Amen [p. 52]**

---

1. When this entry was originally written by Oliver Cowdery, the date was left blank, but it was later supplied by Joseph Smith.
2. Handwriting of Frederick G. Williams.
3. According to Geauga County, Ohio, tax records, Elijah Smith owned 273 acres of land in Kirtland; Josiah Jones, 78 acres; Austin Loud, 2 1/2 acres; Azariah Lyman, 8 acres; and Andrew Bardslee, 30 acres. In addition, Loud and Lyman jointly owned a sawmill, a gristmill, and 17 acres.

/¹31 January 1834 · Friday

it is my prayer to the Lord that three thousand subscriber[s] may be added to the Star in the term of three yea[rs]

26 February 1834 · Wednesday

Started from home to obtain volenteers for Zion²

27 February 1834 · Thursday

~~startted~~ **Started Stayed at Br Roundays³**

28 February 1834 · Friday

stayed at a strangers who entertained us very kindly ⟨in⟩ Westleville [Wesleyville, Erie County, Pennsylvania]

1 March 1834 · Saturday

arived at Br [Job] Lewis and on the 2d [March 1834] the Sabath Brother Barly [Parley Pratt] preached in this place and I preached in the evening had a good [p. 53] meeting there is a small church in this place⁴ tha[t] seem to be strong in th[e] faith Oh may God keep them in the faith and save them and lead them to Zion—

3 March 1834 · Monday

this morning intend[ed] to start on our Journy to ⟨the⟩ east ⟨But did not start⟩⁵ O may God bless us with the gift of utterance to accomplish the Journy and the Errand on which

---

1. Handwriting of Frederick G. Williams.
2. A 24 February revelation had designated Joseph Smith and Parley Pratt to travel together to solicit funds and volunteers "to assist in redeeming Zion," restoring the Saints driven from Jackson County, Missouri, to their homes and property. (See D&C 103:37.)
3. Shadrach Roundy at Elk Creek, Erie County, Pennsylvania.
4. Westfield, Chautauqua County, New York.
5. Insertion by Parley Pratt.

**we are sent and return soon to the land of Kirtland [p. 54]
and ⟨find⟩ my Family all well O Lord bless my little children
with health and long life to do good in th[is] generation for
Christs sake Amen —**

/¹Kirtland Geauger [Geauga County] Ohio
Thom[p]son [Geauga County] —
Springfield Erie [County] Pensy[l]vania
Elkcrick [Elk Creek, Erie County]
Westfield [Chautauqua, New York] —
Laona Chautauque N york
Silver Creek [Chautauqua, New York] —
Perrysburgh Cateragus [Cattaraugus County, New York]
Collins Genesee [County, New York]
China [Genesee County, New York] [p. 55]
Warsaw [Genesee County, New York] —
Geneseeo Levingston [Geneseo, Livingston County, New
York]
Sentervill [Centreville, Allegany County, New York]
Cattlin Alleghany
Spafford ~~Spafford~~ Onondaga [County, New York]

John Gould payed me on papers — $ 1.50

/²Journal of P[arley Pratt] and J[oseph Smith]

4 March 1834 · Tuesday

took our Journy from Westfield [Chatauqua County, New
York] ⟨accompanyed By Br [John] gould⟩ rode 33 miles arrived
in **Vilanova** s⟨t⟩aid all night with a Brother [Reuben] Mc Bride,
next morning went 4 m[ile]s³ to Br Nicisons [Freeman Nick-

---

1. Itinerary of Joseph Smith and Parley Pratt to obtain volunteers for the aid
of Zion. Unidentified hand.
2. Handwriting of Parley P. Pratt.
3. The MS. here and twice under the entry of 11 March reads "m;s."

erson][1] found him and [p. 56] his house hold full of faith and of the holy spirit we cald the church together and Related unto them what had hapened to our Brethren in Zion opened to them the prophesyes and revelations con-cerning the order of the gethering of Zion and the means of her Redemtion and Brother Joseph Prophesyed to them and the spirit of the Lord came mightily upon them and with all redyness the yo[u]ng and midle aged volenteered for Zion [p. 57] same evening held 2 meetin⟨gs⟩ 3 or 4 miles Apart. next day

6 March 1834 · Thursday

held another Meeting at Bro Nicisons the few un Believeers that atended were outragious and the meeting ended in com-pleet confusi⟨on⟩

7 March 1834 · Friday

started ~~toards~~ on our Journy accompany⟨ed⟩ By Br Nicison Leaving Brs goold [John Gould] and Mathews[2] to Prepare ⟨and gether up⟩ the companys in the churches in that region and meet us in Ohio Reddy for Zion the first of May we arrived after dark to the [p. 58] county seat of Cataraugus cald Eli-cutville [Ellicottville] tryed every tavern in the place But Being Court time we found no room But were compeled to ride on in a ~~d~~ dark muddy rainy night we found shelter in rideing 1 mile Paid higher for our fare than tavern price

8 March 1834 · Saturday

continued our journy came to Palmersville [Farmersville] to the house of Elder Mc gown [Marcellus McKown] were Invited to go to Esq **walkers**—[3] to spend the evening [p. 59]

---

1. At Perrysburg, Cattaraugus County, New York.
2. Possibly David Matthews.
3. The 1830 census lists Leonard Walker, Thomas B. Walker, and Billings Walker living near Marcellus McKown at Farmersville.

we found them verry frien⟨dly⟩ and somewhat Believeing tarryed allnight

9 March 1834 · Sunday

held meeting in a school house had grea⟨t⟩ attentian found a few desyples who were firm in faith and after meeting found many Believeing and could hardly get away from them we apointed A meeting in freedom [Cattaraugus County, New York] for Monday 10th [March 1834] and are now at Mr [Warren A.] Cowderyes in the full Enjoyment of ⟨all⟩ the Blessings Both temporal and spiritual [p. 60] of which we stand in need or are found worthy to receive held meting on Monday ~~moved~~ Preachd to crowd[ed] ⟨congregat[ion]⟩ at eve preacht again to a hous crowded full to overflowing after meting I proposed if any wished to obey if they would make it manifest we would stay to administer at another meeting a young man of the methodist order arose and testified his faith in the fulness of ⟨the⟩ gospel and desired to Be Baptised we Appointed another meting and the next [p. 61] day tuesday 11th [March 1834] held meeting and Baptised Heman hide[1] after which we rode 9 m[ile]s Put up with...... ⟨**Stewards tavern**⟩ next day rode 36 m[ile]s to fauther [Edmund] Bosleys.[2]

13 March 1834 · Thursday

held meting I Prea⟨chd⟩

---

1. Parley Pratt recalled, "We visited Freedom . . . tarried over Sunday, and preached several discourses, to which the people listened with great interest; we were kindly and hospitably entertained among them. We baptized a young man named Heman Hyde; his parents were Presbyterians, and his mother, on account of the strength of her traditions, thought that we were wrong, and told me afterwards that she would much rather have followed him to an earthly grave than to have seen him baptized. Soon afterwards, however, herself, her husband, and the rest of the family, with some thirty or forty others, were all baptized and organized into a branch of the Church." (Parley P. Pratt, Jr., ed., *Autobiography of Parley P. Pratt* [Salt Lake City: Deseret Book Company, 1961], 109–10.)

2. At Livonia, Livingston County, New York.

14 March 1834 · Friday

in F[ather Alvah] Beamans[1]

15 March 1834 · Saturday

at Father Beamans and Brother Sidny [Rigdon] and Lyman [Wight] arived at his house to ⟨the⟩ Joy of our Souls in Lyvona [Livonia, Livingston County, New York]

16 March 1834 · Sunday

Brother Sidney preached to a very large congregation in ⟨Geneseo⟩

17 March 1834 · Monday

Brother ~~Ba~~ [p. 62] ~~Bro~~ Parly preached in the afternoon[2]

18 March 1834 · Tuesday

Stayed at Father Boslys [Edmund Bosley] all day

19 March 1834 · Wednesday

Started for home arrived at Brother Whitheys [Isaac McWithy][3] **tarried all night &c**

---

1. Parley Pratt noted, "Among those whose hospitality we shared in that vicinity was old father Beeman and his amiable and interesting family. He was a good singer, and so were his three daughters; we were much edified and comforted in their society, and were deeply interested in hearing the old gentleman and brother Joseph converse on their early acquaintance and history. He had been intimate with Joseph long before the first organization of the Church; had assisted him to preserve the plates of the Book of Mormon from the enemy, and had at one time had them concealed under his own hearth." (Pratt, *Autobiography*, 110.)

2. On this day Joseph Smith and Parley Pratt attended a conference of elders at Alvah Beaman's in Avon, New York, in preparation for Zion's Camp. The purpose of the meeting was to establish procedures for obtaining men to "assist in the redemption of Zion according to the commandment" and money to help the church in Missouri and Ohio. (Kirtland Council Minutes, 17 March 1834.)

3. At Bennington, Genesee County, New York.

20 March 1834 · Thursday

Started on ⟨our⟩ Journy at noon took dinner at Brother Joseph Holbrooks,[1] and at night ~~we~~ tryed three times to git keept in the name of Deciples, and could not be kept, [p. 63] after night we found a man who would keep us for mony thus we see that there ⟨is⟩ more ~~pl~~ place for mony than for Jesus ⟨Deciples or⟩ the Lamb of God, the name of the man is ~~Wilson Rauben Wilson~~ — Reuben Wilson[2] that would not keep us without mony he ⟨lived in China [Genesee County, New York]⟩ &c. —

21 March 1834 · Friday

came to a man by the name of Starks 6th miles East of Springville[3] [Erie County, New York] [p. 64]

22 March 1834 · Saturday

came and tarri[e]d with vincen nights [Vinson Knight] in ~~P~~ Perrysburg Co — of Cattaraugus —

23 March 1834 · Sunday

came to Father [Freeman] Nickersons Perrysburg the same Co[unty] NY held a meeting &c.

24 March 1834 · Monday

this ⟨day⟩ am not able to start for ~~he~~ home but feel determined to go on the morrow morning —

---

1. At Wethersfield, Genesee County (now Wyoming County), New York.
2. The 1830 Federal Census lists Reuben Wilson (in his sixties) and family of seven living in China, Genesee County, New York.
3. The 1830 Federal Census lists Joseph Starks (in his thirties) and family of seven living at Sardinia, Erie County, about six miles east of Springville.

25 March 1834 · Tuesday

came from Father Nickerson to Father Leweses [Job Lewis] in [p. 65] Westfield [Chautauqua Co., New York] Father Nickerson came with me

26 March 1834 · Wednesday

Came from Westfield to Elk kreek [Erie County, Pennsylvania] stayed with Elder Hunt on free cost

27 March 1834 · Thursday

Came to springfield [Erie Co., Pennsylvania] found Brother Sidney and came to within 16 miles from Painsville [Lake Co., Ohio]

28 March 1834 · Friday

Came home found my Family all well and the Lord be praised for this blessing

29 March 1834 · Saturday

at home had much [p. 66] Joy with ⟨my⟩ Family

30 March 1834 · Sunday

Sabb⟨a⟩th at home and went to hear Brother Sidney Preach the word of life &c. —

31 March 1834 · Monday

Monday this day came to Sharden [Chardon, Geauga County, Ohio] to tend the Court against Docter P Hurlbut &c

1 April 1834 · Tuesday[1]

this day at Brother Riders[2] and the Court has not braught on our tryal yet we are ingaged in makeing out some supenies [subpoenas] &c — for witnesses this is ~~m~~ [p. 67] ~~this~~ Ap[r]el 1st Tusday my soul delighteth in the Law of the Lord for he forgiveth my sins and ⟨will⟩ confound mine Enimies the Lord shall destroy him who has lifted his heel against me even that wicked man Docter P. H[u]rlbut he ⟨will⟩ deliver him to the fowls of heaven and his bones shall be cast to the blast of the wind ⟨for⟩ he lifted his ⟨arm⟩ against the Almity therefore [p. 68] the Lord shall destroy him

/[3]2 April 1834 · Wednesday

attended court at Chardon, Thursday the same. Friday morning returned home. Saturday returned to Chardon ⟨as witness for fath[er] Johnson⟩[4] in the evening returned home. Mr. Bussle [Benjamin Bissel] the State's Att'y for Portage County called on me this evening: He is a gentlemanly appearing man, and treated me with respect.

/[5]7 April 1834 · Monday

Bros Newel [Whitney] Oliver [Cowdery] Frederick [Williams] Heber [Kimball] and myself met[6] [p. 69] in the counsel room and bowed down befor[e] the Lord and prayed that he would furnish the means to deliver the firm from debt and ⟨be⟩ set at liberty and also that I may prevail against that wicked Hurlbut and that he be put to shame accordingly on the 9

---

1. MS. reads "~~32d~~ Tusday."
2. Probably Ezekiel Rider.
3. Handwriting of Oliver Cowdery.
4. On 5 April 1834 John Johnson was granted a license to keep a tavern in Kirtland. Joseph Smith testified before the court on Johnson's qualifications. (Geauga County, Ohio, Common Pleas Court, 5 April 1834, Book M, 184.)
5. Handwriting of Frederick G. Williams.
6. MS.: "meet"

[April 1834] after an impartial trial the Court decided that the said Hurlbut was bound over under 200 dollars [p. 70] bond to keep the peace for six month[s] and pay the cost which amounted to near three hundred dollars all of which was in answer to our prayer for which I thank my heavenly father[1]

Remember to carry the bond between A S—Gilbert & N K Whitney and have them exchang⟨d⟩ when I go to Zion[2]

10 April 1834 · Thursday

had a co[u]ncel [p. 71] of the united firm at which it was agreed that the firm should be desolv[ed] and each one have their stewardship set off to them[3]

11 April 1834 · Friday

attended meeting and restored Father Tyler[4] to the Church

12 April 1834 · Saturday

went to the lake [Erie] and spent the day in fishing and visiting the brethren in that place and took my horse from Father [John] Johnson and let brother Frederick [G. Williams] have him to keep.

13 April 1834 · Sunday

was sick and could not attend meeting [p. 72]

14 April 1834 · Monday

purch[as]ed some hay and oats and got them home

---

1. According to the court record, at the Hurlbut trial, beginning 2 April 1834, it was ruled that Joseph Smith "had ground to fear that the said . . . Hurlbut would wound, beat or kill him, or destroy his property." Hurlbut was ordered to post a $200 bond "to keep the peace" for six months and to pay the court costs, which amounted to $112.59. (Geauga County, Ohio, Common Pleas Court, 9 April 1834, Book M, 193.)

2. In the MS. this sentence is enclosed with a pen line.

3. See D&C 104.

4. Possibly Andrew Tyler.

15 April 1834 · Tuesday

drawed a load of hay & ⟨on Wensday 16 [April 1834]⟩ plowed and sowed oats for Brother Frederick and on

17 April 1834 · Thursday

attended a meeting agreeable to appoint[ment] at which time the important subjects of the deliverence of Zion and the building of the Lords house in [p. 73] Kirtland[1] by bro Sidney after which bro Joseph arose and requested the brethren and sisters to contr[i]bute all the money they could for the deliverence of Zion and recei⟨v⟩ed twenty nine dollars and sixty eight cts

/²18 April 1834 · Friday

left Kirtland in company with brothers Sidney Rigdon, Oliver Cowdery, ⟨and⟩ Zebedee Coltrin for New Portage to attend a conference. Travelled to W[illiam]. W. Williams in [p. 74] Newburgh [Cuyahoga County, Ohio] and took dinner, after which we travelled on, and after dark were hailed by a man who desired to ride. We were checked by the Spirit and refused: he professed to be sick; but in a few minutes was joined by two others who followed us hard, cursing and swearing, but we were successful in escaping their hands through the providence of the Lord, and stayed at a tavern where we were treated with civility. Next morning,

---

1. In December 1832, less than two years after Joseph Smith arrived in Kirtland, a revelation commanded the building of "a house of learning, a house of glory, a house of order, a house of God." (D&C 88:119.) Begun in 1833 and finished in 1836, the structure was built at great sacrifice to the Latter-day Saints. In referring to the edifice, the Joseph Smith journal interchangeably uses "temple" "Temple of the Lord," "house of the Lord," "house of God," and "chapel." (See Cook, *Revelations of the Prophet Joseph Smith*, 183–85; Backman, *The Heavens Resound*, chapter 9.)
2. Handwriting of Oliver Cowdery.

19 April 1834 · Saturday

started, and arrived at brother Joseph Bozworth's [Bosworth] ⟨in⟩ Cop [p. 75] Copley, Medina County, [Ohio] where we took dinner. Bro. J. Bozworth was strong in the faith—he is a good man and may, if faithful, do much good. After resting a while, we left, and soon arrived at brother Johnathan Tayler's [Jonathan Taylor], in Norton, where we were received with kindness.

We soon retired to the wilderness where we united in prayer and suplication for the blessings of the Lord to be given unto his church: We called upon the Father in the name of Jesus to go with the breth[r]en who were [p. 76] going up to the land of Zion, to give brother Joseph strength, and wisdom, and understanding sufficient to lead the people of the Lord, and to gather back and establish the saints upon the land of their inheritances, and organize them according to the will of heaven, that they be no more cast down forever. We then united and laid on hands: Brothers Sidney, Oliver, and Zebedee [Coltrin] laid hands upon bro. Joseph, and confirmed upon him all the blessings necessary to qualify him to do ⟨stand⟩ before the Lord in his high calling; and [p. 77] he return again in peace and triumph, to enjoy the society of his breth[r]en. Brothers Joseph, Sidney, and Zebedee then laid hands upon bro. Oliver, and confirmed upon him the blessings of wisdom and understanding sufficient for his station; that he be qualified to assist brother Sidney in arranging the church covenants which are to be soon published;[1] and to have intelligence in all things to do the work of printing. Brother[s] Joseph, Oliver, Zebedee then laid [p. 78] hands upon bro. Sidney, and con-

---

1. After the destruction of the Missouri print shop interrupted publication of the Book of Commandments, at a meeting of the Kirtland high council, September 24, 1834, Joseph Smith, Oliver Cowdery, Sidney Rigdon, and Frederick Williams were appointed a committee to "arrange the items of doctrine" of the Church and publish them as a "book of covenants." The others were to continue this labor while Joseph Smith traveled to Missouri with Zion's Camp.

firmed upon him the blessings of wisdom and knowledge to preside over the Church in the abscence of brother Joseph, and to have the spirit to assist bro. Oliver in conducting the Star, and to arrange the Church covenants, and the blessing of old age and peace, till Zion is built up & Kirtland established, till all his enemies are under his feet, and of a crown of eternal life at the ⟨in the⟩ Kingdom of God with us. [p. 79] We, Joseph, Sidney, and Oliver then laid hands upon bro. Zebedee, and confirmed the blessing of wisdom to preach the gospel, even till it spreads to the islands of the sea, and to be spared to see three score years and ten, and see Zion built up and Kirtland established forever, and even at last to receive a crown of life. Our hearts rejoiced, and we were [p. 80] comforted with the Holy Spirit, Amen.

20 April 1834 · Sunday[1]

Brother Sidney Rigdon entertained a large congregation of saints, with an interesting discourse upon the "Dispensation of the fulness of times," &c.

21 April 1834 · Monday

Attended conference and had a glorious time, some few volunteered to go to Zion, and others donated $66.37 for the benefit of the scattered breth[r]en in Zion. Returned to Kirtland on the 22d and found all well. [p. 81]

23 April 1834 · Wednesday

Assembled in council[2] with breth[r]en Sidney, Frederick, Newel, John Johnson and Oliver and united in asking the Lord to give bro. Zebedee Coltrin influence over our bro. Jacob Myre [Myers], and obtain from him the money which he has gone

---

1. In the MS. "18" has been crossed out preceding "20" in the date.

2. At this meeting, the revelation recorded in D&C 104 was given to the Church.

to borrow for us, or cause him to come to this place & give it himself.

/¹30 April 1834 · Wednesday

this day paid the ~~amount~~ ⟨sum⟩ of fifty dollars on the following memorandom to the [p. 82] following persons viz

Milton Holmes	$15.00
Henry Herriman	7.00
Sylvester Smith	10.00
Wm Smith	5.00
Harvey Stanl[e]y	5.00
William Smith	5.00
N K Whitney	3.00
	$50.00

Money received of the following brethren consecrated for the deliver[y] of Zion

By letter from East	$10.00
Do [ditto] "	50.00
Do "	100.00 [p. 83]
By Letter	$07 00
Wm Smith	.5 00
Wm Cahoon	.5 00
Harvey Stanley	.5 00
Received of Martin Harris	47 00
/²Rec[e]ived of Dexter Stillman	10.
Do of Lyman Johnson	5.00
Do of Sophia Howe	7.60 [p.84]

/³21 August 1834 · Thursday

This day brother Frederick Williams returned from Cleveland and told us concerning the plague,⁴ and after much con-

---

1. Handwriting of Frederick G. Williams.
2. Unidentified handwriting.
3. Handwriting of Oliver Cowdery. A half page preceding this entry is blank in the MS.
4. Reference to the cholera epidemic.

sultation we agreed that bro. Frederick should go to Cleveland and commence administering to the sick, for the purpose of obtaining ~~means~~ ⟨blessings for them, and⟩ for the ~~work of~~ ⟨glory of⟩ the Lord: Accordingly we, Joseph, Frederick, and Oliver united in prayer before the Lord for this thing. [p. 85.]

Now, O Lord, grant unto us this[1] blessings, in the name of Jesus Christ, and thy name shall have the glory forever; Amen.

30 August 1834 · Saturday

Received of the Church by the hand of Jared Carter from the east of consecrated money $3.00

4 September 1834 · Thursday

This day Edward [Edmund] Bosley said that if he could obtain the management of his property in one year he would put it in for the printing of the word of the Lord. [p. 86]

29 November 1834 · Friday

This evening Joseph and Oliver united in prayer for the continuance of blessings, after giving thanks for the relief which the Lord had lately sent us by opening the hearts of certain brethren from the east to loan us $430.

After conversing and rejoicing before the Lord on this occasion we agreed to enter into the following covenant with the Lord, viz:—

That if the Lord will [p. 87] prosper us in our business, and open the way before ⟨us⟩ that we may obtain means to pay our debts, that we be not troubled nor brought into disrepute before the world nor his people, that after that of all that he shall give us we will give a tenth, to be bestowed upon the poor in his Church, or as he shall command, and that we will

---

1. "this" written over "those" in MS.

be faithful over that which he has entrusted to our care ~~and~~ that we [p. 88] may obtain much: and that our children after us shall remember to observe this sacred and holy covenant: ~~after us.~~ And that our children and our children's [children] may know of the same we here subscribe our names with our own hands before the Lord:

Joseph Smith Jr
/¹Oliver Cowdery.

And now, O Father, as thou didst prosper our father Jacob, and bless [p. 89] him with protection and prosperity where ever he went from the time he made a like covenant before and with thee; and as thou didst, even the same night, open the heavens unto him and manifest great mercy and favor, and give him promises, so wilt thou do by us his sons; and as his blessings prevailed above the blessings of his Progenitors unto the utmost bounds of the [p. 90] everlasting hills, even so may our blessings prevail ~~above~~ ⟨like⟩ his; and may thy servants be preserved from the power and influence of wicked and unrighteous men; may every weapon formed against us fall upon the head of him who shall form it; may we be blessed with a name and a place among thy saints here, and thy sanctified when they shall rest. Amen. [p. 91]

*30 November 1834 · Sunday*²

While reflecting upon the goodness and mercy of the Lord, this evening, a prophecy was put into our hearts, that in a short time the Lord would arrange his providences in a merciful manner and send us assistance to deliver us from debt and bondage. [p. 92]

---

1. Handwriting of Oliver Cowdery.
2. MS. reads "Sabbath evening, November 30, 1834."

5 December 1834 · Friday[1]

According to the directions of the Holy Spirit breth[r]en Joseph Smith Jr. Sidney, Frederick G. Williams, and Oliver Cowdery, assembled to converse upon the welfare of the Church, when brother Oliver Cowdery was ordained an assistant President of the High and Holy Priesthood[2] under the hands of brother Joseph Smith Jr. saying, "My brother, in the name of Jesus Christ who died was crucified for the sins of the world, I lay my hands upon thee, and ordain thee an assistant President of the high and holy priesthood in the Church of the Latter Day Saints["]
[p. 93]

/[3]Please to send the Paper that Has formerly Been sent to John C[..]p[..]ton send it Now to Nathan Chase at West Lodi Cataraugus County N. Y

Received of Elisha C Hubbard one Dollar for Papers Perysburgh[4] [p. 103]

Hazard Andr[e]ws 1 paper Fairview Postoffi[ce] Cattaragus County

---

I have sent the money 25 cents by David Mo[.]t[..] as he

---

1. MS. reads, "Friday Evening, December 5, 1834."
2. Hyrum Smith received this office in 1841, in the place of Oliver Cowdery (see D&C 124:94–96); no other men were ever called as assistant presidents.
3. Unidentified handwriting.
4. The 1830 Federal Census lists Elisha Hubbard, in his fifties, at Perrysburg, Cattaraugus County, New York. "Perysburgh" has been added in pencil.

was to send the paper to Mis Taylor to Rushford but I wish to have it come in my name as above

---

Direct Samuel Mcbride & James Mcbride['s] Papers to Nashville Post office Shitauqua County[1]

I wish you to send me one more Paper monthly and send one Monthly Paper to Eleazer & Samuel & Richard Nickerson South Dennis in the County of Barnstable Massachusetts[2]

J[ohn] Nickerson [p. 104]

/[3]The voice of the Spirit is, that brother Sidney speak to the congregation this day, first, Brother Joseph next, bro. Oliver and if time bro Zebedee [Coltrin][4]

Joseph Smith Jr

Oliver Cowdery [p. 105]

---

1. Samuel and James McBride are listed in the 1830 Federal Census at Villanova, Chautauqua County, New York.
2. The 1830 Federal Census lists Eleazer, Samuel, and Richard Nickerson at Yarmouth, Barnstable County, Massachusetts.
3. Handwriting of Oliver Cowdery.
4. This statement, written in light pencil in contrast to the ink used in the diary, probably refers to the conference held at Norton, Medina County, Ohio, on 12 April 1834.

OHIO JOURNAL,
1835–1836

MS. Joseph Smith Papers, LDS Church Archives, Salt Lake City, Utah.

Editorial Note

Among the journals of Joseph Smith this one is the largest, and the last one that contains substantial direct input from his own pen. Although only four pages are in his handwriting, most of the volume was evidently dictated by him. Covering a six-month period from September 1835 to March 1836, the journal contains glimpses of his life as president of the Church as well as insight in to personal and family concerns. It reveals his interest in education and languages, gives a report of his First Vision as told to a stranger who visited him in November 1835, describes events leading to the dedication of the Kirtland temple, and ends with an account of his vision in the temple in April 1836.

This journal measures 12 1/2 × 8 1/16 inches and is bound with a pressboard cover with marble design paper glued to it. The spine is covered with brown leather. The book contains 112 leaves, 99 of which contain handwriting. It was originally used for work on the Joseph Smith Bible revision. Two pages — one at the back of the book (originally the front), and one at the front — contain references to "Scriptures relating to Repentence," and "Scriptures relating to the Sabbath day." Written on the front cover in black ink are the words "Sabbath Day" and under it, "No 9." Turning the volume over so that the back becomes the front, the title "Repentence" and a large "D" are written in black ink. Above the "D" the faded words, "Sketch Book." This side is the front of the journal, which is written entirely in brown ink, on 193 pages (97 leaves). Glued to the spine is a piece of white paper with "1835–6 Journal" carefully hand-printed upon it.

/[1]Sketch Book for the use of Joseph Smith, jr.

22 September 1835 · Tuesday

This day Joseph Smith, jr. labored with Oliver Cowdery, in obtaining and writing blessings.[2] We were thronged a part of the time with company, so that our labor, in this thing, was hindered; but we obtained many precious things, and our souls were blessed. O Lord, may thy Holy Spirit be with thy servants forever. Amen.

23 September 1835 · Wednesday

This day Joseph Smith, Jr. was at home writing blessings for my most beloved Brotheren ⟨I⟩ have been hindered by a multitude of visitors but the Lord has blessed our Souls this day. May Godd grant ⟨to⟩ continue his mercies unto my house, this ⟨night⟩ day for Christ sake. This day my Soul has desired the salvation of Brother Ezra, Thayr [Thayer]. Also Brother Noah, Packard. Came to my house and let the Chappel Committee[3] have one thousand dollers, by loan, for the

---

1. Handwriting of Oliver Cowdery.

2. According to Oliver Cowdery, on 18 December 1833, Joseph Smith, as the "first elder and first patriarch of the Church," had given blessings "by the spirit of prophecy" to members of his family, including his father and his brothers Hyrum, Samuel, William, and Don Carlos. The Prophet also pronounced blessings upon associates in the Church leadership, Oliver Cowdery, Frederick Williams, and Sidney Rigdon—people who had "long been employed in the work of the Lord, and were personally known to him." Cowdery wrote the blessings at the time they were given. Then, in September 1835, Cowdery began to copy the blessings for permanent preservation in a large, leather-bound record book. On 22 September 1835 Joseph Smith gave blessings to David Whitmer, John Whitmer, John Corrill, and William W. Phelps. The same day, Cowdery, having desired "to know the mind of the Spirit" concerning his friend and brother, Joseph Smith, and after fasting and prayer, noted that the heavens were opened, and he (Oliver) wrote a lengthy blessing which was "part of that which was shown and declared should come upon my brother." (See Patriarchal Blessing Book 1, 8–16, MS., LDS Church Archives.)

3. In June 1833, Hyrum Smith, Reynolds Cahoon, and Jared Carter were appointed a committee to direct the construction of the Kirtland Temple. Workers on the temple received economic help through Bishop Newel K. Whitney, who supervised the committee's storehouse. (Backman, *The Heavens Resound,* chapter 9; *History of the Church,* 2:333.)

Sketch book for the use of
Joseph Smith, jr

September 22, 1835. This day Joseph Smith, jr
labored with Oliver Cowdery, in obtaining and
writing blessings. We were thronged a part of the
time with company, so that our labor, in this thing
was hindered; but we obtained many precious things, and
our souls were blessed. O Lord, may thy Holy Spirit be with
thy servants forever. Amen.

September 23d. This day Joseph Smith, Jr. was at home
writing blessings for my most beloved Brotheren, I have
been hindered by a multitude of visitors but the Lord
has blessed our souls this day. May God grant to continue his mercies unto my house, this night, for Christ
is sake. This day my soul has desired the salvation of Brother Ezra Thayr. Also Brother Noah
Packard. Came to my house and let the Chappel Committee have one thousand dollers, by loan,
for the building the house of the Lord; Oh may
God bless him with an hundred fold even of the
things of the Earth, for this ritious act. My heart is full of
desire to day, to be blessed of the God, of Abraham
with prosperity, untill I will be able to pay all
my depts; for it is the delight of my soul to be honest
Oh Lord that thou knowes right well I will help me
and I will give to the poor —

September 23d 1835 This day Brothers William
Tibbets John, and Joseph Tibbets started for
Mosoura the place designated for Zion or the
Saints gethering they came to bid us farewell
the Brotheren came in to pray with them and
Brother David Whitmer acted as spokesman
he prayed in the spirit a glorious time suc-
=ceeded this pray Joy filled our heart and we

Joseph Smith, Ohio Journal, 1835–1836, p. 1. LDS Church Archives.

building the house of the Lord; Oh may God bless him with an hundred fold! even of the ⟨things of⟩ Earth, for this ritious act. My heart is full of desire to day, to ⟨be⟩ blessed of the God, of Abraham; with prosperity, untill I will be able to pay all my depts; for it is ⟨the⟩[1] delight of my soul to ⟨be⟩ honest. Oh Lord that thou knowes[t] right well! help me and I will give to the poor. —[2]

This day Brothers William, ~~Tibbets~~ John, and Joseph Tibbits [Tippets] Started for Mosoura[3] the place designated for Zion or the Saints gathering[4] they Came to bid us farewell the Brotheren Came in to pray with them and Brother David Whitmer acted as spokesman he prayed in the spirit a glorious time succeded his prayr Joy filled our hearts and we [p. 1] blessed them and bid them God speed ~~and~~ and promiced them a safe Journy and took them ⟨by the hand⟩ and bid them farewell for ⟨a⟩ season Oh! may God grant them long life and good days these blessings I ask ⟨upon them⟩ for Christ sake Amen[5]

24 September 1835 · Thursday

This day the high Council[6] met at my house to take into conside[r]ation the redeemtion of Zion and it was the voice

---

1. "the" written over "my" in the MS.

2. In this paragraph in the MS., Joseph Smith wrote capital letters over lowercase letters in the sentences beginning with "May," "This," "Also," and "My."

3. On 28 November 1834, the Kirtland high council met to consider a letter presented to them by John and Joseph Tippets, members of the Church from Lewis, Essex County, New York, listing money and property totaling $848.40 being sent by the Church in Essex County to purchase land in Missouri. Desiring the counsel of the Church leaders on the matter, the two men were advised to remain in Kirtland during the winter and make part of their money available for use of the Church there, to be repaid with interest the following year. At a high council meeting on 24 August 1835, the Tippetses were appointed to go to Missouri the coming fall "to purchase land for the church in Essex, New York." This entry in the diary marks the departure of these men. (Kirtland Council Minutes, 28 November 1834; 24 August 1835.)

4. D&C 57:1–3.

5. In the MS., the date "September 23d 1835," is repeated at the beginning of this paragraph.

6. The first high council of the Church was organized at Kirtland, Ohio, on

of the spirit of the Lord that we petition to the Governer[1] that is those who have been driven out ⟨should⟩ ~~to~~ do so to be set back on their Lands next spring and we go next season to live or dy ~~to this end so the dy is east~~ in Jackson County we truly had a good time and Covena[n]ted to strugle for this thing u[n]till death shall desolve this union and if one falls that the rest be not ~~dis ha~~ discouraged but pe[r]sue this object untill it is acomplished which may God grant u[n]to us in the name of Christ our Lord

    This day drew up an Arti⟨c⟩le of inrollment for the redemtion of Zion that we may obtain volenteers to go ~~me~~ next Spring to ⟨Mo—⟩[2] I ask God in the name of Jesus that we may obtain Eight hundred men ⟨or one thousand⟩ well armed and that they may acomplish this great work even so Amen—[3] [p. 2]

---

17 February 1834. The council consisted of twelve high priests and was organized for the purpose of "settling important difficulties which could not be settled by the church or the bishop's council to the satisfaction of the parties." In addition to its judicial function, the high council played an important administrative role in the early church. (The organizing minutes of the high council are found in D&C 102.)

    1. Daniel Dunklin, governor of Missouri.

    2. John Whitmer wrote of the meeting in which this transaction took place: "We met in counsel at the house of J. Smith, Jr., the seer, where we according to a previous commandment given, appointed David Whitmer captain of the Lord's Host, and Presidents F. G. Williams and Sidney Rigdon his assistants and President W. W. Phelps, myself and John Corrill, as an assistant quorum, and Joseph Smith, Jr., the seer, to stand at the head and be assisted by Hyrum Smith and Oliver Cowdery. This much for the war department, by revelation." (John Whitmer, "The Book of John Whitmer: Kept by Commandment," chapter 17, MS., RLDS Church Archives, Independence, Missouri, published in F. Mark McKiernan and Roger D. Launius, eds., *An Early Latter Day Saint History: The Book of John Whitmer* [Independence, Missouri: Herald House, 1980].)

    3. In the MS. the date, September 24th 1835, is repeated at the beginning of this paragraph. After the expulsion of the Latter-day Saints from Jackson County, Missouri (Zion), in the fall of 1833, an effort was made the following year to restore the Saints to their lands. A revelation (D&C 103) called for the organization of a force of men to travel to Missouri for that purpose. When Zion's Camp, a group of some 200 armed men led by Joseph Smith, left Kirtland in May 1834, they were strengthened by the promise of the governor for state support. However, after the Camp arrived in Missouri and was confronted by

/¹25 September 1835 · Friday

This day I remained at home: nothing of note transpired. ~~The twelve all returned from the east to day.~~

26 September 1835 · Saturday

This evening, the twelve having returned from the east this morning,[2] we met them, and conversed upon some matters of difficulty which ware existing between some of them, and president Rigdon, and all things were settled satisfactorily.[3]

---

an armed mob, the governor withdrew his promised support. A short time later, following a violent storm that dispersed the mob and an outbreak of cholera that claimed the lives of fourteen of the Camp, the Prophet delivered a revelation disbanding the Camp. (D&C 105; see also Peter Crawley and Richard L. Anderson, "The Political and Social Realities of Zion's Camp," *BYU Studies* 14 [Summer 1974]: 406–20.)

The revelation that disbanded Zion's Camp in June 1834 advised the elders of the Church to wait "a little season" until "endowed with power from on high" before they again attempted to redeem their Zion. (D&C 105:9–12.) Consequently, Church leaders decided to wait until after the temple was finished, and the "endowment" received, before again turning their attention to reclaiming their Missouri land. It is evident that as of 24 September 1835, the Prophet intended to return to Missouri the next spring with an enlarged "Zion's Camp." However, by April of 1836, the plan had changed. (See note 1, p. 204.)

1. Handwriting of Oliver Cowdery.

2. The Council of Twelve had been called on 14 February 1835. As one of the presiding quorums of the Church, the Twelve were designated as "special witnesses of the name of Christ," to build up and regulate the affairs of the Church "in all nations." The Twelve were designated as "twelve traveling councilors," to distinguish them from the "standing high councils" with presiding jurisdiction in the stakes. (D&C 107:23, 33, 36.) On 12 March 1835, less than a month after the Council of Twelve had been organized, they were called on a mission to the eastern states to "hold conferences in the vicinity of the several branches of the Church for the purpose of regulating all things necessary for their welfare." The Twelve left Kirtland on 4 May and returned 26 September 1835. ("A Record of the Transactions of the Twelve Apostles of the Church of Christ," 4, MS. For an account of the mission and its aftermath see Ronald K. Esplin, "The Emergence of Brigham Young and the Twelve to Mormon Leadership, 1830–1841" [Ph.D. diss., Brigham Young University, 1981], 164–70.)

3. On this date the presidency of the Church, consisting of Joseph Smith, Sidney Rigdon, Hyrum Smith, and Oliver Cowdery, and the presidency in Missouri, David Whitmer, William Phelps, and John Whitmer, met to consider two charges against the Twelve: one from a Warren A. Cowdery letter containing

27 September 1835 · Sunday

Attended meeting: brethren, Thomas B. Marsh, David W. Patten, Brigham Young and Heber C. Kimball preached and broke bread. The Lord poured out his Spirit, and my soul was edified.

28 September 1835 · Monday

High council met and tried brother Gladden Bishop:[1] he was reproved, repented, and was reordained. The next was Lorenzo L. Lewis for fornication: he was cut off from the Church.

29 September 1835 · Tuesday

High Council met to-day and tried brother Allen Avery:[2] he was acquited from any charge. Also Brother Phineas H. Young, who was also acquited:[3] also bro. Lorenzo Young, who confessed his error and was forgiven.[4] In all these I acted on

---

reports "derogatory to the character and teaching" of the Twelve while on their mission to the East, and another from William McLellin and Orson Hyde expressing dissatisfaction with Sidney Rigdon. The charges growing out of the Cowdery letter were found to be false, and the McLellin and Hyde matter was satisfactorily resolved. (Kirtland Council Minutes, 26 September 1835. See also Journal of Joseph Smith, 16 January 1836.)

1. On this date Bishop was charged with "advancing heretical doctrines . . . derogatory to the character of the Church." (Kirtland Council Minutes, 28 September 1835.) For a treatment of the Church court system see Edwin Brown Firmage and Richard Collin Mangrum, *Zion in the Courts: A Legal History of the Church of Jesus Christ of Latter-day Saints, 1830–1900* (Urbana and Chicago: University of Illinois Press, 1988).

2. The charge against Avery was for rebelling against the decision of the elder's council that took away his license. However, Avery came forward, readily complied with the requisitions of the high council, and was restored to his office. (Kirtland Council Minutes, 29 September 1835.)

3. Phineas was accused of "unchristian like conduct" in transactions involving the transfer of copies of the Book of Mormon during an 1835 proselyting journey, but the council found no cause for action, and he was acquitted. (Kirtland Council Minutes, 29 September 1835.)

4. A charge had been brought against Lorenzo by W. W. Phelps in 1835 for teaching that "poor men ought not to raise up seed or children" but that marriage relations were nevertheless acceptable. After Lorenzo confessed, the charge was dismissed. (Kirtland Council Minutes, 29 September 1835.)

the part of the defence for the accused to plead for mercy.[1] The Lord blessed my soul, and the council was greatly blessed, also. Much good will no doubt, result from our labors during the two days in which we were occupied on the business of the ~~CCh~~ Church.

30 September 1835 · Wednesday

Stayed at home and visited many who came to enquire after the work of the Lord.

1 October 1835 · Thursday

This after noon labored on the Egyptian alphabet,[2] in company with brsr. O. Cowdery and W. W. Phelps: The system of astronomy was unfolded.[3]

---

1. In cases of individuals tried before the high council, the accused was to be represented by half the council, not necessarily to "plead for mercy" but rather "to prevent insult or injustice." (D&C 102:12–18.)

2. In July 1835 the Kirtland Saints purchased Egyptian mummies and papyrus from one Michael Chandler, who had come to Kirtland from the East after hearing of Joseph Smith's notoriety as a translator. A "Grammar & Alphabet of the Egyptian Language," in the handwriting of William W. Phelps and Warren Parrish, appears to have been a product of early study of the papyrus. (History of the Church, 2:235–36; "Grammar and Alphabet of the Egyptian Language," 1 vol., MS., LDS Church Archives.) Another product of the study of these materials was the book of Abraham, first published beginning in the Times and Seasons 3 (1 March 1842): 703ff, and eventually included as one of the canonized scriptures of the Church. (See also Stanley B. Kimball, "New Light on Old Egyptiana: Mormon Mummies 1848–71," Dialogue 16 [Winter 1983]: 72–90; Hugh Nibley, "The Meaning of the Kirtland Egyptian Papers," BYU Studies 11 [Summer 1971]: 350–99; Nibley, The Message of the Joseph Smith Papyri: An Egyptian Endowment [Salt Lake City: Deseret Book Company, 1975]; Edward H. Ashment, "The Facsimiles of the Book of Abraham: A Reappraisal," Sunstone 4 [December 1979]: 33–48; Nibley, "The Facsimiles of the Book of Abraham: A Response by H. W. Nibley to E. H. Ashment," Sunstone 4 [December 1979]: 49–51; Nibley, Abraham in Egypt [Salt Lake City: Deseret Book Company, 1981].)

3. When this entry was incorporated into Joseph Smith's History, it was clarified to read, "the principles of astronomy as understood by Father Abraham and the ancients unfolded to our understanding, the particulars of which will appear hereafter." (History of the Church, 2:286; see also Abraham 3.)

2 October 1835 · Friday

To-day wrote a letter to be published in the Messenger and Advocate.[1] [p. 3]

/²3 October 1835 · Saturday

held a high council on the case of Elder John Gould for giving credence to false and slanderous reports instigated to Injure bro Sidney Rigdon and also Dean Gould for thretning bro Sidney Rigdon and others in authority of the Elders. after due deliberation the[y] both confessed and wer[e] acquited.[3] In the afternoon waited on the twelve most of them at my house and exhibited to them the ancient reccords in my possession[4] and gave explanation of the same thus the day passed off with the blessings of the Lord

4 October 1835 · Sunday

started early in the morning with brother J. Carrell [John Corrill] to hold a meeting in Perry [Geauga County, Ohio] when about a mile from home we saw two Dears playing in the field which diverted our minds by giving an impatus to our thoughts upon the subject of the creation of God we con-

---

1. Commencing in the September issue of the *Messenger and Advocate*, a Kirtland paper under the editorship of John Whitmer, Joseph Smith produced three letters that were published in successive issues, with the intent "that perhaps the elders traveling through the world . . . may be aided in a measure, in doctrine, and in the way of their duty." ("To the Elders of the Church of Latter Day Saints," *Messenger and Advocate*, 1 (September 1835): 179–82; 2 (November 1835): 209–12; 2 (December 1835): 225–30; *History of the Church*, 2:253–72.)

2. Handwriting of Frederick G. Williams.

3. The council considered charges against the two Goulds by Reynolds Cahoon—John for "making expressions . . . calculated to do injury to the . . . cause . . . and manifesting a very strong dissatisfaction against the teachings of the Presidency of the Church"; and Dean for "using wrong expressions and threatening the Elders of the Church," specifically Sidney Rigdon. At this meeting "the wound was healed." (Kirtland Council Minutes, 3 October 1835.)

4. See note 2, p. 45.

versed upon many topicks and the day passed off in a very agreeable manner and the Lord blessed our souls when we arived at Perry we were disappointed of a meeting through misarangements but conversed freely ~~upon~~ with Bro John Correls relatives which allayed much prejudice as we trust may the lord have mercy on their souls

5 October 1835 · Monday

returned home being much fatiegued riding in the rain spent the remainder of the day in reading and meditation &c and [p. 4] in the evening attend[ed] a high councel of the twelve apostles. had a glorious time and gave them many instruction[s] concerning their duties for time to come. told them that it was the will of God they should take their families to Missouri next season,[1] also attend this fall the solemn assembly[2] of the first Elders for the organization of the school of the

---

1. The intention was that the Twelve and their families would move to Missouri as part of the renewed effort to redeem Zion the following spring, but these instructions were later changed. (See note 3, p. 42; p. 203; Ronald K. Esplin, "The Emergence of Brigham Young and the Twelve," 193–95, 203–4; and Marvin S. Hill, *Quest for Refuge: The Mormon Flight from American Pluralism* [Salt Lake City: Signature Books, 1989], 53–54.)

2. A December 1832 revelation promised a "solemn assembly" in which an "endowment" of spiritual power, a day of Pentecost, would be poured out upon faithful "first laborers" in the kingdom. The assembly, to be held upon completion of the Kirtland Temple, was to be preceded by a period of preparation, which would include instruction, ordinances of washing and anointing, and a renewal of personal commitment. The experience was calculated to increase faith and unity and to strengthen participants in their responsibilities and prepare them "to overcome all things." The period between 17 January and 1 May 1836 was one in which spiritual gifts were frequently manifest in various gatherings of the Saints. Joseph Smith said "it was a Pentecost and an endowment indeed, long to be remembered . . . a year of jubilee, and time of rejoicing to the saints of the Most High God." (See D&C 88:70; 105:33; the Joseph Smith journal entries of 12 November 1835, 21 January and 30 March 1836; and Lyndon Cook, *Revelations of the Prophet Joseph Smith*, 182–83; Backman, *The Heavens Resound*, chapter 16; and Karl Ricks Anderson, *Joseph Smith's Kirtland* [Salt Lake City: Deseret Book Company, 1989], chapter 16.)

prophets,[1] and attend to the ordinence of the washing of feet[2] and to prepare the[i]r hearts in all humility for an endowment with power from on high to which they all agreed with one accord, and seamed to be greatly rejoiced may God spare the lives of the twelve with one accord to a good old age for Christ the redeemers sake amen

6 October 1835 · Tuesday

At home ~~father or~~ Elder Stevens[3] came to my house and loaned F G Williams and Co[4] six hundred Dollars which greatly

---

1. To better qualify the elders of the Church for their responsibilities, and to prepare them for the anticipated "solemn assembly," a school known as the "school of the prophets" or "school of the elders" was organized in Kirtland. A December 1832 revelation outlined rules governing the school (D&C 88:118–41). Beginning in 1833, instruction continued during four winter seasons. The 1835–36 session of the school met between 2 November and 29 March. An important part of the school, which generally convened in the printing office, was the study of Hebrew. (Cook, *Revelations of the Prophet*, 185–91; Backman, *The Heavens Resound*, 264–72; Karl Ricks Anderson, *Joseph Smith's Kirtland*, 115–19.)

Heber Kimball noted that four hundred attended the school in the winter of 1835. He wrote, "Some studied grammar and other branches. We also employed the celebrated Hebrew teacher Mr. Seixas, who gave us much insight in a short time, into that language. . . . The Elders and church had been previously commanded to seek learning and study the best books, and get a knowledge of countries, kingdoms, languages &c., which inspired us with an untiring thirst after knowledge." (Heber C. Kimball, "Journal and Record of Heber Chase Kimball an Apostle of Jesus Christ of Latter Day Saints," 34–35, MS.)

2. The revelation that announced the formation of the School of the Prophets in Kirtland stated that candidates for the school were to be received by the ordinance of the washing of feet, a symbol of unity and cleanliness, and to be "clean from the blood of this generation." (D&C 88:138–40; also journal entry of 12 November.)

3. Possibly Jonathan Stevens, who, along with his two sons, Uzziel and Lyman, and his son-in-law, John E. Page, was directed by the Kirtland high council in August 1835 to settle his family in Kirtland and then go forth to preach the gospel. (Kirtland Council Minutes, 24 August 1835.)

4. In 1831 a "literary firm" had been organized to oversee Church publications. Two years later, after the destruction of the Church press in Missouri, Oliver Cowdery established another press in Kirtland, Ohio under the firm name "Frederick G. Williams and Company." 1835 was a busy year for the printing company. The press published the first edition of the Doctrine and Covenants,

releaved us out of our present difficulties may God bless and preserve his soul for ever— Afternoon called to visit my father who was very sick with a fever some better towards evening spent the rest of the day in reading and meditation

7 October 1835 · Wednesday

went to visit my fathe[r] find him very low administered some mild herbs agreeable to the commandment[1] may God grant to restore him immediately to health for christ the redeemers sake Amen This day bro N K Whitney and Bro Hyrum Smith started for buffalo [New York] to purchase good[s] to replenish the committe store[2] by land in the stage may God grant in the name of Jesus that their lives may [p. 5] be spared and they have a safe Journey and no accident or sickness of the least kind befall them that they may return in health and in safety to the bosom of their families—

Blessed of the lord is bro [Newel] Whitney even the bishop of the church of the latter day saints, for the bishoprick shall never be taken away from him while he liveth and the time cometh that he shall overcome all the narrow mindedness of his heart and all his covetous desires that so easily besetteth him and ⟨he⟩ shall deal with a liberal hand to the poor and the needy the sick and the afflicted the widow and the fatherless and marvi[l]ously and miraculously shall the Lord his God provid for him, even that he shall be blessed with ⟨all the ~~the~~⟩ a fullness of the good things of this earth and his seed after him from generation to generation and it shall come to pass

---

and was printing a hymn book and three newspapers, the *Latter Day Saints' Messenger and Advocate, The Northern Times* (a political paper supporting Andrew Jackson), as well as reprinting *The Evening and the Morning Star*, published earlier in Missouri. By October 1835 heavy expenses and minimal returns had brought the company to the brink of collapse. (Cook, *Joseph Smith and the Law of Consecration*, 47–51; Backman, *The Heavens Resound*, 70–71.)

1. See D&C 42:43; 89:10.
2. See note 3, p. 39.

that according to[1] the measure that he meeteth out with a liberal hand unto the poor so shall it be measured to him again by the hand of his God even an hundred fold Angels shall guard ⟨his⟩ house and shall guard the lives of his posterity, and they shall become very great and very numerous on the earth, whomsoever he blesseth they shall be blessed. whomsoever he curseth they shall be cursed. and when his enemies seek him unto his hurt and distruction let him rise up and curse and the hand of God shall be upon his enemies in Judgment [p. 6] they shall be utterly confounded and brought to dessolation, therefor he shall be preserved unto the utmost and his ⟨life⟩ day shall be precious in the sight of the Lord he shall rise up and shake himself as a lion riseth out of his nest and roareth untill he shaketh the hills and as a lion goeth forth among the lesser beasts, so shall the goings forth of him ⟨be⟩ whom the Lord hath anointed to exalt the poor and to humble the rich, therefore his name shall be on high and his rest among the sanctified[2] this afternoon recommenced translating the ancient reccords[3]

/⁴8 October 1835 · Thursday

at home nothing of note transpired of as we now recollect. I attended on my Father with feelings of great anxiety —

9 October 1835 · Friday

at home nothing worthy of note transpired on this day waited on ⟨my Father⟩

---

1. "to" repeated in MS.
2. A handwritten copy of the preceding blessing, probably written at the time, is introduced with these lines: "The following blessing was given by president Joseph Smith, Jr. through the Urim and Thummim, according to the spirit of prophecy and revelation, on Wednesday, the 7th of October, 1835, and written by president Frederick G. Williams, who acted as Clerk."
3. See note 2, p. 45.
4. Handwriting of Warren Parrish to page 38 of the MS.

10 October 1835 · Saturday

at home, visited the house of my Father found ⟨him failing very fast⟩ —

11 October 1835 · Sunday

visited my Father ⟨again⟩ who was verry sick ⟨in secret prayer in the morning the Lord said my servant thy father shall live⟩ I waited on him all this day with my heart raised to god in the name of Jesus Christ that he would restore him to health again, that I might be blessed with his company and advise esteeming it one of the greatest earthly blessings, to be blessed with the society of Parents, whose mature years and experience renders them capable of administering the most wholsom advise; at Evening Bro. David Whitmer came in we called on the Lord in mighty prayer in the name of Jesus Christ, and laid our hands on him, and rebuked the diseas[e] and God heard and answered our prayers to the great Joy and satisfaction of our souls, our aged Father arose and dressed himself shouted and praised the Lord called [p. 7] Br Wm Smith who had retired to rest that he might praise the Lord with us by joining in Songs of praise to the most High

12 October 1835 · Monday

rode to Willoughby in company with my wife to purchase some goods at W[indsor P]. Lyons Store on our return we found a Mr. Bradly lying across the road he had been thrown ~~from~~ from his waggon [and] was much injured by the fall

13 October 1835 · Tuesday

visited my Father who was verry much recovered from his sickness indeed, which caused us to marvel at the might power and condesension of our Heavenly Father in answering our prayers in his behalf

14 October 1835 · Wednesday

at home

15 October 1835 · Thursday

Laboured in Fathers orchard gathering apples

16 October 1835 · Friday

was called into the printing ⟨office⟩ to settle some difficulties in that department, at evening on the same day I baptised Ebenezer Robinson the Lord poured out his spirit on us and we had a good time[1]

17 October 1835 · Saturday

called my family together and aranged my domestick concerns and ~~domestic~~ dismissed my boarders

18 October 1835 · Sunday

attended meeting in the chapel confirmed several who had been baptised[2] and blessed several ~~blessings~~ children with the

---

1. Of his baptism by Joseph Smith, Robinson wrote, "At dinner that day, (Oct. 16, 1835) Joseph Smith, Jr. finished his meal a little before the others at the table, and went and stood in the doorway (the door being open, it being a warm pleasant day,) with his back to the door jamb, when we arose and went and stood before him, and looking him in the face said, 'do you know what I want?' when he replied, 'No, without it is to go into the waters of Jordan.' We told him that was what we wanted, when he said he would attend to it that afternoon. We then went to the printing office together, he to his council room which adjoined the room where we worked, and we to our work in the printing office. We worked until well on to the evening, feeling very anxious all the time, for it seemed that we could not live over night without being baptized; after enduring it as long as we could, went to the door of their room, and gently opened it, (a thing we had never presumed to do before.) As soon as Mr. Smith saw us he said, 'yes, yes, brethren, Brother Robinson wishes to be baptized, we will adjourn and attend to that.' We repaired to the water, (the Chagrin river which flows through Kirtland,), and, after a season of prayer, Brother Joseph Smith, jr., baptized us by immersion." (Ebenezer Robinson, "Items of Personal History of the Editor," *The Return* [Davis City, Iowa] 1:74.)
2. One of those confirmed on 18 October was Ebenezer Robinson.

blessings of the new and everlasting covenant Elder Parley P. Pratt preach[e]d in the fore noon, and Elder John F. Boynton in the after noon, we had an interesting time

19 October 1835 · Monday

at home, exibited the records of[1] antiquity to a number who called to see them

20 October 1835 · Tuesday

at home preached at night in the School-house.

21 October 1835 · Wednesday

at home nothing [p. 8] of note transpired

22 October 1835 · Thursday

at home attending to my domestick concerns

23 October 1835 · Friday

at home ~~attended the prayer meeting~~ ⟨see page 50⟩[2]

24 October 1835 · Saturday

Mr Goodrich and his lady ~~called~~ called to see the antient Records also called at Doct. F G. Williams to see the mummies, Brs. Hawks[3] & Carpent⟨er⟩ from Michigan visited us & taried over Sunday and attended meeting—

---

1. "of" repeated in MS.
2. In the MS. the insertion is written before the date. A prayer offered this day was recorded following the 27 November 1835 diary entry on pages 50–51 of the manuscript. (See p. 90.)
3. Possibly Joseph B. Hawkes (1799–1862), born at Buxton, New York. Family records show him in Pontiac, Oakland County, Michigan, in 1834, and in Far West, Caldwell County, Missouri, in 1836. (Family Group Records Collection.)

25 October 1835 · Sunday

attended meeting President Rigdon preached in the fore noon, Elder Lyman Johnson in the afternoon, after which Elder S. Bronson [Seymour Brunson] joined Br. Wm Perry & Sister Eliza Brown in matrimony, and I blessed them with long life and prosperity in the name of Jesus Christ, at evening I attended Prayer meeting opened it and exorted the brethren & Sister[s] about one hour, the Lord pourd out his spirit and some glorious things were spoken in the gift of toungs, and interp[r]eted concerning the redemption of Zion

26 October 1835 · Monday

went to Chardon to attend the county Court in company with Brs Hyrum Samuel & Carloss Smith, Br. Samuel was called in question before this Court for not doing military duty, and was fined because we had not our conference minuets with us for testimony to prove that F G. Williams was clerk of the conference – this testimony we should have carried with us had it not been for the neglect of our Council, or Lawyer, who did not put us in possession of this information this we feel was a want of fidelity to his client, and we concider it a base insult ⟨practised⟩ upon us on the account of our faith, that the ungodly might have unlawful power over us and trample us under their unhallowed feet; & in consequence of this neglect a fine was imposed on Br Samuel [p. 9] of $20. including costs, for which ~~Lawsuit~~ he was obliged to sell his cow, to defray the expenses of the same, and I say in the name of Jesus Christ that the money that they have thus unjustly taken shall be a testimony against them and canker & eat their flesh as fire[1]

---

1. The Militia Act of 1792 had required the enrollment of every free, white male citizen between the ages of eighteen and forty-five to serve in his state militia. This service required the attendance of each member of the militia, equipped at his own expense, at a muster lasting from one to six days, depending

27 October 1835 · Tuesday

in the morning I was called to visit at Br Samuel Smiths
his wife was confined an⟨d⟩ in a verry dangerous situation, Br.
Carloss [Don Carlos Smith] took one of my horses and went
to Chardon after Doct. [Frederick] Williams I went out into
the field and bowed before the Lord and called upon him in
mighty prayer in her behalf the word of the Lord came unto
me saying my Servant Fredrick shall come and shall have
wisdom given him to deal prudently and my handmaden shall
be delivered of a living child & be spared, he come in a bout
one hour after that and in the course of about 2 hours she was
delivered[1] and thus what God had manifested to me was fulfilled every whit, on the night of the same day I preached in
the School house to a crowded congregation

28 October 1835 · Wednesday

at home[2] attending to my family concerns &c

---

upon the state, for purposes of training. Failure to comply resulted in a fine,
which was the means of enforcing compulsory military service. However, the
law exempted all those employed in conveying the mail, sailors at sea, and "all
persons who now are or may hereafter be exempted by the laws of the respective
states." Most states exempted state and local officials, clergymen, teachers, and
students in college. (U.S., *Statutes at Large*, vol. 1, 264–65, 271–72; William
H. Riker, *Soldiers of the States: The Role of the National Guard in American
Democracy* [Washington, D.C.: Public Affairs Press, 1957], 27–29; Lena London,
"The Militia Fine, 1830–1860," *Military Affairs* 15 [1951]: 133–44; Robert
Reinders, "Militia and Public Order in Nineteenth Century America," *Journal
of American Studies* 11 [April 1977]: 81–101.)

In October 1835 the case of *George Metcalf, Paymaster of the 1st Brigade,
2nd Regiment, 9th Division, Ohio Militia, vs. Samuel H. Smith* came before the
court at Chardon, Geauga County, Ohio. At a court of inquiry held 25 September
1833 Smith had been fined $1.75 for failing to attend company and regimental
musters in 1833. Represented by his attorney, Benjamin Bissel, Samuel Smith
sought dismissal of the charges against him on various technical grounds and
contended that he was a minister of the gospel, and hence not subject to the
military requirement. However, the court sustained the charges against Smith
and ordered him to pay the fine and court costs. (Geauga County, Ohio, Court
of Common Pleas, Final Record, Book S, 95–101.)

1. Susanna Bailey Smith (1835–1905), the first child of Samuel and Mary
Bailey Smith.
2. MS. reads "holm"

29 October 1835 · Thursday

Br W. Parish [Warren Parrish] commenced writing for me. Father & Mother Smith visit[ed] us and while we set writing Bishop Partrige [Edward Partridge] passed our window just returned from the East —[1] Br Parish commenced writing for me at $15.00 pr month I paid him $16.00 in advance out of the committee Store Br Parrish agrees to board himself, for which I agree to ⟨allow him⟩ four Dollars more pr. month making $19.00. I was then called to appear before the high Council which was [p. 10] setting to give my testimony in an action brought against Br. David Eliot for whiping his Daughter unreasonably my testimony was in his favour, returned to our writing room, went to Dr. Williams after my large Journal,[2] made some observations to my Scribe concerning the plan of the City which is to be built up hereafter on this ground consecrated for a stake of Zion[3] while at the Doct[or's] Bishop E Pa[r]trige came in, in company with President Phelps, I was much rejoiced to see him, we examined the mumies, returned

1. In January 1835 Partridge went on a proselyting mission to the eastern states and New England, returning to Kirtland 29 October.

2. The "large Journal" referred to here later became volume A-1 of the manuscript of the *History of the Church*. The involvement of Frederick Williams, Warren Parrish, and Warren A. Cowdery in writing Joseph's "large Journal," its format and content, and its discontinuance and later use for the Church history are described in *The Papers of Joseph Smith* 1: 15, 17, 113–14, 265–66.

3. A discussion of Joseph Smith's master plan for Kirtland is found in Parkin, *Conflict at Kirtland*, 210–12; and Ronald K. Esplin, "The Emergence of Brigham Young and the Twelve to Mormon Leadership," chapter 5.

According to Wilford Woodruff in connection with a later visit to Kirtland, "Joseph presented us in some degree the plot of the city of Kirtland . . . as it was given him by vision. It was great, marvelous and glorious. The city extended to the east, west, north, and south. Steam boats will come puffing into the city. Our goods will be conveyed upon railroads from Kirtland to many places and probably to Zion. Houses of worship would be reared unto the most high. Beautiful streets was to be made for the saints to walk in, Kings of the earth would come to behold the glory thereof, and many glorious things not now to be named would be bestowed upon the saints." (Diary of Wilford Woodruff, 6 April 1837. Published in Scott G. Kenney, ed., *Wilford Woodruff's Journal*. 9 vols. [Midvale, Utah: Signature Books, 1983].)

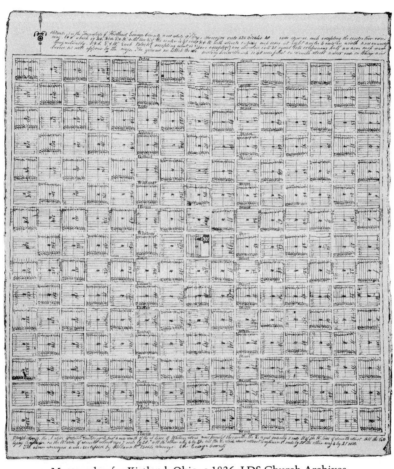

Master plan for Kirtland, Ohio, c.1836. LDS Church Archives.

home and my scribe commenced writing in ⟨my⟩ Journal a history of my life, concluding President Cowdery['s] 2d letter to W. W. Phelps, which president Williams had begun[1] Bishop Whitney & his wife with his Father & Mother[2] called to Visit us, his parents having lately arived here from the East called to make enquiry concerning the coming forth of the book of Mormon, Bishop Partrige & some others came in I then set down and ~~taught~~ ⟨related to⟩ them the history of the coming forth of the book the administration of the Angel to me the rudiments of the gospel of Christ &c they appeared well satisfyed & I expect to baptise them in a few days, or this is my feelings upon the subject altho they have not made any request of this Kind at present, went to the council, the Presidency arose and adjourned on my return Elder Boynton observed that long debates were bad.[3] I replyed that it was generally the case that to[o] much altercation was ~~generally~~ indulged in, on both sides and their debates protracted to an unprofitable length; we were ~~seated~~ called to super, after being seated around the table Bishop Whitney observed to Bishop Partrige that ⟨the⟩ thought had just occured to his mind that perhaps in about one yea[r] from this time they might be seated together around a table ~~in~~ on the land of Zion [p. 11] ~~Sister Emma~~ ⟨my wife⟩ observed that she hoped it might be the case that not only they but the rest of the[4] company present might be seated around her table in the land of promise; the same sentiment was reciprocated from the company round the table and my heart responded amen God grant it, I ask in the name of Jesus Christ, after super I went to the high council in company with my wife and some others that belong to my house hold I was solicited to take a seat with the presidency and preside in a

---

1. See *The Papers of Joseph Smith*, 1:43 for the place referred to.
2. Samuel and Susanna Kimball Whitney, from Marlborough, Vermont.
3. MS.: "had."
4. "of the" repeated in MS.

case of Sister Eliots I did so my Mother was called as testimony and began to relate circumstances that had been brought before the church and settled I objected against such testimony the complainant Br. William Smith arose and accused me of invalidating or doubting my mothers testimony which I had not done nor did I desire to do I told him he was out of place & asked him to set down he refused I repeated my request he become enraged I finally ordered him to set down he said he would not unless I knocked him down I was agitated in my feeling on the account of his stubournness and was about to ~~call~~ leave the house, but my Father requ[e]sted me not to ⟨do so⟩ I complyed[1] the house was brought to order after much debate upon the subject and we proceded to buisness & br. Eliot & his wife were both cleared from the charges prefered against them

30 October 1835 · Friday

at home Mr. Fransis Porter[2] ~~called~~ from Jefferson Co. New York a member of the Methodist Church, called to make some inquiry about lands in this place whether there is any farmes for sale that are valuable and whether [p. 12] a member of our church could move into this vicinity and purchase lands and enjoy his own possessions & property without making it common Stock, he had been requested to do so by some brethren who live in the town of Leroy Jeff[erson] Co N. Y I replyed that I had a valuable farm joining the Temple Lot that I would sell & that there is other lands for sale in this place and that we have no common stock business among us, that every man

---

1. Joseph Smith's volatile younger brother, William, a man of considerable energy and talent, frequently clashed with Joseph and with fellow members of the Quorum of Twelve. His ambition and temperament were inappropriate given his position as younger brother and junior member of the Quorum of Twelve, leading to several serious confrontations.

2. The 1830 Federal Census lists a Francis Porter (in his forties) and his family of eleven, at LeRoy, Jefferson County, New York.

enjoys his own property, or can if he is disposed, consecrate liberally or illiberally to the support of the poor & needy, or the building up of Zion, he also enquired how many members there are in this church I told him that there is about five or six hundred who commune at our chapel and perhaps a thousand in this vicinity; at evening I was presented with a letter from Br. Wm Smith the purport of which is that he is censured by the brethren on the account of what took place at the council last night and wishes to have the matter settled to the understanding of all, that he may not be censured unjustly, concidering that his cause was a just one, and that he had been materially injured; I replied that I thought we parted with the best of feelings, that I am not to blame on the account of the dissatisfaction of others. I invited him to call and talk with me, and that I would ~~give~~ ⟨talk with⟩ him in the spirit of meekness and give him all the satisfaction I could — this reply was by letter copy retained

31 October 1835 · Saturday

in the morning br. Hyram Smith came in and said he had been much troubled all night and had not slept any [p. 13] that something was wrong while talking br. Wm Smith came in according to my requ[e]st last night br. Hyram observed that he must go to the Store I invited him to stay he said he would go and do his business & return he did so while he was gone br. William introduced the subject of our difficulty at the council, I told him I did not want to converse upon the subject untill Hyrum returned, he soon came in I then proposed to relate the occurrences of the council before named and wherein I had been out of the way I would confess it and ask his forgivness, and then he should relate his story and make confession wherein he had done wrong ~~he said he had not done wrong~~ and then leave it to br. Hyrum Smith & br. Parish to decide the matter between us and I would agree to the decission & be satisfyed there with; he observed that he had not done wrong, and that I was always determined to carry my points whether right or wrong and there fore he would not stand an equal chance with me; this was an insult, but I did not reply to him in a harsh manner knowing his inflamatory disposition, but tryed to reason with him and show him the propriety of a complyance with my request, I finally succeeded with the assistance of br. Hyrum in obtaining his assent to the proposition that I had made. I then related my story and wherein I had been wrong I confessed it and asked his forgivness after I got through he made his statements justifying himself throughout in transgressing the order of the council & treating the authority of the Presidency with contempt; after he had got through br. Hyrum began to make [p. 14] some remarks, in the spirit of meekness, he became enraged, I joined my brother in trying to calm his stormy feelings, but to no purpose he insisted that we intended to add abuse to injury, his passion increased, he arose abruptly and declared that he wanted no more to do with ~~them~~ us or the church and said we might take his licence for he would have nothing to do with us, he rushed out at the door we tryed to prevail on him to stop, but all to no purpose, he went away in a passion, and soon sent his licence to me, he went home and spread the levvin of iniquity among my brethren and especially prejudiced the mind of br. Samuel as I soon learned that he was in the street exclaiming against me, which no doubt our enemys rejoice at, and where the matter will end I know not, but I p[r]ay God to forgiv[e] him and th[e]m, and give them humility and repentance, the feelings of my heart I cannot express on this occasion. I can only pray my heavenly Father to open their eyes that they may discover where they stand, that they may extricate themselves from the snare they have fallen into— after dinner I rode out in company with my wife and children, br. carloss & some others, we went to visit br. Roundy & family who live near Willoughby, we had an interesting visit at br. Roundy['s] as soon as I returned I was called upon to baptise Samuel Whitney & his Wife and Daughter[1] after baptism we returned to their house and offered our thanks, in prayer I obtained a testimony that Br. William would return ~~and~~ to the church and repair the wrong he had done [p. 15]

1 November 1835 · Sunday

Verily thus Saith the Lord unto me, his servant Joseph Smith jr min[e] anger is kindle[d] against my servant Reynolds Cahoon because of his iniquities his covetous and dishonest principles in himself and family and he doth not purge them away and set his house in order therefore if he repent not chastisment awaiteth him even as it seemeth good in my sight therefore go and declare unto him these words I went imediately and del[i]vired this message according as the Lord commanded me I called him in & read what the Lord had said concerning him, he acknowledged that it was verily so & expressed much humility—I then went to meeting Elder Carrill [John Corrill] preached a fine discourse, in the afternoon President Phelps continued the servises of the day by reading the 5th chapt. of Mathew also the laws regulating the High Council and made some remarks upon them after which sacrament was administered I then confirmed a number who had been baptised & blessed a number of children in the name of Jesus Christ with the blessings of the new and everlasting covenant, notice was then given that the Elders School[2] wou[l]d commence on the[3] morrow, I then dismissed the meeting.

2 November 1835 · Monday

was engaged in regulating the affairs of the School, I then had my team prepared & Sidney Oliver Frederick ~~and~~ my scribe

---

1. The parents and sister of Newel K. Whitney, who had arrived in Kirtland on 29 October.
2. See note 1, p. 48.
3. "on the" repeated in MS.

and a number of others went to Willoughby to Hear Doct[or] Piexotto [Daniel Peixotto] deliver a lecture on the ~~profession~~ theory & practice of Physic [medicine] [p. 16] we called at Mr. [Nathan] Cushmans, had our horses put in the Stable took dinner, attended the lecture was treated with great respect throughout; returned home Lyman Wight came from Zion to day;[1] — George & Lyman Smith also from the East[2] the question was agitated whether Frederick G. Williams or Oliver Cowdery Should go to New York to make arangements respecting a book bindery they refered to me for a decision, and thus cam[e] the word of the Lord unto me saying it is not my will that my servant Frederick should go to New York, but inasmuch as he wishes to go and visit his relatives that he may warn them to flee the wrath to come let him go and see them, for that purpose and let that be his only business, and behold in this thing he shall be blessed with power ~~while~~ to overcome their prejudices, Verily thus saith the Lord Amen.

3 November 1835 · Tuesday[3]

Thus came the word of the Lord unto me ~~saying~~ concerning the Twelve ⟨saying⟩ behold they are under condemnation, because they have not been sufficiently humble in my sight, and in consequence of their covetous desires, in that they have not dealt equally with each other in the division of the moneys which came into their hands, never⟨the⟩less some of them dealt equally therefore they shall be rewarded, but verily I say unto

---

1. Wight had left Missouri in September 1835 and arrived in Kirtland, Ohio, on 2 November to attend the School of the Prophets.

2. On 5 June 1835 George A. and his second cousin, Lyman Smith, had been sent on a proselyting mission: "We traveled about two thousand miles on foot, without purse or scrip, through the eastern part of Ohio, the western part of Pennsylvania and New York; held about eighty meetings, baptized eight, and preached from house to house continually." The two missionaries arrived back in Kirtland on 2 November. ("Sketch of the Autobiography of George Albert Smith," *Deseret News*, 18 August 1858.)

3. MS. reads "~~Thus came~~ Tuesday 3d."

you they must all humble themselves before me, before they will be accounted worthy to receive an endowment to go forth in my name unto all nations, as for my Servant William let the Eleven humble themselves in prayer and in faith [p. 17] and wait on me in patience and my servant William shall return, and I will yet make him a polished shaft in my quiver, in bringing down the wickedness and abominations of men and their shall be none mightier than he in his day and generation, nevertheless if he repent not spedily he shall be brought low and shall be chastened sorely for all his iniquities he has commited against me. nevertheless the sin which he hath sined against me is not even now more grevious than the sin with which my servant David W. Patten and my servant Orson Hyde and my servant Wm E. McLellen have sinned[1] against me, and the residue are not sufficiently humble before me, behold the parable which I spake concerning a man having twelve Sons,[2] for what man amon[g] you having twelve Sons and is no respecter to them and they serve him obediantly and he saith[3] unto the one be thou clothed in robes and sit thou here, and to the other be thou clothed in rags[4] and sit thou there, and looketh upon his sons and saith I am just, ye will answer and say no man, and ye answer truly, therefore Verely thus saith the Lord your God I appointed these twelve that they should be equal in their ministry and in their portion and in their evangelical rights, wherefore they have sin[n]ed a verry grevious sin, in asmuch as they have made themselves unequal and have not hearkned unto my voice therfor let them repent speedily and prepare their hearts for the solem[n] assembly [p. 18] and for the great day which is to come Verely thus saith the Lord Amen.[5]

---

1. MS.: "sinded"
2. D&C 38:26.
3. "saith" written over "sayeth" in MS.
4. MS.: "rages"
5. At the time this revelation was given, the Twelve had served together as

I then went to assist in organizing the Elders School called to order and I made some remarks upon the object of this School, and the great necessity there is of our rightly improving our time and reigning up our minds to ~~the~~ a sense of the great object that lies before us, viz, that glorious endowment that God has in store for the faithful I then dedicated the School in the name of the Lord Jesus Christ. after the School was dismissed I attended a patriarchal meeting at Br Samuel Smiths, his wifeses parents[1] were blessed also his child & named Susanah, at evening I preach[e]d at the School-house to a crowded congregation

4 November 1835 · Wednesday

in morning, at home attended school ~~all~~ during the school hours, made rapid progress in our studies, in the evening, lectured on grammar, at home on this day King Follet arived at this place from Zion

5 November 1835 · Thursday

attended School ~~all day~~ Isaac Morley came in from the east[2] this morning I was called to visit Thomas Burdick who was sick, I took my scribe with me and we p[r]ayed for and laid our hands on him in the ⟨name⟩ of the Lord Jesus and rebuked his affliction — Wm E. McLellen & Orson Hyde came in and desired to hear the revelation concerning the Twelve, my scribe read to ~~him~~ them they expressed some little dis-

---

a quorum less than ten months. Ronald K. Esplin has noted, "This was a collection of individuals not yet molded into a unit and often without a clear view of its role and purpose. Neither tradition nor precedent defined for them their mission or suggested how they accomplish it. Scriptural models and [Joseph] Smith's instructions provided guidelines, but the precise bounds of their authority and methods of their work could only be the product of shared experiences." (Esplin, "The Emergence of Brigham Young and the Twelve," 151. For a more detailed discussion of the context of the revelation see his entire chapter 4.)

1. Joshua Bailey and Hannah Boutwell Bailey.
2. See entry of 7 November 1835.

satisfaction but after examining their own hearts, they acknowledged it to be the word of the Lord [p. 19] and said they
were satisfied;[1] after School Brigham Young came in and desired also to hear, it read ~~also~~ after hearing it he appeared
perfectly satisfied; in the evening lectured on Grammar

6 November 1835 · Friday

at home. attended School during the school hours returned
and spent the evening at home I was this morning introduced
to a man from the east, after hearing my name he ~~replied~~
remarked that I was nothing but a man: indicating by this
expression that he had supposed that a person, ⟨to⟩ whom the
Lord should see fit to reveal his will, must be something more
than a man, he seems to have forgotten the saying that fell
from the lips of St. James, that Elias was a man of like passions
like unto us, yet he had such power with God that He in answer
to his prayer, shut the heavens that they gave no rain for the
space of three years and six months, and again in answer to
his prayer the heavens gave forth rain and the earth brought
forth fruit;[2] and indeed such is the darkness & ignorance of
this generation that they look upon it as incredible that a man
should have any intercourse with his Maker.

7 November 1835 · Saturday

spent the day at home attending to my domestic concerns;
The word ⟨of the Lord⟩ came to me saying, behold I am well
pleased with my servant Isaac Morley and my servant Edward
Partridge, because of the integrity of their harts in laboring in
my vinyard for the salvation of the souls of men,[3] Verely I say

---

1. See entry of 3 November 1835.
2. James 5:17–18.
3. Partridge and Morley had been sent on a proselyting mission in the East
in May 1835. They had left Kirtland on 2 June and returned in late October
having baptized three and preached eighteen times.

unto you their sins are [p. 20] forgiven them, therefore say unto them in my name that it is my will that they should tarry for a little season and attend the school, and also the solem assembly for a wise purpose in me, even so amen

8 November 1835 · Sunday

went to meeting in the morning at the us[u]al hour, Z[erubbabel]. Snow preached a verry interesting discourse, in the after noon J[oseph]. Young preached; after preaching Isaac Hill came forward to make some remarks by way of confession, he had been previously excommunicated from the church for lying & for an attempt to seduce a female; his confession was not satisfactory to my mind ⟨Uncle⟩ John Smith arose and made some remarks respecting the dealings of the high council on the case of said Hill, that is that he should make a public confession of his crime and have it published in the messenger and Advocate, he proposed that Mr Hill should now make his confession before the congregatio⟨n⟩ and then immediately observed that he had forgiven Mr Hill, which was in contradiction to the sentiment he first advanced, this I attributed to an error in Judgment not in design President Rigdon then arose and verry abruptly militated against ⟨the sentiment of⟩ Uncle John, which had a direct tendency to destroy his influence and bring him into disrepute in the eyes of the church, which was not right, he also misrepresented Mr Hills case ~~wh~~ and spread darkness rather than light upon the subject a vote ~~was then called~~ of the church was then called on his case and he was restored without any further confession; that he should [p. 21] be received into the church by babtism which was administered acordingly. after I came home I took up a labour with uncle John and convinced him that he was wrong & he made his confession to my satisfaction; I then went and laboured with President Rigdon and succeded in convincing him also of his error which he confessed to my satisfaction.

The word of the Lord cam[e] unto me saying that President Phelps & President J[ohn]. Whitmer are under condemnation before the Lord, for their errors ⟨for which they made satisfaction the same day⟩;[1] I also took up a labour with John Carrill [Corrill] for ~~leaving the meeting before~~ ⟨not partaking of the⟩ sacrament, he made his confession; also my wife for ~~the same~~ leaving the meeting before sacrament she made no reply, but manifested contrition by weeping

9 November 1835 · Monday

after breckfast ~~Sister~~ ⟨Mary⟩ Whitcher came in and wished to see me, ~~she~~ I granted her request she gave a relation of her griveances which were, unfathonable at present, and if true sore indeed, and I pray my heavenly Father to bring the truth of her case to light, that the reward due to evil doers may be given them, and ⟨that⟩ the afflicted & oppressed may be delivered; — while setting in my house between the hours of ten & 11 this morning a man came in, and introduced himself to me, calling ⟨himself⟩ by the name of Joshua the Jewish minister [Robert Matthias], his appearance was some thing singular, having a beard about 3 inches in length which is quite grey, also his hair is long and considerably silvered with age [p. 22] I should think he is about 50 or 55 years old, tall and strait slender built of thin visage blue eyes, and fair complexion, he wears a sea green frock coat, & pantaloons of the same, black fur hat with narrow brim, and while speaking frequently shuts his eyes with a scowl on his countinance: I made some enquiry after his name but received no definite answer; we soon commenced talking upon the subject of religion and after I had made some remarks concerning the bible I commenced giving him a relation of the circumstances connected with the coming forth of the book of Mormon, as follows — being wrought up

---

1. This insertion, in the hand of William W. Phelps, was probably added at a time later than the surrounding text.

in my mind, respecting the subject of religion and looking at[1] the different systems taught the children of men, I knew not who was right or who was wrong and I considered[2] it of the first importance that I should be right, in matters that involve eternal consequ[e]nces; being thus perplexed in mind I retired to the silent grove and bow[e]d down before the Lord, under a realising sense that he had said (if the bible be true) ask and you shall receive knock and it shall be opened seek and you shall find and again, if any man lack wisdom let him ask of God who giveth to all men libarally and upbradeth not; information was what I most desired at this time, and with a fixed determination to obtain it, I called upon the Lord for the first time, in the place above stated or in other words I made a fruitless attempt to p[r]ay, my toung seemed to be swolen in my mouth, so that I could not utter, I heard a noise behind me like some person walking towards me, I strove again to pray, but could not, the noise of walking seemed to draw nearer, I sprung up on my feet, and [p. 23] and looked around, but saw no person or thing that was calculated to produce the noise of walking, I kneeled again my mouth was opened and my toung liberated, and I called on the Lord in mighty prayer, a pillar of fire appeared above my head, it presently rested down upon me[3] head, and filled me with Joy unspeakable, a personage appeard in the midst of this pillar of flame which was spread all around, and yet nothing consumed, another personage soon appeard like unto the first, he said unto me thy sins are forgiven thee, he testifyed unto me that Jesus Christ is the Son of God; ⟨and I saw many angels in this vision⟩ I was about 14 years old when I received this first communication; When I was about 17 years old I saw another vision of angels in the night season after I had retired to bed I had not been a

---

1. "at" written over "upon" in MS.
2. "I considered" written over "considering" in MS.
3. "me" written over "my" in MS.

sleep, ~~when~~ but was meditating upon my past life and experience, I was verry concious that I had not kept the commandments, and I repented hartily for all my sins and
transgression, and humbled myself before Him ⟨whose eyes are
over all things⟩, all at once the room was iluminated above the
brightness of the sun an angel appeared before me, his hands
and feet were naked pure and white, and he stood between the
floors of the room, clothed with ~~in~~ purity inexpressible, he said
unto me I am a messenger sent from God, be faithful and keep
his commandments in all things, he told me of a sacred record
which was written on plates of gold, I saw in the vision the
place where they were deposited, he said the Indians were the
literal descendants of Abraham he explained many ~~things~~ of
the prophesies to [p. 24] me, one I will mention which is ~~this~~
in Malachi 4 chapt. behold the day of the Lord cometh &c.
also that the Urim and Thumim, was hid up with the record,
and that God would give me powre to translate it, with the
assistance of this instrument he then gradually vanished out
of my sight, or the vision closed, while meditating on what I
had seen, the angel appeard to me again and related the same
things and much more, also the third time bearing the same
tidings, and departed; during the time I was in this vision I
did not realize any thing ~~else~~ around me except what was
shown me in this communication: after the vision had all
passed, I found that it was nearly day-light, the family soon
arose, I got up also: — on that day while in the field at work
with my Father he asked me if I was sick I replyed, I had but
little strenght, he told me to go to the house, I started and
went part way and was finally deprived ~~deprived~~ of my strength
and fell, but how long I remained I do not know; the Angel
came to me again and commanded me to go and tell my Father,
what I had seen and heard, I did so, he wept and told me that
it was a vision from God to attend to it I went and found the
place, where the plates were, according to the direction of the
Angel, also saw them, and the angel as before; the powers of

darkness strove hard against me. I called on God, the Angel told me that the reason why I could not obtain the plates at this time was because I was under transgression, but to come again in one year from that time, I did so, but did not obtain them [p. 25] also the third and the fourth year, at which time I obtained them, and translated them into the english language, by the gift and power of God and have been preaching it ever since.

While I was relating this brief history of the establishment of the Church of Christ in these last days, Joshua seemed to be highly entertained after I had got through I observed that, the hour of worship & time to dine had now arived and invited him to tarry, which he concented to,

After dinner the conversation was resumed and Joshua proceded to make some remarks on the prophesies, as follows:

He observed that he was aware that I could bear stronger meat than many others, therefore he should open his mind the more freely:— Daniel has told us that he is to stand in his proper lot, in the latter days according to his vision he had a right to shut it up and also to open it again after many days, or in the latter times; Daniels Image[1] whose head was gold, and body, armes, legs and feet was composed of the different materials described in his vision represents different governments, the golden head was ⟨to represent⟩ Nebuchadnazer King of Babylon, the other parts other kings & forms of government, which I shall not now mention in detail, but confine my remarks, more particularly to the feet of the Image: The policy of the wicked spirit, is to separate what God has joined togather and unite what He has separated, which he has succeded in doing to admiration, in the present state of society, which is like unto Iron and clay, there is confusion in all things, both [p. 26] both Political and religious, and notwithstanding all the efforts that are made to bring about a union, society re-

---

1. Daniel 2.

mains disunited, and all attempts to ⟨unite her⟩ are as fruitless, as to attemp[t] to unite Iron & Clay.

The feet of the Image, is the government of these united States, other Nations & Kingdoms are looking up to her, for an example, of union fre[e]dom and equal rights, and therefore worship her, like as Daniel saw in the vision, although they are begining to loose confidence in her, seeing the broils and discord that distract, her political & religious horizon; this Image is characteristic of all governments and institutions or most of them; as they begin with a head of gold and terminate in the contemp[t]ible feet of Iron & clay: making a splendid appcarancc at first, proposing to do much more than the[y] can perform, and finally end in degradation and sink, in infamy; we should not only start to com[e] out of Babylon but leav[e] it entirely lest we are overthrown in her ruins, we should keep improving and reforming; twenty-four hours for improvement now, is worth as much as a year, a hundred years ago; the spirit of the Fathers that was cut down, or those that were under the altar, are now rising, this is the first resurection the Elder that falls first, will rise last; we should not form any opinion only for the present, and leave the result of futurity with God: I have risen up out of obscurity, but was looked up to when but a youth, in temporal things: It is not necessary that God should give us all things at first or in his first commission to us, but in his second. John saw the angel deliver the gospel in the last days,[1] which would not be necessary if [p. 27] it was already, in the world, this expression would be inconsistent, the small lights that God has given, is sufficient to lead us out of babylon, when we get out we shall have the greater light. I told Jo[s]hua that I did not understand him concerning the resurection and wishd him to be more explanitory on the subject; he replied that he did not feell impressed

---

1. Revelation 14:6.

by the spirit to unfold it further at present, but perhaps he might at some other time.

I then withdr[e]w to do some buisness with another gentleman that called to see me. He [Joshua] informed my Scribe that he was born in Washington County Town of Cambridge New York. he says that all the railroads canals and other improvements are performed by spirits of the resurection.

The silence spoken of by John the Revelator which is to be in heaven for the space of half an hour,[1] is between 1830 & 1851, during which time the judgments of God will be poured out after that time there will be peace.

Curiosity to see a man that was reputed to be a Jew, caused many to call during the day and more particularly at evening Suspicions were entertained that said Joshua was the noted [Robert] Mathias of New York, spoken so much of in the public prints on account of the trials he underwent in that place before a court of justice, for murder manslaughter comtempt of court whiping his Daughter &c for the two last crimes he was imprisoned, and came out about 4 months [p. 28] since, after some, equivocating he confessed that he was realy Mathias: after supper I proposed that he should deliver a lecture to us, he did so sitting in his chair; he commenced by saying God said let there be light and there was light, which he dwelt upon through his discource, he made some verry exelent remarks but his mind was evidently filled with darkness, after he dismissed his meeting, and the congregation disperced, he conversed freely upon the circumstances that transpired in New York. His name is Robert Mathias, he say[s] that Joshua, is his priestly name.

During all this time I did not contradict his sentiments, wishing to draw out all that I could concerning his faith; the next morning

---

1. Revelation 8:1.

10 November 1835 · Tuesday

I resumed the conversation and desired him to enlighten my mind more on his views respecting the resurection, he says that he posses[ses] the spirit of his fathers, that he is a litteral decendant of Mathias the Apostle that was chosen in the place of Judas that fell[1] and that his spirit is resurected in him, and that this is the way or schem[e] of eternal life, this transmigration of soul or spirit from Father to Son: I told him that his doctrine was of the Devil that he was in reality in possession of [a] wicked and depraved spirit, although he professed to be the spirit of truth, itself, ⟨& he said⟩ also that he possesses the soul of Christ; he tarried until Wednesday 11th, after breckfast I told him, that my God told me that his God is the Devil, and I could not keep him any longer, and he must depart, and so I for once cast out the Devil in bodily shape, & I believe a murderer [p. 29] on monday th[e] 9th Mr. Beeman [Alvah Beman] of N. Y came here to ask advice of me concerning purchasing lands, whether it is best for him to purchase in this vicinity and move into this church, or not, he says that he cannot arrange his buisness so as to go to the Missouri next spring; I advised him to come here, and settle untill he could move to Zion

11 November 1835 · Wednesday

at home attended School during school Hours, returned home and spent the evening, around my fire-side, teaching my family the science of grammar; it commensed snowing this afterno[o]n, the wind is verry heavy indeed

12 November 1835 · Thursday

attended School again, during school Hours, rain & snow is still falling, it is about one inch in dept[h], the wind is verry

---

1. Acts 1:15–26.

heavy, and the weather extremly unpleasant, the labour[er]s who commenced finishing the out side of the ~~house~~ Chappel[1] were oblieged to brake off from their buisness at the commencement of this storm viz on the 11th they commenced plasturing and finishing the outside on monday the 2. Inst. this job is let to A[rtemus]. Millet & L[orenzo] Young, ⟨at $1,000⟩ they have progressed rapidly since they commenced.

J[acob]. Bump has the job of plastering the inside of the house through out at $15.00, he commenced on Monday the 9th and is continueing it notwithstanding the inclemency of the weather. This evening viz the 12th at 6 oclock met[2] with the council of 12. by their request, 9 of them were present [p. 30] council opened by singing & prayer, and I made some remarks as follows: — I am happy in the enjoyment of this opportunity of meeting with this council on this occasion, I am satisfyed that the spirit of the Lord is here, and I am satisfied with all the breth[r]en present, and I need not say that you have my utmost confidence, and that I intend to uphold, you to the uttermost, for I am well aware that you ~~do and delight in so doing~~ have to sustain my character ~~my character~~ against the vile calumnies and reproaches of this ungodly generation and that you delight in so doing: — darkness prevails, at this time as it was, at the time Jesus Christ was about to be crucified, the powers of darkness strove to obscure the glorious sun of righteousness that began to dawn upon the world, and was soon to burst in great blessings upon the heads of the faithful, and let me tell you brethren that great blessings awate us at this time and will soon be poured out upon us if we are faithful in all things, for we are even entitled to greater blessings than they were, because the[y] had the person of Christ with them, to instruct them in the great plan of salvation, his personal presence we have not, therefore we need great faith on

---

1. I.e., the temple.
2. MS.: "meet"

account of our peculiar circumstances and I am determined to do all that I can to uphold you, although I may do many things ⟨inadvertently[1]⟩ that are not right in the sight of God; you want to know many things that are before you, that you may know how ~~how~~ to prepare your selves for the [p. 31] great things that God is about to bring to pass; but there is on[e] great deficiency or obstruction, in the way that deprives us of the greater blessings, and in order to make the foundation of this church complete and permanent, we must remove this obstruction, which is to attend to certain duties that we have not as yet attended to; I supposed I had established this church on a permanent foundation when I went to the Missouri and indeed I did so, for if I had been taken away it would have been enough, but I yet live, and therefore God requires more at my hands: — The item to which I wish the more particularly to call your attention to night is the ordinance of washing of feet, this we have not done as yet but it is necessary now as much as it was in the days of the Saviour, and we must have a place prepared, that we may attend to this ordinance, aside from the world; we have not desired much from the hand of the Lord, with that faith and obediance that we ought, yet we have enjoyed great blessings, and we are not so sensible of this as we should be: when or wher[e] has God suffered one of the witnesses or first Elders of this church to fall? never nor nowhere amidst all the calamities and judgments that have befallen the inhabitants of the earth his almighty arm has sustained us, men and Devils have raged and spent the[ir] malice in vain. [p. 32] we must have all things prepared and call our solem assembly as the Lord has commanded us, that we may be able to accomplish his great work: and it mu[s]t be done in Gods own way, the house of the Lord must be prepared, and the solem assembly called and organized in it according to the order of the house of God and in it we must attend to

---

1. MS.: "invertarilly"

the ordinance of washing of feet; it was never intended for any but official members, it is calculated to unite our hearts, that we may be one in feeling and sentiment and that our faith may be strong, so that satan cannot over throw us, nor have any power over us, — the endowment you are so anxious about you cannot comprehend now, nor could Gabriel explain it to the understanding of your dark minds, but strive to be prepared in your hearts, be faithful in all things that when we meet in the solem assembly that is such as God shall name out of all the official members, will meet, and we must be clean evry whit, let us be faithful and silent brethren, ⟨and⟩ if God gives you a manifestation, keep it to yourselves, be watchful and prayerful, and you shall have a prelude of those joys that God will pour out on that day, do not watch for iniquity in each other if you do you will not get an endowment for God will not bestow it on such; but if we are faithful and live by every word that procedes forth from the mouth of God I will venture to prophesy that we shall get a [p. 33] blessing that will be worth remembering if we should live as long as John the Revelator, our blessings will be such as we have not realized before, nor in this generation. The order of the house of God has and ever will be the same, even after Christ comes, and after the termination of the thousand years it will be the same, and we shall finally roll into the celestial Kingdom of God and enjoy it forever: — you need an endowment brethren in order that you may be prepared and able to over come all things, and those that reject your testimony will be damned the sick will be healed the lame made to walk the deaf to hear and the blind to see through your instrumentality; But let me tell you that you will not have power after the endowment to heal those who have not faith, nor to benifit them, for you might as well expect to benefit a devil in hell as such an one, who is possessed of his spirit and are willing to keep it for they are habitations for devils and only fit for his society but when you are endowed and prepared to preach the gospel to all nations kindred and

77

toungs in there own languages you must faithfully warn all and bind up the testimony and seal up the law and the destroying angel will follow close at your heels and execute his tremendeous mission upon the children of disobediance, and destroy [p. 34] the workers of iniquity, while the saints will be gathered out from among them and stand in holy places ready to meet the bride groom when he comes. —

I feel disposed to speak a few words more to you my brethren concerning the endowment, all who are prepared and are sufficiently pure to abide the presence of the Saviour will see him in the solem assembly.

The brethren expressed their gratifycation for the instruction I had given them, we then closed by prayer. — I then returned home and retired to rest

13 November 1835 · Friday

attended school during school hours, returned home after School; Mr Messenger[1] of Bainbridge Chenango Co. N[ew]. Y[ork]. came in to make some enquiry about H[ezekiah]. Peck's family he is a Universalian minister we entered into conversation upon religious subjects, we went to President Rigdon's and spent the evening in conversation, we preachd the gospel to him, and bore testimony to him of what we had seen and heard, he attempted to raise some objections but the force of truth bore him down, and he was silent, although unbelieving; returned home and retired to rest

14 November 1835 · Saturday

Thus came the word of the Lord unto me saying: verily thus saith the the Lord unto my servant Joseph concerning

---

1. Possibly William Messenger, born at Linklean, Chenango County, who was a merchant in South Otselic, Chenango County, New York in 1830–34. By 1841 he was a trustee in the Methodist Episcopal Church at Linklean. (James Hadden Smith, *History of Chenango and Madison Counties, New York* [Syracuse, 1874], 477, 487.)

my servant Warren [Parrish] behold [p.35] his sins are forgiven him because of his desires to do the works of righteousness therefore in as much as he will continue to hearken unto my voice he shall be blessed with wisdom and with a sound mind even above his fellows, behold it shall come to pass in his day that he shall ⟨see⟩ great things shew forth themselves unto my people, he shall see much of my ancient records, and shall know of hiden things, and shall be endowed with a knowledge of hiden languages, and if he desires and shall seek it at my hand, he shall be privileged with writing much of my word, as a scribe unto me for the benefit of my people, therefore this shall be his calling until I shall order it otherwise in my wisdom and it shall be said of him in a time to come, behold Warren the Lords Scribe, for the Lords Seer whom he hath appointed in Israel: Therefore ⟨if he will⟩ keep my commandments he shall be lifted up at the last day, even so Amen

A Gentleman called this after noon by the name of Erastus Holmes of Newbury Clemon [Newberry, Clermont] Co. Ohio, he called to make enquiry about the establishment of the church of the latter-day Saints and to be instructed more perfectly in our doctrine &c I commenced and gave him a brief relation of my experience while in my [p. 36] juvenile years, say from 6 years old up to the time I received the first visitation of Angels which was when I was about 14. years old and also the[1] visitations that I received afterward, concerning the book of Mormon, and a short account of the rise and progress of the church, up to this, date he listened verry attentively and seemed highly gratified, and intends to unite with the Church he is a verry candid man indeed and I am much pleased with him.

15 November 1835 · Sunday

he went with me to meeting, which was held in the School-house on account of the Chappel not being finished plastering.

---

1. "the" repeated in MS.

President Rigdon preached on the subject of men's being called to preach the gospel and their qualifications &c we had a fine discourse it was verry interesting indeed. Mr. Holmes was well satisfied, he came home with me and dined.

Said Holmes has been a member of the Methodist Church, and was excommunicated for receiving, the Elders of the church of the latter-day Saints into his house

Went to meeting in the afternoon, before partaking of the sacrament Isaac Hills case was agitated again, and settled after much controversy, and he retained in the church by making an humble acknowled[g]ement before the church, and concenting to have his confession published in the Messenger and advocate, after which the ordinance of the Lord['s] Supper was administered, and the meeting closed, verry late, — returned home and spent the evening. — [p. 37]

16 November 1835 · Monday

at home, dictated a letter for the Advocate,[1] also one to Harvey Whitlock. Father [Alvah] Beeman called to council with me Elder [Elial] Strong and some others

/[2]Copy of the Letter from Harvey Whitloc[k]

Dear sir having a few leisure moment[s] I have at last concluded to do what my own Judgment has long dictated would be right but the allurements of many vices has long retarded the hand, that would wield the pen to make intelligent the communication that I wish to send to you: And even now that ambition which is a prevaling and predominent principles among the great mass of natural men even now forbids that plainness of sentiment with which I wish to ~~unbosom my feelings~~ write. For know assuredly sir to you I wish to unbosom my feelings, and unravil the secrets of my heart: as before the omnicient Judge of all the earth.

---

1. See note 1, p. 46.
2. Handwriting of Frederick G. Williams.

Be not surprised when I declare unto you, as the spirit will bear record that my faith is firm and unshaken in the things of the everlasting gospel as it is proclaimed by the servants of the latter-day saint[s].

Dear brother Joseph (If I may be allowed the expression) when I considder the happy times and peaseful moments, and pleasant seasons I have enjoyed with you, ~~and~~ and this people; contrasted with my now degraded state; together with the high, and important station I have held before [p. 38] God: and the abyss into which I have fallen, is a subject that swells /[1] my heart to big for utterance, and language is overwhelmed with feeling, and looses its power of description. and as I desire to know the will of God concerning me; Believing it is my duty to make known unto you my real situation.

I shall therefore, dispasionately procede to give a true and untarnished relation; I need not tell you that in former times, I have preached the word; and endeavored to be instant in season [and] out of season, to reprove rebuke exhort and faithfully to discharge that trust reposed in me. But oh! with what grief & lamentable sorrow and anguish do I have to relate that I have fallen, from that princely station where unto our God has called me. Reasons why are unnecessary. May the fact suffice; and believe me when I tell you, that I have sunk myself, (since my last separation from this boddy) in crimes of the deepest dye, and that I may the better enable you to understand what my real sins are, I will mention (although pride forbids it) some that I am not guilty of, my ⟨hands⟩ have not been stained with inocent blood; neither have I lain couched around the cottages of my fellow men to seize and carry off the booty; nor have I slandered my neighbor, nor bourn fals testimony, nor taken unlawful hire, nor oppressed the widdow nor fatherless, neither have I persecuted the Saints. But my hands are swift to do iniquity, and my feet are fast running in the

---

1. Handwriting of Warren Parrish to page 87 of the MS.

paths of vice and folly; and my heart [p. 39] quick to devise wicked imaginations: nevertheless I am impressed with the sure thought that I am fast hastning into a ~~whole~~ world of disembodied beings, without God & with but one hope in the world; which is to know that to er[r] is human, but to forgive is divine: much I might say in relation to myself and the original difficulties with the church, which I will forbear, and in asmuch as I have been charged with things that I was not guilty of I am now more than doubly guilty. and am now willing to forgive and forget only let me know that I am within the reach of mercy; If I am not I have no reflections to cast, but say that I have sealed my own doom and pronounced my own sentence. If the day is passed by with me may I here beg leave to entreat of those who are still toiling up the ruged assent to make their way to the realms of end less felicity, and delight, to stop not for anchors here below, follow not my example. but steer your course onward in spite of all the combined powers of earth and hell, for know that one miss step here is only retrievable by a thousand groans and tears before God. Dear Brother Joseph, let me entreat you on the reception of this letter, as you regard the salvation of my soul, to enquire at the hand of the Lord in my behalf; for I this day in the presence of God, do covenant to abide the word that may be given, for I am willing to receive any [p. 40] chastisement that the Lord sees I deserve.

Now hear my prayer and suffer me to break forth in the agony of my soul. O ye Angels! that surround the throne, ⟨of God⟩ Princes of heaven, that excell in strength, ye who are clothed with transcendant brightness, plead O plead for one of the most wretched of the sons of men. O ye heavens! whose azure arches rise immensely high and strech immeasurably wide, grand ampitheater of nature, throne of the eternal God bow to hear the prayer of a poor wretched bewildered way wanderer to eternity. O thou great Omnicient & omnipresent Jehovah, thou who siteth upon the throne, before whom all things are present, thou maker moulder & fashioner of all things visible and invisable breath o breath into the ears of thy servant the Prophet, words suitably adapted, to my case, and situation, speak once more, make known thy will concerning me, which favours I ask in the name of the Son of God Amen

N.B I hope you will not let any buisiness prevent you from answering this letter in hast[e]

Yours Respectfully
Harvey Whitlock

to Joseph Smith [p. 41]

Copy of a Letter sent Harvy Whitlock in answer to his
Kirtland Nov. 16th 1835

Bro Harvey Whitlock

I have received your letter of the 28th Sept. 1835, and I have read it twice, and it gave me sensations that are better imagined than discribed; let it suffice, that I say the verry floodgates of my heart were broken up: I could not refrain from weeping. I thank God, that it has entered into your heart, to try to return to the Lord, and to his people; if it so be, that he will have mercy upon you.

I have inquired of the Lord concerning your case, these words came to me

Verily thus saith the Lord unto you: let him who was my servant Harvey, return unto me; — and unto the bosom of my Church, and forsake all the sins wherewith he has offended against me and persue from hence forth a virtuous and upright life, and remain under the direction of those whom I have appointed to be pillars, and heads of my church, and behold, saith the Lord, your God; his sins shall be blotted out from under heaven, and shall be forgotten from among men, and shall not come up in mine ears, nor be recorded as ⟨a⟩ memorial against him, but I will lift [p.42] him up as out of deep mire, and he shall be exalted upon the high places, and shall be counted worthy to stand ammong princes, and shall yet be made a polished shaft in my quiver, of bringing down the strong holds of wickedness, among those who set themselves up on high, that they may take council against me, and against annointed ones in the last days.

Therefore let him prepare himself speedily and come unto you; even to Kirtland and inasmuch as he shall harken unto all your council from henceforth he shall be restored unto his former state, and shall be saved unto the uttermost, even as the Lord your God livith Amen.

Thus you see my dear Brother the willingness of our heavenly Father to forgive sins and restore to favour all those who are willing to humble themselves before him, and confess their sins and forsake them, and return to him with full purpose of heart (acting no hypocrisy) to serve him to the end.

Marvle not that the Lord has condescended to speak from the heavens and give you instructions whereby you may learn your duty: he has heard your prayers, and witnessed your humility; and holds forth the hand of paternal affection, for your return; the angels rejoice over you, while the saints are willing to receive you again into fellowship.

I hope on the recept of this, you will ~~not~~ loose ~~any~~ no time in coming to [p. 43] Kirtland: for if you get here in season, you will have the privilege of attending the School of the prophets, which has already commenced and, also receive instruction in doctrine, and principle, from those whom God has appointed whereby you may be qualified to go forth, and declare the true doctrines of the Kingdom according to the ~~true doctrines of the~~ mind and, will of God. and when you come to Kirtland, it will be explained to you why God has condescended to give you a revelation according to your request.

Please give my respects to you[r] family, and bee assured I am yours in the bonds of the new and everlasting covenant

Joseph Smith Jun

on this evening, viz the 16th [November 1835] a council was called at my house to council with ~~Father~~ Alva Beeman on the subject of his mooving to the Missourie; I had previously told him that the Lord had said that he had better go to the Missourie, next Spring: however he wished a council, called, the council met President D[avid]. Whitmer arose and said the spirit manifested to him that it was his duty to go; also others bore the same testimony.

The same night ~~that~~ I received the word of the Lord on Mr. H[o]lmes case, he had desired that I would inquire at the hand of the Lord whether it was [p. 44] his duty to be baptised here, or wait until he returned home: — The word of the Lord came unto me saying, that Mr. Holmes had better not be baptised here, and that he had better not return by water, also that there were three men that were seeking his destruction, to be ware of his ene[m]ys

17 November 1835 · Tuesday

exibited ⟨the Alphabet⟩ ~~some~~ of the ancient records to Mr. Holmes and some others, went with him to F G. Williams to see the Mumies, we then took the parting hand, and he started for home, being strong in the faith of the gospel of Christ and determined to obey the requirements of the same.

I returned home and spent the day dictating and comparing letters.

This has been a fine pleasant day although cool, this Evening at early candlelight I pr[e]ached at the School house, returned home and retired to rest,

18 November 1835 · Wednesday

at home in the fore noon, untill about 11 oclock. I then went to Preserved Harris's, to preach his fathers[1] funeral Ser-

---

1. Nathan Harris (1758–1835).

mon, by the request of the family I preached on the subject
of the resurection, the congregation were verry attentive My
wife my mother and my scribe went with me to the funeral,
we rode in a waggon, had a pleasant ride, the weather was
pleasant, when we went, but cloudy and cool when we returned
[p. 45]

at evening Bishop Whitney his wife Father and Mother,
and Sister in law, came in and invited me and my wife to go
with them & visit Father Smith & family my wife was unwell
and could not go; however I and my Scribe went, when we got
there, we found that some of the young Elders, were about
engaging in a debate, upon the subject of miracles, the
q[u]estion was this; was or was it not the design of Christ to
Establish his gospel by miracles.

After an interesting debate of three hours or more, during
which time much talent was displayed, it was desided by the
presidents of the debate in the negative; which was a righteous
descision I discovered in this debate, much warmth displayed,
to much zeal for mastery, to much of that enthusiasm that
characterizes a lawyer at the bar, who is determined to defend
his cause right or wrong. I therefore availed myself of this
favorable opportunity, to drop a few words upon this subject
by way of advise, that they might improve their minds and
cultivate their powers of intellect in a proper manner, that they
might not incur the displeasure of heaven, that they should
handle sacred things verry sacredly, and with due deference to
the opinions of others and with an eye single to the glory of
God. [p. 46]

19 November 1835 · Thursday

went in company with Doct. Williams & my scribe to see
how the workmen prospered in finishing the house;[1] the ma-

---

1. I.e., the temple.

sons on the inside had commenced puting on the finishing coat of plastureing. on my return I met Loyd [Lloyd] & Lorenzo Lewis and conversed with them upon the subject of their being disaffected.[1] I found that they were not so, as touching the faith of the church but with some of the members:

I returned home and spent the day in translating the Egyptian records: ~~on~~ this has been a warm & pleasant day —

20 November 1835 · Friday

in morning at home: the weather is warm but rainy, we spent the day in translating, and made rapid progress

At Evening, President Cowdery returned from New York, bringing with him a quantity of Hebrew books for the benefit of the school, he presented me with a Hebrew bible, lexicon & grammar, also a Greek Lexicon and Websters English Lexicon.

President Cowdery had a prosperous journey, according to the prayers of the saints in Kirtland

21 November 1835 · Saturday

at home, spent the day in examining my books and studying ⟨the⟩ ~~my~~ hebrew alphabet, at evening met with our hebrew class to make some arrangments about a Teacher, it was decided by the voice of the School to send [p.47] to N. York for a Jew to teach us the language, if we could get released from the engagement we had made with Doct. Piexotto [Peixotto] to teach the language, having asertained that he was not qualified to give us the knowledge we wish to acquire

22 November 1835 · Sunday

went to meeting at the us[u]al hour. Simeon Cater [Carter] preached from the 7th Chapt of Mathew; President Rigdon's

---

1. See entry of 28 September 1835.

brother in Law & Some other relatives were at meeting, in the after noon the meeting was held in the School-house also in the evening had a meeting, and Elder [Andrew Jackson] Squires who had withdrawn from the Church made application, to return after giving him a severe chastisment, he was recieved, and his licence restored to him; when the case of Elder Squires was introduced, we organized into a regular council. Sylvester Smith was chosen Clerk and after conciderable altercation upon the subject & keen rebuke he was restored by the voice of the council & church & the clerk ordered to give him his licence as above stated.[1] On this night we had a snow storm

23 November 1835 · Monday

Several brethren called to converse with me, and see the records; rec'd a letter from Jared Carter, spent the day in conversing, and in studying, the hebrew, language

This has been a stormy day [p. 48]

24 November 1835 · Tuesday

at home, spent the fore noon instructing those that called to inquire concerning the things of God, in the last days: in the after-noon, we translated some of the Egyptian, records; I had an invitation to attend a wedding at Br. Hiram Smith's in the evening also to solemnize the matrimonial ceremony, ⟨between Newell Knight & Lydia Goldthwaite⟩ I and my wife, went, when we arrived a conciderable company, had collected, the bridegroom & bride came in, and took their seats, which

---

1. After joining the Church in the early 1830s, Squires "preached the gospel successfully," then joined the Methodists for a time, and now desired to return to fellowship in the Church. At this council convened to hear his case, Joseph Smith spoke on the "impropriety of turning away from the truth," and Sidney Rigdon spoke on the "folly of fellowshipping any doctrine or spirit aside from that of Christ." After a repentant expression, Squires was again restored to fellowship and his office as elder. (Kirtland Council Minutes, 22 November 1835.)

gave me to understand that they were ready. I requested[1] them to arise and join hands. I then remarked that marriage was an institution of h[e]aven instituted[2] in the garden of Eden, that it was necessary that it should be Solemnized by the authority of the everlasting priesthood, before joining hands however, we attended prayers. I then made the remarks above stated; The ceremony was original ⟨with me⟩ it was in substance as follows. You covenant to be each others companions through life, and discharge the duties of husband & wife in every respect to which they assented. I then p[r]onounced them husband & Wife in the name of God and also ~~pronounced~~ the blessings that the Lord confered upon adam & Eve in the garden of Eden, that is to multiply and replenish the earth, with the addition of long life and prosperity; dismissed them and returned home. —[3] The weather is freezing cold, some snow on the ground [p. 49]

---

1. MS.: "requesteded"
2. MS.: "institude"
3. This was the first marriage performed by Joseph Smith. Newel Knight wrote: "In order to fulfil the gentile law it was necessary to obtain a licence from the County Clerk to get married. I took a horse & rode nine miles to obtain the licence & returened a bout three in the evening. Both myself & Lydia had desired that the Prophet might seal the bond of matrimony for us, but had not made our desires known to any save the Lord. As Bro. Hiram [Hyrum Smith] was going to invite the guests, I requested him to ask Elder S[eymour] Brunson to come to marry us, not expecting Brother Joseph would attend to that ordinance, as he never had married any one, he haveing no licence from the State. the State refused to give such licence to the Elders of this Church on the ground that they were not considered by the State to be preachers of the gospel, & if any attempted to marry with out such licence they would & did cause them to pay a penalty. . . . But . . . when Brother Hiram invited the Prophet & his family he observed that [he] was going to invite Brunson to marry us, Joseph replied stop I will marry them my self, this was good news to us; it seemed that the Lord had granted unto us the desire of our hearts, suffice it to say the feast was prepared, the guests were ready, the Prophet & his Council were there, we received much Instruction from the Prophet concerning matrimony, and what the ancient order of God was, & what it must be again concerning marriage. In the name of the Lord, & by the authority of the priesthood which he held he joined us in the bonds of matrimony." (Newel Knight, Autobiography and Journal, MS., LDS

25 November 1835 · Wednesday

spent the day in Translating. To-day [David] Harvey Redfield & Jesse Hitchcock arived here from Missourie; the latter
says that he has no doubt, but that a dose of poison was
administered to him in a boll of milk but God deli⟨vered him⟩

26 November 1835 · Thursday

at home, we spent the day in transcribing Egyptian characters from the papyrus. — I am severely afflicted with a cold. —
to day Robert Rathbone [Rathbun] and George Morey arrived
from Zion

27 November 1835 · Friday

much afflicted with my cold, yet able to be about and I am
determined to overcom in the name of the Lord Jesus Christ, —
spent the day in ~~stud~~ reading Hebrew at home.

The weather continues cold and unpleasant. — Br. Parrish
my scribe being afflicted with a cold, asked me to lay my hands
on him in the name of the Lord I did so, and in return I asked
him to lay his hands on me & we were both relieved. —

⟨See page 9th⟩ Copy of a prayer offered up on the 23d day
of Oct 1835, by the following individuals, at 4 oclock P.M.
viz. Joseph Smith Jn, Oliver Cowdery, David Whitmer, Hirum
Smith John Whitmer, Sidn[e]y Rigdon, Samuel H. Smith, Frederick G. Williams, and Wm. W. Phelps, assembled and united

---

Church Archives.)

Lydia Knight noted that at the time of the marriage, the Prophet stated, "Our
Elders have been wronged and prosecuted for marrying without a license. The
Lord God of Israel has given me authority to unite the people in the holy bonds
of matrimony. And from this time forth I shall use that privilege and marry
whomsoever I see fit." (*Lydia Knight's History* [Salt Lake City: Juvenile Instructor
Office, 1883], 31.)

Seymour Brunson, the Mormon elder who had been initially considered to
solemnize the Bailey/Knight marriage, had received a license to bind civil marriages while visiting the southern part of the state, where anti-Mormon prejudice
was not so intense. (See Max Parkin, "Conflict at Kirtland," 174–77.)

in prayer, with one voice before the Lord for the following blessings:

That the Lord will give us means sufficient to deliver us from all our afflictions and difficulties, wherein we are placed by means of our debts; that he will open the way and deliver Zion in the appointed [p. 50] time and that without the shedding of blood; that he will hold our lives precious, and grant that we may live to the common age of man, and never fall into the hands nor power of the mob in Missourie nor in any other place; that he will also preserve our posterity, that none of them fall even to the end of time; that he will give us the blessings of the earth sufficient to carry us to Zion, and that we may purchase inheritances in that land, even enough to carry on ⟨and accomplish⟩ the work unto which he was appointed us; and also that he will assist all others who desire, according to his commandments, to go up and purchase inheritances, and all this easily and without perplexity, and trouble; and finally, that in the end he will save us in his Celestial Kingdom. Amen.

Oliver Cowdery   Clerk

28 November 1835 · Saturday

at home, spent the morning in compareing our journal. —

~~This~~ Elder Josiah Clark called this morning to see me, he lives in Cam[pb]el County K.Y[Kentucky] about three miles above Cincinate.

I am conciderably recovered from my cold, & I think I shall be able in a few days to translate again, with the blessing of God. — The weather is still cold and stormy, the snow is falling, & winter seems to be closing in ~~verry fast~~, all nature shrinks before the chilling blasts of rigid winter. —

Elder Clark above mentioned, has been biten by a mad dog some three or four [p. 51] years since, has doctered much, and received some benefit by so doing, but is much afflicted notwithstanding, he came here that he might be benefited by the prayers of the church, accordingly we prayed for and layed our hands on him, in the name of the Lord Jesus Christ and anointed him with oil, and rebuked his affliction, praying our heavenly Father to hear and answer our prayers according to our faith

29 November 1835 · Sunday

went to meeting at the us[u]al hour Elder Morley preachd and Bishop Partridge in the afternoon; their discourses were well adapted to the times in which we live, and the circumstances under which we are placed, their words were words of wisdom, like apples of gold in pitchers[1] of silver, spoken in the simple accents of a child, yet sublime as the voice of an angels, the saints, appeared to be much pleased with the beautiful discourses of these two fathers in Israel; after these servises closed, three of the Zion brethren came forward and recieved their blessing

Solon Foster was ordained to the office of an Elder; the Lord's supper was then administered, and the meeting closed.

returned home and spent the evening. The storm continues, the weather is verry cold [p. 52]

30 November 1835 · Monday

yet the snow is falling, and is sufficiently deep for ~~slay~~ sleighing, this is an uncommon storm for this country, at this season of the year spent the day in writing a letter for the Messenger & Advocate on the Subject of the Gathering; —[2] this afternoon, Henry Capron called to see me, he is an old acquaintance of mine, from Manchester New York, shewed him the Egyptian records

---

1. MS.: "pictures"
2. See *Messenger and Advocate* 2 (December 1835): 225–30. This was the last of a three-part installment. See note 1, p. 46.

1 December 1835 · Tuesday

at home spent the day in writing, for the M & Advocate, the snow is falling and we have fine sleighing.

2 December 1835 · Wednesday

a fine morning I made preparation, to ride to Painsvill[e], with my wife and ~~children~~ family, also my Scribe, we had our sleigh and horses prepared and set out, when we ~~arived~~ were passing through Mentor Street, we overtook a team with two men on the sleigh. I politely asked them to let me pass, they granted my request, and as we passed them, they bawled out, do you get any revelation lately, with an adition of blackguard that I did not understand, this is a fair sample of the character of Mentor Street inhabitants, who are ready to abuse and scandalize, men who never laid a straw in their way, and infact those whos faces they never saw, and cannot bring an acusation, against, either [p. 53] of a temporal or spir[i]tual nature; except our firm belief in the fulness of the gospel and I was led to marvle ~~that God~~ at the long suffering and condescention of our heavenly Father, in permitting, these ungodly wretches, to possess, this goodly land, which is ~~the~~ indeed as beautifully situated, and its soil as fertile, as any in this region of country, and its inhabitance, ~~as~~ wealthy even blessed, above measure, in temporal things, and fain, would God bless, them with, ~~with~~ spiritual blessings, even eternal life, were it not for their evil hearts of unbelief, and we are led to ~~cry in our hearts~~ mingle our prayers with those saints that have suffered the like treatment before us, whose souls are under the altar crying to the Lord for vengance upon those that dwell upon the earth and we rejoice that the time is at hand when, the wicked who will not repent will be swept ⟨from the earth⟩ with the besom of destruction and the earth become an inheritance for the poor and the meek. —

when we arived at Painsvill[e] we called at Sister Harriet

How[e']s, and left my wife and family to visit her while we rode into Town to do some buisness, ~~returned~~ called and visited H. Kingsbury—Returned and dined with Sister How[e], and returned home, had a fine ride the sleighing is ~~fine~~ ⟨good⟩ and weather pleasant—[p. 54]

3 December 1835 · Thursday

at home, wrote a letter to David Dort, Rochester Michigan, another to Almyra Scoby [Almira Mack Scobey Covey] Liberty Clay co., Mo. at home all day,— at evening, was invited with my wife, to attend, at Thomas Caricoes, to join W[arren]. Parrish & Martha H. Raymond in mattrimony, we found a verry pleasant and respectable company waiting when, we arived, we opened our interview with singing & prayer, after which, I delivered an address, upon the subject of matrimony, I then invited the ⟨parties⟩ ~~couple~~ to arise, who were to be joined in wedlock, and, solemnized the institution in a brief manner, and pronounced them husband and wife in the name of God according to the articles, and covenants of the ⟨Church of the⟩ latter day saints,[1] closed by singing and prayer, took some refreshment, and retired; having spent the evening, agreeably

4 December 1835 · Friday

to day, in company with Vinson Knights, we drew, three hundred and fifty Dollars, out of Painsvill[e] Bank, on three

---

1. The "Articles and Covenants," a statement of fundamental principles, beliefs, and practices for the Church, served as a constitution, a standard of conduct and procedure. It was routinely read at early Church conferences, used by lay members as a standard for behavior, and carried by missionaries to teach procedure and policy. The revelation was eventually published in the Doctrine and Covenants and is today's section 20. (See Robert J. Woodford, "The Historical Development of the Doctrine and Covenants" [Ph.D. diss., Brigham Young University, 1974], 1:286–351. On its larger impact see David J. Whittaker, "The 'Articles of Faith' in Early Mormon Literature and Thought," in *New Views of Mormon History: A Collection of Essays in Honor of Leonard J. Arrington*, edited by Davis Bitton and Maureen U. Beecher [Salt Lake City: University of Utah Press, 1987], 63–92.)

months credit, for which we gave, the names of F G. Williams
& Co N. K. Whitney John Johnson, & ~~Newel~~ Vinson Knights,
I also settled with Br. Hiram Smith, and V. Knights, and paid
said [K]nights ~~$2045~~ two hundred and forty five dollars, I also
paid, or have it in my power to pay, J. Lewis for which, blessing,
I feel hartily, to thank my heavenly Father, and ask him, in
the name of Jesus Christ, to enable us to extricate [p. 55]
ourselves, from all ~~the~~ embarasments whatever that we may
not be brought into disrepute, in any respect, that our enemys
may not have any power over us; — spent the day at home,
devoted some time in studying ⟨the⟩ hebrew language. — this has
been a warm day with, some rain; our snow is melting verry
fast, — This evening, a Mr. John Holister of Portage County
Ohio called to see me on the subject of religion, he is a member
of the close communion baptise Church, he said he had come
to enquire concerning the faith of our church having heard
many reports of the worst character about us, he seemed to
be an honest enqui[r]er after truth. I spent the evening in
talking with him, I found him to be an honest candid man,
and no particular peculiarities about him, only his simplisity,
he tarried over night with me, and acknowledged in the ⟨morn-
ing⟩ that although he had thought he knew something about
religion he was now sensible that he knew but little, which
was the greatest, trait of wisdom that I could discover in him

5 December 1835 · Saturday

the weather is cold and freezing, and the snow is falling
moderately, and there is a prospect of sleighing again, spent
the forenoon in studying, hebrew with Doct. Williams & President Cowdery, I am labouring under some indisposition of
health. laid down and slept a while, and [p. 56] and arose
feeling tolerable well through the blessings of God. — I received
a letter to day from Reuben McBride, Vilanova [Chautauqua

Co.] N. Y also another from Parley Pratts mother in law[1] from Herkimer Co. N. Y of no consequence as to what it contained, but cost me 25 cents for postage, I mention this as it is a common occurence, and I am subjected to a great deal of expence in this way, by those who I know nothing about, only that they are destitute of good manners, for if people wish to be benefited with information from me, common respect and good breeding wou[l]d dictate, them to pay the postage on their letters. —[2]

6 December 1835 · Sunday

went to meeting at the us[u]al hour. G. Carter preached a splendid discourse, in the after ⟨noon⟩ we had an exortation, and communion. — Br. Draper insisted on leaving the meeting, some 2 or 3 weeks since, before communion, and would not be prevailed upon to tarry a few moments although, we invited him to do so as we did not wish to have the house thrown into confusion, he observed that he would not if we excluded him from the church, to day, he attempted to make a confession, but it was not satisfactory to me, and I was constrained

---

1. Thankful Cooper Halsey.

2. On this date, Joseph Smith inserted a notice in the *Messenger and Advocate* to inform his friends and all others "that whenever they wish to address me thro' the Post Office, they will be kind enough to pay the postage on the same. My friends will excuse me in this matter, as I am willing to pay postage on letters to hear from *them*; but am unwilling to pay for insults and menaces, — consequently, must refuse all, unpaid."

Between 1816 and 1845 the cost for sending a single-sheet letter less than 30 miles was 6 cents; not over 80 miles, 10 cents; not over 150 miles, 12 1/2 cents; and not over 400 miles, 18 3/4 cents. Greater distances cost 25 cents. Letters of two or more sheets required additional postage in proportion. If a letter weighed more than an ounce, the postage quadrupled. For many, postal communication was a luxury. Prior to 1847, when postage stamps were authorized, the option of collecting postage from the addressee had led to many abuses, including the payment by the addressee for letters containing offensive and insulting messages. (Arthur E. Summerfield, *U.S. Mail: The Story of the United States Postal Service* [New York: Holt, Rinehart and Winston, 1960], 45–46; Clyde Kelly, *United States Postal Policy* [New York and London: D. Appleton and Co., 1932], 57–58.)

by the spirit to deliver him over to the bufetings of satan untill he should humble himself, and repent, of his sins, and make a satisfactory confession before the church— [p. 57]

7 December 1835 · Monday

received a letter from Milton Holmes, and was much rejoiced to hear from, him, and of his prosperity in proclaiming the gospel, wrote him a letter requesting, him to return to this place,

Spent the day in reading the hebrew. Mr. John Hollister called and to take the parting hand with me, and remarked that he had been in darkness all his days, but had now found the light and intended to obey it. also a number of brethren called this Evening to see the records. I exibited and explained them to their satisfaction. We have fine Sleighing

8 December 1835 · Tuesday

at holm spent the day in reading hebrew in company with, President Cowdery Doct. Williams Br. H[yrum]. Smith & O[rson]. Pratt.

In the evening I preached, as us[u]al at the School House, had great liberty in speaking the congregation, were attentive, after the servises closed the brethren proposed to come and draw wood for me

9 December 1835 · Wednesday

at home, the wind is strong and chilly, from the South, and their is a prospect of a storm Elder [Noah] Packard came in this morning and made me a present, of 12 dollars which he held in a note against me,[1] may God bless him for his

---

1. The settlement of debt in a largely barter economy required that one who performed services or supplied goods to another keep a record of each transaction. When two people settled their accounts, each brought his or her own record, and both signed the resulting settlement. Often when a debt was acquired, a hand-

liberality, also James Aldrich, sent me my note by the hand of Jesse Hitchcock, on which [p. 58] there was 12 dollars due, and may God bless him for his kindness to me

also the brethren whose names are written below opened the[ir] hearts in great liberality and payed me at the committee Store the sums set oposite their respective names

John Corrill	$5.00
Levi Jackman	3.25
Elijah Fordham	5.25
James Em[m]ett	5.00
Newel Knight	2.00
Truman Angell	3.00
Wm Felshaw	3.00
Emer Harris	1.00
Truman Jackson	1.00
Samuel Rolph	1.25
Elias Higbee	1.00
Albert Brown	3.00
Wm F. Cahoon	1.00
Harlow Crosier	.50
Salmon Gee	.75
Harvey Stanley	1.00
Zemira Draper	1.00
George Morey	1.00
John Rudd	.50
Alexander Badlam	1.00
	40.50.
with the adition of the 2 notes above	24.00

written record was made on a scrap of paper. These notes became a sort of scrip and circulated until retired by cash, labor, or barter. As in this case, the debt could be settled by the creditor presenting his copy of the note as a gift to the debtor. (See James M. McCabe, "Early Ledgers and Account Books: A Source for Local Vermont History," *Vermont History* 37 [Winter 1969]: 5–12.)

My heart swells with gratitude inexpressible w⟨h⟩en I realize the great condescention of my heavenly Fathers, in opening the hearts of these, my beloved brethren [p. 59] to administer so liberally, to my wants and I ask God in the name of Jesus Christ, to multiply, blessings, without number upon their heads, and bless me with much wisdom and understanding, and dispose of me, to the best advantage, for my brethren, and the advancement of thy cause and Kingdom, and whether my days are many or few whether in life or in death I say in my heart, O Lord let me enjoy the society of such brethren

To day Elder Tanner[1] brought me the half of a fat[e]ned hog for the be[ne]fit of my family.

And a few days since Elder S[hadrach]. Roundy brought me a quarter of beef and may all the blessings, that are named above, be poured upon their heads, for their kindness toward me —

10 December 1835 · Thursday

a beautiful morning indeed, and fine sleighing, this day my brethren meet according, to previous arangement, to chop and haul wood for me, and they have been verry industrious, and I think they have supplyed me with my winters wood, for which I am sincerely grateful to each and every, one of them, for this expression of their goodness towards me And in the name of Jesus Christ I envoke the rich benediction of heav[e]n to rest upon them even all and their families, and I ask my heavenly Father [p. 60] to preserve their health's and those of their wives and children, that they may have strength of body to perform, their labours, in their several ocupations in life, and the use and activity of their limbs, also powers of intellect

---

1. Probably John Tanner (1778–1850), born in Hopkinton, Rhode Island, and living in Warren County, New York, when converted after the miraculous healing of his leg in 1832. He gave substantial sums of money for the benefit of the Church in Kirtland. (Andrew Jenson, *Latter-day Saint Biographical Encyclopedia* [Salt Lake City: Deseret News Press, 1914], 2:799–802.)

and understanding hearts, that they may treasure up wisdom, and understanding, ~~until~~ and inteligence, above measure, and be preserved from plagues pestilence, and famine, and from the power of the adversary, and the hands of evil designing, men and have power over all their enemys; and the way be prepared before them, that they may journey to the land of Zion and be established, on their inheritances, to enjoy undisturbe[d] peace and happiness for ever, and ultimately to be crowned with everlasting life in the celestial Kingdom of God, which blessings I ask in the name of Jesus of Nazareth. Amen

I would remember Elder Leonard Rich who was the first one that proposed to the brethren to assist me, in obtaining wood for the use of my family, for which I pray my heavenly Father, to bless ⟨him⟩ with all the blessings, named above, and I shall ever remember him with much gratitude, for this testimony, of benevolence and respect, and thank the great I am,[1] for puting into his heart to do me this kindness, and I say in my heart, I will trust in thy goodness, and mercy, forever, for thy wisdom and benevolence ⟨O Lord⟩ is unbounded and beyond the comprehension of men and all of thy ways cannot be found out [p. 61]

This afternoon, I was called in company with President David Whitmer, to visit Sister Angeline Works, who lives at Elder Booths[2] we found her verry sick, and so much deranged, that She did not recognize her friends, and intimate acquaintences we prayed for and layed hands on her[3] in the name of Jesus Christ, and commanded her in his name to receive he[r] senses, which was immediately restored ~~to her~~ we also ~~asked~~

---

1. A reference to Deity. See Exodus 3:14; John 8:58.
2. Possibly Lorenzo Dow Booth (1807–1847), a resident of Kirtland who was a member of the first quorum of seventies and had participated in the march of Zion's Camp. (Susan E. Black, "Membership of the Church of Jesus Christ of Latter-day Saints, 1830–1848" [Provo, Utah: Religious Studies Center, Brigham Young University, 1984], 6:164–65.
3. "her" repeated in MS.

a healing blessing prayed that she might be restored to health, she said she was better. – On our return we found the brethren engaged, in putting out the board kiln which had taken fire, and after labouring for about one hour, against this distructive, element they succeded in conquering it, and, probably will save about one fourth part of the lumber, that was in it, how much loss the committee have sustained by this fire I do not know but it is conciderable as there was much lumber in the kiln

There was about 200 brethren engaged on this occasion and displayed, much activity, and interest, for which they deserve much credit.

This evening I spent at hom[e], a number of brethren called to see the records which I exibited to them, and they were much pleased with their interview [p. 62]

11 December 1835 · Friday[1]

a fire broke out in a shoe-makers shop owned by Orson Johnson, but was soon, extinguished, by the active exertions of the brethren, but the family were much alarmed, the shop being connected with their dwelling house, they carryed their furniture into the street, but not much damage was sustained. – This is a pleasant morning, and their is a prospect of a thaw

Spent the day at home, in reading, and instructing those who called for advise. – today Elder Dayly[2] & his wife left for home.

12 December 1835 · Saturday[3]

at home, spent the fore noon in reading, at about 12 o clock a number of young person[s] called to see the records

---

1. MS. reads "Thursday Friday morning the 11th"
2. Probably Moses Daley (1794–1865), born at Wallkill, Orange County, New York. Died at Riverside, Riverside County, California. (Black, "Membership of the Church," 13:79–82.)
3. MS. reads "Friday Saturday morning 12th"

Egyptian records I requested my Scribe to exibit them, he did so, one of the young ladies, who had been examining them, was asked if they had the appearance of Antiquity, she observed with an air of contempt that they did not, on hearing this I was surprised at the ignorance she displayed, and I observed to her that she was an anomaly in creation for all the wise and learned that had ever examined them, without hesitation pronounced them antient, I further remarked that, it was downright wickedness ignorance bigotry and superstition that caused her to make the remark, and that I would put it on record, and I have done so because it is a fair sample of the prevailing spirit of the times [p. 63] showing that the victims of priestcraft and superstition, would not believe though one should rise from the dead.

At evening attended a debate,[1] at Br. Wm. Smiths, the question proposed to debate upon was, as follows.—was it necessary for God to reveal himself to man, in order for their happiness.—I was on the affirmative and the last one to speak on that side of the question,—but while listning, with interest to the, ingenuity displayed, on both Sides of the qu[e]stion, I was called, away to visit, Sister Angeline Work[s], who was suposed to be dangerously sick, Elder Corrill & myself went and prayed for and layed hands on her in the name of Jesus Christ, She appeard to be better,—returned home

---

1. Lyceums, mechanics' institutes, and agricultural societies flourished in Jacksonian America. During this period hundreds of informal associations were established for the purpose of improving the social, intellectual, and moral fabric of society. The lyceum movement, with its lectures, dramatic performances, class instruction, and debates, contributed significantly to the education of adult Americans in the nineteenth century and provided the cultural framework for the Kirtland, Ohio, debates and schools. See Edward W. Stevens, Jr., "Science, Culture, and Morality: Educating Adults in the Early Nineteenth Century," in *"Schools and The Means of Education Shall Forever Be Encouraged:" A History of Education in the Old Northwest, 1787–1880*, edited by Paul H. Mattingly and Edward W. Stevens, Jr. (Athens, Ohio: Ohio University Libraries, 1987): 69–83; Carl Bode, *The American Lyceum: Town Meeting of the Mind* (New York: Oxford University Press, 1956).

13 December 1835 · Sunday

at the us[u]al hour for meeting viz. at 10 ocl[oc]k attended meeting, at the School house on the flats, Elder J[esse]. Hitchcock preachd a verry feeling discourse indeed, in the afternoon Elder Peter Whitmer, related his experiance, after which President F G. Williams related his also, they both spoke of many things connected with the rise and progress of this church, which were interesting, and the Saints, listened with much attention, after these serv[ic]es closed, the sacrament of the Lords Supper was administered, under the superintendance of President D. Whitmer, who presided over the meeting during the day. I then made som[e] remarks respecting [p. 64] prayer meetings and our meeting was brought to a close, by invoking the blessings of heaven.

We then returned home. I ordered my horse saddled and myself and Scribe, rode to Mr. E[benezer]. Jennings, where I joined Eb[e]nezer Robinson and Angeline Works, in matrimony, according to previous arangements. Miss ⟨Works⟩ had so far recoverd from her illness, that she was able to sit in her easy chair while I pronounced the mariage ceremony. —

We then rode to Mr. [Isaac] McWithy's a distance of about 3 miles from Town, where I had been Solicited, to attend and solemnize, the matrimonial covenant betwen Mr. E[dwin]. Webb & Miss E[liza]. A. McWithy, the parents and many of the connections of both parties were present, with a large and respectable company of friends, who were invited as guests; and after making the necessary arangements the company come to order, and the Groom & bride, with the attendants politely came forward, and took their seats, and having been requested, to make some preliminary remarks upon the subject of matrimony, touching the design of the All Mighty in this institution, also the duties of husbands & wives towards eac[h] other, and after opening our interview with singing and prayer, I delivered a lecture of about 40 minuits in length, during this time all seemed to be interested, except one or two individuals, who manifested, a spirit of grovling contempt, which I was constrained to reprove and rebuke sharply, after I had ~~been~~ closed my remarks, I sealed the matrimonial [p.65] ceremony in the name of God, and pronounced the blessings of heaven upon the heads of the young married couple we then closed by returning thanks.

A sumptuous feast was then spread and the company were invited to seat themselves, at the table by pairs, male & female commencing with the oldest, and I can only say that the interview was conducted with propriety and decorum, and our hearts were made to rejoice, while together, and ~~all~~ cheerfulness prevailed, and after spending the evening agreeably untill 9, oclock, we pronounc[e]d a blessing, upon the company and withdrew, and returned home

To day the board kiln, took fire again

14 December 1835 · Monday

this morning a number of brethren from New York call[ed] to visit me, and see the Egyptian records. Elder [Martin] Harris also returned this morning from Palmyra N. York. Br. Frazier Eaton, of the same place called and paid me a visit, a verry fine man also Sister Harriet How[e] called to pay us a visit

After dinner we went to attend the funeral of Sylvester Smiths youngest child.[1] in the evening met[2] according to notice previously given to make arangements to guard against fire, and organized a company for this purpose, counciled also on other affairs of a temporal nature.

To day Samuel Branum [Brannan] came to my house, much afflicted with a swelling on his left arm, which was oc-

---

1. Sylvester M. Smith died at the age of eleven weeks and four days. (Early Church Information File, LDS Church Family History Library, Salt Lake City, Utah.)
2. MS.: "meet"

casioned by a bruise [p. 66] on his elbow, we had been called to pray for him and anoint him with oil, but his faith was not sufficient to effect a cure, and my wife prepared a poultice of herbs and applyed to it and he tarryed with me over night

Spent the day at home reading hebrew, and visiting friends who called to see me.

~~To day I received a letter form Elder Orson Hyde from his own hand~~

15 December 1835 · Tuesday

spent the day at home, and as us[u]al was blessed with much company, some of which called to see the records Samuel Brannum [Brannan], is verry sick in consequence of his arm, it being much inflamed

This afterno[o]n Elder Orson Hyde, handed me a Letter, the purport of which is that he is dissatisfyed with the committee,[1] in their dealings, with him in temporal affairs, that is that they do not deal as liberally ~~in~~ ⟨with⟩ him as they do with Elder William Smith, also requested me to reconcile the revelation, given to the 12,[2] since their return from the East,

That unless these things and others named in the letter, could be reconciled to his mind his honour would not stand united with them. — this I believe is the amount of the contents of the letter although much was written, my feelings on this occasion, were much laserated, knowing that I had dealt in righteousness with him in all things and endeavoured to promote his happiness and well being, as much as lay in my power, and I feel that these reflections are [p. 67] ungrateful and founded in jealousy and that the adversary is striving with all his subtle devises and influence to destroy him by causing a division amon[g] the twelve that God has chosen to open

---

1. The committee consisted of Hyrum Smith, Reynolds Cahoon, and Jared Carter. See note 3, p. 39.
2. See entry of 3 November 1835.

the gospel Kingdom in all nations,[1] but I pray my Heavenly Father in the name of Jesus of Nazareth that he may be delivered from the power of the destroyer, and that his faith fail not in this hour of temptation, and prepare him and all the Elders to receive an endument [endowment], in thy house, even according to thine own order from time to time as thou seeest them worthy to be called into thy Solemn Assembly [p. 68][2]

16 December 1835 · Wednesday

the weather is extremely cold, this morning I went to the council room, to lay before the presidency the letter that I received yesterday from Elder O. Hyde, but when I arived, I found that I had lost said letter, but I laid the substance of it as far as I could recollect before the council, but they had not time to attend to it on the account of other buisness, accordingly we adjourned untill Monday Evening the 20th Inst.

Returned home Elder McLellen Elder B. Young and Elder J[ared]. Carter called and paid me a visit, with which I was much gratified. I exibited and explaind the Egyptian Records to them, and explained many things to them concerning the dealings of God with the ancients and the formation of the planetary System, they seemed much pleased with the interview.

This evening according to adjournment I went to Br. Wm. Smiths, to take part in the debate that was commenced on Saturday evening last. — after the debate was concluded, and a desision given in favour of the affirmative of the question, some altercation took place, upon the impropr[i]ety of continueing the school fearing that it would not result in good.

Br. Wm oposed these measures and insisted on having another question proposed, and at length become much en-

---

1. For the text of the Hyde letter see the entry of 17 December.
2. Half page left blank in MS. at this point.

raged particularly at me and used [p. 69] violence upon my person, and also upo[n] Elder J. Carter and some others, for which I am grieved beyond expression, and can only pray God to forgive him inasmuch as he repents of his wickedness, and humbles himself before the Lord

17 December 1835 · Thursday

at home. — quite unwell. — This morning Elder Orson Hyde called to see me, and presented me with a copy of the letter that he handed me on Tuesday last, which I had lost

The following is a copy

Dec. 15th 1835

President Smith

Sir you may esteem it a novel circumstance to receive a written communication from me at this time.

My reasons for writing are the following. I have some things which I wish to communicate to you, and feeling a greater liberty to do it by writing alone by myself, I take this method; and it is generally the case that you are thronged with buisness and not convenient to spend much time in conversing upon subjects of the following nature. Therefore let these excuses paliate the novelty of the circumstance and patiently hear my recital.

After the committee had received their stock of fall and winter goods, I went to Elder Cahoon and told him that I was destitute of a cloak and wanted him to trust me until Spring for materials to make one. He told me that [p. 70] he would trust me until January, but must then have his pay as the payments for the goods become due at that time. I told him that I know not from whence the money would come and I could not promise it so soon.

But in a few weeks after I unexpectedly obtained the money to buy a cloak and applyed immediately to Elder C for one and told him that I had the cash to pay for it, but he said that the materials for cloaks were all sold and that he could not accommodate me, and I will here venture a guess that he has not realized the cash for one cloak pattern.

A few weeks after this I called on Elder Cahoon again and told him that I wanted cloth for some shirts to the amount of 4 or 5 Dollars I told him that I would pay him in the spring and sooner if I could.

He told me let me have it not long after, my school was established and some of the hands who laboured on the house attended and wished to pay me at the Committee Store for their tuition. —I called at the Store to see if any nego⟨ti⟩ation could be made and they take me off where I owed them, but no such negotiation could be made. These with some other circumstances of like character called forth the following reflections.

In the first place I gave the committee $275 in cash besides some more and during the last season have traveled thro the Middle and Eastern states to suport and uphold the Store and in so doing have reduced myself to nothing in a pecuniary point. Under [p.71] these circumstances this establishment refused to render me that accomodation which a worldlings establishment would have gladly done, and one too, which never ⟨received⟩ a donation from my me nor in whose favour I never raised my voice or exerted my influence.

But after all this, thought I, it may be right and I will be still—Un[t]il not long since I asertained that Elder Wm Smith could go to the Store and get whatever he pleased, and no one to say why do ye so, until his account has amounted to seven Hundred Dollars or there abouts and that he was a silent partner in the conce[r]n, yet not acknowledged ⟨as⟩ such fearing that his creditors would make a hawl upon the Store.

While we were abroad this last season we strain[e]d every nerve to obtain a little something for our familys and regularly divided the monies equally for ought that I know, not knowing that William had such a fountain at home from whence he drew his support. I then called to mind the revelation[1] in which myself, McLellen and Patten were chastened and also the quotation in that revelation of the parable of the twelve sons: as if the original meaning referd directly to the twelve apostles of the church of the Latter day Saints. I would now ask if each one of the twelve has not an equal right to the same accomodations from that Store provided they are alike faithful. If not, with such a combination [p. 72] mine honor be not thou united.

If each one has the same right, take the baskets off from our noses or put one to Williams nose or if this cannot be done, reconcile the parable of the twelve sons with the superior priveleges that William has.

Pardon me if I speak in parables or parody.

A certain shepherd had twelve sons and he sent them out one day to go and gather his flock which were scattered upon the mountains and in the vallies afar off they were all obedient to their fathers mandate, and at Evening they returned with the flock, and one son received wool enough to make him warm and comfortable and also rec[eive]d of the flesh and milk of the flock, the other eleven received not so much as one kid to make merry with their friends

These facts with some others have disqualified my mind for studying the Hebrew Language at present, and believing, as I do, that I must sink or swim, or in other words take care of myself, I have thought that I should take the most efficient means in my power to get out of debt, and to this end I p[r]oposed taking the school,[2] but if I am not thought competent to take the charge of it, or worthy to be placed in that station, I must devise some other means to help myself; altho having been ordained to that office under your own hand with

---

1. See entry of 3 November 1835.
2. I.e., the School of the Prophets, or School of the Elders at Kirtland.

a p[r]omise that it should not be taken from me. — [p. 73] Conclusion of the whole matter is sutch I am willing to continue and do all I can provided we can share equal benefits one with the other, and upon no other principle whatever. If one has his suport from the "publick crib" let them all have it. But if one is pinched I am willing to be, provided we are all alike.

If the principle of impartiality and equality can be observed by all I think that I will not peep again —

If I am damned it will be for doing what I think is right. — There have been two applications made to me to go into business since I talked of taking the school, but it is in the world and I had rather remain in Kirtland if I can consistently

All I ask is Right I Am Sir with Respect Your obt. servt.

Orson Hyde

To President J. Smith jn
Kirtland Geauga Co. Ohio [p. 74]

Elder O. Hyde called and read the foregoing letter himself and, I explained upon the objections, he had set forth in it, and satisfyed his mind upon every point, perfectly and he observed after I had got through, that he was more than satisfyed, and would attend the hebrew school, and took the parting hand with me with every expression of friendship that a gentleman, and a Christian could manifest, which I felt to reciprocate, with ~~the~~ cheerfulness and entertain, the best of feeling for him, and most cheerfully forgive him the ingratitude which was manifisted in his letter, knowing that it was for want of corect information, that his mind was disturbed as far as his reflections related to me.

But on the part of the committe, he was not treated, right in all thing[s], however all things, are settled amicably, and no hardness exists between us or them

My Father & Mother called this evening to see me upon the subject of the difficulty, that transpired at their house on wednesd[a]y evening between me and my Br. William, they were sorely afflicted in mind on the account of that occurrence. I conversed with them, and ~~showed~~ convinced them that I was not to blame in taking the course I did, but had acted in righteousness, in all thing[s] on that occasion

I invited them to come and live with me, they concented to do so as soon as it is practicable [p. 75]

18 December 1835 · Friday

at home Br. Hyrum Smith called to see me and read a letter ~~to me~~ that he received from William, in which he asked, his [—] ~~for~~ forgivness for the abuse he offered to him, at the debate, he tarried, most of the fore noon, and conversed freely with me, upon the subject, of the difficulty, existing between me and Br. William, he said that he was, perfectly satisfied, with the course I had taken, with him, in rebuking, him in his wickedness, — but he is wounded to the verry soul, with the conduct of William, and altho he feels the tender feelings of a brother, toward him yet he can but look upon his conduct as an abomination in the sight of God

And I could pray in my heart that all my brethren were like unto my beloved brother Hyrum, who posseses the mildness of a lamb, and the integrity of a Job and in short the meekness and humility of Christ, and I love him with that love that is stronger than death; for I never had occasion to rebuke him, ~~and~~ nor he me which he declared when he left me to day [p. 76]

18th Inst. [December 1835]

Copy of a letter from Br. William Smith

Br. Joseph —

Though I do not know but I have forfeited all right and title to the word brother, in concequence of what I have done, for I concider myself, that I am unworthy to be called one, after coming to myself and concidering upon what I have done

111

I feel as though it was a duty, to make a humble confession to you for what I have done or what took place the other evening—but leave this part of the subject at present.—I was called to an account by the 12, yesterday for my conduct; or they desired to know my mind or determination and what I was going to do I told them that on reflection upon the many difficulties that I had had with the church and the much disgrace I had brought upon myself in concequence of these things and also that my health would not permit me to go to school to ⟨make⟩ any preperations for the endument [endowment] and that my health was such that I was not able to travel, I told them that it would be better for them to appoint one in the office that would be better able to fill it, and by doing this they would throw me into the hands of the church, and leave me where I was before I was chosen—

Then I would not be in a situation [p. 77] to bring so much disgrace upon the cause, when I fell into temptation, and perhaps by this I might obtain Salvation you know my passions and the danger of falling from so high a station, and thus by withdrawing from the office of the apostleship while their is salvation for me, and remaining a member in the church; I feel a fraid if I do'nt do this it will be worse for me, some other day

And again my health is poor and I am not able to travel and it is necessary that the office should not be idle— And again I say you know my passions and I am a fraid it will be worse for me, by and by

do so if the Lord will have mercy on me and let me remain as a member in the church, and then I can travel and preach, when I am able— do not think that I am your enemy for what I have done, perhaps you may say or ask why I have not remembered the good that you have done to me— When I reflect upon the ingury I have done you I must confess that I do not know what I have been doing about— I feel sorry for what I have done and humbly ask your forgiveness— I have

112

not confidence as yet to come and see you for I feel ashamed of what I have done, and as I feel now I feel as though [p.78] all the confessions that I could make verbally or by writing would not be sufficient to atone for the transgression — be this as it may I am willing to make all the restitution you shall require. If I can stay in the church as a member — I will try to make all the satisfaction possible —

yours with respect
William Smith

Do not cast me off for what I have done but strive to save me in the church as a member I do repent of what I have done to you and ask your forgiveness — I concider the transgression the other evening of no small magnitude, — but it is done and I cannot help it now — I know brother Joseph you are always willing to forgive.

But I sometimes think when I reflect upon the many inguries I have done you I feel as though a confession was not hardly sufficient — but have mercy on me this once and I will try to do so no more —

The 12, called a council yesterday and sent over after me and I went over

This council rem[em]ber was called together by themselves and not by me

Wm S [p. 79]

Kirtland Friday Dec 18th 1835

Answer to the foregoing Letter from Br. William Smith a Copy

Br. William having received your letter I now procede to answer it, and shall first procede, to give a brief naration of my feelings and motives, since the night I first came to the knowledge, of your having a debating School, which was at the time I happened in with, Bishop [Newel K.] Whitney his Father and Mother &c — which was the first that I knew any thing about it, and from that time I took an interest in them, and was delighted with it, and formed a determination, to attend the School for the purpose of obtaining information, and with the idea of imparting the same, through the assistance of the spirit of the Lord, if by any means I should have faith to do so; and with this intent, I went to the school on ⟨last⟩ Wednesday night, not with the idea of braking up the school, neither did it enter into my heart, that there was any wrangling or jealousy's in your heart, against me;

Notwithstanding previous to my leaving home there were feelings of solemnity, rolling across my breast, which were unaccountable to me, and also these feelings continued by spells to depress my ~~feelings~~ ⟨spirit⟩ and seemed to manifest that all was not right, even after the ~~debate~~ school commenced, and during the debate, yet I strove to believe that all would work together for good; I was pleased with the power of the arguments, that were aduced, and did [p. 80] not feel to cast any reflections, upon any one that had spoken; but I felt that it was ~~my~~ ⟨the⟩ duty of old men that set as presidents to be as grave, at least as young men, and that it was our duty to smile at solid arguments, and sound reasoning, and be impresed with solemnity, which should be manifest in our countanance, when folly and that which militates against truth and righteousness, rears its head

Therefore in the spirit of my calling and in view of the authority of the priesthood that has been confered upon me, it would be my duty to reprove whatever I esteemed to be wrong fondly hoping in my heart that all parties, would concider it right, and therefore humble themselves, that satan might not take the advantage of us, and hinder the progress of our School.

Now Br. William I want you should bear with me, notwithstanding my plainness —

I would say to you that my feelings, were grieved at the interuption you made upon Elder McLellen, I thought, you should have concidered your relation, with him, in your apostle ship, and not manifest any division of sentiment, between you, and him, for a surrounding multitude to take the advantage of you: — Therefore by way of entreaty, on the account of the anxiety I had for your influence and wellfare, I said, unto you, do not have any feeling, or something to that amount, why I am thus particular, is that if you, have misconstrued, my feelings, toward you, you may be corrected. — [p. 81]

But to procede — after the school was closed Br. Hyrum, requested the privilege, of speaking, you objected, however you said if he would not abuse the school, he might speak, and that you would not allow any man to abuse the school in your house. —

Now you had no reason to suspect that Hyrum, would abuse the school, therefore my feelings were mortifyed, at those unnecessary observations, I undertook to reason, with you but you manifested, an inconciderate and stubourn spirit, I then dispared, of benefiting you, on the account of the spirit you manifested, which drew from me the expression that you was as ugly as the Devil.

Father then commanded silence and I formed a determination, to obey his mandate, and was about to leave the house, with the impression, that you was under the influence of a wicked spirit, you replyed that you, would say what you pleased in your own house, Father replyed, say what you please, but let the rest hold their toungs, then a reflection, rushed through my mind, of the, anxiety, and care I ha[ve] had for you and your family, in doing what I did, in finishing your house and providin[g] flour for your family &c and also father had possession in the house, as well, as your self; and when at any time have I transgressed, the commandments of my father? or sold my birthright, that I should not have the privilege of speaking in my fathers house, or in other words in my fathers family, or in your house, [p. 82] (for so we will call it, and so it shall be,) that I should not have the privilege of reproving a younger brother, therefore I said I will speak, for I built the house, and it is as much mine as yours, or something to that effect, (I should have said that I helped finish the house,) I said it merely to show that it could not be, the right spirit, that would rise up for trifling matters, and undertake to put me to silence, I saw that your indignation was kindled against me, and you made towards me, I was not then to be moved, and I thought, to pull off my loose coat, least it should tangle me, and you be left to hurt me, but not with the intention, of hurting You, but you was to soon for me, and having once fallen into the hands of a mob, and ~~now~~ been wounded in my side,[1] and now into the hands of a brother, my side gave way, and after having been rescued, from your grasp, I left your house, with feelings that were indiscriba[b]le, the scenery had changed, and all those expectations, that I had cherished, when going to your house, of brotherly kindness, charity forbearance and natural affection, that in duty binds us not to make each others offenders for a word.

But alass! abuse, anger, malice, hatred, and rage ⟨with a lame side⟩ with marks, of violence heaped upon ~~my body~~ me by a brother, were the reflections of my disapointment, and with these I returned home, not able to sit down, or rise up, without help, but through the blessings of God I am now better. — [p. 83] I have received your letter and purused it with care. I have not entertained a feeling of malice, against you, I am, older than you and have endured, more suffering, have been mar[r]ed by mobs, the labours of my calling, a series of persecution, and injuries, continually heaped upon me, all serve to debilitate, my body, and it may ⟨be⟩ that I cannot boast of being stronger, than you, if I could, or could not, would this be an honor, or dishonor to me, — if I could boast like David of slaying a Goliath, who defied the armies of the living God,[2]

---

1. Probably a reference to the mobbing at Hiram, Ohio, on 24 March 1832.
2. 1 Samuel 17:10.

or like Paul, of contending with Peter face to face,[1] with sound arguments, it might be an honor, But to mangle the flesh or seek revenge upon one who never done you any wrong, can not be a source of sweet reflection, to you, nor to me, neither to an honorable father & mother, brothers, and sisters, and when we reflect, with what care ~~our parents~~ and with what unremiting diligence our parents, have strove to watch over us, and how many hours, of sorrow, and anxiety, they have spent over our cradles and bedsides, in times of sickness, how careful we ought to be of their feelings in their old age, it cannot be a source of swe[e]t reflection to us to say or do any thing that will bring their grey hairs down with sorrow to the grave.

In your letter you asked my forgivness, which I readily grant, but it seems to me, that you still retain an idea, that I have given you reasons to be angry or disaffected with me.

Grant me the privilege of saying then, [p. 84] that however hasty, or harsh, I may have spoken, at any time to you, it has been done for the express purpose of endeavouring, to warn exhort, admonish, and rescue you, from falling into difficulties, and sorrows which I foresaw you plunging into, by giving way to that wicked spirit, which you call your passions, which you should curbe and break down, and put under your feet, which if you do not you, never can be saved, in my view, in the Kingdom of God.

God requires the will of his creatures, to be swallowed up in his will.

You desire to remain in the church, but forsake your apostleship, this is a stratigem of the evil one, when he has gained one advantage, ~~your~~ he lays a plan for another, but by maintaining your apostleship in rising up, and making one tremendious effort, you may overcome your passions, and please God and by forsaking your apostleship, is not to be willing, to make that sacrafice that God requires at your hands

---

1. Galatians 2:11.

117

and is to incur his displeasure, and without pleasing God do not think, that it will be any better for you, when a man falls one step he must regain that step again, or fall another, he has still more to gain, or eventually all is lost.

I desire brother William that you will humble yourself, I freely forgive you and you know, my unshaken and ~~unshaken~~ unchangable disposition I ~~think~~ know in whom I trust, I stand upon [p. 85] the rock, the floods cannot, no they shall not overthrow me, you know the doctrine I teach is true, and you know that God has blessed me, I brought salvation to my fathers house, as an instrument in the hand of God, when they were in a miserable situation, you know that it is my duty to admonish you when you do wrong this liberty I shall always take, and you shall have the same privilege, I take the privilege, to admonish you because of my birthright, and I grant you the privilege because it is my duty, to be humble and to receive rebuke, and instruction, from a brother or a friend.

As it regards, what course you shall persue hereafter, I do not pretend to say, I leave you in the hands of God and his church. Make your own desision, I will do you good altho you mar me, or slay me, by so doing my garments, shall be clear of your sins, and if at any time you should concider me to be an imposter, for heavens sake leave me in the hands of God, and not think to take vengance on me your self.

Tyrany ursurpation, and to take mens rights ever has and ever shall be banished from my heart.

David sought not to kill Saul, although he was guilty of crimes that never entered my heart.

And now may God have mercy upon my fathers house, may God take [p. 86] away enmity, from betwen me and thee, and may all blessings be restored, and the past be forgotten forever, may humble repentance bring us both to thee ⟨O God⟩ and to thy power and protection, and a crown, to enjoy the society of father mother Alvin Hyrum Sophron[i]a Samuel

Catharine Carloss Lucy the Saints and all the sanctified in peace forever, is the prayer of

~~This from~~ Your brother
Joseph Smith Jun

To William Smith—

19 December 1835 · Saturday

at home wrote the ⟨above⟩ letter to Br. Wm. Smith **I have had many ~~sollam~~ ⟨solemn⟩ feelings this day Concerning my Brothe[r] William and have prayed in my heart to fervently that the Lord will not ~~him~~ ⟨cast him⟩ off but he may return to the God of Jacob and magnify his apostleship and calling may this be his happy lot for the Lord of Glorys Sake Amen**

20 December 1835 · Sunday

At home all day and took solid[1] Comfort with my Family had many serious reflections also Brothers [Ambrose] Palmer and Tailor [Jonathan Taylor] Came to see me I showed them the sacred record to their Joy and sati[s]faction O may God have mercy upon these men and keep them in the way of Everlasting life in the name of Jesus Amen [p. 87]

21 December 1835 · Monday

At home Spent this [day] in indeavering to treasure up know[l]edge for the be[n]ifit of my Calling the ⟨day⟩ pas[s]ed of[f] very pleasantly for which I thank the Lord for his blessings to my soul his great mercy over my Family in sparing our lives O Continue thy Care over me and mine for Christ sake

---

1. MS.: "solled"

*22 December 1835 · **Tuesday***

At home ~~this~~ Continued my studys O may God give me learning even Language and endue[1] me with qualifycations to magnify his name while I live I also deliv[er]ed an address to the Church this Evening the Lord blessed my Soul, my scribe[2] also is unwell O my God heal him and for his kindness to me O my soul be thou greatful to him and bless him and he shall be blessed ~~of for ever~~ of God forever I believe him to be a faithful friend to me therefore my soul delighteth in him Amen

Joseph Smith Jr

*/[3]23 December 1835 · **Wednesday***

In the forenoon at home stud[y]ing the greek Language and also[4] waited upon the brethren who came in and exhibiting to them the papirus, in the afternoon visited brother Leonard Rich with the relatives of bro Oliver Cowdery had not a very agreeable visit for I found them [p. 88] filled with prejudice against the work of the Lord and their minds blinded with superstition & ignorence &c

*24 December 1835 · **Thursday***

At home in the forenoon in the afternoon assisted in running ⟨out⟩ a road across my farm by the commissionor[s] who were appoint[e]d by the court for the same —

*25 December 1835 · **Friday***

At home all this day and enjoyed myself with my family it being Chris⟨t⟩mas day the only time I have had this privilege so satisfactorily for a long time

---

1. MS.: "indo"
2. Warren Parrish.
3. Handwriting of Frederick G. Williams.
4. MS.: "aslo"

26 December 1835 · Saturday

commenced studeing the Hebrew Language in company with bros [Warren] Parrish & [Frederick G.] Williams in the mean time bro Lyman Sherman came in and requested to have the word of the lord through me for said he I have been wrought upon to make known to you my feelings and desires and was promised ~~to have~~ that I should have a revelation ~~and~~ which should make known my duty

last evening a brother from the east called upon me for instruction whose name is Jonathan Crosby[1] also in the course of the day two gentlemen called upon me while I was cutting wood at the door and requested an interview with the head of the church which I agreed to grant to them on Sunday morning the 27 Inst [p. 89] The following is a revelation given to Lyman Sherman this day 26 Dec 1835

Verily thus saith the Lord unto you my servant Lyman your sins are forgiven you because you have obeyed my voice in coming up hither this morning to receive councel of him whom I have appointed

Therefore let your soul be at rest concerning your spiritual standing, and resist no more my voice, and arise up and be more careful henceforth in observing your vows which you have made and do make, and you shall be blessed with exceding great blessings. Wait patiently untill the time when the solemn assembly shall be called of my servants then you shall be

---

1. In an autobiography written later in his life, Crosby recalled arriving in Kirtland in the evening and going to see the Prophet "first of all." Although Joseph was entertaining several people at the time, he made the stranger welcome and put him up for the night. "We had a very plesent time, drank peper and sider and had supper. I thought he was a quear man for a Prophet, at first, he didnt appear exactly as I exspected to see a Prophet of God, however I was not stumbled at all. I found him to be a friendly cheerful pleasent agreable man. I could not help likeing him." (Jonathan Crosby, "A Biographical Sketch of the Life of Jonathan Crosby written by Himself," 13, MS., Utah Historical Society.)

numbered with the first of mine elders and receive right by ordination with the rest of mine elders whom I have chosen

Behold this is the promise of the father unto you if you continue faithful – and it shall be fulfilled upon you in that day that you shall have right to preach my gospel wheresoever I shall send you from henceforth from that time. Therefore strengthen your brethren in all your conversation in all your prayers, and in all your exhortations, and in all your doings, and behold and lo I am with you to bless you and deliver you forever Amen[1]

27 December 1835 · Sunday

at the us[u]al hour, attended meeting at the School house, President Cowdery delivered a verry able and interesting discourse – in the after part of the day Br. [p. 90] Hyrum Smith & Bishop Partri⟨d⟩ge, delivered each a short and ⟨interesting⟩ lecture, after which the sacrament of the Lords supper ⟨was administered⟩ and dismissed our meeting –

Those Gentlemen that proposed to have an interview with me on this morning, did not come, and I conclude they were trifling characters

28 December 1835 · Monday

having prefered a charge against Elder Almon Babbit for traducing my character, he was this morning called before the High Council, and I attended, with my witnesses, and substantiated my charge against him and he in part acknowledged his fault but not satisfactory to the council, and after parleying with him a long time, and granting him every indulgence, that righ[t]eousness require the council adjourned without obtaining a full confession from him –[2]

---

1. Published in D&C 108.
2. Babbitt was brought before the high council for traducing the character of Joseph Smith. His case was not resolved until 2 January 1836, when he reconciled his difficulty and was "restored to fellowship." (Kirtland Council Minutes, 28 December 1835; 2 January 1836.)

On this day the council of the seventy met[1] to render an account of their travels and ministry, since they were ordained to that apostleship,[2] the meeting was interesting indeed, and my heart was made glad while listning to the relations of those that had been labouring, in the vinyard of the Lord with such marvelous success, and I pray God to bless them with an increas[e] of faith, and power, and keep them [p. 91] all with the indurance of faith in the name of Jesus Christ, to ~~Amen~~ the end

29 December 1835 · Tuesday

at home untill about 10. oclock I then went to attend a blessing meeting at Oliver Olneys, in company with my wife, & father and mother who had come to live with me, also my scribe went with us a large company assembled and Father Smith arose and made some preliminary remarks, which were verry applicable, on occasions of this kind, after which ~~he opened the meeting by~~ a hymn was sung and he opened the meeting by prayer about 15 persons then received a patriarchal blessing under his hands —[3] the servises were then dismissed, as they commenced, viz. by singing and prayer. — a table was then spread and crowned with the bounties of nature, and after invoking the benediction of heaven upon the rich repast, we fared sumptuously, and suffice it to say that we had a glorious

---

1. MS.: "meet"
2. The organization of the seventy in the Church had occurred on 28 February 1835, two weeks after the Quorum of Twelve was organized. The revelation that outlined the duties of various priesthood offices stated that the seventy were "called to preach the gospel, and to be especial witnesses unto the Gentiles and in all the world," and that they were "to act . . . under the direction of the Twelve." (D&C 107:25, 34.)
3. Joseph Smith, Sr., had been ordained patriarch to the Church on 18 December 1833. The giving of patriarchal blessings derived from the ancient practice among Old Testament patriarchs (Genesis 27, 49). The blessings, which included words of comfort, counsel, and instruction, also designated the recipients' lineage from one of the tribes of Israel. Among those who received blessings at this time were Lyman Wight, Ezra Hayes, and George Morey.

meeting, through out and I was much pleased with the harmony and decorum that existed among the brethren and sisters, we returned home and ~~spent the evening~~ — at early candlelight I went and pr[e]achd at the school house to a crowded congregation, who listened [p. 92] with attention, while I delivered a lecture of about 3, hours in length, I had liberty in speaking, some presbyterians were present, as I after learned, and I expect that some of my sayings set like a garment that was well fited, as I exposed their abominations in the language of the scriptures, and I pray God that it may be like a nail in a sure place, driven by the master of assemblies. Col. Chamberlains[1] Son called to day

30 December 1835 · Wednesday

spent the day in reading hebrew at the council room, in company with my scribe which gave me much sattisfaction, on the account of his returning health, for I delight in his company

31 December 1835 · Thursday[2]

at home, after attending to the duties of my family, retired to the council room, to persue my studies, the council of the 12 convened in the ⟨upper⟩ room in the printing office directly over the room wher⟨e⟩ we were convened, in our studies, they sent for me and the presidency, (or part of them,) to receive council from us on the subject of the council, which is to be held on Saturday next

In the after noon I attended at the Chapel to give directions, concerning [p. 93] the upper rooms, and more especially the west room which I intend ocupying, for a translating room, which will be prepared this week

---

1. Possibly Solomon Chamberlain (1788–1858).
2. "~~Friday morning Jany. 1st 1836~~" appears in MS. prior to this entry.

1 January 1836 · Friday

this being the beginning of a new year, my heart is filled with gratitude to God, that he has preserved my life and the lives of my family while another year has rolled away, we have been, sustained and upheld in the midst of a wicked and perverse generation, and exposed to all, the afflictions temptations and misery that are incident to human life, for which I feel to humble myself in dust and ashes, as it were before the Lord — but notwithstanding, the gratitude that fills my heart on retrospecting the past year, and the multiplyed blessings that have crowned our heads, my heart is pained within me because of the difficulty that exists in my father's family, the Devil has made a violent attack on Br. Wm [Smith] and Br Calvin [Stoddard] and the powers of darkness, seeme lower over their minds and not only theirs but cast a gloomy shade over the minds of my ~~my parents and some of my~~ brothers and sisters, which prevents them from seeing things as they realy are, and the powers of Earth & hell seem combined to overthrow us and the church by [p. 94] causing a division in the family, and indeed the adversary is bring[ing] into requisition all his subtlety to prevent the Saints from being endowed, by causing division among the 12, also among the 70, and bickerings and jealousies among the Elders and official members of the church, and so the leaven of iniquity foments and spreads among the members of the church.

But I am determined that nothing on my part shall be lacking to adjust and amicably dispose of and settle all family difficulties, on this day, that the ensuing year, and years, be they many or few may be spent in righteousness before God, and I know that the cloud will burst and satans kingdom be laid in ruins with all his black designs, and the saints come forth like gold seven times tried in the fire, being made perfect throug[h] sufferings, and temptations, and the blessings of heaven and earth multiplyed upon our heads which may God grant for Christ sake Amen—

Br. William came to my house and Br. Hyrum, also, Uncle John Smith, we went into a room in company with father and Elder Martin Harris, ~~and~~ father, Smith then opened our interview by prayer after which, he expressed his feelings on the ocasion in a verry feeling and pathetic manner even with all the sympathy of a father whose feeling[s] were wounded deeply on the [p. 95] account of the difficulty that was existing in the family, and while he addressed us the spirit of God rested down upon us in mighty power, and our hearts were melted Br. William made an humble confession and asked ~~our~~ my forgiveness for the abuse he had offered me and wherein I had been out of the way I asked his forgivness, and the spirit of confession and forgiveness, was mutual among us all, and we covenanted with each other in the sight of God and the holy angels and the brethren, to strive from hence forward to build each other up in righteousness, in all things and not listen to evil reports concerning each other, but like brethren, indeed go to each other, with our grievances in the spirit of meekness, and be reconciled and thereby promote our own happiness and the happiness of the family and in short the happiness and well being of all.—my wife and mother, ~~Uncle John~~ & my scribe was then called in and we repeated the covenant to them that we had entered into, and while gratitude swelled our bosoms, tears flowed from our ey[e]s.— I was then requested to close our interview which I did with prayer, and it was truly a jubilee and time of rejoiceing [p. 96]

2 January 1836 · Saturday

acording to previous arangement, I went to council at 9 oclock.—this council was called, to set in judgment, on a complaint, prefered against Br. William, by Elder Orson Johnson[1] the council organized and opened by prayer and proceded to buisness, but before entering on the trial Br. William arose and humbly confessed the charges prefered against him and asked the forgivness of the council and the whole congregation a vote was then called to know whether his confession was satisfactory, and whether the brethren would extend the hand of fellowship to him again, with cheerfulness the whole congregation raised their hands to receive him

Elder Almon Babbit also confessed ~~his~~ the charges which I prefered against him in a previous council,[2] and was received into fellowship, and some other buisness was transacted, in union and fellowship and the best of feelings seemed to prevail among the brethren, and our hearts were made glad on the occasion, and there was joy in heaven, and my soul doth magnify the Lord for his goodness and mercy endureth forever—council adjourned with prayer as usual—

3 January 1836 · Sunday

went to meeting at the us[u]al hour President Rigdon, delivered a fine lecture upon the subject of revelation, in the afternoon I confirmed about 10 or 12 persons who [p. 97] had been baptised, among whom was M[arvel] C. Davis who was baptized at the intermission to day—Br William Smith made his confession to the church to their satisfaction, and was cordially received into fellowship again, the Lords supper was administered, and br. William gave out an appointment to preach in the evening, at early candlelight, and preach[e]d a fine discourse, and this day has been a day of rejoicing to me, the cloud that has been hanging over us has burst with bless-

---

1. On 29 December 1835, Johnson had brought charges against William Smith of "unchristian like conduct in speaking disrespectfully of President Joseph Smith . . . and the revelations & commandments given through him" and for "attempting to inflict personal violence." (Kirtland Council Minutes, 29 December 1835.)
2. See entry of 28 December 1835.

ings on our heads, and Satan has been foiled in his attempts to destroy me and the church, by causing jealousies to arise in the hearts of some of the brethren, and I thank my heavenly father for, the union and harmony which now prevails in the Church

4 January 1836 · Monday

met[1] and organized our hebrew School according to the arangements that were made on saturday last, we had engaged Doct[or] Piexotto [Peixotto] to teach us in the hebrew language, when we had our room prepared, we informed him that we were ready and our room prepared and he agreed to wait on us on this day and deliver his introductory lecture yesterday he sent us word that he [p. 98] could not come untill wedensday next a vote was called to know whether we would, submit to such treatment or not and carried in the negative, and Elder Sylvester Smith appointed as clerk to write him on the subject and inform him that his servises, were not wanted, and Elders Wm E McLellen & Orson ⟨Hyde⟩ Johnson despached to Hudson Semenary,[2] to hire a teacher, they were appointed by the voice of the School, to act for in their behalf — however we concluded to go on with our school and do the best we can untill we can obtain a teacher, and by the voice of the school I concented, to render them all the assistance I am able to, for the time being — we are ocupying the translating room for the use of the School untill another room can be prepared, this is the first day that we have ocupied ⟨it⟩ this room which is the west room

1. MS.: "meet"
2. The Western Reserve College at Hudson, Summit County, Ohio, about twenty-eight miles south of Kirtland, was founded in 1826. The curriculum of the college in the 1830s was theology, languages, philosophy, and mathematics. (William H. Perrin, ed., *History of Summit County, Ohio* [Chicago, 1881], 446–66.)

in the upper part of the Chappel,[1] which was concecrated this morning by prayer offered up by father Smith

This is a rainy time and the roads are extremely mudy met[2] this evening at the Chapel to make arangements for a Singing School after some altercation, a judicious arangement was made, a comittee of 6 was chosen, to take charge of the singing department, [p. 99]

5 January 1836 · Tuesday

attended the Hebrew School, divided them into classes, had some debate with Elder Orson Pratt, he manifested a stubourn spirit, which I was much grieved at

6 January 1836 · Wednesday

attended School again, and spent most of the fore noon in setling, the unplesant feelings that existed in the breast of Elder O. Pratt and after much controversy, he confessed his fault and asked the forgivness of the whol[e] school and was cheerfully forgiven by all

Elder McLellen returned from Hudson, and reported to the school that he had hired a Teacher, to teach us the term of 7. weeks for $320. that is 40. Schollars for that amount, to commence in about 15. days hence. — he is highly celebrated as a hebrew schollar,[3] and proposes to give us sufficient knowledge in the above term of time to read and translate the language [p. 100]

Conference Minuits

at a conference held at the School house on Saturday the 2d Jan 1836 the following individuals were appointed by the voice of the conference to be ordained to the office of Elders

---

1. See Kirtland Temple drawing, *The Papers of Joseph Smith* 1:195.
2. MS.: "meet"
3. Reference to the hiring of Joshua Seixas.

in the church of the latter day saints under the hands of President Joseph Smith Jr

Sidney Rigdon Clerk —

Vincent [Vinson] Knight
Thomas Grover
Elisha [Elijah] Fordham
Hyram Dayton   Eldrs
Samuel James
John Herrott [Herritt]

7 January 1836 · Thursday

attended a sumptuous feast at Bishop N K. Whitneys this feast was after the order of the Son of God the lame the halt and blind wer[e] invited according to the in[s]truction of the Saviour

our meeting was opened by singing and prayer offered up by father Smith, after which Bishop Whitneys father & mother were bless[ed] and a number of others, with a patriarchal blessing, we then received a bountiful refreshment, furnished by the liberality of the Bishop the company was large, — before we parted we had some of the Songs of Zion sung, and our hearts were made glad while partaking of an antipast of those [p. 101] Joys that will be poured upon the head of the Saints w[h]en they are gathered together on Mount Zion to enjoy each others society forever more even all the blessings of heaven and earth ~~and~~ where there will be none to molest nor make us afraid —

returned home and spent the evening

8 January 1836 · Friday

Spent the day in the hebrew School, and made rapid progress in our studies

9 January 1836 · Saturday

attended School in the fore noon at about 11. oclock received the following note

Thus saith the voice of the spirit to me, if thy Brother Joseph Smith jn will attend the feast at thy house this day (at 12 ocl) the poor & lame will rejoice at his presence & also think themselves honored—

Yours in friendship & Love

9th Jany 1836   N[ewel] K. W[hitney]

I dismissed the School in order to attend to this polite invitation, with my wife father & mother

We attended the feast, a large congregation assembled a number was blessed under the hands of father Smith, and we had a good [p. 102] time, returned home and spent the evening

10 January 1836 · Sunday

went to the meeting at the us[u]al hour Elder Wilber Denton & Elder [Wilkins] J[enkins]. Salisbury, preached in the fore noon, in the after noon Br. Samuel & Br. Carloss Smith, they all did well concidering their youth,[1] and bid fair to make useful men in the vinyard of the Lord, administered the sacrament and dismissed

at the intermission to day 3, were baptised by Elder Martin Harris—

returned home and spent the evening—

11 January 1836 · Monday

at home There being no school I spent the day at home, many brethren called to see me, among whom was Alva Bea-

---

1. Salisbury was 26, Samuel Smith, 27, and Don Carlos Smith, 19.

mon from New York Genesee[1] Co. he has come to attend the Solemn Assembly, — I delight in the society of my friends & brethren, and pray that the blessings of heaven and earth may be multiplyed upon their heads

12 January 1836 · Tuesday

at home, — this ⟨day⟩ I called on the presidency of the church, and made arangements to meet tomorrow at 10, oclock A.M [p. 103] to take into concideration the subject of the Solemn Assembly — This after noon, a young man called to see the Egyptian manuscripts, and I exibited them to him, he expressed great satisfaction, and appeared verry anxious to obtain a knowledge of the translation. — also a man was introduced to me by the name of Russel We[a]ver from Cambria[2] Niagary Co. N. Y. this man is a preacher, in the church that is called Christian or Unitarian, ~~some~~ he remarked that he had but few minuits to spend with me, we entered into conversation, and had som[e] little controversy upon the subject of prejudice, but soon come to ~~the~~ an understanding, he spoke of the gospel and said he believed it, adding that it was good tidings of great joy — I replyed that it was one thing, to proclaim good tidings and another to tell what those tidings are, he waived the conversation and withdrew — he was introduced by Joseph Rose —

13 January 1836 · Wednesday

at 10, oclock A. M met[3] in council with all the presidency of Kirtland and Zion ~~that~~ together with ⟨all⟩ their councilors that could be found in this place[4] however some of the councellors were absent, both of Kirtland and Zion

---

1. MS.: "Jenesee"
2. MS.: "Cambray"
3. MS.: "meet"
4. The presidency in Kirtland consisted of Joseph Smith, Sr., Sidney Rigdon, and Hyrum Smith, and at Zion (Missouri) of David Whitmer, John Whitmer, and William W. Phelps. (History of the Church, 2:364.) Another report of the meeting is in Kirtland Council Minutes, 13 January 1836.

The presidency of the Seventy were also present, and many more [p. 104] of the Elders of the church of the latterday Saints — come to order, sung Adam-ondi-ahman and opened by prayer offered up by Joseph Smith Sen —

I ~~President John Smith~~ presided on the occasion

After the council was organized and opened ~~President Joseph Smith jr~~ I made some ~~verry pertinent~~ remarks in my introductory lecture before the authority of the church, this morning, in general terms, laying before them, the buisness of the day which was to suply some deficiencies in the ~~council~~ Bishop['s] coun[c]il in this place ⟨also in the high *council*⟩ after some altercation upon the most proper manner of proc[e]ding Elder Vinson Knight was nominated by the Bishop and seconded by the presidency vote called of that body and caried vote was then called from the high council of Zion and carried vote was then called from the twelve and carried — vote then called from the council of the Seventy and carried — vote then called from the Bishop and his council from Zion and carried — Elder Knight was received by the universal voice and concent of all the authority of the Church as a councilor in the Bishops council ⟨in⟩ this place, to fill the place of Elder Hyrum Smith, who is ordained to the [p. 105] Presidency of the high council of Kirtland

He was then ordained under the hands of Bishop N K. Whitney to the office of a councillor also to that of high priest

Council adjourned for one hour by singing the song, come let us rejoice in the day of Salvation

Council assembled at one oclock P. M organized and proceded to buisness The first buisness this afternoon was to supply some deficiencies in the high council in Kirtland, the stake of Zion John P. Greene was nominated and seconded by the presidency vote taken and carried in his favour by the unanimous voice of ~~the~~ all the authority of the church — he supplyes the place of President O. Cowdery who is elected to the presidency of the high council in this place

Elder Thomas Grover was nominated to supply the place of Luke Johnson who is chosen and ordained one of the twelve Apostles—the nomination was seconded and vote carried in his favour by all the authority present and he is received as a councilor in the high council in Kirtland

Elder Noah Packard was next nominated and seconded to supply the place of Sylvester Smith[1] who is ordained to the presidency of the Seventy—vote called and carried [p. 106] in his favour and Elder Packard was received by the unanimous vote of all the authority present as a high councilor in Kirtland

Elder John Page was nominated, but was not present and his name droped

Elder Joseph Kingsbury was nominated and seconded, to fill the place of Orson Hyde, who is chosen and ordained one of the twelve, vote called and carried unanimously and Elder Kingsbury was received as a hi[g]h councilor in Kirtland

Elder Samuel James, was nominated and seconded to fill the place of Joseph Smith Sen—vote called and carried unanimously in his favour and Elder James was received as a high councilor in Kirtland

The new elected councilors were then called forward in order as they were elected, and ordained under the hands of President's Rigdon, Joseph Smith Sen and Hyrum Smith to the office of High Priests and councilors in this place, viz. Kirtland the Stake of Zion. — many great and glorious blessings were pronounced upon the heads of thes[e] councilors by president S. Rigdon who was spokesman on the occasion

Next proceded to supply the deficiencies in the Zion high council [p. 107] which were two viz. Elder's John Murdock and Solomon Hancock who were absent—Elder's Alva Bemon and Isaac McWithy were nominated and seconded, to s[u]pply their place for the time being vote taken of the whole assembly

---

1. In the Kirtland high council.

and carried in their favour, to serve as councilors in the high council of Zion, for the present

Elder Nathaniel Miliken and Thomas Carrico, were nominated and seconded to officiate as doorkeepers in the house of the Lord, vote called and carried, by the unanimous voice of the assembly

President's Joseph Smith Jn S. Rigdon W. W. Phelps D. Whitmer H. Smith, were nominated and seconded to draft rules and regulation[s] to govern the house of the Lord vote called and carried by the unanimous voice of the whole assembly

The question was agitate[d] whether whispering, should be allowed in our councils and assemblys

A vote was called from the whole assembly and carried in the negative, that no whispering shall be allowed nor any one allowed (except he is called upon or asks permission,) to speak [p. 108] loud in our councils or assemblies, upon any concideration whatever, and no man shall be interupted while speaking unless he is speaking out of place, and every man, shall be allowed to speak in his turn—Elder Miliken objected to officiate in the house of the Lord as door keeper on account of his health, and was released by the voice of the assembly

The minuits of the council were then read, and council adjourned untill Friday the 15th Inst. at 9. ocl A. M. at the ⟨west⟩ school room in the upper part of the Chapel

President S. Rigdon made a request to have some of the presidency lay their hands upon him and rebuke a severe affliction, in his face which troubles him most at night—Eldr's H. Smith and D. Whitmer by my request laid hands upon him and prayed for him and rebuked his disease in the name of the Lord Jesus Christ, —the whole assembly said responded—Amen

Elder D W. Patten also made a request in behalf of his wife for our prayers for her, that she might be healed. —I offered

135

up a pray[er] for her recovery, the assembly responded Amen [p. 109]

President Rigdon then arose and made some verry appropriate remarks touching the enduement, and dismissed the assembly by prayer—

W Parrish   Scribe

This has been one of the best days that I ever spent, there has been an entire unison of feeling expressed in all our p[r]oceedings this day, and the Spirit of the God of Israel has rested upon us in mighty power, and it has ⟨been⟩ good for us to be here, in this heavenly place in Christ Jesus, and altho much fatiegued with the labours of the day, yet my spiritual reward has been verry great indeed

Returned home and spent the evening

14 January 1836 · Thursday

at 9. oclock, met[1] the hebrew class at the school room in the Chapel, and made some arangements, about our anticipated Teacher Mr J. Sexias [Joshua Seixas] of Hudson, Ohio—[2]

I then retired to the council room in the printing office, to me[e]t, my colleagues who were appointed, with my self to draft rules and regulations to be observed in the house of the Lord in Kirtland built by the Church of the latter day saints, in the year of our Lord 1834 which are as follows [p. 110]

1st—It is according to the rules and regulations of all regular and legal organized bodies to have a president to keep order.—

2nd—The body thus organized are under obligation to be in subjection to that authority—

3rd—When a congregation assembles in this house they

---

1. MS.: "meet"
2. See entry of 6 January 1836.

shall submit to the following rules, that due respect may be payed to the order of worship—viz.

1st—no man shall be interupted who is appointed to speak by the presidency of the Church, by any disorderly person or persons in the congregation, by whispering by laughing by talking by menacing Jestures by getting up and running out in a disorderly manner or by offering indignity to the manner of worship or the religion or to any officer of said church while officiating in his office in any wise whatever by any display of ill manners or ill breeding from old or young rich or poor male or female bond or free black or white believer or unbeliever and if any of the above insults are offered such measures will be taken as are lawful to punish the aggressor or aggressors and eject them out of the house

2nd—An insult offered to the presiding Elder of said church, shall be considered an insult to the whole [p. 111] body, also an insult offered to any of the officers of said church while officiating shall be considered an insult to the whole body—

3rd—All persons are prohibited from going up the stairs in times of worship

4th—All persons are prohibited from exploring the house except waited upon by a person appointed for that purpose—

5th—All persons are prohibited from going into the several pulpits except the officers who are appointed to officiate in the same

6th—All persons are prohibited from cutting marking or maring the inside or outside of the house with a knife pencil or any other instrument whatever, under pain of such penalty as the law shall inflict—

7th—All children are prohibited from assembling in the house above or below or any part of it to play or for recreation at any time, and all parents guardians or masters shall be ameneable for all damage that shall accrue in consequence of their children—

8th – All persons whether believers or unbelievers shall be treated with due respect by the authorities of the Church – [p. 112]

9th – No imposition shall be practised upon any member of the church by depriving them of their ⟨rights⟩ in the house – council adjourned sini di [sine die]

returned home and spent the after no[o]n, – towards evening President Cowdery returned from Columbus, the capital of this State,[1] I could not spend much time with him being under obligation to attend at Mrs. Wilcox[']s to join Mr. John Webb and Mrs Catharine Wilcox in matrimony also Mr. Thos Carrico and Miss Elizabeth Baker at the same place, I found a large company assembled, the house was filled to overflowing, we opened our interview by singing and prayer suited to the occasion after which I made some remarks in relation to the duties that are incumbent on husbands and wives, in particular the great importance there is in cultivating the pure principles of the institution, in all its bearings, and connexions with each other and Society in general

I then invited them to arise and join hands, and pronounced the ceremony according to the rules and regulations of the Church of the latter day Saints

~~Closed~~ after which I pronounced such blessings upon their heads as the Lord put into my heart ~~even~~ the blessings of Abraham Isaac and Jacob, and dismissed by singing and prayer

we then took some refreshment [p. 113] and our hearts were made glad with the fruit of the vine, this is according to pattern, set by our Saviour himself, and we feel disposed to patronize all the institutions of heaven

---

1. On 10 October 1835, Oliver Cowdery had been elected by the Geauga County Democratic Convention as a delegate to the state convention held at Columbus on 8 January 1836. He left Kirtland on 3 January. (Diary of Oliver Cowdery for dates indicated. The diary is published in Leonard J. Arrington, "Oliver Cowdery's Kirtland, Ohio, 'Sketch Book,' " *BYU Studies* 12 [Summer 1972]: 410–26.)

I took leave of the congregation and retired

15 January 1836 · Friday

at 9 oclock A.M met[1] in council agreeably to the adjournment, at the council room in the Chapel[2] organized the authorities of the church agreeably to their respective offices in the same, I then made some observation respecting the order of the day, and the great responsibility we are under to transact all our buisness, in righteousness before God, inasmuch as our desisions will have a bearing upon all mankind and upon all generations to come

Sung the song Adam-ondi-ahman and open[ed] by prayer — & proceeded to buisness, by reading the rules and regulations to govern the house of the Lord in Kirtland, — The vote of the presidency was called upon these rules, and ~~carried~~ passed by the unanimous voice of this presidency ⟨viz.⟩ of the high council, some objections were raised by president Cowdery, but waived, on an explination

The privilege of remarking upon the rules above named, was next granted [p. 114] to ⟨the⟩ high councillors of Kirtland, and after much altercation, their vote was called and unanimously passed, in favour of them

The investigation was then thrown before ~~the~~ the ⟨high⟩ council of Zion, some objections or inquiry, was made upon some particular items, which were soon settled, and their vote called ~~called~~ and passed unanimously in favour of them —

The twelve next investigated the subject of these rules,[3] and their vote called and passed unanimously in favour of them — Counsel adjourned for an hour — 1 oclock P. M in council, come to order, and proceded to buisness

---

1. MS.: "meet"
2. I.e., the temple.
3. The following day Joseph Smith explained why the high council had received priority over the Twelve on this occasion, while considering the rules governing the house of the Lord in Kirtland. (See p. 143)

The subject of the rules to govern the house of the Lord, come next in order before the counsel of the Seventy, their vote called and carried unanimously

The vote of the Bishop ⟨of Zion⟩ and his counsillors was then called, and after some debate was passed unanimously

The question was then thrown before the Bishop in Kirtland and his counsellors their vote called and carried in their favour — The above rules hav[e] now passed through the several quorums, in their order, and passed by the unanimous vote of the whole, and are therefore received and established as a law to govern the house of the Lord in this place, — In the investigati[o]n of this subject, I found that many who had deliberated upon this subject [p. 115] were darkened in their minds, which drew forth, some remarks from me, respecting the privileges of the authorities of the church, that they should, each speak in his turn, and in his place, and in his time and season, that their may be perfect order in all things, and that every man, before he, makes an objection to any, item, that is thrown before them for their concideration, should be sure that they can throw light upon the subject rather than spread darkness, and that his objections be founded in righteousness which may be done by applying ourselves closely to study the mind and will of the Lord, whose Spirit always makes manifest, and demonstrates to the understanding of all who are in possession, of his Spirit —

Elder [Don] Carloss Smith was nominated and seconded, to be ordained to the high priesthood[1] — also to officiate as president to preside over that body in ~~this place~~ Kirtland — The vote was called of the respective quorums in their order

---

1. A revelation "on priesthood" dated 28 March 1835 stated that there were two divisions of priesthood in the Church — the Melchizedek and Aaronic. The Melchizedek, or "greater" priesthood, "holds the right of presidency, and has power and authority over all the offices in the church . . . to administer in spiritual things." The Aaronic, or "lesser" priesthood "has power in administering outward ordinances." The revelation stated further that "high priests, after the order of the Melchizedek priesthood, have a right to officiate in their own standing, under the direction of the presidency, in administering spiritual things, and also in the office of an elder, priest, . . . teacher, deacon and member." (D&C 107:1–10.)

and passed through the whole house by their unanimous voice—

Elder Alva Beemon [Alvah Beman], was nominated and seconded to officiate as president of the Elders in Kirtland[1] Elder Beemon arose and asked permission to speak, and made the following remarks—Brethren you [p. 116] know that I am young and I am old and ignorant[2] and kneed much instructions, but I wish to do the will of the Lord—The vote of the several authorities was then called and carried unanimously—

William Cowdery was nominated and seconded to officiate as president over the priests of the Aaronic priesthood[3] in Kirtland, the vote of the assembly was called, beginning at the Bishops council and passing through the several authorities untill it come to the presidency of the high counsel in Kirtland and received their sanction having ⟨been⟩ carried, unanimously in all the departments, below

Oliver Olney was nominated and seconded to preside over the teachers[4] in Kirtland ~~and~~ The vote of the assembly was called and passed unanimously

---

1. Church revelations stated that it was the function of elders to conduct meetings and "administer in spiritual things" in the absence of a high priest. (D&C 20:45; 107:11–12.)

2. This is probably an inadvertent scribal error and should read "you know that you are young and I am old and ignorant." Alvah Beman was born in 1775.

3. The priest's responsibility was "to preach, teach, expound, exhort, and baptize, and administer the sacrament, and visit the house of each member, and exhort them to pray vocally and in secret, and attend to all family duties: and he may also ordain other priests, teachers, and deacons—and he is to take the lead of meetings when there is no elder present . . . [and] assist the elder if occasion requires." (D&C 20:46–52.)

4. The duty of the office of teacher in the Aaronic priesthood was "to watch over the church always, and be with, and strengthen them, and see that there is no iniquity in the church, neither hardness with each other; neither lying, backbiting, nor evil speaking; and see that the church meet together often, and also see that all the members do their duty—and he is to take the lead of meetings in the absence of the elder or priest and . . . warn, expound, exhort, and teach, and invite all to come unto Christ." The teacher did not have authority to baptize, administer the sacrament, or confer the gift of the Holy Ghost. (D&C 20:53–58.)

Ira Bond was nominated and seconded to preside over the deacons[1] in Kirtland–vote called and passed unanimously

Eld[e]r Carloss Smith was called forward to the seat of the presidency and ordained to the office's whereunto he was elected and many blessings pronounced [p. 117] upon his head, by Joseph Smith Jr. S. Rigdon and Hyrum Smith who were appointed to ordain him

Also Eld[e]r Beemon received his ordination under the hands of the same, to the office whereunto he had been elected, and many blessings pronounced upon his head

Bishop Whitney ⟨and his counselors⟩ then proceded to ordain Wm. Cowdery to the office whereunto he had been called, viz. to preside over the priests of the Aaronic priesthood in Kirtland, many blessings were sealed upon his head—

also Oliver Olney to preside over the teachers, in Kirtland with many blessings — also Ira Bond to preside over the deacons in Kirtland, with many blessings upon his head

next proceeded to nominated doorkeepers in the house of the Lord the officers of the several quorums were nominated seconded and carried that each should serve in their turn as doorkeepers, also ~~that~~ Nathaniel Miliken Thomas Carrico Samuel Rolph and Amos R. Orton were elected to the office of doorkeepers [p. 118]

nominated and seconded that the presidency of the high counsel hold the keys of the outer and inner courts of the Lords house in Kirtland, except one of the vestries ⟨keys⟩ which is to be held by the Bishopric of the Aaronic Priesthood[2]

---

1. The office of deacon in the Aaronic priesthood was to assist the teachers and "warn, expound, exhort, and teach, and invite all to come unto Christ." As with the teachers, the deacons did not have authority to baptize, administer the sacrament, or confer the gift of the Holy Ghost. (D&C 20:57–59.)

2. One of the functions of the bishopric, consisting of the bishop and his counselors, was to preside over the Aaronic priesthood in administering the temporal affairs of the Church. The bishop was also appointed to be "a judge in Israel," to "sit in judgment upon transgressors." (D&C 107:13–15, 68, 72–74.)

the vote of the assembly called and carried unanimously

nominated and seconded that John Carrill [Corrill] be appointed to take charge of the house of the Lord in Kirtland immediately The vote of the assembly called and passed unanimously

President Rigdon then arose and delivered his charge to the assembly, his remarks were few and appropriate—adjourned by ~~singing and~~ prayer[1]

W. Parrish *Scribe*

16 January 1836 · Saturday[2]

by request I meet with the council of the 12 in company with my colleagues F G Williams and S. Rigdon

Council organized and opened by singing and prayer offered up by Thomas B. Marsh president of the 12

He arose and requested the privilege in behalf of his col-

---

1. The purpose of this meeting, and the one two days previous which constituted a gathering of the entire Church leadership, was to fill gaps in the organization of the Church leadership, and, since the first temple was nearing completion and would soon be dedicated, make regulations to govern the conduct of those who entered that holy edifice.

According to the minutes of the Kirtland High Council, after the meeting convened, Joseph Smith "proceeded to give many good instructions in relation to the order & manner of conducting the council and also delivered a solemn charge to the counsel after which he opened by prayer and presided as before."

"President J. Smith Junr one of the committee to draft rules for the regulation of the House of the Lord, made the report of said committee by reading the rules they had drafted three times. They were approved and unanimously adopted, and the counsil adjourned one hour."

"Met at the expiration of the time aforesaid and proceeded to business without ceremony. Motioned and seconded that the Laws regulating the house of the Lord go into effect from this time, and that Elder John Corril take it upon him to see that they are enforced, giving him the privelege of calling as many as he choose to assist him." (Kirtland Council Minutes, 15 January 1836.)

Oliver Cowdery summarized the events of 15 January in his diary: "The several Quorums of the authorities of the Church met today, and transacted important business preparatory to the endowment. The Spirit of the Lord was in our midst." (Diary of Oliver Cowdery, 15 January 1836; published in Leonard J. Arrington, "Oliver Cowdery's Kirtland, Ohio, 'Sketch Book.' ")

2. MS. reads "Saturday morning the 16th"

leagues of speaking, each in his turn without being interupted; which was granted them—Elder Marsh proceeded [p. 119] to unbosom his feelings touching the mission of the 12, and more particularly respecting a certain letter which they received from the presidency of the high council in Kirtland, while attending a conference in the ~~East~~ State of Maine—also spoke of being plased in our council, on Friday last below the council's of Kirtland and Zion having been previously placed next [to] the presidency, in our assemblies—also observed that they were hurt on account of some remarks made by President H. Smith on the trial of Gladden Bishop[1] who had been previously tried before the council of the 12, while on their mission in the east,[2] who had by their request thrown his case before the high council in Kirtland for investigation, and the 12 concidered that their proceedings with him were in some degree, discountenanced—[3]

~~The remaining~~ Elder Marsh then gave way to his brethren and they arose and spoke in turn untill they had all spoken acquiessing in the observations of Elder Marsh and mad[e] some additions to his remarks which are as follows—That the letter in question which they received from the presidency, in which two of their numbers were suspended, and the rest severely chastened, and that too upon testimony which was

---

1. See entry of 28 September 1835.

2. Reference is made to the 4 May–26 September 1835 mission of the Twelve in which they traveled through the eastern states and New England holding conferences and regulating the affairs of the Church. (See entry of 26 September 1835.)

3. The March 1835 revelation that defined and established the interrelationship between the presiding quorums of the Church designated the First Presidency, the Quorum of Twelve, and the stake high councils as "equal in authority in the affairs of the church, in all their decisions." (D&C 107:22–24, 36–37.) For a time after their appointment as a quorum, as the nature and scope of their apostolic calling was being defined, the Twelve, individually and collectively, confronted Joseph Smith with issues that concerned their relationship to him, the First Presidency, and the high council. The meeting on 16 January was an attempt to resolve some of these issues. (For a discussion of this context see Esplin, "The Emergence of Brigham Young and the Twelve," chapter 4.)

unwarantable, and particularly stress was laid upon a certain letter which the presidency had received from Dr. [p. 120] W[arren]. A. Cowdery of Freedom New York in which he prefered charges against them which were false,[1] and upon which they ⟨we⟩ (the presiders) had acted in chastning them and therefore, the 12, had concluded that the presidency had lost confidence in them, and that whereas the church in this place, had carressed them, at the time of their appointment, to the appostleship they now treated them coolly and appear to have lost confidence in them also —

They spoke of their having been in this work from the beginning almost and had born[e] the burden in the heat of the day and passed through many trials and that the presidency ought not to have suspect their fidelity nor loose confidence in them, neither have chastised them upon such testimony as was lying before before them — also urged the necessity of an explanation upon the letter which they received from the presidency, and the propriety of their having information as it respects their duties, authority &c that they might come to ⟨an⟩ understanding in all things, that they migh[t] act in perfect unison and harmony before the Lord and be prepared for the endument [endowment] — also that they had prefered a charge against Dr [Warren] Cowdery for his unchristian conduct which the presidency had disregarded — also that President O. Cowdery on a certain occasion had made use of language to one of the [p. 121] twelve that was unchristian and unbecoming any man, and that they would not submit to such treatment

---

1. While the Twelve were on their mission to the East in 1835, they were censured by the Presidency for neglecting "to teach the Church in Freedom, New York the necessity of contributing of their earthly substance for the building of the House of the Lord" in Kirtland. The censure was based upon a letter sent them by Warren Cowdery. In a note of reconciliation, published in the February 1836 *Messenger and Advocate*, Cowdery apologized, stating that he had afterward learned that his observations were ill-founded.

The remarks of all the 12 were made in a verry forcible and explicit manner yet cool and deliberate, /¹ I arose

I observed that we had heard them patiently and in turn should expect to be heard patiently also; and first I remarked that it was necessary that the 12 should state whether they were determined to persevere in the work of the Lord, whether the presidency are able to satisfy them or not; vote called and carried in the affirmative unani⟨m⟩ously; I then said to them that I had not lost confidence in them, and that they had no reason to suspect my confidence, and that I would be willing to be weighed in the scale of truth today in this matter, and risk it in the day of judgment; and as it respects the chastning contained in the letter in question which I acknowledge might have been expressed in too harsh language; which was not intentional and I ask your forgiveness in as much as I have hurt your feelings; but nevertheless, the letter that that Elder Mclellen wrote back to Kirtland while the twelve were at the east was harsh also and I was willing to set the one against the other; I next proceeded to explain the subject of the duty of the twelve; and their authority which is next to the present presidency, and that the arangement of the assembly in this place on the 15 inst /²in placing the high councils of Kirtland and next [to] the presidency was because the buisness to be transacted was buisness that related to that body in particular which was to [p. 122] fill the several quorum's in Kirtland; not beca[u]se they were first in office, and that the arangement was most Judicious that could be made on the occasion also the 12, are not subject to any other than the first presidency; viz. myself S. Rigdon and F G. Williams — I also stated to the 12, that I do not continue countinanc[e] the harsh language of President Cowdery to them neither in myself nor any other man, although I have sometimes spoken to harsh from the

1. Possibly the handwriting of Jesse Hitchcock.
2. Handwriting of Warren Parrish.

impulse of the moment and inasmuch as I have wounded your feelings brethren I ask your forgivness, for I love you and will hold you up with all my heart in all righteousness before the Lord, and before all men, for be assured brethren I am willing to stem the torrent of all opposition, in storms in tempests in thunders and lightning by sea and by land in the wilderness or among fals[e] brethren or mobs or wherever God in his providence may call us and I am determined that neither hights nor depths principalities nor powers things present or to come nor any other creature shall separate me from you; and I will now covenant with you before God that I will not listen too nor credit, any derogatory report against any of you nor condemn you upon any testimony beneath the heavens, short of that testimony which is infalible, untill I can see you face to face and know of a surity [p. 123] and I do place unlimited confidence in your word for I believe you to be men of truth, and I ask the same of you, when I tell you any thing that you place equal confidence in my word for I will not tell you I know anything which I do not know — but I have already consumed more time than I intended to when I commenced and I will now give way to my colleagues

President Rigdon arose next and acquiessed in what I had said and acknowledged to the 12, that he had not done as he ought, in not citing Dr. Cowdery to trial on the charges that were put into his hands by the 12, that he had neglected his duty in this thing, for which he asked their forgiveness, and would now attend to it if they desired him to do so, and ~~Elder~~ ⟨Presdt⟩ Rigdon also observed to the 12 ~~that~~ ⟨if he⟩ ~~he might~~ had spoken, or reproved too harshly, at any time and had injured their feelings by so doing he asked their forgivness. —

President Williams arose and acquiessed in the above sentiments expressed by myself and President Rigdon, in full and said many good things

The President of the 12, then called a vote of that body to know whether they were perfectly satisfied with the [p. 124]

explenation which we had given them and whether they would enter into the covenant we had proposed to them, which was most readily manifested in the affirmative by raising their hands to heaven, in testimony of their willingness and desire to enter into this covenant and their entire satisfaction with our explanation, upon all the difficulties that were on their minds, we then took each other by the hand in confirmation of our covenant and their was a perfect unison of feeling on this occasion, and our hearts over flowed with blessings, which were pronounced upon each others heads as the Spirit gave us utterance my scribe is included in this covenant with and blessings with us, for I love him, for the truth and integrity that dwelleth in him and may God enable us all, to perform our vows and covenants with each other in all fidelity and rightiousness before Him, that our influence may be felt among the nations of the earth in mighty power, even to rend the Kingdom of darkness in sunder, and triumph over priestcraft and spiritual wickedness in high places, and brake in pieces all other Kingdoms that are opposed to the Kingdom of Christ, and spread the light and truth of the everlasting gospel from the rivers to the ends of the earth

Elder Beemon call[ed] for council upon the subject of his returning home he wished to know whether it was best for him to return before the Solemn Assembly [p. 125] or not, after taking it into concideration the council advised him to tarry we dismissed by singing and prayer and retired

W. Parrish   Scribe

17 January 1836 · Sunday[1]

/[2]Attended meeting at the schoolhouse at the usual hour a large congregation assembled; I proceeded to organize the several quorums present; first, the presidency; then the twelve,

---

1. MS. reads "Sunday morning the 17th"
2. Possibly handwriting of Jesse Hitchcock.

and the seventy all who were present also the counsellors of Kirtland and Zion. President Rigdon then arose /[1]and observed that instead of preaching the time would be occupied, by the presidency and twelve in speaking each in their turn untill they had all spoken, the Lord poured out his spirit upon us, and the brethren began to confess their faults one to the other and the congregation were soon overwhelmed in tears and some of our hearts were too big for utterance, the gift of toungs, come upon us also like the rushing of a mighty wind, and my soul was filled with the glory of God.

In the after noon I joined three couple in matrimony, in the publick congregation, whose names are as follows — Wm F. Cahoon and Maranda [Miranda] Gibbs ~~Larona Cah~~ Harvy Stanly [Harvey Stanley] and Larona Cahoon — also Tunis Rap[p]leye and Louisa Cutler, — We then administered the Lord['s] supper and dismissed the congregation; ⟨which⟩ was so dense that it was [p. 126] verry unpleasant for all — we were then invited to Elder Cahoons to a feast which was prepared on the occasion, and had a good time while partaking of the rich repast that was spread before us, and I verily realized that it was good for brethren to dwell together in unity, ~~even~~ like the dew upon the mountains of Israel, where the Lord commands blessings, even life for ever more,

Spent the evening at home

18 January 1836 · Monday

attended the hebrew school, — This day the Elders School was removed into the Chapel in the room adjoining ours — nothing very special transpired

Copy of a Letter
Willoughby January 5th 1836

To Elder W. Parrish

---

1. Handwriting of Warren Parrish.

Sir I have received an open note from Mr. Sylvester Smith informing me that your School concidered itself dissolved from all ingagements with me, for this I was not unprepared. But he adds that I must excuse him for saying that I appear to be willing to trifle with you in regard to appointments time, &c—

This insinuation is unworthy of me beneath my sence of honour, and I [p. 127] could hope unwaranted by any mean suspicion of your whole body—I wrote for books to New York by Mr. Cowdery–not but I could I could not have taught the rudiments without them–but because I wished to make my instruction philosophically availing as well as mere elementary. In this object I thought myself confirmed by *you*, my books have not come as yet & are probably lost—of the pecuniary value I seek not. —I borowed a book of Elder Boynton, & told him, believing him to be responsible that Wednesday would be best for me to deliver a publick lecture owing to my engagements here. I here was *officially* informed when the School was to be *opened* by me. —

The addition of insult to wrong may be gratifying to small minds—mine is above it, scorns and repud[i]ates it. —

I am verry respectfully Your verry ob. Servt.

Daniel L M. Piexotto [Peixotto]

/¹The Answer

Kirtland Jan 11th 1836

Dr. Piexotto,

Sir, I received yours of the 5th Inst in which you manifested much indignation and considered your hounour highly insulted by us as a body, if not by me as an individual, and deprecated our conduct because we informed you that you appear[e]d willing to trifle with us, as it [p. 128] respects our engagement with you to teach our Hebrew class I have acted in this matter as agent for the School; the time agreed upon

---

1. Possibly handwriting of Jesse Hitchcock.

for you to commence, was not to be protracted, at farthest later than Dec 15th and the class have ever till now, considered themselves bound by the engagement I made with you. — When Elder Cowdery and myself called, you set a time that you would come over to Kirtland and have our agreement committed to writing, but did not come, some were displeased, I excused you; some days passed without our hearing from you: at length Dr Williams called and you specified another time that you would come, (which is some 2 or 3 weeks since) the class were again disappointed, I again plead an excuse for you; on last saturday week, or in other words on the 2 Inst our class met and agreed to organize ~~the~~ on Monday morning the 4 Inst, at 9 oclock A.M. and by the voice of the school I was appointed to wait on you, and advertize your honour that we were ready, and should expect you to attend at that ~~hau~~ hour; presuming that you would be ready at this late period to fulfill your engagement if you ever intended to; and accordingly I called, and informed you of the arang⟨e⟩ments we had made, but on account of your arang⟨e⟩ments at the *Medical University* I was willing to exceed my instructions, and let you name the hour that you would wait on us on that day, which was at 4 oclock P.M.

Sunday the 3 inst, I learned from Elder Boyanton [Boynton] that it would be most convenient for you to call on Wedensday, the school knew nothing of this as a body, on Monday morning we met, and I was called upon to report which I did; I also stated what I had [p. 129] heard from Elder Boyanton, the voice of the class was called to know, whether they considered themselves any longer under obligation to you, and whether they would wait any longer for you, and carried in the negative.

Now sir, what could I say in your behalf? I answer, nothing; I should have considered it an insult to have asked 40 men who had laid by every other consideration to attend this school, to lay upon their oars 3 days longer with the impression on their minds, (and justly too) that it would be altogether uncertain whether you would come then or not.

With these things lying before us, we are told by your *honour* that it may be gratifying to small minds to add *insult* to *wrong*; and you also informed me in your note, that you was not unprepared for the inteligence it contained, which is virtually saying that you intended the abuse you have heaped upon us.

I assure you sir that I have ever entertained the best of feelings towards you, and have recognized you as a friend in whom I could repose unlimited confidence and with[1] whom I have acted in good faith, and I am not a little surprized on this occasion, that you should treat us with such marked contem⟨pt⟩ and then upbraid us with adding insult to wrong; small as you may consider our minds, we have sufficient discernment to discover this insult, although offered by your *honour*, and sufficient good manners not to insult or wrong any man.

Respectfully your most obedient humble servant
Warren Parrish

P.S. The note that we sent you, was well sealed when it was put into the hands of the messenger; which you informed me you recieved open, yours

W. P. [p. 130]

/[2]~~Monday morning the 18th at 9 oclock, attended the hebrew school, nothing special transpir[e]d on this day—spent the evening at home with my family—~~

19 January 1836 · Tuesday

spent the day at school, the Lord blessed us in our studies.— this day we commenced reading in our hebrew bibles with much success, it seems as if the Lord opens our minds, in a marvelous manner to understand his word in the original

---

1. MS.: "whith"
2. Handwriting of Warren Parrish.

language, and my prayer is that God will speedily endue[1] us with a knowledge of all languages and toungs, that his servants may go forth for the last time, to bind up the law and seal up the testimony

Form of Marriage Certificate—
I hereby certify that agreeably to the rules and regulations of the Church of Christ of Latter-Day Saints, on matrimony, were joined in marriage Mr. William F. Cahoon and Miss Nancy M. Gibbs, both of this place, on Sabbath the 17th instant.

Joseph Smith Jun
Presiding Elder of said Church [p. 131]

Kirtland Ohio Jan. 18th 1836

20 January 1836 · Wednesday[2]

attended school at the us[u]al hour, and spent the day in reading and lecturing, and made some advancement in our studies, — At evening I attended at John Johnsons with my family, on a matrimonial occasion, having been invited to do so, ~~and~~ to join President John F. Boynton and Miss Susan Lowell in marriage, a large and respectable company assembled, and were seated by Eldr's O. Hyde & W. Parrish in the following order— The presidency and their companions in the first seats the twelve apostles in the second the 70, in the third, and the remainder of the congregation seated with their companions

After the above arangments were made Eldr Boynton & his Lady with their attendants, came in and were seated in front of the presidency—a hymn was sung, after which I adressed a throne of grace, —I then arose and read aloud a licence granting any minister of the gospel the priviledge of solem-

---

1. MS.: "indu"
2. MS. reads "Wednesday morning 20th"

nizing the rights of matrimony, and after calling for objection if any there were, against the anticipated alliance between Eldr Boynton & Miss Lowell and waiting sufficient time, I observed that all forever after this must hold their peace —

I then envited them to join hands and I pronounced the ceremony according to the rules and regulations of the church of the Latter-day Saints, in the name of [p. 132] God, and in the name of Jesus Christ I pronounced upon them the blessings of Abraham Isaac and Jacob and such other blessings as the Lord put into my heart, and being much under the influence of a cold I then gave way and President S. Rigdon arose and delivered a verry forcible address, suited to the occasion, and closed the servises of the evening by prayer. — Eldr O. Hyde Eldr L. Johnson & Eldr W. Parrish who served on the occasion, then presented the presidency with three servers filled with glasses of wine, to bless, and it fell to my lot to attend to this duty, which I cheerfully discharged, it was then passed round in order, then the cake, in the same order, and suffise it to say our hearts were made ~~cheerful and~~ glad, while partaking of the bounty of the earth, which was presented, untill we had taken our fill, and Joy filled every bosom, and the countenances of old, and young, alike, seemed to bloom with the cheerfulness and smiles of youth and an entire unison of feeling seemed to pervade the congregation, and indeed I doubt whether the pages of history can boast of a more splendid and inocent wedding and feast than this for it was conducted after the order of heaven, who has a time for all thing[s] and this being a time of rejoicing, we hartily embraced it, and conducted ourselves accordingly — Took leave of the [p. 133] company and returned home. —

21 January 1836 · Thursday[1]

This morning a minister from Conneticut by the name of John W. Olived called at my house and enquired of my father

---

1. MS. reads "Thursday morning the 21st"

if ~~Smith~~ the pro[p]het live's here he replied that he did not understand him. Mr. Olived asked the same question again and again and recieved the same answer. he finally asked if Mr. Smith lives here, father replyed O yes Sir I understand you now. — father then stept into my room, and informed me that a gentleman had called to see me, I went into the room where he was, and the first question he asked me, after passing a compliment, was to know how many members we have in our church, I replyed to him, that we hav[e] ~~about~~ between 15 hundred and 2,000 in this branch. — [1] He then asked me wherein we differ from other christian denomination[s] I re-plyed that we believe the bible, and they do not. — however he affirmed that he believed the bible, I told him then to be bap-tised, — he replied that he did not realize it to be his duty — But when [I] laid ~~him~~ before him the principles of the gospel, viz. faith and repentance and baptism for the remission ⟨of sins⟩ and the laying on of hands for the reseption of the Holy Ghost ⟨he manifested much surprise⟩ — I then observed that the [p. 134] hour for school had arived, and I must attend The man seemed astonished at our doctrine but by no means hostile

At about 3. oclock P. M I dismissed the school and the presidency, retired to the loft of the printing office, where we attended to the ordinance of washing our bodies in pure water,[2] we also perfumed our bodies and our heads, in the name of

---

1. At this time there was no way to accurately determine Church member-ship. In October 1835 Joseph Smith had told a visitor there were "about five or six hundred" who communed at the chapel in Kirtland and "perhaps a thousand" church members in the vicinity. (See entry of 30 October 1835.) Milton Backman has estimated the LDS Kirtland population in 1836 at about 1,300. In 1843 the Prophet told an inquirer, "There are no correct data by which the exact number of members comprising this . . . Church . . . can be known." (Backman, *The Heavens Resound*, 139–40; Dean Jessee, "The Beginning of Mormon Record Keeping," in *The Prophet Joseph: Essays on the Life and Mission of Joseph Smith*, by Larry C. Porter and Susan Easton Black, eds. [Salt Lake City: Deseret Book Company, 1988], 144.)

2. A sanctifying ordinance in preparation for the endowment. (See Cook, *Revelations*, 216–17.)

the Lord at early candlelight, I met[1] with the presidency, at the west school room in the Chapel[2] to attend to the ordinance of annointing our heads with holy oil—also the councils of ~~Zion~~ Kirtland and Zion, met in the two adjoining rooms, who waited in prayer while we attended to the ordinance,— I took the oil in my ⟨left⟩ ~~right~~ hand, father Smith being seated before me and the rest of the presidency encircled him round about. — we then streched our right hands to heaven and blessed the oil and concecrated it in the name of Jesus Christ—we then laid our hands on our aged fath[er] Smith, and invoked, the blessings of heaven,—I then annointed his head with the concecrated oil, and sealed many blessings upon him, ~~head,~~ the presidency then in turn, laid their hands upon his head, beginning at the eldest, untill they had all laid their hands on him, and pronounced such blessings, upon his head as the Lord put into their hearts — all blessing him to be our patriarch,[3] ~~and~~ ⟨to⟩ annoint our [p. 135] heads, and attend to all duties that pertain to that office.—I then took the seat, and father annoint[ed] my head, and sealed upon me the blessings, of Moses, to lead Israel in the latter days, even as moses led him in days of old,—also the blessings of Abraham Isaac and Jacob. — all of the presidency laid their hands upon me and pronounced upon my head many prophesies, and blessings, many of which I shall not notice at this time, but as Paul said, so say I, let us come to vissions and revelations,—[4]The heavens were opened upon us and I beheld the celestial kingdom of God, and the glory thereof, whether in the body or out I cannot tell,—I saw the transcendant beauty of the gate ~~that enters~~, through which the heirs of that Kingdom will enter, which was like unto circling flames of fire, also the blasing throne of

---

1. MS. here and three lines below reads "meet."
2. I.e., the temple.
3. MS.: "patraark"
4. Beginning at this point a portion of this entry is published as D&C 137.

God, whereon was seated the Father and the Son, — I saw the beautiful streets of that Kingdom, which had the appearance of being paved with gold — I saw father Adam, and Abraham and Michael and my father and mother, my brother Alvin that has long since slept, and marvled how it was that he had obtained ~~this~~ an inheritance ⟨in⟩ that[1] Kingdom, seeing that he had departed this life, before the Lord ⟨had⟩ set his hand to gather Israel ⟨the second time⟩ and had not been baptised for the remission of sins — Thus ~~said~~ came the voice ⟨of the Lord un⟩to me saying all who have [p. 136] died with[out] a knowledge of this gospel, who would have received it, if they had been permited to tarry, shall be heirs of the celestial kingdom of God — also all that shall die henseforth, with⟨out⟩ a knowledge of it, who would have received it, with all their hearts, shall be heirs of that kingdom, for I the Lord ⟨will⟩ judge all men according to their works according to the desires of their hearts — and ~~again I also beheld the Terrestial Kingdom~~ I also beheld that all children who die before they arive to the years of accountability, are saved in the celestial kingdom of heaven — I saw the 12, apostles of the Lamb, who are now upon the earth who hold the keys of this last ministry, in foreign lands, standing together in a circle much fatiegued, with their clothes tattered and feet swolen, with their eyes cast downward, and Jesus ⟨standing⟩ in their midst, and they did not behold him, the Saviour looked upon them and wept — I also beheld Elder McLellen in the south, standing upon a hill surrounded with a vast multitude, preaching to them, and a lame man standing before him, supported by his crutches, he threw them down at his word, and leaped as an hart,[2] by the mighty power of God

Also Eld[er] Brigham Young standing in a strange land, in the far southwest, in a desert place, upon a rock in the midst

---

1. "that" written over "this" in MS.
2. MS.: "heart"

of about a dozen men of colour, who, appeared hostile [p. 137] He was preaching to them in their own toung, and the angel of God standing above his head with a drawn sword in his hand protec[t]ing him, but he did not see it, — and I finally saw the 12 in the celestial kingdom of God, — I also beheld the redemption of Zion, and many things which the toung of man, cannot discribe in full. — Many of my brethren who received this ordinance with me, saw glorious visions also, — angels ministered unto them, as well as my self, and the power of the highest rested upon, us the house was filled with the glory of God, and we shouted Hosanah to the God and the Lamb

I am mistaken, concerning my receiving the holy anointing first after father Smith, we received ⟨it⟩ in turn according to our age, (that is the presidency,)

My Scribe also recieved his anointing ⟨with us⟩ and saw in a vision the armies of heaven protecting the Saints in their return to Zion — & many things that I saw

The Bishop of Kirtland with his counsellors and the Bishop of Zion with his counsellors, were present with us, and received their, annointing under the hands of father Smith and confirmed by the presidency and the glories of heaven was unfolded to them also —

We then invited the counsellors of Kirtland and Zion and Kirtland into our room, and President Hyrum [p. 138] Smith annointed the head of the president of the counsellors in Kirtland and President D. Whitmer the head of the president, of the counsellors of Zion —

The president of each quorum then annointed the heads of his colleagues, each in his turn beginning, at the eldest

The vision of heaven was opened to these also, some of them saw the face of the Saviour, and others were ministered unto by holy angels, and the spirit of prop[h]esy and revelation was poured out in mighty power, and loud hosanahs and glory to God in the highest, saluted the heavens for we all communed with the h[e]avenly host's, — and I saw in my vision all of the presidency in the Celestial Kingdom of God, and, many others who were present[1]

Our meeting was opened by singing and prayer offered up by the head of each quorum, and closed by singing and invoking the benediction of heaven with uplifted hands, and retired between one and 2. oclock in the morning [p. 139]

22 January 1836 · Monday

attended at the school room at the us[u]al hour. – But insted of persuing our studies /²we ~~commenced~~ spent the time in rehearsing to each other the glorious scenes that transpired on the preceding evening, while attending to the ordinance of holy anointing. – At evening we met at the same place, with the council of the 12 and the presidency of the 70 who were to receive this ordinance; the high councils of Kirtland and Zion were present also: we called to order and organized; the Presidency then proceeded to consecrate the oil; we then laid our hands upon Elder Thomas B. Marsh who is the president of the 12 and ordained him to the authority of anointing his brethren, I then poured the concecrated oil upon his head in the name of Jesus Christ and sealed such blessings upon him as the Lord put into my heart; the rest of the presidency then

---

1. Oliver Cowdery also recorded the events of 21 January: "At about three o'clock P.M. I assembled in our office garret, having all things prepared for the occasion, with presidents Joseph Smith, jr. F.G. Williams, Sidney Rigdon Hyrum Smith, David Whitmer, John Whitmer and elder John Corrill, and washed our bodies with pure water before the Lord, preparatory to the annointing with holy oil. After we were washed, our bodies were perfumed with a sweet smelling oderous wash. At evening the presidents of the Church, with the two bishops and their counsellors, and elder Warren Parrish, met in the presidents' room, the high councils of Kirtland and Zion in their rooms. Those named in the first room were annointed with the same kind of oil and in the man[ner] that were Moses and Aaron, and those who stood before the Lord in ancient days, and those in the other rooms with annointing oil prepared for them. The glorious scene is too great to be described in this book, therefore, I say, that the heavens were opened to many, and great and marvelous things were shown." (Oliver Cowdery Diary, 21 January 1836.)

2. Possibly handwriting of Jesse Hitchcock.

laid their hands upon him and blessed him each in their turn beginning at the eldest; he then anointed ⟨and blessed⟩ his brethren from the oldest to the youngest, I also laid my hands upon them and prounounced many great and glorious [blessings] upon their heads; the heavens were opened and angels ministered unto us.

The 12 then proceeded to anoint and bless the presidency of the 70 and seal upon their heads power and authority to anoint their brethren; the heavens were opened upon Elder Sylvester Smith and he leaping up exclaimed, The horsemen of Israel and the chariots thereof. ~~President Rigdon arose~~ /[1]Br. [Don] Carloss Smith was also, annointed and ~~ordained~~ blessed to preside over the high priesthood. — President Rigdon, arose to conclude the servises of the evening [p. 140] by invoking the benediction of heaven ~~of heaven~~ upon the Lords anointed ⟨which he did⟩ in an eloquent manner the congregation shouted a loud hosannah the gift of toungs, fell upon us in mighty pow[e]r, angels mingled ~~themselves~~ their voices with ours, while their presence was in our midst, and unseasing prasis swelled our bosoms for the space of half an hour, — I then observed to the brethren that it was time to retire, we accordingly ⟨closed⟩ our interview and returned home at about 2. oclock in the morning /[2]& the spirit & visions of God attended me through the night[3]

---

1. Handwriting of Warren Parrish.
2. Handwriting of Sylvester Smith.
3. Of 22 January Oliver Cowdery wrote, "At evening met in the president's room where were the presidents, the twelve, the presidents of the 70, the high councils of Kirtland and Zion, and the bishops and their counsellors. The presidents proceeded and annointed Thomas B. Marsh, the president of the twelve, and he annointed the other eleven. The Twelve then proceeded, president Marsh taking the lead, and annointed the presidents of the Seventy. Elder Don Carlos Smith was ordained and annointed president of the high priesthood of the Melchisedek priesthood, by the presidents of the Church. Near the close of the meeting, 2 o'clock in the morning, almost all present broke out in tongues and songs of Zion." (Oliver Cowdery Diary, 22 January 1836.)

23 January 1836 · Saturday

attended at the school room as usual & we came together filled with the spirit as on the past evening & did not fe[e]l like studying but commenced conversing upon heavenly things & the day was spent agreably & profitably—⟨Elder⟩ ~~& other~~ Alvah Beaman had been tempted to doubt the things which we recd. on saturday evening & he made an humble confession & asked forgiveness of the school whi[c]h was joyfully given— & the ~~old man~~ said he would try to resist Satan in [the] future

24 January 1836 · Sunday

Met the several quorems in the room under the printing office & after organizing & op[e]ning by prayer called upon the High council of Kirtland to proceede and confess their sins as th[e]y might be directed by the spirit—& they occupied the first part of the day and confessed & exhorted as the spirit led.— P.M. attended again & saw ⟨the⟩ Bread & wine administered to the quorems & brethren who were present—

In the evening met the Presidency in the room over the printing room & counseled on the subject of endowment & the preperation necessary for [p. 141] the solemn Assembly which is to be called when the House of the Lord is finished[1]

25 January 1836 · Monday

Recd a line from my scribe informing me of his ill health as follows—

Brother Joseph, My great desire to be in your company &

---

1. According to Oliver Cowdery, "The quorums met today: we had a good season. At evening met the presidency in the upper room in the printing office, and conversed upon the time of, and preparation and sanctification for the endowment." (Oliver Cowdery Diary, 24 January 1836; see also the Joseph Smith journal entries of 5 October 1835, note 2, p. 47, and 27–30 March 1836.)

in the Assembly of the Saints where God opens[1] the heavens & exhibits the treasures of eternity is the only thing that has stimulated me for a number of days past to leave my house; for be assured, dear brother, my bodily affliction is severe; I have a violent ⟨cough⟩ more especially nights, which deprives me of my appetite, & my strength fails, & writing has a particular tendency to injure my lungs while I am under the influence of such a cough I therefore, with reluctance send your journal to you untill my health improves

Yours in haste[2]
Warren Par⟨r⟩ish

P.S. Brother Joseph, pray for me, & ask the prayers of the class on my account also.

Appointed Elder Sylvester Smith acting Scribe for the time being or till Eld[er]. Parrish shall recover his health — spent the day at home receiving visiters &c

26 January 1836 · Tuesday

Mr. Seixas arived from Hudson to teach the hebrew Langu[a]ge & I attended upon the organizing of the class for the purpose of receiving his lectures in hebrew grammar — his hours of instruction are from ten to eleven A.M. & from two to three P.M. his introduction pleased me much. I think he will be a help to the class in learning the hebrew

27 January 1836 · Wednesday

attended school as usual & other matters which came before me to attend to [p. 142]

---

1. MS.: "opnes"
2. MS. reads "heart"

28 January 1836 · Thursday

attended school at the usual hours In the evening met the quorems of High Priests in the west room of the upper loft of the Lord,s house & in company with my council of the presidency— consecrated & anointed the cou[n]sellors of the President of the High priesthood & having instructed them & set the quorem in order I left them to perform the holy anointing— & went to the quorem of Elders in the other end of the room. I assisted in anointing the counsellors of the President of the Elders & gave them the instruction necessary for the occasion & left the President & his council to anoint the Elders while I should go to the adjoining room & attend to organizing & instructing of the quorem of the Seventy—

I found the Twelve Apostles assembled with this quorem & I proceeded with the quorem of the presedincy to instruct them & also the seven presidents of the seventy Elders to call upon God with uplifted hands to seal the blessings which had been promised to them by the holy anointing As I organized this quorem with the presedincy in this room, Pres. Sylvester Smith saw a piller of fire rest down & abide upon the heads of the quorem as we stood in the midst of the Twelve.

When the Twelve & the seven were through with their sealing prayers I called upon Pres. S. Rigdon to seal them with uplifted hands & when he[1] had done this & cried hossannah that all [the] congregation should join him & shout hosannah to God & the Lamb & glory to God in the highest—It was done so & Eld[er]. Roger [p. 143] Orton saw a ~~flaming~~ ⟨mighty⟩ Angel riding upon a horse of fire with a flaming sword in his hand followed by five others—encircle the house & protect the saints even the Lords anointed from the power of Satan & a host of evil spirits which were striving to disturb the saints—

Pres. Wm Smith one of the Twelve saw the h[e]avens

---

1. "he" repeated in MS.

op[e]ned & the Lords host protecting the Lords anointed. Pres. Z Coltrin one of the seven saw the saviour extended before him as upon the cross & [a] little after crowned with a glory upon his head above the brightness of the sun after these things were over & a glorious vision which I saw had passed I instructed the seven presidents to proceede & anoint the seventy & returned to the room of the High Priests & Elders & attended to the sealing of what they had done with uplifted hands, the Lord had assisted my bro. Carloss the Pres. of the High Priests to go forward with the anointing of the High priests so that he had performed it to the acceptance of the Lord, notwithstanding he was verry young & inexperienced in such duties & I f[e]lt to praise God with a loud hossannah for his goodness to me & my fathers family & to all the children of men — praise the Lord all ye his saints — praise his holy name after these quorems were dismissed I retired to my home filled with the spirit & my soul cried hossannah to God & the Lamb through ⟨the⟩ silent watches of the night & while my eyes were closed in sleep the visions of the Lord were sweet unto me & his glory was round about me praise the Lord. [p. 144]

29 January 1836 · Friday

attended school & read hebrew — recd the following line from the Presidency of the Elders —

Kirtland Jany. 29. AD. 1836
To the Presidents of the Church of Latter day saints. Beloved Bret[hren]. feeling ourselves amenable to you for our proceedings as the presidency of the first quorem of Elders in Kirtland, & believing that we are to be govorned by you; we desire to know if we are to receive all those who are recommended to us by Elders for ordaination, or shall we receive none only those who have written recommendations from you. please answer our request

E. M. Green Clk

Alvah Beman   Pres.
Reuben Hadlock [Hedlock]
John Morton   Counsel

Answered the above verbally & attended to various duties. P.M. I called in all my father,s family & made a feast— ⟨& related my feeling towards them⟩ My father pronounced the following Patriarchial blessings

Henry Garrett, born in Deerfield, Onieda Co. N. Y. Sept 5. A D. 1814—Bro. I bless thee by the authority of the Priesthood Lord had eye upon thee, Satan seek destruction relatives also I seal thee unto life. power to tread the adversa[r]y under thy feet & be useful reclaim friends. be a son of God, an heir jointly with Jesus Christ. stand on the earth if faithful till thou hast recd. all the desires of thy heart which are in righteousness, the Lord shall bless thy chil[dren] after thee with the blessings of Abraham Isaac & Jacob, shall walk with companion to the [p. 145] House of God & see his glory fill the house & thou shalt receive all the blessings which thy heart can desire—I seal these blessings upon thee in the name of Jesus Amen—

Charles H. Smith born in Potsdam St. Lawrence Co Ny. April 16. 1817—Thou art in thy youth—satan will lay many snares for thee but I secure thee by the power of the holy priesthood from his grasp, thou hast no father—an orphan. The Lord shall watch over thee & keep thee & thou shalt receive the priesthood & be mighty in word, save fathers house receive all the blessings of the Earth even of A[braham] I[saac]. & Jacob—stand on earth till Redeamer com[es] & do all that the power of the holy priesthood can qualify thee for. I seal these blessings upon thee in the name of Jesus Amen—

Marietta Carter born in Benson, Rutland Co. Vt. April 1. AD. 1818—Thou art an orphan & the Lord shall bless thee more than thy own father could do if he had not been taken from thee—thy name is written in the Book of life—become a companion & a mother—Lord bless thy children & some of them shall prophecy—thy father laid down his life for the redemption of Zion—his spirit watches over thee—thy heart shall be filled with light not sleep in the dust—see thy Redeamer come in the clouds of heaven. & be caught up to meet him & be ever with him—these blessings I seal upon thee in the name of Jesus Amen [p. 146]

Angeline Carter born in Benson Rutland Co. V.t. Aug[u]st 26 ⟨1823⟩ Thou art a child—thy heart is pure & Satan shall have no power over thee because of thy blessing God shall be thy father, an heir with Jesus—observe the words of thy friends who care for thee & seek to please them. The Lord will give thee children & wisdom to teach them righteousness, & they shall be blest of the Lord & call thee blessed, a daughter of Abraham live till satisfied with life. I seal the[e] up unto eternal life in the name of Jesus Amen—

Joanna Carter born in Putnam Ny[1]—Nov. 26. AD. 1824— I seal the blessings of a father, thy father is no more. blessings of Abraham Isaac & Jacob. strength health healed of all infirmities. Satan have no power to afflict—Lord guard thee by his holy Angels—name written in heaven—eyes opened to see visions Angels minister unto thee—a companion—lead thee to the house of God—see the glory of God fill the house—see the end of this generation—have power to stand against all the power of satan & overcome through the faith which is in Jesus. I seal thee up unto eternal life in the name of the Lord Jesus Amen—

Nancy Carter born in Benson Rutland Co. V.t— Feby. 26 AD. 1827—Thou art a child—the Lord loves thee Satan shall seek in vain to destroy thee—Lord raise friends for thee which shall guard thee from the destroyer. thy name is written in heaven live to see the winding up of this generation [p. 147] Angels shall watch over thee in thy youth Eyes op[e]ned—see

---

1. Family records give her birthplace at Benson, Rutland County, Vermont.

thy God — raise children in righteousness & they shall be blest & call thee blessed because of thy diligence in teaching them the doctrine of the kingdom. I seal all these blessings upon thee in the name of Jesus Amen[1] Written & recorded by

Sylvester Smith scribe

This was a good time to me & all the family rejoiced together — we continued the meeting till about eight oclock in the evening & related the goodness of God to us in op[e]ning our eyes to see the visions of heaven & in sending his holy Angels to minister unto us the word of life — we sang the praise of God in animated strains & the power of love & union was felt & enjoyed —

30 January 1836 · Saturday

Attended school as usual, & waited upon several visiters & showed them the record of Abraham — Mr Seixas our hebrew teacher examined them[2] with deep interest & pronounced them to be original beyound all doubt, he is a man of excellent understanding — & has a knowledge of many languages which were spoken by the Ancients[3] — he is an honorable man so far as I can judge as yet — in the evening went to the upper rooms of the Lord's house & set the different quorems in order — instructed the Presidents of the seventy concerning the order of their anointing & requested them to proceed & anoint the seventy having set all the quorems in order I returned [p. 148] to my house being weary with continual anxiety & labour in puting all the Authorities in & in striving to purify them for the solemn assembly according to the commandment of the Lord

---

1. Marietta, Angeline, Joanna, and Nancy Carter were daughters of John S. Carter, a member of the Kirtland high council who died of cholera during the march of Zion's Camp to Missouri in 1834.
2. I.e., the Egyptian papyri.
3. MS.: "antints"

31 January 1836 · Sunday

Attended divine service in the schoolhouse organized the several quorems of the Authoraties of the church — appointed door keepers to keep order about the door because of the crowd & to prevent the house from being excessively crowded — The high council of Zion occupied the first part of the day in speaking as they were led & relating experi[e]nces trials &c. — P.M. house came to order as usual & Pres. Sidney Rigdon delivered a short discours[e] & we attended to the breaking of bread the season was as interesting as usual — In the evening my father attended to the blessing of three Brethren at Pres. O. Cowderies — spent the evening at home

1 February 1836 · Monday

attended scholl as usual — & in company with the other committe organized another class of 30 to receive Mr Seixas Lectures on the hebrew — in the evening attended to the organizing of the quorems of High priests — Elders — Seventy & Bishops in the uper rooms of the house of the Lord & after blessing each quorem in the name of the Lord I left them & returned home had an other interview with Mr. Seixas our hebrew teacher & related to him some of the dealings of God to me — & gave him some of the evidences of the work of the latter days — he listned candidly & did not oppose [p. 149]

2 February 1836 · Tuesday

Attended school as usual & various duties went to the schoolhouse in the evening & heard an animated discourse delivered by Pres. S. Rigdon he touched the outlines of our faith — showed the scattering & gathering of lsrael from the scriptures & the stick of Joseph in the hands of Eaphraim & The law of Eaphraim aside from that of Moses It was an interesting meeting — the spirit bore record that the Lord was well pleased! —

3 February 1836 · Wednesday

attended our hebrew lecture P. M. & studied with O. Cowdery & Sylvester Smith P. M.—received many visiters & showed the records of Abraham—my father blest three with a patriarchial blessing— Eld[er]. A[lvah]. Beman handed in the names of seventy of his quorem—designed for another seventy if God will—

4 February 1836 · Thursday

attended school & assisted in forming a class of 22 to read at 3.o clock P.m. the other 23 reads at 11 o.clock the first class recit[e]s at a quarter before 10 ⟨Am⟩ & the second at a quarter before 2–p.m. we have a great want of books but are determined to do the best we can—may the Lord help us to obtain this language that we may read the scriptures in the language in which they were given

5 February 1836 · Friday

Attended school & assisted the committe to make arangements for supplying the third & fourth classes with books—concluded to divide a bible into several parts for the benefit of said classes continued my studies in the hebrew—rec[eive]d several visiters & attended various duties—[p. 150]

6 February 1836 · Saturday

called the anointed together to receive the seal of all their blessings. The High Priests & Elders in the council room as usual—The Seventy with the Twelve in the second room & the Bishop in the 3—I laboured with each of these quorems for some time to bring [them] to the order which God had shown to me which is as follows—first part to be spent in solemn prayer before god without any talking or confusion & the conclusion with a sealing prayer by Pres. Sidney Rigdon when all the quorems are to shout with one accord a solemn

169

hosannah to God & the Lamb with an Amen–amen & amen–& then all take seats & lift up their hearts in silent prayer to God & if any obtain a prophecy or vision to rise & speak that all may be edified & rejoice together I had considerable trouble to get all the quorems united in this order– I went from room to room repeatedly & charged each separately–assuring them that it was according to the mind of God yet notwithstanding all my labour–while I was in the east room with the Bishops quorems I f[e]lt by the spirit that something was wrong in the quorem of Elders in the west room– & I immediately requested Pres. O. Cowdery & H. Smith to go in & see what was the matter–The quorem of Elders had not observed the order which I had given them & were reminded of it by Pres. [Don] Carloss Smith & mildly requested to observe order & continue in prayer & requested– some of them replied that they had a teacher of their own & did not wish to be troubled by others this caused the spirit of the Lord to withdraw [p. 151] This interrupted the meeting & this quorem lost th[e]ir blessing in a great measure–[1] the other quorems were more careful & the quorem of the seventy enjoyed a great flow of the holy spirit many arose & spok[e] testifying that they were filled with the holy spirit which was like

---

1. The elders quorum minutes give this perspective: "Met to proceed with the anointing of the Elders of the Most High. Counselor Morton organized those who were anointed in order for supplications. President Beman finished the anointing. The first presidency came and sealed our anointing by prayer and shout of Hosanna. The first counselor organized those who had been anointed in order for supplication. They gave us some instructions and left us. President Beman spoke to the assembly. Sever[al] spoke and there seemed to be a cloud of darkness in the room. Pres. O. Cowdery & H. Smith came and gave some instructions and the cloud was broken and some shouted, Hosanna and others spake with tongues. The first president (J. Smith jr) returned and reprimanded us for our evil deeds which was the cause of our darkness. He prophesied saying this night the key is turned to the nations, and the angel John is about commencing his mission to prophesy before kings, and rulers, nations tongues and people. The assembly was dismissed with prayer." ("A Record of the First Quorum of Elders Belonging to the Church of Christ: in Kirtland Geauga Co. Ohio," pp. 4–5. MS. RLDS Church Archives, Independence, Missouri.)

fire in their bones so that they could not hold their peace but were constrained to cry hosannah to God & the Lamb & glory in the highest. Pres. Wm Smith one of the twelve saw a vision of the Twelve & seven in council together in old England & prophecied that a great work would be done by them in the old co[u]ntries & God was already beginning to work in the hearts of the p[e]ople — Pres. Z. Coltrin one of the seven saw a vision of the Lords Host — & others were filled with the spirit & spake in tongues & prophecied — This was a time of rejoicing long to be remembered! praise the Lord —

/¹7 *February 1836 · Sunday*

attended ~~the~~ meeting at the us[u]al hour the quorums, were seated according to their official standing in the church, — The Bishop of Zion and his counsellors ocupied the fore noon in confession and exortation — The Bishop of Kirtland and his counsellors, occupied, the stand in the after noon, — the discourses of these two quorums were verry interesting, a number of letters of commendation were presented and read, a vote called and all received into the church in Kirtland. — bread was broken and blessed, and while, it was passing President Rigdon, commenced speaking from Acts 2d [chapter] and continued about 15, minuits. his [p. 151]² reasoning was cogent, — the wine was then blessed and passed after which meeting, dismissed — at evening meet with the presidency in the loft of the Printing-office, in company with the presidency of the 70, to chose other 70. also — Blessed one of the Zion brethren, — dismissed and retired —

8 *February 1836 · Monday*³

attended School at the us[u]al hour. — nothing worthy of note transpired — in the afternoon lectured in upper room of

---

1. Handwriting of Warren Parrish.
2. This and the previous page of the MS. are numbered 151.
3. MS. reads "Monday morning the 8th"

the printing office with some of the brethren, — at evening ~~Mr~~ visited Mr Seixas, in company with President's Rigdon & Cowdery, he converses freely, is an interesting man — This day Elder Parrish my scribe, received my journal again, his health is so much improved that he thinks he will be able, with the blessing of God to perform this duty[1]

9 February 1836 · Tuesday

spent the day in studying the hebrew language, — we have pleasant weather and fine sleighing —
Spent the evening at home

10 February 1836 · Wednesday[2]

at home at 10. oclock met at School room to read hebrew
In the afternoon, read in the upper room of the printing-office — at 4. oclock called at the School room in the chapel, to make some arrangments, concerning the classes — on my return home I was informed that Br. Hyrum Smith had cut himself [p. 152] I immediately repaired to his house and found him badly wounded in his ⟨left⟩ arm, he had fallen on his axe, which caused a wound about 4 or 5 inches in length Dr. Williams was sent for immediately ~~and~~ who when he came in sewed it up and dressed it, and I feel to thank God that it is no worse, and I ask my heavenly Father in the name of Jesus Christ to heal my brother hyrum ~~Smith~~ of his wound, and bless my fathers family one and all, with peace and plenty, and ultimately eternal life —

/³8 February 1836 · Monday

Met in council, meeting opened with prayer by President Hyrum Smith; Levi Jacks⟨on⟩[4] supplied the place ~~of~~ of Joseph Coe.

---

1. See entry of 25 January 1836.
2. MS. reads "Wednesday morning the 10th"
3. Possibly handwriting of Jesse Hitchcock.
4. Probably Levi Jackman.

Sister [*blank*] entered a complaint against Joseph Keeler, after hearing the testimony the Councillors proceeded to give their council after which Pres. Hyrum Smith arose and made some remarks, the same was agreed to by President David Whitmer after which the Presidency gave room for the parties to speak both of which made a few remarks, the Pres[ident] then decided that Joseph Keeler be acquited a vote of the council was called, the council agreed to the decision of the Presidency.

Jesse Hitchcock   Clerk.

/[1]*11 February 1836 · Thursday*[2]

at home — attended the School and read hebrew with the morning Class — spent the afternoon in reading, and exibiting the Egy[p]tian records to those who called to see me and heavens blessings have attended me. — [p. 153]

12 February 1836 · Friday

spent the day in reading hebrew, and attending to the duties of my family, and the duties of the church, nothing very special transpired meet this evening to make arangements concerning ⟨ordinations⟩[3]

13 February 1836 · Saturday

spent the fore noon in reading Hebrew. — at noon I prepared a horse and sleigh, for Professer Seixas, to go to Hudson to visit his family

14 February 1836 · Sunday

attended to the ordinance of baptism, before meeting — at the us[u]al hour attended meeting, the presidents of the 70,

---

1. Handwriting of Warren Parrish.
2. MS. reads "Thursday mornin[g] 11th"
3. 12 February entry continues following entry of 14 February.

expressed their feelings, on the occasion, and their faith in the book of Mormon, and the revelations, — also their entire confidence in ⟨all⟩ the quorums that are organized in the church of Latter day Saints—had a good time. the spirit of God rested upon the congregation; — administered the Sacrament and confirmed, a number who had been baptised, and dismissed

12 February 1836 · Friday

I met in the School room in the chapel in company with the several quorums to take into concideration the subject of ordinations, as mentioned at the top of this page

opened by singing and prayer I then arose and made some remarks upon the object of our meeting, which were as follows— first that many are desiring to be ordained to the ministry, who are [p. 154] not called and consequ[e]ntly the Lord is displeased— Secondly, many already have been ordained who ought [not] to hold official stations in the church because they dishonour themselves and the church and bring persecution swiftly upon us, in consequence of their zeal without k[n]owledge—I requested the quorum's to take some measures to regulate the same. I proposed some resolutions and remarked to the brethren that the subject was now before them and open for discussion

The subject was taken up and discussed by President's S. Rigdon O. Cowdery Eldr. M. Harris and some others, and resolutions drafted, by my scribe who served as clerk on the occasion—read and rejected—it was then proposed that I should indite resolutions which I did as follows

1st—Resolved that no one be ordained to any office in the church in this stake of Zion at Kirtland without the unanimous voice of the several ~~quorums~~ bodies that constitute this quorum who are appointed to do church buisness in the name of said church—viz the presidency of the church & council [of] the 12. apostles of the Lamb and 12 high counsellors of Kirtland the 12, high counsellors of Zion, the Bishop of Kirtland & his counsellors the Bishop of Zion and his counsellors— the 7 presidents of the Seventies; untill otherwise ordered by the said quorums.—[p. 155]

2nd—And further resolved that no one be ordained in the branches of said church abroad unless they are recommended by the ~~church~~ voice of the respective branches of the church to which they belong to a general conference appointed by the heads of the church, and from that conference receive their ordination—[1]

15 February 1836 · Monday

attended the Hebrew School at the usual hour,—spent the afternoon in reading hebrew, and receiving and waiting upon visitors—on this day we commenced translating the Hebrew language, under the instruction of Professor Seixas, and he acknowledg's that we are the most forward of any class he ever taught, the same length of time[2]

---

1. Meeting on 13 February, the Twelve accepted the first resolution but presented this amendment to the second: "That none be ordained to any office in the branches to which they belong to a general conference, appointed by those, or under the direction of those who are designated in the Book of Covenants as having authority to ordain and set in order all the Officers of the church abroad & from that conference receive their ordination." On 17 and 18 February the Kirtland and Zion high councils met and unanimously adopted the amendment of the Twelve. However, after deliberating upon the matter with the Presidency of the Church on February 22, the original resolutions were adopted without amendment. (Kirtland Council Minutes, 13, 17, 18, 22 February 1836.)

2. According to Oliver Cowdery, Professor Seixas was still absent on 15 February: "Att. Heb. School. The profess[or] being abscent, our class appointed myself to look over them for the time. After, assisted pres. Smith to overlook the 11 o'clock [class]. In the afternoon met pres's. J. Smith, jr. S. Rigdon, W.W. Phelps John Whitmer and elder S. James in the office study and united in prayer for Professor Seixas and his family, pres. Smith taking the lead: The items asked for were in substance as follows: That the Lord will have mercy upon the man whom we have employed to teach us the Hebrew language; that all evil prejudice may be taken from his heart, and that the Spirit of God may visit him continually by night and by day, that he may be lead to embrace the gospel and believe the book of Mormon; that he will give him the spirit of humility and meekness that

16 February 1836 · Tuesday

atten[d]ed School at the usual hour and resumed our translating and made rapid progress many called to day to see the
House of the Lord, and to visit me and see the Egy[p]tian
manuscripts—we have [p. 156] extremely cold weather and
fine sleighing

17 February 1836 · Wednesday

attend[ed] the school and read and translated with my class
as usual, and my soul delights in reading the word of the Lord
in the original, and I am determined to persue the study of
languages untill I shall become master of them, if I am permitted to live long enough, at any rate so long as I do live I
am determined to make this my object, and with the blessing
of God I shall succed to my sattisfaction, — this evening Elder
Coe called to make some arangements about the Egyptian
records and the mummies, he proposes to hire a room at J[ohn].
Johnsons Inn and exibit them there from day to day at certain
hours, that some benefit may be derived from them — I complied with his request, and only observed that they must be
managed with prudence and care especially the manuscripts

18 February 1836 · Thursday

spent the day as usual in attending to my family concerns,
~~and~~ receiving and waiting upon those who called for instruction
and attending to my studies,

---

we may become his teachers in the things of salvation, that he may come forth
and be baptized into the Church of Christ, that we may be benefitted with the
knowledge he has of languages: and that the Lord will have mercy upon his
family, and visit them with his Holy Spirit and cause them to embrace the fulness
of the gospel, that they may be saved with him. We do not ask to become his
teachers only that he may become our brother in the faith of the gospel, that
his soul may be saved: all of which are asked in the name of the Lord Jesus
Christ. Amen." (Oliver Cowdery Diary, 15 February 1836. The Diary is published
in Arrington, "Oliver Cowdery's Kirtland, Ohio, 'Sketch Book.' ")

19 February 1836 · Friday

    attended with the morning class and translated—professor Seixas [p. 157] handed me the names of a few whom he had selected from the first class, and requested us to meet together this afternoon and lecture, which we did in the upper room of the printing-office—The names are as follows President's S. Rigdon O. Cowdery W. W. Phelps—Bishop E. Partridge Eldr's [William] E. McLellen O. Hyde O. Pratt Sylvester Smith myself and Scribe— these professor Seixas requested to meet one hour earlyer on the following morning—I conversed with Mr. Seixas upon the subject of religion, at my house this afternoon, he listened with attention and appeared interested with my remarks, and I believe the Lord is striving with him, by his holy spirit, and that he will eventually embrace the new and everlasting covenant, for he is a chosen vessel unto the Lord to do his people good, —but I forbear lest I get to prophesying upon his head—this evening President Rigdon and myself called at Mr. Seixas lodgings and conversed with him upon the subject of the School, had a pleasant interview[1]

20 February 1836 · Saturday

    at home attending to my domestick concerns, at 9 oclock attended the school and translated with the morning class— spent the after-noon with my class in the printing-office— spent the evening at home [p. 158]

21 February 1836 · Sunday

    Spent the day at home, in reading meditation and prayer— I reviewed my lessons in Hebrew—On this day some 3 or 4 persons were baptised and the powers of darkness seem to be giving way on all sides. many who have been enemies to the

---

1. Oliver Cowdery was also present: "We found him weary with his labors in teaching the school." (Oliver Cowdery Diary, 19 February 1836.)

work of the Lord are beginning to enquire in to the faith of the Latter day Saints and are friendly

22 February 1836 · Monday

translated Hebrew with the 1st class in the morning — returned home and, made out my return to the county clerk on 11. marriages which I have solemnized within 3. months past 8, by license from the clerk of the court of common pleas in Geauga county Ohio, and 3, by publishment, sent them to chardon by Elijah Fuller — I baptised John O. Waterman. I spent the afternoon translating at with my scribe Eldr W. Parrish at his house at 4. oclock. meet, Professor Seixas and the school committee at [the] printing office to make some arangements for the advancement of the several classes

The lower room of the chapel is now prepared for painting —

This afternoon the sisters met to make the veil of the Temple[1] Father Smith presided over them and gave them much good instruction, closed by singing & prayer [p. 159]

23 February 1836 · Tuesday

read and translated Hebrew — This afternoon the sisters met again at the chapel to work on the ve[i]l toward the close of the day I met with the presidency & many of the brethren in the house of the Lord — I made some remarks from the pulpit upon the rise and progress of the church of Christ of Latter day Saints and pronounced a blessing upon the Sisters for the liberality in giving their servises so cheerfully to make the veil for the Lord's house also upon the congregation and dismissed

---

1. Made of white canvas curtains that could be raised or lowered, the veil of the Kirtland temple divided the main assembly room into four sections, allowing four separate meetings to be held simultaneously. (E. R. Snow, *Biography and Family Record of Lorenzo Snow* [Salt Lake City, 1884], 12.)

24 February 1836 · Wednesday

attended to my studies as us⟨u⟩al — at evening met the quo-rums at the school-room in the chapel to take into concider-ation the propriety or impropriety of ordaining a large number of individuals who wish to be ordained to official stations in the church — each individuals nam[e] was presented and the voice of the assembly called and all of them except 7. were rejected — [1] Their ordinations defered untill another time — O. Hyde O. Cowdery and Sylvester Smith were nominated and seconded to draft and ⟨make⟩ regulations concerning licenses [2] — vote of the assembly called and unanimously passed [3]

Thomas Burdick nominated and seconded to officiate as clerk to record licenses, and receive pay for his servises ac-cordingly [p. 160] vote called and passed unanimously also nominated and seconded that the 12, and presidents of the 70, be see that the calls for preaching in the region round about

---

1. At this meeting the names of several men were presented for ordination to priesthood offices in the Church: William Wightman, Charles Wightman, David Cluff, Truman Jackson, Reuben Barton, and Daniel Miles were received as elders, and Moses Daley as a high priest; nineteen others whose names were presented for ordination were rejected. (Kirtland Council Minutes, 24 February 1836.)

2. One of the earliest revelations governing Church administration stated that each person ordained to an office in the priesthood was to take a certificate from the person who ordained him, which "when presented to an elder, he is to give him a license, which shall authorize him to perform the duty of his calling." (D&C 20:64.) Subsequently, licenses were issued to those ordained to the priesthood as tangible evidence of authority and legitimate association with the Church. By 1836, because of imperfect record keeping, it became necessary to regulate the dispensing of licenses, and Orson Hyde, Oliver Cowdery, and Sylvester Smith were appointed a committee to draft necessary rules. The presentation of the committee rules and the action of the Church regarding them took place on 3 March. (Donald Q. Cannon, "Licensing in the Early Church," *BYU Studies* 22 (Winter 1982): 96–105; Jessee, "The Beginning of Mormon Record Keeping.")

3. Oliver Cowdery recorded his appointment, along with Orson Hyde and Sylvester Smith, "to draft resolutions to be adopted as a rule of Church, regulating the recording of licenses, and conference minutes." (Oliver Cowdery Diary, 24 February 1836.)

Kirtland be attended to, and filled by judicious Elders of this church—

adjourned, and closed by singing and prayer—

25 February 1836 · Thursday

attended to my studies as usual, and made some proficiency.— in the afternoon I was called upon by President Rigdon to go and visit his wife who was verry sick,—I did so in company with my scribe, we prayed for ~~her~~ and annointed her in the name of the Lord and she began to recover from that verry hour—Returned home and spent the evening

26 February 1836 · Friday

attended and read hebrew with the first class in the morning— spent the afternoon in the printing office—settled som[e] misunderstanding between Br. Wm Smith and professor Seixas—

27 February 1836 · Saturday

I prepared my horse and sleigh for Mr Seixas to ride to Hudson to visit his family, he is to return on monday next— attended with my class at the printing office [p. 161] both in the fore and afternoon, and lectured on, and translated Hebrew—we have cold weather and fine sleighing[1]

28 February 1836 · Sunday

This morning two gentlemen late from Scotland called to see me, to make inquiry about the work of the Lord in these

---

1. Oliver Cowdery adds this: "Professor Seixas left this morning to visit his family at Hudson, Ohio. I was called to lay hands upon pres. T. B. Marsh, in company with pres. J. Smith, jr. and also upon my brother-in-law, Peter Whitmer, jr. the latter was very sick of a Typhus fever, and was immediately heald and arose from his bed. I heard the other was better. In the afternoon and evening met pres. Orson Hyde and Sylvester Smith in committee and dictated resolutions to be introduced Thursday evening for the consideration of the quorums." (Oliver Cowdery Diary, 27 February 1836.)

last days, they treated me with respect, and the interview was pleasing to me, and I presume interesting to them, they attended our meeting, with me, and expressed a satisfaction in what they heard

They spoke of Irvin[1] the oriental reformer and his prop[h]esies — after meeting, I returned home and spent the after part of the day and evening in reading and translating the Hebrew

29 February 1836 · Monday

spent the day in studying as usual. — A man called to see the house of the Lord in company with another gentleman, on entering the door they were politely invited by the gent[l]eman who has charge of the house to take of[f] their hats one of them complyed with the request unhesitatingly while the other observed that he would not take of[f] his hat nor bow to Jo Smith but that he had made Jo bow to him at a certain time — he was immediately informed by Eldr Morey the keeper of the house that his first buisness was to leave it ~~the house~~ for when [p. 162] a man imposed upon me he was imposed upon himself, the man manifested much anger, but left the house. — for this independence and resolution of Eldr Morey I respect him and for the love he manifests toward me, and may Israels God bless him and give him an ascendency over all his enemies —

This afternoon Professor Seixas returned from Hudson, and brought a few more bibles and one grammar of his 2d edition. — the weather is warm & our sleighing is failing fast

1 March 1836 · Tuesday

attended School, in the fore noon in the afternoon at the printing office and read and translated with my class untill 4. oclock — returned home and attended to my domestic concerns

---

1. Edward Irving, the Church of Scotland minister, whose teachings became the basis of the religious movement known as Irvingism, later the Catholic Apostolic Church.

We have fine sleighing which is uncommon in this country at this season of the Year

2 March 1836 · Wednesday

persued my studies as usual — at 7 oclock in the evening, the first class met, agreeably to the request of Mr. Seixas at Eldr O. Hydes to spend one hour in translating, — dismissed and returned home

3 March 1836 · Thursday

attended to my studies in the hebrew. — some misunderstanding, took place between [p. 163] Professor Seixas and some of the schollars respecting the sale of some Bibles, — his feelings were much hurt appearantly, he made some remarks concerning it to each class at noon he called on the school committee with his feelings much depressed — we gave him all the satisfaction we could in righteousness, and his feelings were measurbly allayed

/[1]This evening the several quorums met agreeably to adjour[n]ment and were organized according to their official standing in the church.[2]

I then arose and made some remarks on the object of our meeting which are as follows.

1st To receive or reject certain resolutions that were drafted by a commitee chosen for that purpose at a preceeding meeting respecting licenses for elders and other official members.

2nd To sanction by the united voice of the quorum[s] certain resolutions respecting ordaining members; that had

---

1. Possibly handwriting of Jesse Hitchcock.
2. The authorities of the Church assembled at the temple were the Presidency, Quorum of Twelve, the high councils of Kirtland and Zion, the bishoprics of Kirtland and Zion, the seven presidents of the seventy, and the presidencies of the high priests, elders, priests, teachers, and deacons. The purpose of the assembly was to consider the work of the committee appointed 24 February to draft resolutions governing the licensing of official members of the Church.

passed through each quorum seperately ~~for~~ without any alteration or amendment except⟨ing⟩ in the quorum of the twelve.

The council opened by singing and prayer. President O. Cowdery then arose and read the resolutions respecting licenses[1] three times, the third time he read the ~~article~~ ⟨resolutions⟩

---

1. The resolutions read by Oliver Cowdery, chairman of the committee, were as follows: "Whereas the records of the several conferences, held by the Elders of the church, and the ordinations of many of the official members of the same, in many cases have been imperfectly kept since its organization, to avoid ever after, any inconvenience, difficulty or injury in consequence of such neglect your committee recommend.

1st. That all licenses hereafter granted by these authorities assembled as a quorum or by general conference held for the purpose of transacting the business of the church, be recorded at full length, by a clerk, appointed for that purpose in a book to be kept in this branch of the church until it shall be thought advisable by the heads of the church, to order other books and appoint other clerks to record licenses as above. And that said recording clerk be required to endorse a certificate under his own hand and signature on the back of said licenses, specifying the time when & place where such license was recorded, and also a reference to the letter and page of the Book containing the same.

2d. That this quorum appoint two persons to sign Licenses given as afore said, one as chairman, and the other as clerk of conference, and that it shall be the duty of said person appointed to sign licenses as clerk of conference immediately thereafter, to deliver the same into the hands of the recording Clerk.

3d. That all general conferences abroad give each individual, whom they ordained a certificate signed by the chairman & Clerk of said conference and stating the time and place of such conference, and the office to which the individual has been ordained, and that when such certificate has been forwarded to the person hereafter authorized to sign licences as clerk of conference, such person shall together with the chairman of conference, immediately sign a license, and said clerk of conference shall, after the same has been recorded forward it to the proper person.

4th. That all official members in good standing & fellowship in the various branches of this church, are requested to forward their present licenses accompanied by a certificate of their virtues & faithful walk before the Lord, signed by the chairman and clerk. of a general conference, or by the clerk of the branch of the church in which official member resides, by the advice & direction of such Church, to the clerk of conference whose duty it shall be to fill a new license as directed in the 3d article. And that all licenses signed recorded and endorsed, as specified in the first article shall be considered good and valid to all intents & purposes in the business, and spiritual affairs of this church as a religious society, , or before any court of record of this or any other country wherein preachers of the Gospel are entitled to special privileges, answering in all respects as an original record without the necessity of refering to any other document.

5. That the recording clerk be required to publish quarterly in a paper published

he gave time and oppertunity after reading each article for objections to be made if any there were; no objections were made—I then observed that these resolutions must needs pass through each quorum seperately begining at the presidency /¹and concequently it must first be thrown into the hands of the president of the Deacon[s] & his council as equal rights & privileges are my motto, and one [p. 164] man is as good as another, if he behaves as well, and that all men should be esteemed alike, without regard to distinction's of an official nature,—the resolutions passed through the quorum of the Deacons by their unanimous voice

It was then thrown before the president of the Teachers and his council and passed unanimously—

Next into the hands of the President of the priests & his council and passed unanimously

Then into the hands of the Bishop's council of Kirtland & passed unanimously

from them to the Bishop of Zion & his council & passed unanimously—

Next into the hands of the president of the ~~high priests & his~~ Elders & his council & passed unanimously

From them into the hands of the president of the High-Priests & his council and passed unanimously

Next into the hands of the presidents of the 70. & passed unanimously

---

by some member or members of this church, a list of the names of the several persons for whom he has recorded licenses within the last quarter.

6. That this quorum appoint two persons to sign as chairman and clerk of conference, Pro. Tempre licenses for the standing chairman and clerk who shall be appointed as named in the 2d article and also to act in their absence in signing other licenses. as specified in the foregoing article

Oliver Cowdery
Orson Hyde   Committee   Kirtland Feb. 27. 1836
Sylvester Smith
(Kirtland Council Minutes, 3 March 1836.)
1. Handwriting of Warren Parrish.

from them to the high council of ⟨Zion⟩ ~~Kirtland~~ & passed unanimously—

from them to the high council of Kirtland & passed unanimously—

~~& Lastly in~~ and then into the hands of the 12, & passed unanimously

& lastly into the hands of the presidency of the Church & all the quorums and rec[eive]d their sanction.—having now passed through all the quorums, the resolutions are received as a Law to govern the Church [p. 165]

I was nominated & seconded for a standing chairman & F. G. Williams for clerk to is[s]ue licenses to the official members of the church S. Rigdon for chairman protem & O. Cowdery clerk—vote called from the several quorums in their order & passed unanimously

I then made some remarks on the amendment of the 12. upon the resolutions recorded on pages 155 & 156. President T. B. Marsh made some observations after me, & then called a vote of his quorum, to asertain whether they would repeal their amendment or not 9. of the 12. vote[d] in the affirmative & 3. in the negative,[1] and the original bill was passed, which is recorded on the pages above named—dismissed by prayer & retired 1/2 past 9. oclock[2]

4 March 1836 · Friday[3]

attended school as usual—The sleighing is failing fast, the icy chains of winter seem to be giving way under the influence

---

1. See entry of 12 February. All of the Twelve voted to recall their previous amendment to the resolution except John F. Boynton, Orson Pratt, and Lyman Johnson. (Kirtland Council Minutes, 3 March 1836.)

2. Oliver Cowdery summarized the day's activities: "Att. Heb. School, met the quorums in the evening in the Lord's house, and read the committee's report previously drawn, which was adopted without amendment, except a small addition in the last article, extending the power of certain conference[s] further, in signing licenses. I confess the hand of God in this matter, in giving me his Holy Spirit, to indite this valuable article, as by it the elders will enjoy their privileges as citizens, and the churches be freed from imposition." (Oliver Cowdery Diary, 3 March 1836.)

3. MS. reads "Friday the 4th ~~Feby~~ ⟨March⟩ 1836"

of the returning Sun, & spring will soon open to us with all his charms

5 March 1836 · Saturday

Attended School—in the afternoon the board kiln to[ok] fire & the lumber principally consumed—this is the 5 or 6 time it has burnt this winter if my memory serves me co-rectly—[1]

6 March 1836 · Sunday

Spent the day at home in the enjoyment ⟨of the society⟩ of my family, around the social fireside[2] [p. 166]

7 March 1836 · Monday[3]

Spent the day in attending to my studies

At Evening met with my class at Professor Seixas['s] Room, & translated the 17th chapter of Genesis,—after the class was dismissed I was requested to tarry with the rest of the School committee, to make some arangements about paying Mr. Seixas for his ~~tuition~~ instruction, & to engage him for another q[uarte]r. we did not arive at any thing definite upon this point,—however ~~he~~ Mr Seixas has agreed to ~~stay~~ ⟨teach us⟩ 3,

---

1. In the evening of 5 March, Joseph Smith met with Oliver Cowdery, Sidney Rigdon, the Twelve, and Warren Cowdery in the upper room of the printing office. According to Cowdery, "the Twelve had profered a charge against my brother for a letter he wrote last summer upon the subject of their teaching while at the Freedom conference. My brother confessed his mistake, upon the testimony of the Twelve, and said he was willing to publish that they were not in the fault, but that he was satisfied they delivered those instructions which he had supposed they had not." (Oliver Cowdery Diary, 5 March 1836.) The resolution of the matter was the publication of the Warren Cowdery statement in the *Messenger and Advocate* of February 1836. (See note 1, p. 145.)

2. Joseph's apparent absence from meetings may be explained from Oliver Cowdery's entry for the day: "Did not attend meeting in consequence of there not being sufficient room for so many in the small houses occupied for meetings." (Oliver Cowdery Diary, 6 March 1836.)

3. "~~March the 7th Monday~~" precedes the date of this entry.

weeks longer, after having a vacation of 2, weeks at the expiration of this course, & perhaps a q[uarte]r.

8 March 1836 · Tuesday

Attended school & translated most of the 22. chapter of Gen. after my class were dismissed, retired to the printing office and translated 10. verses of Ex 3d [chapter] which with the 1st & 2nd Psalms are our next lesson

9 March 1836 · Wednesday

Attended School as usual — ~~This day the snow is falling~~

10 March 1836 · Thursday

Attended School, in the morning, in the afternoon, read Hebrew in the office at evening went down to [the] Professor['s] room to be instructed by him, in the language on the account of the storm the class did not meet. [p. 167]

11 March 1836 · Friday

meet with the morning class,.at 9. oclock, — at 10. went into the office and made a divission of our class for private studies for our better accommodation, & advancement in the language we are persuing

Presidents Rigdon Phelps & Cowdery and myself meet at the printing office Eldr's O. Pratt Sylvester Smith & Bishop Partri[d]ge, at L[uke] Johnson's

Eldr's McLellen O. Hyde & W. Parrish on the flats — [1] this evening our class met at Mr Seixas['s] room & spent an hour in our studies, — class dismissed & retired except the school committee, who tarried and made some arangements with Mr

---

1. The low area of Kirtland lying north of the temple in the vicinity of the Newel K. Whitney store.

Seixas about continuing longer with us & bringing his family to this place

This has been a very stormy day and the snow is, still falling fast, & the prospect is fair for another run of sleighing which is uncommon for this country at this season of the Year

12 March 1836 · Saturday

engaged a team to go to Hudson after Mr Seixas['s] family ⟨& goods⟩ also a Horse and cutter for himself & wife, — we have cold weather & fine sleighing—I was informed to day that a man by the name of Clark froze to death last night near this place, who was under the influence of ardent spirits: O my God how long will this monster intemperance [p. 168] find it's victims on the earth, me thinks until the earth is swept with the wrath and indignation of God, and Christ's Kingdom becomes universal. O come Lord Jesus and cut short thy work in rightieousness.

Eldr Solomon Hancock received a letter to day, from Missouri bearing the painful inteligence, of the death of his wife.[1] May the Lord bless him and comfort him in this hour of affliction

13 March 1836 · Sunday

met with the presidency & some of the 12, and counseled with them upon the subject of removing to Zion this spring, we conversed freely upon the importance of her redemption, and the necessity of the presidency removing to that place, that their influence, might be more effectually, used in in gathering the saints to that country, and we finally come to the resolution to emigrate on or before the 15th of May next, if kind providence smiles, upon us and openes the way before us

---

1. Solomon Hancock's wife, Alta Adams Hancock, died 18 January 1835 in Clay County, Missouri.

14 March 1836 · Monday

Attended School as usual Professor Seixas returned from Hudson with his ⟨family⟩

15 March 1836 · Tuesday

At School in the forenoon in the afternoon, met in the printing office, recd, and waited upon those who caIled to see me, and attended to my domestick concerns — at evening met in the printing office & recd a lecture, on grammar [p. 169]

16 March 1836 · Wednesday

persued my studies in the Hebrew language, — at evening met the quorum of singers in the chapel, they performed admirably, concidering the advantages they have had

17 March 1836 · Thursday

At school in the morning, in the afternoon in the office at evening, met with the quorums in the west school-room of the Lord's House to receive or reject certain individuals whose names were presented for ordination's a number were received, by the united voice of the assembly[1]

18 March 1836 · Friday

attended School with the morning class. — at 10. oclock, went to the school house to attend the funeral of Susan Johnson, daughter of Esekiel Johnson, she is a member of the church of Latter day Saints & remained strong in the faith, untill, her spirit, took it's exit from time to eternity

May God bless and comfort her afflicted parents, family

---

1. Erastus B. Wightman, Osmon M. Duel, Chapman Duncan, Joshua Bosley, and Heman Hyde were sustained for ordination; four others were rejected. (Kirtland Council Minutes, 17 March 1836.)

connexions, and friends—President Rigdon delivered a fine discourse on the occasion, and much solemnity prevailed

19 March 1836 · Saturday

Read Hebrew with the morning class.—Spent the day in attending [p. 170] to my domestick concerns, and the affairs of the church

20 March 1836 · Sunday

attended the house of worship, as usual the quorum of high priests, delivered short addresses to the congregation, in a very feeling, and impressive manner,—at the intermission at noon one individual was baptised—in the afternoon, administered the Lords Supper, as we are wont to do on every Sabath, and the Lord blessed our souls with the out pouring of his spirit, and we were made to rejoice in his goodness,

21 March 1836 · Monday

At school in the morning—after school went to the printing office and prepared, a number of Elders licinces, to send by Elder [Ambrose] Palmer to the court [in] Medina County in order to obtain licenses to marry, as the court in this county will not grant us this privelege.—To day 10 persons were baptized, in this place

22 March 1836 · Tuesday

read Hebrew with the morning class,—to day 5, young men were received into the church by baptism, in this place— This is a stormy day, the snow is nearly a foot deep, an uncommon storm, for this season of the year [p. 171]

23 March 1836 · Wednesday

Attended School—This is a pleasant day and fine sleighing—2, more were received into the church by baptism

24 March 1836 · Thursday

Attended School as usual in the evening, met with my class at the printing office, and recd a lecture from Professor Seixas upon the Hebrew language

After we were dismissed, we called at the School-room to hear the ⟨choir⟩ ~~quire~~ of Singers perform, which they did admirably

On this day 5. more were recd into the Church by baptism —

25 March 1836 · Friday

Attend[ed] School with the morning class — also at 5 oclock P.M and recd a lecture upon the Hebrew Grammar — We have pleasant weather and good sleighing —

26 March 1836 · Saturday

At home attending to my domestick concerns in the morning. — after brekfast met with the presidency to make arangements for the solemn assembly which occupied the remainder of the day[1]

27 March 1836 · Sunday

The congregation began to assemble ⟨at the chapel⟩ at about 7 oclock one hour earlier than the doors were to be opened many brethren had come in from the region's [p. 172] round about to witness the dedication of the Lords House and share in his blessings and such was the anxiety on this occasion that some hundreds, (probably five or six,) assembled ~~collected~~ before the doors were opened —

---

1. Oliver Cowdery reported: "We prepared for the dedication of the Lord's house. I met in the president's room, pres. J. Smith, jr. S. Rigdon, my brother W.A. Cowdery & Elder W. Parrish, and assisted in writing a prayer for the dedication of the house." (Oliver Cowdery Diary, 26 March 1836.)

The presidency entered with the door ke[e]pers and aranged them at the inner and outer doors also placed our stewards to receiv[e] donations from those who should feel disposed to contribute something to defray the expenses of building the House of the Lord—⟨we also dedicated the pulpits & consecrated them to the Lord⟩ The doors were then opened President Rigdon President Cowdery and myself seated the congregation as they came in, ~~we received about~~ and according to the best calculation we could make we received between 9 ⟨hundred⟩ and 10,00 which is as many as can be comfortably situated we then informed the door keepers that we could rec[e]ive no more, and a multitude were deprived of the benefits of the meeting on account of the house not being sufficiently capacious to receive them, and I felt to regret that any of my brethren and sisters should be deprived of the meeting, and I recommended them to repair to the School-house and hold a meeting which they did and filled that house ⟨also⟩ and yet many were left out—

The assembly were then organized in the following manner.— viz.[1] [p. 173]

West end of the. house—

Presdt. F G. Williams Presdt. Joseph Smith, Sen and Presdt. W W. Phelps occupied the 1st pulpit for the Melchisedic priesthood— Presdt. S. Rigdon myself and Presdt Hyrum Smith in the 2nd— Presdt. D. Whitmer Presdt. O. Cowdery and Presdt.

---

1. At this point in the MS., the following material was crossed out and a fresh start made: "President F G. Williams Presdt. Joseph Smith, Sen ~~father~~ and Presdt W W. Phelps occupied the first pulpit ⟨in the west end of the house⟩ for the Melchisedec priesthood, Presdt. S. Rigdon, Myself, and Prest. Hyrum Smith the 2nd— Presdt D. Whitmer Presdt O. Cowdery and Presdt John Whitmer the 3d— The 4th was [p. 173] occupied by the president of the high priests and his counsellors, and 2 choiristers— The 12. apostles on the right, the high council of Kirtland on the left, The pulpits ⟨in the east end of the house⟩ for the Aaronic priesthood were occupied in the following manner— The Bishop of Kirtland and his counsellors in the first pulpit— the Bishop of Zion and his counsellors in the 2nd— the presdt. of the priest[s] and his counsellors in the 3d— the presdt. of the Teachers and his counsellors in the 4th— ~~the 7 presdt of the seventies~~ The high council of Zion on the right, the 7. presdt of the Seventies on the left."

J. Whitmer in the 3d—The 4th was occupied by the president of the high-priests and his counsellors, and 2 choiresters— The 12. Apostles on the right in the 3 highest seats—The presdt of the Eld[e]rs his clerk & counsellors in the seat immediatly below the 12—The high council of Kirtland consisting of 12, on the left in the 3, first seats— the 4th seat below them was occupied by ~~the presidency's~~ Eldr's W A. Cowdery & W. Parrish who served as scribes.—The pulpits in the east end of the house for the Aaronic priesthood were occupied as follows.—The Bishop of Kirtland and his counsellors in the 1st pulpit.—The Bishop of Zion and his counsellors in the 2nd—The presdt. of the priests and his counsellors in the 3d—The presdt. of the Teachers and his counsellors ⟨& one choirister⟩ in the 4th—The high council of Zion consisting of [p. 174] 12 counsellors on the right—The presdt of the Deacons and his counsillors in the seat below them— The 7 presdts of the Seventies on the left—The choir of singers were seated in the 4 corners of the room in seats prepared for that purpose—rec[eive]d by contribution $960.00[1]

9 oclock A. M the servises of the day were opened by Presdt S. Rigdon by reading 1st the 96 Psalm secondly the 24th Psalm—the choir then sung hymn on the 29th page of Latter day Saints collection of hymn's—prayer by Presdt Rigdon choir then sung hymn on 14th page[2] Presdt Rigdon then ⟨read⟩ the 18, 19, & 20, verses of the 8th Chapter of Mathew and preached more particularly from the 20th verse.—his prayer and address were very forcible and sublime, and well adapted to the oc-

---

1. In the MS. "recd by contribution $960.00" appears to have been written in the same hand sometime after the text that surrounds it. Ira Ames, who was in charge of the donations at the door during the temple dedication, noted, "There were three large tin pans full of gold & silver. . . . A great many strangers came from the country to see it [the temple] and all donated freely." (Ira Ames, Autobiography and Journal, 1836. MS., LDS Church Archives, Salt Lake City, Utah.)

2. The two hymns referred to are "Ere Long the Veil Will Rend in Twain," by Parley P. Pratt, and "O Happy Souls, Who Pray," by William W. Phelps.

casion. — after he closed his sermon, he called upon the several quorums commenceing with the presidency, to manifest by rising up, their willingness to acknowledge me as a prophet and seer and uphold me as such by their p[r]ayers of faith, all the quorums in their turn, cheerfully complyed with this request he then called upon all the congregation of Saints, also to give their assent by rising on their feet which they did unanimously

After an intermission of 20, minutes the servises of the day were resumed, by singing Adam ondi ahman.[1] /[2]I then made a short address and called upon the several quorums, and all the congregation of saints to acknowledge the Presidency as Prophets and Seers, and uphold them by their prayers, they all covenanted to do so by rising; I then called upon the quorums and congregation of saints to acknowledge the 12 [p. 175] Apostles who were present as Prophets and Seers and special witnesses to all the nations of the earth, holding the keys of the kingdom, to unlock it or cause it to be done among ~~all nations~~ them; and uphold them by their prayers, which they assented to by rising, # I then called upon the quorums and congregation of saints to acknowledge the high council of Kirtland in all the authorities of the Melchisedec priesthood and uphold them by their prayers which they assented to by rising. I then called upon the quoru⟨ms⟩ and congregation of saints to acknowledge and upho⟨ld⟩ by their prayer's the Bishops of Kirtland and Zion and their counsellors, ~~the Presidents of the Priests~~ in all the authority of the Aaronic priesthood, which they did by rising. I then called upon the quorums and congregation of saints to acknowledge the high-council of Zion, and uphold them by their prayers in all the authority of the

---

1. "This Earth Was Once a Garden Place," by William W. Phelps. (See *Hymns of the Church of Jesus Christ of Latter-day Saints* [Salt Lake City: The Church of Jesus Christ of Latter-day Saints, 1985], no. 49.)

2. Possibly handwriting of Jesse Hitchcock.

high priesthood which they did by rising. I next called upon the quorums and congregation of saints to acknowledge the Presidents of the seventys who act as their represent[at]ives as ⟨Apostles and⟩ special witnesses to the nations to assist the 12 in opening the gospel kingdom, among all people and to uphold them by their prayer's which they did by rising—I then called upon the quorums and all the saints to acknowledge [the] president of the Elders and his counsellors and uphold them by their prayers which they did by rising—The quorums and congregation of saints were then called upon to acknowledge and uphold by their prayers the Presidents of the Priests, Teachers, and Deacons and their counsellors, which they did by rising.

N. B. The Presidents ~~were~~ of the seventy's were acknowledged first after the 12 Apostles [p. 176]

The hymn on the hundred and 14 page was then sung,[1] after which I offered to God the following dedication prayer.[2]

Prayer,

At the dedication of the Lord's House in Kirtland Ohio March 27, 1836.—by Joseph Smith, jr. President of the Church of the Latter Day Saints.

Thanks be to thy name, O Lord God of Israel, who keepest covenant and shewest mercy unto thy servants, who walk uprightly before thee with all their hearts; thou who hast commanded thy servants to build an house to thy name in this place. (Kirtland.) And now thou beholdest, O Lord, that so thy servants have done, according to thy commandment. And now we ask the[e], holy Father, in the name of Jesus Christ, the Son of thy bosom, in[3] whose name alone salvation can be administered to the children of men: we ask the[e], O Lord, to accept of this house, the workmanship of the hands of us,

---

1. "How Pleased and Blessed Was I to Hear the People Cry," by Isaac Watts.
2. See D&C 109.
3. "in" repeated in MS.

thy servants, which thou didst command us to build; for thou knowest that we have done this work through great tribulation: and out of our poverty we have given of our substance to build a house to thy name, that the Son of Man might have a place to manifest himself to his people.

And as thou hast said, in a revelation given unto us, calling us thy friends, saying—"Call your solemn assembly, as I have commanded you; and as all have not faith, seek ye diligently and teach one another words of wisdom; yea, seek ye out of the best books words of wisdom: Seek learning; even by study, and also by faith,

"Organize yourselves; prepare every ~~thing~~ needful thing, and establish a house, even a house of prayer, a house [of] fasting, a house of faith, a house of learning [p. 177] a house of glory, a house of order, a house of God: that your incomings may be in the name of the Lord, that your outgoings may be in the name of the Lord: that all your salutations may be in the name of the Lord, with uplifted hands to the Most High."[1]

And now, Holy Father, we ask thee to assist us, thy people with thy grace in calling our solemn assembly, that it may be done to thy honor, and to thy divine acceptance, and in a manner that we may be found worthy in thy sight, to secure a fulfilment of the promises which thou hast made unto us thy people, in the revelatio[n]s given unto us: that thy glory may rest down upon thy people, and upon this thy house, which we now dedicate to thee; that it may be sanctified and consecrated to be holy, and that thy holy presence may be continually in this house; and that all people who shall enter upon the threshold of the Lord's house may feel thy power and be constrained to acknowledge that thou hast sanctified it, and that it is thy house, a place of thy holiness.

And do thou grant, holy Father, that all those who shall worship in this house, may be taught words of wisdom out of

---

1. D&C 88:117–20.

the best books, and that they may seek learning, even by study, and also by faith, as thou hast said; and that they may grow up in thee and receive a fulness of the Holy Ghost, and be organized according to thy laws, and be prepared to obtain every needful thing and that this house may be a house of prayer, a house of fasting, a house of faith, a house of glory, and of God, even thy house: that all the incomings of thy people, into this house, may be in the name of the Lord; that all their outgoings, from this house, may be in the name of the Lord; that all their salutations may be in the name of [p. 178] [the] Lord, with holy hands uplifted to the Most High;[1] and that no unclean thing shall be permitted to come into thy house to pollute it.

And when thy people transgress, any of them, they may speedily repent and return unto thee, and find favour in thy sight, and be restored to the blessings which thou hast ordained, to be poured out upon those who shall reverance thee in this thy house.

And we ask, holy Father, that thy servants may go forth from this house, armed with thy power, and that thy name may be upon them and thy glory be round about them, and thine angels have charge over them, and from this place they may bear exceeding great and glorious tidings, in truth, unto the ends of the earth, that they may know that this is thy work, and that thou hast put forth thy hand, to fulfil that which thou hast spoken by the mouths of thy prophets concerning the last days.

We ask the[e], holy Father, to establish the people that shall worship and honorably hold a name and standing in this thy house, to all generations, and for eterni⟨ty⟩ that no weapon formed against them shall prosper; that he who diggeth a pit for them shall fall into the same himself; that no combination of wickedness shall have power to rise up and prevail over thy

---

1. D&C 88:118–20.

people, upon whom thy name shall be put in this house: and if any people shall rise against this people, that thine anger be kindled against them: and if they shall smite this people, thou wilt smite them—thou wilt fight for thy people as thou didst in the day of battle, that they may be delivered from the hands of all their enimies.

We ask thee, holy Father, to confound, and astonish and bring to shame, and confusion, all those who have [p. 178][1] spread lying reports abroad over the world against thy servant or servants, if they will not repent when the everlasting gospel shall be proclaimed in their ears, and that all their works may be brought to nought, and be swept away by the hail, and by the judgments, which thou wilt send upon them in thine anger, that their may be an end to lyings and slanders against thy people: for thou knowest, O Lord, that thy servants have been innocent before thee in bearing record of thy name for which they have suffered these things, therefore we plead before thee for a full and complete deliverence from under this yoke. Break it off O Lord: break it off from the necks of thy servants, by thy power, that we may rise up in the midst of this generation and do thy work!

O Jehovah, have mercy upon this people, and as all men sin, forgive the transgressions of thy people, and let them be blotted out forever. Let the anointing of thy ministers be sealed upon them with power from on high: let it be fulfilled upon them as upon those on the day of Pentacost: let the gift of tongues be poured out upon thy people, even cloven tongues as of fire, and the interpretation thereof. And let thy house be filled, as with a rushing mighty wind, with thy glory.

Put upon thy servants the testimony of the covenant that where they go out and proclaim thy word, they may seal up the law, and prepare the hearts of thy saints for all those judg⟨e⟩ments thou art about to send, in thy wrath, upon the

---

1. This and the previous page of the MS. are numbered 178.

inhabitants of the earth because of their transgressions, that thy people may not faint in the day of trouble. [p. 179]

And whatever city thy servants shall enter, and the people of that city receive their testimony let thy peace and thy salvation be upon that city, that they may gather out from that city the righteous, that they may come forth to Zion, or to her stakes, the places of thine appointment, with songs of everlasting joy,—and until this be acomplished let not thy judgements fall upon that city.

And whatever city thy servants shall enter, and the people of that city receive not their testimony of thy servants, and thy servants warn them to save themselves from this untoward generation let it be upon that city according to that which thou hast spoken, by the mouths of thy prophets; but deliver thou, O Jehovah, we beseech thee, thy servants from their hands, and cleanse them from their blood. O Lord, we delight not in the destruction of our fellow men: their souls are precious before thee; but thy word must be fulfilled: — help thy servants to say, with thy grace assisting them, thy will be done, O Lord, and not ours.

We know that thou hast spoken by the mouth of thy prophets, terrible things concerning the wicked in the last days, that thou wilt pour out thy judgements, without measure; therefore, O Lord, deliver thy people from the calamity of the wicked, enable thy servants to seal up the law and bind up the testimony, that they may be prepared against the day of burning.

We ask thee, holy Father, to remember those who have been driven by the inhabitants of Jackson county Missouri, from the lands of their inheritance, and break off, O Lord, this yoke of affliction [p. 180] that has been put upon them. Thou knowest, O Lord, that they have been greatly oppressed and afflicted, by wicked men, and our hearts flow out in sorrow because of their grevious burdens. O Lord, how long wilt thou suffer this people to bear this affliction, and the cries of the innocent ones to ascend up in thine ears, and their blood to come up in testimony before thee and not make a display of thy power in their behalf?

Have mercy, O Lord, upon that wicked mob, who have driven thy people, that they may cease to spoil, that they may repent of their sins, if repentance is to be found; but if they will not, make bare thine arm, O Lord, and redeem that which thou didst appoint a Zion unto thy people,

And if it cannot be otherwise, that the cause of thy people may not fail before thee, may thine anger be kindled and thine indignation fall upon them that they may be wasted away, both root and branch from under heaven; but inasmuch as they will repent, thou art gracious and merciful, and will turn away thy wrath, when thou lookest upon the face of thine anointed.

Have mercy, O Lord, upon all the nations of the earth: have mercy upon the rulers of our land may those principles which were so honorably and nobly defended: viz, the constitution of our land, by our fathers, be established forever. Remember the kings, the princes, the nobles, and the great ones of the earth, and all people; and the churches: all the poor, the needy and the afflicted ones of the earth, that their hearts may be softened when thy servants shall go out from thy house, O [p. 181] Jehovah, to bear testimony of thy name, ⟨that⟩ their prejudices may give way before the truth, and thy people may obtain favour in the sight of all, that all the ends of the earth may know that we thy servants have heard thy voice, and that thou hast sent us, that from among all these thy servants, the sons of Jacob, may gather out the righteous to build a holy city to thy name, as thou hast commanded them.

We ask thee to appoint unto Zion other stakes besides this one, which thou hast appointed, that the gathering of thy people may roll on in great power and majesty, that thy work may be cut short in righteousness.

Now these words, O Lord, we have spoken before thee, concerning the revelations and commandments which thou hast given unto us, who are i[de]ntified with the Gentiles; — But thou knowest that we have a great love for the children of Jacob who have been scattered upon the mountains; for a long time in a cloudy and dark day.

We therefore ask thee to have mercy upon the children of Jacob, that Jerusalem, from this hour, may begin to be redeemed; and the yoke of bondage may begin to be broken off from the house of David, and the children of Judah may begin to return to the lands which thou didst give to Abraham, their father, and cause that the remnants of Jacob, who have been cursed and smitten, because of their transgression, to be converted from their wild and savage condition, to the fulness of the everlasting gospel, that they may lay down their weapons of bloodshed and cease their rebellions. And may [p. 182] all the scattered remnants of Israel, who have been driven to the ends of the earth, come to a knowledge of the truth, believe in the Messiah, and be redeemed from oppression, and rejoice before thee.

O Lord, remember thy servant Joseph Smith jr. and all his afflictions and persecutions, how he has covenanted with Jehovah and vowed to thee O mighty God of Jacob, and the commandments which thou hast given unto him, and that he hath sincerely strove to do thy will. — Have mercy, O Lord, upon his wife and children, that they may be exalted in thy presence, and preserved by thy fostering hand. — Have mercy upon all their immediate connexions, that their prejudices may be broken up, and swept away as with a flood, that they may be converted and redeemed with Israel and know that thou art God.

Remember, O Lord, the presidents, even all the presidents of thy church, that thy right hand may exalt them with all their families, and their immediate connexions, that their names may be perpetuated and had in everlasting remembrance from generation to generation.

Remember all thy church, O Lord, with all their families,

and all their immediate connexions, with all their sick and afflicted ones, with all the poor and meek of the earth, that the kingdom which thou hast set up without hands, may become a great mountain and fill the whole earth, that thy church may come forth out of the wilderness of darkness, and shine forth fair as the moon, clear as the sun, and terrible as an army with banners, and be adorned as a bride for that day when [p. 183] thou shalt unveil the heavens, and cause the mountains to flow down at thy presence, and the valleys to be exalted, the rough places made smooth, that thy glory may fill the earth. That when the trump shall sound for the dead, we shall be caught up in the cloud to meet thee, that we may ever be with the Lord, that our garments may be pure, that we may be clothed upon with robes of righteousness, with palms in our hands, and crowns of glory upon our heads, and reap eternal joy for all our sufferings.

O Lord, God Almighty, hear us in these our petitions, and answer us from heaven, thy holy habitation, where thou sittest enthroned, with glory, honour, power majesty, might, dominion, truth, justice judgement, mercy and an infinity of fulness, from everlasting to everlasting.

O hear, O hear, O hear us, O Lord, and answer these petitions, and accept the dedication of this house, unto thee, the work of our hands, which we have built unto thy name; and also this church to put upon it thy name. And help us by the power of thy spirit, that we may mingle our voices with those bright shining seruphs, around thy throne with acclamations of praise, singing hosanna to God and the Lamb: and let these thine anointed ones be clothed with salvation, and thy saints shout aloud for joy. Amen and Amen.

/[1]Sung Hosanah to God and the Lamb[2] after which the Lords supper was administered

---

1. Handwriting of Warren Parrish.
2. "The Spirit of God Like a Fire is Burning," by William W. Phelps. (*Hymns*, no. 2.)

I then bore testimony of the administering of angels. —
Presdt Williams also arose and testified that while Presdt Rigdon was making [p. 184] his first prayer an angel entered the window and ⟨took his⟩ seated ~~himself~~ between father Smith, and himself, and remained their during his prayer Presdt David Whitmer also saw angels in the house

We then sealed the proceedings of the day by a shouting hosanah to God and the Lamb 3 times sealing it each time with Amen, Amen, and Amen and after requesting all the official members to meet again in the evening we retired — [1] met in the evening and instructed the quorums respecting the ordinance of washing of feet which we were to attend to on wednesday following

28 March 1836 · Monday

Attended school — nothing worthy of note transpired

29 March 1836 · Tuesday

Attended school, which was the last day of our course of lectures in Hebrew by Professor Seixas, — ~~After we dismissed made some arrangements for our meeting on the morrow, attended to my domestick concirns, nothing very special transpired~~

~~At evening I met with the presidency in the Temple of the Lord and the Lord commanded us to tarry and san[c]tify ourselves by washing our feet~~

At 11 oclock A. M. Presidents Joseph Smith Jun Frederick G. Williams, Sidney Rigdon, Hyrum Smith, and Oliver Cowdery met in the most holy place in the Lords house and sought for a revelation from Him to teach us concerning our going to Zion, and other im-[p. 185]portant matter[s] after uniting in

---

1. Oliver Cowdery's report of the Kirtland Temple dedication, which adds a report of Sidney Rigdon's address, was published in *Messenger and Advocate* 2:274–81.]

prayer, the voice of the Spirit was that we should come into this place three times, and also call the other presidents, the two Bishops and their councils (each to stand in his place) and fast through the day and also the night and that during this, if we would humble ourselves, we should receive further communication from Him.[1]

After this word was received, we immediately sent for the other brethren who came. The presidency proceeded to ordain George Boosinger to the high priesthood and annoint him.

This was in consequence of his having administered unto us in temporal things in our distress. And also because he left the place just previous to the dedication of the Lords house to bring us the temporal means previously named.

Soon after this, the word of the Lord came to us through Presdt J. Smith Jun that those who had entered the holy place must not leave the house untill morning but send for such things as were necessary, and also, that during our stay we must cleans[e] our feet and partake of the sacrament that we might be made holy before Him, and thereby be qualified to officiate in our calling upon the morrow in washing the feet of the Elders.[2]

Accordingly we proceeded and cleansed our faces and our feet, and then proceeded to wash each others feet. — president S. Rigdon first washed presdt J. Smith jun and then in [p. 186] turn was washed by him — after which president Rigdon washed presdt J. Smith Sen. and Hyrum Smith ⟨prsdt⟩ J. Smith Jun washed presdt F. G Williams, and then pres. Hyrum Smith washed president David Whitmer's feet and president Oliver

---

1. Prior to this the Church presidency and Twelve had determined to move to Zion (Missouri) with their families by 15 May 1836. A contemplated revelation concerning their removal to Zion is not found in the pages that follow. (See journal entries of 24 September 1835 and 13, 30 March 1836; also Esplin, "The Emergence of Brigham Young and the Twelve to Mormon Leadership, 1830–1841," 194–96.)

2. On the ordinance of washing of feet see the entries of 5 October and 12 November 1835.

Cowdery's, then pres D. Whitmer washed pres. W. W. Phelps feet and in turn pres Phelps washed pres John Whitmers feet.

The Bishops and their councils were then washed: After which we partook of the bread and wine. The Holy S[p]irit rested down upon us and we continued in the Lords house all night prophesying and giving glory to God

/¹30 March 1836 · Wednesday²

According to appointment the presidency, the 12, the seventies, the high ~~co(u)neils~~ councils, the Bishops and their entire quorums, the Elders, and all the official members in this stake of Zion amounting to about 300 met in the temple of the Lord to attend to the ordinance of washing of feet, I ascended the pulpit and remarked to the congregation that we had passed through many trials and afflictions since the organization of this church and that this is a year of Jubilee to us and a time of rejoicing, and that it was expedient for us to prepare bread and wine sufficient to make our hearts glad, as we should not probably leave this house until morning; to this end we should call on the brethren to make a contribution, the stewards passed round and took up a liberal contribution and messengers were dispatched for bread and wine, tubs [of] water and towels were prepared and I called the house to order, and the presidency proceeded to wash the feet of the 12 pronouncing many prophecy's and blessings upon them in the name of the Lord Jesus, the brethren began to prophesy [p. 187] upon each others heads, and cursings upon the enimies of Christ who inhabit Jackson county Missouri continued prophesying and blessing and sealing them with Hosanna and Amen until nearly 7 oclock P.M. the bread ⟨& wine⟩ was then brought in, and I observed that we had fasted all the day, and lest we faint; as the Saviour did so shall we do on this occasion, we shall

---

1. Possibly handwriting of Jesse Hitchcock.
2. MS. reads "Wednesday morning 8 o clock March 30 1836"

bless the bread and give it to the 12 and they to the multitude, after which we shall bless the wine and do likewise; while waiting ~~for the wine~~ I made the following remarks, that the time that we were required to tarry in Kirtland to be endued would be fulfilled in a few days, and then the Elders would go forth and each must stand for himself, that it was not necessary for them to be sent out two by two as in former times; but to go in all meekness in sobriety and preach Jesus Christ & him crucified not to contend with others on the account of their faith or systems of religion but pursue a steady course, this I delivered by way of commandment, and all that observe them not will pull down persecution upon ~~your~~ ⟨their⟩ heads, while those who do shall always be filled with the Holy Ghost, this I pronounced as a prophesy sealed with a Hosanna & amen. Also that the seventies are not called to serve tables or preside over churches to settle difficulties, but to preach the gospel and build them up, and set others who do not belong to these quorums to preside over them who are high priests—the twelve also are not to serve tables, but to bear the keys of the kingdom to all nations, and unlock them and call upon the seventies to follow after them and assist them. The 12 are at liberty to go wheresoever they will [p. 188] and if one shall say, I wish to go to such a place let all the rest say Amen.

The seventies are at liberty to go to Zion if they please or go wheresoever they will and preach the gospel and let the redemtion of Zion be our object, and strive to affect it by sending up all the strength of the Lords house whereever we find them, and I want to enter into the following covenant, that if any more of our brethren are slain or driven from their lands in Missouri by the mob that we will give ourselves no rest until we are avenged of our enemies to the uttermost, this covenant was sealed unanimously by a hosanna and Amen. — I then observed to the quorums that I had now completed the organization of the church and we had passed through all the necessary ceremonies, that I had given them all the instruction they needed and that they now were at liberty after obtaining their lisences to go forth and build up the kingdom of God, and that it was expedient for me and the presidency to retire, having spent the night previous in waiting upon the Lord in his temple, and having to attend another dedication on the morrow, or conclude the one commenced on the last sabbath for the benifit of those of my brethren and sisters who could not get into the house on the former occasion but that it was expedient for the brethren to tarry all night and worship before the Lord in his house I left the meeting in the charge of the 12 and retired at about 9 o clock in the evening; the brethren continued exhorting, prophesying and speaking in tongues until 5 o clock in the morning—the Saviour made his appearance to some, while angels minestered unto others, and it was a penticost and enduement indeed, long to be remembered for the sound shall go forth from this place into all the [p. 189] world, and the occurrences of this day shall be hande[d] down upon the pages of sacred history to all generations, as the day of Pentecost, so shall this day be numbered and celebrated as a year of Jubilee and time of rejoicing to the saints of the most high God.

31 March 1836 · Thursday[1]

This day being set apart to perform again the ceremonies of the dedication for the benifit of those who could not get into the house on the preceeding sabbath I repaired to the temple at 8 o clock A.M. in company with the presidency, and arranged our door-keepers and stewards as on the former occasion, we then opened the doors and a large congregation entered the house and were comfortably seated, the authorities of the church were seated, in their respective order and the services of the day were commenced prosecuted and termi-

---

1. MS. reads "Thursday morning 8 o clock March 31st"

nated in the same manner as at the former dedication and the spirit of God rested upon the congregation and great solemnity prevailed.

/¹1 April 1836 · Friday

At home most of the day, many brethren called to see me, some on temporal & some on spiritual buisiness, among the number was Leeman [Leman] Copley, who testified against me in a suit I brought against Doctor P. Hulbut for threatning my life, he confessed that he bore a fals[e] testimony against me, in that suit but verily thought at the time that he was right but on calling to mind a̶l̶l̶ all the circumstances connected t̶h̶e̶ with the things that transpired at the time he was [p. 190] convinced that he was wrong, and humbly confessed it and asked my forgivness, which was readily granted, he also wished to be received into the church again by baptism, and was received according to his desire, he gave me his confession in writing

/²2 April 1836 · Saturday

Transacted business (although of a temporal nature), in company with S. Rigdon, O. Cowdery, J. Whitmer F. G. Williams, D. Whi[t]mer & W. W. Phelps, which was to have a bearing upon the redemption of Zion. The positive manner in which he [Joseph Smith] expressed himself on this, ⟨his⟩ favorite theme, was directly calculated to produce conviction in the minds of those who heard him, that his whole soul was engaged in it, notwithstanding on a superficial view of the same subject they might differ from him in judgement. It was determined in council, after mature deliberation, that he and O. Cowdery should act in concert in raising funds for the accomplishment of the aforesaid object. As soon as the above plan was settled,

---

1. Handwriting of Warren Parrish.
2. Handwriting of Warren A. Cowdery.

he and O. Cowdery set out together, and their success was such in one half day, as to give them pleasing anticipations, ~~and~~ assure them that they were doing the will of God and that his work prospered in their hands

3 April 1836 · Sunday

He attended meeting in the Lords House, assisted the other Presidents of the Church in seating the congregation and then became an attentive listener to the preaching from the Stand. T. B. Marsh & D. W. Patten spoke in the A.M. to an attentive audience of about 1000 persons. In the P.M. he assisted the other Presidents in distributing the elements of the Lords Supper to the church, receiving them from the ~~Hands~~ "Twelve" whose privilige it was to officiate in the sacred desk this day. After having performed this service to his brethren, he retired to the pulpit, the vails being dropped, [p. 191] and bowed himself with O. Cowdery, in solemn, but silent prayer to the Most High. After rising from prayer the following vision was opened to both of them.

The vail was taken from their minds and the eyes of their understandings were opened. They saw the Lord standing upon the breast work of the pulpit before them, and under his feet was a paved work of pure gold, in color like amber: his eyes were as a flame of fire; the hair of his head was like the pure snow, his countenance shone above the brightness of the sun, and his voice was as the sound of the rushing of great waters, even the Voice of Jehovah, saying, I am the first and the last, I am he who liveth, I am he who was slain. I am your Advocate with the Father. Behold your sins are forgiven you. You are clean before me, therefore, lift up your heads and rejoice, let the hearts of your brethren rejoice and let the hearts of all my ~~brethren~~ ⟨people⟩ rejoice, who have with their might, built this house to my name. For behold I have accepted this house and my name shall be here; and I will manifest myself to my people, in mercy, in this House, yea I will appear unto my servants and speak unto them with mine own voice, if my people will keep my commandments and do not pollute this Holy House. Yea the hearts of thousands and tens of thousands shall greatly rejoice in consequence of the blessings which shall be poured out, and the endowment with which my servants have already been endowed and shall hereafter be endowed in this House. And the fame of this House shall spread to foreign lands, and this is the beginning of the blessing, which shall [p. 192] be poured out upon the heads of my people. even so Amen.[1]

After this vision closed, the Heavens were again opened unto them and Moses appeared before them and committed unto them the keys of the gathering of Israel from the four parts of the Earth and the leading of the ten tribes from the Land of the North.[2] After this Elias appeared and committed the dispensation of the gospel of Abraham, saying, that in them and their seed all generations after them should be blessed. After this vision had closed, another great and glorious vision burst upon them, for Elijah, the Prophet, who was taken to Heaven without tasting death, also stood before them, and said, behold the time has fully come which was spoken of by the Mouth of Malachi, testifying, that he should be sent before the great and dreadful day of the Lord come, to turn the hearts of the Fathers to the children, and the children to the fathers, lest the whole earth be smitten with a curse. Therefore, the keys of this dispensation are committed into your hands, and by this ye may know that the great and the dreadful day of the Lord is near, even at the doors [p. 193]

---

1. See D&C 110.

2. Keys refer to the right of presidency, the authority to direct and control the use of the priesthood. A March 1832 revelation stated that the keys of the kingdom had been given to Joseph Smith, "which belong always to the presidency of the high priesthood." (D&C 81:1–2.) However, the keys of the kingdom were not all given at once. Periodically, prophets from the past restored to Joseph Smith the authority, or keys, pertaining to particular functions over which they had jurisdiction, as on the occasion here.

MISSOURI JOURNAL, 1838, MARCH TO SEPTEMBER

MS. Joseph Smith Papers, LDS Church Archives, Salt Lake City, Utah.

Editorial Note

This journal covers six months from 13 March to 10 September 1838 — a critical time in Mormon history. It begins with the arrival of Joseph Smith at Far West, Caldwell County, Missouri, after dissension and threats of violence had forced his departure from Kirtland, Ohio. In 1833, following the expulsion of the Latter-day Saints from Jackson County, Missouri, where they had sought to establish Zion, they moved north across the Missouri River to Clay County. Three years later, in the face of rising discontent among the old settlers, they migrated still farther north, and east, to Caldwell County. This journal records Joseph Smith's attempt to establish a new gathering place and headquarters city in Caldwell County during the spring and summer of 1838. It also records the beginnings of the deterioration of that effort, which resulted in the expulsion of the Latter-day Saints from Missouri by the following spring. Except for the first page, which appears to have been dictated by the Prophet, almost the entire journal was written by George W. Robinson as he copied letters, minutes, and revelations and observed the comings and goings of the Church Presidency. Robinson had been appointed clerk and recorder for the Church and secretary for the First Presidency on 4 April 1838. In addition to Robinson's writing in the journal, James Mulholland, another of the Prophet's clerks, copied in a revelation and a lengthy letter written by Joseph Smith from the jail at Liberty, Missouri, in December 1838.

The journal measures 13 × 8 1/4 inches and consists of 182 leaves (364 pages) bound in a brown, hard-cover, leather binding. The inside

211

front cover is blank. Page 1 has "General" written at the top; on pages 2–14 are recorded "Names of members of the Church in Missouri then situated most in Caldwell County commencing in June 1838." Pages 15 to 83 contain the 1838 Missouri Journal; 85 to 100 are numbered blank pages; 101 to 108 contain a handwritten copy of Joseph Smith's letter to the Church from the Liberty jail in Clay County, Missouri, dated 16 December 1838; 109 to 110 are numbered and blank except that page 110 has "Recor" written on the top line. Then follow 55 unnumbered blank pages. At a later date the book was turned over and used to record 197 pages of patriarchal blessings. From the blessing side of the book the spine is labelled with a "5," designating the volume number of patriarchal blessings. From the journal side, the cover of the volume is labeled with a large handprinted letter "G."

The Scriptory Book–
of Joseph Smith Jr–
President of the Church of
Jesus Christ, of Latterday Saints
In all the World.
Far West April 12th 1838.

Kept by Geo. W. Robinson Recorder of the Church of Jesus Christ of Latter Day Saints

[part of page blank]

The following is a letter from Prest Smith[1] [p. 15]

13 March 1838 · Tuesday

On the 13th day of March I with my family and some others arrived within 8 miles[2] of Far West[3] and put up at brother

---

1. See letter of 4 September 1837 on p. 216.
2. MS. reads "milds"
3. The town of Far West, in Caldwell County, Missouri, was founded by Latter-day Saints in 1836. By the summer of 1838 the town consisted of 150 houses, four dry goods stores, three groceries, a half dozen blacksmith shops, two hotels, and a printing office. In 1837 preparations were made to build a

Barnerds [John P. Barnard][1] to tarry for the night. Here we ware met[2] by an escort of bretheren from the town who came to make us welcome to their little Zion. On the next day as we ware about entering the town Many of the bretheren came out to meet us who also with open armes welcomed us to their boosoms. We were immediately received under the hospitable roof of George W. Harris who treated us with all kindness possible. here we refreshed ourselves with much sattisfaction after our long and tedious Journey and the bretheren braught in such necessaries as we stood in need of for our presant comfort and necessities.

After being here two or three days my Brother Samuel [Smith] arrived with his family an[d] shortly after his arrival while walking with him & cirtain other bretheren the following sentements occured to my mind. —

Motto of the Church of Christ of *Latterday Saints*.

The Constitution of our country formed by the Fathers of Liberty.

---

temple in Far West, and on 4 July 1838 the cornerstone was laid. Between March 1838, when Joseph Smith arrived in the town, and the expulsion of the saints in 1839, Far West was headquarters of the Church. At its height approximately 2,000 people lived there. (Andrew Jenson, *Encyclopedic History of the Church of Jesus Christ of Latter-day Saints* [Salt Lake City, 1941], 245–46.)

1. In the night of 12 January 1838, Joseph Smith and Sidney Rigdon left Kirtland, Ohio, on horseback to escape mob violence. They traveled to Norton, Medina County, where they stayed with friends until their families arrived, and then continued their journey in covered wagons. Inclement weather, lack of provisions, and the pursuit of enemies complicated their trip. After leaving Paris, Illinois, the two families traveled different routes due to illness among the Rigdons. (*History of the Church*, 3:1–3.)

At a meeting of the Missouri high council at Far West on 24 February 1838, a committee was appointed "to obtain two waggons and teams and money to go and meet the Brethren J. Smith jr & S. Rigdon and assist them" on their journey. John P. Barnard traveled to Huntsville, Missouri, in his carriage to bring Joseph Smith and his family to Far West. (Donald Q. Cannon and Lyndon W. Cook, eds., *Far West Record: Minutes of The Church of Jesus Christ of Latter-day Saints, 1830–1844* [Salt Lake City: Deseret Book Company, 1983], 141–44; Elden Jay Watson, *Manuscript History of Brigham Young, 1801–1844* [Salt Lake City: 1968]: 27.)

2. MS.: "meet"

Peace and good order in society Love to God and good will to man.

All good and wholesome law's; And virtue and truth above all things

And Aristarchy[1] live forever!!!

But Wo, to tyrants, Mobs, Aristocracy, Anarchy and Toryism:[2] And all those who invent or seek out unrighteous and vexatious lawsuits under the pretext or color of law or office, either religious or political.

Exalt the standard of Democracy! Down [p. 16] with that of Priestcraft, and let all the people say Amen! that the blood of our Fathers may not cry from the ground against us.

Sacred is the Memory of that Blood which baught for us our liberty.

Signed	Joseph Smith Jr.
Geo, W. Robinson	Thomas B. Marsh
	D. W. Patten
	Brigham Young
	Samuel H. Smith
	George M. Hinkle
	John Corrill. —

Quest. on Scripture.[3]

1st. Who is the stem of Jessee spoken of in the 1st 2d 3d 4th and 5th verses of the 11th Chap. of Is[a]iah.

Ans. Verely thus saith the Lord It is Christ

Q. 2d. What is the Rod spoken of in the 1st verse of the 11th Chap. that shou[l]d come of the stem of Jessee.

---

1. A body of good men in power, or government by excellent men.

2. Joseph Smith's sentiments here are best understood in light of events in Kirtland that had forced the Prophet to leave that place to save his life (see note 2, p. 216). In his letter of 29 March 1838, copied in this journal, the Prophet refers to the Kirtland dissenters, or Parrishites, as "Aristocrats or Anarchys." See p. 221.

3. The following answers to questions are in D&C 113.

Ans. Behold thus saith ⟨the Lord⟩ it is a servant in the hands of Christ who is partly a decendant of Jessee as well as of Ephraim or of the house of Joseph, on whome thare is laid much power.

Qest 3d. What is the Root of Jessee spoken of in the 10th verse of the 11th Chap.

Ans. Behold thus saith the Lord; it is a decendant of Jessee as well as of Joseph unto whom rightly belongs the Priesthood and the kees of the Kingdom for an ensign and for the geathering of my people in the Last days.–[p. 17]

Questions by Elias Higby

1st Q. What is ment by the command in Is[a]iah 52d Chap 1st verse which saith Put on thy strength O Zion and what people had I[sa]iah referance to

A. He had reference to those whome God should call in the last day's who should hold the power of Priesthood to bring again zion and the redemption of Israel. And to put on her strength is to put on the authority of the priesthood which she (Zion) has a right to by lineage: Also to return to that power which she had lost

Ques. 2d. What are we to understand by Zions loosing herself from the bands of her neck 2d verse.

A. We are to understand that the scattered remnants are exorted to[1] return to the Lord from whence they have falen which if they do the promise of the Lord is that he will speak to them or give them revelation See 6th 7th and 8th verses The bands of her neck are the curses of God upon her or the remnants of Israel in their scattered condition among the Gentiles.

The following letter I wrote previous to my leaving Kirtland and sent by the hand of T. B. Marsh

---

1. "to" repeated in MS.

Sept 4th A.D. 1837
Kirtland Geauga Co. Ohio

Joseph Smith Jr. Prest of the Church ⟨of Christ⟩ of Latter Day Saints in all the world To John Corroll [Corrill] & the whole Church in Zion [p. 18] Sendeth Greeting, Blessed be the God of and father of our Lord Jesus Christ Who has blessed you with many blessings in Christ, And who has delivered you many times from the hands of your enemies And planted you many times in an heavenly or holy place, My respects & love to you all, and my blessings upon all the faithfull & true harted in the new & everlasting covenant & for as much as I have desired for a long time to see your faces & converse with you & instruct you in those things which have been revealed to me pertaining to the Kingdom of God in the last days, I now write unto you offering an appolegy, My being bound with bonds of affliction by the workers of iniquity and by the labours of the Church endeavoring[1] in all things to do the will of God, for the salvation of the Church both in temporal as well as spiritual things. Bretheren we have waided through a scene of affliction and sorrow thus far for the will of God, that language is inadequate to describe pray ye therefore with more earnestness for our redemption, you have undoubtedly been informed by letter & otherwise of our difficulties in Kirtland which are now about being settled[2] and that you may have a

---

1. MS.: "endeaveroung"
2. Following the dedication of the Kirtland temple in 1836, Joseph Smith had turned his attention to the building up of Kirtland as a gathering place of the Latter-day Saints. However, by the summer of 1837, in the wake of the collapse of the Kirtland Bank, misunderstanding of the Prophet's mission, manifest by an unwillingness to comply with his authority in temporal matters, was a cause of much dissent in the Church. Prophetic involvement in the economic, social, and political affairs of life was the focus of opposition against Joseph Smith that extended to the presiding councils of the Church. Dissenters openly opposed his policies and leadership. Eyewitnesses said "the hearts of many of the strong trembled," and conditions deteriorated to the point that "a man's life was in danger the moment he spoke in defence of the Prophet."
At the 3 September 1837 Kirtland conference, the minutes of which are copied

knowlege of the same I subscribe to you the following minuits of the comittee, of the whole Church of Kirtland the authorities &c. refering you to my brother Hyrum & br T. B. Marsh for further particulars also that you [p. 19] may know how to proceed to set in order & regulate the affairs of the Church in Zion whenever they become disorganized The minuits are as follows; Minuits of a Conference assembled in committee of the whole Church on the 3rd of Sept. 1837 9 O Clock A.M. G. W. Robinson was called upon to take the minuits of the conference, S. Rigdon then presented Joseph Smith Jr to the Church to know if they still looked upon & would still receive & uphold him, as the Prest. of the whole Church And the vote was unanymous in the affirmative: Prest Smith then presented S. Rigdon & F. G. Williams for his councilors and to constitute with himself the three first Prest of the Church. Vote unanymous in the affirmative, Prest. Smith then introdused O. Cowdery, J. Smith Sen.–Hiram Smith & John Smith for assistant Councilors.[1] These last four together with the three fi⟨r⟩st are to be concidred the heads of the Church, Carried unanymously. Voted that N. K. Whitney hold his office as

---

here, and at later meetings that fall, in Kirtland and Far West, Missouri, efforts were made by the Prophet to resolve the problems that had undercut the unity of the Church. But before the end of the year, dissension flared anew. Under the leadership of Warren Parrish, who had been Joseph Smith's secretary, approximately thirty prominent men of the Church, including a member of the First Presidency, several of the Twelve, high council, First Council of Seventy, and witnesses of the Book of Mormon, had renounced Joseph Smith and the Church and had established a new organization — the Church of Christ. During this time of apostasy, approximately three hundred left the Church, representing about 15 percent of the Kirtland membership. The dissenters, commonly referred to as the "Parrishites," or "the old standard," contributed to events that forced the Prophet and others loyal to him to flee Kirtland for their lives. (See Backman, *The Heavens Resound*, chapter 17; Esplin, "The Emergence of Brigham Young and the Twelve to Mormon Leadership, 1830–1841," chapters 5–7; Marvin S. Hill, "Cultural Crisis in the Mormon Kingdom: A Reconsideration of the Causes of Kirtland Dissent," *Church History* 49 [September 1980]: 286–97; and Parkin, "Conflict at Kirtland," chapter 10.)

1. This was the first appointment of assistant counselors in the Church.

Bishop & continue to act as such in Kirtland & that R Cahoon & V Knight continue to act as councilors to the Bishop The Twelve Apostles were then presented one by one When T. B. Marsh D. W. Patten B. Young H. C. Kimble O. Hyde P. P. Pratt O. Prat Wm Smith Wm E McLellin, were received unanymously in their Apostleship Luke & Lyman Johnson & J. F. Boynton were rejected & cut off though privileged with conffesing and making sattisfaction, Elder Boynton (which was the only one present at the time) arose and endeavoured to confess, Justifying himself in his former conduct by reason of the failure of the Bank &c his conduct was strongly protested by Elder [p. 20] Brigham Young in a plain and energetic manner, Stating various reasons why he would or could not receive him into fellowship until a hearty conffession and repentance was manifested, He was followed by Elder Marsh who acquiesed in testimony & resolution Elder Boynton again arose & still attributed his difficulties to the failure of the Bank, Stating that he had understood the Bank was instituted by the will of God, and he had been told that it never should fail let men do what they would Prest Smith then arose and stated that if this had been declared, no one had authority from him for so doing, For he had allways said unless the institution was conducted on righteous[1] principals it would not stand, A Vote was then taken to know if the congregation was sattisfied with Boyntons confession Voted in the negative Conf—Adjourned for one hour—

Conference assembled at 2 O Clock P M. Opened by reading singing & prayer, The Prest then arose & said he would call upon the Church to know if they were sattisfied with their High Council and should proceed to name them individualy John Johnson Joseph Coe Joseph Kingsbury & Martin Harris were objected to,[2] also John P Green but this case put over

1. MS.: "richeous"
2. See note 2 on p. 216.

untill he should be present, Noah Packard Jared Carter Samuel H Smith, These were voted to retain their office Oliver Granger Henry G. Atwood Wm Marks Mahew Hillman Harlow Readfield [Redfield] Asa[h]el Smith Phinehas Richards & David Dort were chosen to fill the place of those objected to, The Prest. then called upon the congregation to know if the recent appointed presidents of the Seventies Should Stand in their calling Voted that John Gaylord James Foster Salmon Gee Daniel S Miles Joseph Young Josiah Butterfield [p. 21] & Levi Handcock [Hancock] Should retain th[e]ir office as Prests of the Seventies John Gould was objected. The Pres then arose and made some remarks concerning the former Prests of the Seventies, the callings and authorities of their Priesthood &c. &c. Voted that the old Presidents of the Seventies be refered to the quorum of High Priests,[1] And also that if any of the members of the quorum of the Seventies Should be disattisfied & would not submit to the Present order, and receive these last Presidents that they Should have power to demand their Lisence & they should no longer be concidered members of the church

Conference Closed by Prayer by the President

~~Joseph Smith Jr Prest Geo W. Robinson Clerk~~

G W Robinson   Clk   Joseph Smith Jr   Prest

Dear Brotheren

Oliver Cowdery has been in transgression, but as he is now chosen as one of the Presidents or Councilors I trust that he

---

1. At the 6 April 1837 conference of the Church in Kirtland, it was noted that all but one of the original presidents of the Seventy, appointed in 1835, had been ordained high priests. "This was declared to be wrong, and not according to the order of heaven." Furthermore, a revelation on priesthood had stated that the presidents of the seventy should be "chosen out of the number of the seventy." (D&C 107:93.) Hence, new presidents of the seventy were selected and those previously ordained high priests were referred to the quorum of high priests. [Messenger and Advocate 3 [April 1837]: 486–87; also, History of the Church, 2: 475–77.]

will yet humble himself & magnify his calling but if he should not, the Church will soon be under the necessaty of raising their hands against him Therefore pray for him, David Whitmer Leonard Rich & others have been in transgression but we hope that they may be humble & ere long make sattisfaction to the Church otherwise they cannot retain their standing, Therefore we say unto you beware of all disaffected Characters for they come not to build up but to destroy & scatter abroad,[1] Though we or an Angel from Heaven preach any other gospel or introduce [any] order of things ⟨than⟩ those things which ye have received and are authorised to received from the first Presidency let him be accursed, May God Almighty Bless you all & keep you unto the coming & kingdom of our Lord and Savior Jesus Christ; Yours in the Bonds of the new ⟨Covenent⟩– J. Smith Jr. [p. 22]

Samu[e]l James was objected to by reason of his absence on a mission and circumstances such that it is impossible for him to attend to the duties of this office

~~J. Smith Jr Prest Geo W Robinson Clk~~

Revelation to Joseph Smith Jr Given in Kirtland Geauga Co. Ohio Sept 4th 1837 Making known the transgression of John Whitmer [and] W. W. Phelps

Verily thus Saith the Lord unto you my Servent Joseph. My Servents John Whitmer & William W Phelps have done those things which are not pleasing in my sight Therefore if they repent not they shall be removed out of their places Amen —

J Smith Jr

The above letter & revelation relative to the transgression and removal from office D. Whitmer O. Cowdery J. Whitmer & W. W. Phelps has been fulfiled as will be Seen in the following Sequence

---

1. See note 2 on p. 216.

Far West March 29th A.D. 1838

To the ~~first~~ Presidency of the Church of Jesus Christ of Latter Day Saints in Kirtland

Dear & well beloved brotheren. Through the grace & mercy of our God, after a long & tedious journey of two months & one day, I and my family arrived in the City of Far West Having been met at Huntsville 120 miles from this [place] by brotheren with teams & money to forward us on our Journey When within eight miles of the City of Far West We were met by an [p. 23] escort of bretheren from the City who were T. B. Marsh John Corril Elias Higby [Higbee] & severel others of the faithfull of the West who received us with open armes and warm hearts and welcomed us to the bosom of their sosciety On our arrival in the City we were greeted on every hand by the saints who bid us welcom[e]; welcome; to the land of their inheritance Dear bretheren you may be assured that so friendly a meeting & reception paid us well for our long Seven years of Servitude persecution & affliction in the midst of our enimies in the land Kirtland yea verily our hearts were full and we feel greatfull to Almighty God for his kindness unto us. The particulars of our Journey brotheren cannot well[1] be writen but we trust that the same God w⟨h⟩o has protected us will protect you also, and will sooner or later grant us the privilege of seeing each other face ⟨to⟩ face & of rehersing all our sufferings We have herd of the destruction of the printing office which we presume to believe must have been occasioned by the Parrishites or more properly the Aristocrats or Anarchys as we believe.[2] The saints here

---

1. MS.: "weell"
2. In January 1838, shortly after Joseph Smith and Sidney Rigdon departed from Kirtland, the Church printing office in Kirtland was burned. Grandison Newell, a non-Mormon, had filed a suit against the Church Presidency for an unpaid debt. On 15 January the printing office was attached and sold at public auction to pay the debt. The following night it was burned. Apostates claimed Church members had burned the establishment because they had lost it; the Saints blamed dissenters, claiming the attachment of the building for debt could not legally stand, therefore it was burned to keep the Church from getting it

have provided a room for us and daily necessary's which is brought in from all parts of the Co. to make us comfortable, so that I have nothing to do but to attend to my spiritual concerns or the spiritual affairs of the Church The difficulties of the Church had been a[d]justed before arrival here by a Judicious High Council with T. B. Marsh & D W Patton [David W. Patten] who acted as Pres. Pro. Tem. of the Church of Zion being appointed by the voice of the Council & Church Wm. W. Phelps & John Whitmer having been cut off from the Church, D Whitmer remains as yet[1] The saints at this time are in union & peace & love prevails throughout, in a word Heaven smiles upon the saints in Caldwell. Various & many have been the falshoods writen from thence[2] [p. 24] to this place, but have prevailed nothing. We have no uneasiness about the power of our enemies in this place to do us harm Br. Samuel H Smith & family arrived here soon after we did in go[o]d health. Br B Young Br D[aniel]. S. Miles & Br L[evi]. Richards arrived here when we did. They were with us on the last of our journey which aded much to our sattisfaction. They also are well They have provided places for their families & are now about to break the ground for seed. Being under the hand of wicked vex⟨at⟩ious lawsuits for seven years past my buisness was so dangerous that I was not able to leave it, in

---

back. (See Hepzibah Richards to Willard Richards, 18 January 1838, as cited in Kenneth W. Godfrey, Audrey M. Godfrey, and Jill Mulvay Derr, *Women's Voices: An Untold History of the Latter-day Saints* [Salt Lake City: Deseret Book Company, 1982], 71; Backman, *The Heavens Resound*, 349–50; Parkin, "Conflict at Kirtland," 322–23; see also note 2 on p. 216.)

1. On 26 January 1838 charges had been brought against the presidency of the Church in Zion (Missouri) — David Whitmer, John Whitmer, and William W. Phelps — for having sold their land in Jackson County, Missouri, contrary to the council of the Church, and for infractions against the Word of Wisdom (D&C 89). The position of the accused was that "they would not be controlled by an ecclesiastical power or revelation whatever in their temporal concerns." At a meeting of the Missouri council on 10 March 1838, Phelps and John Whitmer were both excommunicated for unchristian-like conduct. (The case is recorded in Cannon and Cook, *Far West Record*, 135–50.)

2. I.e., from Kirtland.

as good a situation as I had antisipated, but if there are any wrongs, they shall all be noticed so far as the Lord gives me ability & power to do so,[1] Say to all the brotheren that I have not forgotten them, but remember them in my prayers, Say to Mother Beaman[2] that I remember her, Also Br Daniel Carter Br St[r]ong & family Bro Granger & family, Finally I cannot innumerate them all for the want of room I will just name Br [Vinson] Knights the Bishop &c. My best respects to them all for the want of room & I commend them and the Church of God in Kirtland to our Heavenly Father & the word of his grace, which is able to make you wise unto Salvation I would just say to Br. [William] Marks that I saw in a vision while on the road that whereas he was closely persued by an in-

---

1. Joseph Smith's opponents often used legal harassment as a tool to counteract his growing influence. According to Eber D. Howe, editor of the Painesville, Ohio, *Telegraph*, "Many of our citizens thought it advisable to take all the legal means within their reach to counteract the progress of so dangerous an enemy in their midst, and many law suits ensued." (E. D. Howe, *Autobiography and Recollections of a Pioneer Printer* [Painesville, Ohio: Telegraph Steam Printing House, 1878], 45, as cited in Parkin, "Conflict at Kirtland," 265.) At the conclusion of an 1837 trial against the Prophet in Geauga County, Ohio, a local newspaper reported: "This is said to be the thirteenth prosecution which has been instituted against Joseph Smith, Jr. for the prejudice against him, he has never in a single instance been convicted, on a final trial. This fact shows on the one hand, that a spirit of persecution has existed, and on the other hand it certainly furnishes some evidence that he has for some reason, been falsely accused, and that he is indeed and in truth better than some of his accusers." (*Painesville Telegraph*, 26 May 1837, as cited in Firmage and Mangrum, *Zion in the Courts*, 56.)

Litigation connected with the Kirtland Safety Society bank, and unpaid debt, accounted for much of the legal hositility against Joseph Smith in Ohio. Careful research by Hill, Rooker, and Wimmer has shown that Joseph Smith's cumulative indebtedness in the period 1835–37 was a little over $100,000; that $60,000, and possibly much more, of this debt was finally settled; and that he had assets to sufficiently cover all his debts had there been sufficient liquid capital and a continuing prosperity. Furthermore, years later and hundreds of miles away, the Prophet continued to settle his Kirtland debts, which suggests that his sudden flight from Kirtland, in the face of numerous lawsuits and threats upon his life, was not an attempt to evade his obligations. (Marvin S. Hill, C. Keith Rooker, Larry T. Wimmer, "The Kirtland Economy Revisited: A Market Critique of Sectarian Economics," *BYU Studies* 17 [Summer 1977]: 391–482.)

2. Sally Burtts, wife of Alvah Beman.

numerable concource of enimies and as they pressed upon him hard as if they were about to devour him, & had seemingly attained some degre of advantage over him But about this time a chariot of fire came and near the place and the Angel of the Lord put forth his hand unto Br. Marks & said [p. 25] unto him thou art my son come *here*, and immediately he was caught up in the Chariot and rode away triumphantly out of their midst and again the Lord said I will raise th[ee] up for a blessing unto many people Now the particulars of this whole matter cannot be writen at this time but the vision was evidently given to me that I might know that the hand of the Lord would be on his behalf   J Smith Jr

I transmit to you the folowing motto of the Church of Jesus Christ of Latter day Saints Recorded on Pages 16 & 17 of J Smith Jr Scriptory Record Book A.[1] We left Pres. Rigdon 30 miles this side of Parris Illinois in consequence of the sickness of Br. G[eorge]. W. Robinsons wife, on yesterday br Robinson arrived here who informed us that his father in law (S. Rigdon) was at Huntsville detained there on account of the ill health of his wife. They will proba[b]ly be here soon.[2] Choice seeds of all kinds of fruit also Choice breed of Cattle would be in much demand also best blood of horses garden seeds of every description also hay seed of all sorts, all of these are much needed in this place

Verry respe[c]tfully I subscribe myself your servent in Christ our Lord & Savior

Joseph Smith Jr
Prest of the Church of Jesus
Christ of Latterday Saints

Pleasent Park Mo.

---

1. See p. 213.
2. Sidney Rigdon arrived at Far West on 4 April 1838. (*History of the Church*, 3: 449.)

March 31st 1838

Respected Sir

Permit me to introduce to your acquaintance Mr Henry Root of Dewit near this place on Misso⟨u⟩ri river[1] His buisness I am unacquainted with, Though any thing he may say to you, you may put the most implisit confidence in, as I have allways found him to be a man of truth & honor, neither have I ever [p. 26] known him to give a misrepresentation of any part. He is a merchant and I suppose doing a moderate buisness his place is now, onley laid out about a year since a beautifull sight to the river, and a first rate landing And Sir permit me to say to you, if you could make it convenient or for your advantage to settle in this County, I would let you have part of my land There is yet to enter adjoining my land, as good land [as] is in the world. I have no doubt you can do as well[2] here in forming a settlement and probaly better than any place in the state The facilities of the river will be of great servise to in settling this uper country besides some of the knowing ones have arrived to uproot you, but here you can break them down in turn, I will join you in the speculation if necessary and if possible the Church I will have after paying for *1600*

---

1. David Thomas, the writer of this letter, and Henry Root, were owners of extensive land holdings in the area of DeWitt, Carroll County, Missouri. DeWitt presented a convenient place of settlement for Latter-day Saints arriving in Missouri, and since it was located at the confluence of the Grand and Missouri Rivers, a settlement there would provide a port of entry from whence goods could be sent to the Saints in Caldwell County and other locations in northwestern Missouri. Sometime after the date of this letter, Church leaders met with Thomas and Root and agreed upon a settlement at DeWitt. The first Church members moved there in July 1838. Their number grew substantially with the arrival of several hundred Saints from Canada under the direction of John E. Page in September. But a short time later the community was abandoned due to mob violence. (See Andrew Jenson, "De Witt," *The Historical Record* 7 (July 1888): 603–8; Leland H. Gentry, "A History of the Latter-day Saints in Northern Missouri from 1836 to 1839" [Ph.D. diss., Brigham Young University, 1965], 163–66; and statement of Sidney Rigdon in *History of the Church*, 3: 450–52.)

2. MS.: "weell"

acres of land $4,000. If they pay me in Far West. Enough give my respects to Mrs Smith & accept for yourself a friends respect

David Thomas

Elder Joseph Smith Jr

N.B. P.S. Further I own a Section of land in Monroe near the forks of Salt river, and if necessary [to] sell or make a settlement there I know of no man in the world I would rather entertain than yourself I would be glad if you would find whether my debt is secure in that place, and let me know Please to help me if you can do so without being oppressive to your feelings or interest there I do not wish you violate[d] for me Mr Root is my confidential friend anything [you] may say to him is safe, if you cannot come [p. 27] a line from you at any time will be thankfully Received through the mail or otherwise. D.T.

I expect Mr Root is on the buisness which I have named to you in this. We have consulted on this buisness by others —

David Thomas

Letter Sent to John Whitmer in consequence of witholding the records of the Church in the ~~Sta~~ City of Far West when called for by the Clerk[1] &c

Far West April 9th 1838

Mr J. Whitmer

Sir. We were desireous of honouring you by giving publicity to your notes on the history of the Church of Latter day Saints,

---

1. John Whitmer had been appointed Church historian on 8 March 1831, and he commenced writing a history of the Church (D&C 47). After his excommunication on 10 March 1838, he retained the history in his possession. A copy of the history was later obtained for the LDS Church by Andrew Jenson in 1893, when he visited George Schweich, brother-in-law to David Whitmer. (See Andrew Jenson, *Autobiography of Andrew Jenson* [Salt Lake City: Deseret News Press, 1938], 209.) The manuscript of the Whitmer History is currently housed in the RLDS Church archives in Independence, Missouri. It has been most recently published in McKiernan and Launius, eds., *An Early Latter Day Saint History: The Book of John Whitmer*.

after such corrections as we thought would be necessary; knowing your incompetency as a historion, and that your writings coming from your pen, could not be put to the press, without our correcting them, or elce the Church must suffer reproach; Indeed Sir, we never supposed you capable of writing a history; but were willing to let it come out under your name notwithstanding it would realy not be yours but ours. We are still willing to honour you, if you can be made to know your own interest and give up your notes, so that they can be corrected, and made fit for the press. But if not, we have all the materials for another, which we shall commence this week to write[1]

Your humble Servents

Joseph Smith Jr
Sidney Rigdon
E. Robinson   Clerk

Presidents of the whole Church of Latterday Saints
N.B. * over— [p. 28]

*The preceding letter to John Whitmer was entered through a mistake occupying a space not belonging to it. ~~not standing in its place~~

Minuits of a Conf. of the authorities of the Church of Latter day Saints Assembled at their first quarterly Conference in the City of Far West April 6th 1838 for the aniversary of the organization of the Church, Also to transact Church buisness, Presidents Joseph Smith Jr & Sidney Rigdon Presiden[c]y 2nd George Morey & Demick Huntington, were appointed Sexton and door keepers John Corril & Elias ~~Higby~~ Higbee ⟨Historians⟩ & T[homas]. B. Marsh, D[avid]. W. Patten, & B[righam]. Young of the twelve were appointed Presidents Pro. Tem of the ~~City of Far West,~~ ⟨Church of Christ of L.D. Saints in Missouri⟩ as the former Pres. D[avid]. Whitmer W[illiam]. W.

---

1. Three weeks later the Church presidency began writing the manuscript of the *History of the Church*. See entry of 30 April 1838.

Phelphs [Phelps] John Whitmer had been put out of their office 4th George W. Robinson was elected as general Church Clerk & Recorder to keep a record of the whole Church also as Scribe for the first Presidency 5th Ebinezer Robinson was Chosen Clerk & Recorder for the ~~City Far West~~ ⟨~~High Council~~ Church in Mo.⟩ also for the High Council[1]

The remainder of the proceedings will be seen in the record kept by E Robinson Also the trial of the expresidents as will be seen by the following abridgement

Charge prefered against O. Cowdery before the high Council in Far West Mo. — by Elder Seymour Bronnson [Brunson],

To the Bishop and Council of the Church of Jesus Christ of Latter Day Saints, [p. 29] I do hereby prefer the following charges against Oliver Cowdery, which consists of nine in number. 1st For persecuting the bretheren, by urging on vexatious lawsuits against the Bretheren and thus distressing the inocent. 2nd For seeking to destroy the Character of Pres. Joseph Smith Jr by falsly insinuating that he was guilty of adultery &c.[2] 3rd By treating the Church with contempt by not attending meeting. 4th For virtually denying the faith by declaring that he would not be governed by any eclesiasticle authority nor revelation whatever in his temporal affairs.[3] 5th For selling his lands in Jackson Co. Contrary to the revelations.[4] 6th For writing and sending an insulting letter to Pres.

---

1. The record kept by George W. Robinson is this journal. Ebenezer Robinson continued to keep the minutes of Church councils and conferences in Missouri known as the Far West Record. Cannon and Cook, eds., *Far West Record*, 157–59 give a more complete report of the 6 April conference.

2. Cowdery's accusation of adultery no doubt derived from his knowledge of the beginnings of plural marriage. There is evidence that the principle was revealed to Joseph Smith as early as 1831, that the Prophet had taken his first plural wife in Kirtland, and that rumors growing from this had contributed to the opposition against him. (See Parkin, "Conflict at Kirtland," 163–74; Danel W. Bachman, "New Light on an Old Hypothesis: The Ohio Origins of the Revelation on Eternal Marriage," *Journal of Mormon History* 5 [1978]: 19–32.)

3. See note 2, p. 216.

4. Shortly after receiving news that a mob had destroyed Church property at

T. B. Marsh while on the high Council attending to the duties of his office as president of the Council and ⟨by⟩ insulting the high Council with the contents of said letter: 7th For leaving his Calling in which God had appointed him by revelation for the sake of filthy lucre & turning to the practice of Law. 8th For disgrasing the Church by being Connected in the Bogus buisness as common report says.[1] 9th For dishonestly retaining Notes after they had been Paid,[2] and finally for lea⟨v⟩ing or forsaking the cause of God and returning to the begerly elements of the world, neglecting his high and holy Calling Contrary to his profession

April 11th 1838—

The Bishop and high Council assembled at the Bishops

Independence, Jackson County, Missouri, the site designated by revelation for their city of Zion, and that the mob had tarred and feathered Bishop Edward Partridge and forced the signing of an agreement that the Saints would leave the county the coming year, Joseph Smith wrote to the Church leadership in Missouri: "We have had the word of the Lord . . . that not one foot of land purchased should be given to the enemies. . . . Know assuredly that every foot of ground that falls into the hands of the enemies with consent is not easy to be obtained again." Four months later, after learning that the Missouri Saints had been driven from Jackson County, the Prophet wrote Bishop Partridge that "this is my council that you retain your lands even unto the uttermost. . . . All those that keep their inheritances notwithstanding they should be peeled and driven shall be likened unto the wise virgins who took oil in their lamps. But all those who are unbelieving and fearful, will be likened unto the foolish virgins, who took no oil in their lamps; and when they shall return, and say unto the saints, give us of your lands, behold there will be no room found for them." (Joseph Smith to William Phelps and others, 18 August 1833; Smith to Partridge, 10 December 1833; published in Jessee, *The Personal Writings of Joseph Smith*, 288, 310. [Spelling has been corrected.])

It should be noted that the charge against Oliver Cowdery of selling his lands in Missouri was not sustained by the council that heard his case. (See Cannon and Cook, *Far West Record*, 169.)

1. Joseph Smith testified before the council that Cowdery had taken a printing press and type from Kirtland, and that a nonmember had reported that a warrant was about to be issued against Cowdery for involvement in counterfeiting. Joseph and Sidney Rigdon confronted Cowdery and told him if he was guilty he should leave the country, but if innocent, he should stand trial and absolve himself. A short time later Cowdery departed. (See Cannon and Cook, *Far West Record*, 168–69.)

2. See note 1, p. 97.

office, in trial of the above Charges April 12th 1838 After the organization of the Council the above Charges were read. Also a letter from O. Cowdery, as will be found recorded in the Church record of the City of Far West Book A.[1] The 1st 2nd 3rd 7th 8th & 9th Charges were Sustained [p. 30] The 4th & 5th Charges were rejected & the 6th withdrawn. Consequently he (O. Cowdery) was concidered no longer a member of the Church of Jesus Christ of Latterday Saints Voted by the high Council that Oliver Cowdery be no longer a Committee to select locations for the gathering of the Saints—[2]

The following Charges were prefered against David Whi[t]mer before the high Council which assembled on the 13th of April 1838 for the purpose of attending to such Charges, whi[c]h Charges are as follows 1st For not observing the words of Wisdom,[3] 2nd For unchristianlike conduct in neglecting to attend to meetings in uniting with and possesing the same spirit of the dessenters 3rd In writing letters to the dessenters in Kirtland unfaivorable to the Cause, and to the Character of Joseph Smith Jr. 4th In neglecting the duties of his calling and sepperating himself from the Church while he has a name among us. 5th For signing himself Pres. of the Church of Christ after he had been cut off, in an insulting

1. The Cowdery letter, dated 12 April 1838, to "Rev. Edward Partridge" is published in Cannon and Cook, *Far West Record,* 164–66; also *History of the Church,* 3: 17–18.)

2. A more complete account of the proceedings in the Cowdery case is in Cannon and Cook, *Far West Record,* 162–71.

3. The revelation known as the Word of Wisdom, regulating the use of tobacco, alcoholic beverages, and other substances, was given 27 February 1833. Although the revelation was taken seriously, its observance in the 19th century was characterized by moderation rather than strict adherence. Not until the 20th century did compliance become a test of fellowship—to be a member in good standing. (Backman, *The Heavens Resound,* 257–61; Paul H. Peterson, "An Historical Analysis of the Word of Wisdom" [M.A. thesis, Brigham Young University, 1972.]; Leonard J. Arrington, "An Economic Interpretation of the Word of Wisdom," *BYU Studies* 1 [Winter 1959]: 37–49; Thomas G. Alexander, "The Word of Wisdom: From Principle to Requirement," *Dialogue* 14 [Fall 1981]: 78–88.)

letter to the High Council, After reading the above charges together with a letter sent to the Pres. of said Council, (a ~~copying~~ copy of which may be found recorded in Far West record Book A.)[1] The Council considered the charges sustained and consequently considred him no longer a member of the Church of Jesus Christ of Latterday Saints. — [2]

Also the same day and date a Charge was prefered against Lyman E Johnson Consisting of 3 Charges ~~which~~ which were read together with a letter from him in answer to them which will be ⟨found⟩ recorded in Far West record [p. 31] Book A.[3] The charges were sustained and he was consequently cut off from the Church. — [4]

Revelation to D. W. Patten. given April 11th 1838 Verily thus Saith the Lord, it is wisdom in my Servant D. W. Patten, that he settle up all his buisness, as soon as he possibly can, and make a disposition of his merchandise, that he may perform a mission unto me next spring, in compa[n]y with ~~with~~ others even twelve including himself, to testify of my name and bear glad tidings unto all the world, for verrily thus saith the Lord that inasmuch as there are those among you who deny my name, others shall be planted in their stead and receive their bishoprick[5] Amen. — [6]

Revelation given to Brigham Young at Far West April 17th 1838. Verrily thus Saith the Lord, Let my Servant Brigham Young go unto the place which he has bought on Mill Creek and there provide for his family until an effectual door is

---

1. See Cannon and Cook, *Far West Record*, 164–66.
2. A more complete account of the proceedings in the Whitmer case is in Cannon and Cook, *Far West Record*, 176–79.
3. See Cannon and Cook, *Far West Record*, 173.
4. A more complete account of the proceedings in the Lyman Johnson case is in Cannon and Cook, *Far West Record*, 172–76.
5. A charge of instructing and governing in spiritual concerns.
6. This revelation is D&C 114.

op[e]ned for the suport of his family untill I shall command
to go hence, and not to leave his family untill they are amply
provided for   Amen. —

Revelation given in Far West, April 26th 1838. Making
known the will of God, concerning the building up of this place
and of the Lord's house &c— Verrily thus Saith the Lord unto
you my Servant Joseph Smith Jr. and also my Servant Sidney
Rigdon, and also my Servant Hyrum Smith, and your coun-
silors who are and who shall be hereafter appointed, and also
unto my Servant Edward Partridge and his Councilors, and
also unto my faithfull Servants, who are of the ~~Hiugh~~ High
Council of my Church in Zion (for thus it shall be called) and
unto all the Elders and people of my Church of Jesus Christ
of Latter Day Saints, scattered abroad [p. 32] in all the world,
For thus shall my Church be called in the Last days even the
Church of Jesus Christ of Latter Day Saints, Verrily I say unto
you all; arise and shine forth ~~frth~~ that thy light may be a
standard for the nations and that thy gathering to-gether upon
the land of Zion and upon her stakes may be for a defence
and for a reffuge from the storm and from wrath when it shall
be poured out without mixture upon the whole earth, Let the
City Far West, be a holy and consecrated land unto me, and
⟨it shall⟩ be called ⟨most⟩ holy for the ground upon which thou
standest is holy Therefore I command you to build an house
unto me for the gathering togethe~~ring~~ of my Saints that they
may worship me, and let there be a begining of this work; and
a foundation and a preparatory work, this following Summer;
and let the begining be made on the 4th day of July next; and
from that time forth let my people labour diligently to build
an house, unto my name, and in one year from this day, let
them recommence laying the foundation of my house; thus
let them from that time forth laibour diligently untill it shall
be finished, from the Corner Stone thereof unto the top thereof,
untill there shall not any thing remain that is not finished.

Verrily I say unto you let not my Servant Joseph neither my Servant Sidn[e]y, neither my Servant Hyrum, get in debt any more for the building of an house unto my name. But let my house be built unto my name according to the pattern which I will shew unto them, and if my people build it not according to the pattern which I shall shew unto their presidency, I will not accept it at their hands. But if my people do build it according to the pattern which I shall shew unto their presidency, even my servant Joseph and his Councilors; then I will accept it at [p. 33] the hands of my people. And again; Verrily I say unto you it is my will, that the City Far West should be built up spedily, by the gathering of my Saints, and also that other places should be appointed for stakes in the regions round about as they shall be manifested unto my Servant Joseph from time to time. For behold I will be with him and I will sanctify him before the people for unto him have I given the Keys of this Kingdom and ministry even so— Amen. — [1]

27 April 1838 · Friday

This day was chiefly spent in writing a history of this Church from the earliest period[2] of its existance up to this date,[3] By Presidents, Joseph Smith Jr & Sidney Rigdon, myself[4] also ~~my~~ engaged in keeping this record—

28 April 1838 · Saturday

This morning Prests Smith & Rigdon & myself, were invited ~~un~~to attend the High Council; and accordingly attended.

---

1. This revelation is D&C 115.
2. MS.: "perion"
3. This marks the beginning of the History later published as *History of the Church of Jesus Christ of Latter- day Saints, Period I, History of Joseph Smith, the Prophet*, edited by B. H. Roberts, 7 vols. (Salt Lake City: Deseret Press, 1964). See Dean C. Jessee, "The Writing of Joseph Smith's History," *BYU Studies* 11 (Spring 1971): 439–73, and *The Papers of Joseph Smith*, 1:230–31, 265–67.
4. I.e., George W. Robinson.

The buisness before the high Council, was the trial of an case appealed, from the branch of the Church near G[u]ymans horse mill; Whereas [Henry][1] Jackson was plantiff, and Aaron Lyon defendant. Council called to order. T[homas]. B. Marsh & D[avid]. W. Patten, Presiding, It appeared in calling the council to order, that some of the seats were vacated; the council then proceeded to fill those seats: &c. And as there appeared to be no persons to fill Said Seats, Eligible to that office, Presidents Smith & Rigdon, were strongly solisited to act as councilors, or to Preside, and let the then presiding officers sit on the council; &c. They accepted of the former proposal, and accordingly Prest. Smith was choosen to act on the part of the defence, and to speak upon the case, togeth[er] with Geo. W. Harris. And Prest. Rigdon, was chosen to act on the part of the prossecution, and to speak upon the case together with Geo. M. Hinkle, After the council was organized, and op[e]ned by prayer; the notorious case of Aaron Lyon, was called in question; After some Arbitrarious[2] Speeches, to know whether witnesses Should be admitted, to testify against A, Lyon, or whether he should have the privilege of confessing his own Sins, It was desided; that witnesses should be admited, and also the writen testimony [p. 34] of the said wife of Said Jackson. Now as to this man Lyon, it is a well known ⟨fact⟩ and without contradiction, that he has been in transgression ⟨ever⟩ Since he first came into Kirtland, which is some four, or five years since, as appeared this day, by different witnesses, which are unimpeac[h]ible. Witnesses against this man Lyon, were these 1,st Sarah Jackson, wife of said plaintiff, Jackson, one Br. Best: also Br. [Shadrach] Roundy. Br John P. Brand Barnard: also Br. Thomas Girmon [Guyman]; also Br Benjamin, and the plantiff; Which testimony Says, Whereas, the plantiff, had some time last season, sent his wife from Alton, Illinois, to

---

1. The MS. is blank here.
2. Not governed by any fixed rules or order.

this country as he himself could not come, at that time, accordingly his wife Mrs Jackson, came and settled in the branch first above mentioned, Now this man Lyon had settled in this branch also, and was their presiding high priest, and had gained to himself great influence in and over that branch, and it also appears that this man had great possessions, and (if we may judge from testimony given this day) calculates to keep them let the Saints ~~of g[...] necessity~~ necessities be what they may, and it also appears that this man was in want of a wife (if actions bespeak the desires of any man) consequently set his wits to work to get one, he commences by getting (as he said,) revelations from God, that he must marry Mrs Jackson, or that she was the woman ~~for~~ to make his wife, and it appeared that these revilations were frequently received by him, and shortly introdused ~~them~~ to Mrs. Jackson, It also was manifested that the old man had sagasity enough to know, that unless he used his priestly office, ~~he~~ to assist him in accomplishing his desighns, ⟨he would fail in the attempt;⟩ he therefore told Mrs. Jackson that he had had a revelation from god that her husband was dead &c. and that she must concent to marry him, or she would be forever miserable; for he had seen her future state of existance, and that she must remember, that whoom soever he blessed, would be blessed, and whom soever he cursed, would be cursed, [p. 35] influencing her mind if possible, to believe his power was sufficient, to make her forever miserable; provided she complied not with his request. &c. Accordingly, they came to an agreement, and were soon to be married, but fortunately or unfortunately for both parties previous to the ~~nuptial~~ arrival of the nuptial day, Behold!! to the asstonishment of our defendant, the husband of Mrs. Jackson arrived at home, and consequently, disanuled the proceedings of the above alluded parties, the old gentleman Lyon, at this time (if not before,) knew verry well, that his god who gave ~~his~~ these revelations, (if ~~any~~ revelations he had,) must of course be no less than the devil, and in order to paliate the justice of his crime, sadled the whole burden upon the devil, that in scourging the person, who had previously befriended him, and counseled him in his [-][1] former days; peradventure he might extricate himself from the Snare, of his own setting, and dictation. But, alass. to[o] late for the old man, the testimony, being closed, and the S⟨w⟩ord of Justice, began to be unsheathed, which fell upon the old man like a scourge of ten thousand lashes, wielded by the hand of President S. Rigdon & George M. Hinkle, inspired by the spirit of justice, accompanied with a flow of elequence, which searched for the feelings, like the sting of so many scorpions, which served to atone for past iniquity. there were no feelings that were not felt after, there were no sores that were not probed, there were no excuses rendred that were not exceptionable. After justice had ~~s~~ ceased to weild [-][2] ⟨its⟩ sword, Mercy then advanced to rescue its victom, which inspired the heart of President J. Smith Jr, & Geo W. Harris who, with profound elequence with ⟨a⟩ deep & sublime thought, with clemency of feeling, spoke in faivour of ~~mercy~~ the defendant, but in length of time, while mercy appeared to be doing her utmost, in contending against justice, the latter ~~even~~ at last gained the ascendency, and took full ~~power over~~ ⟨possession of⟩ the mind of [p. 36] the speaker, who leveled a voley of darts, which came upon the old man, like a huricane upon the mountain tops, which seemingly, was about to sweep the victom entirely out of the reach of mercy, but amidst the clashing of the sword of Justice, mercy still cla⟨i⟩med the victom, and saved him still in the church of Jesus Christ of Latter Day Saints, and in this last kingdom Happy is it for those whose sins (like this mans) goes before them to Judgement, that they may yet repent and be saved in the Kingdom of our God. Council desided, that inasmuch as this man, had confessed his sins, and asked for forgiveness, and promised to mark well

---

1. Illegible crossed-out word in MS.
2. Illegible crossed-out word in MS.

the path of his feet, and do, (inasmuch as lay in his power.) what God, Should required at his hands. accordingly, it was decided, that he give up his license as High Priest, and stand as a member in the Church, this in consequence of his being concidered not capable of dignifying that office, &c Council Adjourned

Geo. W. Robinson, Scribe

29 April 1838 · Sunday

This day was spent chiefly in meeting with the saints. in this place, and in administering unto them, the word of life.

30 April 1838 · Monday

This day was spent by the first Presidency in writing the history of the Church; and in resitation of grammer lessions, which ressitations is attended to, ~~in the~~ ⟨each⟩ morning previous to writing.

1 May 1838 · Tuesday

This day was also spent in writing Church History, by the first Presidency

2 May 1838 · Wednesday

This day was also spent in writing history, and ⟨receiving⟩ lectures on grammer. by President Rigdon. [p. 37]

3 May 1838 · Thursday

This day also was spent in Writing & passing and in administering to the Sick.

4 May 1838 · Friday

This day also was spent in studying, & writing history, by the presidency. also ⟨a⟩ letter from J. E. Page.

5 May 1838 · Saturday

This day was spent, by the Presidency, in writing for the Elders Journal.[1] Also receiveded intelligence from Cannada, by one br Bailey. who called upon Pres. Smith, and stated that two hundred Wagons, with families; would probably be here in three weeks. The presidency also attended an address, delivered by Gen. Willson [Robert Wilson]. upon Politicks Political ⟨matters⟩ General Willson. is a candidate for Congress. ⟨being a Federalist.⟩

6 May 1838 · Sunday

This day, President Smith. delivered a discourse. to the people. showing, or setting forth the evils that existed, and would exist, by reason of hasty Judgement or dessisions upon any subject, given by any people or in judgeing before they hear both sides of the question, He also cautioned them against men,[2] who should come here whining and growling about their money, because they had helpt the Saints and bore some of the burden with others. and thus thinking that others, (who are still poorer and who have still bore greater burden than themselves) aught to make up their loss &c. And thus he cautioned them to beware of them for here and there they throw[3] out foul insinuations, to level as it were a dart to ⟨the⟩ best interests of the Church, & if possible to destroy the Characters of its Presidency He also instructed the Church, in the

---

1. The monthly *Elder's Journal* was first published at Kirtland, Ohio, in October 1837 as a continuation of the *Messenger and Advocate*. The first issue was edited by Joseph Smith and printed by Thomas B. Marsh and Don C. Smith. After the Kirtland printing office was destroyed by fire in November 1837, publication of the *Journal* did not resume until July 1838 at Far West, Missouri. Only one issue of the paper was published in Missouri in 1838 before violence disrupted the printing. The type used on the *Journal* was later used in publishing the *Times and Seasons* at Nauvoo, Illinois. (Jenson, *Encyclopedic History*, 218.)
2. "men" repeated in MS.
3. MS.: "through"

Mistories of the Kingdom of God; giving them a history of the Plannets &c. and of Abrahams writings upon the Plannettary System &c. In the after part of the day Prest. Smith spoke upon different Subjects he dwelt some upon the Subject of Wisdom, & upon the word of Wisdom. &c. — [p. 38]

7 May 1838 · Monday

This day was spent in company with Judge Morain [Josiah Morin] one of our neighbouring County Judges, also the Democratic candidate for the State Senate. & in company with Elder [Reynolds] C⟨a⟩hoon & P[arley]. P. Pratt, who this day arrived in this place, the former from Kirtland. and the latter from the City of New York; where he had been preaching for some time past; And our hearts were made glad with the pleasing inteligence of ⟨the⟩ gathering of the Saints flocking from all parts of the world to this land; to avoid the destructions which are coming upon this generation, as spoken by all the holy Prophets Since the world began

8 May 1838 · Tuesday

This day Presidents, J[oseph]. Smith Jr. & S[idney]. Rigdon spent the day with Elder [Reynolds] Cahoon in visiting the place he had selected to live, also in some ~~pry~~ private buisness of their own, also in the after part of the day, in answering the questions proposed in the Elders Journal. Vol. 1st No. 2nd Pages 28th, & 29th[1] On yesterday ~~our beloved Brother~~ Thomas B. Marsh, lost his Son James who died near the close of the day,[2] This ~~lad~~, brother though young, ~~and~~or⟨n⟩ed his profession as a Saint of God, and died in the faith of the everlasting Gospel; —

---

1. The questions and answers are published in *History of the Church*, 3:28–30.
2. James G. Marsh was fourteen years old when he died. (*History of the Church*, 3:28.)

9 May 1838 · Wednesday

This day, the Presidency, attended the funeral of James Marsh, And Prest. Smith was requested to preach the funeral discourse, and accordingly complied, and we were greatly edified upon the occasion,

10 May 1838 · Thursday

This day, President S. Rigdon, deliverd an address in the Schoolhouse in the South west quarter of the City, upon the subject of the Political policy of our Nation, to a large concourse of People, from all quarters of the County, and even from other Counties [p. 39]

Although, he being verry hoarse, with a ~~bad~~ ⟨Severe⟩ cold, yet being assisted, by the spirit, and power, of Allmighty God, was enabled to elucidated the policy, to the understanding of all present, Both of the Federal party, and also of the Democratic party, from the time of their first appearance in our country; endeavering to give an impartial hearing on both Sides of the question, In consequence of One Gen. [Robert] Willsons speech, delivered upon Politics in the same place, a short time previous to this:[1] who touched upon one side of the matter only; He being a Federalist, and knowing that for the good of his cause, and for the safety of his Electionereing campaign: it would be policy for him to dwell on one side of the question onley; But the Politics of this Church (with but few exceptions onley,) are that of ~~the~~ Democracy; which is ~~th~~ also the feelings of the speaker ⟨who spoke⟩ this day, and ⟨all⟩ of ⟨~~all~~⟩ the first presidency, It is my principles also. Prest Smith, and myself attended the Delivery of Said speech and were highly edified—

11 May 1838 · Friday

This day, the presidency attend[ed] the Council of the Bishop in case of the trial of Wm E. McLellin & Doctor

---

1. See entry of 5 May 1838.

McCord, who were found in transgression. Mr. McCord, arose, and Said, he was sorry to troubl[e] the council on his account, for he had intended to withdraw from the Church, before he left the place. he also stated, he had no confidence in the work of God, neither in his Prophet, which he ⟨has⟩ raised up in these last days, and consequently should go his own way, he accordingly gave up his license, and departed Wm. E. McLellin, also said the Same. He further Said he had no confidence in the heads of the Church, beleiving they had transgressed, and got out of the way, and consequently ⟨he⟩ left of[f] praying and keeping the commandments of God, and went his own way, and indulged himself in his lustfull desires. But when he he⟨a⟩rd that [p. 40] the first presidency, had made a general settlement and acknowleged their sins, he then began to pray again, and to keep the commandments of God. Though when interogated by Prest Smith he said he had seen nothing out of the way himself, but it was heresay, and thus he judges from heresay. But we are constrained to say, O!! Foolish Man! what excuse is [it] that thou renderest, for thy sins, that because thou hast heard of some mans transgression, that thou Shouldest leave thy God, and forsake thy prayers, and turn to those things that thou knowest to be contrary to the will of God, we say unto thee, and to all Such, beware! beware! for God will bring the[e] into Judgement for thy sins. — [1]

12 May 1838 · Saturday

This day Prests. Smith & Rigdon together with myself, attended the High Council[2] to Lay before ~~them~~ it, some buisness pertaining to themselves directly, and individually. The presidency laid before ~~them~~ high Council, their situation, as

---

1. Neither this journal nor the Far West Record indicates what action was taken regarding William E. McLellin at this time. He later dated his disaffection with what he termed the excesses of the Church in Kirtland. By the fall of 1838 he was actively associated with dissenters from the Church.
2. The Far West Record dates this council meeting 13 May 1838.

to maintaining the(i)r families in the situation & relation they stood to the Church. spending, as they have, for eight years, their time ~~and~~ tallents & property in the service of the Church, and are now reduced as it were, to absolute begery, And still were detained in service of the Church, and it now become[s] necessary that something should be done for their support. ~~an~~ either by the Church, or else they must do it themselves, of their own labours, and if the Church said help yourselves, they would thank them, and immediately do so, but if the Church said serve us, then some provisions must be made for them. The subject was taken into concideration, by the Council, (who acts for the Church), and thouroughly investigated. Whereupon [p. 41] the Council voted to authorize the Bishop, to give or to make over to Prests. Joseph Smith Jr & Sidney Rigdon each an eighty of land, situate[d] adjacent to the City Corporation which land is the property of the Church. Also voted that a committee of three, be appointed, of the Council, to contract with said presidency to their sattisfaction, for their se[r]vices, this present year, Not for preaching or for receiving the word of God by revelation, neither for instructing the saints in richteousness, but for services rendered in the Printing establishment, in translating the ~~words~~ ancient records &c. &c. The Committee, which consisted of Geo. W. Harris, Elias Higbee & Simeon Carter, who agreed that Prests Smith & Rigdon Should be entitled to, & receive for this year [*blank*][1] as a just remuneration for their Services.[2]

---

1. The published *History of the Church* supplies the figure $1100.
2. According to Ebenezer Robinson much later, the committee recommended to the high council at a later meeting a stipend of $1100 per annum for each member of the presidency. The council approved the recommendation by a vote of eleven to one, but when word of the action became known, "the members of the church, almost to a man, lifted their voices against it. The opposition was so strong that at the next meeting of the council the resolution was rescinded." ("Items of Personal History," *The Return* 1 [August 1889]: 115–21.)

13 May 1838 · Sunday

Today Prest R[eynolds]. Cahoon (late Prest of Kirtland) delivered a discourse to the Saints, in the former part of the day, and Prest Rigdon, preached the funeral Sermon of Swain Williams,[1] son of F. G. Williams in the after part of the day. —

14 May 1838 · Monday

Prest Smith spent this day in ploughing for, himself in his garden. Prest Rigdon spent the day in correcting and prepareing matter for the press, and also ⟨spent a short time⟩ in Company with Elder Harlow Readfield [Redfield], who arrived this day from Kirtland Ohio. And I have spent this day in helping Prest Smith, and also in writing.

18 May 1838 · Friday

To day Presidents J Smith Jr & S Rigdon and T. B. Marsh D. W. Patten Bishop E[dward] Partridg[e] E[lias] Higbee, S[imeon]. Carter, A. Rigsley [Alanson Ripley], myself and many others, left Far West to visit the north countries for the purpose of laying off stakes of Zion, making locations & laying claims for the gathering of the Saints for the benefit of the poor, and for the upbuilding of the Church of God, We traveled this day to the mouth of Hon[e]y Creek, which [p. 42] is a tribuitary to [the] Grand River, where we camped for the knight, we passed this day a beautifull Country of land, a majority of which is Prarie which signifies untimbered land and thickly covered with grass and weeds, there is a plenty of wild game in this land, such as Deer, Turkey, Hens, Elk, &.c. we saw a large black wolf, Prest Smith put on his dog after the wolf and ⟨we⟩ followed on after, but the wolf out run us and we lost Him[2] ~~wolf~~ we have nothing to fear in camping out except Rattle

---

1. Joseph Swain Williams was nineteen years old at the time of his death.
2. "Him" written over "the" in MS.

Snakes which are ~~peculiar~~ ⟨natural⟩ to this country, though not verry numerous, we turn our horses loose and let them feed in the prairie,

19 May 1838 · Saturday

The next morning we struck our tents, and marched crossed Grand River at the mouth of Honey Creek at a place called Nelsons ferry, Grand River is a large beautifull deep and rapid stream and will undoubtedly admit of steam Boat[s] and other water craft navigation, and at the mouth of honey creek is a splendid harbour for the safety of such crafts, and also for landing freight We next kept up the river mostly in the timber for ten miles, untill we came to Col. Lyman Wights[1] who lives at the foot of Tower Hill, a name appropriated by Prest Smith, in consequence of the remains of an old Nephitish Alter an[d] Tower, ~~In the after~~ where we camped for the sabath. In the after part of the day, Prests. Smith and Rigdon and Myself,[2] went to Wight's Ferry about a half mile from this place up the river, for the purpose of selecting and laying claims to [a] city plott near said Ferry, in Davis County Township 60, Range 27 & 28, and Sections 25, 36, 31, 30, which was called Spring Hill a name appropriated by the bretheren present, But afterwards named by the mouth of [the] Lord and was called Adam Ondi Awmen,[3] because said he it [p. 43] is the place where

---

1. After his return to Missouri from Kirtland, Ohio, in 1836, Lyman Wight established a ferry on the Grand River.

2. I.e., George W. Robinson.

3. Adam-ondi-Ahman in Daviess County, Missouri, was located about 25 miles north of Far West, Caldwell County. The following revelations suggest why the Saints attached such importance to it: D&C 78:15; 107:53–57; 116:1, and Daniel 7:13–14. (Descriptions of the area, with its altar, or altars, and tower, are in John H. Wittorf, "An Historical Investigation of the Ruined 'Altars' at Adam-ondi-Ahman, Missouri," *Newsletter and Proceedings of the SEHA*, No. 113 [Published by The Society for Early Historic Archeology, Brigham Young University, 15 April 1969], 1–8; Robert J. Matthews, "Adam-ondi-Ahman," *BYU Studies* 13 [Autumn 1972]: 27–35.)

On 28 June 1838, the settlement at Adam-ondi-Ahman became the third stake of the Church, with John Smith as president and Reynolds Cahoon and Lyman Wight as counselors. (Jenson, *Enyclopedic History*, 4–5. A description of Adam-ondi-Ahman is found in *History of the Church*, 3:39–40.)

Adam shall come to visit his people, or the Ancient of days shall sit as spoken of by Daniel the Prophet.[1]

20 May 1838 · Sunday

Sunday was spent principally at Adam Ondi Awmen, but at the close of the day we struck our tents and traveled about six miles north and camped for the knight, we had in company at this place Judge Morain [Morin] and company traveling also to the north,

21 May 1838 · Monday

in the morning after making some Locations in this place which is in Township 61 Range 27, & 28, we next returned to Robinsons Grove about two miles in order to secure some land near grand river which we passed the day previous, and finding a mistake in the ⟨former⟩ survey concluded to send the surveyor south 5 or 6 miles to obtain [a] correct survey, we did so, and some of us taried to obtain water for the camp

In the evening we held a council, to consult the bretheren upon the subject of our journey to know whether it is wisdom to go immediately into the north country or to tarry here and about here to secure the land on grand river &.c. The Bretherin spoke their minds verry freely upon the subject, Prest Smith said he felt impressed to tarry and secure the land near by, all that is not secured between this and Far West especially on grand river, Prest Rigdon said if they should go to [the] north in this expedition he thought it best to go immediately to that place, but thought it best by all means, to secure the land near by on the river &c, The question was put by Prest Smith and carried unanymously in favour of having the land secured on the river and between this place and Far West.

---

1. See D&C 116.

22 May 1838 · Tuesday

The next day Prest Rigdon with a company went to the east of the camp and selected some of the best locations in the county, and returned with news of good locations in that vicinity yet [p. 44] to be secured, ~~in that vicinity~~ Prest Smith and myself followed on in their course, but could not find them and consequently returned to the camp in Robinsons Grove, we next scouted west in order to obtain some game to suply our necessities but found or killed none, we [found] some ancient antiquities about one mile west of the camp, which consisted of stone mounds, appearently laid up in square[1] piles, though somewhat decayed and obliterated, by the almost continual rains Undoubtedly these were made to seclude some valuable treasures deposited by the aborigionees of this land

23 May 1838 · Wednesday

The next day we all traveled and located lands East, on Grove Creek and near the City of Adam Ondi Awman, towards Knight Prests Smith & S. Rigdon went to Col. Wights and the remainder returned to the tents,

24 May 1838 · Thursday

The next morning the company returned to Grove Creek to finish the survey, Prest. Rigdon and Col. Wight also returned to the surveying, and Prst Smith returned to Far West

25 May 1838 · Friday

this day our compa[n]y went up the river and made some locations, in the after part of the day we struck our tents, and mooved to Col. Wights

---

1. MS.: "squire"

26 May 1838 · Saturday

The next day we surveyed land across the river opposite *Adam-Ondi-Awmen*

27 May 1838 · Sunday

was spent principally at Col. [Lyman] Wight's.

28 May 1838 · Monday

The next morning we started for home *Far West*. About noon we met ⟨Prests⟩ J Smith Jr and Hyram Smith, and Some 15 or 20 others, who were going to seek locations in the *north*, We continued our way home where we arived Monday evening and found our families well &c.

30 May 1838 · Wednesday

Prest Hyram Smith returned ⟨to⟩ Far West.

1 June 1838 · Friday

Prest J Smith Jr returned on account of his wifes sickness who was delivered of a son[1]

4 June 1838 · Monday

Prests. J Smith Jr S. Rigdon [p. 45] Hyram Smith & myself and others left this place [Far West] for Adam Ondi Awman, we stayed this knight at br. Moses ~~Dayleys~~ Daileys [Daley],

5 June 1838 · Tuesday

the next morning we went to Col. Wight's it rained and was somewhat wet We continued surveying and building houses &c for some time day after day, the Surveyors run out

---

1. Joseph Smith's fifth son, Alexander Hale Smith, was born 2 June 1838 at Far West, Missouri.

the City plott and we retur[n]ed to Far West This day was spent in diverse labors for the Church together with a greater share of this month and the ensuing one

4 July 1838 · Wednesday

This day was spent in Cellebrating the 4 of July in commemoration of the decleration of ⟨the⟩ Independance of the United States of America, and also to make our decleration of Independance from all mobs and persecutions which have been inflicted upon us time after time ⟨un⟩till we could bear it no longer, being driven by ruthless mobs and enimies of the truth. from our homes our property confiscated our lives exposed and our all jeopardized by such conduct. We therefore met on this day in Far West Mo. to make our decleration of independance, and to lay the corner stones of the house of the Lord agreeably to the commandment of the Lord unto us given April 26th 1838, as recorded on Pages. 32, 33, & 34 Book A. — [1]
An address was def delivered by Prest. S[idney]. Rigdon, Prest J[oseph] Smith Jr Prest of the day, Prest H[yrum]. Smith Vice Prest. & Prest. S[idney]. Rigdon Orator, R[eynolds]. Cahoon Chief Marshial G[eorge]. M. Hinkle, & J[efferson]. Hunt, asst. Marshial, and myself[2] commanded the Regiment, The order of the day was most splendid and beautifull Several thousands of spectators were present to witness the s[c]ene, The address w was delivred on the public square[3] under the hoisted flagg representing the Liberty and independence [p. 46] of these United States of America.[4]

---

1. D&C 115:7–10.
2. I.e., George W. Robinson.
3. MS.: "squire"
4. Rigdon's oration was given against a backdrop of the expulsion of the Latter-day Saints from Jackson County and the failure of the state to reinstate them to their property and homes, and it no doubt reflected the views of the Church Presidency. A segment of the speech, interpreted out of context, became an emotional war cry in igniting opposition against the Saints in the months that followed. (A reprint is in Peter Crawley, "Two Rare Missouri Documents," *BYU Studies* 14 [Summer 1974]: 518–27. On the context of the speech see Richard L. Anderson, "Atchison's Letters and the Causes of Mormon Expulsion from Missouri," *BYU Studies* 26 [Summer 1986]: 14–15; Marvin S. Hill, *Quest for Refuge*, 77–84.)

Shortly after Prests. J. Smith Jr S. Rigdon H. Smith and myself, left this place for Adam Ondi Awman we saw a deer or two on the way. Prest Smith set his dogs after them one of which was a gray hound which cau[gh]t the deer but could not hold him, although he ~~through thorough~~ ⟨threw⟩ him down, yet he injoured the dog so badly that he let him go, and we lost him, The race was quite amusing indeed.

I would mention or notice something about O[liver]. Cowdery David Whitmer Lyman E Johnson and John~~son~~ Whitmer who being guilty of bace iniquities and that to manifest in ~~all~~ the eyes of all men, and being often entreated[1] would continue in their course seeking the lives of the First Presidency and to overthrow the Kingdom of God which they once testified off. Prest Rigdon preached one Sabbath upon the salt that had lost its savour, that it is henceforth good for nothing but to be cast out, and troden under foot of men, And the wicked flee when no man pursueth, These men took warning, and soon they were seen bounding over the prairie like the scape Goat to carry of[f] their own sins[2] we have not seen them since, their influence is gone, and they are in a miserable condition, so also it [is] with all who turn from the truth to lying cheating defrauding & Swindeling

Some time past was spent in trying to obtain pay from these men who are named above, who have absconded, and endeavered to defraud their creditors[3] [p.47]

---

1. "June" penciled sideways in the margin opposite these lines, evidently by a later hand.

2. Leviticus 16:21–22.

3. Dissension in the Church in Missouri was an extension of the same spirit that had manifest itself in Kirtland. (See note 2, p. 216.) Some of the leading Missouri dissenters were Oliver Cowdery, David and John Whitmer, William W. Phelps, and Lyman E. Johnson. Their influence was such as to constitute a threat to the function and order of the Church there. On 17 June 1838, Sidney Rigdon delivered at Far West what became known as the "salt sermon," proclaiming that if the salt had lost its savour it was good for nothing, but to be cast out, and trodden under the feet of men. Rigdon's discourse was followed by a letter with 84 signatures ordering the dissenters to leave the county or face the consequences. Within a few days they had departed. (See Donna Hill, *Joseph Smith*, 225–27; Leonard and Allen, *Story of the Latter-day Saints*, 120–22.)

11 July 1838 · Friday

This day received a letter from Orson Hyde & Heber C Kimball Two of the Twelve Apostles of the Lamb in these last Days, who having been on a mission to England just returned to Kirtland Ohio[1] and dated same place, Directed to Prest J. Smith Jr.

Dear Brother Joseph

In health peace & safty we arrived in this place on Monday last, from the scene of our labor during the past year after a passage of 31 days. We cannot give a full account of our labors now, but suffise it to say the standard of truth is reared on the other side of the great waters, and hundreds are now fi[gh]ting the good fight of faith, beneath the shade of its glorious banner. We have fought in the name of the Lord Jesus, and under the shadow of the cross we have conquered, Not an enimy has risen up against us, but that has fallen for our sakes, Every thing we have done has prospered, and the God of the Holy Prophets has been with us, and to him belongs the praise. Our brethren in the East are poor yet rich in faith and the peace of our God abides upon them, we have not interfered with the priests at all except when we have been assalted by them, We have preached repentance & baptism & baptism & repentance, We have strictly attended to our own buisness and have let others alone We have experienced the truth of Solomons words which are as follows When a mans ways please the Lord he maketh his enimies that they are at peace with him[2] our enimies have seen their entire insufficiency to stand against the

---

1. Hyde, Kimball, and others had left New York on a proselyting mission to England on 28 June 1837 and arrived back in Kirtland, Ohio, on 22 May 1838. Their mission, which marked the introduction of Mormonism in Europe, resulted in more than 1500 convert baptisms. Kimball reached Far West, Missouri, 25 July. (Stanley B. Kimball, *Heber C. Kimball: Mormon Patriarch and Pioneer* [Urbana, Chicago, London: University of Illinois Press, 1981], 41–53.)

2. Proverbs 16:7.

power of truth manifest through us, and have gone away and left us in ~~peaceb~~ peacefull possession of [p. 48] the field, Concerning the Nicholatine Band of which you warned us against we would say God is not there, and we are not there, they deal in sand stone & bogus, but we in faith hope & Charity[1] We have not means to situate our families in f Far West at present and as we have not been chargable to the Church hitherto, we do not like to be⟨c⟩ome a burthen to them in the extreme state of poverty to which they are reduced, We can preach the gospel when the Lord is with us, and by it we can live, and the time will come when we shall have means to settle with the Saints. Kirtland is not our home, it looks dolefull here, We shall go westward as soon as we can, the folks here tell many dark and pittifull tales about yourself, & others. but the faults of our bretheren is poor entertainment for us, We have no accusation to bring for the Lord has shown us that he has taken the matter into his own hands, and every secret shall be braught to light and every man chastened for his sins, untill he confess[es] and forsake[s] them—and then he shall find mercy Therefore we can say we are at peace with God and with all mankind, and if any creature has aught against us, we have naught against him, and we say forgive us for Christ['s] sake, We should be glad to see all our bretheren of the Twelve, and we s[h]all as we can consistantly, our good wishes and best respects to them To yourself Bro. Sidney and families, and to all the faithfull bretheren and sisters in Christ Jesus our Lord, Will you or some other of the bretheren write us soon and let us know the true state of things in Far West, We have been gone allmost a year and have heard but very little, but we now hear much, We would like to know if a spirit of union prevails &c. &c.

---

1. Many dissenters from the Church were still in Kirtland when Kimball and Hyde arrived back there in May 1838. Apparently Joseph Smith had equated them with the biblical heretical Nicolaitan sect (Revelation 2:6, 15; G. W. Bromiley, *The International Standard Bible Encyclopedia* [Grand Rapids, Michigan: William B. Eerdmans Publishing Company, 1979] 3:533–34.)

We are as ever your bretheren in the bonds of the Everlasting Covenant,

H.C. Kimball

Orson Hyde

We are one [p. 49]

To Prest J. Smith Jr.

The following is [a] letter from Don C. Smith

Nine Miles from Terre Haute Ind.

Bro. Joseph

I sit down to inform you of our situation at the present time.[1] I started from Norton Ohio the 7th of May, in company with Father, Wm., [Wilkins] Jenkins Salsbury, Wm McClerry [McCleary] & Lewis Rob[b]ins, and families, also Sister [Margaret] Singl[e]y is one of our number, we started with 15 horses seven wagons, & two Cows, we have left two horses by the way sick one with a swelling on his shoulder, a 3rd horse (as it were our dependance) was taken lame, last evening and is not able to travel, and we have stoped to docter him We were disappointed on every hand before we started, in getting money, we got no assistance whatever only as we have taken in sister Singly and she has assisted us as far as her means extends, we had when we started $75 dollars in money, we sold the 2 cows for $13.50 per cow we have sold of your goods to the amt of $45.74 and now we have only $25 dollars to carry 25 souls & 13 horses, 500 miles, we have lived very close and camped out knight [nights], notwithstanding the rain & cold,

---

1. This letter notes the departure of Don Carlos Smith and others of the Smith family, including their parents, from Kirtland, Ohio. Following the departure for Missouri of Joseph Smith and other Church leaders from Kirtland in January 1838, others of the faithful Saints followed throughout the spring and summer. The largest contingent, designated the Kirtland Camp, consisted of more than 500 people under the direction of the seventy. It left Kirtland 6 July and arrived in Far West, Missouri, on 2 October 1838. An account of the Kirtland Camp expedition is in History of the Church, 3:87–148.

& my babe only 2 weeks old when we started,[1] Agness [C. Smith] is very feeble Father & Mother are not well but verry much fatigued, Mother has a severe cold, and it is nothing in fact but the prayer of faith and the power of God, that will sustain them and bring them through, our carriage is good and I think we shall be brought through, I leave it with you and Hyram to devise some way to assist us to some more expence money, we have had unaccountable bad roads, had our horses down in the mud, and broke of[f] one wagon tongue [p. 50] and thills,[2] and broke down the carriage twice and yet we are all alive and camped on a dry place for allmost the first time. Poverty is a heavy load but we are all obliged to welter under it, it is now dark and I close, may the Lord bless you all and bring us together is my prayer Amen

All the arrangements that bro. Hyram left for getting money failed, they did not gain us one cent

To J. Smith Jr.

Don C. Smith

8 July 1838 · Sunday

The following Revelations were read in the Congregation this day, which was given in Ohio — [3]

Revelation Given at the French Farm in Kirtland ~~Geaga~~ ⟨Geauga⟩ Co. Ohio. In the presence of J. Smith Jr., S. Rigdon V. Knight & Geo. W. Robinson January 12th 1838. —

When inquiry was made of the Lord relative to the trial of the first Presidency of the Church of Christ of Latter Day Saints, For transgressions according to the item of law, found

---

1. Sophronia, child of Don C. and Agnes Coolbrith Smith.

2. MS. reads "fills". Thills: shafts between which a single animal is harnessed.

3. A penciled notation written sideways in the margin (not part of the original journal) reads "over looked in its place."

in the Book of Covenants 3rd Section 37 Verse[1] Whether the descision of such an Council of one Stake, Shall be conclusive for Zion and all her stakes

Thus saith the Lord, Let the first Presidency of My Church, be held in full fellowship in Zion and all her Stakes, untill they shall be found transgressors, by such an high Council as is named in the above alluded Section, in Zion, by three witnesses standing against each member of said Presidency, and these witnesses shall be of long and faithfull standing, and such also as cannot [p. 51] be impeached by other witnesses before such Council, and when a descision is had by such an Council in Zion, it shall only be for Zion, it shall not a⟨n⟩swer for her stakes, but if such descision be acknowledged by the Council of her stakes, then it shall answer for her stakes, But if it is not acknowledged by the stakes, then such stake may have the privilege of hearing for themselves or if such descision shall be acknowledeged by a majority of the stakes, then it shall answer for all her stakes And again,

The Presidency of my Church, may be tried by the voice of the whole body of the Church in Zion, and the voice of a majority of all her Stakes And again

Except a majority is had by the voice of the Church of Zion and a majority of all her stakes, The charges will be concidered not sustained and in order to sustain such charge or charges, before such Church of Zion or her stakes, such witnesses must be had as is named above, that is the witnesses to each President, who are of long and faithfull standing, that cannot be immpeached by other witnesses before the Church of Zion, or her stakes, And all this saith the Lord because of wicked and asspiring men, Let all your doings be in meekness and in humility before me even so Amen—

Revelation Given the same day January 12th 1838, upon

---

1. D&C 107:7–8.

an inquiry being made of the Lord, whether any branch of the Church of Christ of Latter Day Saints can be concidered a stake of Zion, untill they have acknowledged the authority of the first Presidency by a vote of such Church

Thus saith the Lord, Verrily I Say unto ~~nay~~ [p. 52] you Nay

No stake shall be appointed, except by the first Presidency, and this Presidency be acknowledged, by the voice of the same, otherwise it shall not be counted as a stake of Zion and again except it be dedicated by this presidency it cannot be acknowledged as a stake of Zion, For unto this end have I appointed them in Laying the foundation of and establishing my Kingdom Even so Amen.

Revelation Given the same day January 12th 1838. Thus Saith the Lord, let the Presidency of my Church, take their families as soon as it is practicable, and a door is open for them, and moove to the west, as fast as the way is made plain before their faces, and let their hearts be comforted for I will be with them, Verrily I say unto you, the time has come, that your labors are finished in this place for a season. Therefore arise—and get yourselves, into a land which I shall show unto you, even a land flowing with milk & honey. You are clean from the blood of this ~~generation~~ people, And wo, unto those who have become your enimies, who have professed my name saith the Lord, for their Judgement lingereth not, and their damnation slumbereth not. Let all your faithfull friends arise with their families also, and get out of this place, and gather themselves together unto Zion and be at peace among yourselves, O Ye inhabitants of Zion, or their shall be no safty for you. *Even so Amen.*[p. 53]

It hap[pe]ned about these times [July 1838] that some excitement was raised in the adjoining Counties, that is Ray & Clay, against us, in consequence of the suden departure of these wicked character[s], of the apostates from this Church, into that vicinity reporting false stories, and statements, but when they come to hear the other side of the question their feeling[s] were all allayed upon that subject especially. The emigration to this land is verry extensive, and numerous, some few are troubled with the *ague and fever*, The first Presidency are chiefly engaged in counciling and settling the emigrants to this land, The prophecies[1] are ~~fulling~~ fulfilling very fast upon our heads, and in our day and generation, They are gathering from the North & from the South from the East & from West, unto Zion, for safety against the day of wrath, which Is to be poured out without mixture upon this generation according to the prophets. —

The following Revelation was given in Far West Mo July 8th 1838, and read this day in the congregation of the Saints,

Revelation Given to the Twelve Apostles July 8th 1838 in Far West Mo in the presence of J[oseph] Smith Jr. S[idney]. Rigdon, H[yrum]. Smith, E[dward]. Partridge I[saac]. Morly J[ared]. Carter, S[ampson]. Avard T[homas].B. Marsh & G[eorge]. W. Robinson

Making known the will of the Lord concerning the Twelve Show unto us thy will O. Lord concerning the Twelve.

Verily thus saith the Lord, Let a conference be held immediately, Let the Twelve be organized. Let men be appointed to supply the places of those who [have] fallen.[2] Let my servent Thomas [B. Marsh] remain for a season in the land of Zion, to publish my word let the residue continue to preach from that hour, and if they will do this in all Lowliness of heart in meekness and pureness and long suffering I the Lord God give unto them a promise, that [p. 54] I will provide for their fam-

---

1. MS.: "Prophets"
2. Members of the Quorum of Twelve who had fallen away were John F. Boynton, Luke and Lyman Johnson, and William E. McLellin.

ilies, and an effectual door shall be op[e]ned for them, from
henceforth, And next spring let them depart to go over the
great waters, and there promulge my gospel in the fullness
thereof, and to bear record of my name. Let them take l[e]ave
of my Saints in the City Far West, on the Twenty sixth day
of April next, on the building spot of mine house saith the
Lord, Let my servent *John Taylor*, and also my servant *John
E Page*, and also my servent *Willford Woodruff* and also my
servent *Willard Richards* be appointed to fill the places of those
who have fallen, and be officially Notified of their appointment
even so Amen[1]

Revelation Given the same day, and at the same place, and
read the same day in the congregations of the saints
Making known the duty of *F. G. Williams & Wm W. Phelps*
Verrily thus Saith the Lord in consequence of their
transgressions, their former standing has been taken away
from them[2] And now if they will be saved, Let them be ordained
as Elders, in my Church, to preach my gospel and travel abroad
from land to land and from place to place, to gather mine Elect
unto me Saith the Lord, and let this be their labors from hence
forth *Even So Amen* — [p. 55]

Revelation, Given the same day and read at the same time,
of the preceeding ones July 8th 1838
O! Lord, show unto thy servents how much thou requirest
of the properties of thy people for a Tithing?[3]

---

1. See D&C 118.
2. Frederick G. Williams had been a counselor to Joseph Smith in the Church
presidency, and William W. Phelps had been one of the presidents of the Church
in Missouri. Both returned to the Church and died in the faith but never again
held high office.
3. Although a law to regulate the economic needs of the Latter-day Saints,
based upon principles of consecration and stewardship of property, had been
introduced in February 1831 (D&C 42), a lack of funds to meet its operating
costs continued to plague the Church. In September 1837, in a letter to "the

Answer. Verrily thus saith the Lord, I require all their surpluss property to be put into the hands of the Bishop of my Church of Zion, for the building of mine house, and for the Laying the foundation of Zion, and for the priesthood, and for the debts of the presidency of my Church, and this shall be the begining of the tithing of my people. and after that, those, who have thus been tithed, shall pay one tenth of all their interest anually. And this shall be a standing Law unto them forever, for my holy pr⟨ie⟩sthood saith the Lord. Verrily I say unto you, it shall come to pass, that all those who gather unto the land of Zion, shall be tithed of their surpluss properties, and shall observe this Law, or they shall not be found worthy to abide among you. And I say unto you, if my people observe not this Law, to keep it holy, and by this law sanctify the Land of Zion unto me, that my Statutes and my Judgements, may be kept thereon that it may be most holy, behold verrily I say unto you, it shall not be a land of Zion unto you, and this

---

saints scattered abroad," Bishop Newel K. Whitney and his counselors at Kirtland lamented that exertions of antagonists to destroy the "kingdom," the building of the temple, publication costs, and a large population of poor had shackled the Church with "great expense." In urging the Saints to "exert themselves with energy to send on means to build up Zion," the bishop noted that "the great work of the last days was to be accomplished by the tithing of His Saints." (Whitney, Cahoon, and Knight to the Saints, 18 September 1837, in *History of the Church,* 2:515–18.)

In December 1837, Bishop Partridge and his counselors, as a committee on Church revenue, appointed by the general council in Missouri, proposed a plan whereby the Church "may voluntarily raise means by tithing themselves to be a fund ready at all times to assist the poor . . . compensate the servants of the Lord for their services in attending to the business of the church and for other necessary purposes." The proposal stipulated that widows and the poor "should not be required to tithe themselves," and that at the beginning of each year "the high council together with the Bishop and his Council shall agree upon, and make known to the church the amount of percentage necessary to be raised the following year." It was estimated that a tithe of "two cents upon the dollar" would raise a sufficient sum to take care of the Church operating costs for 1838. There is no indication that the proposal was adopted, but the initiative for a 2 percent tithing helps place the question raised by Joseph Smith on 8 July in its context. (See Cannon and Cook, *Far West Record,* 129–32; Cook, *Joseph Smith and the Law of Consecration,* chapter 3.)

shall be an ensample unto all the stakes of Zion, *even so Amen.*[1]

[p. 56]

Revelation Given the same day July 8th 1838 Making known the desposition of the properties tithed, as named in the preceeding revelation —

Verrily thus saith the Lord, the time has now come that it shall be disposed of, by a council composed of the first Presidency of my Church and of the Bishop and his council and by ⟨my⟩ high Council, and ⟨by⟩ mine own voice unto them saith the Lord, even so Amen.[2]

Revelation Given to Wm. Marks, N[ewel]. K. Whitney Oliver Granger & others. ⟨Given⟩ in Zion. *July 8th 1838*

Verrily thus saith the Lord unto my servent Wm. Marks, and also unto my servent N. K. Whitney, Let them settle up their buisness spedily, and Journey from the land of Kirtland before I the Lord sendeth the snows again upon the ground, Let them awake and arise and come forth and not tarry for I the Lord command it, therefore if they tarry, it shall not be well with them, let them repent of all their sins and of all their covetous desires, before me saith the Lord. For what is property unto me saith the Lord. Let the properties of Kirtland be turned out for debts saith the Lord, ~~the Lord~~ Let them go; saith the Lord, and whatsoever remaineth let it remain in your hands saith the Lord, for have I not the fowls of heaven and also the fish of the sea, and the bea[s]ts of the mountains, have I not made the earth, do I not hold the destinies of all the armies of the Nations of the earth, therefore will I not make the solitary places to bud, and to blossom, [p. 57] and to bring forth in abundence saith the Lord, Is there not room enough upon the

---

1. See D&C 119.
2. See D&C 120.

mountains of Adam Ondi Awmen, and upon the y̶ plains of Olah Shinehah,[1] or in the land where Adam dwelt; that you should not covet that which is but the drop, and neglect the more weighty matters, Therefore come up hither unto the Land of my people, even Zion, let my servent Wm. Marks, be faithfull over a few things, and he shall be a ruler over many. Let him preside in the midst of my people in the City Far West and let him be blessed with the blessings of my people. Let my servent N. K. Whitney be ashamed of the Nicholatine band,[2] and of all their secret abominations, and of all his littleness of soul before me saith the Lord and come up unto the land of Adam Ondi Awman, and be a bishop unto my people saith the Lord, not in name but in deed saith the Lord.[3] And again verrily I say unto you I r̶e̶m̶b̶e̶r̶ remember my servent Oliver Granger, behold Verrily I say unto him, that his name shall be had in sacred rememberance from Generation to Generation *for ever and ever*, saith the Lord. Therefore let him contend ernestly for the redemption of the first presidency of my Church saith the Lord, and when he falls he shall rise again for his sacrafice shall be more sacred unto me, than his increase saith the Lord, Therefore, let him come up hither spedily unto the land of Zion, and in due time he shall be made a merchent unto my name saith the Lord, for the benefit of my people, Therefore let no man despise my servent Oliver [p. 58] Granger, but let the blessings of my people be upon him forever and ever, and again verily I say unto you, let all my servents in the Land of Kirtland rem[em]ber the Lord their God, and mine house also, to keep and preser[v]e it holy, and to overthrow the money Changers in mine own due time saith the Lord, Even so Amen—[4]

---

1. See Abraham 3:13.
2. See note 1, p. 251.
3. In December 1831, Whitney had been appointed a bishop of the Church at Kirtland, Ohio. (See D&C 72:1–8.)
4. See D&C 117.

26 July 1838 · Thursday

This day the first presidency, High Council, & Bishops Court, ~~to~~ met to take into concideration, the disposing of the publick properties in the hands of the Bishop, in Zion, for the people of Zion have commenced liberally to consecrate agreeably to the revelations, and commandments of the Great I am of their surpluss properties &c.[1]

It was agreed that the first presidency keep all their properties, that they can dispose of to their advantage and support, and the remainder be put into the hands of the Bishop or Bishops, agreeably to the commandments, and revelations,

1st. Mooved seconded & carried unanymously, That the first presidency shall have their expences defrayed in going to Adam Ondi Awman, and also returning therefrom That the Bishop of Zion pay one half, and the Bishop of Adam Ondi Awman the other half

2nd. Mooved seconded & carried unanymously–that all the traveling expences of the first presidency, shall be defrayed in traveling at any time or place [p. 59]

3rd. Mooved seconded & carried unanymously That the Bishop be authorized to pay orders coming from the east inasmuch as they will consecrate liberally, but this to be done under the inspection of the first presidency

4th That the first presidency shall have the prerogative to say to the Bishop whose orders, shall or may be paid by him in this place or in his Jurisdiction. Carried unanymously

5th. Mooved seconded and carried That the Bishop of Zion receive all consecrations, east, west, & south, who are not in the Jurisdiction of a Bishop of any other stake.

6th Mooved & carried, that we use our influence to put a stop to the selling of Liquior in the City Far West or in our

---

1. The 8 July revelation had required the Saints to consecrate all of their surplus property, and after that to "pay one-tenth of their interest annually." See p. 258.

midst, That our streets may not be filled with drunkeness and that we use our influence to bring down the price of provisions. —

7th. Mooved, seconded & carried unanimously that *br. Wm W. Phelps*, be requested to draw up a petition to remove the county seat to Far West

27 July 1838 · Friday

Some time past the bretheren or saints have come up day after day to consecrate, and to bring their offerings into the store house of the lord, to prove him now herewith and se[e] if he will not pour us out a blessing that there will not be room enough to contain it,[1] They have come up hither [p. 60] Thus far, according to the ⟨Revelater⟩ order of the Danites, we have a company of Danites in these times, to put to right physically that which is not right, and to cleanse the Church of verry great evils which hath hitherto existed among us inasmuch as they cannot be put to right ᵐ by teachings & persuasyons, This company or a part of them exhibited on the fourth day of July

They come up to consecrate, by companies of tens, commanded by their captain over ten.[2]

28 July 1838 · Saturday

President Smith and Prest Rigdon left Far West, for Adam Ondi Awman to transact some important buisness, and to

---

1. See Malachi 3:10.

2. The part of this entry following page 60 has been crossed out in the original MS., evidently by a later hand. The Danites were originally an orthodox term for Mormon militia in Caldwell County in 1838, that also served in public service functions of the LDS social order as well as military affairs. Eventually the name came to be associated exclusively with the secret doings of Sampson Avard (one of its officers) and his band. (See David J. Whittaker, "The Book of Daniel in Early Mormon Thought," in *By Study and Also by Faith: Essays in Honor of Hugh Nibley*, edited by John M. Lundquist and Stephen D. Ricks [Salt Lake City and Provo, Utah: Deseret Book Company and Foundation for Ancient Research and Mormon Studies, 1990] 1:155–201; and Dean C. Jessee and David J. Whittaker, "The Last Months of Mormonism in Missouri: The Albert P. Rockwood Journal," *BYU Studies* 28 [Winter 1988]: 5–41; Leland H. Gentry, "The Danite Band of 1838," *BYU Studies* 14 [Summer 1974]: 421–50.)

settle some Cannadian bretheren, in that place, as they are emegrating numerously to this land from all parts of the County. Elder Babit [Almon W. Babbitt] from Cannada with his company, has arrived, brother [Theodore] Turley is with him —

29 July 1838 · Sunday

This day Elder Orson Hyde & Heber C Kimball Preached. They have just returned from England from a mission of some thing over a years duration,[1] They bring glad tidings of great joy from that people, They baptised between one and two thousand and left greater prospects than they had ever before seen Ord[a]ined a large number of Elders, Priests Teachers & Deacons, & thus the work is spreading rappedly throug[h] the country, A large majority of the saints in Kirtland have and are arriving here every day, Kirtland has been broken up by those who have professed the name of Latter Day Saints and have denied the faith [p. 61] which they once preached and by their preaching gathered many saints into this land, and now have betrayed them, O Justice! where hast thou fled, And thou administrations whither hast thou concealed thyself, —

30 July 1838 · Monday

This day the circuit court of our ~~courcuit~~ circuit sits in this place commencing today. Judge [Austin A.] King presiding Judge, quite a number of Lawyers were here, from Liberty & Richmond &c. They have Just returned from [the] Davis County session, Prst. Hyram Smith & myself attended court, —

---

1. Heber C. Kimball left England on 20 April and arrived in Kirtland on 22 May 1838.

31 July 1838 · Tuesday

This day was spent principaly in Court by most of the Presidency. Judge King. waited upon President J. Smith Jr and spent a short time with him. Counselor [Thomas C.] Burch, who is also the Circuit Attorney called upon Prest. Rigdon this day, and had a short interview with him, soleseting him verry hard, to preach this evening as he said those gentlemen of his profession wished to hear him, as also did Judge King, but being quite fatigued in consequence of his absence and labors, returning last evening with Prest. Smith, from Adam Ondi Awman, Cou⟨r⟩t adjourned for its regular sessions. –

1, 2, 3, August 1838 · Wednesday–Friday

were all spent by the first Presidency at home, being somewhat fatigued, in consequence of insesant labors, therefore nothing of importance transpired during this time, we saw the publication of the Oration delivered by [p. 62] Prest. Rigdon on the 4th day [of] July 1838 it was published in the Far West, a paper published in Liberty Clay County Mo.

5 August 1838 · Sunday

The first presidency attended meeting this day, at the usual place of worship Erastus Snow preached a discourse. Prest Smith made some observations immediately after, by way of instructions to the Elders in particular relative [to] wisdom &c. Prest Rigdon delivered a short discourse in the after part of the day and at the Close thereof Elder Simeon Carter and Myself were called upon to administer unto several by the laying on of hands for their confermation and the giving of the Holy Ghost. Br. F. G. Williams was among the number, who being rebaptized a few days since was this day confirmed. –

6 August 1838 · Monday

This day is the day for General Election throughout the state for officers, office seekers from without the Church who depend verry much on our help, begin to flatter us with smooth stories but we understand them verry well through the wisdom of God given unto us they cannot deceive us for God is with us and very near us, for he speaks often unto us, through the means he has appointed

Met in the morning in Council with the first presidency at Prest. Smiths house, to take into concideration the conduct of certain Cannada bretheren, who had gone contrary to council and settled at the forks of Grand River¹ whereupon it was agreed that they must return to Adam Ondi Awman according to the Council of God, or they would not be concidered one among us [p. 63] just as the Lord has said in a revelation to us Given July 8th 1838.

In the after part of the day a meeting was held in the school house as follows

At meeting of the Citizens of Caldwell County assembled in the City Far West, The meeting was called to order, by calling Judge Elias Higbee to the Chair and appointing Geo. W. Robinson Secretary

After some remarks made by the Chairman relative to the object of this meeting, [consideration was given to] the resignation of the present Post Master Wm. W. Phelps, and in appointing his successor

Mr. S. Rigdon was nominated seconded and carried unanymously to succeed Wm. W. Phelps in the post office department, and that he be recommended to the Post Master Gen. as the person of our choice, as citizens of this City, and

---

1. This was Almon Babbitt's company of Canadian immigrants that had arrived in Far West on 28 July 1838 and had been directed to settle at Adamondi-Ahman.

also worthy of our sufferage. Dated Far West Mo. August 6th 1838—

Geo. W. Robinson. *Secretary.*
Elias Higbee Cha[i]r.

This afternoon the citizens of Far West assembled in the school house in the S. W. q[uarte]r. of the Town.

The meeting was opened by Calling Judge Elias Higbee to the Chair, and appointing Geo W Robinson Secretary

1st. Whereupon it was unanimously agreed that the Citizens of the Counties of Caldwell & Davis [p. 64] aught and [s]hould have a weekly News paper published for their information upon the news of the day. Prest. Smith said the time had come when it was necessary that we should have som[e] thing of this nature to unite the people and aid in giving us the news of the day &c.

Whereupon it was unanimously agreed that Prest. S. Rigdon should Edit the same

2nd That a petition be drawn up to remove the County Seat to this place

Some remarks were made by Prest. Rigdon upon the subject,—showing the great necessity of so doing.

3d And that it is the duty of the bretheren to come into Cities to build and live and Carry on their farms out of the City Prest. Smith spoke upon the same subject of mooving into Cities to live, according to the order of God, he spoke quite lengthy and then Prest. H. Smith spoke and endeavoured to impress it upon the ~~same sa~~ minds of the Saints,[1]

---

1. In June 1832 Joseph Smith had sent a "plat of the city of Zion" to the Saints in Missouri—his plan for an ideal city. The city, a mile square, was to be laid out in ten-acre blocks intersected by uniformly wide streets. Each block was to be divided into half-acre lots containing one house to a lot—the lots positioned in such a way that no house would face another across the street. The houses, built of brick or stone, would be located twenty-five feet back from the street, leaving space in front for a "small yard . . . to be planted in a grove, according to the taste of the builder." The remainder of the lot would be used

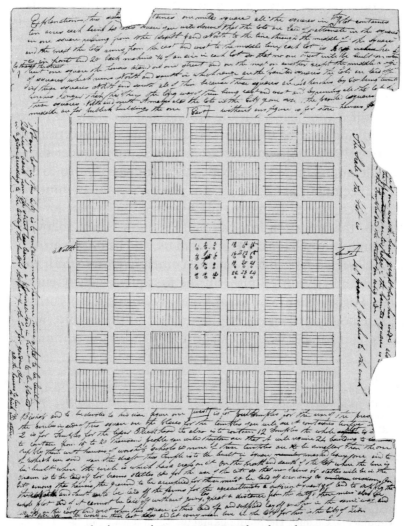

Plat for city of Zion, 1833. LDS Church Archives.

7 August 1838 · Tuesday

This morning an alarm come from Galliton the County Seat of Davis County. that during the Election on yesterday at that place some two or three of our bretheren were killed in consequence of the Malignity of the Missourians, it was reported that the citizens of Daviess County who were opposed to our religion, did endeavor to prohibit the bretheren from voting at the election in that place, and that, the men who were killed were left upon the ground and not suffered to be intered, and that the majority of that County were determined to drive the [p. 65] bretheren from the County,[1] under these conciderations quite a number of us volunteered to go to the assistance of our bretheren in that place accordingly some 15 or 20 men started from this place armed and equipt for our defence the bretheren from all parts of the County, followed after and continued to come and join us, and before we arrived at Col. Wights we had quite a large company Prests Smith and Rigdon and H[yrum] Smith, all the first presidency, General [Elias] Higbee, Gen. [Sampson] Avard myself and ma⟨n⟩y others to[o] tedious to mention at this time or in this record, were in the company. it was put upon me[2] to take the command

---

for gardens. Blocks in the middle of the city would contain public buildings. Barns, stables, and farming land was to be located outside the residential area. The city as a whole would contain fifteen to twenty thousand people. "When this square is thus laid off and supplied, lay off another in the same way, and so fill up the world in these last days." The plan was intended to provide the cities' inhabitants equal access to the advantages of both rural and urban life, and to minimize the disadvantages of both. (*History of the Church,* 1:357–59.)

The concept of the "City of Zion" became a distinguishing characteristic of the "Mormon village" in the American West. (See Richard H. Jackson, "The Mormon Village: Genesis and Antecedents of the City of Zion Plan," *BYU Studies* 17 [Winter 1977]: 223–40; and Richard H. Jackson, "Righteousness and Environmental Change: The Mormons and the Environment," in *Essays on the American West, 1973–74,* Charles Redd Monographs in Western History, No. 5, ed. Thomas G. Alexander [Provo, Utah: Brigham Young University Press, 1975], 21–42.)

1. Although several were wounded, no one was killed in the fight.
2. I.e., George W. Robinson.

in consequence of my holding the office of *Colonel*. whose duty it is to command one regiment, we marched without much intermision untill we reached Col. Wights, however some of our small parties were attacked, I think on twice in going over, but, no serious injury done, we reached Col. Wights that same evening found some of the bretheren assembled for to receive council upon what to do ac [&c] as a number of the men who were at the battle the day before, were there and I believe all of them, and were threatened with vengence by some of their enimies, some of the bretheren were wounded badly but none killed, quite a number of the Missourians were badly wounded some with their sculs cracked as reported, about 150 Missourians faut against from 6 to 12 of our bretheren, our bretheren faut like tigers they cl[e]ared the ground at that time, in knocking down and draging out, the principal men who faught so bravely were John L Butler, Hyram Nelson,[1] [p. 66] whose names aught to be immortalized, from the courage they possessed and their determination in this thing and for the victory they gained[2]

---

1. Possibly Price Nelson (1822–1850), a brother, since Hiram Nelson (1829–1856) was only eight years old at the time. (Family Group Records Collection.)

2. The election-day fight at Gallatin, Missouri, on 6 August 1838 marked the beginning of the so-called Mormon War, which culminated in the Governor's extermination order, the arrest and imprisonment of Church leaders, and the driving of the Latter-day Saints from the state. Poor communication and exaggerated rumors on both sides helped escalate the violence. Rumors quickly turned skirmishes into massacres, further inflaming passions.

According to Sidney Rigdon, the fracas at Gallatin followed when William Peniston, a Whig candidate for the Missouri house of representatives, faced the prospect of not being elected if Mormons voted. Peniston arrived at his conclusion after contacting Lyman Wight, an uncompromising Daviess County Mormon Democrat. Then on the morning of the election Peniston delivered an inflammatory speech at the election site denouncing the character of the Latter-day Saints, which incited the violence. (Rigdon to Col. Sterling Price, 8 September 1838, MS. draft, LDS Church Archives; and *An Appeal to the American People* [Cincinnati, 1840], 15–17. Eyewitness accounts of the Gallatin fight are in Reed C. Durham, Jr., "The Election Day Battle at Gallatin," *BYU Studies* 13 [Autumn 1972]: 36–61; William G. Hartley, *John Lowe Butler: History and Autobiography of a Mormon Frontiersman,* chapter 6, forthcoming book.)

We tarried all knight at that place and in the morning[1] we called to se[e] squire Adam Black who was manifestly[2] an enimy of ours, for the evidences were before us that he did last summer unite himself to a band of mobers to drive our brethern from the County and to prohibit them from settleing in the County and that [he] personally warned many of said bretheren to leave in a certain given time or they should be further delt with, he was obliged to confess this when interrogated upon the subject and in consequences of the violation of his oath as a magistrate in the County of Daviess, we required him to give us some sattisfaction so that we might know whether he was our friend or enimy, and whether he would adm[in]ister the laws of our country or not in justice for people, we presented him with a paper to sign which was an article of peace, but he being Jealous of us would not sign it but said he would draw one himself and sign it to our sattisfaction, he did so,[3] and we left him in peace, The same evening some of ~~our~~ the citizens of the County came to visit us to sue for peace, we told them we would [meet] their principal men in a committee on the next day[4] at that place at twelve O,Clock, accordingly we did so, and entered into a covenant of peace with their principal men of said County for inst[ance] Judge [Josiah] Morin Mr. [John D.] Williams Mr. [James B.] Turner Mr. [Jacob S.] Rogers and many others [p. 67] The covenant of peace was to preserve each others rights,

---

1. 8 August 1838.
2. MS.: "mainfstly"
3. Black's agreement read: "I, Adam Black, a Justice of the Peace of Daviess county do here by sertify to the People, caled Mormin that he is bound to suport the Consticution of this State & the united State & he is not attached to eny mob, nor willnt attach his self to eny such people and so long as they will not molst me I will not molest them. Adam Black, J.P. This the 8 day of august 1838." (John Taylor, *A Short Account of the Murders, Roberies, Burnings, Thefts, and Other Outrages Committed by the Mob and Militia of the State of Missouri, upon the Latter Day Saints* [Springfield, Ill., 1839?], 2; see also, *History of the Church*, 3:59–60.)
4. 9 August 1838.

and stand in their defence, that if men should do wrong they, neither party should uphold them or endeavour to secret them from Justice but they shall be delivered up even all[1] offendrs to be delt with according to law and Justice Upon these terms we parted in peace, and soon every man left the ground and returned to his habitation, We came home the same knight arrived at home about 12 Oclock at knight, and found all well in Far West—

10 August 1838 · Friday

Nothing of importance transpired this day the presidency were at home, being somewhat fatigued did not leave their houses to transact much buisness.—

11 August 1838 · Saturday

This morning the first presidency left this place for the forks of Grand river, in company with Elder Almon Babbit, to visit Elder Babbits Company who came on with him from Cannada, and settled contrary to council on the forks of Grand river, to give such council as is needed. This afternoon a committe from Ray County came into this place to inquire into the procedings of our sosciety in going armed into the County of Daviess, as complaint had been entered by Adam Black and others in said county of Ray[2] And said committee desired to

---

1. "all" repeated in MS.
2. On 10 August, William Peniston, the prime mover behind the election day fight of 6 August, signed an affidavit before the circuit judge, Austin A. King. He charged that the company sent by the Mormons on the 7th to check rumors that some of their people had been killed, and which, incidentally, had visited Adam Black to determine his support of justice in the face of his previous record, was "a large body of armed men, whose movements and conduct are of a highly insurrectionary and unlawful character; that they consist of about five hundred men, and that they, or a part of them, to the number of one hundred and twenty, have committed violence against Adam Black, by surrounding his house, and taking him in a violent manner, and subjecting him to great indignities by forcing him, under threats of immediate death, to sign a paper writing of a very disgraceful character . . . and that the body of men now assembled do intend to commit great violence to many of the citizens of Daviess county, and . . . that Joseph Smith, Jun., and Lyman Wight are the leaders of this body of armed men. . . . " (See *History of the Church,* 3:61.)

confer with a committee that might be appointed by our Citizens, Accordingly a meeting was called of the Citisens of Caldwell County to meet in the City Hall in the City Far West At 6 Oclock P.M. The following are the minuits of a meeting held in Far West in the City Hall [p. 68]

At a meeting of the Citisens of Caldwell County, Met in the City Hall, in Far West August 11th 1838. To take into concideration certain movements on the part ⟨of the citisens⟩ of the County Ray, wherein they have accused the people of our sosciety of breaking the peace, even in defending our rights and those of our bretheren i̶n̶ of late in the County of Daviess

Meeting called to order by calling Bishop E[dward]. Partridge to the *Chair*, and appointing Geo. W. Robinson *Secretary*

1st Resolved That a committee of seven be appointed on the part of the Citisens of Caldwell to confer with and wait on the Committee on the part of the Citisens of the County of Ray

2nd Resolved That this committee with th[e]ir secretary, have power to answer such questions and interrogatories as shall be put by the committee of the County of Ray, and as are named in the document presented to this meeting purporting to be the preamble and resolutions and resolves, of said meeting of said Citisens of Ray

3rd Resolved–That whereas the document presented as above named had no date or signiture either as *Chairman* or Secretary That this committee shall sattisfy themselves of the fact or reasons given, and act accordingly

4th Resolved That this Committee report again to this meeting as soon as may be [possible] together with all information received

Geo. W. Robinson *Secretary*.

Edward Partridge *Chair*. [p. 69]

12 August 1838 · Sunday

This day the first presidency were in the north country, not having returned from the forks of Grand river, to which place they went with Elder Babbit. I[1] remained in Far West during this Journey taken by them.

13 August 1838 · Monday

This day was spent as usual, the first Presidency returned at evening all sound and well, though some what fatigued with the Journey, they were chased some 10 or 12 miles ~~Mi~~ by some evil designing persons but escaped out of their hands, Men were sent to notify them, that a writ had been ishued by Judge [Austin A.] King the circuit Judge to aprehend Prest. Joseph Smith Jr & Lyman Wight for defending their rights &c.[2] They met ~~them~~ the presidency about 8 miles from this place and all returned ⟨safe⟩ to this place.

14 August 1838 · Tuesday

This day was spent by the presidency in secular buisness of their own

15 August 1838 · Wednesday

was also spent in the same manner

16 August 1838 · Thursday

was spent principally at home, the sheriff of Daivess County[3] acompanied by Judge [Josiah] Morin: called on Prest.

---

1. I.e., George W. Robinson.
2. The writ served on Joseph Smith and Lyman Wight grew out of a charge by Adam Black that he had been intimidated by members of the Mormon posse that visited him the 8th of August, two days after the election day fight at Gallatin, and forced him to sign the instrument that bore his name on that date. See note 3, p. 270.
3. William Morgan.

Smith and notified him that he had a writ for [to] take him into Daviess County and try him, for visiting that County as before stated, Prest. Smith did not refuse to be taken, as some people had reported that he would not be taken nor submit to the Law, but he said he would or calculated always to submit to the Laws of our Country, But he told the Sheriff that he wished to be tried in his own County as the Citisens of Daviess County were [p. 70] highly exasperated toward him, he further stated that the Laws of our Country gave him this privilege, the Sheriff did not serve his writ upon hearing this, and said he would go to Richmond and see Judge King upon the subject, Prest. Smith told him he would remain at home untill he should return. etc. The Sheriff accordingly returned and found Prest. Smith at home where he had been during his absence The Sheriff informed him very gravely that he (Prest Smith) was out of his jurisdiction and that he (said Sheriff) could not act in this County he therefore returned as light as he came

20 August 1838 · Monday

This day the inhabitants of the different parts of the Town or County met to organize themselves into companies called agricultural Companies, the presidency were there and took a part in the same, one Company was established called the western agricultural Com[pan]y who voted to take in one field for grain Containing twelve Sections which is Seven thousands six hundred & eighty acres of land Another Company was organised Called the Eastern Agricultural Company the number of acres is not yet asertained, the next day[1] another Company was organized Called the Southern Agric. Comp[an]y field to be as large as the first one.

---

1. 21 August 1838.

22 August 1838 · Wednesday

This day was spent part of the time in counciling with several bretheren upon different subjects, Bretheren continue to gather into Zion daily

23 August 1838 · Thursday

This day was spent in such municipal[1] labors as they saw was necessary, in this place

24 August 1838 · Friday

This day was spent at home by the first Presidency as also was the 25, 26, 27, 28, 29 & 30,th (see page 74) [p. 71]

/[2]A Revelation given [at] Kirtland July 23rd 1837.
The word of the Lord unto Thomas, B. Marsh concerning the twelve Apostles of the Lamb.[3]
Verily thus saith the Lord unto you my servant Thomas[,] I have heard thy prayers[,] and thine alms have come up as a memorial before me[,] in behalf of those thy brethren who were chosen to bear testimony of my name and to send it abroad among all nations[,] kindreds[,] tongues and people[,] and ordained through the instrumentality of my servants. [2] Verily I say unto you[,] there have been some few things in thine heart and with thee, with which I the Lord was not well pleased; nevertheless inasmuch as thou hast abased thyself thou shalt be exalted: therefore all thy sins are forgiven thee. Let thy heart be of good cheer before my face[,] and thou shalt bear record of my name[,] not only unto the Gentiles, but also unto the Jews; and thou shalt send forth my word unto the

---

1. In the MS. "municipal" crossed out, evidently by a later hand.
2. Handwriting of James Mulholland in MS.
3. Brackets in the following revelation indicate inked editorial changes, made by a later hand. Wherever "your" precedes an inserted "[thy]" it was crossed out by this later editor.

ends of the earth. [3] Contend thou therefore morning by morning[,] and day after day let thy warning voice go forth; and when the night cometh[,] let not the inhabitants of the earth slumber because of thy speech. [4] Let thy habitation be known in Zion[,] and remove not thy house, for I the Lord have a great work for ~~you~~ ⟨thee⟩ to do, in publishing my name among the children of men[:][1] therefore gird up ~~your~~ [thy] loins for the work. Let ~~your~~ [thy] feet be shod also for thou art chosen, and thy path[2] lyeth among the mountains and among many nations, and by thy word many high ones shall be brought low; and by thy word many low ones shall be exalted, thy voice shall be a rebuke unto the transgressor, and at thy rebuke let the tongue of the slanderer cease its perverseness. Be thou humble and the Lord thy God shall lead thee by the hand and give thee an answer to thy prayers. I know thy heart and have heard thy prayers concerning thy brethren. Be not partial towards them in love above many others, but let ~~your~~ [thy] love be for them as for ~~your~~[thy]self, and let ~~your~~ [thy] love abound unto all men and unto all who love my name. And pray for ~~your~~ [thy] brethren of the twelve. Admonish them sharply for my name's sake, and let them be admonished for all their sins, and be ye faithful before me unto my name; and after their temptations and much tribulation behold I the Lord will feel after them, and if they harden not their hearts and stiffen not their necks against me they shall be converted and I will heal them. Now I say unto you, and what I say [p. 72] unto you, I say unto all the twelve. Arise and gird up your loins, take up your cross, follow me, and feed my sheep. Exalt not yourselves; rebel not against my servant Joseph for Verily I say unto you I am with him and my hand shall be over him;

---

1. The colon was written over a comma in the MS.

2. A "printer's take" (a mark designating an interruption or break for a typesetter) appears at this point in the MS. Evidently type was set from this manuscript for the 1844 edition of the Doctrine and Covenants. (See D&C, 1844 ed., section 104.)

and the keys which I have given him, and also to youward shall not be taken from him untill I come.

Verily I say unto you my servant Thomas, thou art the man whom I have chosen to[1] hold the keys of my kingdom (as pertaining to the twelve) abroad among all nations, that thou mayest be ~~thy~~ my servant to unlock the door of the kingdom in all places where my servant Joseph, and my servant Sidney, and my servant Hyrum, cannot come[;][2] for on them have I laid the burden of all the Churches for a little season: wherefore whithersoever they shall send you, go ye, and I will be with you[,] and in whatsoever place ye shall proclaim my name[,] an effectual door shall be opened unto you[,] that they may receive my word. [8] Whosoever receiveth my word receiveth me, and whosoever receiveth me receiveth those (the first presidency) whom I have sent, whom I have made counsellors for my name's sake unto you. [8] And again I say unto you, that whosoever ye shall send in my name, by the voice of your brethren the twelve, duly recommended and authorized by you, shall have power to open the door of my kingdom unto any nation whithersoever ye shall send them, inasmuch as they shall humble themselves before me and abide in my word[,] and hearken to the voice of my spirit.

[9] Verily[,] verily[,] I say unto you, darkness covereth the earth and gross darkness the ~~people~~ minds of the people[,] and all flesh has become corrupt before my face! Behold vengeance cometh speedily upon the inhabitants of the earth[;] A day of wrath[;][3] A day of burning[;] A day of desolation[;] of weeping[;] Of mourning and of lamentation[,] And as a whirlwind it shall come upon all the face of the earth[,] saith the Lord. [10] And upon my house shall it begin[;] and from my house shall it

---

1. A "printer's take" appears at this point in the MS.
2. A semicolon is written over a comma in the MS.
3. This and each of the four following editorial corrections were written over an exclamation mark in the MS.

go forth saith the Lord. First among those among you saith the Lord; who have professed to know my name and have not known me[,] and have blasphemed against me in the midst of my house saith the Lord.

[11] Therefore see to it that you trouble not yourselves concerning the affairs of my Church in this place[,] saith the Lord[;] but purify your hearts before me[,] and then go ye into all the world and preach my gospel unto every creature[,] who have not received it[,] and he that believeth and is baptized shall be saved, and he that believeth not, and is not baptized[,] [p. 73] shall be damned[: 12] For unto you (the twelve) and those (the first presidency) who are appointed with you to be your counsellors and your leaders, is the power of this priest-hood given for the last days and for the last time, in the which is the dispensation of the fulness of times, which power you hold in connection with all those who have received a dispen-sation at any time from the beginning of the creation[:] for verily I say unto you the keys of the dispensation which ye have received[,] have came down from the fathers: and last of all[,] being sent down from heaven unto you. [13] Verily I say unto you, Behold how great is your calling. Cleanse your hearts and your garments, lest the blood of this generation be required at your hands. Be faithful untill I come for I come quickly and my reward is with me to recompense every man according as his work shall be. I am Alpha and Omega:—Amen.[1]

/[2]The above revelation was given in Kirtland, and was not here in time to insert in its proper Sequence
G. W. R. Recorder.

31 August 1838 · Friday

Prest. Joseph spent some considerable time this day in conversation with br. John Corril, in consequence of some

---

1. See D&C 112. A "printer's take" appears at this point in the MS.
2. Handwriting of George W. Robinson in MS.

expressions made by him in pressence of some considerable number of bretheren pressent, who might perhaps be weak in the faith, as they had not been long in the place, therefore consequently were made verry unwisely. Bro. Corril's conduct for some time past, has been verry unbecoming indeed especially [for] a man in whoom so much confidence has been placed. He has been difficulted to keep track and walk step, by step, with the great wheal which is propelled by the arm of the great Jehovah, he says he will not yeald his Judgement, to any thing proposed by the Church, or any individuals of the Church, or even the voice of the great (I am,) given through the appointed organ, as revelation, but will always act upon his Judgement [p. 74] let him believe in whatever religion he may, he says he will always say what he pleases, for he says he is a republican, and as such he will do, say, act, and believe, what he pleases. Let the reader marrk such republicanismism as this, That a man should oppose his own Judgment to the Judgment of God, and at the same time profess to believe in the same God, when that God has said, the wisdom of God, is foolishness with men, and the wisdom or Judgment of men is foolishness with God. Prest. Rigdon also made some observations to br. Corril, which he afterwards acknowleged were correct, and that he understood things different after the interview, from what he did before.

1 September 1838 · Saturday

The first Presidency their Scribe & Judge Higbee (as surveyor,) Started this morning for the halfway house (as it is called) kept [by] br. [Waldo] Littlefield, some 14 or 15 miles from Far West directly north,[1] For the purpose of appointing a city of Zion, for the gathering of the saints in that place, for safety and from the storm which will soon come upon this

---

1. Near the Caldwell/Daviess County line.

genneration, and that the bretheren may be together in the hour of the coming of the son of Man and that they may receive instructions to prepare them for that great day which will come upon this generation as a thief in the knight. There is great exitement at present among the Misourians seeking if possible an ~~oet~~ occasion against us they are continually chafing us, and provoking us to anger if possible, one sene of threatning after an-other. but we do not fear them [p. 75] For the Lord God the eternal Father is our God and Jesus the mediator is our Saviour, and in the great I am, is our strength and confidence we have been driven time after time and that without cause and smitten again and again, and that without provocation, untill we have prooved the world with kindness, and the world proved us, that we have no designs against any man or set of men that we injure no man. That we are peaceable[1] with all men, minding our own buisness, and our buisness only, we have Suffered our rights and our liberties to be taken, from us, we have not avenged ourselves of those wrongs, we hav[e] appealed to magistrates, to Sheriffs, to Judges, to Govonours and to the President of the United States, all in vain, yet we have yealded, peacibly to all these things, we have not complained at the great God, we murmured not, but peacibly left all, and retired into the back Country in the broad and wild Prairie, in the barren & desolate plains, and there commenced anew, we made the desolate places to bud and blosom as the rose, and now the fiend like race[2] are disposed to give us no rest. Their Father (the Devil) is hourly calling upon them to be up and doing, and they like willing and obedient children need not the second admonition. But in the name of Jesus Christ the Son of the Living God we will ~~do it~~ & endure it no longer, if the Great God will arm us with courage, with strength and with power, to resist them in their

---

1. MS.: "peasibl"
2. MS.: "rase"

persecutions. We will not act on the offensive but always on the defensive, our rights and[1] [p. 76] our liberties shall not be taken from us, and we peacibly submit to it, as we have done heretofore, but we will avenge ourselves of our enimies, inasmuch as they will not let us alone, But to return again to our subject We found the place for the city, and the bretheren were instructed to gather immediately into it, and soon they should be organised according to the Laws of God. A more particular history of this city will be given hereafter, perhaps at the ⟨at its⟩ organization and dedication. —[2] We found a new route home saving I should think 3 or 4 miles, we arrived at Far West about Day light dawn[3]

2 September 1838 · Sunday

The first Presidency attended worship as usual the fore part of the Day. Prest. ⟨Smith⟩ and myself did not attend in the after part of the day, but retired to Prest. Smiths to examine the church records Br. Joseph spent some considerable part of the afternoon in company with a gentleman[4] from Livingston County, who had become considerable ex[c]ited, on account of a large collection of people saying to take Joseph Smith Jr. & Lyman Wight, for going to one Adam Black's as has been previously stated, and recorded in this record, and as they said Prest. Smith and Col. Wight, had resisted the officer, who had endeavoured to take them etc. and accordingly these men were assembling to take them (as they said) They are collecting from every part of the Country to Daviess County. report says they are collecting from Eleven Counties, to help take two men [p. 77] who had never resisted the Law or officer, neither

---

1. "our rights and" repeated in MS.
2. This sentence was written in the MS. at the bottom of page 77 and keyed for insertion here. Penciled changes by later editors alter the wording to: "history of this city may be expected hereafter . . . "
3. MS.: "down"
4. MS.: "gentlemen"

thought of doing so, and this they knew at the same time, or many of them at least. This looks a little to[o] much like mobocracy, it foretells some evil intentions, the whole uper Missouri is all in an uproar and confusion. This evening we sent for General [David] Atchison of Liberty Clay County, who is the Major General of this division. We sent for him to come and counsil with us, and to se[e] if he could not put a stop to this collec[t]ion of people, and to put to a stop to hostilities in Daviess County, we also sent a letter to Judge King containing a petition, for him to assist in putting down and scattering the mob, which are collecting at Daviess.[1]

3 September 1838 · Monday

Nothing of importance transpired this day, onley reports concerning the collection of the mob in Daviess County which in part has been collecting and collected ever since the election in Daviess which was on the sixth of August last as has been heretofore mentioned. This evening General [David R.] Atchison arrived in Town[2]

4 September 1838 · Tuesday

This day was spent in council with the Gen. He says he will do all in his power to disperce the mob. &c.– We employed him and [Alexander W.] Doniphan (his partner) as our Lawyer

---

1. In the MS. the following penciled alterations in this day's entry were made by those who later edited the text for inclusion in the History of the Church: "Adam Black's in Davies County and as they said Prest. Smith . . . and accordingly these men were assembling to take them (as they say) . . . This evening I sent for General Atchison . . . Major General of this division, to come and counsil with us. . . . I also sent a letter to Judge King. . . . "

2. In the MS. the following penciled alterations in this day's entry were added by those who later edited the text for inclusion in the History of the Church: "mob in Daviess County which has been collected . . . since the election in Daviess on the sixth of August last I was at home most of the day. This evening General Atchison arrived at Far West." The sentence "I was at home most of the day" is derived from the parallel entry of the same date in the journal James Mulholland kept for Joseph Smith that follows this one (see p. 300).

and counselor in Law, They are concidered the first Lawyers in the Uper Missouri, Prest. Rigdon & myself[1] commenced this day the studay of Law under Generals Atchison & Doniphon [p. 78] They think by dilligent application we can be admitted to the bar in twelve months. The result of the council was, that, Prest. Smith & Col. Wight volunteer and be tried by Judge King in Daviess County[2] (Col Wight) being present being previously notified to attend the council. Accordingly Thursday next was appointed for the trial, and word to that amount, was sent to Judge King (who had previously agreed to volunteer and try the case) to meet all at br. [Waldo] Littlefields near the county line south of Daviess, ~~We all return~~[3]

5 September 1838 · Wednesday

Judge King come to town, on his way to Daviess, to meet the above named engagement Gen. Atchison had gone before Judge King arrived, the Judge stayed all knight,

6 September 1838 · Thursday

Prest. Smith repaired to br. Littlefields to stand trial, he was accompanied by several of the bretheren among whoom was Prest. Hyram Smith Judge E[lias]. Higbee & myself[4] &c. &c. Prest Smith thought it not wisdom to make his appearance before the public in consequence of the many threats made against him and the high state of exitement in that place,[5] The trial could not go on in consequence of the absence of the

---

1. I.e., George W. Robinson.
2. On the charges originating with Adam Black. See entry of 11 August 1838.
3. In the MS. the following penciled alterations in this day's entry were added by those who later edited the text for inclusion in the History of the Church: "in council with the Gen. . . . as our Lawyers and counselors . . . the studay of Law under the instruction of Generals Atchison . . . that myself & Col. Wight volunteer . . . near the county line in the southern part [of] Daviess,"
4. I.e., George W. Robinson.
5. At Gallatin, the Daviess County seat.

Plaintiff[1] and lack of testimony, consequently the court adjourned till tomorrow at 10 Oclock at A Mr. [John] Raglin's some 6 or 8 miles farther south, and also he is a real mob Character, he lives within [p. 79] one half mile of Caldwell County line. We all returned this evening to Far West.

7 September 1838 · Friday

We all met at Raglins agreeable to adjournment. We did not know but there would be a distirbance among the mob characters, today, we accordingly had an army of men placed at the County line so as to be ready at a minuits warning if there should be any difficulty at the trial, the trial commenced Mr. Penningston [William Peniston] who was the prossecutor had no witnesses but Adam Black who contrived to swear a great many things that never had an exista[n]ce untill he swore them and I presume, never entered the heart of any man And in fine I think he swore by the Job. (as he was employed so to do by Penningston.)

The witnesses on the part of the defence was Dimick B. Huntington, Gideon Carter Adam Lightner & myself. The Judge bound Prest Smith & Col. Wight over to court in a five hundred dollar bond, there was no proof against them criminal, but it is suposed he did it to pasify as much as possible the feelings of the mobers. he (the Judge) stating after in my presence that there was nothing proven against them worthy of bonds, but they submitted without murmuring a word, gave the bonds with sufficient securities, and all returned home the same evening,[2] We found two persons in Daviess at the trial,

---

1. Adam Black.
2. At this hearing Joseph Smith and Lyman Wight were bound over to appear at the next term of the Daviess circuit court on 29 November, "to answer to an indictment to be prefered against them for a misdemeanor." The preliminary hearing for other defendents in the Adam Black case did not occur until 18 September, after Alexander Doniphan and David Atchison had brought militia to protect the court. (State vs. J. Smith Jr. & L. Wight, MS., Brigham Young University Library.)

which[1] Gentlemen were sent from Charriton County as a committe[e] to enquire into all this matter. as the mobers had sent [p. 80] to that place for assestance, they said to take Smith & Wight, but their object was to drive the brethren from the County of Daviess as was done in Jackson County, They said the people in Charriton did not se[e] proper to send help without knowing for what purpose they were doing it, and this they said was their errand, They came home with us, to hold a council with us, in order to learn the facts of this great exitement, which is as it were turning the world up side down,[2]

8 September 1838 · Saturday

The Presidency met in Council with the committe above named, from Charriton County, together with General Atchison, where a relation was given of this whole matter, the present state of exitement and the cause of all this confusion, These Gentlemen expressed their fullest sattisfaction upon this matter considering they had been outrageously imposed upon, in this matter. They left this afternoon appearantly perfectly sattisfied with the interview, News came this evening that the mob were to attack Adam Ondi Awman,[3]

---

1. In the MS. "from" inadvertently precedes "which"
2. In the MS. the following penciled changes in this day's entry were added by those who later edited the text for inclusion in the History of the Church: "we accordingly had a company of men . . . Wm. P. Penniston who was the prossecutor . . . (and that he was employed so to do by Penniston.) . . . Adam Lightner and Geo. W. Robinson. The Judge bound Col. Wight & myself over to court . . . no proof against us to criminate us but . . . the Judge stated afterwards in presence of Geo. W. Robinson that . . . but we submitted without murmuring . . . at the trial, which Gentlemen . . . They accompanied us to Far West to hold a council with us. . . . "
3. The following penciled alterations in this day's entry were added by those who later edited the text for inclusion in the History of the Church: "Council with the committe from Charriton County . . . was given of the whole matter . . . the cause of all the confusion, . . . fullest sattisfaction upon the subject considering . . . the mob were to attack Adam Ondi Awman and a few of the brethren started for to assist the brethren to defend that place,"

9 September 1838 · Sunday

This morning a company in addition to what went last evening went to Adam Ondi Awmon to assist the bretheren there in their defence against the ~~bot~~ mob. Capt. Wm Al[l]red took a company of ten men, all mounted, and went to entrsect a team with guns and amunition from Richmond for the mob in Daviess, they found the wagon broke down and the boxes of guns drawn into the high grass near by the wagon [p. 81] no one present that could be discovered, on a short time two men [on] horse back came from towards the camp of the mob and immediately behind them was a man with a wagon, they all come up, and were taken by virtue of a writ supposing them to be the men who were abetting the mob, in carrying the guns and amunition to those murderers, yea and murderers to[o]! in cool blood, The men were taken together with the guns to Far West the guns were destributed among the bretheren for their defence, and the prisoners were held in custody,[1] This was a glorious day indeed the plans of the mob were frustrated in loosing their guns, and all th[e]ir efforts appeared to be blasted, or blast before carried into effect,[2] The mob continue to take prisioners at their pleasure, some they keep and some they let go. they try all in their power to make us commit the first act of violence they frequently send in word that they are tortureing the prisioners to death, in the most agravating man-

---

1. MS.: "custorday."
2. When news reached Far West that arms and ammunition were being sent from Ray County to Daviess County to be used against the Mormons, Elias Higbee, a justice of the Caldwell County court, authorized William Allred, a Caldwell militia captain, to take volunteers and intercept the arms shipment, which he did. Three gun-runners, John B. Comer, William L. McHaney, and Allen Miller, were brought before Albert Petty, a Far West justice of the peace, and charged with transporting firearms. When it was found that the weapons were government arms deposited at Richmond, they were distributed among the Mormon militia. Eventually, the arms were collected and returned to Richmond, and the prisoners released. (See Gentry, "A History of the Latter-day Saints in Northern Missouri," 186–88.)

ner, but we understand all their ways, and their cunning and wisdom is not past finding out[1]

10 September 1838 · Monday

Today we proceeded to trial of those prisioners they said they wished for an opportunity of getting bail so as to obtain Counsil; they were given to understand that no bail could be taken, for this purpose, but that he could have a sufficient time to send for counsil if he wished, the court accordingly adjourned untill Wendnessday [p. 82] following, The Prisioners names were John B. Comer Al[l]en Miller Wm L. McHaney, They were brought before Albert Petty a Justice of the Peace in Far West

11 September 1838 · Tuesday [p. 83]

[pages 84–100 blank]

Editorial Note

The three months that elapsed between the foregoing journal and the letter that follows marked the end of the Latter-day Saint quest for Zion in Missouri in 1838. Following the election-day fight at Gallatin, Daviess County, on 6 August, opposition against the Latter-day Saints increased to a point that brought open conflict and eventual expulsion from the state. The conflict came to a head in the last week of October when state militia, activated by an extermination order from the Governor, massacred seventeen Mormons in a remote settlement on Shoal Creek. The Mormon force at Far West surrendered, and Church leaders, including Joseph Smith, were taken into captivity. After a hearing at Richmond, Ray County, the Prophet and several others were charged with "overt acts of treason" and other crimes and imprisoned at Liberty, in Clay County, to await trial. It was there on 16 December 1838 that Joseph Smith wrote the following letter, with the memory of recent events,

---

1. In the MS. the following penciled alterations, in this day's entry, were added by those who later edited the text of the journal for inclusion in the History of the Church: "murderers to[o] in cool blood . . . appeared to be blasted. The mob. . . . "

including betrayal by trusted friends, fresh upon his mind. The letter is written in the hand of James Mulholland, who served as a clerk to the Prophet in Missouri in the fall of 1838 and again after he arrived in Illinois in 1839. (A summary of the expulsion from Missouri and the events that led to it is in Allen and Leonard, *The Story of the Latter-day Saints*, chapter 4.)

Liberty Jaol Missouri
16th December 1838

To the Church of Latter day Saints in Caldwell County, and all the Saints who are scattered abroad, and are persecuted, and made desolate, and are afflicted in divers manners for Christ's sake, and the Gospel, — and whose perils are greatly augmented by the wickedness and corruption of false brethren,[1] may grace mercy and the peace of God be and abide with you, and notwithstanding all your sufferings, we assure you, that you have our prayers, and fervent desires for your wellfare and salvation both day and night We believe that that God who seeth us in this solitary place, will hear our prayers and reward you openly; know assuredly, Dear Brethren that it is for the testimony of Jesus, that we are in bonds and in prison. But we say unto you, that we consider that our condition is better, (notwithstanding our sufferings,) than those who have persecuted and smitten us, and borne false witness against us, and we also most assuredly believe that those who bear false witness against us, do seem to have a great triumph over us for the present. But we want you to remember Haman and Mordacai,[2] you know Haman could not be satisfied so long as he saw Mordicai at the King's gate, and he saught the life of Mordicai and the people of the jews. But God so ordered,

---

1. Dissenters from the Church in Missouri included Thomas B. Marsh, Orson Hyde, William W. Phelps, Sampson Avard, John Corrill, John Cleminson, Reed Peck, George Hinkle, David Whitmer, and John Whitmer. The testimony of some of these was a factor in Joseph Smith's imprisonment.

2. Esther 2–8.

that Haman was hanged upon his own gallows, So shall it come to pass with poor Haman in the last days, those who have saught by their unbelief and wickedness, and by the principle of mobocracy to destroy us, and the people of God, by killing and scattering them abroad, and wilfully and maliciously delivering us into the hands of murderers, desiring us to be put to death, thereby having us dragged about in chains and cast into prison, and for what cause? It is because we were honest men, and were determined to defend the lives of the Saints at the expence of our own, I say unto you that those who have thus vilely treated us like Haman, shall be hanged upon their own gallows, or in other words, shall fall into their own ~~snare~~ gin and snare and ditch and trap which they have prepared for us, and shall go back [p. 101] wards and stumble and fall, and ⟨their⟩ name shall be blotted out, and God shall reward them according to all their abominations; Dear Brethren do not think that our hearts faint, as though some strange thing had happened unto us, for we have seen and been assured of all these things beforehand, and have had an assurance of a better hope than that of our persecutors, therefore God hath made broad our shoulders for the burden. We glory in our tribulations because we know that God is with us, that he is our friend; and that he will save our souls. We do not care for them that kill the body; they cannot harm our souls, we ask no favors, at the hands of mobs, nor of the world, nor of the Devil, nor of his emissaries the Dissenters, and those who love and make and swear falsehoods, to take away our lives. We have never dissembled, nor will we for the sake of our lives for as much then as we know that we have been endeavoring with all our minds, mights and strength, to do the will of God, and all things whatsoever he hath commanded us, and as to our light observations from time to time they have nothing to do with the fixed purposes of our hearts, therefore it sufficeth us to say, that our souls were vexed from day to day. We refer you to Isai[a]h who considers those who make a man an offender for a word, and lay a snare for him that reproveth in the gate[1] We believe that the old Prophet verily told the truth, we have no retraction to make, we have reproved in the gate, and men have laid snares for us, we have spoken words and men have made us offenders, and notwithstanding all this our minds are not yet darkened but feel strong in the Lord, But behold the words of the saviour "If the light which is in you become darkness, behold how great is that darkness,"[2] look at the dissenters. Again if you were of the world, the world would love its own, Look at Mr [George M.] Hinkle a wolf in sheep's clothing, Look at his Brother, John Corrill Look at the beloved Reed Peck, who aided him ~~by~~ ⟨in⟩ leading us as the Saviour was led, into the camp as a lamb prepared for the slaughter,[3] as a sheep dumb before his shearers, so we opened not our mouths. But these men like Balaam[4] being greedy for reward sold us into the hands of those who loved them for the world loves his own. I would remember W. W. Phelps who comes up before us as one of Jobs destroyers,[5] God suffered

---

1. Isaiah 29:21.

2. Matthew 6:23.

3. On 31 October 1838, when a bloody confrontation seemed imminent between Mormon and non-Mormon militia units facing each other at Far West, Caldwell County, Missouri, a delegation under the direction of George Hinkle, commander of the Mormon force, arranged for a conference with Missouri militia commander, Samuel Lucas, and Church leaders, under a flag of truce in the hope of working out a settlement of the conflict. However, instead of a discussion to resolve differences, the meeting became a surrender and marked the beginning of more than five months imprisonment for the Prophet and others. Joseph Smith regarded Hinkle's action as a betrayal. In November, Hinkle testified as a witness for the state in the preliminary hearing before Judge King at Richmond that retained the Prophet in prison to face trial on a charge of treason. Other members of the truce committee, John Corrill and Reed Peck, also testified for the state against their former associates at the Richmond hearing. (See *History of the Church*, 3: 188–89; *Document Containing the Correspondence, Orders, &C.*, 72–75; 110–113; 116–20; 125–29; Corrill, *A Brief History of the Church of Christ of Latter Day Saints*, 40–42.)

4. Numbers 22:5ff.

5. After siding with dissenters, William Phelps, one of the presidents of the Church in Missouri, was rejected by a vote of the Saints in February 1838. He was among those who testified for the state against Church leaders at the Rich-

such [p. 102] kind of beings to afflict Job, but it never entered into their hearts that Job would get out of it all. This poor man who professes to be much of a Prophet, has no other dumb ass to ride only David Whitmer,[1] to forbid his madness when he goes up to curse Israel, and this ass not being of the same kind of Balaam's therefore the angel notwithstanding he appeared unto him, yet he could ⟨not⟩ penetrate his understanding, sufficiently so, but what he brays out cursings instead of blessings, Poor Ass, who ever lives to see it, will see him and his rider perish like those who perished in the gainsaying of Core, or after the same condemnation, Now as for these and the rest of their company, we will not presume to say that the world loves them, but we presume to say that they love the world and we classify them in the error of Balaam, and in the gainsaying of Core, and with the company of Cora, Dathan & Abiram.[2]

Perhaps our brethren may say because we thus write, that we are offended at those Characters! If we are it is not for a word neither because they reproved in the gate, but because they have been the means of shedding innocent blood. Are they not murderers then at heart, are not their consciences seared as with a hot iron. We confess we are offended, but the

---

mond hearing in November. (Cannon and Cook, *Far West Record*, 135–41; *Document Containing the Correspondence, Orders, &C.*, 120–25.)

In the published version of this letter in *History of the Church*, 3:228, William E. McLellin's name appears in the place of William W. Phelps's.

1. Whitmer, who had been president of the Church in Missouri, was excommunicated in April 1838 for allying himself with the Kirtland dissenters, and for "separating himself from the cause." (Cannon and Cook, *Far West Record*, 176–78.) William W. Phelps had been a counselor to Whitmer in the Missouri Church presidency. In 1837 dissenters had attempted to put Whitmer forward to replace the Prophet.

2. Numbers 16:1–3, 31–35; Jude 11.

The actions of dissenters in Kirtland and Missouri, and the testimony of some of them at the November hearing in Richmond, were an important factor in the imprisonment of Church leaders, and in the driving of the Saints from Missouri in the winter of 1838–39. An awareness of this helps place Joseph Smith's strong feelings here in context.

saviour said, ["]it must needs be that offences come, but wo unto them by whom they come, and again blessed are ye, when men shall revile you and persecute you and shall say all manner of evil falsly for my sake. Rejoice and be exceeding glad for great is your reward in Heaven for so persecuted they the Prophets which were before you."[1] Now brethren if any men ever had reason to claim this promise, we are the men, for we know that the world not only hates us, but they speak all manner of evil of us falsely for no[2] other reason than that we have been endeavouring to teach the fulness of the gospel of Jesus Christ. After we were bartered away by Hinkle and were taken into the militia camp, we had all the evidence we could have asked for, that the world hated us.[3] If there were Priests among them of all the different sects they hated us, and that most cordially too, If there [were] Generals they hated us,[4] If there were Colonels they hated us, and the soldiers and officers of all classes hated us, and the most profane blasphemers and drunkards and whoremongers hated us, they all hated us most cordially and now what did they hate us for, purely because of the testimony of Jesus Christ; Was it because we ar[e] liars, We know that is reported [p. 103] by some; but it is reported falsely. Was it because we have committed treason against the

---

1. Matthew 18:7; 5:11.

2. "no" repeated in MS.

3. One of the men taken prisoner with Joseph Smith described the moment of surrender: "We were marched into camp surrounded by thousands of savage looking beings, many of whom were dressed and painted like Indian warriors. These all set up a constant yell, like so many bloodhounds let loose upon their prey. . . . If the vision of the infernal regions could suddenly open to the mind, with thousands of malicious fiends, all clamoring, exulting, deriding, blaspheming, mocking, railing, raging and foaming like a troubled sea, then could some idea be formed of the hell which we had entered." (Pratt, *Autobiography*, 186.)

4. Exceptions were David R. Atchison and Alexander W. Doniphan. Doniphan had refused an order to take the prisoners into the Far West town square the morning after their arrest and shoot them. His humanity on this and other occasions during the sojourn of the Latter-day Saints in Missouri ingratiated him in the eyes of the Latter-day Saints. (See *History of the Church*, 3:190–91; and Anderson, "Atchison's Letters.")

state in Daviess County, or of burglary or of larceny or Arson, or any other unlawful act in Daviess County. We know that Priests and certain lawyers, and certain Judges who are the instigators aiders and abittors of a certain gang of murderers and robbers who have been carrying on a scheme of Mobocracy to uphold their priestcraft against the saints of the last days for a number of years, and who have by a well contemplated and premeditated scheme to put ⟨down⟩ by physical operation a system of religion that all the world by all their mutual attainments and any fair means whatever were not able to resist. Hence mobbers were encouraged by Priests and Levites, by the Pharisees and the Sadducees, and Essinees and the Herodians and every other "E" and "ite" egging[1] on the most ruthless, abandoned, and debauched and lawless & inhumane and beastly set of men that the earth can boast of and indeed a parallel cannot be found any where else, to gather to gether to drive to steal and to plunder to starve and to exterminate and burn the houses of the Mormons. These are the characters that by their treasonable and overt acts, have desolated and laid waste Daviess County These are the characters that would fain make all the world believe that we are guilty of the abov-enamed acts, but they represent us falsely, We stood in our own defence and we believe that no man of us acted only in a just a lawful and righteous retaliation against such marauders. We say unto you that we have not committed treason, neither any other unlawful act in Daviess County.[2] Was it for

---

1. MS. reads: "other E and ite agging"
2. The charges against Joseph Smith and other Latter-day Saints followed acts of Mormon retaliation after a long period of antagonism and violence had driven the Saints from three Missouri counties and threatened to drive them again. At the conclusion of the Richmond hearing, Joseph Smith and a few others had been charged with "overt acts of treason in Daviess County" and confined in prison to await trial. According to the Prophet's History, their treason consisted of "having whipped the mob out of Daviess county and taking their cannon from them." ("State of Mo. vs. Jos. Smith Jr. et al.," Daviess County Circuit Court Papers, MS., State Historical Society of Missouri, Columbia, Missouri, copy at

murder in Ray County against Mob Militia who was a wolf in ~~sheep's~~ first instance, Hide and hair, teeth legs and tail, who afterwards put on a Militia sheep skin well tanned with the wool on, who could sally forth in the day time into the flock & snarl and show his teeth, and scatter and devour the flock and satiate himself upon his prey, and then sneak back into the brambles in order that he might conceal himself in his well tryed skin with the wool on. We are well aware that

---

Brigham Young University Library; "A History of the Persecution of the Church of Jesus Christ of Latter Day Saints in Missouri," *Times and Seasons* 1 [September 1840]: 164.)

Even non-Mormons understood that the one-sided Richmond charges ignored the severe provocations that drove the Mormons, finally, to "acts of desperation": On 25 September 1838 General H. G. Park wrote Governor Boggs that upon his arriving at the scene of conflict he found a large body of men from adjoining counties "armed and in the field, for the purpose . . . of assisting the people of this county against the Mormons, without being called out by the proper authorities." Two days later, David Atchison wrote the Governor, "I have no doubt your Excellency has been deceived by the exaggerated statements of designing or half-crazy men. I have found there is no cause of alarm on account of the Mormons." (Parks to Boggs, 25 September 1838; Atchison to Boggs, 27 September 1838, cited in *Document Containing the Correspondence, Orders, &c.*, 32–34.)

Not until the middle of October, after all hope for legal recourse was exhausted and the Latter-day Saints faced the prospect of being driven again, did the Saints retaliate. Requesting arms from the federal garrison at Ft. Leavenworth on 27 October, Generals Atchison and Doniphan wrote that the citizens of the northern counties had "raised mob after mob for the last two months for the purpose of driving a community of fanatics, (called Mormons) from those counties and from the State. Those things have at length goaded the Mormons into a state of desperation that has now made them aggressors instead of acting on the defensive. This places the citizens of this whole community in the unpleasant attitude that the civil and decent part of the community have now to engage in war to arrest a torrent that has been let loose by a cowardly mob." (Atchison and Doniphan to Mason, Commanding at Leavenworth, 27 October 1838, MS., National Archives.) Later, Atchison wrote the U.S. adjutant general that "the imprudent conduct of a part of the citizens in the upper counties, have brought about the present difficulties; goading the Mormons to acts of desperation; even bloodshed and plunder, laying waste and devastating a whole county." (Atchison and Doniphan to Mason, Commanding at Leavenworth, 27 October 1838, MS., National Archives; Atchison to Jones, 6 November 1838, MS. On the nature of the conflict in Missouri see Gentry, "A History of the Latter-day Saints in Northern Missouri," chapter 10; and Richard L. Anderson, "Atchison's Letters and the Causes of Mormon Expulsion from Missouri.")

there is a certain set of Priests and satellites and mobbers that would fain make all the world believe that we are the dogs that barked at this howling wolf that made such havoc among the sheep, who when he retreated he howled and bl[e]ated at such a ~~rate~~ desperate rate, that if one could have been there he would have thought that all the wolves whether wrapped up in sheep skins or in goat skins or in any other skins, and [p. 104] in fine all the beasts of the forest were awfully alarmed and catching the scent of innocent blood, they sallied forth with one tremendous howl and crying of all sort, and such a howling and such a tremendous havoc never was known, Such a piece of inhumanity and relentless cruelty and barbarity cannot be found in all the annals of history, These are the characters who would make the world believe that we had committed murder by making an attack upon this howling wolf while we were at home and in our beds and asleep, and knew nothing of the transaction, any more than we know what is going on in China while we are within these walls.[1] Therefore we say again unto you in these things they have represented us falsely. Was it for committing adultry, we are aware that false slander has gone abroad for it has been reiterated in our ears. These are falsehoods also.

Renegade Mormon Dissenters run abroad into the world and spread various false and libelous reports against us thinking thereby to gain the friendship of the world because they

---

1. The metaphor of the howling wolf evidently has reference to the battle at Crooked River on 25 October 1838. Two days earlier Samuel Bogart, commander of a company of Ray County militia, had written his superior, General Atchison, that in consequence of Mormon retaliation in Daviess County, he had mustered his company to patrol the border between Ray and Caldwell Counties as a protective measure, and to await further orders. But Bogart, failing to confine his surveillance to his own county, crossed into Caldwell and took hostages. When a Mormon militia unit, under the command of David Patten, came to free the hostages, a battle ensued at Crooked River in which at least four men were killed and several wounded. Joseph Smith was not a participant in the battle. (Anderson, "Atchison's Letters," 32; Gentry, "A History of the Latter-day Saints in Northern Missouri," 264–73.)

know that we are not of the world, and that the world hates us, therefore they make a toast of these characters, by them try to do all the injury they can, and after that they hate them worse than they do us, because they find them to be base traitors and sycophants. Such characters God hates, we cannot love them, the world hates them, and we sometimes think that even Satan ought to be ashamed of them.

We have heard that it is reported by some, that some of us should have said that we not only dedicated our property but our families also to the Lord, And Satan taking advantage of this, has transfigured it into licentiousness such as a community of wives, which is an abomination in the sight of God— When we consecrate our property to the Lord, it is to administer to the poor and the needy for this is the law of God. It is not for the purpose of the rich those who have no need. And when a man consecrates or dedicates his wife and children he does not give them to his neighbour nor to his brother, for there is no such law, for the law of God is that thou shalt not commit adultery thou shalt ⟨not⟩ covet thy neighbour's wife, He that looketh on a woman to lust after her, has committed adultery ⟨already⟩ in his heart. Now for a man to consecrate his property and his wife and children to the Lord is nothing more or less, than to feed the hungry clothe the naked visit the widow and the fatherless, the sick, and the afflicted and do [p. 105] all he can to administer to their relief in their afflictions. And for him and his house to serve the Lord. In order to do this he and all his house must be virtuous and must shun the very appearance of evil.[1]

Now if any person has represented anything otherwise than what we now write he or she is a liar and has represented us falsely and this is another manner of evil which is spoken against us falsely.

1. On the principle of consecration see Cook, *Joseph Smith and The Law of Consecration*.

We have learned also since we have been prisoners that many ⟨false⟩ and pernicious things which were calculated to lead the saints far astray and to do them great injury as coming from the Presidency, taught by Dr [Sampson] Avard,[1] and we have reason to fear ~~that~~ many other designing and corrupt characters like unto himself, which the Presidency never knew of being taught in the Church by anybody untill after they were made prisoners, which if they had known of, they would have spurned them and their authors from them as they would the very gates of hell. Thus we find there have been frauds and secret abominations and evil works going on, leading the minds of the weak and unwary into confusion and distraction, and pawning it all the while upon the Presidency, while mean time the Presidency were ignorant as well as innocent of those things which were practicing in the Church in their name, and were attending to their own Secular and family concerns, weighed down with sorrow, in debt, in poverty, in hunger assaying to be fed, yet finding themselves receiving deeds of

---

1. Avard led a maverick contingent of Danites in Daviess County during the last stages of the 1838 conflict in Missouri. He had organized his company with secret oaths and sinister intentions, and he claimed authorization from the Church Presidency. Lyman Wight wrote that Avard "invented schemes and plans to go against mobocracy, which were perfectly derogatory to the laws of this State [Missouri] and of the United States. . . . More than once did he raise a conspiracy against them (the Presidency) . . . Now when he was brought before the court he swore that all these treasonable purposes . . . originated with us." After his deeds were discovered he was excommunicated. Avard was the first witness to testify on behalf of the State at the Richmond hearing, claiming that Joseph Smith was "the prime mover and organizer" of his Danite band. His testimony went far in establishing the treason charge that imprisoned the Prophet. In searching for evidence for the court of inquiry, John B. Clark, the Missouri militia commander, wrote that not until he captured Avard was he able to obtain any "useful facts" for the hearing. "No one disclosed any useful matter until he was captured and brought in." Prior to his testimony, Avard had told Oliver Olney that if he wished to save himself, he must "swear hard against the heads of the Church." (*Document Containing the Correspondence, Orders, &C.*, 90, 97; Journal of Lyman Wight, as quoted in *The History of the Reorganized Church*, 2: 298; Gentry, "A History of the Latter-day Saints in Northern Missouri," 229–42; *History of the Church*, 3: 209–10.)

charity but inadequate to their subsistence and because they received those deeds we were envied and hated by those who professed to be our friends.

But notwithstanding we thus speak, we honor the church when we speak of the Church, as a Church, for their liberality, kindness, patience and long suffering, and their continual kindness towards us. And now brethren we say unto you, what more can we enumerate? is not all manner of evil of every description spoken of us falsely, yea we say unto you falsely, we have been misrepresented and misunderstood and belied and the purity and integrity and uprightness of our hearts have not been known, and it is through ignorance, yea the very depth of ignorance is the cause, of it, and not only ignorance but on the part of some gross wickedness and hypocracy also, who by a long face and sanctimonious prayers and very pious sermons had power to lead the minds of the ignorant and unwary and thereby obtain such influence that when we approached their [p. 106] iniquities the Devil gained great advantage, would bring great sorrow and trouble on our heads, and in fine we have waded through an ocean of tribulation and mean abuse, practised upon us by the illbred and the ignorant, such as Hinkle, Corrill, Phelps, Avard, Reed Peck, [John] Cleminson and various others who are so very ignorant that they cannot appear respectable in any decent and civilized society, and whose eyes are full of adultery and cannot cease from sin. Such characters as M'Lellin, John Whitmer, D. Whitmer, O. Cowdery, & Martin Harris who are too mean to mention and we had like to have forgotten Marsh and Hyde whose hearts are full of corruption,[1] whose cloak of hypocracy was

---

1. Contributing to the evidence used to expel the Latter-day Saints from Missouri and imprison their leaders was an affidavit dated 20 October 1838 signed by apostles Thomas B. Marsh and Orson Hyde, who had become disaffected by that time. Written at the request of a committee of citizens of Ray County, the document outlined Mormon retaliatory forays against the mob in Caldwell and Daviess counties, and it claimed that Joseph Smith had advocated

not sufficient to shield them or to bear them up in the hour of trouble, who after having escaped the pollutions of the world through the knowledge of our Lord and Saviour Jesus Christ became again entangled and overcome, their latter end is worse than the beginning. But it has happened ⟨unto them⟩ according to the words of the Saviour, "The dog has returned to his vomit, and the sow that was washed to her wallowing in the mire.["][1] Again if we sin wilfully after we have received the knowledge of the truth, there remaineth no more sacrifice for sin but rather a certain fearful looking of judgement and fiery indignation to come which shall devour these adversaries. For he who despised Moses' Law, died without mercy under two or three witnesses, of how much sorer punishment suppose ye shall he be thought worthy who hath sold his brother and denied the new and everlasting covenant by which he was sanctified calling it an unholy thing, and doing despite the unto the spirit of grace.

And again we say unto you, inasmuch as there be virtue in us, and the holy priesthood hath been conferred upon us, and the keys of the kingdom have not been taken from us. For verily thus saith the Lord! "Fear not, but be of good cheer. For the keys of which I gave unto you are yet with you"! Therefore we say unto you, Dear Brethren in the name of the Lord Jesus Christ, we deliver these Characters unto the buffetings of Sa-

---

death for any Mormon who refused to take up arms. The affidavit also claimed that the Prophet intended taking the state of Missouri, the United States, and eventually the whole world, and that he would "tread down his enemies, and walk over their dead bodies; that if he was not let alone he would be a second Mohamet to this generation, and that he would make it one gore of blood from the Rocky Mountains to the Atlantic Ocean." However, upon later returning to the Church, both Hyde and Marsh admitted their actions were not based on first-hand knowledge. (*Document Containing the Correspondence, Orders, &C.*, 57–59; see also Esplin, "The Emergence of Brigham Young and the Twelve," 339–43; and Esplin, "Thomas B. Marsh As President of the First Quorum of Twelve, 1835–38," in *Sidney B. Sperry Symposium* [Sandy, Utah: Randall Book, 1984], 167–90.)

  1. 2 Peter 2:22.

tan, untill the day of redemption, that they may be dealt with according to their works, and from henceforth their works shall be made manifest. And now Dear and Wellbeloved Brethren And when we say Brethren, we mean those who have continued faithful in Christ; Men, Women and Children, we feel to exhort you in the name of the Lord Jesus, to be strong in the faith of the new and [p. 107] everlasting covenant, and nothing frighted at your enemies. For what has happened unto us is an evident token to them of damnation, but unto us of Salvation, and that of God. Therefore hold on even unto death, for he that seeks to save his life shall loose it, but he that looseth his life for my sake and the gospel's shall find it, sayeth Jesus Christ.

Brethren from hencforth let truth and righteousness abound in you; and in all things be temperate, abstain from drunkenness, and from swearing, and from all profane language, and from every thing which is unrighteous or unholy, also from enmity and hatred, and covetousness, and from every unholy desire, Be honest one with another, for it seemeth, that some have come short of these things, and some have been uncharitable, and have manifested greediness because of their acts (debts) towards those who have been persecuted and dragged about in chains without cause and imprisoned. Such characters God hates, and shall have their turn of sorrow in the rolling of the great wheel for it rolleth and none can hinder. Zion shall yet live, though she seemeth to be dead. Remember that whatsoever measure you meet out to others, it shall be measured unto you again. We say unto you Brethren be not afraid of your adversaries. Contend earnestly against mobs, and the unlawful works of dissenters and of darkness, and the very God of peace shall be with you, and make a way for your escape from the adversary of your Souls.

We commend you to God, and the word of his grace which is able to make you wise unto Salvation. Amen.

Joseph Smith Jr. [p. 108]

MISSOURI JOURNAL, 1838, SEPTEMBER TO OCTOBER

MS. Joseph Smith Papers, LDS Church Archives, Salt Lake City, Utah.

Editorial Note

This small record, in the handwriting of Joseph Smith's clerk, James Mulholland, can be divided into three parts: The first two pages contain a listing of scriptural references keyed to the 1835 edition of the Doctrine and Covenants, and miscellaneous notes, probably for Mulholland's own use. On pages 3 to 5 is recorded a sketchy journal kept for Joseph Smith by Mulholland from 3 September to 6 October 1838, a period when opposition was mounting against the Latter-day Saints in Caldwell and Daviess Counties, Missouri. After having been previously forced from their lands in Jackson and Clay Counties, by 1838 the Saints had moved northeast to the Counties of Caldwell and Daviess in the hope of establishing a permanent place of gathering. But less than a month after this journal ends, Joseph Smith was in custody, his people had been ordered to leave the state, and the prospects for building Zion in Missouri appeared to have vanished. The remainder of the record—pages 6 to 11—contains a diary of Mulholland's own activities after resumption of his clerical work for Joseph Smith and the Church in Illinois following the Prophet's arrival there from Missouri in April 1839. The Mulholland diary covers the period from 22 April to 20 October 1839, during which the Prophet moved his people from their temporary refuge at Quincy, Adams County, Illinois, to their new place of settlement at Commerce (later named Nauvoo), Hancock County. Although the Mulholland diary is not a record of Joseph Smith's own activity, as is the Missouri journal that precedes it, it is included here to preserve the literary context of the Missouri journal, and because it provides a parallel account of Mulholland's clerical activity for comparison with the journal he kept for the Prophet in Illinois that follows this one.

This record was made by folding six 8 × 10-inch yellow sheets of paper to make a 4 × 10-inch booklet of twenty-four pages. The text is written in brown ink on the first eleven pages; the remainder of the booklet is blank. On the back cover at the top of the page are the words "James Mulholland / M / Joseph Smith / Journal." Below that, in the middle of the page written sideways, is "James Mulholland / for / Joseph Smith / 1838." Opposite page 7, written sideways in the middle of the page, is the notation "Mulholland, James / Journal kept for / Joseph Smith jun. / 1839" in the handwriting of Andrew Jenson, a former assistant Church historian.

Page 175 withdrew my Spirit and I do his will[1]
His word ye shall receive as if from mine own mouth Page 177—[2]
Be patient in afflictions for thou shalt have many. Page 111[3]
according to this pattern 112 page[4]
The Song of the righteous page 179[5]
Thou shalt not command him who is at thy head— page 181[6]
Contrary to church covenants 182[7]
in glory even as I am—page 113[8]
and none else   Do [ditto]—
because of their agency P–115[9]
even that same death Do [ditto] Do[10]
even as many as would believe Do [ditto] Do[11] [front page]
                    [third of page blank]

---

1. See D&C 19:20, 24.
2. D&C 21:5.
3. D&C 24:8.
4. D&C 24:19.
5. D&C 25:12.
6. D&C 28:6.
7. D&C 28:12.
8. D&C 29:12.
9. D&C 29:10.
10. D&C 29:41.
11. D&C 29:43.

Ideas &c &c &c[1]

When Juda[2] is gathered, the Lord will also bring again the assyrian captivity viz: Israel.

The Spirit poured out upon all flesh but your sons & daughters shall prop[h]ecy. Joel[3]

promise, book of Mormon page 541 & 34th[4]

no impostor would attempt to make such–for instance the promise of the Holy Ghost—

Another angel–a falling away come

Saviour did not come untill his time came

so also the book of Mormon

Proof that Gentiles were not the other sheep that is. The Saviour Said I am not sent save to the lost sheep of the house of Israel—

Jealousy of the Chinese, hid up 6 million Children of Israel—

In England 1000 souls in 9 months[5]

Unbelief close the way to knowledge

Ephraimites to be the hunters & fishers —[6]

Testimony of the Spirit will seal the destiny of men—

The difference between Saints & world is that Saints know, the world do not. [*third of page blank*] [p. 2]

Commenced to write for President

---

1. The following brief notes are possibly ideas Mulholland preserved from the teachings of Joseph Smith and other Church leaders.

2. "Juda" written over "Israel" in MS.

3. Joel 2:28.

4. This reference was the subject of a discourse on the Book of Mormon by John E. Page on 7 July 1839. (See p. 322.) Depending upon which edition of the Book of Mormon was being used, page 541 in the 1830 edition corresponds with Ether 2:4–13 in the current edition; page 541 in the 1837 edition, corresponds with 3 Nephi 29:4–30. Both references contain promises.

5. Reference to the beginning of missionary work in Britain by the Latter-day Saints in 1837.

6. See Jeremiah 16:16.

Joseph Smith Junr
on Monday the 3rd September 1838
Memorandum &c &c

3 September 1838 · Monday

At home all or greater part of day[1]

4 September 1838 · Tuesday

Breakfast with him[2] 1/2 past 7 oclock, ~~dined~~ at home for dinner a little before noon, & again in the evening between 5 & 6 oclock.

5 September 1838 · Wednesday

At home[3] for breakfast at ⟨1/2 past 7⟩ also for dinner from 1 to 2 oclock at home in the evening about 6 oclock.

6 September 1838 · Thursday

~~He rode out on Horseback~~ He left home a horseback 1/2 past 7. morning At home again the even[in]g before dark.

7 September 1838 · Friday

Saw him leave home about sun rising and heard, and saw him at home between 10 and 11 oclock same night.

8 September 1838 · Saturday

At home about 8 oclock morn[ing] at home between 2 & 3 oclock Afternoon.

---

1. Mulholland is referring, of course, to Joseph Smith.

A comparison of the journal entries of 3 to 10 September written here by James Mulholland, with overlapping entries of the same date in the previous journal (pp. 282–85) recorded by George W. Robinson, reveals how little detail Mulholland recorded at a crucial time.

2. Third-person references in this and following entries are to Joseph Smith.

3. I.e., Joseph Smith.

No men around from 8th to 14[1]

14 September 1838 · Friday

At home about 3 P.M & all the evening.

15 September 1838 · Saturday

At home early in morning for breakfast & dinner say 9–2 oclock

16 September 1838 · Sunday

At home all day

17 September 1838 · Monday

Saw him early morning again at 9 oclock forenoon also afternoon

18 September 1838 · Tuesday

At home all day & unwell. in better health towards evening. – [p. 3]

19 September 1838 · Wednesday

At home in the morning for breakfast. about 8 oclock. – also for dinner about 1 oclock and in the evening before bed time.

20 September 1838 · Thursday

At home from morning untill about 10 oclock went out on horseback[2] & returned at about sunset or rather before it– at home all evening

---

1. Word had come to Far West that a mob was about to attack the Saints at Adam-ondi-Ahman which may explain the absence of men. (See the entries of 8 and 9 September on pp. 285–87.)

2. I.e., Joseph Smith.

21 September 1838 · Friday

Saw him at home at breakfast

22 September 1838 · Saturday

At home early in the morning & at breakfast about 1/2 past 7 oclock saw him ride out a hors[e]back about 9 oclock.

24 September 1838 · Monday

At home at breakfast and before, saw him ride out a horse-back about 1/2 past 8 oclock morning.
Returned home about 5 oclock evening

25 September 1838 · Tuesday

At home for breakfast about 8 oclock saw him go out a horseback saw him again between 11 & 12 oclock at which he was untill about 1/2 past 5 evening saw him at home in evening about 1/2 past 6.

26 September 1838 · Wednesday

At home morning early also at breakfast between 7 & 8 oclock. Saw him ride out between 10 & eleven oclock and saw him at home again 9 oclock evening

27 September 1838 · Thursday

At home before & at breakfast 8 ocl[oc]k saw him again at 4 oclock in the evening & between 5 and 6 oclock in the City. [p. 4]

28 September 1838 · Friday

At home for breakfast about 8 oclock. Saw him walk out about nine, saw him again between one and two at home all afternoon, saw him ride out about sunset.

29 September 1838 · Saturday

Did not see him untill about 3 oclock afternoon, saw him then come home a horseback. at home all evening.

30 September 1838 · Sunday

At home for breakfast and u[n]till ten oclock, went from home at that time.

1 October 1838 · Monday

Not at home untill about 5 oclock afternoon, at home all the evening.

2 October 1838 · Tuesday

At home for breakfast about 1/2 past 7 oclock saw him again in the ev[en]ing about 1/2 past four oclock, again at supper about 1/2 past 6 oclock[1]

3 October 1838 · Wednesday

At home before and at breakfast also about one oclock afternoon.

4 October 1838 · Thursday

Saw him at home about sunrise, all the forenoon, and at noon. In the evening again about 8 oclock.

5 October 1838 · Friday

Saw him early in the morning say 7 oclock, again about 10 oclock, did not see him all the afternoon, understood that he went from home.[2]

---

1. On this date the Kirtland Camp, consisting of a large body of the Kirtland, Ohio, Saints arrived in the vicinity of Far West and was met by the First Presidency and others, including Joseph Smith, who escorted them into the town.

2. While searching out a townsite in lower Caldwell County on 5 October, Joseph Smith heard that the Mormon settlement at DeWitt, in Carroll County, was under siege by a mob. Traveling there, he confirmed the report and helped evacuate the inhabitants after efforts for their protection had failed. (See *The Papers of Joseph Smith*, 1:213–14; Gentry, "A History of the Latter-day Saints in Northern Missouri," 194–212.)

6 October 1838 · Saturday

[*blank*]

An acct of my labors last fall I have received pay for 2 month[s] at $20 pr — $40.[1] [p. 5]

Contra acct	
April 22nd 1839	$
Laid out for Pen ink & paper —	0.50
May 5th Do [ditto] Do paper —	0.25
14th quills & ink powder —	0.37 1/2
	$1.12 1/2
July 16th To steel pens —	$1.25
Do [ditto] Sand & Caster —	0.75
	0.50

[*half page blank*]

[p. 6]

Commenced again to write for the Church on Monday the 22nd Aprile 1839.[2]

April 22nd	$–0
Received in money from Elder Green[3] —	0.12 1/2
May 4th	
Do [ditto] from Bishop [Vinson] Knights —	0.50
14th	
Do [ditto] from President Smith —	0.50
	$ 1.12 1/2
Do [ditto] from Do [ditto]	75

---

1. These two lines written upside down at the bottom of p. 5 in the MS. In addition to his writing in this journal, James Mulholland did other clerical work for Joseph Smith. See for example the revelation and the lengthy letter of 16 December 1838 copied into the previous journal (see pp. 275–78; 288–300).

2. The following entries are a record of Mulholland's own activities, including his clerical work. See pp. 318ff. for the journal he kept for Joseph Smith that covers the same period. A comparison of the two parallel records adds some clarity to the activities of both men.

3. Probably John P. Greene.

All this time busy for Church

9 May 1839 · Thursday

accompanied President Smith to Commerce Illinois. returned on the 14th[1] and again returned with my wife to Commerce on Sunday evening the 19th.[2]

20 May 1839 · Monday

spent part of the day assisting br [Alanson] Ripley to survey.

21 May 1839 · Tuesday

spent in same manner—

22 May 1839 · Wednesday

⟨sick⟩ Thursday & Friday writing. Saturday at council
Committee &c Cr. on account of late services
By Sundries as per account— $ 5.64 ⟨Cts⟩

27 May 1839 · Monday

writing all day for Church[3]

28 May 1839 · Tuesday

writing &c about 3/4 of the time

---

1. "14th" written over "15th" in MS.
2. This sentence refers to Mulholland's returning to Quincy on the 14th and
back to Commerce on the 19th. Joseph Smith evidently remained in Commerce
after arriving there on the 10th, because Wilford Woodruff visited him and his
family in Commerce on the 18th. (Diary of Wilford Woodruff, 18 May 1839;
see also the entry in the next journal for 10 May 1839.)
3. Mulholland's writing for the Church in the Nauvoo period includes the
entire extant text of the draft and fifty-nine pages of the final manuscript of the
History of the Church, volume A-1 (see *Papers of Joseph Smith* 1:230–31; 265,
267, 324.), and seventy-three pages of the Joseph Smith's 1838–43 letterbook.
His clerical tenure ended with his death on 3 November 1839.

29 May 1839 · Wednesday

Do [ditto] about 1/3 of the day, rest unwell

30 May 1839 · Thursday

writing and examining papers &c. Six oclock evening commenced to work on Lot
30th received of Br [Vinson] Knights on acct $ 1.00 cts
Friday & Saturday writing—

3, 4 June 1839 · Monday, Tuesday

writing for Church

5, 6 June 1839 · Wednesday, Thursday

writing & working for myself

7, 8 June 1839 · Friday, Saturday

for Church

10–13 June 1839 · Monday–Thursday

⟨writing &c for Church history⟩ 13th received cash $ 10.00

14, 15 June 1839 · Friday, Saturday

for Church

16 June 1839 · Sunday

at meeting, Br Bosiers [Squire Bosier] [p. 7]

17, 18 June 1839 · Monday, Tuesday

writing history,

19 June 1839 · Wednesday

forenoon unwell, afternoon writing history—

20 June 1839 · Thursday

forenoon studying ⟨for⟩ history— afternoon unwell,

21 June 1839 · Friday

unwell.

22 June 1839 · Saturday

copying in Letter book

23 June 1839 · Sunday

at home

24 June 1839 · Monday

all this week Copying letters &c &c

30 June 1839 · Sunday

at home

1 July 1839 · Monday

writing letters &c

2 July 1839 · Tuesday

to myself across the river

3 July 1839 · Wednesday

forenoon to myself Afternoon writing history—

4–6 July 1839 · Thursday–Saturday

forenoon writing for the Church Afternoon to myself

7 July 1839 · Sunday

at Meeting

8 July 1839 · Monday

forenoon writing afternoon unwell

9, 10 July 1839 · Tuesday, Wednesday

writing

11 July 1839 · Thursday

went to Quincy received on acct cash of Mr S. $ 3.00

16, 17 July 1839 · Tuesday, Wednesday

Left Quincy on Tuesday 16th and arrived home at Commerce on Wednesday noon.

18 July 1839 · Thursday

–moved to Brother [Theodore] Turleys

19, 20 July 1839 · Friday, Saturday

unwell

21 July 1839 · Sunday

at home rather unwell ⟨end of first Quarter⟩

22 July 1839 · Monday

commenced again to write

23, 24 July 1839 · Tuesday, Wednesday

writing

25 July 1839 · Thursday

Idle from the extreme heat, and sultriness. [p. 8]

26 July 1839 · Friday

writing & recording history.

27 July 1839 · Saturday

for myself—

28 July 1839 · Sunday

at meeting home &c

29 July 1839 · Monday

and all the week working and writing for myself.
Received cash $ 20.00
Pantaloons—
Paper at sundries white & blue 2 quire, sewing silk— 12 1/2
Potatoes 1/2 bushel 25

4 August 1839 · Sunday

at meeting &c

5 August 1839 · Monday

and all the week writing & working for myself

11 August 1839 · Sunday

at meeting also

12 August 1839 · Monday

& all the week for myself

18 August 1839 · Sunday

at meeting also

19 August 1839 · Monday

and all the week at home attending my wife who was sick

25 August 1839 · Sunday

and all the week at home my wife still sick

31 August 1839 · Saturday

recd 1 Box pills— $ 1.50

1 September 1839 · Sunday

and all the week at home, wife recovering: —27 lb pork at
9 cts—$ 2.16
1/2 bushel corn— 0.25

8 September 1839 · Sunday

at home wife much better

9–13 September 1839 · Monday–Friday

writing &c &c for Church [p. 9]
Friday received cash. of J. S. [Joseph Smith] $ 1.00

14 September 1839 · Saturday

at home—

15 September 1839 · Sunday

at home

16 September 1839 · Monday

at home
4 3/4 lb hogs lard at [*blank*] pr lb

17, 18 September 1839 · Tuesday, Wednesday

writing

19 September 1839 · Thursday

doing business for T[heodore] Turley received 12 lb pork at [*blank*] cts per
ferriage across river— 0.25

20, 21 September 1839 · Friday, Saturday

writing

22 September 1839 · Sunday

at meeting with wife
Flour per br Markam [Stephen Markham] 41 lb at 3.50 per hundred— $ 1.43 1/2
All this week writing &c for J. S Jr

29 September 1839 · Sunday

at meeting at br J's [Joseph Smith's]

30 September, 1 October 1839 · Monday, Tuesday

writing &c

2 October 1839 · Wednesday

forenoon at home afternoon writing

3 October 1839 · Thursday

Forenoon writing
recieved 12 lb meat at [*blank*] per
Do [ditto] 1/2 bushel corn .25
house logs pr J Holman 30.0

4 October 1839 · Friday

3 hours work of 2 men

5 October 1839 · Saturday

unwell

6 October 1839 · Sunday

unwell

7 October 1839 · Monday

Ditto —

8 October 1839 · Tuesday

forenoon writing afternoon writing also —

9–12 October 1839 · Wednesday–Saturday

Do [ditto] Do
1 Bowl full of Honey— First payment on lot— $ 30.00

13 October 1839 · Sunday

at meeting in grove

14 October 1839 · Monday

and all the week writing &c [p. 10]
recieved 10 lb beef at 4 1/2 per lb $ 00.45
1/2 bushel corn

20 October 1839 · Sunday

at meeting in the evening

21–23 October 1839 · Monday–Wednesday

about half time unwell [p. 11]

ILLINOIS JOURNAL, 1839

MS. Joseph Smith Papers, LDS Church Archives, Salt Lake City, Utah.

Editorial Note

This journal covers the period from 16 April to 15 October 1839, beginning with the arrival of Joseph Smith at Quincy, Illinois, after five months of imprisonment in Missouri. It reports the Prophet's removal to Commerce, Illinois, in May and the beginnings of Mormon settlement there. The journal is in the handwriting of James Mulholland, who had been engaged in clerical work for Joseph Smith during the previous autumn. The journal is a record of Mulholland's observations of the Prophet intermixed with his own activity, and a few entries possibly dictated by the Prophet. Mulholland's use of first person, sometimes referring to himself and sometimes to Joseph Smith, requires careful reading to avoid confusion.

The journal was fashioned by folding eight 8 × 10-inch sheets of white paper in half to form a booklet of thirty-two pages handstitched along the fold. The text of the journal, in brown ink, is in the handwriting of James Mulholland on the first fifteen pages; the remaining seventeen are blank. The cover was made by folding a 10 × 16-inch sheet of heavy blue paper in half. The front cover has the words "Minute Book, 1839, J. Smiths Journal, Escape from Prison" in four lines written in black ink by James Mulholland. On the back cover written sideways near the top in two lines are the words "Joseph Smith's Journal Escape from Prison 1839" in black ink.

Minute Book.

1839

J. Smiths Journal

Escape from Prison [*Front Cover*]

1839

Escaped Aprile 16th[1]

22 April 1839 · Monday

President Smith and his fellow prisoners, arrived safe at Quincy Ill.[2] on ~~Tuesday~~ ⟨Monday⟩ the 22nd of April and spent all next day [Apr. 23] greeting and receiving visits from his brethren and friends—

24 April 1839 · Wednesday

In the evening of the 24th met in council with the Church[3]— when a committee was appointed to go to Ioway &c. of which he was one. Went to Ioway made purchases & returned on friday the 3rd May—[4]

---

1. While being taken under guard from Gallatin, Daviess County, to Columbia, Boone County, Missouri, in compliance with a change of venue in their case, Joseph Smith, Hyrum Smith, Alexander McRae, Lyman Wight, and Caleb Baldwin were allowed by their captors to escape near Yellow Creek in Chariton County. For more detail see Jessee, " 'Walls, Grates and Screeking Iron Doors': The Prison Experience of Mormon Leaders in Missouri, 1838–1839," in *New Views of Mormon History*, Davis Bitton and Maureen U. Beecher, eds. (Salt Lake City: University of Utah Press, 1987):19–42. *History of the Church*, 3:319–20 indicates the escape took place on 15 April.

2. Upon their expulsion from Missouri the Latter-day Saints received a friendly and sympathetic reception from the citizens of Quincy, Illinois, during the winter and spring of 1838–39. Through meetings and committees, the people of Quincy provided the necessities of life until the Saints were able to establish themselves more permanently at Commerce (later Nauvoo), Hancock County, Illinois.

3. Minutes of the meeting are recorded in Joseph Smith Letter Book, 2:139–40, and published in *History of the Church*, 3:335–36.)

4. The committee organized to "visit Iowa Territory immediately, for the purpose of making a location for the Church" was comprised of Joseph Smith, Newel Knight, and Alanson Ripley. The initial acquisition of land in the area later known as Nauvoo occurred on 30 April and consisted of 123 acres purchased from Hugh White and 47 acres from Isaac Galland. (*History of the Church*, 3:342; David E. Miller and Della S. Miller, *Nauvoo: The City of Joseph* [Santa Barbara and Salt Lake City: Peregrine Smith, Inc., 1974], 27.)

4 May 1839 · Saturday

presided at general Conference near Quincy Ill.[1]

5 May 1839 · Sunday

Do [ditto] continued.

6 May 1839 · Monday

met in Council with the twelve [an]d others Quincy Ill—

7 May 1839 · Tuesday

Do [ditto]— Do Do

10 May 1839 · Friday

Moved with his family To Commerce Hancock Co. Ill.[2]

13 May 1839 · Monday

Transacted various business with Br [Oliver] Granger &c[3] at home attending to general business—

---

1. Wilford Woodruff noted that the conference was held at the Presbyterian camp ground two miles north of Quincy. (Diary of Wilford Woodruff, 4 May 1839. Minutes of the conference are recorded in Joseph Smith Letter Book, 2:140–44 and published in *History of the Church*, 3:344–47.)

2. Commerce (later named Nauvoo), Hancock County, Illinois, was situated on a large bend in the Mississippi River 53 miles north of Quincy. The area was the site of a Sac and Fox Indian village in 1824 when obtained by Captain James White, a native of Ohio. In 1834 the town of Commerce was laid out, and in 1839, Hugh White, the son of James, sold the first land purchased by the Latter-day Saints in the area. When Joseph Smith arrived on 10 May, he settled in a log house on the bank of the river about a mile south of Commerce. According to the Prophet's History, when he arrived "there were one stone house, three frame houses, and two block houses, which constituted the whole city of Commerce." (Jenson, *Encyclopedic History*, 560–62; Robert Flanders, *Nauvoo: Kingdom on the Mississippi* [Urbana, Illinois: University of Illinois Press, 1965], 39–41; *History of the Church*, 3:375.)

3. At the conference held in Quincy, Illinois, on 4 May 1839, Oliver Granger had been appointed to oversee the affairs of the Church in Kirtland, Ohio. On 13 May the First Presidency wrote a letter of attorney declaring that Granger had been appointed to "engage in vast and important concerns as an agent for the Church." (*History of the Church*, 3:350–51.)

14 May 1839 · Tuesday

Do [ditto] ~~Wednesday~~, Do On the 14 I returned to Quincy so kept no ~~record~~ ⟨Minute⟩ of course, I got back here Sunday evening the 19th May.[1] [p. 1]

20 May 1839 · Monday

this week at home and employed dictating letters and attending to the various business of the Church[2]

25 May 1839 · Saturday

met in Conference with the twelve, and others of the Church Wm Smith['s] case disposed of—[3]

26 May 1839 · Sunday

at home, Elder O. Pratt & John Taylor preached—

27 May 1839 · Monday

and beginning of the week at home, latter part of week he, (President Smith) went to Quincy with others of the Presidency and returned on Wednesday 5th June ~~Spent greater part of latter part study and~~ Latter part at home

---

1. The reference here is to Mulholland (who is writing the journal for Joseph Smith) traveling to Quincy, not Joseph Smith. Wilford Woodruff wrote that he visited the Prophet in Commerce on the 18th. (Diary of Wilford Woodruff, 18 May 1839.)

2. Wilford Woodruff moved his family from Quincy, Illinois, to Montrose, Iowa, on 18 May. On the 21st he wrote of riding through the area for several miles around Montrose with the First Presidency, including Joseph Smith and three of the Twelve, and that Joseph's horse ran with him at great speed before he stopped it. (Diary of Wilford Woodruff, 18, 21 May 1839.)

3. Because of vindictive statements he made against his brother Joseph in Missouri, William Smith had been suspended from Church fellowship. Wilford Woodruff noted on the 25th that the Twelve spent the day receiving counsel from Joseph Smith and that William Smith was restored to the Quorum of Twelve. (Woodruff Diary, 25 May 1839.)

9 June 1839 · Sunday

at meeting with wife and family at Brother Bosiers [Squire Bosier] — Elder [John E.] Page pr[each]ed —

10 June 1839 · Monday

began to study & prepare to dictate history — [1] ⟨Elder Page baptized one woman⟩

11 June 1839 · Tuesday

Commenced to dictate and I to write history — [2]

12–14 June 1839 · Wednesday–Friday

Generally so employed[3]

15 June 1839 · Saturday

left home with his family on a visit[4] [p. 2]

16 June 1839 · Sunday

Meeting held br [Squire] Bosiers Brs Rose[5] and [Theodore] Turley presiding I was present and considered that Br Rose ⟨spoke⟩ not ⟨in⟩ acco[r]dance with the doctrines of the Church, nor with the Spirit of God Others thought so too — [6]

---

1. This marks the resumption of work on the History of the Church. (See the Joseph Smith Journal entries of 30 April to 4 May 1838 for the beginning of that work.)

2. Surviving pages of a draft of the beginning manuscript pages of the History of the Church is in the handwriting of James Mulholland, as is the first 59 pages of the finished MS., book A-1. See *The Papers of Joseph Smith* 1: 230–31; 265–67.

3. I.e., working on the history.

4. The Prophet visited his brothers William at Plymouth, Hancock County, and Don Carlos, near Macomb in McDonough County, Illinois.

5. Possibly Joseph Rose.

6. Here it is Mulholland who attends the meeting; Joseph was still visiting his family in Macomb.

President Rigdon preached at Montrose—[1]
Bishop [Newel] Whitney arrived here—

17 June 1839 · Monday

Bishop [Vinson] Knight arrived returned to Quincy on [*blank*][2]

18 June 1839 · Tuesday

Br Rose baptised one man named [*blank*] at P[re]st Rigdon's place

15 June 1839 · Saturday

Started on Saturday morning ⟨15th June⟩ with my family— on a visit to Br Carlos met Br Wm on the prairie, found him in good spirits—went with him to his house ⟨in Plymouth–C.⟩, found his family all well Staid over night, and had a very satisfactory visit. Next day went on to Br Don C[arlos] Smiths, McDonough Co. near ⟨the village of⟩ McComb. Staid there untill Monday, and there met with br Sam[ue]l Smith, who I had not before seen since our deliverance from prison.

18 June 1839 · Tuesday

went to the house of a man by the name of Mathews,[3] during the [p. 3] evening the neighbors came in, and I gave them a short discourse,

---

1. Montrose, Iowa, was the site of a U.S. military garrison established in 1834, located in Lee County, Iowa, across the river west of Commerce (Nauvoo), Illinois. At the time of the Mormon exodus from Missouri, a number of Saints found temporary shelter in the deserted military barracks at Montrose, and soon after, substantial land was purchased in the area. Wilford Woodruff, one of the occupants, described the population of the place in May 1839 as consisting of half Mormons and half non-Mormons, including a lawless element. (Jenson, *Encyclopedic History*, 530; Diary of Wilford Woodruff, 20 May 1839.)

2. *History of the Church*, 3:378, indicates Knight returned the same day.

3. Possibly Anson Mathews (1787–1870).

20 June 1839 · Thursday

Thursday following went to Elder Zebedee Coulters [Coltrin's], from there were invited to visit a brother [at] br Vance's[1] place which wee did and there gave to the brethren and friends of the Neighborhood, a brief history or account of the coming forth of the Book of Mormon,

22 June 1839 · Saturday

We returned to Don C[arlos]'s place, and on Sunday [June 23] went to Br Wilcox's[2] and there preached to a very crowded congregation and so eager were they to hear that a part of them stood out in the rain during the sermon, and ⟨in⟩ general they all expressed good satisfaction as to what they had heard.

24 June 1839 · Monday

Started for home and got as far as Br Parkins [Ute Perkins], near Fountain Green, Hancock Co—when they insisted that we should tarry, and on Tuesday [June 25] we held meeting, and spoke with considerable liberty to a large congregation,

26 June 1839 · Wednesday

Arrived all safe & sound, at home, Commerce Ill.,

27 June 1839 · Thursday

Attended a conference [p. 4] of the Twelve[3]—at which time Br Orson Hyde, made his confession and was restored to the

---

1. Possibly John Vance (1794–1882).
2. Possibly Benjamin Wilcox.
3. Joseph Smith's reunion with the Quorum of Twelve following his Missouri imprisonment became a watershed of instruction to prepare them for their first mission abroad and a more exalted leadership role in the Church. At the meeting on the 27th Wilford Woodruff wrote of "the vast number of the keys of the Kingdom" presented to them that day. (Diary of Wilford Woodruff, 27 June 1839; see also Willard Richards's Pocket Companion, same date. On the relationship between Joseph Smith and the Twelve at this time see Ronald K. Esplin, "The Emergence of Brigham Young and the Twelve to Mormon Leadership," 1830–1841, chapter 9.)

Priesthood again,[1]

28 June 1839 · Friday

transacting business of various kinds, Counseling the brethren &c &c —

29 June 1839 · Saturday

At home principally

30 June 1839 · Sunday

at meeting at Br [Squire] Bosiers Bore testimony to a crowded audience concerning the truth of this work & also of the truth of the Book of Mormon &c. &c.

1 July 1839 · Monday

Spent the day principally counseling with the Brethren —

2 July 1839 · Tuesday

Spent this day on the Iowa side of the river Forenoon went in company with Elders [Sidney] Rigdon & H[yrum] Smith, Bishops [Newel K.] Whitney & [Vinson] Knights and others to visit a purchase lately made by brother Knights as a location for a town,

Advised that a town be built there,[2]

---

1. Orson Hyde's departure from the Church and testimony against the Saints the previous year had been a factor in the arrest and imprisonment of LDS Church leaders in Missouri. Upon Hyde's return, Woodruff wrote of him, "a more humble and penitant man I never saw." (Diary of Wilford Woodruff, 25 June 1839. For details on Hyde's disaffection see Esplin, "The Emergence of Brigham Young and the Twelve," 341–42, 399.)

2. In June 1839 the Church, through Bishop Vinson Knight, had bought a large tract of land west of Montrose in Lee County, Iowa. The proposed settlement was named Zarahemla and was intended to eventually embrace Montrose and become a sister city to Nauvoo across the river. In 1841, 326 church members were reported at Zarahemla, but the town did not prosper. (Jenson, *Encyclopedic History*, 971–72.)

Afternoon, met with the twelve & some of the Seventies who are about to proceed on their mission to Europe the nations of the earth, and the Islands of the sea.[1] The meeting was [p. 5] opened by singing and prayer after which The Presidency proceeded to bless two of the Twelve, who had lately been ordained into that quorum viz: Wilford Woodruff & George ⟨A⟩ Smith & one of the Seventies viz Theodore Turley after which a̶ blessings were also pronounced by them on the heads of the wives of ⟨some of⟩ those about to ⟨go⟩ abroad. The meeting was then addressed by President Hyrum Smith, by way of advice to the Twelve &c &c chiefly concerning the nature of their mission, their practicing prudence & ~~charity tow~~ humility in their plans ⟨or subjects⟩ for preaching, the necessity of their not trifling with their office, and of holding on strictly to the importance of their mission & the authority of the priesthood. — I— (President Joseph Smith Jr) then addressed them, and gave much instruction calculated to guard them against self sufficiency, self-righteousness & self importance, touching upon many subjects of importance & value to all who wish to walk humbly before the Lord, but especial[l]y teaching them [p. 6] to observe charity wisdom, & fellow feeling with love, one towards another in all things & under all circumstances.[2]

3 July 1839 · Wednesday

Baptized Dr Isaac Galland & confirmed him by the water edge–about two hours afterwards, ordained him to the office of an elder.

---

1. The Twelve were about to depart for England on their first mission abroad in response to the July 1838 revelation that had directed them "to go over the great waters, and there promulgate my gospel." (D&C 118:4; on the significance of the mission see Esplin, "The Emergence of Brigham Young and the Twelve to Mormon Leadership," chapter 10.)

2. Wilford Woodruff gives a more extensive report. (Diary of Wilford Woodruff, 2 July 1839; see also Willard Richards's Pocket Companion, same date.)

Afternoon dictating History—

4, 5 July 1839 · Thursday, Friday

(assisted by Br Newel Knight) dictating History

6 July 1839 · Saturday

also at home Studying Church records &c &c

7 July 1839 · Sunday

Meeting held in the open air as a large assemblage was expected to ~~witness~~ ⟨lis[ten] to⟩ the farewell addresses of the 12 who were then about to take their departure on this most important mission, viz to the nations of the earth, and the Islands of the sea Elder John E. Page, being the first of the 12 present, opened the meeting by addressing a few words ⟨of gen[eral]⟩ introductory nature after which singing and prayer were observed, when Elder Page, delivered a very interesting discourse on the subject of the Book of Mormon recapitulating in short terms the subjects of a former discourse on the same subject [p. 6][1] and afterwards proceeded to read portions from the Bible and Book of Mormon concerning the best criterions whereby to judge of its authenticity. And then went on to show that no impostor would ever attempt to make such promises as are contained [on] pages 541 and 34th[2] — which he did in a very satisfactory manner. ⟨& then bore testimony⟩ ~~after which the meeting adjourned for~~ one
hour, — Afternoon —
The meeting was again opened by prayer &c Elder John Taylor spoke on the subject of this dispensation— The other angel which John saw— having the everlasting gospel to preach

1. Two pages are inadvertently numbered "6" in the MS.
2. The reference corresponds to 3 Nephi 30:2 if Page was using the 1837 edition of the Book of Mormon.

&c &¹ ⟨he then bore testimony of the truth of the Book of Mormon &c &c⟩

Elder Woodruffs address went chiefly to exhortation to the Saints to perseverance after which he bore his testimony also. Elder Orson Hyde next came forward and having alluded to his own late fall, exhorted all to perseverance in the things of God, expressed himself one with his brethren and bore testimony to his knowledge of the truth and the misery of falling from it.

Elder Brigham Young made some very appropriate remarks, and also bore testimony to the truth of these [p. 7] things, and gave an invitation to come forward and be baptised when three manifested their determination to renounce the world, and take upon themselves the name of Jesus Christ.

One brother was then confirmed after which President S. Rigdon addressed the meeting in a very feeling manner, showing that it must be no small matter which ⟨could⟩ induce men to leave their families and their homes to travel over all the earth, amidst persecutions and trials such as always followed the preaching of this gospel; he then addressed himself to the twelve and gave them some cou[n]sel and consolation—as far as in his power. after which I (JS.) requested their prayers & promised to pray for them &c &c²

The meeting was large & respectable a large number were present who did not belong to our Church The most perfect order prevailed throughout. The meeting dismissed about 1/2 past five oclock, when we repaired to the water and the three candidates were baptised & confirmed. [p. 8]

---

1. See Revelation 14:6.

2. Wilford Woodruff reported Joseph's brief remarks in his journal: "Joseph addressed us in few words & says remember brethren that if you are imprisiond Brother Joseph has been imprisiond before you. if you are placed whare you can ownly see your Brethren through the grates of a window while in Irons because of the gospel of Jesus Christ remember Brother Joseph has been in like circumstances." (Diary of Wilford Woodruff, 7 July 1839.)

8–10 July 1839 · Monday–Wednesday

Selecting Hymns, with the 12[1]
About this time sickness began to manifest itself much amongst the brethren as well as among the inhabitants of the place, so that this week and next was generally spent in visiting the sick, and ministering unto them, some had faith enough and were healed, others had not,[2]

21 July 1839 · Sunday

no meeting on account of much rain, and much sickness. however, many of the sick were ⟨on⟩ this day, raised up by the powe[r] of God, through the instrumentality of the Elders of Israel ministering to them in the name of Jesus Christ

22, 23 July 1839 · Monday, Tuesday

⟨also⟩ the sick were ministered unto, with great success but many still remain sick & new cases occurring daily.

---

1. Wilford Woodruff noted that he "spent the day in Commerce with Joseph & some of the Twelve in aranging a selection of Hymns for the Church." (Diary of Wilford Woodruff, 10 July 1839.) This selection of hymns was taken by Brigham Young and others of the Twelve when they left for England later in the year, with the intent of publishing them there. However, on 27 October 1839, the Nauvoo high council voted that "Emma Smith select and publish a hymn-book for the use of the Church, and that Brigham Young be informed of this action and he not publish the hymns taken by him from Commerce." (*History of the Church*, 4:17–18.) And yet some of the hymns selected in July 1839 may have found their way into the publication the following year in England of *A Collection of Sacred Hymns for the Church of Jesus Christ of Latter-day Saints* by Brigham Young, Parley P. Pratt, and John Taylor.
2. The illness was due to the malaria that infested the swamp lands upon which Nauvoo was partially built. In his autobiography Wilford Woodruff wrote that large numbers of Latter-day Saints driven from Missouri "were flocking into Commerce; but had no homes to go into, and were living in wagons, in tents, and on the ground. Many therefore, were sick through the exposure they were subjected to. Brother Joseph had waited on the sick, until he was worn out and nearly sick himself." Woodruff noted that on 22 July, the Prophet, after reflecting upon the situation of the Saints and praying, the power of God "rested upon him mightily," and he went forth and healed many of the sick on both sides of the river. (See Woodruff, *Leaves From My Journal*, 62–65.)

28 July 1839 · Sunday

meeting held as usual B[r.] P[arley]. P. Pratt, preached,[1] on the gathering of Israel, and in the ~~evening~~ afternoon Orson Pratt addressed the Church, on the necessity of keeping the commandments of God. [p. 9] After which I spoke & admonished the Church individually to set his house in order, to make clean the insid[e of] the platter, and to meet on the next sabbath to partake of sacrament in order that by our obedience to the ordinances, we might be enabled to prevail with God against the destroyer, and that the sick may be healed. —

All this week chiefly spent among the sick, who in general are gaining strength, and recovering health

4 August 1839 · Sunday

Church came together for prayer meeting and sacrament. Exhorted the Church at length concerning the necessity of being righteous and clean at heart before the Lord, many others also spoke, especially some of the twelve who were present, professed their willingness to proceed on their mission to Europe, without either purse or Scrip &c &c &c

the sacrament was administered a spirit of humility and harmony prevailed, and the church passed a resolution that the 12 proceed as soon as possible and that they would provide for their families— [p. 10]

11 August 1839 · Sunday

At meeting forenoon
A Sermon by P. P. Pratt. Afternoon 1 baptized and 4 confirmed viz Br [Davidson] Hibbard his wife & little son & daughter. ⟨& sacrament administered⟩

---

1. Parley Pratt had arrived in Commerce on 19 July after eight months imprisonment in Missouri. On Pratt's imprisonment and escape see his *Autobiography*, 209–80.

This week chiefly spent visiting the sick, sickness much decreased —

News from Kirtland By D[imick]. Huntington [*blank space*]

18 August 1839 · Sunday

not at meeting Self and wife rode out— forenoon
Sermon by Orson Pratt on the order & plan of creation 3 baptized
Afternoon three confirmed and one ordained an Elder
This week chiefly spent among the sick also,
New purchase made[1]

25 August 1839 · Sunday

at meeting Sickness decreasing

1 September 1839 · Sunday

at meeting also, Spoke concerning some errors [p. 11] in br P. P. Pratts works[2] &c &c &c This week sickness much decreased

8 September 1839 · Sunday

[*blank*]

9 September 1839 · Monday

& greater part of week visiting the sick and attending to business of the new town &c &c

---

1. Reference is to the purchase of 80 acres in Nauvoo known as the William White purchase, north of the land obtained from Hugh White.

2. Possible reference to Parley Pratt's *A Voice of Warning*, published in 1837, and his *Mormonism Unveiled*, printed in 1838, both of which contained ideas corrected by Joseph Smith.

13 September 1839 · Friday

at noon left home for Brother Wm Smiths place[1] returned home Saturday evening

15 September 1839 · Sunday

Visiting the sick

16 September 1839 · Monday

~~and greater part of the went to Burlington and returned~~ and greater part of the week arranging business of town lots &c

18 September 1839 · Wednesday

went to Burling[ton], I[owa] T[erritory] and returned on Thursday evening

20, 21 September 1839 · Friday, Saturday

at home

22 September 1839 · Sunday

attended & presided at meeting–Spoke concerning the ⟨other⟩ Comforter[2] &c &c &c
This week transacting various business at home greater part of time except when visiting the sick, all in general ~~except~~ recovering but some very slowly—

29 September 1839 · Sunday

Meeting at own house After others had spoken, spoke and explained concerning uselessness of preaching [p. 12] to the world about great judgements but rather to preach the simple

---

1. At Plymouth, Hancock County, Illinois.
2. See John 14.

gospel–Explained concerning the coming of the Son of Man &c that all will be raised to meet him but the righteous will remain with him in the cloud whilst all the proud and all that do wickedly will have to return to the earth and suffer his vengeance which he will take upon them this is the second death &c &c

Also that it is a false idea that the saints will escape all the judgements whilst the wicked suffer–for all flesh is subject to suffer–and "the righteous shall hardly escape" still many of the saints will escape–for the just shall live by faith–yet many of the righteous shall fall a prey to disease to pestilence &c by reason of the weakness of the flesh and yet be saved in the kingdom of God So that it is an unhallowed principle to say that such and such have transgressed because they have been preyed upon by disease or death for all flesh is subject to death and the Saviour has said, "Judge not lest ye be judged".

All the fore part of this week at home and preparing for conference

3 October 1839 · Thursday

met in council and on

5 October 1839 · Saturday

met in general conference which continued Saturday and Sunday–the assemblage [p. 13] was very large–a great deal of business was transacted, and great instruction given

See Conference Minutes — [1]

Week beginning Sunday 6th october After Conference busied in attending to general affairs of the Church–principally about home

---

1. Minutes of the conference were recorded in Joseph Smith Letter Book 2, 164–67, 197–200, and are published in *History of the Church*, 4:12–14.

13 October 1839 · Sunday

at meeting in the Grove[1] meeting small on account of cold weather—

15 October 1839 · Tuesday

Afternoon went to Quincy in company with Br Hiram [Hyrum Smith] J[ohn].S. Fulmer and Bishop [Vinson] Knight– Quite a number of families moving in— [p. 15]

---

1. An outdoor meeting place on the hill near the temple.

ILLINOIS JOURNAL, 1841–1842

MS. *Archives of the First Presidency, LDS Church, Salt Lake City, Utah.*

Editorial Note

This journal primarily chronicles Joseph Smith's experience during 1842, a year marked by important developments in his own life, in the Church, and within the community at Nauvoo. It was the year he was elected mayor of the city; established the Female Relief Society; introduced the temple endowment; was arrested for alleged complicity in the shooting of the ex-governor of Missouri, Lilburn Boggs; became the object of bitter attack from former associate and confidant John C. Bennett; commenced publication of the book of Abraham; and, in addition, actively directed most Church and Nauvoo affairs.

The gap of more than two years that separates the previous journal from this one was due to circumstances, according to the History, that prevented Joseph Smith from "handing down to posterity a connected memorandum of events." (*History of the Church*, 4:470.) Less than three weeks after the conclusion of the 1839 journal, his clerk, James Mulholland, a young man of thirty-five, suddenly died while the Prophet was en route to Washington, D.C., to seek redress from the federal government for Missouri losses of his people. After his return to Nauvoo in March 1840, the Prophet lamented that he had depended upon Robert Foster, a recent convert, who had accompanied him to Washington, D.C., to keep his journal for him during the trip: "but he has failed me." (*History of the Church*, 4:89.) Later that year, Robert B. Thompson, who had written for the Quincy *Argus* and had been employed as a clerk at the Quincy courthouse, was appointed general Church clerk to succeed George W. Robinson. In February 1841 Thompson was also named Nauvoo city recorder. Thompson did substantial writing for Joseph Smith in the Prophet's correspondence and history but died of tuberculosis on 27 August 1841 at age thirty. (*History of the Church*, 4:411.) It was not until after Willard Richards was appointed Joseph Smith's personal secretary in December 1841 that the Prophet succeeded in renewing work on his journal.

Richards's work on the journal commenced on 13 December 1841 and continued until the Prophet's death on 27 June 1844, with the exception of about six months when Richards was absent from Nauvoo. During that time William Clayton and two others, as yet unidentified, took his place. Written at the request of Joseph Smith, the journal contains copies of letters and other documents as well as reports of speeches in addition to its account of daily activity. Although some journal entries are in first person, it is doubtful any of it was actually dictated by Joseph Smith.

The journal is written in a large leather-bound book measuring 11 5/8 × 17 inches, containing 477 pages. Besides the journal, the book contains copies of revelations and a record of donations for the building of the temple at Nauvoo, Illinois. The first three leaves of the book are blank; the fourth contains the title "The Book of the Law of the Lord" in very ornate hand lettering in black ink. Pages 3–25 contain copies of Doctrine and Covenants revelations. The journal begins on page 26 and ends on page 215 but is interspersed with pages that contain lists of donations which then continue unbroken from page 216 to the end of the volume. The front and back covers are unmarked, but the spine of the book is labeled "Law of the Lord."

/¹13 December 1841 · Monday

A conference was held at Ramus² on the 4 & 5th of December 1841, over which the patriarch of the church, Hyram Smith Presided, and Joseph Johnson acted as clerk; Brigham Young. Heber C. Kimball, Willard Richards & John Taylor of

---

1. Handwriting of Willard Richards in MS.
2. Ramus, Hancock County, Illinois, located 22 miles southeast of Nauvoo, was settled by Latter-day Saints arriving in Illinois from their Missouri expulsion in 1839. By July 1840 the Saints in the area numbered about 110 living on 5,200 acres of land. The population eventually increased to around 500. The place was platted for the Church by William Wightman in August 1840 and was incorporated as a town by the state legislature in 1843. Ramus was later known as Macedonia, and, after the Saints left Illinois in 1846, was renamed Webster. (Jensen, *Encyclopedic History*, 690–91; Flanders, *Nauvoo: Kingdom on the Mississippi*, 138–39.)

the Quorum of the twelve being present, when it was unanimously Resolved by the whole conference that the organization of the Church at Ramus as a stake be discontinued, & that John Lawson be presiding Elder over the Branch, & Joseph Johnson Clerk; And that William Whiteman [Wightman], The Bishop, transfer all the Church property in Ramus to the Sole trustee in trust Joseph Smith, President of the whole church.[1]

This day Joseph the Seer, and President of the church, appointed Willard Richards. Recorder. for the Temple,[2] and the scribe for the private office of the President. Just opened in the upper story of the New Store,[3] and the recorder entered

---

1. Joseph Smith's involvement in buying and selling land, so prevalent in his Nauvoo journals, was due to his position as treasurer and Trustee-in-Trust for the Church. On 20 October 1839 the Nauvoo High Council had named the Prophet as treasurer of the Church, with power to buy and sell land. James Mulholland was appointed sub-treasurer to serve as clerk for recording land contracts. However, in June 1840 the Prophet memorialized the High Council to relieve his involvement "in the temporalities of the Church" and appoint someone "to take charge of the city plot, and attend to the business transactions" so that he could devote himself "exclusively to those things which relate to the spiritualities of the Church." Although the council appointed Henry G. Sherwood (Mulholland had died in the meantime) to take charge of the city plot and act as clerk, they knew of no way to relieve the Prophet of his responsibility and requested him to continue as treasurer. On 24 January 1841 Joseph Smith was elected sole Trustee-in-Trust for the Church with power "to receive, acquire, manage or convey property, real, personal, or mixed, for the sole use and benefit of said Church," in compliance with Illinois law governing business transactions of religious corporations. (*History of the Church*, 4:16–17, 136–37, 141, 144, 286–87; and Flanders, *Nauvoo: Kingdom on the Mississippi*, 119–27.)
2. The Nauvoo temple was built on an eminence overlooking the Mississippi River in response to a revelation of 19 January 1841 (D&C 124). The cornerstones were laid on 6 April 1841. Built at an approximate cost of one million dollars, the grey sandstone structure measured 128 by 88 feet, with walls 65 feet high and a 165-foot tower. The temple was finished and dedicated in April 1846 as the Latter-day Saints were beginning to leave Nauvoo for the West. A fire partially destroyed the building on 9 October 1848, and the remaining structure was demolished by a tornado on 25 May 1850. (See Jenson, *Encyclopedic History*, 563–64.)
According to the published notice of Richards's appointment, it was his responsibility to "receive all property devoted to the building of the Temple and enter the same, at the Recorder's office in the lower room of the new store." (*Times and Seasons* 3 [15 December 1841]: 638.)
3. See p. 337. The Joseph Smith red brick store, a two-story structure located

Joseph Smith Store, Nauvoo, Illinois.
Photograph, Brigham H. Roberts, 1885. LDS Church Archives.

on the duties of his office.[1]

14 December 1841 · Tuesday

Joseph commenced opening, unpacking, and assorting goods in the large front room on the seckond floor of the new store, situated on the corner of the Lot. bounded north by water street, & West by Granger Street, this 14th day of December A.D. 1841. The building being yet unfinished, the Joiners and Masons. are prosecuting their labors in the lower part thereof. —

17 December 1841 · Friday

Brigham Young, President of the Quorum of the twelve, arrived at his house in Nauvoo, July 1st 1841. from England, having been absent from his family since the 14th of September 1839,[2] and the following Revelation was given at his house in

"Nauvoo City, July 9th 1841.

Dear & well beloved Brother, Brigham Young, Verily thus saith the Lord unto you my servant Brigham it is no more required at your hand to leave your family as in times past for your offering is acceptable to me I have seen your labor and toil in journeyings for my name. I therefore command you to

---

at the intersection of Granger and Water Streets in Nauvoo, was one of the important buildings of the town. In addition to being used as a store, it served as a main location for business, civic, educational, and church gatherings until the temple and other Nauvoo buildings were completed. It was the location of a school, recording room for the temple committee and tithing office, Joseph Smith's private office, meetings of the Nauvoo Masonic Lodge, the Female Relief Society, and priesthood quorums, and it was the place where the temple endowment was first introduced. (See Roger D. Launius and F. Mark McKiernan, *Joseph Smith Jr.'s Red Brick Store* [Macomb, Illinois: Western Illinois University, 1985]; Lisle G. Brown, "The Sacred Departments for Temple Work in Nauvoo: The Assembly Room and the Council Chamber," *BYU Studies* 19 [Spring 1979]: 361–74.)

1. In the MS. both this and the previous paragraph are dated 13 December.
2. This refers to Brigham Young's return from the mission of the Twelve to England.

send my word abroad and take special care of your family from this time henceforth and forever, Amen. Given to Joseph Smith this day."[1] [p. 26]

[pp. 27–30, *donations*][2]

15 December 1841 · Wednesday

In reply to enquiries concerning Almon Babbitt. the Printing Press. Kirtland, &c contained in a letter written at Kirtland, Nov 16th 1841, by[3] Lester Brooks & Zebedee Coltrin, acting Prests—& Thomas Burdick, Bishop. & council. To. Presidents Joseph Smith & Brigham Young &c.[4] it was decided as follows;

"It remains for Almon Babbitt to offer satisfaction, if he wishes so to do, according to the minutes of the Conference.[5] *You are doubtless all well aware that all the stakes except those in Hancock, Co. Illinois, & Lee county Iowa. were discontinued some time Since by the First Presidency, as published in the Times and Seasons;*[6] but as it appears that there

---

1. Published in D&C 126.
2. References to *donations* interspersed in the pages of the journal are a record of consecrations and tithing donated to the Church for the building of the Nauvoo Temple.
3. "by" repeated in MS.
4. The letter stated, "we had great hopes that Kirtland would rise from its former desolation to honor the cause of the Lord in common with Nauvoo." It added that in support of this hope, they had established a printing office in Kirtland, and concluded, "We have gone so far, that it would rather seem a loss to abandon the undertaking now. Nevertheless, . . . we shall be guided by your counsel." (Brooks, Coltrin, Burdick, and Winters to the First Presidency and Twelve, 16 November 1841, MS., LDS Church Archives.)
5. The minutes reported that "contrary to the revelations . . . and detrimental to the interests of the Church," Almon Babbitt had used his influence to entice migrating Saints to settle at Kirtland, Ohio (where he served as stake president), rather than proceed to the appointed places of gathering in Illinois and Iowa. At the October 1841 Church conference Babbitt was disfellowshipped "until he shall make satisfaction." (*History of the Church*, 4:424.)
6. A little more than a month after the cornerstones of the Nauvoo Temple were laid, the First Presidency, "anxious to promote the prosperity" of the Church, urged the Saints residing outside of Hancock County, Illinois, "to make

are many in Kirtland who desire to remain there and build up that place, and as you have made great exertions, according to your letter, to establish a printing press, & take care of the poor, &c since that period, you may as well continue operations according to your designs, & go on with your printing, & do what you can in Righteousness to build up Kirtland but do not suffer yourselves to harbor the Idea that Kirtland will rise on the ruins of Nauvoo. It is the privilege of brethren emigrating from any quarter to come to this place, and it is not right to attempt to persuade those who desire it, to stop short."[1] (Extract from the letter of the presidents in reply: Dec 15th 1841.)

16 December 1841 · Thursday

This day William Wightman, of Ramus, deliverd to Prest. Joseph Smith, sole Trustee in Trust, the *deed* for the unsold ⟨& bonded⟩ Lots of land in the town of Ramus, bearing date Decr 8th 1841: also the plat of the "first addition To Ramus." and the notes which have been received of Individuals who have purchased lots. and the Bonds of William Miller. Sept 21. 1840; & of Uti [Ute] Perkins Nov 26th 1840: & of Wm G. Perkins, Nov 7. 1840, & of John F. Charles Nov 16. 1841. for lots of land adjoining Ramus. and which may hereafter be added. to the Town plat; (a part of the land included in Wm Millers Bond is included in the first addition to Ramus;) The

---

preparations to come in without delay. This is important, and should be attended to by all who feel an interest in the prosperity of this corner-stone of Zion. Here the Temple must be raised, the University built, and other edifices erected which are necessary for the great work of the last days, and which can only be done by a concentration of energy and enterprise. Let it therefore be understood, that all the stakes, excepting those in this county, and in Lee county, Iowa, are discontinued, and the saints instructed to settle in this county as soon as circumstances will permit." ("To the Saints Abroad," *Times and Seasons* 2 [1 June 1841]:434; see also *History of the Church*, 4:362.)

1. On LDS involvement in Kirtland after the body of the Latter-day Saints left there in 1838 see Davis Bitton, "The Waning of Mormon Kirtland," *BYU Studies* 12 (Summer 1972): 455–64; and Backman, *The Heavens Resound*, chapter 19.

above described property in Ramus. & the Notes ⟨were⟩ is transferred to the sole Trustee in trust. for the benefit of the whole church, (by a vote of the Ramus Conference Decr 4 & 5th 1841.) after applying sufficient of said property to liquidate the claims of those from whom the Town was purchased, and also paying two notes given by Wm Wightman for money borrowed to pay for the above property, viz, To Lyman prentice [Prentiss] $11.45: & James Cummin[g]s $50.00 and some other small demands against said Wightman which have been contracted for the benefit of the church in Ramus.

5 January 1842 · Wednesday

William Wightman. signed over & delivered the Town Plat of Ramus to the sole trustee in Trust Joseph Smith. [p. 31]

[p. 32, *donations*]

11 December 1841 · Saturday

Late this evening. Joseph, the prop⟨h⟩et, and trustee in trust for the Temple, Commanded Brigham Young. President of the twelve, while sitting in the New store, to go immediately and instruct the building committee in their duty, & forbid their receiving any more property for the building of the Temple Until they received it of himself, and if the committee did not give heed to the instruction, and attend to their duty to put them in the way so to do:

And on monday morning, Decr 13th, Brigham delivered the above message to Reynolds Cahoon and Elias Higby while in the committee House. in Presence of Heber C. Kimball, Willford Woodruff. and Willard Richards.

13 December 1841 · Monday

Some time in the fall of 1839. Daniel S. Witter, of the Steam mill at Warsaw,[1] solicited the First Presidency of the

---

1. Warsaw, Hancock County, Illinois, located on the Mississippi River fifteen

church to make a settlement on the school section, No. 16, 1 mile south of Warsaw: and the solicitations were continued by D. S. Witter. Mark Aldrich & others, from time to time, Till the spring or summer of 1841. when articles of Agreement were entered into between Calvin A. Warren. Esqr Witter, Aldrich & others, owners of the school Section; and the First Presidency; giving the saints the privilege of settling on the school. section, which had been surveyed & laid out in town Lots. & called. *Warren,* in certain conditions; and willard Richards went to Warsaw on the 8th of September. and spent several weeks to prepare for the reception of Emigrants;[1] in the meantime the inhabitants of Warsaw. attempted to form an Anti-Mormon Society. & were much enraged because that Esquire [Jacob C.] Davis, (who had spoken favorably of the Saints) was appointed clerk of the county by Judge [Stephen A.] Douglass. In Novr about 200 saints arrived at Warsaw, from England, led by Joseph Fielding, and were visited on the 24th of Novr by Richards & Taylor, of the Quorum of the twelve, & counselled to Tarry at Warsaw. according to the instruction of the first Presidency,

December 13th Isaac Decker. Presiding Elder at Warsaw, stated to the Presidency at Nauvoo, that Mr Witter had risen $1. per barrel on flour, and sold the sweepings of his mill to

---

miles south of Nauvoo, was founded in 1834 by John R. Wilcox, Mark Aldrich, John Montague, and John W. Vineyard. By 1845 the town had a population of 472. (Thomas Gregg, *History of Hancock County, Illinois* [Chicago: Charles C. Chapman & Co., 1880], 637–38.)

1. An epistle of the Twelve notified British Saints of the prospects for settlement at Warren: "The church has commenced a new city 20 miles below this [Nauvoo], and 1 mile below Warsaw, called, Warren, where many city lots, and farms in the vicinity, can be had on reasonable terms; and it will be wisdom for many of the brethren to stop at that place, for the opportunity for erecting temporary buildings will be greater than at this place, also the chance for providing food, will be superior, to those who wish to labor for it.

"Warsaw is at the foot of the Desmoine Rapids, and one of the best locations for mercantile purposes, there is in this western country." ("An Epistle of the Twelve," *Times and Seasons* 3 [15 November 1841]: 602.)

the Saints at $2.25 per cwt; and that Witter & Aldrich had forbid the brethren the priviledge of getting the old wood on the school section, which they had full liberty to get; that the price of wood on the wharf had fallen, 25 cents per cord since the arrival of the Saints; that the citizens had risen on their rents; &c, and the First Presidency decided that ~~that~~ the saints should remove from Warsaw to Nauvoo immediately, & that the proceedings at Warsaw be published in the Times & Seasons.[1] [p. 33]

[pp. 34-35, *donations*]

December 1841

Nauvoo December 1841.
Elder Amos Fuller, of Zarahemla stated to President Joseph Smith that he had settled all his debts, and made all necessary provision for his family, and desired to know the will of God concerning himself. —

December 22d 1841. Verily thus saith the Lord unto my servants the Twelve, Let them appoint unto my servant Amos Fuller, a mission to preach my gospel unto the children of men, as it shall be manifested unto them by my Holy Spirit. *Amen.*

22 December 1841 · Wednesday

Nauvoo, — Dec[e]mber 22d 1841.
The word of the Lord came unto Joseph the Seer, verily thus saith the Lord, Let my servant John Snider [Snyder] take a mission to the Eastern continent,[2] unto all the conferences now sitting in that region, and let him carry a package of

---

1. For a history of the brief settlement at Warren, see Marshall Hamilton, " 'Money-Diggersville' — The Brief, Turbulent History of the Mormon Town of Warren," *John Whitmer Historical Association Journal* 9 (1989): 49-58.
2. I.e., the British Isles.

Epistles that shall be written by my servants the Twelve, making known unto them their duties concerning the building of my houses[1] which I have appointed unto you saith the Lord, that they may bring their gold, & their silver, and their precious stones, and the box-tree, and the Fir-tree, and all fine wood to beautify the place of my sanctuary saith the Lord; and let him return speedily with all means which shall be put into his hands, even so; *Amen.*

This day commenced receiving the first supply of Groceries at the new store. 13 waggons arrived from Warsaw loaded with sugar, molasses, glass, salt, tea, coffee, &c purchased in St Louis.– The original stock purchased in New Orleans having been detained at St Louis by Holbrook, Inn-keeper under false pretences; & on this evening Joseph the Seer commenced giving instructions to the scribe concerning writing the Proclamation to the Kings of the earth mentioned in the Revelation given January 19, 1841.[2] [p. 36]

[pp. 37–38, *donations*]

24 December 1841 · Friday

Elder Truman Gillet Junr returned from a short mission to Van Beuren Co, Iowa, where he baptized 14, bringing $20. as a donation to the building of the Temple from James Mo[o]re whom, he baptized.– Bro Gillet having been disfellowshiped by the elders quorum, is again restored by the first Presiden⟨c⟩y, & the decision of the Quorum revoked.

Christmas eve, 11 o'clock. While conversing with Brigham Young and N. K. Whitney about sending an Agent to England. to establish a cheap & expeditious conveyance for the saints & merchandize to this place. President Joseph said in the name

---

1. The Nauvoo House and the Nauvoo Temple.
2. D&C 124:3–4. In the MS. both this and the previous paragraph are dated 22 December.

of the Lord we will prosper if we go forward in this thing.–
Private Office.[1]

26 December 1841 · Sunday

The public meeting of the saints was at President Joseph
Smiths house, on Sunday evening Dec 26th and after Patriarch
Hyram & Elder Brigham had spoken on the principles of faith
and the gifts of the spirit, President Joseph read the 13th chap
of 1st Corinthians and a part of the 14 chap, and remarked
that the gift of Tongues was necessary in the church; but That
if satan could not speak in tongues he could not tempt a
Dutchman, or any other nation, but the English, for he can
tempt the Englishman, for he has tempted me, & I am an
Englishman; but the Gift of Tongues, by the power of the Holy
Ghost, in the church, is for the benefit of the Servants of God
to preach to unbelievers, as on the days of Pentecost. when
devout men from evry nation shall assemble to hear of the
things of God. let the ⟨elders⟩ preach to them in their own mother
tongue, whether it is German, French, Spanish or Irish or any
other. & let those interpret who understand the Languages
spoken. in their mother tongue. & this is what the Apostle
meant. in 1. Corinthians 14.27.

27 December 1841 · Monday

Joseph. was with Brigham, Heber C, Willard. & John ⟨Taylor⟩
of the Twelve, at ~~his~~ ⟨my⟩[2] office. instructing them in the principles of the kingdom. & what the twelve should do in relation
to the mission of John Snider [Snyder]. & the European conferences, so as to forward the gathering, means for building

---

1. In the MS. both this and the previous paragraph are dated 24 December.
2. Later penciled alteration in MS.

the Temple & Nauvoo House,[1] & merchandize; that Brigham might go with John on his Mission if he chose. but the object of the mission could be accomplished without.

28 December 1841 · Tuesday

Joseph baptized Sidney Rigdon, for and in behalf of his parents.[2] Reynolds Cahoon and others in the Font. [p. 39]

[pp. 40–42, *donations*]

29 December 1841 · Wednesday

The corner stone of the Nauvoo House was laid by President Joseph Smith. on the 2d of October 1841. (At the commencement of the Last General conference of the church in Nauvoo previous to the finishing of the Temple,) and the following articles were deposited therein by the president. To Wit. —

A Book of Mormon

---

1. The same revelation that initiated the building of a temple at Nauvoo (D&C 124) also commanded construction of a hotel. The building was commenced in the spring of 1841 but was not completed. By the time the Saints left Nauvoo in 1846, the walls were above the second-story windows. After the departure of the Saints, the building became the property of Emma Smith, widow of the Prophet Joseph Smith. Her second husband, Lewis C. Bidamon, remodeled and completed the building on a smaller scale, as a hotel, and he and Emma lived there from 1871 until they died. (See Jenson, *Encyclopedic History*, 562; Linda King Newell and Valleen Tippetts Avery, *Mormon Enigma: Emma Hale Smith* [Garden City, N.Y.: Doubleday & Company, 1984], 259, 286–88.)

2. The concept of vicarious baptism for the dead among the Latter-day Saints was introduced by Joseph Smith in a funeral discourse for Seymour Brunson on 15 August 1840. The first such baptisms were performed in the Mississippi River. In 1841 a font was constructed in the basement of the unfinished Nauvoo Temple. After its dedication on November 8, these ordinances for the dead were performed there. Joseph Smith published an editorial on the subject in the *Times and Seasons* 3 (15 April 1842): 759–61 and wrote epistles to the Church in September 1842 that were later canonized as D&C 127 and 128. (See Andrew F. Ehat and Lyndon W. Cook, eds., *The Words of Joseph Smith* [Provo, Utah: Religious Studies Center, Brigham Young University, 1980], 49; Cook, *Revelations of the Prophet Joseph Smith*, 247.)

A Revelation given January 19th 1841.

The "Times & Seasons" containing the charter of the Nauvoo House. ⟨No. 23. Apr. 21. 1841⟩[1]

Journal of Heber C. Kimball.

The Memorial of Lyman Wight, To the United States' Senate.

A Book of Doctrine & Covenants. - 1st Edition.

No. 35. of the Times and Seasons.

The original Manuscript of the Book of Mormon.[2]

The persecution of the Church in the State of Missouri, published in the "Times & Seasons"

The Holy Bible

1 Half Dollar |

1 Quarter Dollar | Silver Coin

2 Dimes |

2 Half Dimes |

      And

1 copper Coin.

[*donations*]

17 January 1842 · Monday

Brigham Young, Heber C. Kimball, O. Pratt, W. Woodruff. John Taylor. Geo. A Smith. & W. Richards of the Quorum of the Twelve assembled in council at the Presidents office. and decided that Elder Amos B. Fuller take a mission to the city of Chicago. in accordance with the Revelation Page 36.[3] and

---

1. Insertion in MS. added later with purple pencil.

2. The original Book of Mormon manuscript remained in the cornerstone of the Nauvoo House until 1882 when it was removed by Lewis C. Bidamon, who had married Emma Smith following the death of the Prophet. Because of moisture the manuscript had deteriorated, but portions that remained were given to Nauvoo visitors and were nearly all eventually deposited in the LDS Church Archives in Salt Lake City. (See Jessee, "The Original Book of Mormon Manuscript," *BYU Studies* 10 [Spring 1970]: 259–78.)

3. See entry of 22 December 1841.

also, that Elder Henry Jacobs. be subje[c]t to the council & presidency of Bro Fuller & accompany him so far on the mission as Bro Fuller judge expedient. [p. 43]

[donations]

30, 31 December 1841 · Thursday, Friday

Visit

Calvin A. Warren Esqr. Mark Aldrich & Daniel S. Witter visited President Joseph, at his office, and after much explanation, and conversation concerning Warren & Warsaw. in which Esqr Warren manifested the kindest & most confidential feelings, and Aldrich & Witter ~~had~~ expressed their entire approbataion of past proceedings of the Presidency; they all agreed that if Joseph did not succeed in the next attempt to establish and build up Warren. that they would fully excuse him from all censure, & should feel satisfied that he had done all that could reasonably be required of any man in a like case, be the consequence what it might to themselves; and Esqr Warren frankly acknowledged, that his temporal salvation depended on the success of the enterprize, and made liberal proposals. for the benefit of the brethren, to help forward the undertaking.[1] The party retired manifesting the best of feeling. & expressing the most perfect satisfaction with their visit with the president & all concerned.

1 January 1842 · Saturday

January 1st 1842 Joseph commenced placing the goods on the shelves, of the New Store for the first time assisted by Bishop Newel K. Whitney and others; and on wednesday. January 5th the doors were opened for trading for the first time;

---

1. That Calvin A. Warren was badly hurt by the Mormon withdrawal is evident from the fact that he and Aldrich took out bankruptcy less than three months after this conversation. (See Dallin H. Oaks and Marvin S. Hill, *Carthage Conspiracy* [Urbana, Chicago, London: University of Illinois Press, 1975], 54.)

the store was filled continually through the day and Joseph was behind the counter continually waiting upon purchasers. [p. 44]

[pp. 45–47, *donations*]

4 January 1842 · Tuesday

Prophecy

Thursday evening December 30th 1841. at the Presidents office, while conversing with Calvin A. Warren Esqr–about the proceedings at Warsaw, President Joseph prophesied in the name of the Lord, that the first thing toward building up Warsaw was to break it down, to break down them that are there, and that it never would be built up till it was broken down, and after that keep them entirely in the dark concerning our movements; and it is best to let Sharpe [Thomas Sharp] publish what he pleased and go to the Devil, and the more lies he prints, the sooner he will get through;[1] not buy him out or hinder him; and after they have been in the dark long enough, let a certain set of men go there who will do as I tell them, a certain kind of men. some of those capitalists from the eastern states, say from Pensylvania; wise men who will take the lead of business, and go ahead of those that are there before they know what we are about, and the place will prosper, and not till then.

12 January 1842 · Wednesday

Coal Mine

Wednesday January 12th 1842 President Joseph. visited his wood-land, about 7 miles South of his residence, accom-

---

1. On Thomas Sharp's antagonism toward the Latter-day Saints see Marshall Hamilton, "Thomas Sharp's Turning Point: Birth of an Anti-Mormon," *Sunstone* 13:5 (October 1989): 16–22; Annette P. Hampshire, "Thomas Sharp and Anti-Mormon Sentiment in Illinois," *Journal of the Illinois State Historical Society* 72 (May 1979): 82–100.

panied by John Sanders and Peter Maughan, and found and examined a vein of coal about 18 inches thick, apparently of a superior quality for the western country.

14 January 1842 · Friday

Maughan and Sanders further examined the coal mine, and a load of coal was drawn to the presidents office. and the room warmed therewith for the first time

16 January 1842 · Sunday

Maughan and Sanders reported they had continued digging untill the vein of coal was but 6 inches thick, & ceased after getting about 3 waggon loads. [p. 48]

[pp. 49–55, *donations*]

17 January 1842 · Monday

A Revelation given at Far West, July 8,th AD. *1838.*[1]
Verily thus saith the Lord unto my servants, William Marks, and N.K. Whitney; Let them settle up their business speedily and Journey from the land of Kirtland before I, the Lord, sendeth snow ⟨again⟩ upon the ground. Let them awake and arise, and come forth and not tarry for I the Lord commandeth it, — therefore, if they tarry it shall not be well with them. Let them repent of all their sins, and all their covetous desires before me saith the Lord; For what is property unto me saith the Lord. Let the properties at Kirtland be turned out for debts saith the Lord, Let them go saith the Lord; and whatsoever remaineth, let it remain in your hands saith the Lord, for have I not the fowls of Heaven, and also the fish of the Sea, and the beasts of the mountains? Have I not made the earth? ⟨Do I not hold the destinies of all the armies of the

---

1. Published in D&C 117.

nations of the earth?) Therefore will I not make the solitary places to bud and to blossom, and bring forth in abundance saith the Lord? Is there not room enough upon the mountains of Adam Ondi Ahman, or upon the plains of Olea Shinihah, or the land where Adam dwelt, that you should not covet that which is but the dross and neglect the morre weighty matters. Therefore, come up hither, unto the Land of my people, even Zion. Let my Servant William Marks be faithful over a few things, and he shall be ruler over many things. Let him preside in the midst of my people, in the city Far West, and let him be blessed with the blessings of my people. — Let my Servant N. K. Whitney be ashamed of the Nicolitans and of all their secret abominations, and of all his littleness of soul before me saith the Lord, and come up unto the land of Adam ondi Ahman, and be a Bishop unto my people saith the Lord, not in name but in deed saith the Lord. And again, Verily I say unto you I remember my Servant Oliver Grainger [Granger]. Behold, verily I say unto him, that his name shall be had in sacred remembrance from generation to generation, forever and ever Saith the Lord; Therefore let him contend earnestly for the redemption of the First Presidency of my church saith the Lord; and when he falls he shall rise again, for his sacrifice shall be more sacred to me than his increase saith the Lord; Therefore let him come up hither speedily unto the land of Zion, and in due time he shall be made a merchant unto my name saith the Lord for the benefit of my people; Therefore let no man despise my servant Oliver Grainger [Granger], but let the blessings. of my people be upon him forever and ever, *Amen.*

And again I say unto you let all the Saints in the land of Kirtland remember the Lord their God, and mine house to preserve it holy, and to overthrow the money changers in mine own due time. Saith the Lord. [p. 56]

6 January 1842 · Thursday

The New Year

The New Year has been ushered in and continued thus far under the most favorable auspices. and the Saints seem to be influenced by a kind and indulgent Providence in their disposition & means, to rear the Temple of the most High God, anxiously looking forth to the completion thereof as an event of the greatest importance to the Church & the world, making the Saints in Zion to rejoice, and the Hypocrite & Sinner to tremble. Truly this is a day long to be remembered by the saints of the Last Days; a day in which the God of heaven has began to restore the ancient ⟨order⟩ of his Kingdom unto his servants & his people: a day in which all things are concurring together to bring about the completion of the fullness of the gospel, a fulness of the dispensation of Dispensations even the fulness of Times; a day in which God has began to make manifest & set in order in his church those things which have been. and those things, which the ancients prophets and wise men desired to see.–but died without beholding it. a day in which those things begin to be made manifest which have been hid from ⟨before⟩ the foundations of the world, & which Jehovah has promised should be made known in his own due time. unto his servants, to prepare. the earth for the return of his glory, even a Celestial glory; and a kingdom of Priests & Kings to God & the Lamb forever, on Mount Zion,–or the hundred & forty & four thousand whom John the Revelator saw, which should come to pass in the Restitution of all things. [p. 57]

Journal of President Joseph

15 January 1842 · Saturday

Commenced reading the Book of Mormon at page 54. ⟨American⟩ stereotype edition, (the previous pages having been corrected) for the purpose of correcting the plates, or some errors which escaped notice in the first edition.[1]

16 January 1842 · Sunday

Preached at his own house, morning evening, illustrating the nature of sin, and shewing that it is not right to sin that grace may abound.

17 January 1842 · Monday

Was transacting business in the city, procuring means to assist the printer &c dined, in company with the Recorder, at Sister Agnes Smith's; and attended, council of the twelve, (present. B. Young. Prest.–H. C. Kimball, O. Pratt. W. Woodruff. John Taylor. Geo A Smith & W Richards.) at his private office. in the evening.

18 January 1842 · Tuesday

After transacting a variety of business, sleeping an hour from Bodily infirmity, read for correction in the Book of Mormon and Debated, in the evening, with the Mayor [John C. Bennett], concerning the Lamanites. and Negroes. —[2]

---

1. Stereotyping was the process of making metal printing plates by taking a mold of composed type and then taking from the mold a cast in type metal. The first stereotype edition of the Book of Mormon (third American edition) was published in 1840 when Ebenezer Robinson traveled to Cincinnati for that purpose. Hugh Stocks in his study of the publication history of the Book of Mormon determined that although Joseph Smith's journal in 1842 refers to the Prophet's making further corrections in the 1840 stereotype edition for another printing, those corrections were not included when the fourth American printing of the Book of Mormon was published from the same plates as the third edition. Nor has a copy of those corrections been found. (Hugh C. Stocks, "The Book of Mormon, 1830–1879: A Publishing History" [MLA thesis, UCLA, 1979], 12–13; on the stereotyping of the Book of Mormon in Cincinnati see Ebenezer Robinson, "Items of Personal History of the Editor," *The Return* 2 [May 1890]: 257–62.)

2. See entry of 25 January 1842.

19 January 1842 · Wednesday

Read in the Book of Mormon, and in the evening visited Bishop [George] Millers Wife,[1] who was very sick and the Bishop absent.–collecting funds for building the temple & Nauvoo House

20 January 1842 · Thursday

Attended a Special conference of the church ~~at Bro~~ 10 o clock A.M. concerning Dr [Isaac] Galland, The conference voted to sanction the revocation of Dr Galland's Agency dated the 18th of January, as published in the "Times and Seasons." and also, instructed the Trustee in Trust To proceed with Dr Gallands affairs in re⟨l⟩ation to the church, as he shall Judge most expedient. –[2] 6–⟨o'k⟩ evening attended a special council in the upper Room of the New Store.

---

1. Mary Catherine Fry Miller.
2. The largest acquisition of land upon which Nauvoo was to be built occurred in August 1839 when approximately five hundred acres were obtained from Connecticut land speculators Horace R. Hotchkiss, John Gillett, and Smith Tuttle. The purchase totaled $114,500, which included $3,000 in annual interest payments to be paid over a period of twenty years. This, with other demands, created a heavy financial burden for the Saints. To meet these demands Church members in the East were encouraged to obtain Nauvoo land in exchange for their eastern property. In the spring of 1841 Hyrum Smith and Isaac Galland were sent East with means to pay notes that were due and to regulate the eastern land exchange. Illness almost immediately forced Hyrum to return to Nauvoo, and Galland continued alone. In September the Prophet learned that Galland had not paid Hotchkiss. By year's end Galland had returned to his Keokuk, Iowa, home, but had not made an accounting of his trip East. In this context the "special conference" convened on 20 January. Two days prior to the conference Galland's power of attorney, issued 15 February 1841 to transact business for the Church, was revoked. ("Special Notice," *Times and Seasons* 3 [15 January 1842]: 667.) Wilford Woodruff noted that the conference was held to take into consideration Isaac Galland's conduct, "who is wronging the Church out of much property." (Diary of Wilford Woodruff, 20 January 1842.) However, two weeks later, Galland did meet with the Prophet. And although he was thereafter estranged from the Church, no action was taken against him for wrongdoing. (See Lyndon W. Cook, "Isaac Galland – Mormon Benefactor," *BYU Studies* 19 [Spring 1979]: 261–84.)

21 January 1842 · Friday

Reading at the office, General business in store & city, in the office in the evening with Elder Taylor & Recorder, interpreting dreams &c. —

22 January 1842 · Saturday

Was very busy in appraising Tything property.[1] and in the evening revised the rules of the City council, attended council & spoke on their adoption, and was Elected vice Mayor protem of Nauvoo City.[2] 18 of 21 votes. [p. 58]

23 January 1842 · Sunday

With the Recorder in his office most of the day at his house in the eve

24 January 1842 · Monday

This day Reckoned with Wm & Wilson Law in the counting Room & examined the Lots on which they are about to build a grain & Sawmill.

25 January 1842 · Tuesday

Signed the deeds for Bro Laws. transacted a variety of business in the city and office, sent a messenger to Bro John Benbows to inform them, he could not visit them. in the evening debated with J[ohn]. C. Bennet. & others, to shew that the

---

1. On 12 January 1842 Willard Richards, Recorder for the Temple, published a notice stating that the Recorder's Office would be open only on Saturday of each week for the reception of tithing and consecrations in order to give the Trustee (Joseph Smith) and the Recorder (Richards) the necessary time to "arrange the Book of Mormon, New Translation of the Bible, Hymn Book, and Doctrine and Covenants for the press." (*Times and Seasons* 3 [15 January 1842]: 667.)

2. The responsibility of the vice-mayor was to preside over the city council in the absence of the mayor. (*Times and Seasons* 3 [1 February 1842]: 683–84.) Joseph Smith was elected temporary vice-mayor of Nauvoo.

Indians have greater cause to complain of the treatment of the whites than the Negroes or Sons of Cain.

26 January 1842 · Wednesday

Rode out to borrow money to refund for money borrowed of John Benbow as an outfit for Dr Galland in his agency. transacted a variety of business. explained scripture to Elder Orson Spencer in his[1] office. read in Book of Mormon in the evening

27 January 1842 · Thursday

Attending to business in general,–in the afternoon in council with the Recorder or giving some particular instructions concerning the *order* of the kingdom & the management of business. placed the carpet, given by Carlos Granger, on the Floor of the Presidents office.– Cast Lots with the Recorder. and spent the evening in *general council* in the upper Room,[2] in the evening. – In the course of the day B. Young & James Ivins returned a favorable report from Dr Galland.[3] with his Letter of Attorney. Letter & papers which he had received of Joseph & the church.

28 January 1842 · Friday

At the office, Sister Emma [Smith] & Sister [Elizabeth Ann] Whitney spent an hour,– present H. C. Kimball. W. Woodruff. B. Young. & received instruction concerning John Snider [Snyder];[4] & E. Robinson concerning the Times and Seasons as

---

1. "my" later penciled over "his" in MS.
2. "Room" written over "Cham" in same ink in MS.
3. See note 2, p. 354.
4. After having been called by revelation on 22 December 1841 on a mission to England (see entry of 22 December above), Snyder hesitated to act unless the Twelve would finance his way.

Recorded on 64 page.–and also deliverd a message [to] Elias Higby [Higbee] to arise & work and his household [p. 59][1]

29 January 1842 · Saturday

Much engaged with the tythings, in the afternoon in his office councilling various individuals. and in the evening in council with Bro. Young Kimball. Richards and others–shewing forth the kingdom & the order thereof concerning many things & the will of God concerning his servants. –

30 January 1842 · Sunday

preached in the morning after father [Austin] Co⟨w⟩les.–& in the evening, at his house, concerning Spirits their operation & designs. –

31 January 1842 · Monday

Assisted in appraising[2] the tithings of Saturday with Sister Emma. Rec[e]ived many calls, read in *Mormon*[3] and in the ⟨evening⟩ was in council with Brigham, Heber C.–Orson. Willford. & Willard. concerning Bro Snider.[4] & the printing office. spent the evening very cheer[i]ly & retired about 10 oclock. After Dinner visited Bro Chase. who was very sick.

2 February 1842 · Wednesday

In council with Dr Galland and Calvin A. Warren Esqr-

3 February 1842 · Thursday

In council with Calvin A. Warren Esqr–concerning a Settlement with the estate of Oliver Granger and delivered him the ⟨necessary⟩ papers accordingly[5]

---

1. Another entry dated the 28th, which clarifies the references to John Snyder, the *Times and Seasons*, and Elias Higbee, is written several pages further in the MS. See p. 362.
2. MS.: "prising"
3. Mormon in the Book of Mormon.
4. See entry of 28 January.
5. One of the major problems facing Joseph Smith in Nauvoo was monetary.

4 February 1842 · Friday

Instructed an invoice of Galland's scrip to be made out.– closed the contract for the printing office by proxy. –[1] attended a debate in the evening.

10 February 1842 · Thursday

The President was sick, and kept his bed.

11 February 1842 · Friday

Convalescent, was at the store twice a few moments

12 February 1842 · Saturday

attended city council.–in the afternoon. plead. in an action of slander before the Mayor.–in behalf of the city against[2]– [Lyman] O. Littlefield.–and obtained Judgment of $500 bonds to keep the peace.

13 February 1842 · Sunday

Council with the mayor., H. Smith the Patriarch.–Recorder &c and visited Sister S. C. Bennet. in co[mpany] with Wm Law & Lady [p. 60]

14 February 1842 · Monday

At the office transacting a variety of business

Besides the immediate expense of resettlement, debts incurred in Ohio before 1838 remained unpaid, and Church property in Kirtland had become encumbered with legal entanglements. In 1840 the Prophet sent Oliver Granger to Kirtland as agent to regulate the temporal affairs of the Church there. While serving in that capacity, Granger died on 25 October 1841.

1. Ebenezer Robinson transfered to Joseph Smith by Willard Richards the printing establishment consisting of the printing office, stereotype foundery, book bindery, house, and 50 by 58 foot lot on the corner of Water and Bain streets for $6,600. (Ebenezer Robinson, "Items of Personal History of the Editor," *The Return* 2 [October 1890]: 346–48; Diary of Wilford Woodruff, 4 February 1842.)

2. MS.: "againts"

17 February 1842 · Thursday

City council. Special meeting. among other items a A general law licencing marriages in this city. Coun[c]ill in the General office eve. – [1]

18 February 1842 · Friday

Adjourned council.– Spoke at considerable length in committee of the whole. on the great priviliges of the Nauvoo Charter. & specially on the Registry of Deeds for Nauvoo. And prophecyed in the name of the Lord God that Judge Douglass. and no other Judge of the circuit court will ever set aside a law of the City council establishing a Registry of Deeds in this city.–(Nauvoo)[2]

19 February 1842 · Saturday

Engaged in the Registers office on the Tythings[3] & in council in the Presidents office with B. Young & H. C. Kimball & others. –

20 February 1842 · Sunday

Meeting on the Hill.[4]

---

1. Wilford Woodruff noted, "A Special City Council was called & among the business of the day a Law was passed regulating marriage Joseph the Seer made many interesting remarks concerning our privileges Council adjourned to next day evening." (Diary of Wilford Woodruff, 17 February 1842.)
2. Woodruff reported, "City council met at early candle light according to adjournment After some business on roads was performed Joseph the Seer took the floor & followed Gen Bennet concerning law our rights &c. His speach was truly interesting & powerful." (Diary of Wilford Woodruff, 18 February 1842.)
3. Woodruff wrote, "This was a busy day . . . it being tithing day for the temple their was much business done at the store property brought in &c." (Diary of Wilford Woodruff, 19 February 1842.)
4. In the vicinity of the temple site.

21 February 1842 · Monday

Visiting in the city. and transacting business at the office in the P.M. & evening

22 February 1842 · Tuesday

[blank]

23 February 1842 · Wednesday

Settled with and paid Bro. Chases–and assisted in the counting room in settling with E[benezer]. Robinson Esqr–visited the printing office. & gave R. Hadlock [Reuben Hedlock] instructions concerning the cut for the altar & Gods in the Records of Abraham. as designed for the Times and Seasons[1]

24 February 1842 · Thursday

attending to business at the general office. P.M. was explaining the Records of Abraham To the Recorder. Sisters Marinda [Marinda Nancy Hyde] Mary and others present. to hear the Explanations

25 February 1842 · Friday

[blank]

26 February 1842 · Saturday

At the Recorders office engaged in the tything. and at a court at the office of the Patriarch. [p. 61]

[pp. 62–65, *donations*]

23 January 1842 · Sunday

Silenced Elder Daniel Wood. of Pleasant Vale for preaching that the church should unsheath the Sword–and also silenced

---

1. See "A Fac-simile From the Book of Abraham, No. 1," *Times and Seasons* 3 (1 March 1842): 703; and Pearl of Great Price, p. 28.

Elder A[lbert]. Lits. for preaching that the authorities of the church were done away–&c. and sent the Letters by the hand of Elder William Draper Junior who preferred the charges; & cited A Lits to appear before the High council of Nauvoo forth-with.–& published the same in the Times and Seasons.[1] in the name of Joseph Smith. P.C.J.C.L.D.S.[2] and B. Young P.Q T.[3]–W. Richards C[ler]k.

25 January 1842 · Tuesday

A Revelation Given Dcr 2d 1841. N.M. [Marinda Nancy] Hyde

Verily thus saith the Lord unto you my servant Joseph. that inas much as you have called upon me to know my will concerning my handmaid Nancy Marinda Hyde Behold it is my will that she should have a better place prepared for her than that in which she now lives, in order that her life may be spared unto her; Therefore go and say unto my servant Ebenezer Robinson, & To my handmaid his wife,[4] Let them open their doors and take her and her children into their house, and take care of them faithfully and kindly until my servant Orson Hyde returns from his mission[5] or until some other provision can be made for her welfare & safety: Let them do these things and spare not and I the Lord will bless them & heal them. if they do it not grudgingly saith the Lord God. and she shall be a blessing unto them, and let my handmaid Nancy Marinda Hyde hearken to the counsel of my servant Joseph in all things whatsoever he shall teach unto her, and it shall be a blessing upon her and upon her children after her, unto her Justification saith the Lord. [p. 66]

---

1. See "Notice," *Times and Seasons* 3 (15 March 1842): 734.
2. President of the Church of Jesus Christ of Latter-day Saints.
3. President of the Quorum of Twelve.
4. Angeline Robinson.
5. Orson Hyde had left Nauvoo in April 1840 on a mission to the Jews in New York, London, Amsterdam, Constantinople, and the Holy Land.

28 January 1842 · Friday

A Revelation to the twelve concerning the Times and Seasons.

Verily thus saith the Lord unto you my servant Joseph. go and say unto the Twelve That it is my will to have them take in hand the Editorial department of the Times and Seasons according to that manifestation which shall be given unto them by the Power of my Holy Spirit in the midst of their counsel[1]

Saith the Lord. Amen

Joseph decided that Elder John Snider [Snyder] should go out on a mission, and if necessary some one go with him, and raise up a church, and get means to go to England. & carry the Epistles required in the Revelation ~~page~~ ⟨of Dec 22⟩ ~~36~~. —[2] and instructed the Twelve, B. Young H. C. Kimball. W. Woodruff. & W. Richards–being present, to call Elder Snider into their council & instruct him in these things, & if he will not do these things he shall be cut off from the church. & be damned.

Elias Higby [Higbee], of the Temple Committee, came into the Presidents office, and the President said to him The Lord is not well pleased with you, & you must straiten up your loins and do better, & your family also. for you have not been

---

1. In June 1839 Ebenezer Robinson and Don Carlos Smith were given the Church printing press salvaged from the Missouri mobbings, with authorization to publish a paper — the *Times and Seasons* — at their own expense, and to use the profits therefrom to support their families. In December 1840 Smith and Robinson divided their printing business — Smith supervising the *Times and Seasons* and handbill printing, and Robinson the book printing, fancy job printing, stereotype foundry, and book bindery. When Don Carlos died in August 1841, Robinson became the sole proprietor of the enterprise until he sold it to the Church in February 1842. (Ebenezer Robinson, "Items of Personal History of the Editor," *The Return* 2 [5 May 1890]: 257–62; *History of the Church,* 4:239.) At this time John Taylor and Wilford Woodruff were appointed to take charge of the printing establishment. (See Diary of Wilford Woodruff, 3 February 1842.)

2. Alterations penciled later in MS.

diligent as you ought. and as spring is approaching you ⟨must⟩ arise & shake yourself & be active. & make your children industrious, & help build the Temple.[1] [p. 67]

[pp. 68–87, *donations*]

27 February 1842 · Sunday

[*blank*]

28 February 1842 · Monday

offered a settlement to Father [Oliver] Snow by Jenkings [Jenkins] notes. which he declined. choosing to take land in Ramus. Paid Bro Robert pierce $2.700, the balance due him for a farm Dr Galland Bought of Bro Peirce in Brandywine Township, Chester County, Penysvania, for $5000. viz–a deed for Lot 2. Block 94 ⟨$1100.⟩. & Lot 4. Block 95.–⟨$800.⟩ & Lot 4. Block 78. $500. The remainder having been previously paid. the Bond was cancelled & given up. & Bro Peirce expressed his satisfaction of the whole proceedings in the Times & Seasons. —[2]

1 March 1842 · Tuesday

During the fore-noon at his office. & the printing office correcting the first plate or cut. of the Records of father Abraham. prepared by Reuben Hadlock [Hedlock] for the Times &

---

1. In the MS. this paragraph, and the preceding one are each dated as separate entries, 28 January 1842.

2. Pierce wrote, "as it is well known to many, that Dr. Galland, as agent for the church, purchased my farm while I was living in Brandywine township, Chester co. Pa, and many supposed or pretended to suppose, I would get nothing in return;—but I wish to say to all my old friends and enemies in Pennsylvania, through the medium of the "Times and Seasons,"– . . . that I have received my pay in full from the church of Jesus Christ of Latter Day Saints . . . I have the fullest confidence in all the transactions of the church, and I request those papers in Philadelphia who published concerning my sale and loss, with such bitter lamentations to publish this also." (*Times and Seasons* 3 [1 March 1842]: 715.)

Seasons. and in council in his office in the P.M. and in the evening with the Twelve & their wives at Elder Woodruff's.– where he explained many important principles in relation to progressive improvement. in the scale of inteligent existence[1]

2 March 1842 · Wednesday

Read the Proof of the "Times and Seasons" as Editor for the First time, No. 9–Vol 3d[2] in which is the commencement of the Book of Abraham.[3] Paid taxes. to Bagley [Walter Bagby], in the General Business office, for county & State purposes, but refused to pay the Taxes on the City & Town of Commerce.–& Commenced Settlement with Gilbert Granger, & continued in the Presidents office till 9 o clock evening.–also visited by General Dudley from Connecticut.

3 March 1842 · Thursday

Council in the General business office at 9 oclock A.M. in the afternoon continued the settlement with Gilbert Granger. but finally failed to effect any thing but to get Newels Note. Granger refusing to give up the papers to the president, which he had received of his father, the same being church property[4]
[p. 88]

---

1. MS.: "existinc." The occasion was Wilford Woodruff's thirty-fifth birthday celebration at which he served his "best friends" a turkey supper. (See Diary of Wilford Woodruff, 1 March 1842.)
2. The January 28 revelation indicated the Twelve would "take in hand the editorial department" of the *Times and Seasons* (see p. 362). However, Ebenezer Robinson, the previous editor, noted that at the time he sold the paper to the Twelve, "it was not fully decided" whether Joseph Smith would be the editor instead of the Twelve. As it turned out, Joseph Smith did assume editorship. Although the Prophet's name appears as editor on volume 3, no. 8, his actual responsibility as editor began with volume 3, no. 9. (*Times and Seasons* 3 [15 March 1842]: 729.)
3. On 19 February Wilford Woodruff wrote, "I have had the privilege this day of assisting in setting the *TIPE* for printing the first peace of the *BOOK OF ABRAHAM* that is to be presented to the inhabitants of the *EARTH* in the *LAST DAYS*." (Diary of Wilford Woodruff, 19 February 1842.)
4. The settlement pertained to the estate of Oliver Granger, who had served

Segment from Egyptian papyrus purchased by Latter-day Saints in Kirtland, Ohio, 1835. LDS Church Archives.

4 March 1842 · Friday

Exhibeting the Book of Abraham, in the original, To Bro Reuben Hadlock [Hedlock]. so that he might take the size of the several plates or cuts. & prepare the blocks for the Times & Seasons. & also gave instruction concerning the arrangement of the writing on the Large cut.[1] illustrating the principles of Astronomy. (in his office) with other general business

5 March 1842 · Saturday

City Council, among other business of importance the office of Register [registrar] of Deeds was established in the City of Nauvoo & President Joseph Smith chosen Register by the City Council.

6 March 1842 · Sunday

Preached at Elder Orson Spencers on the Hill near the Temple

7 March 1842 · Monday

At the general Business office. Peter Melling. the Patriarch from England, brought to the office cash $⟨13.37⟩ and clothing 3 65.[2] from P. P. Pratt & Amos Fielding of England, and much general business transacted

---

as agent to settle Church affairs in Kirtland, Ohio, before his death in 1841. One of the items of Church property Gilbert Granger refused to give up was a book of patriarchal blessings, containing those given by Joseph Smith and his father. The history of the loss of the book and how it was eventually returned to the Church in 1859 is in Jessee, "Joseph Smith and the Beginning of Mormon Record Keeping," 153–54.

1. See the cut of the Book of Abraham facsimile no. 2, following page 720 in *Times and Seasons* 3 (15 March 1842).

2. "3" written over "to" in MS.

8 March 1842 · Tuesday

Commenced Translating from the Book of Abraham, for the 10 No of the Times and Seasons—and was engaged at his office day & evening

9 March 1842 · Wednesday

Examining copy for the Times & Seasons presented by [John] Taylor & [John C.] Bennet. and a variety of other business in the President[s] office in the morning. in the afternoon continued the Translation of the Book of Abraham. called Bishop [Vinson] Knights & the ~~Post office~~ ⟨Mr Davis's⟩ &c with the Recorder. & continued translating & revising & Reading letters in the evening, Sister Emma being present in the office

10 March 1842 · Thursday

Gave instruction concerning a deed to Stephen Markam. & Shadrach Roundy. & Hiram Clark. and Letter of Attorney ⟨from⟩ Mrs. Smith to E[dward]. Hunter—& a great variety of other Business— & Rode out. & in the evening attended Trial at Patriarch Hiram's office. The City of Nauvoo. vs, ⟨Amos⟩[1] Davis for indecent and abusive Language About Joseph ⟨Smith⟩ while at Mr Davis the day previous The charges were clearly substantiated by the Testimony of Dr [Robert] Foster. Mr & Mrs. [Davidson] Hibbard and others. Mr Davis was found guilty by Jury, & by municipal court bound over to keep the peace 6 month[s] under $100 Bonds,— after which ~~the~~ the President retired to the Printing office with his Lady, ⟨&⟩ Supped, ⟨&⟩ with the twelve who had been at the office. closed the evening. & retired to his habitation[2] [p. 89]

---

1. This, and the following insertion penciled later in MS.
2. The date and the insertion of "Amos" are possibly errors. Wilford Woodruff recorded having attended the court at Hyrum Smith's on March 9 in which "Lysander M. Davis was found guilty of slandering the character of Joseph Smith & was bound over to keep the peace under $100 bond." After the trial Joseph and the Twelve dined on roast turkey with Sister Hyde. (Diary of Wilford Woodruff, 9 March 1842.)

11 March 1842 · Friday

The Nauvoo Legion was on parade commanded by Li[e]utenant Genral Joseph Smith in person[1] The line was formed at 10'oclock A.M. & soon the Legion ma[r]ched from their usual place of parade below the Temple, To Water Street, in front of General Smith's house, where the troops were inspected and after a recess marched west on the bank of the River & taking a circuetous route resumed their usual Post on the parade ground & closed the day in good order & ⟨with⟩ good feelings & to the fullest satisfaction of the commander in chief. —

In the evening the President attended the Trial of Elder Francis G. Bishop at his own house, the Prests house, Elder Bishop appeared before the High council of Nauvoo, on complaint of having received, written & published on or taught certain Revelations & doctrines not consistent with the Doctrine & Covenants of the Church. Mr Bishop refusing to present the written Revelations. the Mayer issued his warrant & brought them before the Council, where parts of the same were Read by Mr Bishop himself. aloud to Council, the whole mass of which appeard to be the extreme of folly, nonsense, absurdity falsehood, & bombastic Egotism, — so much so as to keep the saints al laughing, when not over awed by sorrow & shame, — President Joseph explaind the nature of the case & gave a very

---

1. The Nauvoo Legion, authorized by the Illinois legislature in December 1840, was a body of militia comprising inhabitants of Nauvoo and later Hancock County. The militia was required to perform the same amount of duty as other state militias and was at the disposal of the mayor of the city and the governor of the state. Its officers were commissioned by the governor. At the first election of officers, 4 February 1841, Joseph Smith was chosen Lieutenant General. When first organized, the Legion comprised six companies, and within a year it numbered some 1,500 men; by Joseph Smith's death in 1844, it numbered about 5,000 men. (Jenson, *Encyclopedic History*, 562–63; Hamilton Gardner, "The Nauvoo Legion, 1840–1845 — A Unique Military Organization," *Journal of the Illinois State Historical Society* 54 [Summer 1961]: 181–97; John Sweeney, Jr., "A History of the Nauvoo Legion in Illinois" [Master's thesis, Brigham Young University, 1974].)

clear elucedation of the tendency of such Prop[h]ets & prop[h]ecyings & gave Mr Bishop over to the Buffetings of Satan until he shall learn wisdom. After a few appropriate obse[r]vati[ons] from Patriarch hyram & some of the council, the council voted unanimously, that F. G. Bishop be removed from the fellowship of the church. president Joseph having previously committed the Revelations above referred to, to the flames.[1]

12 March 1842 · Saturday

Lieut. Gen. Joseph Smith. presided over a courtmartial consisting of the officers of the Nauvoo Legion, at his own house for the purpose of deciding upon the Rank & station of the several officers, & the more perfect organization of the Legion[2] [p. 90]

---

1. According to Wilford Woodruff, who attended the trial, "Gladden had set himself up as some great thing for 8 or 9 years & the church had been so much troubled with him by his foolish conduct that he had been cut off a number of times from the church & restored, & he had now set himself up as a prophet & Revelator to the church & a number of his revelations were brought forward & red before the congregations & it was the greatest Bundle of Nonsens ever put together it would have taken Gladden Bishop ten thousand Years to have accomplished the work which he said in his pretended revelations he should perform he took the name of God in vain & his crime was so great in his Blaspheming God in his pretended revelations that Joseph the Seer said that nothing would excuse him in the sight of God & angels in commiting the unpardonable sin ownly because he was a fool & had not sens sufficient for the Holy Ghost to enlighten him." (Diary of Wilford Woodruff, 11 March 1842.)

2. Section 25 of the Nauvoo charter, which authorized the Nauvoo Legion, stated that the "Court Martial . . . shall be composed of the commissioned officers of said Legion, and constitute the law-making department, with full power and authority to make, ordain, establish, and execute all such laws and ordinances as may be considered necessary for the benefit, government, and regulation of said Legion; provided said Court Martial shall pass no law or act, repugnant to, or inconsistent with, the Constitution of the United States, or of this State." (*History of the Church*, 4:244.) At the meeting of the Court Martial on the 12th an ordinance consisting of fourteen sections was passed setting forth provisions for the government and regulation of the Legion. The ordinance is published in *Times and Seasons* 3 (15 March 1842): 733–34.

13 March 1842 · Sunday

[*blank*]

14 March 1842 · Monday

Transacted a great variety of business at the office

15 March 1842 · Tuesday

officiated as grand chaplin at the Installation of the Nauvoo Lodge. of Free Masons. at[1] the Grove. near the Temple, Grand Master [Abraham] Jonas being present. —[2] A Large number of people assembled on the occasion, the day was exceedingly fine, all things were done in order, and universal satisfaction manifested.[3] Admitted a me[m]ber of the Lodge in the evening.

---

1. "at" written over "an"
2. In 1841 Church members who had been masons in other states before they joined the Latter-day Saints petitioned the Grand Lodge of Illinois to establish a lodge at Nauvoo. On 15 October 1841, Abraham Jonas, the Grand Master of the Grand Lodge of Illinois, who also had political aspirations in Illinois, granted a dispensation for the organization of the Nauvoo Lodge. On 29 December 1841, eighteen masons met in the office of Hyrum Smith and organized, and, on 15 March 1842, Grand Master Jonas visited Nauvoo for installation of the Lodge.

By that time fifty-five men had applied for membership. On this date, Joseph Smith and Sidney Rigdon were made "masons on sight" which allowed them to participate in the installation of the Lodge. The same day the two leaders were made Entered Apprentice Masons; the next morning, Fellow Craft Masons; and, in the afternoon, Master Masons. (See Mervin B. Hogan, *The Founding Minutes of Nauvoo Lodge, U.D.* [Des Moines, Iowa: Research Lodge Number 2, 1971]; also, T. Edgar Lyon, "Free Masonry at Nauvoo," *Dialogue* 6 [Spring 1971]: 76–78.)

The Nauvoo lodge was one of five Mormon lodges of freemasonry established in Illinois and Iowa in the early 1840s. The others were the Helm and Nye Lodges in Nauvoo; the Eagle Lodge at Keokuk, Iowa; and the Rising Sun Lodge at Montrose, Iowa. For a brief history of the rise and demise of these lodges see Joseph E. Marcombe, "Freemasonry at Nauvoo," *Journal of History*, 10: 408–39.

3. Wilford Woodruff noted that a procession formed at Joseph Smith's store and marched to the grove in front of the temple for the organization meeting of the 15th; he estimated about 3,000 people were present. (Diary of Woodruff, 15 March 1842.)

16 March 1842 · Wednesday

Continued with the Lodge.

17 March 1842 · Thursday

Assisted in organizing "The Female Relief Society of Nauvoo" in the "Lodge Room" Sister Emma Smith President, & Sister ⟨Elizabeth Ann⟩[1] Whitney & ⟨Sarah M.⟩ Cleveland councillors, ⟨I⟩ Gave much instruction, read in the New Testament, Book of Doctrine & Covenants, concer[n]ing the Elect Lady. & shewed that *Elect* meant to be *Elected* to a *certain work* &c, & that the revelation was then fulfilled by Sister Emma's Election to the Presidency of the Soc[i]ety, she having previously been ordained to expound the Scriptures. her councillors were ordaind by Elder J⟨ohn⟩ Taylor & Emma ⟨was⟩ Blessed by the same. —[2]

---

1. This and the following insertions in this paragraph are later additions in brownish ink.

2. Jill Mulvay Derr has outlined the beginnings of the Female Relief Society of Nauvoo: "Originally a seamstress, a Miss Cook hoped to combine her own skill with the financial resources of her employer, Sarah M. Kimball, in providing shirts for workmen on the Nauvoo Temple. As the two women discussed this charitable partnership, they envisioned and brought together a larger 'ladies society' of the neighborhood women. This group came under the still larger ecclesiastical umbrella when Joseph Smith organized them 'under the priesthood after the pattern of the priesthood.' " (Jill Mulvay Derr, "Strength in Our Union": The Making of Mormon Sisterhood," in *Sisters in Spirit: Mormon Women in Historical and Cultural Perspective*, ed. Maureen Ursenbach Beecher and Lavina Fielding Anderson [Urbana and Chicago: University of Illinois Press], 158. The minutes of the organization are in "A Record of the Organization and Proceedings of The Female Relief Society of Nauvoo," MS., LDS Church Archives.)

Joseph Smith's stated purpose for the Society was to "provoke the brethren to good works in looking to the wants of the poor"; to search after "objects of charity, and in administering to their wants"; to assist in "correcting the morals and strengthening the virtues of the community"; and "to reform persons . . . and by kindness sanctify and cleanse [them] from all unrighteousness." He also saw the Society as a means to help the women prepare for the temple. ("A Record of the Organization and Proceedings of The Female Relief Society," 17 March, 9 June 1842, MS.; see also Jill Mulvay Derr, Janath R. Cannon, Maureen U. Beecher, *Women of Covenant: The Story of Relief Society* [Salt Lake City: Deseret Book Company, 1992], chapter 1.)

371

18 March 1842 · Friday

[blank]

19 March 1842 · Saturday

[blank]

20 March 1842 · Sunday

Baptized 60 or 70 in the River, confirmed them in the grove & baptized in the Font in the P.M.[1]

21 March 1842 · Monday

Commenced a Settlement with Wm Marks[2]

22 March 1842 · Tuesday

At the General Business office (Sarah Ann Whitney's Birth day, ⟨(17 years of age)⟩[3] celebration, at the Lodge Room,[4] co. waited upon by the Recr[5]) home in the eve.

23 March 1842 · Wednesday

At his office in council with H. C. Kimball, Recr &c.

24 March 1842 · Thursday

At his office. waited on the members of the Female Relief Society. & entered a complaint against.[6] Clarissa Marvel

---

1. Wilford Woodruff noted that a large assembly of Saints gathered to hear Joseph Smith speak on the subject of baptism, but "as a young child was dead and his Corpes presented in the assembly" the Prophet changed the topic of his discourse to death and the resurrection. A summary of the speech is in the Woodruff Diary. (See also *Times and Seasons* 3 [15 April 1842]: 751–53.)

2. Marks had periodically loaned money and property to the Church. (*History of the Church*, 4:565.)

3. Insertion added later in brown ink.

4. The general business office or Lodge Room was the upper room in Joseph Smith's Nauvoo store.

5. Recorder, Willard Richards.

6. MS.: "againts"

for Slander[1]

25 March 1842 · Friday

[*blank*]

26 March 1842 · Saturday

[*blank*] [p. 91]

26 March 1842 · Saturday

Elder John Snider [Snyder] Received his final instructions from the President, & received his blessing from Prest B. Young. with the Laying on of the hands of Prest. Joseph. J. E. Page. & W. Richards. & Started for England same day.

27 March 1842 · Sunday

Baptized 107 individuals after speaking on baptism for the Dead[2] and witnessed the landing of 150 English brethren from the Steam boat Ariel[3]

28 March 1842 · Monday

Received P. P. Pratts donations from England. and transacted other business at the office.

29 March 1842 · Tuesday

[*blank*]

30 March 1842 · Wednesday

[*blank*]

---

1. Charges against Clarissa Marvel of slandering Joseph Smith were investigated by the Society on 30 March and continued to the next meeting. ("A Record of the Organization and Preceedings of The Female Relief Society," p. 23.)

2. In his diary of this date Wilford Woodruff summarized this address.

3. According to Wilford Woodruff, the *Ariel* was carrying 170 Mormon converts from England, led by Lyman Wight, and some $3,000 worth of goods for the temple and Nauvoo House when it arrived at Nauvoo. (Diary of Wilford Woodruff, 28 March 1842.)

31 March 1842 · Thursday

In council at his office with Elders Young. Taylor &c. & wrote an Epistle to the Female Relief Society and spoke to the Society in the afternoon.[1]

1 April 1842 · Friday

At the General Business office

2 April 1842 · Saturday

Paid Hugh Rhodes $1150. for a Farm

3 April 1842 · Sunday

[blank]

4 April 1842 · Monday

Transacted business at his house with Josiah Butterfield concerning the Lawrence estates.[2] & closed a settlement with Wm Marks in the Counting Room.

5 April 1842 · Tuesday

Settled with Bro [William] Niswanger

6 April 1842 · Wednesday

With his family. and several of the Twelve. viz. B. Young H. C. Kimball. W. Richards. & gave instructions how to or-

1. The meeting of the Female Relief Society was held on 30 March. A summary of Joseph Smith's remarks is in "A Record of the Proceedings of The Female Relief Society of Nauvoo," MS., pp. 22–23; see also *History of the Church*, 4:570.

2. After the death of Henry Lawrence, a Canadian, and the removal of his family to Nauvoo, Joseph Smith became guardian of the Lawrence estate. See Gordon Madsen, "The Lawrence Estate Revisited: Joseph Smith and Illinois Law Regarding Guardianships," paper read at Nauvoo Symposium, 21 September 1989, at Brigham Young University.

ganize & adjourn the special conference,[1] it being so wet & cold that it was not prudent to continue the meeting & the presidents health would not admit of his going out. at his house also the Patriarch and the Twelve present bore Testimony to the principles of virtue which they had invariably heard taught by Joseph.

7 April 1842 · Thursday

Spoke to the conference in the grove & replied to Elder John E. Page's communication. shewing the cause of his Seperation from Elder Hyde. on his mission to Jerusalem. fi[r]st a covenant to communicate to each other all secrets.[2] [p. 92]

8 April 1842 · Friday

[blank]

9 April 1842 · Saturday

Preached at the Funeral of Bro Ephraim Marks in the Morning.[3] and in the evening attended city council

---

1. Proceedings of the three-day conference are reported in *Times and Seasons* 3 (15 April 1842): 761–63; and *History of the Church*, 4: 583–86. See also Wilford Woodruff Diary. Woodruff reports that 275 elders were ordained in connection with this conference.

2. In April 1840 Orson Hyde and John E. Page had been called on a mission to visit Jewish communities in Europe and the Holy Land. The two men started their mission together but after a time separated—Elder Hyde continuing on to the Holy Land, and Elder Page eventually returning to Nauvoo. At the 1842 April conference, Page was called upon to explain "the nonperformance of his mission." In his remarks he stated that as he and Hyde started their mission they had made a covenant "to stand by each other . . . that if they were insulted, or imposed upon they would stand by each other even unto death, and not separate unless to go a few miles to preach a sermon," and that all money they obtained would "go into one purse, and it did so." He added that they would "often renew the covenant between them." In his comments following Page's remarks, Joseph Smith stated, "it was wrong to make the covenant of confidence referred to by him; that it created a lack of confidence for two men to covenant to reveal all acts of secrecy or otherwise to each other." ("Conference Minutes," *Times and Seasons* 3 [15 April 1842]: 761–63.)

3. Wilford Woodruff's diary summarizes the remarks of Joseph Smith and

10 April 1842 · Sunday

Preached in the grove after Elder Wm Law. had spoken. a[nd] pronounced a curse upon all Adulterers & fornicators & unvirtuous persons. & those who had made use of his name to carry on their iniquitous designs.[1]

11 April 1842 · Monday

In the Lodge & at his house–

12 April 1842 · Tuesday

In the Lodge[2]

13 April 1842 · Wednesday

In the Lodge Mr. Backinstos [Jacob Backenstos]. & [George P.] Stiles. & Robinson [Chauncey Robison] from carthage entered 1st degree & Joseph assisting P.M. S⟨aml⟩ H. Smith. Wm Smith. & Vincen Knight. on 3d degree[3]

Sidney Rigdon at the funeral of Ephraim Marks, son of Nauvoo stake president William Marks. An edited version of the report is in *History of the Church,* 4:587.

1. Wilford Woodruff's diary gives a summary of Joseph Smith's discourse. An edited version is in *History of the Church,* 4:588.

Because of its controversial nature, the doctrine of plural marriage had first been taught by Joseph Smith to only a few of his closest associates. By 1842, unscrupulous individuals in the Mormon community had used their awareness of the doctrine to cover immoral practices, informing their victims that Church leaders sanctioned such acts so long as they were kept secret. When the Prophet learned of the deception, he moved vigorously to counter it. By so doing, the issue was forced into the public spotlight. Nauvoo Mayor John C. Bennett was the most vocal among the exposed deceivers. Following the uncovering of his perfidy, he published and lectured widely against the Church and became one of its most bitter opponents. (See Donna Hill, *Joseph Smith the First Mormon* [Garden City, N.Y.: Doubleday & Company, 1977], chapter 4; John C. Bennett, *History of the Saints: An Expose of Joe Smith and Mormonism* [Boston: Leland & Whiting, 1842].)

2. This was a meeting with the Quorum of Twelve. See MS. minutes under this date; also *History of the Church,* 4:589–93.

3. Minutes of the proceedings are in Hogan, *Founding Minutes of the Nauvoo Lodge, UD.,* 17.

14 April 1842 · Thursday

Calvin A. Warren Esqr arrived and commenced an investigation of the principles of general insolvency.[1]

15, 16 April 1842 · Friday, Saturday

Busily engaged in making out a list of Debtors & invoice of Property to be passed into the hands of the assignee.

17 April 1842 · Sunday

At home

18 April 1842 · Monday

To carthage. in company with. Hyrum Smith Samuel H. Smith, & testified to their lists of insolvency before the clerk of the county commissioners. Sidney Rigdon & many more brethren. were at Carthage on the same day & business. — W. Richards was present.

19 April 1842 · Tuesday

Rode out in the city. & examined some land near the north limits

---

1. In April 1842 Joseph Smith decided to apply for bankruptcy under the federal law that went into effect in February that year. His rationale for taking this action was due to "the embarrassment under which we have labored through the influence of mobs and designing men, and the disadvantageous circumstances under which we have been compelled to contract debts in order to [maintain] our existence, both as individuals and as a society." (*History of the Church*, 4:594–95; 5:7. The Prophet's petition for bankruptcy as also those of his brothers Hyrum and Samuel, and several others, was published in successive issues of *The Wasp* [Nauvoo, Illinois], beginning 14 May 1842. For a review of the process see Dallin H. Oaks and Joseph I. Bentley, "Joseph Smith and Legal Process: In the Wake of the Steamboat *Nauvoo*," *BYU Law Review* 2 [1976]: 735–82; also Firmage and Mangrum, *Zion in the Courts*, 120–24.)

20 April 1842 · Wednesday

assisted in surveying some land in section 25. sold Wm Cross. [p. 93]

21 April 1842 · Thursday

[*blank*]

22 April 1842 · Friday

[*blank*]

23 April 1842 · Saturday

[*blank*]

24 April 1842 · Sunday

Preached on the hill near the Temple. concerning the building of the Temple. and pronounced a curse on the merchants & the rich who would not assist in building it.

25 April 1842 · Monday

Reading meditation &c. mostly with his family

26 April 1842 · Tuesday

"

27 April 1842 · Wednesday

"

28 April 1842 · Thursday

at Two o'clock after-noon met the members of the "Female relief Society" and after presiding at the admission of many new members. gave a lecture on the pries[t]hood shewing how the Sisters would come in possession of the privileges & bless-

ings & gifts of the priesthood & that the signs should follow
them. such as healing the sick casting out devils &c. & that
they might attain unto these blessings. by a virtuous life &
conversation & diligence in keeping all the commandments[1]

29 April 1842 · Friday

was made manifest a conspiracy against the peace of his
househould[2]

30 April 1842 · Saturday

visiting with Judge [James] Adams. & his own family. &
signed deeds to James & Charles Ivins. & many others.

1 May 1842 · Sunday

preached in the grove on the keys of the kingdom charity
&c. – The keys are certain signs & words by which false spirits
& personages may be detected from true.–which cannot be
revealed to the Elders till the Temple is completed.– The rich
can only get them in the Temple. The poor may get them on
the mountain top as did Moses. The rich cannot be saved
without cha[r]ity. giving to feed the poor. when & how God
requires as well as building. There are signs in heaven earth
& hell. the elders must know them all to be endued with power.
to finish their work & prevent imposition. The devil knows
many signs. but does not know the sign of the son of man.
or Jesus. No one can truly say he knows God until he has
handled something. & this can only be in the holiest of Holies.

2, 3 May 1842 · Monday, Tuesday

with his family

---

1. A summary of Joseph Smith's discourse on this date is in the Relief Society
minutes kept by Eliza R. Snow, the diary of Wilford Woodruff at the end of the
year 1842, and *History of the Church*, 4:602–7.

2. "J.C.B." written lightly in the margin by Willard Richards no doubt refers
to John C. Bennett.

4 May 1842 · Wednesday

In council in the Presidents & General offices with Judge Adams. Hyram Smith Newel K. Whitney. William Marks, Wm Law. George Miller. Brigham Young. Heber C. Kimball & Willard Richards. [*blank*] & giving certain instructions concerning the priesthood. [*blank*] &c on the Aronic Priesthood to the first [*blank*] continuing through the day.[1]

5 May 1842 · Thursday

Judge Adams left for Springfield the others continued in Council as the day previous & Joseph & Hyrum were [*blank*][2] [p. 94]

---

1. The blanks indicate erased words.

This marks the beginning of the endowment ceremony as practiced in Latter-day Saint temples. The published *History* indicates Joseph Smith instructed those present "in the principles and order of the Priesthood, attending to washings, anointings, endowments and the communication of keys pertaining to the Aaronic Priesthood, and so on to the highest order of the Melchisedek Priesthood, setting forth the order pertaining to the Ancient of Days, and all those plans and principles by which any one is enabled to secure the fullness of those blessings which have been prepared for the Church of the First Born, and come up and abide in the presence of the Eloheim in the eternal worlds. In this council was instituted the ancient order of things for the first time in these last days. And the communications I made to this council were of things spiritual, and to be received only by the spiritual minded: and there was nothing made known to these men but what will be made known to all the Saints of the last days, so soon as they are prepared to receive, and a proper place is prepared to communicate them, even to the weakest of the Saints; therefore let the Saints be diligent in building the Temple, and all houses which they have been, or shall hereafter be, commanded of God to build; and wait their time with patience in all meekness, faith, perseverance unto the end, knowing assuredly that all these things referred to in this council are always governed by the principle of revelation." (*History of the Church,* 5:2.)

The endowment ceremony consists of instruction, ordinances, and covenants calculated to motivate Church members to high ideals of devotion and morality in this life and to prepare them for the highest blessings in a post-mortal life. Before Joseph Smith's death in 1844, fewer than a hundred members had received the endowment. After his death, and the completion of the upper story of the Nauvoo Temple, more than 5,000 others were endowed before the departure of the Saints from Nauvoo. (See Cook, *Revelations of the Prophet,* 250–51.)

2. The blank indicates an erasure. According to *History of the Church,* 5:3, Joseph and Hyrum Smith received their endowment from those who had received it from the Prophet the previous day.

6 May 1842 · Friday

Attended the officer drill in the morning. & visited Lyman Wight who was sick

7 May 1842 · Saturday

Commanded the Nauvoo Legion through the day. the Legion one year since consisted of 6[1] companies. to day of 26 companies amounting to about Two thousand Troops. The consolidated Staff of the Legion partook of an excellent dinner at the house of the commander in chief between one & three. P.M. The day was very fine. & passed away very harmoniously. without drunkenness. noise or confusion. There was a great concourse of spectators. & many distinguis[h]ed Strangers who expressed much satisfaction.—& the commander in chief in a very appropriate address. remarked that his soul was never better satisfied than on this occasion. after the Legion was dismissed. Rode in Co. with his Lady & others around the Temple.

8 May 1842 · Sunday

Meeting at the grove. Prest Rigdon Preached

9 May 1842 · Monday

With his family.

10 May 1842 · Tuesday

Transacted a variety of business at the Store. printing office &c.

11 May 1842 · Wednesday

Called with the recorder to see a new secretary[2] at Bro Colleges [Joseph W. Coolidge]. dictated various letters & busi-

---

1. "6" written over "two".
2. I.e., a writing desk or cabinet for the temple recorder's office.

ness. called a few moments with Recorder at B. [Vinson] Knights

12 May 1842 · Thursday

Dictated a Letter to President Rigdon, concerning certain difficulties or surmises which existed, & attended the meeting of the Female Relief Society. the house being filled to overflowing. The meeting closed with heavy thunder storm.

13 May 1842 · Friday

Received answer from S. Rigdon after. a variety of current business having been in his garden & with his family much of the day. walked in the evening to the P[ost]. office with the Recorder.[1] & had a private interview with Prest Rigdon with much apparent satisfaction to all parties. concerning certain evil reports put in circulation by F. M. [blank][2] about Prest Rigdons family & others after which the Recorder waited on him to his gate.

14 May 1842 · Saturday

City council. Advocated strongly the necessity of some active measures being taken to suppress houses & acts of infamy in the city; for the protection of the innocent & virtuous–& good of public morals. shewing clearly that there were certain characters in the place who were disposed to corrupt the morals & chastity of our citizens & that houses of infamy did exist. upon which a city ordinance was passed to prohibit such things & published in this days wasp.[3] ⟨I⟩[4] Also. spoke Largely for the repeal of the ordinance of the city licencing

---

1. I.e., Willard Richards.
2. The blank indicates an erasure in the MS. It is filled with "Higbee" in *History of the Church.*
3. *The Wasp* 1 (14 May 1842): 3.
4. Later insertion in MS. in different ink.

merchants. Hawkers[1] Tavern[s] & ordinances. desiring that this might be a free people. & enjoy equal rights & Privileges. & the ordinances were repealed.–Bro Amos Fielding arrived from Liverpool.– after Council worked in his garden. & walked out in the city & borrowed two Sovereign[2] to make a payment This day it was first hinted in Nauvoo that Ex Governor [Lilburn] Boggs of Missouri. had been shot.[3] [p. 95]

[pp. 96–121, *donations*]

15 May 1842 · Sunday

Attended meeting at the grove. Prest Rigdon preached. News of Governor Boggs. confirmed By general Report & published on the stand[4]

16 May 1842 · Monday

Transacting business at the store until 10. A.M. Then at home & in the P.M. at the printing office with Bro. Young Kimball Richards &c in council

---

1. Peddlers, persons who offer their goods for sale by shouting their wares in the street or going from door to door.

2. A gold coin of the United Kingdom, equal to one pound sterling, that went out of circulation after 1914.

3. Boggs, a confirmed enemy of the Church during its years in Missouri, was shot by an unknown assailant on the evening of 6 May while sitting in his home. Although seriously wounded, he recovered. Later in the year, influenced by John C. Bennett, who at the time was venting his wrath against Joseph Smith after being expelled from the Church for immorality, Boggs charged the Prophet and Orrin Porter Rockwell with the attempt on his life and initiated proceedings to have the Prophet extradited to Missouri. (See entries of August 8ff.)

4. Wilford Woodruff, who was present at the meeting, wrote his reaction to the news: "True information has Just reached us that the Noted Governor Boggs of Missouri who By his orders expeled ten thousand Latter Day Saints, Has just Been assassinated in his own house & fallen in his own Blood. . . . Thus this ungodly wretch has fallen in the midst of his iniquity & the vengance of God has overtaken him at last & he has met his Just deserts though by an unknown hand this information is proclaimed through all the papers & By dispatched messengers & hand Bills through the land thus Boggs hath died as a fool dieth & gone to his place to receive the reward of his works." (Diary of Wilford Woodruff, 15 May 1842, MS.) Some time later, Woodruff added a postscript to his entry correcting the first rumor: "Boggs was shot but did not die but has since recovered from his wounds."

17 May 1842 · Tuesday

At home and about the offices through the day. & in the evening called at Bro Sniders to See Clark Leal of Fountain Green about Some land. &c

18 May 1842 · Wednesday

Rode on horse back with the Recorder in co. with clark Leal. To Bro [John] Benbows. & searched out the N.E. Quarter Sec 15. 6 N. 8 W. & contracted for the refusal of the Same at $3 per Acre. owned by Crawford B. Shelden of N York. dined at Bro Benbows. visited Bro Sayres [Edward Sayers]. &c. which with business at the different offices closed the day.

19 May 1842 · Thursday

Rain. At home during A.M.–1. o clock P.M. City council. The Mayor John C. Bennet having resigned his office,[1] Joseph was Elected Mayor & Hyrum Smith Vice Mayor of Nauvoo. While the election was going forward in the council. Joseph[2] recieved & wrote the following Rev[elation]–& threw it across the room to Hiram Kimball one of the Councillors.

"Verily thus saith the Lord unto you my servant Joseph by the voice of my Spirit, Hiram Kimball has been insinuating evil. & forming evil opinions against you with others. & if he continue[s] in them he & they shall be accursed. for I am the Lord thy God & will stand by thee & bless thee. *Amen.*"

After the Election Joseph spoke at some length concerning the evil reports which were abroad in the city concerning himself–& the necessity of counteracting the designs of our enemies. establishing a night watch &c. whereupon the mayor was authorized to establish a night watch by city ordinance,

Dr John C. Bennet, Ex mayor, was then called upon by

1. Bennett resigned his office as mayor on 17 May.
2. "I" penciled later over "Joseph" in MS.

the mayor to state if he knew ought against him.–when Dr. Bennet replied "I know what I am about. & the heads of the church know what they are about. I expect: I have no difficulty with the heads of the church. I publicly avow that any one who has said that I have stated that General Joseph Smith has given me authority to hold illicit intercourse with women is a Liar in the face of God. Those who have said it are damned Liars: they are infernal Liars. He never ⟨either⟩ in public or private gave me any such authority or license, & any person who states it is a scoundrel & a Liar. I have heard it said that I should become a Second [Sampson] Avard by withdrawing from the church, & that I was at variance with the heads ⟨& should use an influence against them⟩ because I resigned the office of mayor [p. 122] This is *false*. I have no difficulty with the heads of the church & intend to continue with you. & hope the time may come when I may be restored to full confidence. & fellowship. & my former standing in the church. & that my conduct may be such as to warrant my restoration.– & should the time ever come that I may have the opportunity to test my faith it will then be known whether I am a traitor or a true man."

Joseph. will you please state definitely whether you know anything against my character either in public or private?

Answer by Gen Bennet, "I do not. in all my intercourse with General Smith. in public & in private he has been strictly virtuous."

Joseph then made some pertinent remarks before the council concerning those who had been guilty of circulating false reports &c & said "Let one twelve months see if Bro Joseph is not calld for to go to every part of the city to keep them out of their groves & I turn the keys upon them from this hour if they will not repent & stop their lyings & surmisings. Let God curse them. & let their tongues cleave unto the roofs of their mouth.

20 May 1842 · Friday

Charges having been preferred against Dr R. {Foster} by Samuel H. {Smith} for abusing the Marshall Henry G. {Sherwood} & abusive language toward said Samuel H. {Smith} The Masonic Brethren met at 1 o clock P.M. when the charges were substantiated confession made by Foster. forgiveness granted. Joseph speaking at conciderable length. to accomplish the decision.

21 May 1842 · Saturday

At the High Council. investigating the case of Robert D. Foster. Chauncey Higby[1] & others. —

22 May 1842 · Sunday

At home. called at the Editors office to have letter copied for Quincy Whig. denying the charge of killing Ex Governor Boggs of Missouri as published in the Quincy whig[2]

---

1. Appearing before the high council on the 21st, Margaret and Matilda Nyman charged Chauncey Higbee with acts of immorality and having claimed he was instructed by Joseph Smith that there was no sin where there was no accuser. (The Nyman affidavits were published in the *Nauvoo Neighbor*, 29 May 1844.)

2. After announcing the 6 May shooting of Missouri ex-governor Lilburn W. Boggs by "an unknown hand," the *Quincy Whig* on 21 May speculated, "There are several rumors in circulation in regard to the horrid affair. One of which throws the crime upon the Mormons — from the fact, we suppose, that Mr. Boggs was governor at the time, and no small degree instrumental in driving them from the State.— Smith too, the Mormon Prophet, as we understand, prophesied a year or so ago, his death by violent means. Hence, there is plenty of foundation for rumor." (*Quincy Whig*, 21 May 1842, p. 3.)

The following day Joseph Smith charged the *Whig* editor with having done him "manifest injustice." He pointed out that Boggs could easily have been the victim of political intrigue and emphasized, "he died not through my instrumentality," adding, "I am tired of the misrepresentation, calumny and detraction heaped upon me by wicked men; and desire and claim only those privileges guaranteed to all men by the Constitution and Laws of the United States and of Illinois." (Smith to Bartlett, 22 May 1842; published in *Quincy Whig*, 4 June 1842, p. 2.)

On the Boggs case see Monte B. McLaws, "Attempted Assassination of Missouri's Ex-Governor, Lilburn W. Boggs," *Missouri Historical Review* 60 (October 1965): 50–62.

23 May 1842 · Monday

A.M. about home. P.M. walked down the River opposite Bro [Davidson] Hibbards with Dr [John F.] Charles. N.K. Whitney W. Woodruff. & Recorder & found a {–} in the water. called a city council. & Elected Dymic [Dimick] B. Huntington Coroner of Nauvoo

24 May 1842 · Tuesday

While the High council were taking depositions of Sarah Miller Sister Nymans [Margaret and Matilda Nyman] & against Chauncey Higby & others for illicit conduct, &c a prosecution was pending between Joseph & Chauncey before E[benezer]. Robinson. in which Chauncey was bound over in $200 Bonds

25 May 1842 · Wednesday

Councilling the Bishops &c. in ferretting out iniquity & much of this week was spent in session by the High Council of Nauvoo.[1] [p. 123]

26 May 1842 · Thursday

Masonic Lodge in the A.M. Dr John C. Bennet confessed the charges preferred against him concerning females in Nauvoo. & was forgiven Joseph plead in his behalf.– Dr Bennet was notified the day previous that the first Presidency. Twelve & Bishops had withdrawn fellowship from him & were about to publish him. but on his humbling himself & requesting it

---

1. Wilford Woodruff participated in these efforts to ferret out iniquity in connection with John C. Bennett and the "spiritual wifery" scandal: "The first Presidency The Twelve & High Council & virtuous part of the Church are making an exhertion abo[u]t these days to clense the Church from Adulterors fornicators & evil persons for their are such persons crept into our midst The high council have held a number of meeting[s] of late & their researches have disclosed much iniquity & a number [have] been cut off from the church." (Diary of Wilford Woodruff, 27 May 1842.)

the withdrawal was withheld from the paper. P.M. Female Relief Society–so full that many could get no admittance.[1]

27 May 1842 · Friday

A billious attack. at home taking medicine

28 May 1842 · Saturday

rather better. walked to the store with Emma. and did some business in the city, called at 8 in the eve at the printing office with the night watch. to see the Wasp. —[2]

29 May 1842 · Sunday

At home

30 May 1842 · Monday

[blank]

31 May 1842 · Tuesday

[blank]

1 June 1842 · Wednesday

Political meetings in the grove for nomination of county officers S. Rigdon. spoke at length. and nominated a general ticket from the county at large. Joseph spoke at length in confirmation of the nomination excepting for Sheriff.

---

1. Joseph Smith's address to the Relief Society on this date was reported by Eliza R. Snow. (See Nauvoo Relief Society Minutes, 26 May 1842; also published in *History of the Church*, 5:19–20.)

2. The 28 May edition of the *Wasp* contained Joseph Smith's petition for bankruptcy.

The Wasp was a weekly Nauvoo newspaper edited by William Smith commencing 16 April 1842. The paper was primarily devoted to news of Nauvoo and current events. On 3 May 1843 the name of the paper was changed to *Nauvoo Neighbor*, with John Taylor as editor; it continued publication until the exodus of the Latter-day Saints from Nauvoo. (Jenson, *Encyclopedic History*, 563, 928–29.)

2 June 1842 · Thursday

Rode out with Bro [John] Bowen & Recorder & Sold Lot. 1. Block 143.

3 June 1842 · Friday

Rode out in city & sold to Bro [Elias] Harmer Lot 1 Block 123–& in the P.M. Rode to Bro Benbows on the Prairie with Sister Emma & others on horse back

4 June 1842 · Saturday

At the printing office in the morning, heard the Letters from the Grand master [Abraham] Jonas Dr [Thomas C.] King & Mr Helme [Meredith Helm] about Bennets expulsion from the Lodge in Ohio.[1] P.M. Paid E. B. Nourse $505. for land bought of [Hugh] McFall. & settled with the heirs of Edward Lawrence at his house. N. K. Whitney & Recorder Present.

5 June 1842 · Sunday

Preached in the morning.[2]

6 June 1842 · Monday

To the Prairie with Bro. [David D.] Yearsly. & Recorder dined at Bro [Cornelius] Lots.

7 June 1842 · Tuesday

Sold Bro Yea[r]sley N.E. 1/4 of Section 15.

---

1. At a meeting of the Nauvoo Lodge on 19 May 1842, Thomas Grover charged "that Dr. John C. Bennett has palmed himself upon the Masonic Brethren in the organization of Nauvoo Lodge U.D. as a regular mason in good standing, when I have reason to believe that he is an expelled mason from a lodge in Fairfield, Ohio, or from Fairfield Lodge, Ohio." (Mervin B. Hogan, "The Confrontation of Grand Master Abraham Jonas and John Cook Bennett at Nauvoo," pp. 8–9, Typescript.)

2. A summary of Joseph Smith's discourse is in the Nauvoo *Wasp* 1 (11 June 1842): 1.

8 June 1842 · Wednesday

Recorder went to Carthage & narrowly escaped with his life. from a fall from on old charley.[1]

9 June 1842 · Thursday

[blank]

10 June 1842 · Friday

Went to Bro Hibbards to purchase some land [p. 124]

11 June 1842 · Saturday

Attended city council

12 June 1842 · Sunday

Home. Brought some poetry to printing office. & got some News papers

13 June 1842 · Monday

A gene[r]al council in Lodge room to devise ways & means to help the poor to labor

14 June 1842 · Tuesday

To the mound with Emma & purchased 3/4 Sections of Land of Hiram Kimball

15 June 1842 · Wednesday

visited in different part of the city. the farm in the Prairie with Recorder & Sister Hyde, & supped at Hiram Kimball's

---

1. Joseph Smith's horse.

16 June 1842 · Thursday

Special Lodge. John C. Bennet made his defense for the last time[1]

17 June 1842 · Friday

This week the recorder was sick & did not take notes.[2]

24 June 1842 · Friday

St Johns day. Rode in masonic procession to the grove where a large Assembly of masons & others listened to an address from Prest Rigdon.[3] dined at Bro [Alexander] Mills.

25 June 1842 · Saturday

Transacted Business with Bro. Hunter. Mr [Almon] Babbit. & sat for the drawing of his profile. for Lithographing on city chart.[4]

26 June 1842 · Sunday

Brigham Young preached. on consecration. or union of action in building up the city & providing labor & food for the

---

1. At this meeting of the Nauvoo Masonic Lodge, evidence was presented that Bennett had previously been expelled from masonry in Ohio. However, upon Bennett's presenting laudatory character references from men in Ohio dated about the time of his expulsion, and claiming that he had never been informed of his expulsion from the Ohio lodge, his case was postponed until the first Thursday in July. (Hogan, *Nauvoo Lodge Minutes*; Hogan, "The Confrontation," pp. 10–11.)

2. One event Willard Richards was unable to report was the meeting of Nauvoo citizens on 18 June in which Joseph Smith, among other things, "spoke his mind in great plainness concerning the iniquity & wickedness" of John C. Bennett, and "exposed him before the public." (Diary of Wilford Woodruff, 18 June 1842.)

3. Masonry's traditional festival of St. John the Baptist. According to Wilford Woodruff, the procession assembled at Joseph Smith's store and marched to the stand near the temple. He estimated 6,000 people were present to hear Rigdon speak. (Diary of Wilford Woodruff, 24 June 1842.)

4. See p. 392. The drawing was made by Sutcliffe Maudsley.

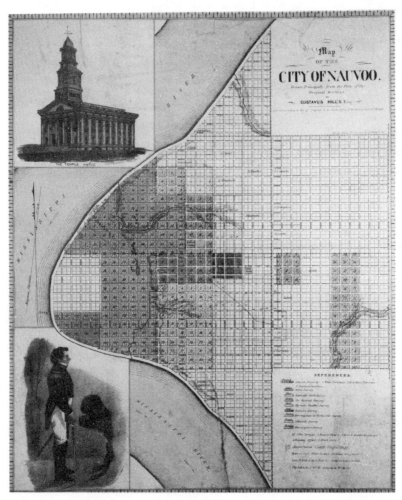

Map of the City of Nauvoo, Drawn Principally from the Plats of the Original Surveys by Gustavus Hill's, Esq. Drawing of Joseph Smith (lower left) by Sutcliffe Maudsley, 1842. LDS Church Archives.

poor. Joseph attended meeting, & council at his house at 6 o clock P.M. present Hyrum Smith. Geo Miller N. K. Whitney. Wm Marks. Brigham Young. Heber C. Kimball. & Willard Richards. To take into consideration the situation of the pine country & Lumbering business[1] and other subjects of importance to the church; after consultation thereon the Brethren united in Solemn prayer that God would make known his will concerning the pine country, & that he would deliver his anointed, his people from all the evil designs of Governor Boggs, & the powers of the state of Missouri, & of Governor [Thomas] Carlin. & the authorities of Illinois, & of all presidents, governors. Judges Legislators & all in authority, and of John C. Bennet.[2] & all mobs & evil designing persons.–so that his people might continue in peace & build up the city of Nauvoo. & that his chosen might be blessed & live to man's appointed age. & that their households. & the household of faith might. continually be blessed with the fost[er]ing care of heaven.–& enjoy the good things of the earth abundantly.– adjourned to monday evening [p. 125]

27 June 1842 · Monday

Transacting business in general through the day. borrowed money of Bros. [Edwin D.] Wooley. Spencer[3] &c. & made payment To Hiram Kimball for the mound. when the council assembled in the evening Brothers. [Edward] Hunter. Ivins

---

1. In 1841 the Church purchased a lumber mill near the falls of the Black River in present-day Jackson County, Wisconsin, from which lumber was supplied to provide Nauvoo building needs, particularly for the Nauvoo House and the temple. (See Don F. Colvin, "A Historical Study of the Mormon Temple at Nauvoo, Illinois" [M.A. thesis, Brigham Young University, 1962], 69–80.)

2. By this time Bennett had begun a vigorous campaign to disparage those who had exposed his immoral schemes. On 8 July the *Sangamon Journal* at Springfield began publication of a series of Bennett letters attacking Joseph Smith and the Church. One weapon in the Bennett arsenal was his repetitions of the allegation that the Prophet was involved in the Boggs assassination attempt earlier in the year.

3. Probably Daniel Spencer.

[Edwin D.] Wooley. [Robert] Pierce & others being present. the adjourned council was pos[t]pon⟨e⟩d till tuesday evening, & Joseph proceed[ed] to Lecture at length on the importance of uniting the means of the brethren for the purpose of establishing manufactories of all kinds, furnishing labor for the poor &c. Brothers Hunter & Wooley offered their goods toward ~~the~~ a general funds & good feelings were generally manifest. This morning Little Frederic G. W. Smith[1]–told his dream to all the house "that the Missourians had got their heads knocked off." –

28 June 1842 · Tuesday

payed Brothers Wooley & Spencer. Bro Hunters goods were rec[e]ived at the store & Bro Robins [Lewis Robbins] consecrated his goods & money to the general funds. the adjourned council of Sunday evening met at the upper Room at Josephs & were agreed that a reinforcement go immediately to the pine country Led by Bro Ezra Chase. & after uniting in Solemn prayer. to God. for a blessing on themselves & families & the church in general. & for the building up of the Temple. & Nauvoo House. & city: for deliverance from their enemies. & the spread of the work of Righteousness: & that Bro Richards (who was expecting to go east tomorrow for his family,)[2] that he might have a prosperous Journey. have power of over the winds & elements, & all opposition & dangers, his life & health

---

1. Joseph Smith's five-year-old son.
2. Less than a year after he joined the Latter-day Saints, Willard Richards was called on a proselyting mission to England with the first missionaries to enter that land. While in England in 1838 he met and married Jeanetta Richards (no relation). Upon returning to America in 1841, Willard left his family with relatives in Massachusetts while he continued on to Nauvoo to prepare a place for them. Because of the press of clerical duties and other responsibilities that came to him there, it was not until the summer of 1842 that he was able to return to Massachusetts for his family. During his travels to the East, Willard was also authorized to collect money for the building of the temple and other Church interests at Nauvoo. (*Times and Seasons* 3 [1 June 1842]: 814.)

be preserved & be speedily returned to this place with his family. that their lives & helth might be preserved & that they might come up in peace to this place. & that Bro Richards might be prospered according to the desire of his heart in all things in relation to his household. & the church. & that the spirit of God might rest upon him continually so that he may act according to the wisdom of heaven, ~~continually~~, the council disposed. Previous to the council President Joseph in company with Bishop Miller, visited Elder Rigdon & his family & had much conversation about J. C. Bennet & others. much unpleasant feeling was manifested by Elder Rigdon's family who were confounded & put to silence by the truth from Prest. Joseph

29 June 1842 · Wednesday

Held a long conversation with Francis Higby [Higbee]. Francis found fault with being exposed. but Joseph told him he spoke of him in self defence. Francis was or appeared humble & promised to reform. Heard the Recorder Read in the Law of the Lord. paid taxes Rode out in the city on business with Brigham Young. The Recorder being about to start east on a Journey committed the Law of the Lord To Wm Clayton to continue this Journal &c in his absence. & the Keys &c to the president. & Clayton

W. Richards/[1] [p. 126]

30 June 1842 · Thursday

In the A.M. spent some time with C[alvin]. A. Warren Eqr from Quincy & others in the private office and in the P.M.

---

1. Willard Richards's handwriting ends at this point in the MS. and William Clayton's begins.

was in the Court martial giving testimony concerning John C Bennett &c.[1]

On the 8th of last November at about 5 o clock in the evening the Baptismal Font was dedicated.[2] In February 1842 Samuel Rolfe washed his hands in the Font being seriously affected with a Fellon, so that the Doctors thought it ought to be cut open; others said it would not be well before spring. After washing in the Font his hand healed in one week. –

On the 25th day of September 1841 a Deposit was made in the south east corner of the Temple. –

2 July 1842 · Saturday

Went out in the city with W. C. [William Clayton] to look at some lots and afterwards rode out to Hezekiah Pecks with sister Emma and others. –

3 July 1842 · Sunday

Preached at the Grove near the Temple on the ancient order of things &c[3]–was at the Grove also in the P.M.

4 July 1842 · Monday

With the Legion in command all day, and at the close expressed his satisfaction with the Legion, and briefly showed the design of its organization viz to defend ourselves and families from mobs &c. He requested any stranger who was present and wished to speak to do so, when Gen. [Ezekiel] Swa[zey]

---

1. The following day Joseph Smith published a statement of "important facts relative to the conduct and character of John C. Bennett . . . that the honorable part of the community may be aware of his proceedings . . . as an imposter and base adulterer." ("To the Church of Jesus Christ of Latter Day Saints, and to all the Honorable Part of Community," *Times and Seasons* 3 [1 July 1842]: 839–43.)

2. Located in the basement of the Nauvoo Temple.

3. According to Woodruff, the Prophet read the 7th chapter of Daniel and "explained about the Kingdom of God set up in the last days." About 6,000 people were present. (Diary of Wilford Woodruff, 3 July 1842.)

from Iowa made some friendly remarks and expressed his satisfaction; also his gratification to see the good discipline of the Legion. —

5 July 1842 · Tuesday

Attended court martial. —

6 July 1842 · Wednesday

In the A.M. attending to business in the city and afterwards rode out to La Harpe with sister Emma and others. —

9 July 1842 · Saturday

Rode out on Prairie with W. C. [William Clayton] & bro [William A.] Gheen to look out some land. Dined on his farm, hoed potatoes &c and in the P.M. returned after which he transacted business in the city

10 July 1842 · Sunday

At the stand, was some sick and could not preach. W. Woodruff preached at home in the P.M. —

11 July 1842 · Monday

With Mr Hunter in the A.M. and in the P.M. was at the printing office reading mail papers. Bought a horse[1] of [Harmon T.] Wilson Deputy Sheriff for aw.$

12 July 1842 · Tuesday

In the lodge consulting concerning Bennetts proceedings and taking Esqr [Daniel H.] Wells affidavit. Bro's [George] Miller & [Erastus] Derby started for Quincy & Mo —[2]

---

1. According to the *History*, Joseph named the horse "Joe Duncan" after Joseph Duncan, former Governor of Illinois, who in his campaign for governor in 1842 spoke vigorously against the Latter-day Saints.

2. Following his exposure and departure from Nauvoo, John C. Bennett pub-

15 July 1842 · Friday

This A.M. early a report was in circulation that O. P. [Orson Pratt] was missing. A letter of his writing was found directed to his wife stating to the effect that he was going away. Soon as this was known Joseph summoned the principal men of the city and workmen on the Temple to meet at the Temple Grove where he ordered them to proceed immediately throughout the city in search of him lest he should have laid violent hands on himself.[1] After considerable search had been made

---

lished a series of letters in the *Sangamon Journal* critical of Joseph Smith and the Church. In a letter dated 2 July, Bennett charged the Prophet with having prophesied the death of ex-Governor Boggs of Missouri and having sent Orrin Porter Rockwell to fulfill the prophecy. (See "Bennett's Second and Third Letters," *Sangamon Journal* [Springfield, Illinois], 15 July 1842.)

On 12 July George Miller and Erastus Derby were sent to Quincy, Illinois, and to Jefferson City, Missouri, to confer with Governors Carlin and Reynolds about rumors that Joseph Smith was soon to be charged with the attempt on Boggs's life and extradited to Missouri. They were to show that John C. Bennett was an instigator in the proceedings and were to place Bennett's charges in the context of his character.

1. After returning in July 1841 from a proselyting mission to England, Orson Pratt confronted the introduction of the practice of plural marriage at Nauvoo in a bizarre scenario that took him briefly out of the Church. By the time Pratt returned from England, Joseph Smith had introduced the practice of plural marriage but had not taught it publicly. One who knew of the practice and had gained the confidence of many of the Saints was was John C. Bennett, who used his knowledge to engage in immoral practices under the guise that such activity was authorized by the Church leadership so long as it was kept secret. After Bennett's treachery was discovered, which resulted in excommunication and his leaving the community in disgrace, he lashed out at Joseph Smith and the Church with a scandalous exposé. In a letter published in the *Sangamo Journal* on 15 July 1842, Bennett charged Joseph Smith with improprieties toward Orson Pratt's wife, Sarah. Faced with statements of his wife and Bennett on one hand, and the Prophet's denial on the other, Orson sided for a time with his wife and Bennett, and, in a moment of despondence, left Nauvoo on 15 July amid rumors of possible suicide, setting off a community alert to find him. Five weeks later he was excommunicated from the Church but by January 1843 learned he had made a faulty judgment and was reinstated in his apostolic calling. On 17 July 1842 Brigham Young wrote Parley Pratt in England: "Br Orson Pratt is in trubble in consequence of his wife, his feelings are so rought up that he dos not know whether his wife is wrong, or whether Josephs testimony and others are wrong and due Ly and he decived for 12 years or not; he is all but crazy about matters."

but to no effect a meeting was called at the Grove where Joseph stated before the public a general outline of J. C. Bennetts conduct and especially with regard to Sis P [Sarah Pratt]. Met again in the P.M. when Hyrum & H. C. Kimball spoke on the same subject after which Joseph arose and said that he would state to those present some things which he had heard respecting Edward & D[avid]. Kilbourn being conspiring with J. C. Bennett in endeavouring to bring [p. 127] a Mob upon us, and as Mr E. Kilbourn was then present he would have the privilege of either admitting or denying it. Question by E. Kilbourn "Who did Bennett tell that I and my brother were conspiring to bring a mob upon you" Answer by Joseph "He told me and he told [blank] Allred and Orson Pratts wife & others." Q by E. Kilbourn "Where did he say we were going to bring a mob from." Ans. by Joseph. "From Galena." Mr. Kilbourn then arose and said. "I was conversing with my brother this morning and he said he had never seen Bennett since he had us before him last year for conspiracy. I have only seen him twice since last fall. I saw ⟨him⟩ once then. I was going to Galena about 2 weeks ago. The Boat I was on stopped at the upper Landing place and I came ashore a little while. The first person I saw was Bennett; we entered into conversation, but there was no mention made of mobs. I have not seen him since. I always regarded Bennett the same as I regard you (Joseph) and thought you were pretty well matched. If anyone says that I have conspired to bring a mob upon you it is false." The meeting was then peaceably dismissed. O. P. [Orson Pratt] returned at night. He was seen about 2 miles this side Warsaw, set on a log. He says he has concluded to do right.

(Brigham Young to Parley Pratt, 17 July 1842; Breck England, *The Life and Thought of Orson Pratt* [Salt Lake City: University of Utah Press, 1985], 74–86; Diary of Wilford Woodruff, 19 January 1843.)

16 July 1842 · Saturday

Rode out on prairie with W. C. [William Clayton] to show some land to Bro Russel[1] from Genesee called at his farm and dined at bro Lots. Afterwards went to hoeing potatoes.

17 July 1842 · Sunday

At the Grove, was sick. At home the remainder of the day.

18 July 1842 · Monday

Rode out to bro Kearn's [Hamilton Henry Kearnes] and to the Farm.

19 July 1842 · Tuesday

Rode out with Dr Foster, Henry Kearns & others to look at Timber Land

22 July 1842 · Friday

A.M. at the stand conflicting with O. P. [Orson Pratt] and correcting the public mind with regard to reports put in circulation by Bennett & others.[2] In the P.M. a petition was prepared and signed[3] by the citizens praying the Governor not to issue a writ for the Prest.[4]

---

1. Possibly Jonathan Russell.
2. The meeting was called to "obtain an expression of the public mind" with respect to the efforts of John C. Bennett to defame Joseph Smith's character. Wilson Law presented a resolution upholding the Prophet's integrity and moral character. The vote was nearly unanimous, but Orson Pratt arose and spoke at length to justify his negative vote, whereupon Joseph publicly asked Pratt, "Have you personally a knowledge of any immoral act in me toward the female sex, or in any other way?" To which Orson replied, "Personally, toward the female sex, I have not." (*Times and Seasons* 3 [1 August 1842]: 869.)
3. MS.: "singed"
4. The petition urging Governor Carlin not to issue a writ for Joseph Smith "to be given up to the authorities of Missouri" in the Boggs case was drawn up by a committee of the city council consisting of John Taylor, William Law, and Brigham Young, assisted by James Sloan, the Recorder. (Nauvoo City Council Minutes, 22 July 1842, MS.; published in *History of the Church*, 5:68–70.)

24 July 1842 · Sunday

In the A.M. at home sick. In the P.M. at the Grove. Spoke concerning bro. [George] Miller having returned with good news. That Bennett could do nothing &c.[1]

26 July 1842 · Tuesday

Sick. Rode to the farm in the P.M.

27 July 1842 · Wednesday

At the Grove, listening to the electioneering candidates. After they had got through spake some

31 July 1842 · Sunday

In council with Bishops Miller & Whitney, B. Young, Jno Taylor &c. concerning Bishop [Vinson] Knights sickness. Bro Knight has been sick about a week and this morning he began to sink very fast untill 12 o clock when death put a period to his sufferings.

3 August 1842 · Wednesday

In the city transacting various business–and in company with General Adams and others.

4 August 1842 · Thursday

In the city learning sword exercise under Col. Brewer from St Louis and attending various other business. [p. 128]

6 August 1842 · Saturday

Went over the river to Montrose to witness the installation of officers of the Rising Sun Lodge, Iowa[2] in company with Col. Brewer Gen. [James] Adams &c

---

1. The entry of 12 July clarifies Miller's mission and message.
2. Masonic lodge.

7 August 1842 · Sunday

At home all day

8 August 1842 · Monday

This A.M the Deputy Sheriff of Adams county[1] in company with two other officers came with a warrant from Governor [Thomas] Carlin and arrested Joseph and O[rrin]. P[orter]. Rockwell. the latter being charged with shooting ex-Governor Boggs of Missouri with intent to kill on the evening of the 6th of May last and Joseph with being accessory. The city council convened immediately and issued a writ of Habeus Corpus to stop them from taking Joseph & Rockwell away without a trial here.[2] The Deputy Sheriff hesitated complying with the writ of Habeus Corpus for some time on the ground (as he said) of not knowing wether this city had authority to issue such writ but after much consultation on the subject they finally

---

1. Probably Thomas C. King.

2. The Nauvoo city charter, which had been ratified by the Illinois legislature in 1840, granted authority to issue writs of habeas corpus, "an order by a court or judge requiring that a person in custody be brought before the court to determine the legality of his or her detention." In anticipation of a possible extradition proceeding in the Boggs case, the Nauvoo city council in July had passed an ordinance declaring that "no citizen of this city shall be taken out of the city by any writs without the privilege of investigation before the municipal court, and the benefit of a writ of habeas corpus." And on 8 August, the day the warrant from Carlin was issued, the city council passed another ordinance stating that in the future any person arrested in the city should be brought before the municipal court on a writ of habeas corpus, and that the court be required to examine "the origin, validity and legality of the writ of process," and if not legally issued, "the court shall discharge the prisoner." And further, if the municipal court determined that the writ was issued "through private pique, malicious intent, or religious or other persecution, falsehood or misrepresentation," contrary to the state and national constitutions, "the writ or process shall be quashed."

The effort of the Latter-day Saints to protect themselves from legal harrassment generated much antagonism against them in western Illinois and contributed to the opposition that eventually resulted in the death of Joseph Smith. (*History of the Church*, 5:57, 87–88; Firmage and Mangrum, *Zion in the Courts: A Legal History of the Church of Jesus Christ of Latter-day Saints, 1830–1890*, 92–105.)

agreed to leave the prisoners in the hands of the city marshall and returned to Quincy to ascertain from the Governor wether our charter gave the city jurisdiction over the case

Received a letter from Post Office which had been broke open and was much grieved at the meanness of its contents.

9 August 1842 · Tuesday

In company with Judge [James H.] Ralston & Lawyer [Stephen] Powers from Keokuk preparing for the return of the Sheriff. Prepared a writ of Habeus Corpus from the Master in Chancery.

10 August 1842 · Wednesday

The Deputy Sheriff returned but could not find Joseph. He endeavoured to alarm sister Emma & the Brethren by his threats, but could not do it they understanding the nature of the Law in that case.

11 August 1842 · Thursday

This A.M. brother Wm Law entered into conversation with the Deputy upon the illegality of the whole proceedings in reference to the arrest. After some remarks from both parties the Sherif acknowledged that he believed Joseph was innocent and that Governor Carlins course which he had pursued was unjustifiable and illegal. During the day Joseph who was at this time at Uncle John Smiths in Zarahemla sent word that he wished to see Sister Emma bro's Hyrum Smith, Wm. Law and others, with instructions to meet on the island between Nauvoo and Montrose after Dark. Whereupon Emma, Hyrum, Wm Law, N. K. Whitney, George Miller, Wm. Clayton & Dimick B. Huntington met at the water side near the Brick Store sometime after dark and proceeded in a skiff to the islands. We proceeded between the islands untill we arrived near the lower end; and then hauled to shore. After waiting a very little while, the skiff arrived from the opposite shore, and in it; Joseph and bro. [Erastus] Derby. A council was then held in the skiffs, and various statements set forth in regard to the state of things. It was ascertained that the Governor of Iowa, had issued a warrant for the apprehension of Joseph, and O. P. Rockwell; and that the sheriff of Lee County, was expected down immediately. Very strong evidence was also manifested that Governor [Thomas] Reynolds of Missouri was not acquainted with these proceedings. That Ex- Governor Boggs had made oath before a justice of the peace or a Judge and that the Judge had made the requisition and not Governor Reynolds. Also that the writ issued by Carlin was illegal and unjustifiable [p. 129]

It is very evident that the whole business is but another evidence of the effects of prejudice, and that it proceeds from a persecuting spirit; the parties having signified their determination to have Joseph taken to Missouri wether by legal or illegal means. It was finally concluded that Joseph should be taken up the river in a Skiff and be landed below the farm called Wiggans' [Ebenezer Wiggins] farm and that he should proceed from thence to brother [Edward] Sayers and their abide for a season. This being concluded upon, the parties separated, Joseph and brother Derby being rowed up the river by brother [Jonathan] Dunham and the remainder crossed over to Nauvoo. It was agreed that brother A[lbert]. P. Rockwood should proceed up the River on shore unto the place where the skiff should stop and there light up two fires as a signal for stopping place. After the Boat had proceeded some distance above the city a fire was discovered on shore. It was concluded that it was the signal and they immediately rowed to shore. When near the shore one of the company hailed a person on the shore but received a very unsatisfactory answer, whereupon they turned about and put to the channel and upon coming near the middle of the river discovered two fires a little higher. They immediately steered towards the fires and was happy to find brother Rockwood awaiting their arrival. They then proceeded through the timber to brother Sayers' house where they were very kindly received and made welcome.

Judge [James H.] Ralston and Lawyer [Stephen W.] Powers departed each for home expressing their perfect willingness to aid us in every possible manner. Judge Ralston also promised to ascertain the state of affairs in Quincy and give us the earliest information

12 August 1842 · Friday

This A.M. it appears still more evident that the whole course of proceedings by Governor Carlin and others is illegal. After some consultation with brother Wm Law sister Emma concluded to dispatch a messenger with a letter to Lawyer Powers of Keokuk to request him to go to Burlington I.T. and there see the Governor of Iowa and endeavor to ascertain a knowledge of the truth as to wether Gov. Reynolds had made any requisition on him for Joseph & Rockwell. Accordingly, Josephs new horse which he rides was got ready and Wm Walker proceeded to cross the river in sight of a number of persons. One cheif design in this procedure was to draw the attention of the Sheriffs and public, away from all idea that Joseph was on the Nauvoo side of the river

At night W. Clayton & John D. Parker left Nauvoo after dark and went to see Joseph and found him chearful and in good spirits.

13 August 1842 · Saturday

This A.M. a letter was received by President Hyrum from brother [David S.] Hollister of Quincy (stating that Gov. Carlin had said that his proceedings was not legal and he should not pursue the subject any further.[)] The letter allso stated that [Edward R.] Ford (the agent to receive Joseph from the hands of the Sheriff and carry him to Missouri) had concluded to

405

take the first Boat and start home: and that he was going to fetch a force from Missouri.[1] All this it is thought. is only a s[c]heme got up for the [p. 130] purpose of throwing us off our guard that they may thereby come unexpected and kidnap Joseph and carry him to Missouri.

In concequence of President Joseph requesting sister Emma to go and see him that they might consult together &c. she concluded to go in the carriage. But when the carriage was being got ready it attracted the attention of the Sheriff and they kept a strict watch for some time. Seeing the difficulty of getting away undiscovered sister Emma concluded to go on foot to Mrs [Elizabeth] Durphy's and wait untill the carriage arrived. Accordingly the cover of the carriage being folded up to shew the Sheriffs that she was not in W. C. [William Clayton] & Lorain [Lorin] Walker started down the river–called at Durphys and then proceeded down the river without being discovered. We went about 4 miles [down] the river road and then turned off towards the Prarie. We went round the city about 2 miles

---

1. In a letter to Governor Reynolds on September 8, Edward Ford summarized his effort to arrest Joseph Smith: "I deemit nesary to in form – you of my proseding I proseded to Burlington with the Demand to gov Cambery which I found it importent to do so. I obtain the Rits – and placed them in the officers Hands in lee – County Iowa the officers conceal them-selves near mont rose I then proseaded my self to Quincy I there in formd the officers and the – govenor of the fact on friday evening layte we left Quincy for nauvoo but unfortunatly for us it rain verry hard and turnd quit dark so that we was compeld to stop we – however started verry earley next morning to nauvoo whe[n] we got there he was gon – thoe Smith was at his House the over night – he was furnish with the informatioun that the officers was A coming he left nauvoo-a-bout seven o clock in the morning and we-a-rived-a-bout nine o clock we then proceded for a carch [search] with five men ondley the officers allso maid and effort in Iowa but his whare a bouts was not found – we carch two Days for Smith and – Rockwell on both sids but and intier failier tho Smith is undoubtely a bout nauvoo it is verry unsearten whether Rockwell is a bout or not govenor Carlin sais all that he can do is to offer a reward of two hundred Dollars for each vilion william Mc. – Daniel sais if you will gave himn the – Apointment that he will undoubtaly take Smithe this is the true statment of my proseadings." (Edward R. Ford to Thomas Reynolds, 8 September 1842, MS., Missouri Historical Society, St. Louis, Missouri.)

from the outskirts and turned into the timber again opposite the Wiggans farm After we got within about a mile from brother Sayers sister Emma left the carriage and proceeded on foot. We soon arrived at brother Sayers and was pleased to find President Joseph in good spirits, although somewhat sick. The carriage returned home after we left it.

A report came over the river that there is seve⟨r⟩al small companies of men in Montrose, Nashville, Keokuk &c in search of Joseph. They saw his horse go down the river yesterday and was confident he was on that side. They swear they will have him. It is said there is a reward of thirteen hundred dollars offered for the apprehension and delivery of Joseph and Rockwell and this is supposed to have induced them to search viz. to get the reward.

The sheriff and Deputy[1] have uttered heavy threats several times saying that if they could not find Joseph they would lay the city in ashes They say they will tarry in the city a month but they will find him.

14 August 1842 · Sunday

Spent the forenoon chiefly in conversation with sister Emma on various subjects, and in reading this history with her. Both felt in good spirits and were very chearful. Wrote the following orders to Major Genl Wilson Law who was reported to be duly elected to that office yesterday,[2] as follows, viz.–

Head Quarters of Nauvoo Legion
Augt 15–1842

Major Gen. Law
D[ea]r General–I take this opportunity to give you some instructions how I wish you to act in case our persecutors should

---

1. James M. Pittman and Thomas King.
2. Wilson Law was elected Major General of the Nauvoo Legion to replace John C. Bennett on 3 August 1842.

carry their pursuits so far as to tread upon our rights as free-born American Citizens. The orders which I am about to give you is the result of a long series of contemplation since I saw you. — I have come fully to the conclusion both since this last difficulty commenced, as before, that I never would suffer myself to go into the hands of the Missourians alive; and to go into the hands of the officers of this state is nothing more nor less, than to go into the hands of the Missourians; for the whole farce has been gotten up, unlawfully and unconstitutionally, as well on the part of the Governor as others; by a mob spirit for the purpose of carrying out mob violence, to carry on mob tolerance in a religious persecution. I am determined therefore, to keep out of their hands, and thwart their designs if possible, that perhaps they may not urge the necessity of force and blood against their own fellow citizens and loyal subjects; and become ashamed and withdraw their pursuits. But if they [p. 131] should not do this and shall urge the necessity of force; and if I by any means should be taken, these are therefore to command you forthwith, without delay, regardless of life or death to rescue me out of their hands. And further, to treat any pretensions to the contrary, unlawful and unconstitutional and as a mob got up for the purpose as religious persecution to take away the rights of men. And further, that our chartered rights and privileges shall be considered by us as holding the supremacy in the premises and shall be maintained; nothing short of the supreme court of this State, having authority to dis-annul them; and the Municipal court having jurisdiction in my case. You will see therefore that the peace of the City of Nauvoo is kept, let who will endeavor to disturb it. You will see also that whenever any mob force or violence is used, on any citizen thereof, or that belongeth thereunto, you will see that that force or violence is immediately dispersed and brought to punishment; or meet it, and contest it at the point of the sword with firm and undaunted and unyeilding valor; and let them know that the spirit of old seventy-six, and of George Washington yet lives, and is contained in the bosoms and blood of the children of the fathers thereof. If there are any threats in the city let legal steps be taken on the part of those that make the threats: and let no man, woman or child be intimidated nor suffer it to be done. Nevertheless as I said in the first place we will take every measure that lays in our power and make every sacrifice that God or man could require at our hands to preserve the peace and safety of the people without collision.[1] And if sacrificing my own liberty for months and years without stooping to the disgrace of Missouri persecution and violence, and Carlins mis-rule and corruption, I bow to my fate with cheerfulness and all due deference in the consideration of the lives, safety and welfare of others. But if this policy cannot accomplish the desired object; let our Charter, and our municipality; free trade and Sailors rights be our motto, and go a-head David Crockett like, and lay down our lives like men, and defend ourselves to the best advantage we can to the very last. You are therefore, hereby authorised and commanded, by virtue of the authority which I hold, and commission granted me by the Executive of this State, to maintain the very letter and spirit of the above contents of this letter to the very best of your ability; to the extent of our lives, and our fortunes; and to the lives and the fortunes of the Legion; as also all those who may volunteer their lives and their fortunes with ours; for the defence of our wives, our children, our fathers and our mothers; our homes; our grave yards, and our tombs; and our dead and their tombstones, and our dear bought American liberties with the blood of our fathers, and all that is dear and sacred to man. Shall we shrink at the onset? No, let every mans brow be as the face of a Lion; let his heart be unshaken as the mighty oak, and his knee confirmed as the sapling[2] of the forrest; and by

---

1. MS.: "colition"
2. MS.: "sappline"

the voice and loud roar of the cannon; and the loud peals and thundering of artillery; and by the voice of the thunderings of heaven as upon mount Sinai; and by the voice of the Heavenly Hosts; and by the voice of the Eternal God; and by the voice of innocent blood; and by the voice of innocence; and by the voice [p. 132] of all that is sacred and dear to man, let us plead the justice of our cause; trusting in the arm of Jehovah the Eloheem who sits enthroned in the heavens: that peradventure he may give us the victory; and if we bleed we shall bleed in a good cause–in the cause of innocence and truth: and from henceforth will their not be a crown of glory for us? And will not those who come after us, hold our names in sacred remembrance? and will our enemies dare to brand us with cowardly reproach? With these considerations, I subscribe myself Yours most faithfully and respectfully with acknowledgements of your high and honored trusts as Major Gen. of the Nauvoo Legion

Joseph Smith–Mayor of the City of Nauvoo

and Lieut Gen. of the Nauvoo Legion of Illinois Militia Wilson Law.

Major Gen. of the Nauvoo Legion. –

P.S. I want you to communicate all the information to me of all the transactions, as they are going on daily, in writing by the hand of my aidecamps. as I am not willing that anything that goes from my hands to you should be made a public matter, I enjoin upon you to keep all things in your own bosom; and I want every thing that comes from you to come through my aids. The bearer of this will be able to pilot them in a way that will not be prejudicial to my safety–

Joseph Smith. –

This letter was put into the hands of Sister Emma with a charge to deliver it to Gen. Law tomorrow. After considerable conversation on various subjects and partaking of dinner Sister Emma accompanied by brother Derby & W. Clayton started for Nauvoo. The morning had been very wet and the roads was very dirty. It was difficult walking. We[1] proceeded to the river and entered a skiff in which we proceeded across the river and then down the side of the islands. Soon after we got on the water the wind began to blow very hard and it was with much difficulty and apparent danger that we could proceed. We continued on as well as we could and after considerable toil arrived opposite the City of Nauvoo. We went between the Islands and crossed over the river to Montrose as soon as we landed the wind abated and we was near calm. Brother Derby wanted to return up the river without the additional toil of crossing to Nauvoo. We was fortunate in happening to meet with bro. Ivins skiff just about to go over to Nauvoo. We got into that skiff and left brother Derby to return at his own leasure. Before we could get over the wind arose again considerable but we arrived home safe and well about 6 o clock P.M. We found Mr [Stephen W.] Powers from Keokuk who had just returned from Burlington. While there he ascertained that there was no writ issued in Iowa for Joseph. The report had evidently originated from the fact of a writ being issued for the apprehension of some horse theives The people enquired if it was not true that Joseph had been commissioned by the United States to visit the Indians and negociate with them for a tract of land, such being the report in circulation. Mr Powers answered that he was not authorised to assert that the report was true but he thought it was not only possible but very probable. [p. 133]

15 August 1842 · Monday

This A.M. several reports were in circulation that the Militia are on their way here, and the same is said to have been stated by the stage driver, but it is supposed that it is only a

---

1. "They" penciled over "we" by a later hand in this and the following sentence of the MS.

scheme to alarm the citizens. Sister Emma presented the forgoing letter to Major Gen. Law to which he responded by the following answer

"Nauvoo City Ill. Augt. 15th Afternoon 1842
Lieut Gen. J. Smith

My Dr friend– I this morning received a line from you by the young man (Walker)[1] respecting the Guns &c. One of them is in the stone Shop by the Nauvoo House. One I expect to get put into Mr Ivins barn and the other I can not get under lock and key any place I know of yet; but I will have them taken the best care of that I can.

I have also received from the hand of your Lady *your orders* at len[g]th respecting matters and things, and I am happy indeed to receive such orders from you, for your views on these subjects are precisely my own. I do respond with my whole heart to every sentiment you have so nobly and so feelingly expressed, and while my heart beats, or this hand which now writes is able to draw and weild a sword you may depend on it being at your service in the glorious cause Liberty and Truth, ready in a moments warning to defends the rights of man both civil and religious. Our *common rights* and *peace* is all we ask and we will use every peaceable means in our power to enjoy these, but our *rights we must have, peace* we must have if we have to *fight* for them.– There has nothing worthy of notice come to my knowledge to day, the *Gentlemen Officers* are seemingly very unhappy and out of humor with themselves more than with any body else, they see we have the advantage of them and that they can not provoke us to break the law, and I think they know if they do that we will use them up the right way. I guess they see that in our patience we possess our souls, and I know that if they shed or cause to be shed a drop of the blood of one of the least amongst us that the lives of

---

1. Lorin Walker.

the transgressors shall atone for it with the help of *our God.* –
I send you the ordinance that was passed by the Court Martial[1]
on Saturday last for your approval or otherwise as it cannot
become a Law without your approbation.

I also send you the returns of the election for Major General, as you ordered the election, you will please order the War
Secretary of the Legion (Col. Sloane) [James Sloan] to send for
a Commission.

With the warmest feelings of my heart I remain most
respectfully, Yours –

Wilson Law."

"P.S. Afternoon 6 o clock

I have just learned that Mr [James M.] Pittman got a letter
about noon and got ready immediately and started off as he
said for Carthage but I think for Quincy giving it up for a bad
job   W. L [Wilson Law]"

About dark brother [Edwin] Woolley returned from Carthage and stated that he had conversed with Chauncey Robison
who informed him that he had ascertained that the Sheriffs
were determined to have Joseph and if they could not succeed
themselves they would bring a force sufficient to search every
house in the [p. 134] city, and if they could not find him there
they would search the state &c. As before stated the Sheriffs
left the City about four o clock saying they were going to
Carthage but brother Woolley did not meet them on the road.
It is believed they are gone to Quincy. In consequence of these
reports it was considered wisdom that some of the brethren
should go and inform Joseph accordingly about 9 o clock Hyrum Geo. Miller, Wm Law, A[masa]. Lyman, Jno D. Parker,
N. K Whitney & Wm Clayton started by different routs, on
foot and proceeded to the place where Joseph was. When the
statement was made the president prepared to leave the city,

---

1. See note 2, p. 369.

expecting he was no longer safe, but upon hearing the whole statement from those present, he said he should not leave his present retreat yet,[1] he did not think he was discovered, neither did he think he was any more unsafe than before He discovered a degree of excitement and agitation manifest in those who brought the report and he took occasion to gently reprove all present for letting report excite them, and advised them not to suffer themselves to be wrought upon by any report, but to maintain an even, undaunted mind Each one began to gather courage and all fears were soon subsided, and the greatest union and good feeling prevailed amongst all present.

Various subjects then was conversed upon and council given by the president which was felt to be both seasonable and salutary. After conversing a while in the grove the company retired into the house and sat and conversed untill 2 o clock at about which time they departed evidently satisfied and much encouraged by the interview It was considered wisdom that the president should have all things in readiness so that if it was necessary he could start immediately for the Pine Country[2] where he would be beyond the reach of his pursuers.

16 August 1842 · Tuesday

Wrote a letter to sister Emma giving her instructions how to proceed in case he had to go to the Pine Country. Also wrote a letter to Wilson Law asking his opinion about the appearance of things and the best course to be pursued. Brother Derby took the letters and is expected back soon. Brother Erastus H Derby is one among the number of the faithful souls, who have taken as yet the greatest interest that possibly could have been imagined for the welfare of president Joseph I therefore record the following blessing from the mouth of the President himself. "Blessed is Brother Erastus H. Derby, and he shall be

---

1. At Edward Sayers'.
2. I.e., the Church lumber operation near Black River Falls, Wisconsin.

blessed of the Lord; he possesses a sober mind, and a faithful heart; the snares therefore that are subsequent to befall other men, who are treacherous and rotten-hearted, shall not come nigh unto his doors, but shall be far from the path of his feet. He loveth wisdom, and shall be found possessed of her. Let there be a crown of glory, and a diadem upon his head. Let the light of eternal Truth shine forth upon his understanding; let his name be had in everlasting remembrance; let the blessings of Jehovah be crowned upon his posterity after him, for he rendered me consolation, in the lonely places of my retreat: How good, and glorious, it has seemed unto me, to find pure and holy friends, who are faithful, just and true, and whose hearts fail not; and whose knees are confirmed and do not faulter; while they wait upon the Lord, in administering to my necessities; [p. 135]

[pp. 136–163, *donations*]

in the day when the wrath of mine enemies was poured out upon me. In the name of the Lord, I feel in my heart to bless them, and to say in the name of Jesus Christ of Nazareth that these are the ones that shall inherit eternal life. I say it by virtue of the Holy Priesthood, and by the ministering of Holy Angels, and by the gift and power of the Holy Ghost. How glorious were my feelings when I met that faithful and friendly band, on the night of the eleventh on thursday, on the Island, at the mouth of the slough, between Zarahemla and Nauvoo. With what unspeakable delight, and what transports of joy swelled my bosom, when I took by the hand on that night, my beloved Emma, she that was my wife, even the wife of my youth; and the choice of my heart. Many were the reviberations of my mind when I contemplated for a moment the many passt scenes we had been called to pass through. The fatigues, and the toils, the sorrows, and sufferings, and the joys and consolations from time to time [which] had strewed our paths

415

and crowned our board. Oh! what a co-mingling of thought filled my mind for the moment, again she is here, even in the seventh trouble, undaunted, firm and unwavering, unchangeable, affectionate Emma. There was Brother Hyrum who next took me by the hand, a natural brother; thought I to myself, brother Hyrum, what a faithful heart you have got. Oh, may the eternal Jehovah crown eternal blessings upon your head, as a reward for the care you have had for my soul. O how many are the sorrows have we shared together, and again we find ourselves shackled with the unrelenting hand of oppression. Hyrum, thy name shall be written in the Book of the Law of the Lord, for those who come after thee to look upon, that they may pattern after thy works. Said I to myself here is brother Newel K. Whitney also, how many scenes of sorrow, have strewed our paths together; and yet we meet once more to share again. Thou art a faithful friend in whom the afflicted sons of men can confide, with the most perfect safety. Let the blessings of the eternal be crowned also upon his head; how warm that heart! how anxious that soul! for the welfare of one who has been cast out, and hated of almost all men. Brother Whitney, thou knowest not how strong those ties are, that bind my soul and heart to thee. My heart was overjoyed, as I took the faithful band by hand, that stood upon the shore one by one. Wm. Law, Wm. Clayton, Dimick B. Huntington, George Miller were there. The above names constituted the little group. I do not think to mention the particulars of the history of that sacred night, which shall forever be remembered by me. But the names of the faithful are what I wish to record in this place. These I have met in prosperity and they were my friends, I now meet them in adversity, and they are still my warmer friends. These love the God that I serve; they love the truths that I promulge; they love those virtuous, and those holy doctrines that I cherish in my bosom with the warmest feelings of my heart; and with that zeal which cannot be denied. I love friendship and truth; I love virtue [p. 164] and Law; I love the God of Abraham and of Isaac and of Jacob, and they are my brethren, and I shall live; and because I live, they shall live also. These are not the only ones, who have administered to my necessity; whom the Lord will bless. There is Brother John D Parker, and Brother Amasa Lyman, and Brother Wilson Law, and Brother Henry G. Sherwood, my heart feels to reciprocate the unwe[a]ried kindnesses that have been bestowed upon me by these men. They are men of noble stature, of noble hands, and of noble deeds; possessing noble and daring, and giant hearts and souls. There is Brother Joseph B. Nobles also, I would call up in remembrance before the Lord. There is brother Samuel Smith, a natural brother; he is, even as Hyrum. There is Brother Arthur Millikin also, who married my youngest sister, Lucy. He is a faithful, an honest, and an upright man. While I call up in remembrance before the Lord these men, I would be doing injustice to those who rowed me in the skiff up the river that night, after I parted with the lovely group; who brought me to this my safe and lonely and private retreat; brother Jonathan Dunham and the other whose name I do not know. Many were the thoughts that swelled my aching heart, while they were toiling faithfully with their oars. They complained not of hardship and fatigue to secure my safety. My heart would have been harder than an adamantine stone, if I had not have prayed for them with anxious and fervent desire. I did so, and the still small voice whispered to my soul, these that share your toils with such faithful hearts, shall reign with you in the kingdom of their God; but I parted with them in silence and came to my retreat. I hope I shall see them again that I may toil for them and administer to their comfort also. They shall not want a friend while I live. My heart shall love those; and my hands shall toil for those, who love and toil for me, and shall ever be found faithful to my friends. Shall I be ungrateful? verily no! God forbid!["] The above are the words, and sentiments, that escaped the lips of President Joseph Smith on this the 16th day of August A.D 1842, in

417

relation to his friends; and has now quit speaking for the moment, but will continue the subject again.

Wm Clayton, Clerk.[1]

17 August 1842 · Wednesday

This day president Joseph and brother Derby went out into the woods for exercise and were accidently discovered by a young man. Various questions were asked him concerning the public feeling, and situation of matters around to all which he answered promptly on being requested not to make it known where they were, he promised faithfully he would not and said time would tell wether he did or no.[2]

Several rumors were afloat in the city, intimating that president Smith's retreat had been discovered, and that it was no longer safe for him to remain at brother Sayers. Consequently sister Emma went to see him at night and informed him of the report. It was considered wisdom that he should remove immediately and accordingly he departed in company with Emma and brother Derby and went to Carlos Grangers who lives on the North East part of the City. Here they were kindly recieved and wel[l]-treated. [p. 165]

19 August 1842 · Friday

This evening President Joseph had a visit from his Aunt Temperance Mack Spent the day mostly in conversation and reading. At night went to the city and concluded to tarry at

---

1. Ink color in the MS. at this point changes from dark brown to blue.

2. The young man who discovered Joseph Smith was Martin Henderson Harris (1820–89), born near Mehoopany, Wyoming County, Pennsylvania. Son of Emer Harris and Debora Lott, and nephew of the Book of Mormon witness Martin Harris. Migrated to Utah in 1850 and settled in Weber County. (See Jenson, *Latter-day Saint Biographical Encyclopedia* 3:105–6; "Martin Henderson Harris, A Utah Pioneer: His Life, Labors, and Posterity," MS., LDS Church Archives.)

home untill something further transpired with regard to the designs of his persecutors.

20 August 1842 · Saturday

Spent the day in the large Room over the Store. Was considerable sick all day. In the evening had an interview with brother Hyrum, Wilson and William Law, N. K. Whitney, & George Miller a few hours, conversing on the illegality of the proceedings of our oppressors &c.

21 August 1842 · Sunday

In the Room over the Store. To day Sidney Rigdon went to the grove near the Temple and there related before the congregation the following incident which took place in his family. He stated that his daughter Eliza [Elizabeth] had been sick unto death all the skill of physicians having been of no avail. She continued to sink untill finally she appeared to die, and went cold. She continually wished to recover and expressed strong desires to live saying she did not want to die &c. He stated that she appeared to die three times and again recover. When she came to the last time she stated that she had something to say to her father, which was to the effect that he must be faithful in the cause, that this was the cause of truth &c. She also said that George W. Robinson had it in his heart to deny the faith but if he did it would be his damnation, also that Nancy [Rigdon] had near denied the faith but if she did she would be damned. She also said that Jno C. Bennett was a wicked man. Elder Rigdon then stated that he felt himself a new man, that his constitution was renewed and his system invigorated. He also bore testimony to the truth of the work; he said he had been in it a number of years and knew for himself that it was the work of God &c. He also said it had been stated that he had said Joseph was a fallen prophet; this he denied in the strongest terms. After he had got through president Hyrum arose and spoke at great length and with great power. He cited Elder Rigdons mind back to the Revelation concerning him, that if he would move into the midst of the city and defend the truth he should be healed &c and showed that what Elder Rigdon felt in regard to the improvement in his[1] health was a fulfilment of the Revelation.[2] He then went on to show the folly of any person's attempting to overthrow or destroy Joseph and read from the Book of Mormon in various places concerning the Prophet who was prophecied should be raised up in the last days, setting forth the work he was destined to accomplish[3] and that he had only just commenced, but inasmuch as wc could plainly see that the former part of the prophecy had been literally fulfilled we might be assured that the latter part would also be fulfilled and that Joseph would live to accomplish the great things spoken concerning him, notwithstanding his enemies might diligently and continualy seek his destruction; hence the danger of any man's lifting his hand against him, for whosoever did it, would surely come to destruction and could not prosper. He asked if it had not already been proven that this was the fact and that all who had persecuted the prophet had come to disgrace and shame; and how should any man prosper whilst seeking to injure him whom God had blessed and promised to protect and concerning whom the prophets had prophecied that he should live to fulfil the work committed to him [p. 166]

He concluded his address by calling upon the saints to take courage and fear not, and also told Elder Rigdon that inasmuch as he had seen the mercy of the Lord exerted in his behalf that it was his duty to arise and stand in defence of the truth and of innocence and of those who were being persecuted inno-

---

1. "his" repeated in MS.
2. See D&C 124:103–4.
3. MS.: "accomplilsh".

cently and finally called for all those who were willing to support and uphold Joseph and who believed that he was doing his duty and was innocent of the charges &c to hold up their right hand whereupon almost every person present was seen with their hands elevated and their countenances beaming with joy. Afterwards he said if there were any who were opposed to Joseph and would not defend him let them manifest it by the same sign but there was not one opposing witness.

It is evident that this meeting was productive of great good and if there was any treachery and secret combinations of evil and designing characters present, the discourse was calculated to show them their true situation and danger and it is very probable would be the means of bringing them to their senses. The whole congregation appeared highly delighted and strengthened by the circumstance and seemed to be inspired with new zeal and courage. During the day Elder Rigdon went over the President Hyrums and conversed upon various subjects and it is evident he intends to arouse his energies and stand in defence of the truth if Satan do[es] not again darken his mind and fill his heart with evil. Orson Pratt has also signified his intention of coming out in defence of the truth and go to preaching/[1]

[remaining half of p. 167 blank]

Goviner Carlin Letters[2]

Quincy June 30th 1842

Dear Sir I recieved by the last mail your letter of the 24 instant, in which you have thought proper to give me a state-

---

1. In MS. William Clayton's handwriting ends and that of Unknown Scribe A begins.

2. The letters of Governor Thomas Carlin to Joseph Smith copied here were written in response to correspondence from the Prophet informing him of the John C. Bennett affair and urging him not to initiate extradition proceedings. Joseph Smith's letters to which Carlin was responding are published in *History of the Church*, 5:42–44, 68–70.

ment of charges against the conduct, and character, of Gen. John C Bennet I can say that I regret that any individual should so far disgrace his obligations to his God, and to his fellow man, as to condesend to the commission of the crimes alledged in your letter to have been perpetrated by Genel, Bennett, it is however in accordance with representations of his character, made to me more than two years since, and which I then felt constrained to believe ware true, since which time I have desired to have as little intercourse with him as possible, No resignation of his commishion as Mj General of the Nauvoo Legion, has reached me, Some weeks since I recieved a short note from him stating, that, you had reason to believe that a conspiracy was getting up in the State of Mo, for the purpose of mobing the Mormons at Nauvoo, and kidnaping you, and taking you to that State, and requested to be informed in case of such mob, whether you would be protected by the authorities of this State &c to which I replied, that as all men ware held[1] ameanable to the Laws, so in like maner the rights of all would be protected, and the dignity of the State maintained to the letter of the constitution and laws, the above is in substance the contents of his note to me and my reply to him, having destroyed his letter as I considered it of no use–should it be retained,

you state that you have heard that I have of late entertained unfavorable feelings towards you (the Mormons) as a people and especially so with regard to yourself &c &c. if this should be true, you would be pleased to know from me the reasons of such hostile feelings,

In reply I can in truth Say that I do not entertain nor cherish hostile or revengeful feelings towards any man or set of men on Earth, but that I may have used strong expressions in reference to yourself, at times when my indignation has been some what aroused by repeated admonitions of my friends

---

1. "held" repeated in MS.

(both before and since the attempt to assassinate ex Gov Boggs) to be upon my guard, that you had prophesied that Boggs should die a violent death–and that I should die in a ditch all this however if true, I looked upon as idle boasting untill since the assassination of Boggs–and even since then in reference to my self, I cannot view it in any other light, because whatever your feelings may have been to-wards Boggs, the mere discharge of an official duty on my part enjoined upon me by the constitution and Laws, of this State, and of the United States could not possibly engender feelings of such deepe malignity, [p. 168] be assured that this matter Gives me no uneasiness nor would the subject now have been mentioned had you not requested a reply to your enquiries. I have seen your denial of the prediction published in the Wasp attributed to you of the death (or assassination) of Gov Boggs, be that true or false, nothing has contributed more towards fixing the belief upon the public mind, that you had made such prediction than the repeated statements of a portion of your followers, that the man[n]er of his death had been revealed to you, and their exultation that it must needs be fulfilled

In reference to your request to be advised how you should act in case a mob should come upon you, I should feel very much at a loss to recommend any course for you to adopt, other than a resort to the first Law of Nature, viz to defend your own rights, because ware I to advise a quiet submission on your part, I could not expect that you would fold your arms, and silently look on whilst those rights ware violated and outraged, as long as you have the power to protect them,

I however have not the most distant thought that there exists at presant, any real caus[e] for the aprehension of a Mob coming upon you, other wise I should feel it my duty to endeavor to arrest it,

very respectfully your obedient servant,
Tho Carlin

General Joseph Smith

Gov Carlins letter
Quincy July 27th 1842

Dear Sir

Your communication of the 25th instant together [with] the petitions of the citizens of the city of Nauvoo both male and female ware delivered to me last evening by Brevet Major General Wilson Law allso a report of James Sloan Esq Sectry of the Nauvoo Legion of the procedings of a court Martial of Brevet Major General had upon charges prefered against Major General John C Bennett upon which trial the court found defendant guilty and sentenced him to be Cashiered all of which have been considered, In reply to your expresscd aprehentions of "the posibility of an attack upon the peaceable inhabitants of the city of Nauvoo and vicinity through the intreagues and false representations of John C Bennett and others" and you[r] request that I would issue official orders to you, to have the Nauvoo Legion ⟨in⟩ readiness to be caled out at a moments warning in defence of the peaceble citizens &c I must say that I cannot concieve of the least probability or scarcely posability of an attack of violence upon the citizens of Nauvoo from any quarter what ever and as uterly imposible that such attack is contemplated by any sufficient number of persons [p. 169] to excite the least appearance of danger or injury, whilst I should consider it my imperative duty to promptly take measures [to] suppress and repell any invasion by violence of the peoples rights, I nevertheless think that it is not my province to interpose my official authority gratuitously where no such exigency exists— From the late disclosures as made by Gen Bennett it is not strange that the ~~citizens~~ aprehension of the citizens of Nauvoo are excited, but so far as I can learn from the expression of public opinion, the excitement is confined to[1] the Mormons them ~~selfs~~ selves, and

---

1. "to" repeated in MS.

only extends to the community at large as a matter of curiosity and wonder,

very respectfully your obedient servent
Tho Carlin

General Joseph Smith jr.

Head Quarters of Nauvoo Legion[1]
August 16th 1842

Major General Law

Beloved Brother and friend those few lines which I recieved from you writen on the 15th was to me like apples of gold in pictures of silver, I rejoice with exceding greatt Joy to be associated in the high and responcible Stations which wee hold whose mind and feelings and heart is so congenial with my own, I love that soul that is so nobly entabernacled in that clay of yours, may God Allmighty grant that it may be satiated with seeing a fullfilment of evry virtuous and manly desire that you possess, may we be able to triumph gloriously over those who seek our destruction and overthrow which I believe we shall, the news you wrote me was more favorable than that which was communicated by the Brethren, they seamed a little agitated for my safety, and advised me for the pine c[o]untry but I succeded admirably [in] calming all their fears, but nevertheless as I said in my former letter I was willing to exile myselfe for months and years if it would be for the safety and wellfare of the people, and I do not know but it would be as well for me to take a trip to the pine countries and remain untill arrangements can be made for my most perfect safety when I returned, these are there fore to confer with you on this subject as I want to have a concert of action in evry thing I do, if I knew that they would oppress me alone and let the rest of you dwell peacably and quietly, I think it would be the

---

1. The letter copied here, Joseph Smith to Wilson Law, 16 August 1842, is in answer to one from Law written 15 August. See entry of the 15th.

wisest plan to absent myself for a little season, if by that means wee could prevent the profusion [of] Blood,– Pleas write and give me your ~~views~~ ⟨mind⟩ on that[1] subject and all other information that has come to hand to day, and what are the signs of the times,– I have no news for I am where I cannot get ~~any news~~ ⟨much⟩ all is quiet and peacible around I [p. 170] therefore wait with ~~P~~ earnest expectation for your advises I [am] anxious to know your opinion on any course ⟨that⟩ I may see proper to take for in the multitude of council there is safety

I add no more but subscribe myselfe your faithful and most obedient servant friend and Brother,

~~Lieutenant~~ Joseph Smith,
Lieutenant General of the Nauvoo
Legion of Illinois Malitea/[2]

To the forgoing letter I received the following answers to wit

Nauvoo City Illinois August 17th 1842

Lieut Gen. J. Smith

Dear Friend–Every thing is moving along in the city in the usual tranquil & industrious manner, there is no change in the appearance of things that a common observer could see, although to one who knows & is acquaint[ed] with the countenances of the thinking few, it is evident that their minds are troubled more than common, and I know by myself that they can not help it, and why should it be otherwise when the Lords anointed is hunted like a Lion of [the] forest by the most wicked & oppressive generation that has ever been since the days of the saviour of the world, indeed every movement of this generation reminds me of the history of the people who crucified Christ, it was nothing but mob law, mob rule and mob violence all the time, the only difference is that the *Governors* then

---

1. In MS. "that" written over "this".
2. In MS. handwriting of Unknown Scribe A ends and William Clayton's resumes.

were more just than the *Governors* now, they were willing to acquit innocent men, but our Governors now despise justice, garble and prevent [pervert] the law, and join in with the mob in pursuit of *innocent blood*. I have been meditating on your communication of yesterday & will just add a thought or so on the subject, respecting particularly your going to the Pine country. I think I would not go there for some time if at all. I do not believe that an armed force will come upon us at all unless they get hold of you first & that we rescue you which we would do under any circumstances with the help of God, but I would rather do it within the limits of the city under the laws of the city, therefore I would think it better to Quarter in the city & not long in one place at once. I see no reason why you might not stay in safety within the city for months without any knowing it only those who ought & that as few as is necessary.

I must close for the present remaining as ever your affectionate friend and obedient servant

Wilson Law.

The following is the one designed especially as answer to President Josephs letter dated August 16th but which through mistake was mislaid and consequently not recorded in the proper place [p. 171]

Nauvoo City Ill. one o clock afternoon Augt 16th 1842
Lieut. Gen. J. Smith

My Dear Friend—I have just received and read yours of to day & hasten to reply. There is no movements of any kind going on to-day amongst the enemy as far as I can see which helps to strengthen me in my opinion of yesterday, but still it might be a calm before a storm and if so we will meet it when it comes. You wish my opinion respecting your absenting yourself for some time from those friends that are dear to you as life, and to whom you are also as dear, & from the place and station to which you are call'd by *Him* who ruleth in the armies of heaven & amongst the inhabitants of the earth. I must confess that I feel almost unworthy to give an opinion on the subject, knowing that your own judgment is far superior to mine, but nevertheless you shall have it freely, it is this I think that if they cannot get you peaceably according to the forms of law, that they will not dare to attempt violence of any kind upon the inhabitants of the city, for they are well aware that they cannot insult us with impunity neither use violence only at the risk of their lives, and there are but few men, who are willing to risk their lives in a bad cause, it is the principles & spirit of Liberty, of Truth, of Virtue, and of Religion & equal rights, that make men courageous and valient & fearless in the day of battle and of strife; and just the contrary with the oppressor for nine times out of ten a bad cause will make a man a coward & he will flee when no man pursueth. Now if I am right in thinking that it is you alone they seek to destroy as soon as they find they can not get you, they will cease to trouble the city except with spies; and if we knew that you were completely out of their reach, we could either laugh at their folly, or whip them for impertinence or any thing else, as the case might be, for we would feel so happy in your safety that we could meet them in any shape. On the whole I think it would be better for you to absent yourself till the next Governor takes the *Chair*, for I do think if you are not here they will not attempt any violence on the city, and if they should they will dis-grace themselves in the eyes of the world, and the world will justify us in fighting for our rights, and then you can come out like a Lion and lead your people to glory and to victory in the name of the *Lord of Hosts*. I know the sacrifice you must make in taking this course, I know it will grieve your noble spirit to do so, for when I think of it myself I feel no desire in life but to fight and to cut off from the earth all who oppress, and to establish that true form of government at once which would guarantee to every man *equal rights*. I

know we have justice on our side in respect of city Laws, &
that the acts of [the] municipal court are legal, but the question
is are we *now* able to *assert* them or had we better wait till
we are more able. The latter course will give us peace *a little*
while, by sacrificing *your liberty* and the feelings of your family
and friends and depriving *us all* of your *society* and *governing
wisdom*. I will only add that I am ready for either course and
may God direct us to do that that is best. [p. 172] If you should
conclude to go away for a while I must see you before you go.
And for the present I will bid you be chearful and make yourself
as happy as you can for the right side of the wheel will soon
be up again. And till then and ever I remain under every circumstance your friend and obt servant
Wilson Law.

On the same day that the foregoing letter was wrote to
Major Gen. Law. President Joseph wrote one to Mrs Emma
in the words following To Wit;

Nauvoo August 16th 1842

My Dear Emma
I embrace this opportunity to express to you some of my
feelings this morning. First of all, I take the liberty to tender
you my sincere thanks for the two interesting and consoling
visits that you have made me during my almost exiled situation. Tongue can not express the gratitude of my heart, for
the warm and true-hearted friendship you have manifested in
these things toward me. The time has passed away since you
left me, very agreeably; thus far, my mind being perfectly reconciled to my fate, let it be what it may. I have been kept from
melancholy and dumps, by the kind-heartedness of brother
[Erastus] Derby, and his interesting chit-chat from time to
time, which has called my mind from the more strong con-
templations of things, and subjects that would have preyed
more earnestly upon my feelings. Last night—in the night—

brother Hyrum, [George] Miller, Law & others came to see us. They seemed much agitated, and expressed some fears in consequence of some manouverings and some flying reports which they had heard in relation to our safety; but after relating what it was, I was able to comprehend the whole matter to my entire satisfaction, and did not feel at all alarmed or uneasy. They think, however, that the Militia will be called out to search the city, and if this should be the case I would be much safer for the time being at a little distance off, untill Governor Carlin could get weary and be made ashamed of his corrupt and unhallowed proceedings. I had supposed, however, that if there were any serious operations taking by the governor; that Judge [James H.] Ralston or Brother [David S.] Hollister would have notified us; and cannot believe that any thing very serious is to be apprehended, untill we obtain information from a source that can be relied on. I have consulted wether it is best for you to go to Quincy, and see the Governor; but on the whole, he is a fool; and the impressions that are suggested to my mind, are, that it will be of no use; and the more we notice him, and flatter him, the more eager he will be for our destruction. You may write to him, whatever you see proper, but to go and see him, I do not give my consent at present. Brother [George] Miller again suggested to me the propriety of my accompanying him to the Pine woods, and then he return, and bring you [p. 173] and the children. My mind will eternally revolt at every suggestion of that kind. More especially since the dream and vision that was manifested to me on the last night. My safety is with you, if you want to have it so. Any thing more or less than this cometh of evil. My feelings and council I think ought to be abided. If I go to the Pine Country, you shall go along with me, and the children; and if you and the children go not with me, I dont go. I do not wish to exile myself for the sake of my own life, I would rather fight it out. It is for your sakes, therefore, that I would do such a thing. I will go with you then, in the same carriage and on Horse back, from time to time, as occasion may require; for I am not willing to trust you, in the hands of those who cannot feel the same interest for you, that I feel; to be subject to the caprice, temptations, or notions of any body whatever. And I must say that I am pre-possessed somewhat, with the notion of going to the Pine Country any how; for I am tired of the mean, low, and unhallowed vulgarity, of some portions of the society in which we live; and I think if I could have a respite of about six months with my family, it would be a savor of life unto life, with my house. Nevertheless if it were possible I would like to live here in peace and wind up my business; but if it should be ascertained to a dead certainty that there is no other remedy, then we will round up our shoulders and cheerfully endure it; and this will be the plan. Let my horse, saddle, saddle-bags, and valice to put some shirts and clothing in, be sent to me. Let brother Derby and Miller take a horse and put it into my Buggy with a trunk containing my heavier cloth[e]s, shoes and Boots &c. and let brother [John] Taylor accompany us to his fathers, and there we will tarry, taking every precaution to keep out of the hands of the enemy, untill you can arrive with the children. Let brother Hyrum bring you. Let Lorain [Lorin Walker] and brother [William] Clayton come along and bring all the writings and papers, books and histories, for we shall want a scribe in order that we may pour upon the world the truth like the Lava of Mount Vesuvius. Then, let all the goods, household furniture, cloth[e]s and Store Goods that can be procured be put on the Boat, and let 20 or 30 of the best men that we can find be put on board to man it; and let them meet us at Prairie Du Chien; and from thence, we will wend our way like larks up the Mississippi untill the towering[1] mountains and rocks, shall reminds us of the places of our nativity, and shall look like safety and home; and then we will bid defiance to the world, to Carlin, Boggs, Bennett, and all their whorish whores,

---

1. MS.: "touring".

431

and motly clan, that [p. 174] follow in their wake, Missouri not excepted; and until the damnation of hell rolls upon them, by the voice, and dread thunders, and trump of the eternal God; then, in that day will we not shout in the victory and be crowned with eternal joys, for the battles we have fought, having kept the faith and overcome the world. Tell the children that it is well with their father, as yet; and that he remains in fervent prayer to Almighty God for the safety of himself, and for you, and for them. Tell Mother Smith that it shall be well with her son, wether in life or in death; for thus saith the Lord God. Tell her that I remember her all the while, as well as Lucy and all the rest; they all must be of good cheer. Tell Hyrum to be sure and not fail to carry out my instructions, but at the same time if the Militia does not come, and we should get any favorable information, all may be well yet. Yours in haste, your affectionate husband until death, through all eternity forevermore,

Joseph Smith

P.S. I want you to write to Lorenzo ⟨D.⟩[1] Wasson, and get him to make affidavit to all he knows about Bennett and forward it. I also want you to ascertain from Hyrum wether he will conform to what I have requested. And you must write me an answer per bearer, giving me all the news you have, and what is the appearance of things this morning

J.S. —

To the foregoing Mrs Emma returned the following answer per hand [of] brother Derby. To Wit;

Dear husband, I am ready to go with you if you are obliged to leave; and Hyrum says he will go with me. I shall make the best arrangements I can and be as well prepared as possible. But still I feel good confidence that you can be protected with-

---

1. Penciled insertion in MS.

out leaving this country. There is more ways than one to take care of you, and I believe that you can still direct in your business concerns if we are all of us prudent in the matter. If it was pleasant weather I should contrive to see you this evening, but I dare not run to[o] much of a risk on account of so many going to see you. General [James] Adams sends the propositions concerning his land, two dollars an acre, payments as follows, assumption of mortgage say about fourteen hundred, interest included. Taxe due, supposed about thirty dollars. Town property one thousand dollars. Balance, money, payable in one, two, three and four years. Brother Derby will tell you all the information we have on hand. I think we[1] will have news from Quincy as soon as tomorrow.

Yours affectionately forever
Emma Smith.

Joseph Smith.–[p. 175]

According to the hint offered by President Joseph in his letter to Sister Emma she wrote the following letter to Governor Carlin which was dated August 16th but ought to have been the 17th.

Nauvoo August 16th 1842

To His Excellency Governor Carlin.

Sir–It is with feelings of no ordinary cast that I have retired after the business of the day and evening too, to address your honor. I am at a loss how to commence; my mind is crowded with subjects to[o] numerous to be contained in one letter. I find myself almost destitute of that confidence, necessary to address a person holding the authority of your dignified, and responsible office; and I would now offer, as an excuse for intruding upon your time and attention, the justice of my cause. Was my cause the interest of an individual or of a

---

1. "we" repeated in MS.

number of individuals; then, perhaps I might be justified in remaining silent. But it is not! Nor is it the pecuniary interest of a whole community alone, that prompts me again to appeal to your excellency. But dear sir, it is for the peace and safety of hundreds I may safely say, of this community, who are not guilty of any offense against the laws of the Country; and also the life of my husband; who has not committed any crime whatever; neither has he transgressed any of the laws, or any part of the constitution of the United States; neither has he at any time infringed upon the rights of any man, or of any class of men or community of any description. Need I say he is not guilty of the crime alleged against him by Governor Boggs.

Indeed it does seem entirely superfluous for me, or any one of his friends in this place, to testify his innocence of that crime; when so many of the citizens of your place, and of many other places in this state, as well as in the Territory; do know positively that the statement of Governor Boggs is without the least shadow of truth; and we do know, and so do many others, that the prosecution against him, has been conducted in an illegal manner; and every act demonstrates the fact, that all the design of the prosecution, is to throw him into the power of his enemies; without the least ray of hope, that he would ever be allowed to obtain a fair trial, and that he would be inhumanly and ferociuosly murdered; no person having a knowledge of the existing circumstances, has one remaining doubt: and your honor will recollect that you said to me that you would not advise Mr. Smith, ever to trust himself in Missouri. And dear Sir, you cannot for one moment indulge one unfriendly feeling towards him, if he abides by your council. Then sir, why is it that he should be thus cruelly pursued? why not give him the privilege of the laws of this State. When I reflect upon the many cruel and illegal operations of Lilburn [p. 176] W. Boggs, and the consequent suffering of myself and family; and the incalculable losses and suffering of many hundreds who survived, and the many precious lives that were lost; all, the effect of unjust prejudice and misguided ambition, produced by misrepresentation and calumny, my bosom heaves with unutterable anguish. And who, that is as well acquainted with the facts as the people at the city of Quincy, would they censure me, if I should say that my heart burned with just indignation, towards our calumniators, as well as the perpetrators of those horrid crimes. But how happy would I now be to pour out my full heart in gratitude to Gov. Boggs if he had rose up with the dignity and authority of the cheif executive of the State, and put down every illegal transaction, and protected the peaceable citizens, and enterprising emigrants, from the violence of plundering out-laws, who have ever been a disgrace to the State, and always will, so long as they go unpunished. Yes I say, how happy would I be to render him not only the gratitude of my own heart, but the cheering effusions of the joyous souls of fathers and mothers, of brothers and sisters, widows and orphans, who he might have saved by such a course, from now drooping under the withering hand of adversity, brought upon them by the persecutions of wicked and corrupt men. And now may I entreat your excellency to lighten the hand of oppression and persecution, which is laid upon me and my family, which materially affect the peace and welfare of this whole community; for let me assure you that there are many whole families that are entirely dependent upon the prosecution and success of Mr Smiths temporal business for their support. And if he is prevented from attending to the common avocations of life, who will employ those innocent, industrious poor people and provide for their wants. But my dear sir, when I recollect the interesting interview, I and my friends had with you when at your place, and the warm assurances you gave us of your friendship and legal protection,[1]

---

1. Emma Smith, accompanied by Eliza R. Snow and Amanda Barnes Smith, had visited Governor Carlin at his Quincy residence in July with a petition from

I cannot doubt for a moment your honorable sincerety; but do still expect you to consider our claims upon your protection from every encroachment upon our legal rights as loyal citizens as we always have been, still are, and are determined always to be a law abiding people; and I still assure myself that when you are fully acquainted with [the] illegal proceedings practised against us in the suit of Gov. Boggs you will recall those writs which have been issued against Mr Smith and Rockwell, as you must be aware that Mr Smith was not in Missouri, and of course he could not have left there; with many other considerations which if duly considered will justify Mr Smith in the course he has taken. And now I appeal to your excellency as I would unto a father, who is not only able but willing to shield me and mine from every unjust prosecution. I appeal to your sympathies [p. 177] and beg you to spare me, and my helpless children. I beg you to spare my innocent children the heartrending sorrow of again seeing their father unjustly drag'ed to prison or to death. I appeal to your affections as a son and beg you to spare our aged mother,—the only surviving parent we have left,—the unsupportable affliction of seeing her son, who she knows to be innocent of the crimes laid to his charge, thrown again into the hands of his enemies who have so long sought for his life; in whose life and prosperity she only looks for the few remaining comforts she can enjoy. I entreat of your excellency to spare us these afflictions and many sufferings which cannot be uttered; and secure to yourself the pleasure of doing good, and vastly increasing human happi-

---

the Female Relief Society soliciting protection for the Prophet. "The Gov. received us with cordiality, and as much affability and politeness as his Excellency is master of, assuring us of his protection, by saying that the laws and Constitution of our country shall be his polar star in case of any difficulty. He manifested much friendship, and it remains for time and circumstance to prove the sincerity of his professions." (Diary of Eliza R. Snow, 29 July 1842, published in Maureen Ursenbach, "Eliza R. Snow's Nauvoo Journal," *BYU Studies* 15 [Summer 1975]: 391–416; see also Newell and Avery, *Mormon Enigma: Emma Hale Smith*, 121.)

ness; secure to yourself the benediction of the aged and the gratitude of the young and the blessing and veneration of the rising generation.

Respectfully your most obedient,
Emma Smith.

⟨P.S.⟩ Sir I hope you will favor me with an answer
E.S.

This letter was sent to Quincy by brother Wm Clayton who presented it to Gov. Carlin on Friday morning the 19th Inst. in presence of Judge Ralston. The Govr read the letter with much attention apparently and when he got through he pased high encomiums on sister Emma and expressed astonishment at the judgement and talent manifest in the manner of her address, He presented the letter to Judge Ralston requesting him to read it. Gov. Carlin then proceeded to reiterate the same language as on a former occasion viz. that he was satisfied there was no excitement anywhere but in Nauvoo "amongst the Mormons themselves" all was quiet and no apprehension of trouble in other places so far as he was able to ascertain. He afterwards stated when conversing on another subject, that "persons were offering their services every day either in person or by letter and held themselves in readiness to come against us whenever he should call upon them, but he never had had the least idea of calling out the Militia neither had he thought it necessary. There was evidently a contradiction in his assertions in the above instances and although he said "there was no excitement but amongst the Mormons" it is evident he knew better. He also said that it was his opinion that if president Joseph would give himself up to the Sheriff he would be honorably acquited and the matter would be ended; but on Judge Ralston asking how he thought the president could go through the midst of his enemies without violence being used towards him and if acquited how he was to get back? the Gov. was evidently at a loss what to say but made light of the matter as though he thought it might be easily done. He took great care to state that it was not his advice that Mr Smith should give himself up but thought it would be soonest decided. It appeared evident that we have no great things to expect from Carlin as it is evident he is no friend. He acknowledged his ignorance of the law touching the case in plain terms. [p. 178]

23 August 1842 · Tuesday

This day president Joseph has renewed the subject of conversation, in relation to his faithful brethren and friends in his own words; which I now proceed to record as follows; "While I contemplate the virtues and the good qualifications and characteristics of the faithful few, which I am now recording in the Book of the Law of the Lord, of such as have stood by me in every hour of peril, for these fifteen long years past; say for instance; my aged and beloved brother Joseph Knight Senr., who was among the number of the first to administer to my necessities, while I was laboring, in the commencement of the bringing forth of the work of the Lord, and of laying the foundation of the Church of Jesus Christ of Latter Day Saints: for fifteen years has he been faithful and true, and even handed, and exemplary and virtuous, and kind; never deviating to the right hand nor to the left. Behold he is a righteous man. May God Almighty lengthen out the old mans days; and may his trembling, tortured and broken body be renewed, and the vigor of health turn upon him; if it can be thy will, consistently, O God; and it shall be said of him by the sons of Zion, while there is one of them remaining; that this man, was a faithful man in Israel; therefore his name shall never be forgotten. There is his son Newel Knight and Joseph Knight whose names I record in the Book of the Law of the Lord, with unspeakable delight, for they are my friends. There are a numerous host of faithful souls, whose names I could wish to record in the

Book of the Law of the Lord; but time and chance would fail. I will mention therefore only a few of them as emblematical of those who are to[o] numerous to be written. But there is one man I would mention namely Porter Rockwell, who is now a fellow-wanderer with myself–an exile from his home because of the murderous deeds and infernal fiendish disposition of the indefatigable and unrelenting hand of the Missourians. He is an innocent and a noble boy; may God Almighty deliver him from the hands of his pursuers. He was an innocent and a noble child, and my soul loves him; Let this be recorded for ever and ever. Let the blessings of salvation and honor be his portion. But[1] as I said before, so say I again while I remember the faithful few who are now living, I would remember also the faithful of my friends who are dead, for they are many; and many are the acts of kindness, and paternal, and brotherly kindnesses which they have bestowed upon me. And since I have been hunted by the Missourians many are the scenes which have been called to my mind. Many thoughts have rolled through my head, and across my breast. I have remembered the scenes of my child-hood. I have thought of my father who is dead, who died by disease which was brought upon him through suffering by the hands of ruthless mobs.[2] He was a great and a good man. The envy of knaves and fools was heaped upon him, and this was his lot and portion all the days of his life. He was of noble stature, and possessed a high, and holy, and exalted, and a virtuous mind. His soul soared above all those mean [p. 179] and grovelling principles that are so subsequent to the human heart. I now say, that he never

---

1. "portion. But" written over "portion; but" in MS.

2. Joseph Smith, Sr., died on 14 September 1840 at age sixty-nine. In the wake of the Kirtland crisis, he had migrated with his family from Ohio to Missouri in 1838, and, following the extermination order that forced the Latter-day Saints from Missouri, he had moved across Missouri to Quincy, Illinois, in the winter of 1839. In the spring he moved to Commerce (later Nauvoo). According to an obituary, he died of consumption brought on from exposures he had suffered. (*History of the Church,* 4:191.)

did a mean act that might be said was ungenerous, in his life, to my knowledge. I loved my father and his memory; and the memory of his noble deeds, rest with ponderous weight upon my mind; and many of his kind and parental words to me, are written on the tablet of my heart. Sacred to me, are the thoughts which I cherish of the history of his life, that have rolled through my mind and has been implanted there, by my own observation since I was born. Sacred to me is his dust, and the spot where he is laid. Sacred to me is the tomb I have made to encircle o'er his head. Let[1] the memory of my father eternally live. ~~Let the faults, and the follies~~ Let his soul, or the spirit my follies forgive. With him may I reign one day, in the mansions above; and tune up the Lyre of anthems, of the eternal Jove. May the God that I love look down from above, and save me from my enemies here, and take me by the hand; that on Mount Zion I may stand and with my father crown me eternally there. Words and language, is inadequate to express the gratitude that I owe to God for having given me so honorable a parentage. My mother also is one of the noblest, and the best of all women. May God grant to prolong her days, and mine; that we may live to enjoy each others society long yet in the enjoyment of liberty, and to breath the free air. Alvin my oldest brother, I remember well the pangs of sorrow that swelled my youthful bosom and almost burst my tender[2] heart, when he died.[3] He was the oldest, and the noblest of my fathers family. He was one of the noblest of the sons of men: Shall his name not be recorded in this book? Yes, Alvin; let it be had here, and be handed down upon these sacred pages, forever and ever. In him there was no guile. He lived without spot

---

1. "Let" written over "that" in MS.
2. "tender" written over "aching" in MS.
3. Joseph Smith was 17 when his brother Alvin died of what his mother said was an overdose of calomel administered by a doctor called in for the emergency of his illness. Alvin's death occurred on 19 November 1823. (Lucy Smith, *Biographical Sketches*, 87.)

from the time he was a child. From the time of his birth, he never knew mirth. He was candid and sober and never would play; and minded his father, and mother, in toiling all day. He was one of the soberest of men and when he died the angel of the Lord visited him in his last moments. These childish lines I record in remembrance of my child-hood scenes. My Brother Don Carlos Smith, whose name I desire to record also, was a noble boy. I never knew any fault in him. I never saw the first immoral act; or the first irreligious, or ignoble disposition in the child. From the time that he was born, till the time of his death; he was a lovely, a good natured, and a kind-hearted, and a virtuous and a faithful upright child.[1] And where his soul goes let mine go also. He lays by the side of my father. Let my father, Don Carlos, and Alvin, and children that I have buried be brought and laid in the tomb I have built.[2] Let my mother, and my brethren, and my sisters be laid there also; and let it be called the Tomb of Joseph, a descendant of Jacob; and when I die, let me be gathered to the Tomb of my father. There are many souls, whom I have loved stronger than death; to them I have proved faithful; to them I [p. 180] am determined to prove faithful, untill God calls me to resign up my breath. O, thou who seeeth, and knoweth the hearts of all men; thou eternal, omnipotent, omnicient, and omnipresent Jehovah, God; thou Eloheem, that sitteth, as sayeth the psalm-

---

1. Joseph Smith's youngest brother, Don Carlos, died on 7 August 1841, at the age of twenty-six. He had led his father's family out of Missouri during the winter of 1839. In making preparation for the publication of the *Times and Seasons* in Nauvoo, it was necessary for him to clean out a cellar through which a spring was constantly flowing, which contributed to the impairment of his health. (*History of the Church*, 4:398–99.)

2. By this time five natural children and one adopted child had preceded Joseph and Emma Smith in death. An unnamed son died shortly after his birth 15 June 1828; unnamed twins, a boy and girl, died the same day they were born, 30 April 1831; an adopted son, Joseph S. Murdock, died in his first year, 29 March 1832; a son, Don Carlos, died on 7 August 1841, less than fourteen months after his birth; and another unnamed son died the day he was born, 6 February 1842.

ist, enthroned in heaven; look down upon thy servant Joseph, at this time; and let faith on the name of thy Son Jesus Christ, to a greater degree than thy servant ever yet has enjoyed, be conferred upon him; even the faith of Elijah; and let the Lamp of eternal life, be lit up in his heart, never to be taken away; and let the words of eternal life, be poured upon the soul of thy servant; that he may know thy will, thy statutes, and thy commandments, and thy judgements to do them. As the dews upon Mount Hermon, may the distillations of thy divine grace, glory and honor in the plenitude of thy mercy, and power and goodness be poured down upon the head of thy servant. O Lord God, my heavenly Father, shall it be in vain, that thy servant must needs be exiled from the midst of his friends; or be dragged from their bosoms, to clank in cold and iron chains; to be thrust within the dreary prison walls; to spend days of sorrow, and of grief and misery their, by the hand of an in-furiated, insensed and infatuated foe; to glut their infernal and insatiable desire upon innocent blood; and for no other cause on the part of thy servant, than for the defence of innocence, and thou a just God will not hear his cry? O, no, thou wilt hear me; a child of woe, pertaining to this mortal life; because of sufferings here, but not for condemnation that shall come upon him in eternity; for thou knowest O God, the integrity of his heart. Thou hearest me, and I knew that thou wouldst hear me, and mine enemies shall not prevail; they all shall melt like wax before thy face; and as the mighty floods, and waters roar; so shall or as the billow-ing earth-quake's, de-vouring gulf; or rolling thunders loudest peal; or vivid, forked lightnings flash; or sound of the Arch-Angels trump; or voice of the Eternal God, shall the souls of my enemies be made to feel in an instant, suddenly; and shall be taken, and ensnared; and fall back-wards, and stumble in the ditch they have dug for my feet, and the feet of my friends; and perish in their own infamy and shame,–be thrust down to an eternal hell, for their murderous and hellish deeds." After writing so much president

Joseph left off speaking for the present but will continue the subject again. He had a very pleasant visit from Mother Smith and Aunt Temperance, who were evidently highly gratified to find him in good spirits and in good health notwithstanding his confinement and lack of exercise. After visiting a-while and hearing read some parts of the Book of the Law of the Lord they departed rejoicing in the blessing and favor of the Almighty. —

In the P.M. president Joseph received a few lines from sister Emma informing him that she would expect him home this evening believing that she could take care of him better at home than elsewhere. Accordingly soon after dark he started for home and arrived safe without being noticed by any person. All is quiet in the city.[1] *Wm Clayton. Clerk.* [p. 181]

24 August 1842 · Wednesday

At home all day. Had a visit from brother Whitney and Isaac Morley

26 August 1842 · Friday

At home all day. In the evening in council with some of the Twelve and others. He gave some very important instructions upon the situation of matters, showing that it was necessary that the officers who could, should go abroad through the States; and inasmuch as a great excitement had been raised, through the community at large, by the falsehoods put in circulation by John C. Bennett and others, it was wisdom in God that the Elders should go forth and deluge the States with a flood of truth; setting forth the mean, contemptible, persecuting conduct of ex-Governor Boggs of Missouri and those connected with him in his mean, and corrupt proceedings in plain terms, so that the world might understand the abusive

---

1. Handwriting at this point in MS. changes from blue to brown ink.

conduct of our enemies, and stamp it with indignation. He advised the Twelve to call a special conference on Monday next to give instructions to the Elders and call upon them to go forth upon this important mission, meantime, that all the affidavits concerning Bennetts conduct be taken and printed, so that each Elder could be properly furnished with correct and weighty testimony to lay before the public. —

27 August 1842 · Saturday

In the large room over the Store with some of the Twelve and others who were preparing affidavits for the press. — [1]

28 August 1842 · Sunday

At home —

29 August 1842 · Monday

This being the [day] appointed for the conference above referred to, the Elders assembled in the grove near the Temple about 10 o clock A.M. President Hyrum introduced the object of the conference by stating "that the people abroad had been excited by John C. Bennetts false statements and that letters had frequently been received inquiring concerning the true nature of said reports; in consequence of which it is thought wisdom in God that every Elder who can, should now go forth to every part of the United States, and take proper documents with them setting forth the truth as it is and also preach the gospel, repentance, baptism & salvation and tarry preaching untill they shall be called home. They must go wisely, humbly setting forth the truth as it is in God, and our persecutions, by which the tide of public feeling will be turned. There are

---

1. A collection of "Affidavits and Certificates, Disproving the Statements and Affidavits Contained in John C. Bennett's Letters" was published at Nauvoo under the date of 31 August 1842. See also *Times and Seasons* 3 (1 August 1842): 869–78.

many Elders here doing little and many people in the world who want to hear the truth. We want the official members to take their staff and go East, (not West) and if a mob should come here they will only have women and children to fight with. When you raise churches send the means you get to build the Temple, and get the people to take stock in the Nauvoo House. It is important that the Nauvoo House should be finished that we may have a suitable house wherein to entertain the great ones of the earth and teach them the truth. We want the Temple built that we may offer our oblations and where we can ask forgiveness of our sins every week, and forgive one another, and offer up our offering & get our endowment [p. 182] The gospel will be turned from the Gentiles to the Jews. Sometime ago almost every person was ordained, the purpose was to have you tried and ready and then to receive their blessings. Everyone is wanted to be ready in two or three days and expects there will be a liberal turnout."

After president Hyrum had got nearly thro⟨u⟩gh president Joseph came up to the stand. The brethren were rejoiced to see him. He had not been seen for three weeks and his appearance amongst the brethren under present circumstances caused much animation and joy, it being unexpected. Some had supposed that he was gone to Europe and some to Washington; and some thought he was in the city, Every one rejoiced to see him once more When president Hyrum had done speaking president Joseph got up and began his remarks by congratulating the brethren on the victory gained over the Missourians once more. "He had told them formerly about fighting the Missourians, and about fighting alone. He had not fought them with the sword nor by carnal weapons; he had done it by stratagem or by outwitting them, and there had been no lives lost; and there would be no lives lost if they would hearken to his council. Up to this day God had given him wisdom to save the people who took council. None had ever been killed who abode by his council. At Hauns Mill the brethren went contrary to his council, if they had not there lives would have been spared.[1] He has been in Nauvoo all the while, and out-witted Bennetts associates and attended to his own business in the City all the time. We want to whip the world mentally and they will whip themselves physically. The brethren cant have the tricks played upon them that were done at Kirtland and Far-west, they have seen enough of the tricks of their enemies and know better." Orson Pratt has attempted to de-stroy himself—caused all the City almost to go in search of him. Is it not enough to put down all the infernal influence of the Devil, what we have felt and seen, handled and evidenced of this work of God? But the Devil had influence among the Jews to cause the death of Jesus Christ by hanging between heaven and earth. O. P and others of the same class caused trouble by telling stories to people who would betray me and they must believe these stories because his wife told him so! I will live to trample on their ashes with the soles of my feet. I prophecy in the name of Jesus Christ that such shall not prosper, they shall be cut down in their own plans. They would deliver me up Judas like, but a small band of us shall overcome. We dont want or mean to fight with the sword of the flesh but we will fight with the broad sword of the spirit. Our enemies say our Charter and writs of Habeus Corpus are worth nothing. We say they came from the highest authority in the States, and we will hold to them. They cannot be disannulled or taken away." He then told the brethren what he was going to do, viz; to send all the Elders away and when the mob came there would only be women and children to fight and they would be ashamed, He said "I dont want you to fight but to go and gather [p. 183] tens, hundreds and thousands to fight for you. If oppression comes I will then shew them that there is a

---

1. Joseph Smith's counsel had been for the Saints living in small groups to gather to larger population centers for safety. (See Gentry, "A History of the Latter-day Saints in Northern Missouri," pp. 289–90.)

Moses and a Joshua amongst us; and I will fight them if they dont take off oppression from me. I will do as I have done this time, I will run into the woods. I will fight them in my own way. I will send bro. Hyrum to call conferences every where through-out the States, and let documents be taken along and show to the world the corrupt and oppressive ⟨conduct⟩ of Boggs, Carlin and others, that the public may have the truth laid before them. Let the Twelve send all, who will support the character of the Prophet–the Lords anointed. And if all who go will support my character I prophecy in the name of the Lord Jesus whose servant I am, that you will prosper in your missions. I have the whole plan of the kingdom before me, and no other person has. And as to all that Orson Pratt, Sidney Rigdon or George W. Robinson can do to prevent me I can kick them off my heels, as many as you can name, I know what will become of them." He concluded his remarks by saying "I have the best of feelings towards my brethren since this last trouble began, but to the apostates and enemies I will give a lashing every oppertunity and I will curse them." During the whole of this address the feelings of the brethren was indiscribable and the greatest joy and good feeling imaginable was manifest. Orson Pratt set behind president Joseph all the time he was speaking. He looked serious and dejected, but did not betray the least signs of compunction or repentance.[1]

About Three hundred and eighty of the brethren volunteered to go out immediately and it is probable they will nearly all be gone in two weeks[2]

---

1. Orson had been excommunicated nine days before, on 20 August, and Amasa Lyman ordained an apostle in his place. Orson was reinstated on 20 January 1843. (England, *Life and Thought of Orson Pratt*, 81, 84–85; Diary of Wilford Woodruff, 19 January 1843.)

2. Wilford Woodruff, who was confined to Nauvoo because of illness between 10 August and 19 September, noted that about 400 elders left to carry out the mission designated by the conference: "their has never at any time been as great a turn out into the vineyard since the foundation of the Church." Because of illness and the need to continue the printing business, only Woodruff and John Taylor of the Twelve did not go on the mission. (Diary of Wilford Woodruff, 10 August 1842.)

30 August 1842 · Tuesday

At home all day—

31 August 1842 · Wednesday

At home in the A.M. In the P.M rode up to the Grove with his lady to attend the Female Relief society's meeting. — [1]

1 September 1842 · Thursday

In the A.M. in the large room over the Store, P.M. at home attending to business.

2 September 1842 · Friday

Spent the day at home. In the P.M. a report came to the effect that the Sheriff[2] with an armed force, was on his way to Nauvoo.

3 September 1842 · Saturday

In the A.M. at home in company with John Boynton: A letter was received from brother [David S.] Hollister to the effect that the Missourians were again on the move and that two requisitions were issued, one on the Governor of this State and the other on the Governor of Iowa. There movements were represented as being very secret and resolute. Soon after 12 o clock [James M.] Pitman the Deputy Sheriff and two other men came into the house.[3] It appeared that they had come up the river side and hitched their horses below the Nauvoo House and then proceeded on foot, undiscovered untill they got into the house. When they arrived president Joseph was in another

---

1. Joseph Smith spoke at the meeting. A report of his address by Eliza R. Snow is in the Relief Society minutes. See also *History of the Church*, 5:139–41.

2. James M. Pittman, Adams County Sheriff.

3. One of the two men who accompanied Pittman was Edward R. Ford. (Ursenbach, "Eliza R. Snow's Nauvoo Journal," 398.)

apartment of the house eating dinner with his family. John Boynton happened to be the first person discovered by the Sheriffs and they began to ask him where Mr Smith was. He answered that he saw him [p. 184] early in the morning; but did not say that he had seen him since. While this conversation was passing, president Joseph passed out at the back door and through the corn in his garden to brother Newel K. Whitney's. He went up stairs and undiscovered. Meantime sister Emma went and conversed with the Sheriffs. Pitman said he wanted to search the house for Mr Smith. In answer to a question by sister Emma he said he had no warrant authorising him to search but insisted upon searching the house. She did not refuse and accordingly they searched through but to no effect. This is another testimony and evidence of the mean, corrupt, illegal proceedings of our enemies Notwithstanding the constitution of the United States says Article 4th "The right of the people to be secure in their persons, houses, papers, and effects, against unreasonable searches and seizures, shall not be violated; and no warrants shall issue, but upon probable cause, supported by oath or affirmation, and particularly describing the place to be searched, and the persons or things to be seized." Yet these men audaciously, impudently, and altogether illegally demanded, and searched the house of president Joseph, even without any warrant or authority whatever. Being satisfied that he was not in the house they departed. They appeared to be well armed, and no doubt intended to take him either dead or alive; which we afterwards heard they had said they would do; but the Almighty again delivered his servant from their blood-thirsty grasp. It is rumored that there are fifteen men in the city along with the Sheriffs and that they dined together to day at Amos Davis's.[1] Soon after sun

---

1. Amos Davis was the proprietor of a store and hotel at the corner of Mulholland and Wells Streets in Nauvoo. (Richard N. Holzapfel and R. Jeffery Cottle, *Old Mormon Nauvoo, 1839–1846* [Provo, Utah: Grandin Book Co., 1990], 40–41.)

down Thos. King and another person arived at the house and demanded to search, which they immediately did; but finding nothing they also went towards Davis's. Some of them was seen about afterwards but at about 10 o clock all was quiet. It is said that they started from Quincey yesterday expecting and fully determined to reach Nauvoo in the night and fall upon the house unawares but report says they lost the road, and got scattered away one from another, and could not get along untill daylight. This in all probability is true as they appeared much fatigued and complained of being weary and sore with riding. President Joseph, accompanied by brother Erastus H. Derby, left brother Whitneys about nine o clock; and went to brother Edward Hunters where he was welcomed and made comfortable by the family, and where he can be kept safe from the hands of his enemies.

I will now proceed to record the following letter from the Governor to sister Emma dated

"Quincy August 24th 1842
"Dear Madam—Your letter of this date has just been handed to me which recalls to my mind your great solicitude in reference to the security and wel-fare of your husband; but I need not say it recalls to my mind the subject matter of your solicitude, because that subject except at short intervals, has not been absent from my mind. I can scarcely furnish you a justifiable apology for delaying a reply so long, but be assured Madam, it is not for want of regard for you, and your peace of mind, that I have post-poned; but a crowd of public business, which has required [p. 185] my whole time; together with very ill health since the receipt of your former letter, and it would be most gratifying to my feelings now, if due regard to public duty, would enable me to furnish such a reply as would fully conform to your wishes—but my duty in reference to all demands made by Executives of other States, for the surrender of fugitives from justice, appears to be plain and simple; con-

sisting entirely of an executive, and not a judicial character leaving me no discretion–or adjudication, as to the innocence, or guilt, of persons so demanded and charged with crime, and it is plain that the constitution and laws of the united States in reference to fugitives from justice, presumes, and contemplates, that the laws of the several States are ample to do justice to all who may be charged with crime. And the statute of this State simply requires, "That when ever the Executive of any other State, or of any Territory of the united States, shall demand of the executive of this State any person as a fugitive from justice, and shall have complied with the requisitions of the act of congress in that case made and provided, it shall be the duty of the executive of this State to issue his *warrant* under the seal of the State, to apprehend the said fugitive" &c. With the Constitution and laws before me, my duty is so plainly marked out, that it would be impossible to err, so long as I abstain from usurping the right of adjudication. I am aware that a strict enforcement of the laws by an executive,–or a rigid administration of them by a judicial tribunal, often results in hardship to those involved, and to you it doubtless appears to be peculiarly so, in the present case of Mr. Smith. If however as you alledge, he is innocent of any crime, and the proceedings are illegal, it would be the more easy for him to procure an acquital. In reference to the remark you attribute to me that I "would not advise Mr Smith ever to trust himself in Missouri" I can only say–as I have heretofore said on many occasions that I never have entertained a doubt that if Mr Smith should submit to the laws of Missouri, that the utmost latitude would be allowed him in his defence, and the fullest justice done him, and I only intended to refer, (in the remark made to you when at my house) to the rabble and not to the laws of Missouri.

Very much has been attributed to me in reference to Genl Smith that is without foundation in truth, a knowledge of which fact, enable[s] me to receive what I hear as coming from him, with great allowance. In conclusion Dear Madam I feel conscious when I assure you, that all my official acts in reference to Mr Smith have been promted by a strict sense of duty, and in discharge of that duty have studiously pursued that course, least likely to produce excitement and alarm, both in your community, and the surrounding public, and I will here add that I much regret being called upon to act at all, and that I hope he will submit to the laws, and that justice will ultimately be done. Be pleased to present my best respects to Mrs–[Amanda Barnes] Smith & Miss [Eliza R.] Snow your companions when at Quincy,[1] and accept of my highest regard for yourself, and best wishes for your prosperity & happiness–

Your obedient servant
Tho. Carlin

Mrs Emma Smith [p. 186]

To the foregoing letter Sister Emma sent the following by way of answer.

"Nauvoo August 27th 1842

"To His Excellency Gov. Carlin

Dear Sir–I received your letter of the 24th in due time, and now tender you the sincere gratitude of my heart, for the interest which you have felt in my peace and prosperity; and I assure you, that every act of kindness, and every word of consolation have been thankfully received and duly appreciated by me and my friends also; and I much regret your ill health, but still hope that you will avail yourself of sufficient time to investigate our cause, and thoroughly acquaint yourself with the illegality of the prosecution instituted against Mr Smith.– And I now certify that Mr. Smith, myself, nor any other person, to my knowledge, has ever, nor do we at this time wish your honor to swerve from your duty, as an executive, in the least.

---

1. See note 1, p. 435.

But we do believe that it is your duty to allow us in this place, the privileges and advantages guaranteed to us by the laws of this State and the United States; this is all we ask, and if we can enjoy these rights unmolested, it will be the ultimate end of all our ambition; and the result will be peace and prosperity to us and all the surrounding country, as far as we are concerned. Nor do we wish to take any undue advantage of any intricate technicalities of law; but honorably and honestly to fulfil all of the laws of this state, and of the United States, and then, in turn, to have the benifits resulting from an honorable execution of those laws. And now, your Excellency will not consider me assuming any unbecoming dictation; but recollect that the many prosecutions that has been got up unjustly, and pursued illegaly against Mr Smith, instigated by selfish and irreligious motives, has obliged me to know something for myself; therefore, let me refer you to the eleventh section of our city Charter. "All power is granted to the City Council, to make, ordain, establish, and execute all ordinances, *not repugnant* to the constitution of the State, or of the United States, or, as they may deem necessary for the peace and safety of said city." Accordingly there is an ordinance passed by the City Council to prevent our people from being carried off by an illegal process. And if any one thinks he is illegally seized, under this ordinance he claims the right of Habeus Corpus, under section 17th of the charter, to try the question of identity, which is strictly constitutional. These powers are positively granted in the charter over your own signature; and now, dear sir, where can be the justice in depriving us of these rights which are lawfully ours, as well as they are the lawful rights of the inhabitants of Quincy and Springfield and many other places where the citizens enjoy the advantages of such ordinances, without controversy. With these considerations, and many more which might be adduced, give us the privilege, and we will show your Honor, and the world besides, if required, that the Mr Smith referr'd to in the demand from Missouri, is not the Joseph Smith of Nauvoo, for he was not in Missouri; neither is he [p. 187] described in the writ, according as the Law requires; and that he is not a fugitive from justice. Why then, be so strenuous to have my husband taken, when you know him to be innocent of an attempt on the life of Governor Boggs, and that he is not a fugutive from justice? It is not the fear of a just decision against him, that deters Mr Smith from going into Missouri; but it is an actual knowledge that it was never intended he should have a fair trial. And now sir, if you were not aware of the fact; I will acquaint you with it now, that there were lying ⟨in⟩ wait, between this place and Warsaw, twelve men from Jackson County, Missouri, for the purpose of taking Mr Smith out of the hands of the officers who might have him in custody. Also those two men from Missouri that were here with Messrs [Thomas C.] King and [James M.] Pi[t]tman, divulg'd the most illegal and infernal calculations concerning taking Mr Smith into Missouri the evidence of which, we can furnish you at any time, if required. And dear Sir, our good feelings revolt at the suggestion that your Excellency is acquainted with the unlawful measures taken by those engaged in the prosecution—measures which, if justice was done to others, as it would be done to us, were we to commit as great errors in our proceedings, would subject all concerned in the prosecution to the penalty of the law, and that without mercy. I admit Sir—that it is next to an impossibility, for any one to know the extent of the tyranny, treachery, and knavery of a great portion of the leading characters of the State of Missouri: yet it only requires a knowledge of the Constitution of the United States, and statute of the State of Missouri; and a knowledge of the outrages committed by some of the inhabitants of that State upon the people called Mormons, and that pass'd unpunished by the administrators of the law; to know that there is not the least confidence to be placed in any of those men that were engaged in those disgraceful transactions.

If the law was made for the lawless and disobedient, and punishment instituted for the guilty, why not execute the law upon those that have transgressed it, and punish those who have committed crime, and grant encouragement to the innocent, and liberality to the industrious & peaceable. And now I entreat your honor to bear with me patiently while I ask, what good can accrue to this State or the United States, or any part of this State or the United States, or to yourself, or any other individual, to continue this persecution upon this people, or upon Mr Smith–a persecution that you are well aware, is entirely without any just foundation or excuse. With sentiments of due respect I am your most obedient servant

Emma Smith

To His Excellency Thomas Carlin
Governor of the State of Illinois

P.S. Sir. You will please tender my best respects and considerations to your wife and family, and tell them I greatly desire to see them with yourself in our place as soon as can be convenient. Emma Smith [p. 188]

4 September 1842 · Sunday

This day President Hyrum Smith & president Wm Law started for the East accompanied by brothers Derby & [Edwin D.] Woolley. President Joseph sent the following letter to W. Clayton by brother Erastus H. Derby. The president wrote it and requested it to be read before the saints when assembled at the Grove near the Temple for preaching which was done according to his request.

"September 1st 1842

"To all the saints in Nauvoo. — [1] Forasmuch as the Lord has revealed unto me that my enemies, both of Missouri and this State were again on the pursuit of me; and inasmuch as they

---

1. See D&C 127.

pursue me without cause, and have not the least shadow, or coloring of justice, or right/[1] on their side, in the getting up of their prosecutions against me; and inasmuch as their pretensions are all founded in falsehood of the blackest die; I have thought it expedient and wisdom in me to leave the place for a short season, for my own safety and the safety of this people. I would say to all those with whom I have business, that I have left my affairs with agents and Clerks, who will transact all business in a prompt and proper manner; and will see that all my debts are cancell'd in due time, by turning out property or otherwise as the case may require, or as the circumstances may admit of. When I learn that the storm is fully blown over, then, I will return to you again: and as for the perils which I am call'd to pass through; they seem but a small thing to me, as the fury and wrath of man have been my common lot all the days of my life; and for what cause, it seems mysterious, unless I was ordained from before the foundation of the world, for some good end, or bad, as you may choose to call it: Judge ye for yourselves, God knoweth all these things whether it be good or bad; but nevertheless, deep water is what I am wont to swim in; it all has become a second nature to me and I feel like Paul, to glory in tribulation, for unto this day, has the God of my fathers delivered me out of them all, and will deliver me from henceforth; for behold and lo! I shall triumph over all my enemies, for the Lord God hath spoken it.

Let all the saints rejoice therefore and be exceeding glad, for Israel's God is their God and he will meet out a just recompence of reward upon the heads of all your oppressors. And again, verily, thus saith the Lord, let the work of my Temple, and all the works which I have appointed unto you, be continued on and not cease; and let your diligence and your perseverance, and patience and your works be redoubled, and

---

1. In MS. William Clayton's handwriting ends and that of Unknown Scribe B begins.

you shall in no wise lose your reward saith the Lord of Hosts. And if they persecute you, so persecuted they the prophets and righteous men that were before you: for all this there is a reward in heaven.

And again, I give unto [you] a word in relation to the baptism for your dead. Verily, thus saith the Lord unto you concerning your dead; Let there be a Recorder, and let him be eye-witness of your baptisms: let him hear with his ears that he may testify of a truth saith the Lord; that in all your re-cordings, it may be recorded in heaven; ⟨that⟩ whatsoever you bind on earth may be bound in heaven, and whatsoever you loose on earth may be loosed in heaven; for I am about to restore many things to the earth pertaining [p. 189] to the Priesthood saith the Lord of Hosts. And again, let all the Rec-ords be had in order, that they may be put in the archives of my holy Temple, to be held in remembrance from generation to generation, saith the Lord of Hosts.

I will say to all the saints, that I desired with exceeding great desire to have address'd them from the Stand, on the subject of baptism for the dead, on the following sabbath: But inasmuch as it is out of my power to do so, I will write the Word of the Lord from time to time, on that subject, and send it you by mail, as well as many other things.

I now close my letter for the present, for the want of more time; for the enemy is on the alert, and as the Savior said, the prince of this world cometh, but he hath nothing in me. Behold! my prayer to God is, that you all may be saved and I subscribe myself, your servant in the Lord, prophet and Seer of the Church of Jesus Christ, of Latter-Day Saints.

Joseph Smith./¹

When this letter was read before the brethren it cheered

---

1. In MS. handwriting of Unknown Scribe B ends and William Clayton's begins.

their hearts and evidently had the effect of stimulating them and inspiring them with courage, and faithfulness.

6 September 1842 · Tuesday

This evening W. C. [William Clayton], Newel K. Whitney, Brigham Young, Heber C. Kimball & Amasa Lyman visited President Joseph, the three latter especially to council concerning their mission &c and the two former concerning a settlement with brother Edward Hunter. The evening was spent cheerfully but nothing of special importance transpired.

7 September 1842 · Wednesday

Early this morning Elder [George J.] Adams and brother [David W.] Rogers from New York visited president Joseph and brought several letters from some of the brethren in that region. One letter from Dr. Willard Richards I will mention in this place.[1] When speaking concerning his interview with Mr James Arlington Bennett Esqr of New York he says "He would be happy to receive a letter of his (president Josephs) own dictation, signed by his own hand." General J. A. Bennett had wrote a letter and sent it by mail which was received a few days ago, and when president Joseph read the foregoing clause in Dr Richards letter he concluded to write him an answer. I will now record the letter from Genl Jas Arlington Bennett which is as follows–

"Arlington House August 16th 1842
"Dear Sir–Your polite and friendly note was handed to me a few days since by Dr W. Richards, who I must say is a very fine specimen of the Mormon people if they are all like him, and indeed I think him a very excellent representative of your-

---

1. Richards, while in the East to get his family, had stopped at Arlington House on Long Island to visit James Arlington Bennet. In April of 1842, Bennet had been appointed inspector-general of the Nauvoo Legion.

self, as I find he is your most devoted admirer and true disciple. He spent two days with me, and from his arguments and extremely mild and gentlemanly demeaner almost made me a Mormon.

You have another representative here, (who spent a day with me some time since) of the name of [Lucien R.] Foster, who is I think president of the church in New York and most unquestionably a most excellent and good man, [p. 190] and would be so if he were Turk, Jew or Saint. He is *ab initio* a good man and to you a most true, enthusiastic and devoted disciple. He has no guile. Dr. [John M.] Bernhisel of New York too, is a most excellent man and true christian. These are men with whom I could associate forever, even if I never joined their church or acknowledged their faith.

General John C. Bennett called on me last friday and spent just two hours when he left as he said for the Eastern States. Being aware that Elder Richards was here he had very little to say. He however proposed to me to aid him, wether serious or not, in arranging materials for publishing "an exposition of Mormon secrets and practices"–which I peremptorily refused on two grounds. 1st. That I had nothing to do with any quarrel that might arise between you and him, as I could not be a judge of the merits or demerits of the matter and 2ndly that inasmuch as he himself had proposed to you and your council to confer on me honors which I never sought, yet which I highly prize, it would be the height of ingratitude as well as inconsistent with every principle of common honesty and pro-priety, for me to join him in an effort to lower *my own honors* by attempting to lower in public estimation the people from whom those honors emanated. He gave Bennett of the Herald his commission which I opposed from the very first, and you now see by that paper the sport which that man has made of it. I tell you there is no dependance on the friendship of that Editor when his interest is at issue. I am assured that J. G. B. [James Gordon Bennett] is going to publish conjointly with J.

ILLINOIS JOURNAL, 1841–1842

C. B. [John C. Bennett] on half profit, the exposition against you and your people, which is going to contain a great number of scandalous cuts and plates. But don't be concerned, you will receive no injury whatever from any thing that any man or set of men may say against you. The whole of this *muss* is only extending your fame and will increase your numbers ten fold. You have nothing to expect from that part of the community who are bigotedly attached to the other churches. They have always believed, and still believe every thing said to your disadvantage; and what General J. C. Bennett is now saying in the papers is nothing more than what was common report before, throughout this whole community, insomuch that I had to contradict it in the Herald under the signature of "Cincinatus",[1] and even requested the Elders at the Mormon Church to do so long ago. You therefore have lost not a whit of ground by it. I must in charity forbear commenting on the course of Genl Bennett in this matter—considering all things, delicacy forbids such a course. There are some things however, I feel very sorely and could wish they had not transpired He and the Herald will make money out of the Book and there the matter will end, as you will find that the Herald will puff it to the skies.[2]

The books which I sent you, you will retain in your hands for the present. My respects to your amiable lady and all friends and believe me as ever, tho, not a Mormon, your sincere friend-
James Arlington Bennett [p. 191]

P.S. I know of no reason why the Wasp was not continued to be sent to me. *I dont like the name*. Mildness should characterise every thing that comes from Nauvoo and even a name

---

1. Bennet's 8 May 1842 letter signed "Cincinnatus," in which he corrects false reports being spread against the Latter-day Saints, was published in the *New York Herald*, 16 May 1842.

2. John C. Bennett's book *The History of the Saints: An Exposé of Joe Smith and Mormonism* was not published by the New York *Herald* but by Leland and Whiting in Boston.

as Paley says in his Ethics[1] has much influence on one side or the other. My respects to your brother its Editor.[2] I would just say that Gen. J. C. Bennett, appeared to me to be in very low spirits, and I find that many communications intended for you from me, has never reached you. Those Books were made over to J C. B. on the presumption that he would in his own name, present them for the benifit of the Temple

J. A. B."

In consequence of president Joseph not having the foregoing with him he concluded to write his answer tomorrow. He however wrote or rather dictated a long Epistle to the Saints which he ordered to be read next sabbath and which will be recorded under that date.[3]

In the P.M. brothers [George J.] Adams & [David W.] Rogers came to visit him again. They conversed upon the present persecution &c president Joseph in his discourse to brothers Adams and Rogers shewed the many great interpositions of the Almighty in his behalf not only during the present trouble, but more especially during the persecution in Missouri &c. The remarks droped on this occasion was truly encouraging and calculated to increase the confidence of those present.

8 September 1842 · Thursday

This A.M president Joseph dictated the following letter to Gen. James Arlington Bennett as before stated—The letter is as follows. —

"Nauvoo September 8th 1842

1. Possibly William Paley, *The Principles of Moral and Political Philosophy* (London: Printed for Baldwyn by J. Haddon, 1821).
2. *The Wasp*, a weekly paper edited by William Smith and John Taylor, was published at Nauvoo, Illinois, beginning 16 April 1842. In April 1843 the name of the paper was changed to *The Nauvoo Neighbor*. (Jenson, *Encyclopedic History,* 928–29.)
3. See entry of 11 September.

Dear Sir–I have just received/[1] your very consoling letter dated August 16th 1842; which I think, is the first letter you ever addressed to me; in which you speak of the arrival of Dr. W. Richards, and of his person very respectfully. In this I rejoice; for I am as warm a friend to Dr. Richards as he possibly can be to me: And in relation to his almost making a Mormon of yourself, it puts me in mind of the saying of Paul in his reply to Agrippa, Acts ch. 26th v. 29th "I would to God that not only thou, but also all that hear me this day; were both almost and altogether such as I am except these bonds." And I will here remark, my dear Sir; that Mormonism is the pure doctrine of Jesus Christ, of which I myself am not ashamed.

You speak also of Elder [Lucien] Foster, President of the Church in New York, in high terms: and of Dr. [John M.] Bernhisel of New York. These men I am acquainted with by information; and it warms my heart, to know that you speak well of them: and as you say, could be willing to associate with them forever, if you never joined their church, or acknowledged their faith. This is a good principle; for when we see virtuous qualities in men, we should always acknowledge them, let their understanding be what it may in relation to creeds and doctrine; for all men are, or ought to be free; possessing un-alienable rights, and the high, and noble qualifications of the laws of nature and of self-preservation; to think, and act, and say as they please; while they maintain a due respect to the rights and privileges of all other creatures; infringing upon none. This [p. 192] doctrine I do most heartily subscribe to and practice; the testimony of mean men, to the contrary, notwithstanding. But Sir, I will assure you, that my soul soars far above all the mean and grovelling dispositions of men that are dispos'd to abuse me and my character: I therefore shall not dwell upon that subject.

---

1. In MS. William Clayton's handwriting ends and that of Unknown Scribe B begins.

In relation to those men you speak of, referred to above; I will only say that there are thousands of such men in this church; who, if a man is found worthy to associate with, will call down the envy of a mean world, because of their high and noble demeanor: and it is with unspeakable delight that I contemplate them as my friends & brethren. I love them with a perfect love; and I hope they love me, and have no reason to doubt but they do.

The next in consideration is John C. Bennett. I was his friend. I am yet his friend; as I feel myself bound to be a friend to all the sons of Adam; whether they are just or unjust, they have a degree of my compassion and sympathy. If he is my enemy it is his own fault; and the responsibility rests upon his own head; and instead of arraigning his character before you, suffice it to say, that his own conduct wherever he goes, will be sufficient to recommend him to an enlightened public, whether for a bad man, or a good one. Therefore whosoever will associate themselves with him, may be assured that I will not persecute them; but I do not wish their association: And what I have said may suffice on that subject, so far as his character is concern'd.

Now in relation to his book that he may write, I will venture a prophecy; that whosoever has any hand in the matter, will find themselves in a poor fix, in relation to the money matters. And as to my having any fears of the influence that he may have against me; or any other man or set of men may have, is the most foreign from my heart; for I never knew what it was, as yet, to fear the face of clay, or the influence of man. My fear, Sir, is before God. I fear to offend him, and strive to keep his commandments. I am really glad that you did not join John C. in relation to his book, from the assurances which I have, that it will prove a curse to all those who touch it.

In relation to the honors that you speak of, both for yourself and James Gordon Bennett of the Herald, you are both strangers to me, and as John C. Bennett kept all his letters, which he receiv'd from you, entirely to himself; and there was no correspondence between you and me, that I knew of; I had no opportunity to share very largely ~~in~~ in the getting up of any of those matters. I could not, as I had not sufficient knowledge to enable me to do so. The whole, therefore, was at the instigation of John C. Bennett, and a quiet submission on the part of the rest, out of the best of feelings. But as for myself, it was all done at a time when I was overwhelm'd with a great many business cares, as well as the care of all the churches. I must be excus'd therefore, for any wrongs that may have taken place, in relation to this matter: And so far as I [p. 193] obtain a knowledge of that which is right shall meet with my hearty approval.

I feel to tender you my most hearty and sincere thanks, for every expression of kindness, you have tendered towards me or my brethren; and would beg the privilege of obtruding myself a little while upon your patience, in offering a short relation of my circumstances. I am at this time persecuted the worst of any man on ⟨the⟩ earth; as well as this people, here in this place; and all our sacred rights are trampled under the feet of the mob.

I am now hunted as an hart by the mob, under the pretence or shadow of law, to cover their abominable deeds. An unhallowed demand has been made from the Governor of Missouri, on oath of Governor Boggs; that I made an attempt to assassinate him on the night of the sixth of May; when on that day, I was attending the officer Drill, and answered to my name when the roll was call'd: and on the seventh, it is well known by the thousands that assembled here in Nauvoo, that I was at my post in reviewing the Nauvoo Legion in the presence of twelve thousand people: And the Governor of the State of Illinois, notwithstanding his being knowing to all these facts, yet he immediately granted a Writ; and by an unhallowed usurpation, has taken away our chartered rights, and denied the right of Habeas Corpus; and has now about thirty of the blood-thirsty kind of men in this place, in search for me; threatening death and destruction, and extermination upon all the Mormons; and searching my house almost continually from day to day; menacing and threatning, and intimidating an innocent wife and children, & insulting them in a most diabolical manner; threatening their lives &c. if I am not to be found, with a gang of Missourians with them; saying they will have me dead or alive; and if alive, they will carry me to Missouri in chains, and when there, they will kill me at all hazards. And all this, is backed up, and urged on, by the Governor of this State, with all the rage of a demon; putting at defiance, the Constitution of this State — our chartered rights — and the Constitution of the United States: For not as yet, have they done *one thing* that was in accordance to them.

While all the citizens of this city, *en mass*, have petitioned the Governor with remonstrances, and overtures, that would have melted the heart of an adamantine *to no effect*. And at the same time, if any of us upon our mouths, to plead our own cause; in the defiance of law and justice, we are instantly threatened with *Militia* and *extermination*. Great God! When shall the oppressor cease to prey and glut itself upon innocent blood! Where is Patriotism? Where is Liberty? Where is the boast of this proud and haughty nation? O humanity! where hast thou fled? Hast thou fled forever?

I now appeal to you Sir, inasmuch as you have subscribed yourself our friend; will you lift your voice and your arm, with indignation against such unhallowed oppression? I must say, Sir that my bosom swells with unutterable anguish, when I contemplate the scenes of horror that we have passed through in the State of Missouri; and then look, and behold and see the storm and cloud [p. 194] gathering ten times blacker; ready to burst upon the heads of this innocent people! Would to God that I were able to throw off the yoke. Shall we bow down and be slaves? Are there no friends of humanity, in a nation that boasts itself so much? Will not the nation rise up and defend

465

us? If they will not defend us, will they not grant to lend a voice of indignation against such unhallowed oppression? Must the tens of thousands bow down to slavery and degradation? Let the pride of the nation arise and wrench these shackles from the feet of their fellow citizens, and their quiet, and peaceable, and innocent and loyal subjects. But I must forbear, for I cannot express my feelings. The Legion would all willingly die in the defence of their rights; but what would this accomplish? I have kept down their indignation and kept a quiet submission on all hands; and am determined to do so at all hazards. Our enemies shall not have it to say, that we rebel against government, or commit treason; however much they may lift their hands in oppression and tyranny, when it comes in the form of government—we tamely submit altho it lead us to the slaughter, and to beggary; but our blood be upon their garments: And those who look tamely on and boast of patriotism, shall not be without their condemnation. And if men are such fools, as to let once the precedent be established, and through their prejudices, give assent to such abomination; then let the oppressor's hand lay heavily throughout the world, until all flesh shall feel it together; and until they may know that the Almighty takes cognizance of such things. And then shall church rise up against church; and party against party; mob, against mob; oppressor against oppressor; army against army; kingdom against kingdom; and people against people; and kindred against kindred. And where, Sir, will be your safety, or the safety of your children; *if my children can be led to the slaughter with impunity by the hands of murderous rebels? Will they not lead yours to the slaughter, with the same impunity?* Ought not then, this oppression Sir, to be check'd in the bud; and to be looked down with just indignation by an enlightened world, before the flame become unextinguishable, and the fire devour the stubble?

But again I say I must forbear, and leave this painful subject. I wish you would write to me in answer to this, and let me know your views. On my part, I am ready to be offered up a sacrifice in that way that can bring to pass the greatest benefit and good, to those who must necessarily be interested in this important matter. I would to God, that you could know all my feelings on this subject, and the real facts in relation to this people, and their unrelenting persecution: And if any man feels an interest in the welfare of their fellow-beings, and would think of saying or doing anything in this matter; I would suggest the propriety of a committee of wise men, being sent to ascertain the justice or injustice of our cause–to get in possession of all the facts; and then make report to an enlightened world, whether [p. 195] we, individually, or collectively, are deserving such high-handed treatment.

In relation to the books that you sent here, John C. Bennett put them into my Store, to be sold on commission; saying, that when I was able, the money must be remitted to yourself. Nothing was said about my consecration to the Temple.

Another calamity has befallen us. Our Post Office in this place, is exceedingly corrupt. It is with great difficulty that we can get our letters to or from our friends. Our papers that we send to our subscribers, are embezzled and burned, or wasted. We get no money from our subscribers, and very little information from abroad; and what little we do get, we get by private means, in consequence of these things: and I am sorry to say, that this robbing of the Post Office of money, was carried on by John C. Bennett; and since he left here, it is carried on by the means of his confederates.

I now subscribe myself your friend, and a patriot and lover of my country, pleading at their feet for protection and deliverance, by the justice of their Constitutions,

I add no more. Your most obedient servant,

Joseph Smith./[1]

---

1. In MS. handwriting of Unknown Scribe B ends and William Clayton's begins.

9 September 1842 · Friday

This P.M. after dark president Joseph received a very pleasant visit from Sister Emma, Wilson Law, Amasa Lyman & George A. Smith.

10 September 1842 · Saturday

This being the Training day for the companies composing the Legion president Joseph kept very close and still; lest on account of the quantity of people passing two and fro he should accidently be discovered. After dark sister Emma sent word by a messinger that she wished him to come home, as she thought he would be as safe at home as any where for the present. Brother Wilson Law also went and carried the same report; consequently the president left for home where he arrived safe and undiscovered. —

11 September 1842 · Sunday

At home all day–At president Josephs request the following letter which himself dictated which read to the saints at the Grove near the Temple./[1]

Journeying, Septr. 6th 1842.
To the Church of Jesus Christ of Latter-day Saints; Sendeth Greeting.[2]

As I stated to you in my letter before I left my place, that I would write to you from time to time, and give you information in relation to many subjects: I now resume the subject of the baptism for the dead as that subject seems to occupy my mind, and press itself upon my feelings the strongest, since I have been pursued by my enemies.

---

1. In MS. handwriting of William Clayton ends and that of Unknown Scribe B begins.
2. See D&C 128.

I wrote a few words of Revelation to you concerning a Recorder. I have had a few additional views in relation to this matter, which I now certify; ie. It was declared in my former letter that there [p. 196] should be a Recorder who should be eye-witness, and also to hear with his ears that he might make a Record of a truth before the Lord. Now, in relation to this matter; it would be very difficult for one Recorder to be present at all times and to do all the business. To obviate this difficulty, there can be a Recorder appointed in each ward of the City,[1] who is well qualified for taking accurate minutes; and let him be very particular and precise in making his Record and taking the whole proceeding; certifying in his Record, that he saw with his eyes, and heard with his ears; giving the date, the names &c. and the history of the whole transaction, naming also some three individuals that are present, if there be any present who can at any time, when call'd upon, certify to the same; that in the mouth of two or three witnesses, every word may be established. Then let there be a general Recorder to whom these other Records can be handed, being attended with certificates over their own signatures; certifying that the Record which they have made, is true. Then the General Church Recorder can enter the Record on the general Church Book with the Certificates and all the attending witnesses, with his own statement that he verily believes the above statements and Records to be true, from his knowledge of the general character and appointment of those men by the Church. And when this is done on the general Church Book; the Record shall be just as holy, and shall answer the ordinance just the same as if he had seen with his eyes and heard with his ears, and made a Record of the same on the general Book.

You may think this Order of things to be very particular: But let me tell you, that they are only to answer the will of

---

1. Nauvoo was divided into four municipal wards on 1 March 1841. (*History of the Church*, 4:305–6.)

God by conforming to the ordinance and preparation, that the
Lord ordained and prepared before the foundation of the world
for the salvation of the dead who should die without a knowledge of the Gospel. And further, I want you to remember that
John the Revelator was contemplating this very subject in
relation to the dead, when he declar'd, as you will find recorded
in Revelations Chap. 20th v. 12; And I saw the dead, small
and great, stand before God: and the books were opened: and
another book was opened, which is the book of Life; and the
dead were judg'd out of those things which were written in
the books, according to their works. You will discover in this
quotation, that the books were opened, and another book was
opened which is the book of Life; but the dead were judg'd out
of those things which were written in the books according to
their works; consequently, the books spoken of, must be the
books which contained the record of their works, and refers
to the Records which are kept on the earth: And the book
which was the book of life, is the Record which is kept in
heaven; the principle agreeing precisely with the doctrine which
is commanded you in the Revelation contained in the letter
which I wrote you previous to my leaving my place, "that in
all your recordings it may be recorded in heaven." Now the
nature of this ordinance consists in the power of the Priesthood
by the revelations of Jesus Christ, wherein it is granted that
whatsoever [p. 197] you bind on earth, shall be bound in
heaven, and whatsoever you loose on earth shall be loosed in
heaven: Or in other words, taking a different view of the translation, whatsoever you record on earth shall be recorded in
heaven; and whatsoever you do not record on earth, shall not
be recorded in heaven; for out of the books shall your dead be
judg'd according to their works, whether they, themselves have
attended to the ordinances in their own *propria persona*, or
by the means of their own agents according to the ordinance
which God has prepared for their salvation, from before the
foundation of the world, according to the records which they

have kept concerning their dead. It may seem to some, to be a very bold doctrine that we talk of; a power which records, or binds on earth, and binds in heaven. Nevertheless, in all ages of the world, whenever the Lord has given a dispensation of the Priesthood to any man, by actual revelation, or any set of men; this power has always been given: Hence, whatsoever those men did in authority, in the name of the Lord, and did it truly and faithfully, and kept a proper and faithful record of the same, it became a law on earth and in heaven; and could not be annull'd according to the decree of the great Jehovah. This is a faithful saying: Who can hear it? And again for a precedent, Matt. chapter 16 verses 18, 19, "And I say also unto thee, that thou art Peter: and upon this rock I will build my church; and the gates of hell shall not prevail against it. And I will give unto thee, the keys of the kingdom of heaven; and whatsoever thou shalt bind on earth, shall be bound in heaven; and whatsoever thou shalt loose on earth, shall be loosed in heaven.["] Now the great and grand secret of the whole matter, and the *summum*[1] *bonum* of the whole subject that is lying before us consists in obtaining the powers of the Holy Priesthood. For him, to whom these keys are given; there is no difficulty in obtaining a knowledge of facts in relation to the salvation of the children of men; both as well for the dead as for the living. Herein is glory, and honor, and immortality and eternal life. The ordinance of baptism by water, to be immers'd therein in order to answer to the likeness of the dead, that one principle might accord with the other to be immers'd in the water, and come forth out of the water is in the likeness of the resurrection of the dead in coming forth out of their graves: hence, this ordinance was instituted to form a relationship with the ordinance of baptism for the dead; being in likeness of the dead. Consequently, the baptismal Font was instituted as a simile of the grave, and was com-

---

1. In MS. "summum" written over "sum and" in darker ink.

manded to be in a place underneath where the living are wont to assemble, to show forth the living and the dead; and that all things may have their likeness, and that they may accord one with another; that which is earthly, conforming to that which is heavenly, as Paul hath declar'd 1st Corinthians, Chap. 15, verses 46, 47 & 48.

"Howbeit, that was not first which is spiritual, but that which is natural, and afterward, that which is spiritual. The first man is of the earth, earthy: the second man, is the Lord from heaven. [p. 198] As is the earthy, such are they also that are earthy: and as is the heavenly, such are they also that are heavenly: And as are the records on the earth in relation to your dead, which are truly made out; so also are the records in heaven. This, therefore, is the sealing and binding power; and in one sense of the word the keys of the kingdom, which consists in the key of knowledge.

And now my dearly and beloved brethren and sisters, let me assure you[1] that these are principles in relation to the dead and the living; that cannot be lightly passed over, as pertaining to our salvation: for their salvation is necessary and essential to our salvation; as Paul says concerning the fathers, "That they without us, cannot be made perfect;" neither can we without our dead, be made perfect. And now, in relation to the baptism for the dead; I will give you another quotation of Paul, I Cor. 15 chap. verse 29 "Else what shall they do which are baptized for the dead, if the dead rise not at all? Why are they then baptized for the dead?" And again in connexion with this quotation I will give you a quotation from one of the prophets, which had his eye fix'd on the restoration of the Priesthood—the glories to be reveal'd in the last days, and in an especial manner, this most glorious of all subjects belonging to the everlasting gospel, viz. the baptism for the dead; for Malachi says, last chap.–verses 5 & 6. "Behold I will send you

---

1. "you" written over "me" in MS.

Elijah the prophet, before the coming of the great and dreadful day of the Lord: And he shall turn the hearts of the fathers to the children, and the hearts of the children to their fathers, lest I come and smite the earth with a curse." I might have rendered a plainer translation to this, but it is sufficiently plain to suit my purpose, as it stands. It is sufficient to know in this case, that the earth will be smitten with a curse, unless there is a welding link of some kind or other, between the fathers and the children, upon some subject or other. And behold! what is that subject? It is the baptism for the dead. For we without them, cannot be made perfect; neither can they, without us, be made perfect. Neither can they or us, be made perfect without those who have died in the gospel also; for it is necessary in the ushering in of the dispensation of the fulness of times; which dispensation is now beginning to usher in, that a whole, and complete and perfect union, and welding together of dispensations and keys, and powers and glories should take place, and be reveal'd, from the days of Adam even to the present time; and not only this, but those things that never have been reveal'd from the foundation of the world; but have been kept hid from the wise and prudent; shall be revealed unto babes and sucklings, in this, the dispensation of the fulness of times.

Now what do we hear in the gospel which we have received? A voice of gladness–a voice of mercy from heaven–a voice of truth out of the earth–glad tidings for the dead; a voice of gladness for the living and[1] the dead; glad tidings of great joy! How beautiful upon the mountains, are the feet of those that bring glad tidings of good things; and that say unto Zion, behold! thy God reigneth. As the dews of Carmel so shall the knowledge of God descend upon them. And again, [p. 199] What do we hear? Glad tidings from Cumorah! Moroni, an angel from heaven, declaring the fulfilment of the prophets–

---

1. "and" repeated in MS.

the book to be reveal'd! A voice of the Lord in the wilderness of Fayette, Seneca County, declaring the three witnesses to bear record of the Book. The voice of Michael on the banks of the Susquehanna, detecting the devil when he appeared as an angel of light. The voice of Peter, James & John, in the wilderness, between Harmony, Susquehanna County, and Colesville, Broom County, on the Susquehanna river, declaring themselves as possessing the keys of the kingdom, and of the dispensation of the fulness of times. And again, the voice of God in the chamber of old father Whitmer in Fayette, Seneca County, and at sundry times, and in divers places, through all the travels and tribulations, of this Church of Jesus Christ of Latter Day Saints. And the voice of Michael the archangel– the voice of Gabriel, and of Raphael, and of divers angels, from Michael or Adam, down to the present time; all declaring, each one their dispensation, their rights, their keys, their honors, their majesty & glory, and the power of their Priesthood; giving line upon line; precept upon precept; here a little and there a little: giving us consolation by holding forth that which is to come and confirming our hope.

Brethren, shall we not go on in so great[1] a cause? Go forward and not go backward. Courage, brethren! and on to the victory. Let your hearts rejoice and be exceeding glad. Let the earth break forth into singing. Let the dead speak forth anthems of eternal praise to the king Immanuel, who hath ordain'd before the world was, that which would enable us to redeem them out of their prisons; for the prisoner shall go free. Let the mountains shout for joy, and all ye vallies cry aloud; and all ye seas and dry lands tell the wonders of your eternal king: And ye rivers, and brooks, and rills, flow down with gladness. Let the woods and all the trees of the field praise the Lord: and ye solid rocks, leap for joy. And let the sun, moon, and the morning stars sing together; and let all the sons of God shout

---

1. "great" written over "good" in MS.

for joy: And let the eternal creations declare his name forever and ever.

And again, I say, how glorious is the voice we hear from heaven proclaiming in our ears, glory and salvation, and honor, and immortality and eternal life. Kingdoms, principalities and powers! behold! the great day of the Lord is at hand, and who can abide the day of his coming, and who can stand when he appeareth? For he is like a refiner's fire, and like fuller's soap: and he shall sit as a refiner and purifier of silver, and he shall purify the sons of Levi, and purge them as gold and silver; that they may offer unto the Lord an offering in righteousness. And let us, present in his holy Temple, when it is finished, a Book, containing the Records of our dead, which shall be worthy of all acceptation.

Brethren, I have many things to say to you on the subject; but shall now close for the present, and continue the subject another time. [p. 200]

I am as ever your humble servant, and never deviating friend,

Joseph Smith./[1]

The important instructions contained in the foregoing letter made a deep and solemn impression on the minds of the saints and they manifested their intentions to obey the instructions to the letter.

12 September 1842 · Monday

At home all day in company with brothers [George J.] Adams & [David W.] Rogers, and councilling brother Adams to write a letter to the Governor. In the P.M sister Emma received a letter from the Governor the following of which is a copy.

---

1. In MS. handwriting of Unknown Scribe B ends and William Clayton's begins.

"Quincy September 7th 1842
Dear Madam — Your letter of the 27th Ultimo was delivered to me on Monday the 5th instant, and I have not had time to answer it untill this evening, and I now appropriate a few moments to the difficult task of replying satisfactorily to its contents, every word of which evinces your devotedness to the interest of your husband and pouring forth the effusions of a heart wholly his. I am thus admonished that I can say nothing, that does not subserve his interest that can possibly be satisfactory to you. And before I proceed I will here repeat, my great regret that I have been officially called upon to act in reference to Mr Smith in any manner whatever. I doubt not your candor when you say you do not desire me "to swerve from my duty as executive in the least" and all you ask is to be allowed the privileges, and advantages guaranteed to you by the constitution and laws. You then refer me to the 11th Section of the Charter of the City of Nauvoo, and claim for Mr Smith the right to be heard by the Municipal Court of said city, under a writ of Habeus Corpus emanating from said court–when he was held in custody under an executive warrant. The charter of the city of Nauvoo is not before me at this time, but I have examined both the charters, and city ordinances upon the subject, and must express my surprise at the extraordinary assumption of power by the board of Aldermen as contained in said ordinance! From my recollection of the charter it authorizes the Municipal Court to issue writs of Habeus Corpus in all cases of imprisonment, or custody, arising from the authority of the ordinances of said city, but that the power was granted, or intended to be granted to release persons held in custody under the authority of writs issued by the courts, or the executive of the State, is most absurd & rediculous, and an attempt to exercise it, is a gross usurpation of power, that cannot be tolerated. I have always expected, and desired, that Mr Smith should avail himself of the benefits of the laws of this State, and of course that he would be entitled

to a writ of Habeus Corpus issued by the circuit court, and entitled to a hearing before said court, but to claim the right of a hearing before the municipal court of the city of Nauvoo is a burlesque upon the charter itself. As to Mr Smiths guilt, or innocence of the crime [p. 201] charged upon him, it is not my province to investigate or determine, nor has any court on earth jurisdiction of his case, but the courts of the State of Missouri, and as stated in my former letter both the constitution and laws presumes that each and every state in this Union, are competant to do justice to all who may be charged with crime committed in said State. Your information that twelve men from Jackson County Mo. were lying in wait for Mr Smith between Nauvoo and Warsaw, for the purpose of taking him out of the hands of the officers who might have him in custody, and murdering him, is like many other marvellous stories that you hear in reference to him—not one word of it true, but I doubt not that your mind has been continually harrowed up with fears produced by that, and other equally groundless stories—that that statement is true is next to impossible, and your own judgment if you will but give it scope will soon set you right in reference to it—if any of the citizens of Jackson had designed to Murder Mr Smith, they would not have been so simple as to perpetrate the crime in Illinois, when he would necessarily be required to pass through to the interior of the State of Missouri, where the opportunity would have been so much better, and the prospect of escape much more certain—that is like the statement made by Mr Smiths first messenger after his arrest, to Messrs [James H.] Ralston and [Calvin A.] Warren—saying that I had stated that Mr Smith should be surrendered to the authorities of Mo. dead or alive—not one word of which was true. I have not the most distant thought that any person in Illinois, or Missouri, contemplated personal injury to Mr Smith by violence in any manner whatever.

I regret that I did not see Genl [Wilson] Law when last at

Quincy. A previous engagement upon business that could not be dispensed with prevented and occupied my attention that evening untill dark. At half past 1 o clock P.M. I came home and learned that the Genl had called to see me, but the hurry of business only allowed me about ten minutes time to eat my dinner and presuming if he had business of any importance that he would remain in the city untill I returned. It may be proper here in order to afford you all the satisfaction in my power, to reply to a question propounded to my wife by Genl. Law in referrence to Mr Smith viz. wether any other, or additional demand had been made upon me by the Govr of Mo. for the surrender of Mr Smith—I answer none, no change whatever has been made in the proceedings. Mr Smith is held accountable only, for the charge as set forth in my warrant under which he was arrested. In conclusion you presume upon my own knowledge of Mr Smiths innocence—and ask why the prosecution is continued against him. Here I must again appeal to your own good judgement and you will be compelled to answer that it is impossible I could know him to be innocent— and as before stated it is not my province to investigate as to his guilt or innocence, but could I know him innocent, and were he my own son, I would nevertheless—(and the more readily) surrender him to the legally constituted authority [p. 202] to pronounce him innocent.

　　With sentiments of high regard and esteem your obt servant
　　　　　　　　　　　　Tho Carlin."
Mrs. Emma Smith.

13 September 1842 · Tuesday

　　At home all day. this day effected a settlement with Mr Edward Hunter

14 September 1842 · Wednesday

　　At home. Mr [Jacob G.] Remick of Keokuk gave president Joseph a Deed for one half of the Land and property he owned in Keokuk amounting to many thousand dollars.[1] Had consultation with C. A. Warren Esqr. In the P.M. received the following letter from Genl. J. Arlington Bennett

"Arlington House Sepr 1–1842

Lieut. Gen. Smith

D[ea]r Sir.–Mrs Smiths letter to Mrs Bennett containing a very lucid account of Dr John C. Bennett has been received and the only thing concerning him that I regard of importance, is, that you found it necessary to expose him. I wish most ardently that you had let him depart in peace, because the public generally think no better of either the one party or the other in consequence of the pretended exposures with which the newspapers have teemed. But then on the long run you will have the advantage, inasmuch as the universal notoriety which you are now acquiring will be the means of adding to Nauvoo three hundred fold.

That you ought to be given up to the tender mercies of Missouri no man in his senses will allow, as you would be convicted on the shadow of evidence when the peoples passions and prejudices are so strongly enlisted against you and under such a state of things how easy it would be to suborn[2] witnesses against you who would seal your fate. Add to this, too, the great difficulty under which an impartial Jury, if such could be found, would labor in their attempt to render an honest verdict, being cohersed by surrounding public prejudice and malice. And yet as you are now circumstanced it will not do to oppose force to force, for your protection, as this in the present case would be treason against the State and would ultimately bring to ruin all those concerned.

Your only plan I think will be to keep out of the way until

---

1. At the April 1843 Church conference, Joseph Smith reviewed his dealings with Jacob G. Remick and the acquisition of Iowa land. (See *History of the Church*, 5:334–36.)
2. MS.: "subern".

this excitement shall have subsided, as from all I can under-stand even from the Dr himself, there is no evidence on which an honest jury could find against you and this opinion I have expressed to him. I most ardently wish that you had one hundred thousand *true* men at Nauvoo and that I had the command of them–*Times and things would soon alter*. I hope to see the day before I die that such an army will dictate times from Nauvoo to the enemies of the Mormon people. I say this in the most perfect candor as I have nothing to gain by the Mormons, nor am I a Mormon in creed, yet I regard them in as favorable a light, (and a little more so) as I do any other sect. In fact I am a Philosophical Christian [p. 203] and wish to see an entire change in the religious world.

I have been long a Mormon in sympathy alone and probably can never be one in any other way, yet I feel that I am a friend of the people as I think them honest and sincere in their faith and these I know as good and honorable men as any other professing Christians.

Dr. Bennett has been the means of bringing me before your people, you will therefore see for *this act* I am in honor bound to say *"Peace to his Mores."* To act otherwise would be un-grateful and dishonorable, both of which qualities are strangers to my nature. Nevertheless by leaving him as he is I can still be your friend, for be assured that nothing I have yet seen from his pen has in the least altered my opinion of you. I well know what allowance to make in such cases.

Docter Bennett, and [Origen] Bachelor are now delivering lectures in New York against you and your doctrines and as-serted practises at Nauvoo. Elder [Lucien] Foster told me this forenoon that the seats have been torn to pieces out of his church in Canal St, and that the congregation had to move to another place. I intimated to you in my last that Bennett of the Herald was about to publish conjointly with the Dr his Book of Exposures but since have learned that it is about to come out in Boston. He expects to make a fortune out of it, and I presume he needs it, but I feel sure that it will only make converts to the Mormon faith. He has borrowed largely from Com. Morris' lacivious Poems.

A general order signed by Hugh McFall, Agt General, and authorised by you has appeared in the Herald, ordering me to repair to Nauvoo to take command of the Legion, and to bring with me Brig. Gen. J. G. Bennett, which states that if the requisition be persisted in blood must be shed. I have assured Bennett of the Herald that I deem it a *hoax* but he insists upon it that it is genuine. My reply to it has appeared to day in that paper. I have there stated that I have written to Govr Carlin for instructions, this is not so, it is only a *rub*. On the whole you will only be made a greater Prophet and a greater man a greater *Emperor* by the affliction and consideration of your good friends. My respects with those of Mrs B. to your lady

I am D[ea]r Sir your sincere friend. James Arlington Bennett.["]

This letter was placed in the hands of Genl. Hugh McFall who immediately wrote a refutation of the clause concerning himself to Governor Carlin, and also one for the Wasp. The general order was not wrote by McFall neither had he a knowledge of its existence untill shown to him in the letter. It is ⟨was⟩[1] evidently got up by our enemies to increase excitement and anger, and is barely another addition to the many slanderous reports put in circulation by evil and designing men. [p. 204]

15 September 1842 · Thursday

In council with Esqr Warren. Also councilled Uncle John Smith and brother Daniel C. Davis to move immediately to Keokuk and help to build up a city.

---

1. Later insertion added to MS. in pencil.

16 September 1842 · Friday

With brother [David W.] Rogers at home. bro R painting

17 September 1842 · Saturday

At home with brother Rogers, painting.

18 September 1842 · Sunday

At home. In the evening had a visit from Mother Smith.

19, 20 September 1842 · Monday, Tuesday

With brother Rogers, painting at his house.

21 September 1842 · Wednesday

In the large room over the store. In the P.M. had a visit from Er John Taylor on[e] of the Quorum of the Twelve who is just recovering from a severe attack of sickness. He councilled Er Taylor concerning the printing office–removing one Press to Keokuk &c. — [1]

22 September 1842 · Thursday

At home. Arrangeing with [Jacob G.] Remick concerning moving printing press to Keokuk; buying paper &c.

23 September 1842 · Friday

At home. Had a visit from Er Taylor.

---

1. Wilford Woodruff noted that prospects had developed at this time for Keokuk, Iowa, to become a Mormon town, and that Joseph Smith had directed him to go there and publish a political paper, while John Taylor would remain in Nauvoo to publish the *Times and Seasons*. These plans did not materialize. On 2 October Woodruff was advised to remain in Nauvoo and assist in the printing office there. (Diary of Wilford Woodruff, 22 September, 2 October 1842.)

Painting of Joseph Smith by David W. Rogers, 1842.
LDS Museum of Church History and Art.

24 September 1842 · Saturday

At home. Had a visit from old Mr [Joseph] Murdock & Lady concerning land &c

25 September 1842 · Sunday

At the Grove. Spake more than two hours chiefly on the subject of his persecution.

26 September 1842 · Monday

In the large room over the Store. —

27, 28 September 1842 · Tuesday, Wednesday

At home. Nothing of importance transpired.

29 September 1842 · Thursday

This day Sister Emma began to be sick with fever; consequently president Joseph kept in the house and with her all day.

30 September 1842 · Friday

Sister Emma no better. president Joseph was with her all day.

1 October 1842 · Saturday

This A.M. president Joseph is sick, having a very severe pain in his left side; was not able to be about in consequence. Sister Emma about as usual. The president had previously sent for the Temple Committee to balance their accounts and ascertain how the Temple business was going on. Some reports had been circulated that the committee was not making a righteous disposition of property consecrated for the building of the Temple and there appeared to be some disatisfaction amongst the laborers. After carefully examining the accounts and enquiring into the manner of the proceedings of Committee president Joseph expressed himself perfectly satisfied with them and their works. The books were [p. 205] ballanced between the Trustee and Committee and the wages of all agreed upon. The president remarked that he was amenable to the state for the faithful discharge of his duties as Trustee in Trust and that the Temple Committee were acco[u]ntable to him and to no other authority; and they must not take notice of any complaints from any source but let the complaints be made to him if any were needed and he would make things right. The parties separated perfectly satisfied and the president said he would have a notice published stating that he had examined their accounts and was satisfied &c. —[1] It was also agreed that the Recorders office should be moved to the Temple, for better convenience.

2 October 1842 · Sunday

About 1 oclock A.M. a messenger arrived from Quincy stating that the Governor had offered a reward of $200 for president Joseph and also $200 for O. P. Rockwell. This report was fully established on receipt of the Mail papers. The Quincy Whig also stated that Governor [Thomas] Reynolds had offered a reward; and published the Governors proclamation offerring a reward of $300 for president Joseph and $300 for O. P. Rockwell. It is not expected that much will be effected by the rewards.

Sister Emma continued very sick to day: the president was with her all day.

3 October 1842 · Monday

Sister Emma a little better. The president with her all day.

---

1. The notice was published in the *Times and Seasons* 3 (1 October 1842): 957.

4 October 1842 · Tuesday

Sister E. is very sick again to day. president Joseph attended with her all the day, himself being somewhat poorly.

5 October 1842 · Wednesday

Sister E. is worse, many fears are entertained that she will not recover. She was baptised twice in the river which evidently did her much good.[1] She grew worse again at night and continues very sick indeed. president Joseph does not feel well, and is much troubled on account of Sister E's sickness. Elder Rigdon called Elder[2] W. Clayton into his office and said he had some matters to make known. He had been at Carthage and had conversation with Judge Douglas concerning Gov. Carlins proceedings &c. He had ascertained that Carlin had intentionally issued an illegal writ expecting thereby to draw president Joseph to Carthage to get acquited by Habeus Corpus before Douglas, and having men there waiting with a legal writ to serve on prest Joseph as soon as he was released under the other one and bear him away to Missouri, without further ceremony. Er Rigdon asked what power the Govrs proclamation gave to any man or set of men who might be disposed to take prest Joseph. He was answered "Just the same power and authority which a legal warrant gave to an officer." It is more and more evident that Carlin is determined to have the president taken to Missouri if he can; but may the Almighty Jehovah shield and defend his servant from all their power, and prolong his days in peace that he may guide his people in righteousness untill his head is white with old age. Amen [p. 206]

---

1. On the practice of baptizing for health, see D. Michael Quinn, "The Practice of Rebaptism at Nauvoo," *BYU Studies* 18 (Winter 1978): 226–32.
2. MS.: "El'r"

6 October 1842 · Thursday

This day sister Emma is better, and although it is the day on which she generally grows worse yet she appears considerably easier. May the Lord speedily raise her to the bosom of her family that the heart of his servant may be comforted. Amen. prest Joseph is comfortable to day.—

7 October 1842 · Friday

This A.M. E'r Elias Higbee stated about the same things as were stated by E'r Rigdon two days ago, and also that he had been informed that many of the Missourians were coming to unite with the Militia of this State, voluntarily and at their own expense; so that after the court rises at Carthage if they dont take prest Joseph there, they will come and search the city &c. It is likely that this is *only* report.

Sister E. is some better.—prest Joseph is cheerful and well.

From the situation and appearance of things abroad President Joseph concluded to leave home, for a short season untill there should be some change in the proceedings of our enemies, accordingly at 20 minutes after 8 o clock P.M. he started away in company with brothers John Taylor, ~~Shadrach Roundey~~ and Wilson Law and John D. Parker. They travelled through the night and part of next day and after a tedious journey arrived at bro. James Taylors well and in good spirits, where he intends to tarry at present.

10 October 1842 · Monday

Er Taylor returned bringing favorable reports concerning prest Josephs health, spirits &c. Sister E. is yet gaining slowly.

15 October 1842 · Saturday

Bro. Jno D. Parker arrived with favorable intelligence from the president. He is well and comfortable.—

20 October 1842 · Thursday

Early this A.M. President Joseph arrived at home on a visit to his family. During the day he was visited by several of the brethren, who rejoiced to see him once more. Sister Emma is still getting better and is able to attend to a little business having this day closed contract, and received pay for a quarter Section of Land of brother Job V. Barnum.

21 October 1842 · Friday

This evening president Joseph returned in company with John D. Parker to father [James] Taylors, judging it wisdom to keep out of the way of his enemies a while longer at least; although all is peace and quiet and a prospect that his enemies will not trouble him much more.

23 October 1842 · Sunday

This day the Temple Committee laid before the Saints the propriety and advantages of laying a temporary floor on the Temple that the brethren could henceforth meet in the Temple to worship instead of meeting in the grove. This was the instructions of president Joseph. The saints seemed to rejoice at this privilege very much. [p. 207]

28 October 1842 · Friday

Soon after day-light this morning president Joseph returned home again to visit his family. He found sister E[mma]. some worse today the remainder of the family are well. In the afternoon he rode out into the city and took a little exercise, From the appearance of things[1] abroad we are encouraged to believe that his enemies wont trouble him much more at present.

This day the brethren finished laying the temporary floor, and seats in the Temple; and its appearance is truly pleasant

---

1. MS.: "thinks".

and chearing. The exertions of the brethren during the past week to accomplish this thing are truly praiseworthy.

29 October 1842 · Saturday

About 10 oclock this morning president Joseph rode up and viewed the Temple. He expressed his satisfaction at the arrangements made and was pleased [with] the progress made in that sacred edifice. After conversing with several of the brethren and shaking hands with numbers who were very much rejoiced to see their Prophet again, he returned home; but soon afterwards went over to the store where a number of brethren and sisters were assembled who had arrived this morning from the neighborhood of New York, Long Island &c. After E[lde]rs Taylor, Woodruff and Samuel Bennett had addressed the brethren and sisters president Joseph spoke to them considerable, showing them the proper course to pursue and how to act in regard to making purchases of land &c. He showed them that it was generally in consequence of the brethren disobeying or disregarding council, that they became dissatisfied and murmered, and many when they arrived here were dissatisfied with the conduct of some of the saints because every thing was not done perfectly right, and they get mad and thus the devil gets advantage over them to destroy them. He said he was but a man and they must not expect him to be perfect; if they expected perfection from him, he should expect it from them, but if they would bear with his infirmities and the infirmities of the brethren, he would likewise bear with their infirmities. He said it was likely he would have again to hide up in the woods, but they must not be discouraged but roll on the city, the Temple &c. When his enemies took away his rights he would bear it and keep out of the way but "if they take away your rights I will fight for you." After speaking considerable and giving them council he blessed them and departed. The company appear to be in good spirits.

30 October 1842 · Sunday

This day the saints met to worship in the Temple and notwithstanding its largeness it was well fill'd. It had been expected that president Joseph would address them, but he sent word that he was so sick that he could not meet with them; consequently Er John Taylor delivered a discourse

In the P.M. president Joseph went to visit sick &c. [p. 208]

31 October 1842 · Monday

This day president Joseph and his children rode out to his farm, and did not return untill after dark.

1 November 1842 · Tuesday

A.M. President & sister E[mma]. rode up to Temple for the benefit of her health she is rapidly gaining. In the P.M. went to see Dr Wd Richards who is very sick;[1] afterwards being accompanied by his children and W. C. [William Clayton] rode out towards the farm. When going down the hill near Caspers the carriage got overbalanced and upset. president Joseph was thrown some distance from the carriage and the children all three almost under it. He arose and enquired if any of the children were killed but upon examination there was no one seriously hurt. Frederic G. W.[2] had his cheek bruised which was about the worst injury received. The horse, so soon as he felt the carriage upset sprang forward but soon entangled himself in some branches and threw himself down on some rails. After some little trouble we succeeded in disengageing the horse from the harness and raising him up. The horse was not much hurt, but the carriage was considerably damaged. It seemed miraculous how we escaped serious injury

---

1. Willard Richards had arrived in Nauvoo from the East with his family on 30 October. (Diary of Wilford Woodruff, 1–5 November 1842.)

2. Joseph Smith's six-year-old son.

from this accident and our escape could not be attributed to any other power than that of divine providence. We felt thankful to God for this instance of his kind and watchful care over his servant and house. Seeing the carriage so much broke it was thought best to return home, accordingly leaving the carriage and part of the harness, and putting the children in bro Stoddards Buggy we returned.

In the evening president Joseph and two children, rode up to the Temple.

2 November 1842 · Wednesday

Spent this A.M in removing the books, desk &c from the store over to the house. In the P.M. rode out to the farm and spent the day in holding plough &c.

3 November 1842 · Thursday

Rode out with E. to the Temple. —

4 November 1842 · Friday

Rode out with Lorain [Lorin] Walker to examine his Timber north of the City This night President Hyrum Smith and William Law returned from their mission to the East. They bring very good reports concerning the public feeling, and say that John C. Bennetts expose has done no hurt but much good. Some of the Twelve also returned from their mission

5 November 1842 · Saturday

On account of the day being wet president Joseph remained at home He had a very pleasant visit from some of the Indians who were accompanied by a negro interpreter. They expressed great friendship with the Mormon people, and said they were their friends. After considerable conversation and partaking of victuals they departed evidently highly gratified with their visit. [p. 209]

491

6 November 1842 · Sunday

At home all day. In the P.M. had a visit from Dr W. Richards.

7 November 1842 · Monday

Spent this A.M. in Council with Patriarch Hyrum and some of the Twelve, and in giving instructions concerning the contemplated Journey to Springfield on the 15th of December next, and what course ought to be pursued in reference to the case of Bankruptcy.[1]

In the P.M. C. A. Warren Esqr arrived, and the president called upon some of the Twelve and others to testify before Esqr Warren what they knew in reference to the appointment of Trustee in Trust &c, shewing also from the records that president Joseph was authorised by the church to purchase and hold property in the name of the church, and that he had acted in all things according to the council given to him.

8 November 1842 · Tuesday

This A.M. called upon Windsor P. Lyons and others to make affidavits concerning the frauds and irregularities practised in the Post office. A petition was drawn and signed by many and sent by Esqr Warren to Judge [Richard M.] Young with a request that the latter should present the petition to the Post Master General and use his influence to have the present post master removed and a new one appointed. president Joseph was recommended for the appointment.[2]

---

1. See note 1, p. 377.
2. George W. Robinson had been appointed Nauvoo postmaster on 21 April 1840. In a letter to Illinois Senator Richard M. Young, accompanying his nomination for that office, Joseph Smith noted that "the citizens generally are suffering severely from the impositions and dishonest conduct of the postmaster and those connected with the postoffice in this city . . . letters had frequently been broken open, money detained, and letters charged twice over, &c, &c., . . . circumstances which caused the people to be anxious for an immediate change." (*History of the Church*, 5:121, 267.)

In the P.M. sat in court at his house as mayor.

9 November 1842 · Wednesday

Paid E[ric] Rhodes $436.93 being the amount of three notes due for the N.W quarter of Section 9–6 North 8 West.

12 November 1842 · Saturday

This day and also friday and the thursday was spent in the city council — [1]

13 November 1842 · Sunday

At home all day

14 November 1842 · Monday

In the city council —

16 November 1842 · Wednesday

Started in company with John D. Parker up the River

22 November 1842 · Tuesday

This day returned home

23 November 1842 · Wednesday

At home all day

26 November 1842 · Saturday

At home nearly all day. Went to visit Er. Brigham Young who was taken sick very suddenly. Tarried 2 or three hours in council &c.

---

1. On this date the Nauvoo city council passed an ordinance "regulating the proceedings on writs of habeas corpus," after which, according to Wilford Woodruff, Joseph Smith "felt secure to stay at home," having spent many weeks in hiding due to efforts to remove him to Missouri in the Boggs affair. (Diary of Wilford Woodruff, 12 November 1842. The ordinance is published in *History of the Church*, 5:185–92.)

27 November 1842 · Sunday

At home. Visited Er B. Young.

28 November 1842 · Monday

At home all day. Some charges having been instituted by the stone cutters against the Temple Committee, at president Josephs request the parties appeared at his house this day to have the difficulties settled. An investigation [p. 210] was entered in to before the prest & his council W. Law. Prest. Hyrum acted as council for defendents. And Er H. G. Sherwood on the part of the accusers. The hearing of testimony lasted untill about 4 o clock at which time the meeting adjourned for half an hour. On coming together again prest. Hyrum addressed the brethren at some length showing the important responsibility of the Committee also the many difficulties they had to contend with. He advised the brethren to have charity one with another and be united &c &c. Er Sherwood replied to prest Hyrums remarks. Prest H. explained some remarks before made. Er Wm Law made a few pointed remarks after which president Joseph arose and gave his decision which was that the Committee stand as before.[1] He likewise showed the brethren that he was responsible to the State for a faithful performance of his office as Sole Trustee in Trust &c. & the Temple Committee were responsible to him and had given bonds to him to the amount of $12000 for a faithful dis-charge of all duties devolving upon them as a Committee &c &c. The trial did not conclude untill about 9 oclock P.M.

---

1. The Temple Committee, Alpheus Cutler, Reynolds Cahoon, and Elias Higbee, had been appointed in October 1840 to oversee building of the Nauvoo Temple. At the time of this trial, Cutler was working at the Church lumber mill in Wisconsin. The principle grievances brought against the committee were an unequal distribution of provisions to those who worked on the temple, and allowing Cahoon's sons more iron and steel tools to work with than others. (Diary of William Clayton, 28 November 1842.)

29 November 1842 · Tuesday

In council with prest Hyrum, Willard Richards & others concerning the Bankruptcy case.[1] P.M. attended court at the trial of Mr [Thomas J.] Hunter before Alderman [Orson] Spencer for Slander.[2] Prest Joseph forgave Hunter the judgement but he was fined $10. for contempt of court.

30 November 1842 · Wednesday

A.M. In council in the large Room over the store preparing evidence in the case of Bankruptcy.

P.M. Had Amos Davis brought before the municipal court for slander but in consequence of the informality of the writ drawn by Esqr [Daniel H.] Wells he was nonsuited.

1 December 1842 · Thursday

This day sister Emma was sick, visited George A. Smith & B. Young of the quorum of the Twelve who were sick. Called on Mr Angels in company with Er Richards to give some council concerning a sick sister. Called on W. W. Phelps to get the historical documents &c. After which he commenced reading and revising history.[3]

---

1. William Clayton was also present, collecting testimony and documents preparatory to the hearing in the case at Springfield, Illinois, in December. (William Clayton Diary, 29 November 1842.)

2. The defendant had been charged with using "ridiculous and abusive language" calculated to deprecate the "moral and religious character" of Joseph Smith. (Complaint of Joseph Smith, City of Nauvoo vs. Thomas J. Hunter, 29 November 1842, MS., privately owned.)

3. For a time following the death of Robert B. Thompson on 27 August 1841, William W. Phelps assisted in writing and compiling the History of the Church. On 16 June 1842 Phelps wrote Parley Pratt, "I am now on the largest amount of business that I have ever undertaken, since I have been in the church: It is to write and compile the History of br. Joseph, embracing the entire history of the church. It will occupy my time and talents for a long time, should nothing intervene." (Phelps to Pratt, 16 June 1842.) After Willard Richards returned to Nauvoo from the East in the autumn of 1842, Phelps's involvement with the History was minimal. The earliest reference to Richards's work on the History

2 December 1842 · Friday

Sat as Mayor in the case of Amos Davis who was fined in the sum of $25. for breach of ordinance by selling spirits by the small quantity. In the evening called on Ers [Willard] Richards & [Newel K.] Whitney to take an appr[a]isal of the printing office establishment, preparatory to a lease to Er's [John] Taylor & [Wilford] Woodruff for the term of five years.[1]

3 December 1842 · Saturday

Called at the Printing Office several times. In the P.M. attended the municipal court in the case of Amos Davis for breach of ordinance &c. [p. 211]

4 December 1842 · Sunday

The day being very wet prest Joseph remained at home all day

5 December 1842 · Monday

A.M. Attended in council with prest Hyrum & others on the Bankrupt case. P.M. had conversation with bro. [William A.] Gheen. In the evening attended the Lodge at which time charges were preferred against George W. Robinson for unmasonic conduct towards prest Joseph.[2]

---

is on 2 December 1842 when he recorded in his diary having written Notes "B" and "C" in the History manuscript. (Jessee, "The Writing of Joseph Smith's History," *BYU Studies* 11 (Summer 1971): 439–71; Diary of Willard Richards, 2 December 1842. Although Richards did not specifically mention Note "A" in his diary, it precedes the other two in his handwriting in the manuscript of the History. See History of the Church, A-1, MS., pp. 1, 3, 5; published in *The Papers of Joseph Smith*, 1:268–69, 273, 276–77.)

1. The inventory on the printing establishment was not completed and a lease agreement signed between John Taylor, Wilford Woodruff, and Joseph Smith until 10 December. (See Diary of Wilford Woodruff, 2–10 December 1842.)

2. Earlier in the year Robinson had left the Church amid accusations of disreputable land dealings; he had also made accusations against Joseph Smith in connection with the practice of plural marriage. (See Flanders, *Nauvoo*, 258;

6 December 1842 · Tuesday

Attended trial of Amos Davis before the municipal Court.

7 December 1842 · Wednesday

This day dined with Er Orson Hyde & family. Er Hyde has this day returned home from his Mission to Jerusalem,[1] his presence was gratifying, spent the day with Er Hyde & drawing wood.

8 December 1842 · Thursday

Had a visit from Er Hyde & wife. Spent the day at home.

9 December 1842 · Friday

This day Prest Joseph went to chopping wood.

On this day President Hyrum started in company with Willard Richards, William Clayton, Henry G. Sherwood, Benjamin Covey, Peter Haws, Heber C. Kimball, Reynolds Cahoon & Alpheus Cutler for Springfield. bro. Covey & prest Hyrum to attend to his case and the others to attend to Prest Josephs case.[2] We arrived at Springfield on tuesday the 13th about 3 P.M. Same evening we were visited by Er William Smith who is a member of the house of Representatives. He stated that

---

Bennett, *The History of the Saints*, 245–49; *The Wasp*, 4 August 1842.)

Heber C. Kimball, who became a mason in 1825, wrote, "No man was admitted into a lodge in those days except he bore a good moral character, and was a man of steady habits; and a member would be suspended for getting drunk or any other immoral conduct. I wish that all men were Masons and would live up to their profession, then the world would be in a much better state than it is now." (Kimball, *Heber C. Kimball: Mormon Patriarch and Pioneer*, 83.)

1. Orson Hyde left Nauvoo in April 1840 on a mission to Europe and the Holy Land. Standing on the Mount of Olives near Jerusalem on 24 October 1841, he dedicated the land of Palestine for the return of the Jews; in August 1842 at Frankfurt, Germany, he published a small work in German about the Church. Hyde returned to Nauvoo on 7 December 1842 after an absence of more than two and a half years. (See *Papers of Joseph Smith*, 1: 402–26.)

2. I.e., Joseph and Hyrum's bankruptcy cases.

the subject of the repeal of our charter had been brought before the house, and the house had referred the subject to the committee on corporations. He had made a spirited speech before the house on the subject; and thought from the appearance of things that the only way to preserve our charter was, to present a resolution to repeal all the Charters in the State, if they repealed the Nauvoo Charter.[1] He stated that we had a many warm friends in both Houses who had determined that if our Charter was repealed all the Charters in the State should, especially Springfield, Quincy & Chicago.[2]

It is evident that there would have been little said on this subject before the Houses, had not Governor Ford in his inaugural address, referred to it in strong terms. In that address he says[3]

---

1. A report of William Smith's speech before the Illinois House of Representatives is in *The Wasp* 1 (14 January 1843), and *History of the Church*, 5: 201–4.

2. Between 1837, when Chicago was chartered as a city by the Illinois general assembly, and 1840, when Nauvoo achieved city status, four other Illinois settlements—Alton, Galena, Springfield, and Quincy—had been chartered. The Nauvoo charter was similar in many respects to the other Illinois city charters. However, the Nauvoo charter did not specify qualifications for public office, whereas other charters required American citizenship. The Nauvoo charter designated a larger number of members for the city council than other charters (four aldermen and nine councilors, which grew to eight aldermen and sixteen councilors by 1841). The Nauvoo charter authorized the city council to not only appoint city officers but remove them from office at will. While the Nauvoo Municipal Court was the third city court authorized by the Illinois General Assembly, the mayor of the city was designated as chief justice of the Nauvoo court with the aldermen as associate justices, whereas appointment of a judge by the governor with approval of the general assembly was the procedure authorized for Chicago and Alton. At Nauvoo, authority to appoint the university board of trustees rested with the city council rather than the state legislature. Furthermore, Nauvoo was granted authority to organize its own militia with its officers commissioned by the governor, independent of other militia units in the state organized on a county level. (See James L. Kimball, Jr., "The Nauvoo Charter: A Reinterpretation," *Journal of the Illinois State Historical Society* 64 [Spring 1971]: 66–78.)

3. In his inaugural address on 8 December, Governor Ford had said: "A great deal has been said about certain charters granted to the people of Nauvoo. These charters are objectionable on many accounts, but particularly on account of the

[space]

It was expected that Govr Ford would not have recommended any alteration in our charter, inasmuch as there is no extraordinary privileges granted to the citizens of Nauvoo, more than is granted by the Springfield Charter, to the citizens of Springfield. Such however was not the case, and his remarks have in some measure added a new stimulus to our enemies to agitate the subject. It is, however, evident that Govr. Ford saw that his remarks were not of the wisest as he said to us afterwards that he regretted he had not recommended a repeal of all the charters in the State at the same time. [p. 212]

We also had an interview with Judge [Stephen A.] Douglas who appeared very friendly and offered to assist us in our business as much as possible. He recommended us to petition the Govr to revoke the writ & proclamation by Ex Gov. Carlin for the arrest of prest Joseph. On Wednesday the 14th we went to see Mr [Justin] Butterfield the U.S. District Attorney. We stated to him our intention of visiting the Govr and our object in so doing. He recommended the course and offered to assist us. We requested Mr Butterfield to prepare a petition which was done & accompanied by an affidavit of each of us present also a copy of the affidavit of Ex-Govr Boggs of Missouri of which the following is a copy: —

"State of Missouri County of Jackson This day personally appeared before me Samuel Weston a Justice of the Peace within and for the County of Jackson the Subscriber Lilburn W Boggs who being duly sworn doeth depose and say that on the night of the sixth day of May 1842 while sitting in his dwelling in the town of Independance in the County of Jackson, he was shot with intent to kill, and that his life was dispaired

---

powers granted. The people of the State have become aroused on the subject, and anxiously desire that those charters should be modified so as to give the inhabitants of Nauvoo no greater privileges than those enjoyed by others of our fellow citizens." (*Sangamon Journal* 12 [15 December 1842]: 1.)

of for several days, and that he believes and has good reason to believe from Evidence and information now in his possession, that Joseph Smith commonly called the Mormon Prophet was accessory before the fact of the intended murder; and that the said Joseph Smith is a Citizen or resident of the State of Illinois and the said deponent hereby applies to the Governor of the State of Missouri to make a demand on the Governor of the State of Illinois to deliver the said Joseph Smith commonly called the Mormon Prophet to some person authorized to receive and convey him to the State and county aforesaid, there to be dealt with according to law.

Lilburn W. Boggs

"Sworn to and subscribed before me this 20th day of July 1842 Samuel Weston J.P."

At 4 o clock P.M. we called upon Mr Butterfield who went with us to see the Govr. Mr Butterfield stated the object of our request and read a communication which he had wrote to E[lde]r Sidney Rigdon last October.[1] He then read our petition and presented the papers to the Govr [Thomas Ford] remarking

---

1. On 20 October 1842, Butterfield had written to Sidney Rigdon expressing his opinion that the requisition of the governor of Missouri upon the governor of Illinois for the surrender of Joseph Smith was illegal, and he had "no doubt but the supreme court of this state would discharge him upon habeas corpus." Butterfield pointed out that the right of the governor of Missouri to demand Joseph Smith, and the duty of the governor of Illinois to give him up, was imposed by the U.S. Constitution: "that a person charged in any state with treason, felony, or other crime, who *shall flee* from justice and be found in another state, shall, on demand of the executive authority of the state from which he fled, be delivered up, to be removed to the state having jurisdiction of the crimes." Butterfield continued, "it can be proved that Joseph Smith was not in the state of Missouri at the time the crime was committed, but was in this state [Illinois]; that it is untrue that he was in the state of Missouri at the time of the commission of the said crime, or has been there at any time since. He could not, therefore, have *fled* from that state since the commission of said crime." He added that unless Joseph Smith had "actually *fled* from the state where the offense was committed, to *another state*, the governor of this state [Illinois] has no jurisdiction over his person, and cannot deliver him up." (The entire letter is in *History of the Church*, 5:173–79.)

at the same time that the arrest was based upon far weaker premises than he had previously supposed, inasmuch as the affidavit of Ex Gov. Boggs said nothing about Joseph having fled from justice, but plainly said he was a resident of the State of Illinois and the Constitution only authorizes the delivery up of a *"fugitive from Justice* to the Executive authority of the State from which he fled." The Govr in his reply stated that he had no doubt but that the writ of Gov. Carlin was illegal, but he doubted as to his authority to interfere with the acts of his predecessor. He finally concluded that he would state the case before the Judges of the Supreme Court at their counsel next day and whatever they decided on shall be his decision. He then stated his reasons for recommending a repeal of the charter and said he regretted that he had not recommended a repeal of all the charters &c.[1] [p. 213]

On thursday the 15th we attended the U.S. District Court being the day appointed for hearing Joseph & Hyrum's cases in Bankruptcy. At our request the cases was not brought on till tomorrow. During the day we endeavored to satisfy Mr Butterfield with security for the payment of a Judgement against Prest Joseph in favor of the United States. That judgement being the only hindrance to Prest Joseph receiving his discharge.[2] In the evening we again waited on Mr Butterfield

---

1. Clayton described Governor Ford as "a very small man apparently weighing about 110 lbs." He added, "The Govr appeared friendly and we think we shall succeed in obtaining a countermand of the writ &c." (Diary of William Clayton, 14 December 1842.)

2. The judgment grew out of the case involving the purchase of a steamboat two years previous. At a public auction in Quincy, Illinois, on 10 September 1840, Lt. Robert E. Lee, acting as agent for the United States, disposed of government property that included two keel-boats and the steamboat *Des Moines*. This equipment was bought by Latter-day Saints to provide river transportation for the settlement of Nauvoo. The promissory note stating terms of the transaction was signed by Peter Haws, Henry W. Miller, George Miller, Joseph Smith, and Hyrum Smith. Rechristened *Nauvoo*, the steamboat had scarcely begun operation by its new owners when it was wrecked and rendered practically useless as a source of income. Complications involving a suit against incompetent steamboat pilots, and the resale of the boat to a third party, resulted in default

who stated that he had attended the council of the Judges, three of whom were[1] of the opinion that the Govr ought to revoke the writ and Proclamation, and three that he ought not to inte[r]fere with the acts of Ex Gov. Carlin. They considered that the present case would be a precedent for cases which might occur hereafter of a similar character consequently it would be best to have it tried on Habeus Corpus.[2] Mr Butterfield said that all the Judges were unanimous in their opinion that pres. Joseph would be acquited on Habeas Corpus, and he thought that would be the best course to be pursued. He said there was no doubt but that the Prest might go to Springfield with safety and would certainly be discharged. On Friday the 16th wc again waited on Mr Butterfield and entered into arrangements in the name of the High Council of the church to secure the payment of the judgement.[3] As soon as this was

---

of payment to the government, whereupon legal proceedings were undertaken for collection of the debt. Responsibility for collection eventually passed to Justin Butterfield, U.S. Attorney for the District of Illinois. Finally, a default judgment was entered against the defendants for the amount of the note, $4,866.38, plus damages and court costs, for a total of $5,212.49 3/4. This judgment then became a lien on all real estate owned by Joseph Smith and the others involved. (See Oaks and Bentley, "Joseph Smith and Legal Process: In the Wake of the Steamboat *Nauvoo*," 735–82.)

1. MS.: "where".

2. Generally, habeas corpus was intended "to determine whether the arrest warrant had been issued correctly and perhaps whether there was probable cause for the arrest, that is, to determine whether the person in custody was being deprived of liberty without due process of law." However, Illinois law at this time evidently enlarged the importance of habeas corpus to a hearing of "the whole merits and facts of the case . . . deciding upon the guilt or rather upon the innocence of the prisoner, and absolutely discharging him without the intervention of a jury, where the court is of opinion that the facts do not sustain the criminal charge." Habeas corpus was used in this manner when Joseph Smith submitted himself to the federal court in Springfield, Illinois, on the Missouri extradition request in the Boggs case in December 1842. (See Firmage and Mangrum, *Zion in the Courts*, 98–99.)

3. The proposition of the high council for payment of the judgment against Joseph Smith, Henry W. Miller, George Miller, and Hyrum Smith by the United States was that a bond would be signed to cover the sum of $5212.49 1/2 by responsible individuals in four equal annual installments with interest and to secure the payment of the bond by mortgage of Illinois real estate worth double the amount of the debt. (Diary of William Clayton, 16 December 1842.)

done he withdrew his objections against Prest Hyrum who immediately obtained his dis-charge. Prest Josephs discharge could not be obtained until Mr Butterfield had wrote to the Solicitor of the U.S. Treasury showing our propositions. If they were accepted a discharge will be immediately obtained.[1]

The meanness and animosity of president Josephs enemies may be perceived by comparing the Affidavit of Ex Govr Boggs and the demand of Govr Reynolds of Missouri, the latter is as follows;

"The Governor of the State of Missouri to the Governor of the State of Illinois Greeting:– Whereas:–it appears by the annexed document (the afft of Boggs) which is hereby certified as authentic, that one Joseph Smith is a fugitive from Justice, charged with being accessary before the fact, to an assault with intent to kill, made by one O. P. Rockwell on Lilburn W Boggs in this State, and it is represented to the Executive Department of this State, has fled to the State of Illinois. Now Therefore I Thomas Reynolds Governor of the said State of Missouri, by virtue of the authority in me vested by the Constitution and Laws of the United States, do by these presents, demand the surrender and delivery of the said Joseph Smith to Edward R. Ford who is hereby appointed as the agent to receive the said Joseph Smith on the part of this State.

"In testimony whereof, I Governor of the State of Missouri have hereunto set my hand, and caused to be affixed the Great Seal of [the] State of Missouri. Done at the city of Jefferson

---

1. Butterfield sent the proposal to U.S. Solicitor Charles B. Penrose on 17 December 1842. In January 1843 Penrose directed Butterfield to reject the Mormon proposal, but in a counteroffer he authorized Butterfield to discharge Joseph Smith in bankruptcy upon immediate payment of one-third of the debt and a confession of judgment for the rest to be paid in three installments. Apparently Butterfield did not receive Penrose's counteroffer. Before the matter could be resolved Joseph Smith was murdered. Consequently, the Prophet was never discharged in bankruptcy. (Oaks and Bentley, "Joseph Smith and Legal Process," 763–66.)

this 22nd day of July in the year of our Lord one thousand eight hundred & forty two of the Independance of the United States the sixty seventh and of this State the twenty-third.

["]By the Governor   Tho Reynolds

["]Jas L. Minon [Minor] Secretary of State."[1] [p. 214]

On Saturday the 17th Govr Ford wrote the following letter to Prest Joseph and sent it by us.[2]

"Springfield Decr 17th, 1842

"Dear Sir:– Your petition requesting me to rescind Govr Carlins proclamation and recall the writ issued against you has been received and duly considered. I submitted your case and all the papers relating thereto, to the Judges of the Supreme Court; or at least to six of them who happened to be present. They were unanimous in the opinion that the requisition from Missouri was illegal and insufficient to cause your arrest, but were equally divided as to the propriety and Justice of my

---

1. William Clayton noted that on the previous evening he and Willard Richards "went to see and had a pleasant interview with Judge Douglas. He stated that he had conversed with Gov. Ford who shewed the feelings of the 6 judges of foresaid. He (Judge Douglas) thought it was best that Joseph should be arrested on the proclamation by some of his friends brought to Springfield and by writ of Habeas Corpus have the case investigated before the Judges of the Supreme Court who he (Douglas) had no doubt would discharge him. He argued that inasmuch as it had been represented that Joseph had defied the Laws of the State &c it would be the surest way to satisfy the public mind & secure Govr. Ford from censure. I asked if their was no danger of treachery &c as a Mason he believed that there was not a particle of doubt but he would immediately receive his discharge The Govr. had said that he should be protected on his way hither to any amount he should desire. Judge Douglas will see the Gov in the morning & request a written authority for Josephs safe conduct here." (Diary of William Clayton, 16 December 1842.)

2. According to Clayton, on the morning of the 17th, he and Richards went to see Judge Douglas, who went with them to see Governor Ford. The governor "expressed his determination not to interfere with the official acts of Carlin in regard to the arrest and proclamation. He advised that Joseph should give himself up and he had no doubt he would be discharged by the Judges of the Supreme Court. At my request the Govr. wrote the following letter to president Joseph." (Diary of William Clayton, 17 December 1842.)

interference with the acts of Governor Carlin. It being therefore a case of great doubt as to my power, and I not wishing ever in an official station to assume the exercise of doubtful powers; and in as much as you have a sure and effectual remedy in the courts, I have decided to decline interfering. I can only advise that you submit to the laws and have a Judicial investigation of your rights. If it should become necessary for this purpose to repair to Springfield I do not believe that there will be any disposition to use illegal violence towards you; and I would feel it my duty in your case, as in the case of any other person, to protect you with any necessary amount of force from mob violence whilst asserting your rights before the courts, going to and returning.

I am most respectfully yours   Thomas Ford."

After receiving this letter we went to see Mr [Justin] Butterfield and shewed him the above letter. He immediately set down and wrote the following. —

"Springfield December 17th 1842
Joseph Smith Esqr. Dear Sir:-
I have heard the letter read which Govr. Ford has written to you, and his statements are correct in relation to the opinion of the Judges of the Supreme Court. The Judges were unanimously of the opinion that you would be entitled to your discharge under a Habeas Corpus to be issued by the Supreme Court[1]–but felt some delicacy in advising Govr Ford to revoke the order issued by Govr Carlin–my advice is, that you come here without delay and you do not run the least risk of being protected while here and of being dis-charged by the Sup. Court by Habeas Corpus–I have also a right to bring the case before the U.S. [District] Court now in Session here, and there you

1. I.e., of the state of Illinois.

are certain of obtaining your discharge–I will stand by you and see you safely delivered from your arrest.

Yours truly J[ustin]. Butterfield"

After receiving these letters we considered it best to return as there was no further prospect of doing any thing further to advantage. From what we could learn there seems to be a good feeling manifested towards Prest Joseph by the citizens of Springfield in general and it is evident we have many friends there.

We started back this day and arrived in Nauvoo on tuesday the 20th all well./[1]

Carried to small memorandum Dr Richards [p. 215]

---

1. In MS. William Clayton's handwriting ends. The following line was written by Willard Richards.

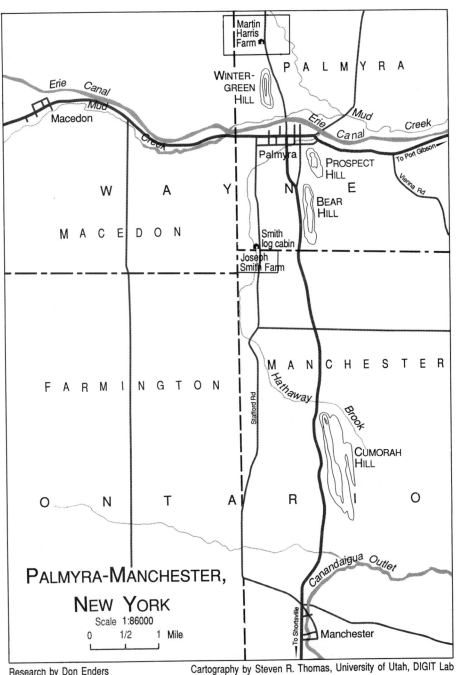

Martin
Harris
Farm

WINTER-
GREEN
HILL

P A L M Y R A

Erie   Canal
Mud
Macedon
Creek

Erie   *Mud*
Canal   *Creek*

Palmyra

To Port Gibson

PROSPECT
HILL

Vienna Rd

W   A   Y   N   E

BEAR
HILL

M A C E D O N

Smith
log cabin

Joseph
Smith Farm

M A N C H E S T E R

F A R M I N G T O N

Hathaway

Stafford Rd

Brook

CUMORAH
HILL

O   N   T   A   R   I   O

Canandaigua   Outlet

PALMYRA-MANCHESTER,
NEW YORK

Scale 1:86000

0   1/2   1 Mile

To Shortsville

Manchester

Research by Don Enders   Cartography by Steven R. Thomas, University of Utah, DIGIT Lab

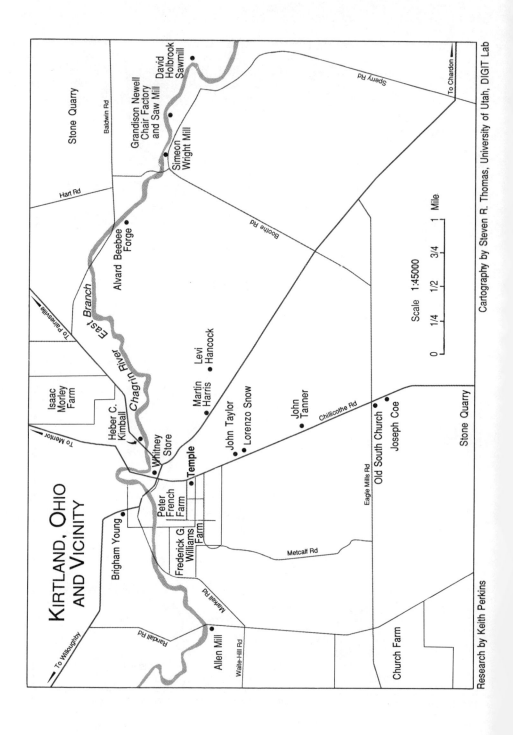

KIRTLAND, OHIO AND VICINITY

To Willoughby

To Painesville

To Mentor

To Chardon

Stone Quarry

Baldwin Rd

Hart Rd

Grandison Newell Chair Factory and Saw Mill

David Holbrook Sawmill

Simeon Wright Mill

Sperry Rd

East Branch

Chagrin River

Alvard Beebee Forge

Boothe Rd

Isaac Morley Farm

Heber C. Kimball

Whitney Store

Levi Hancock

Martin Harris

John Taylor

Lorenzo Snow

Temple

John Tanner

Chillicothe Rd

Old South Church

Joseph Coe

Brigham Young

Peter French Farm

Frederick G. Williams Farm

Eagle Mills Rd

Metcalf Rd

Randall Rd

Markell Rd

Allen Mill

Waite-Hill Rd

Church Farm

Stone Quarry

Scale 1:45000

0   1/4   1/2   3/4   1 Mile

Cartography by Steven R. Thomas, University of Utah, DIGIT Lab

Research by Keith Perkins

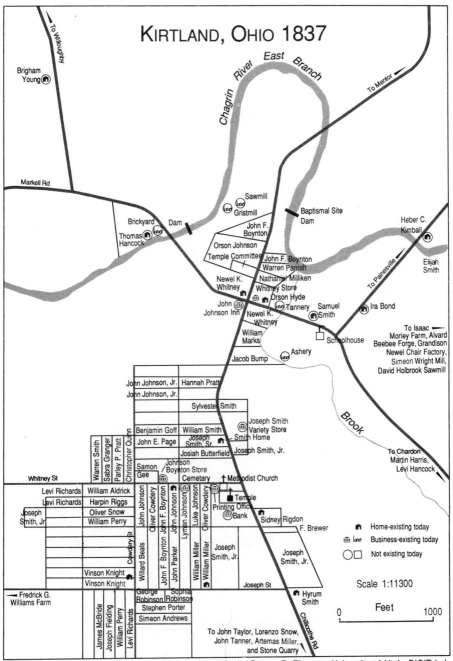

KIRTLAND, OHIO 1837

Cartography by Steven R. Thomas, University of Utah, DIGIT Lab

Research by Keith Perkins

Chagrin River East Branch

To Willoughby

Brigham Young

To Mentor

Markell Rd

Sawmill
Gristmill

Brickyard   Dam
Thomas Hancock

John F. Boynton

Baptismal Site
Dam

Heber C. Kimball

Orson Johnson

Elijah Smith

Temple Committee

John F. Boynton
Warren Parrish

Newel K. Whitney

Nathaniel Milliken
Whitney Store
Orson Hyde

To Painesville

John Johnson Inn

Tannery   Samuel Smith

Ira Bond

Newel K. Whitney

William Marks

Schoolhouse

To Isaac Morley Farm, Alvard Beebee Forge, Grandison Newel Chair Factory, Simeon Wright Mill, David Holbrook Sawmill

Jacob Bump   Ashery

John Johnson, Jr.   Hannah Pratt
John Johnson, Jr.

Sylvester Smith

Brook

Benjamin Goff   William Smith

Joseph Smith Variety Store

John E. Page

Joseph Smith, Sr.

Smith Home

Josiah Butterfield   Joseph Smith, Jr.

Warren Smith
Sabra Granger
Parley P. Pratt
Christopher Quinn

Samon Gee

Johnson Boynton Store

To Chardon
Martin Harris, Levi Hancock

Cemetery   Methodist Church

Whitney St

Levi Richards   William Aldrick
Levi Richards   Harpin Riggs

Joseph Smith, Jr

Oliver Snow
William Perry

John Johnson
Oliver Cowdery
John F. Boynton
John Johnson
Lyman Johnson
Luke Johnson
Oliver Cowdery

Temple
Printing Office
Bank

Sidney Rigdon

F. Brewer

Home-existing today
Business-existing today
Not existing today

Cowdery St

Willard Beals
John F. Boynton
John Parker
William Miller
William Miller

Joseph Smith, Jr.

Joseph Smith, Jr.

Scale 1:11300

Vinson Knight
Vinson Knight

Joseph St

Hyrum Smith

Feet

0   1000

Fredrick G. Williams Farm

George Robinson   Sophia Robinson
Stephen Porter
Simeon Andrews

James McBride
Joseph Fielding
William Perry
Levi Richards

Chillicothe Rd

To John Taylor, Lorenzo Snow, John Tanner, Artemas Miller, and Stone Quarry

MINNESOTA

WISCONSIN

MISSOURI–ILLINOIS REGION

Black
River
Falls

Mississippi

Prairie
du Chien

River

Galena

IOWA

Rock

River

Dixon
LEE
Pawpaw

Des

Moines

River

Burlington

HENDERSON

Monmouth

WARREN

Peoria

VAN
BUREN

Farmington Shokokon

LEE Nauvoo McDONOUGH

Carthage Macomb

Missouri

Grand

DAVIESS

Adam-ondi-Ahman
Gallatin Millport

River

Chariton River

Warsaw
Monticello

HANCOCK

Brooklyn

Rushville

SCHUYLER

Beardstown

Quincy Mt. Sterling
ADAMS

BROWN CASS

SANGAMON

Jacksonville

Haun's Mill
Far West
CALDWELL

LIVINGSTON

Salt

Huntsville

Beverly

Springfield

River

Paris
RALLS

PIKE

MORGAN

SCOTT

River

Ft. Leavenworth

CLAY RAY
Liberty

CARROLL

CHARITON

DeWitt

RAND-
OLPH

MONROE

Atlas

GREENE

Louisiana

PIKE

Carrolton

Richmond

Independence

JACKSON

HOWARD

Columbia

BOONE

Alton

St. Louis

ILLINOIS

Missouri

River

Mississippi

Jefferson
City

MISSOURI

Scale 1:5000000

0   50   100 Miles

River

Cartography by Steven R. Thomas, University of Utah, DIGIT Lab

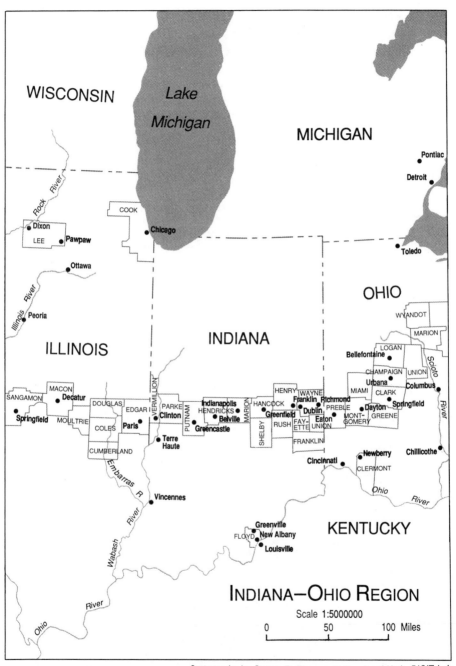

WISCONSIN

Lake Michigan

MICHIGAN

Pontiac

Detroit

COOK

Chicago

Rock River

Dixon

LEE

Pawpaw

Ottawa

Illinois River

Peoria

Toledo

OHIO

WYANDOT

MARION

INDIANA

ILLINOIS

Bellefontaine

LOGAN

CHAMPAIGN UNION

Scioto River

SANGAMON

MACON

Decatur

DOUGLAS

EDGAR

PARKE

VERMILION

HENRY

WAYNE

Urbana

MIAMI

CLARK

Columbus

Franklin Richmond

Indianapolis

HENDRICKS

Belville

MARION

HANCOCK

Greenfield

Dublin

PREBLE

Dayton

Springfield

GREENE

Springfield

MOULTRIE

Clinton

Paris

Greencastle

SHELBY

RUSH

FAY-
ETTE

Eaton

UNION

MONT-
GOMERY

COLES

CUMBERLAND

Terre
Haute

FRANKLIN

Embarras R.

Vincennes

Newberry

Cincinnati

CLERMONT

Chillicothe

Ohio River

Wabash River

Greenville

FLOYD New Albany

Louisville

KENTUCKY

INDIANA–OHIO REGION

Scale 1:5000000

0   50   100 Miles

Ohio River

Cartography by Steven R. Thomas, University of Utah, DIGIT Lab

Map Labels

Water Bodies: Lake Huron, Lake Erie, Lake Ontario

Regions/States: MICHIGAN, CANADA, NEW YORK, PENNSYLVANIA, OHIO, WEST VIRGINIA, VIRGINIA, MD, KY

Ontario Counties: GREY, SIMCOE, DUFFERIN, WELLINGTON, YORK, ONTARIO, PEEL, HALTON, WATERLOO, WENTWORTH, BRANT, HALDIMAND, OXFORD, NORFOLK

New York Counties: ORLEANS, NIAGARA, MONROE, GENESEE, ERIE, WYOMING, LIVINGSTON, ONTARIO, YATES, STEUBEN, ALLEGANY, CATTARAUGUS, CHAUTAUQUA, SENECA, WAYNE, FAYETTE

Ohio Counties: ASHTABULA, LAKE, GEAUGA, CUYAHOGA, SUMMIT, PORTAGE, MEDINA, LORAIN, WAYNE, ASHLAND, RICHLAND, CRAWFORD, WYANDOT, MARION, MORROW, LOGAN, UNION, CABELL, MASON

Cities/Towns (Canada): Toronto, St. Catherines, Brantford, Mt. Pleasant, Colborne, Waterford, Simcoe, NIAGARA

Cities/Towns (Michigan): Pontiac, Detroit

Cities/Towns (New York): Rochester, Macedon, Palmyra, Cambria, Canandaigua, Waterloo, Buffalo, Avon, Bennington, Geneseo, Livonia, Fayette, Warsaw, China, Springville, Perrysburg, Collins, Freedom, Silver Creek, Laona, Westfield, Lodi, Dayton, Centerville, Farmersville, Villanova, Ellicotville, Catlin, Westervelle, Erie, Elk Creek, Springfield

Cities/Towns (Ohio): Cleveland, Newburg, Willoughby, Fairport, Painesville, Kirtland, Thompson, Chardon, Hiram, Nelson, Hudson, Amherst, Copley, Norton, Akron, New Portage, Bucyrus, Galion, Mansfield, Wooster, Columbus, Chillicothe, Guyandott, Perry, Ashtabula

Cities/Towns (Pennsylvania): Pittsburgh, Loysville, Harrisburg

Cities/Towns (Virginia/MD): Washington, D.C.

Rivers: Scioto River, Ohio River, Potomac River

OHIO–NEW YORK REGION

Scale 1:5000000

0   50   100 Miles

Cartography by Steven R. Thomas, University of Utah, DIGIT Lab

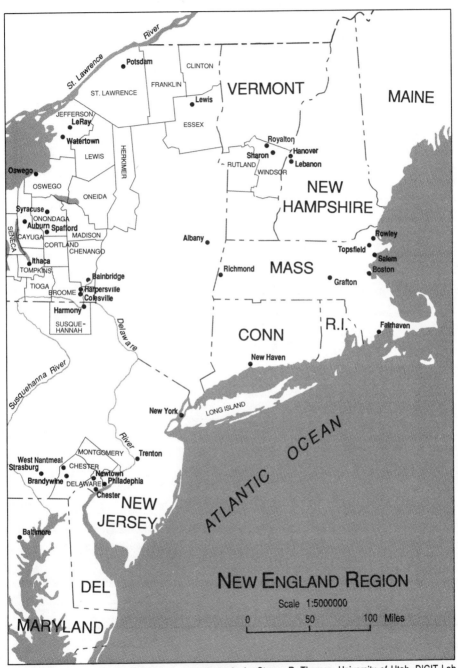

NEW ENGLAND REGION

Scale 1:5000000

0   50   100 Miles

Cartography by Steven R. Thomas, University of Utah, DIGIT Lab

GENTRY

DAVIESS

Grove Creek

Robinson's Grove ×
Adam Black's ×
Lyman Wight Ferry
Adam-ondi-Ahman
Lyman Wight's
Gallatin
Millport
Nelson's Ferry
× Littlefield's
× John Raglin's

Muddy Cr.

Honey Cr.

Grindstone Cr.

DE KALB

BUCHANAN

CLINTON

CALDWELL

Mill Creek ●

Far West ●
Shoal Creek
× Haun's Mill
× Guymon's Horse Mill

× Battle site

PLATTE

RAY

Crooked River

Fishing River

● Ft. Leavenworth

CLAY

● Richmond

Liberty ●

Missouri River

Independence ●

Blue River
L. Blue River

JACKSON

MISSOURI RIVER

Research by James L. Kimball Jr.

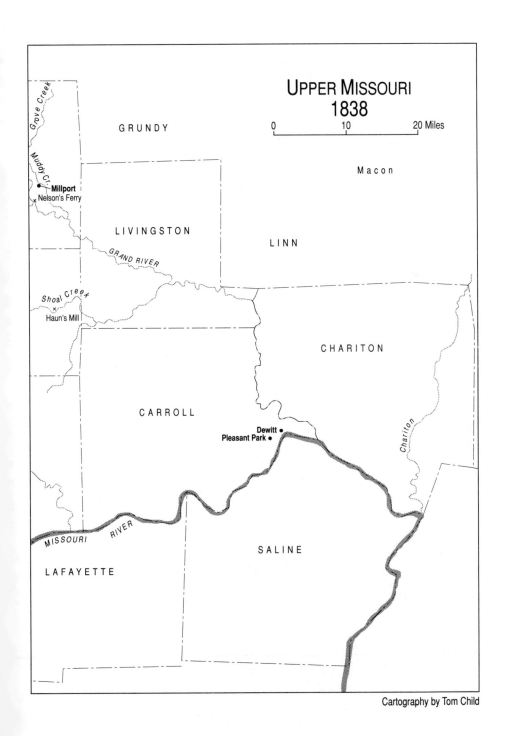

UPPER MISSOURI
1838

0   10   20 Miles

GRUNDY

Macon

Grove Creek

Muddy Cr.

● Millport
× Nelson's Ferry

LIVINGSTON

LINN

GRAND RIVER

Shoal Creek

× Haun's Mill

CHARITON

CARROLL

Chariton

Dewitt ●
Pleasant Park ●

SALINE

MISSOURI   RIVER

LAFAYETTE

Cartography by Tom Child

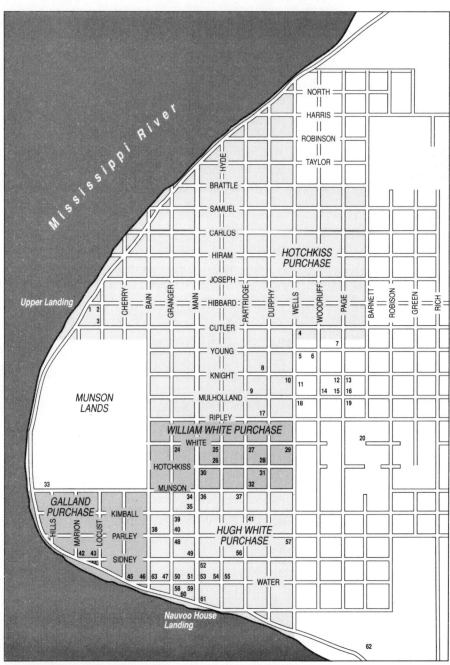

Mississippi River

Upper Landing

MUNSON LANDS

GALLAND PURCHASE

HILLS
MARION
LOCUST

33

42 43
44

45 46

HOTCHKISS PURCHASE

NORTH
HARRIS
ROBINSON
TAYLOR

HYDE
BRATTLE
SAMUEL
CARLOS
HIRAM
JOSEPH
HIBBARD
CUTLER
YOUNG
KNIGHT
MULHOLLAND
RIPLEY

WHITE

CHERRY
BAIN
GRANGER
MAIN
PARTRIDGE
DURPHY
WELLS
WOODRUFF
PAGE
BARNETT
ROBISON
GREEN
RICH

1 2
3

4
7
5 6
8
10
9
11   12 13
14 15 16
18   19
17

WILLIAM WHITE PURCHASE

24   25   27   29
          26   28
HOTCHKISS
          30   31
MUNSON   32

20

KIMBALL

PARLEY

SIDNEY

34 36   37
35

38   39   41
      40
      48   56
      49
52
53 54 55
58 59
60
61

HUGH WHITE PURCHASE

57

63 47 50 51

WATER

62

Nauvoo House Landing

Research by James L. Kimball Jr.

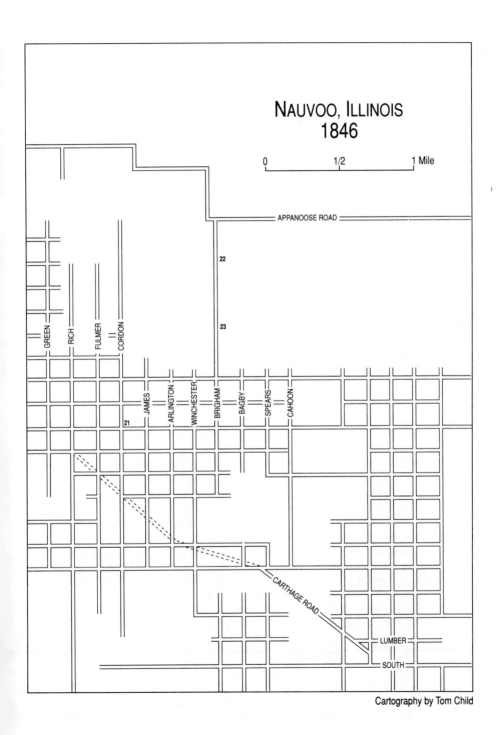

NAUVOO, ILLINOIS
1846

0   1/2   1 Mile

APPANOOSE ROAD

22

23

GREEN
RICH
FULMER
CORDON

JAMES
ARLINGTON
WINCHESTER
BRIGHAM
BAGBY
SPEARS
CAHOON

21

CARTHAGE ROAD

LUMBER

SOUTH

Cartography by Tom Child

NUMERICAL KEY TO MAP OF NAUVOO, ILLINOIS, 1846

1. Upper stone house
2. Willard Richards
3. Hiram Kimball
4. George Fidler
5. Parley Pratt
6. Samuel Bennett
7. Orson Spencer
8. John Eagle
9. Edward Hunter
10. Grove/Stand
11. Nauvoo Temple
12. Robert Foster (Mammoth Hotel)
13. Samuel M. Marr (store)
14. Moses Smith (store)
15. Nauvoo Expositor (probable location)
16. Keystone Store
17. David D. Yearsley
18. Amos Davis (store/home)
19. Frederick Moesser (grocery)
20. James Taylor
21. Edward Sayers
22. Carlos Granger
23. Hyrum Smith (farm)
24. Nauvoo Legion parade ground
25. Theater
26. Orson Hyde
27. Willard Richards (new house)
28. Durphy, Elizabeth
29. Cemetery (old burying ground)
30. Windsor P. Lyon (store/home)
31. Wilford Woodruff
32. Heber C. Kimball
33. Sutcliffe Maudsley
34. Sylvester Stoddard
35. *Times and Seasons*
36. Jonathan Browning
37. Porter Rockwell
38. Seventies Hall
39. Brigham Young
40. John Taylor
41. Elias Harmer
42. Wilson Law (mill)
43. William Phelps
44. William Law (mill)
45. Don Carlos Smith
46. Aaron Johnson
47. William Marks
48. Newel K. Whitney
49. Masonic Hall
50. William Law (store)
51. David W. Rogers
52. Sidney Rigdon
53. Joseph Smith (Mansion House)
54. Theodore Turley (blacksmith shop)
55. James Mulholland
56. Henry Miller
57. John Bowen
58. Joseph Smith (store)
    assembly room
    counting room
    mayor's court
    theater
    president's office
    lodge room
    municipal court
59. Joseph Smith (Homestead)
60. Joseph Smith (smokehouse)
    president's office
61. Nauvoo House
62. Davidson Hibbard
63. Hyrum Smith

ALPHABETICAL KEY TO MAP OF
NAUVOO, ILLINOIS, 1846

Bennett, Samuel, 6
Bowen, John, 57
Browning, Jonathan, 36
Cemetery (old burying ground),
  29
Davis, Amos (store/home), 18
Durphy, Elizabeth, 28
Eagle, John, 8
Fidler, George, 4
Foster, Robert (Mammoth Hotel),
  12
Granger, Carlos, 22
Grove/Stand, 10
Harmer, Elias, 41
Hibbard, Davidson, 62
Hunter, Edward, 9
Hyde, Orson, 26
Johnson, Aaron, 46
Keystone Store, 16
Kimball, Heber C., 32
Kimball, Hiram, 3
Law, William (store), 50
Law, William (mill), 44
Law, Wilson (mill), 42
Lyon, Windsor P. (store/home),
  30
Marks, William, 47
Marr, Samuel M. (store), 13
Masonic Hall, 49
Maudsley, Sutcliffe, 33
Miller, Henry, 56
Moesser, Frederick (grocery), 19
Mulholland, James, 55
Nauvoo *Expositor* (probable
  location), 15
Nauvoo House, 61
Nauvoo Legion parade ground,
  24
Nauvoo Temple, 11

Phelps, William, 43
Pratt, Parley, 5
Richards, Willard, 2
Richards, Willard (new house),
  27
Rigdon, Sidney, 52
Rockwell, Porter, 37
Rogers, David W., 51
Sayers, Edward, 21
Seventies Hall, 38
Smith, Don Carlos, 45
Smith, Hyrum, 63
Smith, Hyrum (farm), 23
Smith, Joseph (Homestead), 59
Smith, Joseph (Mansion House),
  53
Smith, Joseph (store), 58
  assembly room
  counting room
  mayor's court
  theater
  president's office
  lodge room
  municipal court
Smith, Joseph (smokehouse), 60
  president's office
Smith, Moses (store), 14
Spencer, Orson, 7
Stoddard, Sylvester, 34
Taylor, James, 20
Taylor, John, 40
Theater, 25
Times and Seasons, 35
Turley, Theodore (blacksmith
  shop), 54
Upper stone house, 1
Whitney, Newel K., 48
Woodruff, Wilford, 31
Yearsley, David D., 17
Young, Brigham, 39

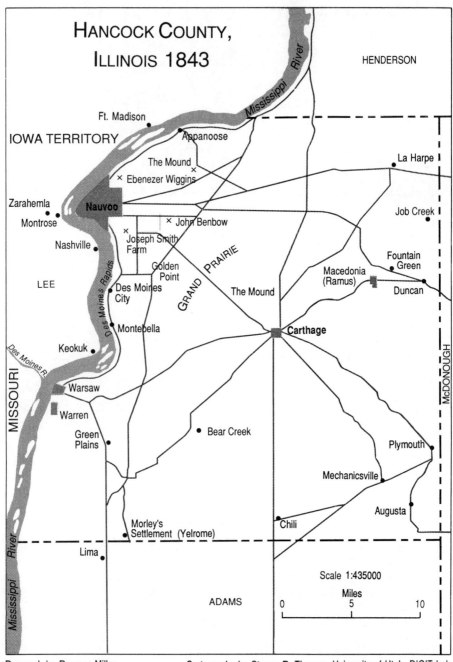

HANCOCK COUNTY, ILLINOIS 1843

HENDERSON

Ft. Madison

IOWA TERRITORY

Appanoose

The Mound ×

× Ebenezer Wiggins

La Harpe

Zarahemla

Nauvoo

Montrose

× John Benbow

Job Creek

× Joseph Smith Farm

Nashville

GRAND PRAIRIE

Fountain Green

Golden Point

LEE

Des Moines City

The Mound

Macedonia (Ramus)

Duncan

Montebella

Carthage

Keokuk

Des Moines Rapids

McDONOUGH

MISSOURI

Warsaw

Des Moines R.

Warren

Green Plains

Bear Creek

Plymouth

Mechanicsville

Augusta

Morley's Settlement (Yelrome)

Chili

Mississippi River

Lima

ADAMS

Scale 1:435000

Miles
0   5   10

Research by Rowena Miller   Cartography by Steven R. Thomas, University of Utah, DIGIT Lab

BIOGRAPHICAL REGISTER

Adams, George Washington Joshua (c.1811–1880), tailor, actor; born at Oxford, Warren County, New Jersey. Adams was a Methodist lay preacher and actor before joining the Latter-day Saints in New York in 1840. Accompanied Orson Hyde on his mission to Palestine in 1841 but did not go farther than Europe. Proselyted in England. Excommunicated in 1845. Affiliated with James J. Strang, 1846–1851. Organized the Church of the Messiah at Springfield, Massachusetts, 1861. Led 156 colonists to Jaffa to prepare Palestine for the return of the Jews in 1866, but the colony ended in failure. Returned to the United States about 1870. Died in Philadelphia. (Peter Amann, "Prophet in Zion: The Saga of George J. Adams," *The New England Quarterly* 37 [December 1964]: 477–500; Reed M. Holmes, *The Forerunners* [Independence, Missouri, 1981].)

Adams, James (1783–1843), lawyer; born at Limsbury, Hartford County, Connecticut. Married Harriet Denton, 1809, and moved to Oswego, New York. To Springfield, Illinois, 1821. Elected justice of the peace in 1823 and probate judge, 1841. Participant in Winnebago and Black Hawk Indian wars, 1827, 1831–1832. Joined the Latter-day Saints in 1836 and was ordained a patriarch. Was appointed deputy grand master of the second Grand Lodge of Illinois, 1840. Instrumental in establishing the Nauvoo masonic lodge in 1842. (*History of the Church*, 6:50–51; Mervin B. Hogan, *Mormonism and Freemasonry: The Illinois Episode* [Salt Lake City, 1980], 308–13; *History of the Early Settlers of Sangamon Co., Ill.* [Springfield, Illinois, 1876], 76].)

Aldrich, Mark (1801–1874), born in Warren County, New York. Married Margaret Wilkinson, 1829, and moved to St. Louis, Missouri, where he received an appointment with the American Fur Company and took charge of the company's station at Keokuk, Iowa. One of the original developers of Warsaw, Hancock County, Illinois, 1832. Elected first postmaster of Warsaw, 1834, and member of the Illinois legislature, 1836. He was a mason and a member of the local militia. Indicted in the murder of Joseph Smith, 1844 but was acquitted. After failing to be elected sheriff of Hancock County in 1846, Aldrich migrated to California during the gold rush. Finally settled in Tucson, Arizona, where he served as the town's first postmaster, a merchant, criminal court judge, Tucson's first American mayor, and for three terms as a representative in the territorial legislature. (Thomas Gregg, *History of Hancock County* [Chicago, 1880], 653–54; Dallin Oaks and Marvin Hill, *Carthage Conspiracy: The Trial of the Accused Assassins of Joseph Smith* [Urbana, 1975], 53–55, 66, 217; C. L. Sonnichsen, *Tucson: The Life and Times of an American City* [Norman, Oklahoma, 1982], 43–47, 59.)

Andrews, Hazard (no information)

Angell, Truman Osborn (1810–1887), carpenter, joiner, architect. Brother-in-law to Brigham Young. Born at Providence, Rhode Island. Married Polly Johnson, 1832. Living in China, New York, when converted to Mormonism, 1833. Moved to Kirtland, Ohio, in 1835 and worked on the temple. Member of the second quorum of seventy. Moved to Missouri, 1837, and Illinois, 1839. Supervised joiner work on Nauvoo Temple. Arrived in Salt Lake Valley with pioneers of 1847. Appointed Church architect; supervised construction of many buildings, including Salt Lake Temple. ("Truman O. Angell—Master Builder," *Our Pioneer Heritage* 10:194–204; Orson F. Whitney, *History of Utah* [Salt Lake City: George Q. Cannon and Sons, 1892–1904], 4:60–61.)

Atchison, David Rice (1807–1886), lawyer; born near Lexington, Fayette County, Kentucky. Graduate of Transylvania University, 1825. Admitted to the Kentucky bar in 1829. In 1830 moved to Clay County, Missouri, where he became a prominent lawyer and was appointed major-general in the Missouri state militia. Was appointed judge of the circuit court of Platte County, 1841. Elected to the Missouri legislature, 1834 and 1838. Served in the U.S. Senate, 1838–1855, where he was frequently president pro-tem, was chairman of the Committee on Indian Affairs, and was influential in framing the Kansas-Nebraska Act of 1854. In 1856 moved to Clinton County, Missouri, where he worked a 1,700-acre farm. Died at Gower, Clinton County. (*The United States Biographical Dictionary*, Missouri volume [New York, 1878], 170–72; Charles Van Doren, ed., *Webster's American Biographies* [Springfield, Massachusetts, 1974], 43–44.)

Atwood, Henry G. (no information)

Avard, Sampson (1803–1869), physician; born at St. Peters on the Isle of Guernsey, Great Britain. His wife, Eliza, was a native of Virginia, and one of their children was born there in 1831. Baptized and ordained an elder by Orson Pratt in Freedom, Beaver County, Pennsylvania, 1835. Moved to Kirtland, Ohio, 1836. Prominent in Missouri Danite activities, 1838. Testimony against Joseph Smith at the 1838 Richmond hearing was a key factor in the Prophet's imprisonment. Excommunicated, 1839. By 1850 he was a practicing physician in Edwardsville, Madison County, Illinois, where he died. (*History of the Church*, 3:181, 192–3, 209–10,

284, 310; U.S. Census, Madison County, Illinois, 1850; James T. Hair, comp., *Gazetteer of Madison County* [Alton, Illinois, 1866], 162.)

Avery, Arvin Allen (1812–1877), born at Spafford, Onondaga County, New York. Married Francis Maria Babbitt 25 September 1835. Living in Nauvoo, Illinois, in 1846. Evidently did not go West with the Latter-day Saints. (Elroy M. Avery and Catharine H. Avery, *The Groton Avery Clan* [Cleveland, 1912], 1:565; "Nauvoo Temple Endowment Register," 1845–1846, 219, Typescript, LDS Church Family History Library.)

Babbitt, Almon Whiting (1813–1856), attorney; born at Cheshire, Berkshire County, Massachusetts. Converted to Mormonism, 1833. Married Julia Ann Johnson, 1834. Participant in the march of Zion's Camp to Missouri later that same year. Proselyting mission to Upper Canada, 1837–1838. Appointed president of Kirtland Stake, 1841. Presiding elder at Ramus, Hancock County, Illinois, 1843. Elected to Illinois state legislature from Hancock County, 1844. Appointed to the committee to sell the property of Latter-day Saints departing from Nauvoo, 1845; and postmaster of Nauvoo, 1846. Crossed the plains to Utah in 1848. Disfellowshipped, 1851. Appointed secretary of Utah Territory, 1852. Killed by Cheyenne Indians in Nebraska. (Lyndon W. Cook, *The Revelations of the Prophet Joseph Smith: A Historical and Biographical Commentary of the Doctrine and Covenants* [Provo, Utah: Seventies Mission Bookstore, 1981], 251–52; Kate B. Carter, ed., "Almon Whiting Babbitt," *Our Pioneer Heritage*, 11:513–72; Jay Donald Ridd, "Almon W. Babbitt, Mormon Emissary" [M.A. thesis, University of Utah, 1953].)

Bacheler, Origen (1799–?), born at Sutton, Worcester, Massachusetts. Married Charlotte Thompson, 1828. Baptist minister. Wrote *Mormonism Exposed, Internally and Externally*, 1838. In New York lecturing against Mormons with John C. Bennett, 1842. (International Genealogical Index.)

Backenstos, Jacob (1811–1857), merchant; born in Dauphin County, Pennsylvania. Married Sarah Lavina Lee, niece of Robert E. Lee, 1836. Living in Sangamon County, Illinois, by 1840. Clerk of the Hancock County, Illinois, circuit court, 1843–1845. Elected to the Illinois legislature, 1844, and Hancock County sheriff, 1845. Backenstos became an army officer in 1846 and participated in the war with Mexico. He became a lieutenant colonel of the 2nd Brigade, Illinois Mounted Rifles, and was wounded in the battle of Chapultepec. Traveled to Oregon with the Mounted Rifles in 1849, resigning in 1851. Living in Oregon City, Clackamas County, 1850. Committed suicide by drowning himself in the Willamette River near Portland in 1857. (Schindler, *Porter Rockwell*, 150–51; *History of the Church*, 7:368; U.S. Census: Oregon City,

Clackamas, Oregon, 1850; *The Carthage Republican*, 8 December 1937.)

Badlam, Alexander (1808–1894), coach maker; born at Norfolk, Norfolk County, Massachusetts. Married Mary Ann Brannan, sister of Samuel Brannan. Participant in Zion's Camp, 1834. Appointed to the first quorum of seventy, 1835. Presided over Boston branch of the Church, 1846–1848. Migrated to Utah, 1850. Mission to California, 1852; studying Chinese in Sacramento, 1853–1855. President of sixth quorum of Seventy. By 1872 he had left the Church. (*History of the Church*, 2:183, 204; Susan Easton Black, "Membership of the Church of Jesus Christ of Latter-day Saints, 1830–1848," [Provo, Utah: Religious Studies Center, Brigham Young University, 1984], 3:146–47; "Journal History of the Church of Jesus Christ of Latter-day Saints," 9 February 1853; 12 January, 4 April 1855; 16 September 1872.)

Bagby, Walter (?–c.1845), one of the early settlers of Carthage, Hancock County, Illinois. Publisher of *The Echo* (Carthage, Illinois), 1837. Treasurer of Hancock County, 1834–1837. School Commissioner of Hancock County, 1840–1841. Member of the Carthage Greys of the Illinois militia. Moved to Louisiana, where he died. (Thomas Gregg, *History of Hancock County*, 688; Siegfried, *History of Hancock County*, 232, 625–26; *History of the Church*, 7:143.)

Baker, Elizabeth, married Thomas Carrico, in Kirtland, Ohio, 1836.

Bardsley/Beardslee, Andrew, born in the 1780s, was living in Kirtland, Ohio, at the time of the 1820–1840 U.S. censuses.

Barnard, John Porter (1803–1874), blacksmith; born at New Hartford, Oneida County, New York. Married Eliza Ann Wycoff, 1826. Converted to Mormonism, 1835. Migrated to Utah, 1848. Died at Harper, Box Elder County, Utah. (Family Group Records Collection.)

Barnum, Job V. (1788–?), hotelkeeper; born at Monkton, Addison County, Vermont. Affiliated with the Latter-day Saints in Nauvoo. Left the Church and in 1857 was an apostle in Charles B. Thompson's Jehovah's Presbytery of Zion. Residing in Nebraska in 1860. (Early Church Information File; *The History of the Reorganized Church of Jesus Christ of Latter Day Saints* [Independence, Missouri: Herald House, 1967], 3:54; U.S. Census, Nebraska Territory, 1860.)

Beman, Alvah (1775–1837), born at New Marlboro, Berkshire County, Massachusetts. Married Sally Burtts in 1796. Moved from Massachusetts to Livonia, Livingston County, New York, 1799. Had a large farm, sheep, cattle; made cloth. Later the family moved to Avon, Livingston County, New York. Among the first to be acquainted with Joseph Smith and his work in Palmyra, New York. Assisted Joseph in concealing Book of Mormon plates from a Palmyra mob. In 1830 he and his family of six, including four daughters, resided at Livonia, New York. Appointed to preside over elders of the Church at Kirtland, 1836. Died at Kirtland,

Ohio. (Milton V. Backman, Jr., *A Profile of Latter-day Saints of Kirtland, Ohio and Members of Zion's Camp* [Provo, Utah: Brigham Young University, 1982], 6; *History of the Church*, 2:370; Mary B. Noble, Autobiography, MS. LDS Church Archives.)

Benbow, John (1800–1874), born at Grendon-Warren, Herefordshire, England. Married Jane Holmes. Baptized by Wilford Woodruff in 1840. Well-to-do farmer who contributed substantially to the Church. Emigrated to America, 1840. Settled on a 160 acre farm on the outskirts of Nauvoo, Illinois. Crossed the plains to Utah in 1848. Living at South Cottonwood at the time of his death. (Diary of Wilford Woodruff, 1840; Arthur B. Erekson, "Whatever Happened to John Benbow?", Typescript.)

Beemer, Philip (1789–?), born at Grimsby, Ontario, Canada. Married Mary Ann Bloomfield, 1816. Militia officer in the War of 1812. Proprietor of a traveler's hostel in Colborne, Norfolk, Ontario, Canada. ("History of Colborne Village," pp. 3–5, MS., LDS Family History Library; E. A. Owen, *Pioneer Sketches of Long Point Settlement* [Toronto, 1898], 474–75, 486–87.)

Bennet, James Arlington (1788–1865), born in New York. A lawyer, studied medicine, lectured on bookkeeping in New York. He was a second lieutenant of artillery in 1814. Appointed inspector-general of the Nauvoo Legion, 1842. Proprietor of the Arlington Academy at New Utrecht, King's County, Long Island, 1843. Joined the Latter-day Saints, 1843, but left the Church soon after the death of Joseph Smith. He was Joseph Smith's first choice as vice-presidential running mate in the 1844 presidential election. Living at Gravesend, King's County, New York, in 1860. (U.S. Census, Gravesend, King's County, New York, 1860; New Utrecht, King's County, New York, 1850; *Boston Transcript*, 4 February 1931; Lyndon W. Cook, "James Arlington Bennet and the Mormons," *BYU Studies* 19 [Winter 1979]: 247–49.)

Bennett, James Gordon (1795–1872), newspaper editor; born at Newmill, Banffshire, Scotland. Emigrated to America in 1819. Correspondent with and editor of various New York newspapers until 1835, when he founded *The New York Herald*. Pioneered many of the methods of modern journalism, including the first financial article, the establishment of European correspondents, and the introduction of a society department. During the Civil War maintained a staff of 63 war correspondents. Throughout his newspaper career he published numerous articles about the Mormons. A resolution of the Nauvoo City Council expressed "lasting gratitude" to the "honorable editor" for his fair treatment of the Mormons. Bennett died in New York City. (*Encyclopedia Britannica*, 15th ed., s.v. "Bennett, James Gordon"; Leonard J. Arrington, "James Gordon Bennett's 1831 Report on 'The Mormonites,'" *BYU Studies* 10 [Spring 1970]: 353–64.)

Bennett, John Cook (1804–1867), physician; born at Fairhaven,

Bristol County, Massachusetts. Living in Ohio when he married Mary Barker, and later separated. Studied medicine and assisted in founding the medical college at Willoughby, 1834. Moved to Illinois, 1838, and practiced medicine. Appointed brigadier general in the Illinois Militia, 1839, and, shortly after, quartermaster general of the state. Moved to Nauvoo and joined the Latter-day Saints, 1840. Instrumental in obtaining the Nauvoo charter. Elected the town's first mayor, chancellor of the University, major-general of the Nauvoo Legion, and assistant president to Joseph Smith. Appointed master in chancery for Hancock County, Illinois. Excommunicated for immorality, 1842. Published and lectured against the Church. Engaged in poultry raising in Massachusetts; developed the Plymouth Rock chicken. Moved to Iowa and practiced medicine until his death in Polk City. (Cook, *Revelations*, 253.)

Bennett, Samuel C. (1810–?) barometer maker; born in England. After joining the Latter-day Saints, he was presiding elder of the branch at Cincinnati, Ohio, in 1840. Elected market inspector and alderman at Nauvoo, Illinois, 1843, and associate justice of the municipal court, 1844. Held commission as doctor in Nauvoo Legion. Among those arrested for destruction of the Nauvoo *Expositor* in June 1844. After the death of Joseph Smith he was associated with Sidney Rigdon and James J. Strang. Editor of Rigdon's *Messenger and Advocate*, 1845. Residing in Allegheny County, Pennsylvania, in 1860. (Black, "Membership of the Church," 4:917; *History of the Church*, 4:204; 6:418, 453, 456, 487; *History of the Reorganized Church*, 3:8, 44; U.S. Census, Ross, Allegheny County, Pennsylvania, 1860.)

Bennett, Selina (1815–?), born in England. Wife of Samuel C. Bennett. (U.S. Census, Ross, Allegheny County, Pennsylvania, 1860.)

Bernhisel, John Milton (1799–1881), physician, political economist, congressional delegate. Born at Lloysville, Perry County, Pennsylvania. Graduated from University of Pennsylvania in medicine. While practicing medicine in New York he joined the Latter-day Saints. Elected bishop in 1841. Moved to Nauvoo, 1843, where he resided in the Mansion House. Married Julia Ann Van Orden, 1845. Crossed the plains to Utah in 1847–1848. Member of the Board of Regents of the University of Deseret, 1850–1858. Between 1849 and 1863 he spent most of his time in Washington, D.C., representing Utah in Congress. After returning to Utah he continued to practice medicine, and was vice-president of ZCMI, a member of the Council of Fifty, and participated in the School of the Prophets and the United Order. He died in Salt Lake City. (Gwynn W. Barrett, "John M. Bernhisel," *Utah Historical Quarterly* 36 (Spring 1968): 144–167; also, Barrett, "John M. Bernhisel: Mormon Elder in Congress," [Ph.D. diss., Brigham Young University, 1968].)

Bishop, Francis Gladden (1809–1878), watch repairer; born at

Greece, Monroe County, New York. After joining the Latter-day Saints in July 1832, he was engaged in extensive missionary work from North Carolina to Canada, 1833–1840, and was president of the branch at Westfield, New York. Heretical tendencies and subsequent repentance resulted in excommunication and readmittance to the Church on three occasions. On 28 September 1835 he was charged with "advancing heretical doctrines . . . derogatory to the character of the Church." Excommunicated in 1842 for purveying his own revelations as doctrine. Later formed a church of his own that existed in Iowa until about 1860. (Kirtland Council Minutes, 28 September 1835; *History of the Church*, 2:284–85; Kate B. Carter, *Our Pioneer Heritage* [Salt Lake City: Utah Printing Company, 1958–1977], 5:335–36; *Messenger and Advocate*, 1:63–64, 167, 186; 2:335; 3:476, 519; *Times and Seasons*, 1:77–78; Richard L. Saunders, "Francis Gladden Bishop and Gladdenism: A Study in the Culture of a Mormon Dissenter and his Movement" [M.S. thesis, Utah State University, 1989].)

Bissel, Benjamin B. (1805–1878), lawyer, judge; born at Hartwick, Otsego County, New York. Moved to Painesville, Geauga County, Ohio. Married Sarah Bright, 1829. One of a dozen attorneys listed in Geauga County tax records for the 1830s. Partner with Noah D. Matoon, a prominent Painesville lawyer. Defended Joseph Smith in July 1834 and helped him escape from a Painesville mob in 1837. While a state senator, 1839–40, he was instrumental in the creation of Lake County, Ohio. He was district or presiding judge, 1842–1846, and was still sitting on the bench in 1857. He died in Painesville. (*Pioneer and General History of Geauga County* [Historical Society of Geauga County, 1880], 67–68; *History of Geauga and Lake Counties, Ohio* [Philadelphia, Williams Brothers, 1878], 30; Mildred E. Hoyes Steed, *Soldiers and Widows of the American Revolution Who Lived in Lake County, Ohio* [Mentor, Ohio, Lakeland Press, 1985], 19–21.)

Black, Adam (1801–?), farmer; born in Henderson County, Kentucky. Moved to Missouri, 1819; elected sheriff of Ray County, 1824. Married Mary Morgan in Ray County, 1825. Moved to Daviess County in 1834 and settled on land that later became the Mormon town of Adam-ondi-Ahman. Served as justice of the peace and County judge in Daviess County and in Gentry County after moving there in 1844. In 1861 moved to Livingston County, where he served as a county judge and was still residing in 1885. (U.S. Census: Daviess County, Missouri, 1840; Gentry County, 1850; International Genealogical Index, LDS Family History Library; *The History of Daviess County, Missouri* [Kansas City, Missouri: Birdsall & Dean, 1882], 355, 648; *History of Caldwell and Livingston Counties, Missouri* [St. Louis: National Historical Company, 1886], 1004–5.)

Boggs, Lilburn W. (1798–1861), born at Lexington, Kentucky.

Served in the War of 1812. Moved to St. Louis, Missouri, about 1816 and engaged in business. After death of first wife, married Panthea Boone, granddaughter of Daniel Boone. Elected lieutenant-governor, 1832, and became governor upon the resignation of his predecessor, Daniel Dunklin. Played a prominent roll in the expulsion of the Mormons from the state in 1838. Severely wounded by an assassin in 1842 and accused Joseph Smith of complicity in the crime. Moved to California in 1846 and became alcalde of the Sonoma district, 1847–1849. He died at Sacramento. (*The National Cyclopedia of American Biography* [New York: James Whites and Company, 1904], 12:303; William M. Boggs, "A Short Biographical Sketch of Lilburn W. Boggs, by his Son," *Missouri Historical Review* 4 [January 1910]: 106–10; Lyndon W. Cook, " 'A More Virtuous Man Never Existed on the Footstool of the Great Jehovah': George Miller on Joseph Smith," *BYU Studies* 19 [Spring 1979]: 405.)

Bond, Ira (1798–1887), farmer; born at Caldwell, Essex County, New Jersey. Married Charlotte Wilcox. After moving to Mendon, New York, he was among the first Mormon converts there in 1832. Called to preside over the deacons in Kirtland, 1836. Owned 178 acres and a dwelling house valued at $465 at Kirtland in 1836. Remained in Kirtland after Mormons left, and died there. ("Journal History of the Church," 14 April 1832; *History of the Church*, 2:371; Geauga County, Ohio, Tax Records; A. E. Sherman, comp., Cemetery Inscriptions, Lake County, Ohio, 22, Typescript, LDS Church Family History Library.)

Boosinger, George (1784–1861), farmer; born in Tennessee. Census records indicate he was in Ohio by 1827 and Missouri by 1837. In 1850 he was living in Macoupin County, Illinois. (U.S. Census: Macoupin County, 1850; Macoupin County, Illinois, Probate Records, 1835–1880.)

Bosier/Bozarth, Squire (1792–1853), born in Hardin County, Kentucky. Participant in the War of 1812. Married Mildred Willis, 1816. Among the pioneer settlers at La Grange, Lewis County, Missouri, 1819. Converted by George Hinkle and moved to Caldwell County about 1836. After the Mormon exodus from Missouri, he was among the earliest settlers at Commerce, Hancock County, Illinois. In December 1839 the Nauvoo high council authorized him to build a sawmill. Died at Woodland, Washington Territory. (Nauvoo Restoration Research File, LDS Church Archives; "Journal History of the Church," 13 December 1839; *History of Lewis County, Missouri*, 26, 62; Mary Alma Kay, Surname Referral File, Keokuk, Iowa.)

Bosley, Edmund (1776–1846), born in Northumberland County, Pennsylvania. Residing in Livonia, Livingston County, New York, 1822–1830. Moved to Kirtland, Ohio, 1833. Living in Missouri by 1838. Migrated with the Latter-day Saints to Illinois in 1839. Died at Winter

Quarters, Nebraska, during the Mormon exodus to Utah. (Lockwood L. Doty, *A History of Livingston County* [Genesee, 1876], 610–11; Lyndon W. Cook and Milton V. Backman, Jr., *Kirtland Elders Quorum Records, 1836–1841* [Provo, Utah: Grandin Press, 1985], 73.)

Bosworth, Joseph (1790–1850), farmer; born at Scituate, Providence County, Rhode Island. Married Lucina Hopkins, 1815. Living in Otsego County, New York, by 1816 and Copley, Summit County, Ohio, by 1818. Joined the Latter-day Saints by 1834. Died at Copley, Ohio. (Family Group Records Collection; U.S. Census: Copley, Summit County, Ohio, 1850; Mary B. Clarke, *Bosworth Genealogy* [San Francisco, 1926], 876–77.)

Bowen, John (1803–1858), farmer; born in Chester County, Pennsylvania. Married Ann Lanbough. In 1847 settled in Montrose, Lee County, Iowa, where he died. (U.S. Census: Montrose, Lee County, Iowa, 1850; "Nauvoo Temple Endowment Register," 1845–1846, Typescript, LDS Church Family History Library; Lee County, Iowa, Probate Records.)

Boynton, John Farnham (1811–1890), merchant, lecturer, scientist, inventor. Born at Bradford (now Groveland), Essex County, Massachusetts. Converted to Mormonism in 1832. Member of the Council of Twelve, 1835–1837. Married Susan Lowell, 1836. Established a mercantile business in Kirtland, Ohio, with Lyman Johnson. Left the Church in 1837. Settled in Syracuse, New York. Lecturer on natural history, geology, and science. Delivered more than four thousand lectures. Sent by U.S. government to California in 1849. Assisted in running boundary line between United States and Mexico. Developed the torpedo that destroyed the Confederate ram Albemarle during U.S. Civil War. Author of thirty-six patents. Avid collector of Boynton genealogy. Died at Syracuse, New York. (Andrew Jenson, *Biographical Encyclopedia*, 1:91; *National Cyclopedia of American Biography*, 4:91–92; John F. Boynton and Caroline H. Boynton, *The Boynton Family* [n.p.: Caroline H. Boynton, 1897], xix–xxxv.)

Brannan, Samuel (1819–1889), born at Saco, York County, Maine. In 1833 he migrated to Kirtland, Ohio, where he worked as a printer. After conversion to Mormonism he served as a missionary. Assisted with Church publication, and presided over the Saints in the eastern states, 1845–1846. Led a group of Saints from New York to San Francisco by ship, 1846–1847. After failing to persuade Brigham Young to settle the migrating Latter-day Saints in California in 1847, he returned to the bay area, where he became one of California's pioneer entrepreneurs. Published the first newspaper in San Francisco. Through extensive merchandising and land holdings he became the state's first millionaire. Excesses led to his excommunication in 1851. Died insolvent in San Diego. (Jenson, *Biographical Encyclopedia*, 3:606–7; Richard Van Wagoner and Steven Walker, *A Book of Mormons* [Salt Lake City: Signature Books, 1982], 19–23; Louis J. Stellman, *Sam Brannan, Builder of San Francisco: A Biography* [New York: Exposition Press, 1954].)

Brooks, Lester (1802–1878), stoveplate molder; born at Lanesboro, Berkshire County, Massachusetts. Married Amy Sophia Hazen, 1828. Counselor in the Kirtland stake presidency, 1841. By 1850 living at Buffalo, Erie County, New York, where he died. (Black, "Membership of the Church," 6:958–59; U.S. Census: Buffalo, Erie, New York, 1850, 1860.)

Brown, Albert (1807–1902), carpenter; born at Windsor, Hartford County, Connecticut. Living in Hoosick, Rensselaer County, New York, in 1830. Converted to Mormonism, 1832. Participant in march of Zion's Camp, 1834. Married Sarah Campbell, 1839. Member of the Nauvoo Legion. Migrated to Utah in 1863. He was a patriarch at time of his death at East Mill Creek, Utah. (Family Group Records Collection; U.S. Census: Rensselaer County, New York, 1830; *Deseret Evening News*, 29 January 1902; Frank E. Esshom, *Pioneers and Prominent Men of Utah* [Salt Lake City: Pioneers Book Publishing Company, 1913], 772.)

Brown, Eliza (1808–?), was born in Chenango County, New York. She married William C. Perry, 1835. Resided among the Latter-day Saints with her family in Missouri and Illinois. (Patriarchal Blessing Index, and "Nauvoo Temple Endowment Register," LDS Church Archives.)

Brunson, Seymour (1798–1840), born at Plattsburgh, Clinton County, New York. Veteran of War of 1812. Married Harriet Gould, 1820. Joined Latter-day Saints in Ohio in 1831. Temporary member of the high council at Far West, Missouri, in 1838, and appointed to the Nauvoo, Illinois, high council the following year. Captain in the 53rd regiment of Missouri militia and colonel in the Hancock County, Illinois, militia. Died at Nauvoo. (Cook, *Revelations*, 153; Family Group Records Collection.)

Bump, Jacob (1791–186?), born at Butternuts, Otsego County, New York, where he lived until 1824. Participant in Zion's Camp, 1834. Married Abigail Pettingill. Contracted to do the plastering on the temple at Kirtland, Ohio. Joined dissenters in Kirtland to depose Joseph Smith in 1837. Used his influence with Kirtland dissenters to prevent mob violence against Mormons leaving Kirtland in 1838. In 1837 associated with William E. McLellin and his Church of Christ in Kirtland; still living there in 1860. (*The Deseret Weekly* [Salt Lake City], 10 February 1858; Black, "Membership of the Church," 7:534–36; "Journal History of the Church," 6 July 1838.)

Burch, Thomas C. (c.1805–1839), lawyer; born in Tennessee. His family moved to Howard County, Missouri, when he was a child. Studied law at Jefferson City. In 1831 he began his practice at Richmond, Ray County. Married Celinary Jacobs, 1834. Appointed judge of the Eleventh

Judicial Circuit, 1838. Died at Keytesville, Chariton County, Missouri. (W. V. N. Bay, *Reminiscences of the Bench and Bar of Missouri* [St. Louis: F. H. Thomas and Company, 1878], 487–88; Ray County Probate Record, 1839.)

Burdick, Thomas (1795–1877), farmer; born at Canajoharie, Montgomery County, New York. Married Anna Higley, 1828. Appointed Church clerk to record membership licenses, February 1836. Kirtland schoolteacher, justice of the peace, and member of the Kirtland high council, 1837. Teaching school at Burlington, Iowa, 1845. In 1846 moved to Council Bluffs, where he was clerk and the first judge of Pottawattamie County; also postmaster at Kanesville. Crossed the plains in 1853 to San Bernardino. Moved to San Gabriel. Member of the board of supervisors of Los Angeles County. Died in Los Angeles. His son, Cyrus, was a cofounder of the city of Pomona. (*An Illustrated History of Los Angeles County California* [Chicago: The Lewis Publishing Company, 1889], 402; J. M. Guinn, *Historical and Biographical Record of Los Angeles and Vicinity* [Chicago: Chapman Publishing Company, 1901], 370; Nellie Johnson, *The Descendants of Robert Burdick* [Syracuse, New York: Syracuse Typesetting Company, 1937], 132–34, 328–30; Smith, *History of the Church*, 2:400, 522; Black, "Membership of the Church," 5:650–51; U.S. Census: Pottowattamie County, Iowa, 1850.)

Burtch, Esther (1816–1896), daughter of Stephen and Margaret Belingar Burtch, born in Mt. Pleasant, Brant County, Ontario, Canada. (*History of Brant County*, 556; Mt. Pleasant Cemetery Record.)

Burtch, Margaret, married Stephen Burtch (b. Balltown, Chautauqua County, New York, 1767) in 1807 in vicinity of Niagara, Canada. Moved with her husband to Mt. Pleasant, Brant County, Ontario, in 1813. Parents of nine children, including Mary and Esther Burtch. (*History of Brant County*, 556.)

Burtch, Mary, daughter of Stephen and Margaret Belingar Burtch, born in Mt. Pleasant, Brant County, Ontario, Canada. (*History of Brant County*, 556.)

Butler, John Lowe (1808–1861), farmer, blacksmith; born in Simpson County, Kentucky. Married Caroline F. Skeen, 1831. Baptized by Mormon missionaries, 1835, and moved to Missouri the following year. Involved in the election-day fight at Gallatin, Daviess County, August 1838. Moved to Quincy, Illinois, in 1839, and to Nauvoo the following year. Served as a bodyguard of Joseph Smith. Crossed the plains to Utah in 1852. Eventually settled at Spanish Fork, Utah County, where he was bishop of the community from 1856 until his death. (Family Group Records Collection; John L. Butler Autobiography, MS., LDS Church Archives; William G. Hartley, *John L. Butler: Autobiography and History of a Mormon Frontiersman* [forthcoming book].

531

Butterfield, Josiah (1795–1871), born at Dunstable, Middlesex, Massachusetts. Married Polly Moulton, 1819. Baptized in Maine by Mormon missionaries, 1833, and moved to Kirtland, Ohio. Member of the Kirtland high council and president of the first quorum of seventy, 1837. Assisted in the migration of the Kirtland Camp to Missouri in 1838. Following the expulsion of the Mormons from Missouri in 1839 he settled at Bear Creek, Adams County, Illinois. After the death of his wife in 1840, he married Margaret Lawrence, mother of Sarah and Maria Lawrence. Excommunicated in 1844; later rebaptized. Joined Reorganized Church, 1865. Died at Watsonville, Santa Cruz County, California. (Cook, *Revelations*, 254–55.)

Butterfield, Justin (1790–1855), lawyer; born at Keene, Cheshire County, New Hampshire. Practiced law in Jefferson County, New York, and New Orleans, Louisiana, before moving to Chicago, Illinois, in 1835. Appointed U.S. district attorney for Illinois in 1841 and commissioner of the General Land Office in 1849. Held the position of land commissioner until disabled by paralysis in 1852. He died in Chicago. (A. T. Andreas, *History of Chicago* [Chicago: A. T. Andreas, 1884], 433–35.)

Cahoon, Larona (1817–1840), born at Harpersfield, Ashtabula County, Ohio. Eldest daughter of Reynolds Cahoon. (Family Group Records Collection.)

Cahoon, Reynolds (1790–1862), farmer, tanner, builder; born at Cambridge, Washington County, New York. Participant in the War of 1812. Married Thirza Stiles, 1810. Among the first converts to Mormonism in Ohio in 1830. Appointed counselor to Bishop Newel K. Whitney at Kirtland, Ohio, 10 February 1832. Member of the committee to oversee building of the Kirtland Temple and, later, the Nauvoo Temple. Moved to Iowa after the 1838 expulsion of the Latter-day Saints from Missouri. Crossed plains to Utah, 1848. Died in South Cottonwood Ward, Salt Lake County. (Cook, *Revelations*, 73; Stella C. Shurtleff and Brent F. Cahoon, *Reynolds Cahoon and his Stalwart Sons* [Salt Lake City: Paragon Press, 1960]; U.S. Census: Salt Lake County, Utah, 1850, 1860; Family Group Records Collection.)

Cahoon, William F. (1813–1893), shoemaker, carpenter, joiner; eldest son of Reynolds Cahoon. Born at Harpersfield, Ashtabula County, Ohio. Baptized at Kirtland, Ohio, in 1830. Proselyting in Ohio, Pennsylvania, and New York, 1833. Participant in Zion's Camp march, 1834. Member of first quorum of seventy, 1835. Married Nancy Miranda Gibbs, 1836. Carpenter on Nauvoo temple, 1844. Migrated to Utah, 1849. President of second quorum of seventy. Died in Salt Lake City. (Jenson, *Biographical Encyclopedia*, 4:687–88; Shurtleff and Cahoon, *Reynolds Cahoon*, 79ff; *Deseret Evening News*, 7 April 1893.)

Capron, Henry (1798–1875), farmer; born in New York. Married Betsey Kent. Veteran of the War of 1812. Spent most of his life at Ava,

Oneida County, New York. He was supervisor and justice of the town for many years. (Daniel E. Wager, ed., *Our County and its People: A Descriptive Work on Oneida County, New York* [Boston: The Boston History Company, Publishers, 1896], 109, 394; U.S. Census: Oneida County, New York, 1830–1850.)

Carlin, Thomas (1789–1852), farmer, governor of Illinois; born in Franklin County, Kentucky. Moved to Missouri in 1803 and Illinois in 1812. Served as a private in the War of 1812 and a captain in the Black Hawk War. Married Rebecca Huitt, 1814. In 1818 settled in Greene County, where he became the first sheriff, and was twice elected a state senator. Moved to Quincy, 1834. Registrar of the land office at Quincy, Illinois, when elected governor on the Democratic ticket in 1838. After his term ended in 1842 he moved to his former home in Carrollton, Greene County, where he died. (Newton Bateman and Paul Selby, eds., *Historical Encyclopedia of Illinois* [Chicago: Munsall Publishing Company, 1900], 79; *Portrait Biographical Album of Peoria County, Illinois* [Chicago, 1890], 135–36.)

Carrico, Thomas (1802–1882), born at Beverly, Essex County, Massachusetts. Baptized in 1834 by John F. Boynton. Settled at Kirtland, Ohio, 1835. Married Elizabeth Baker, 1836. Appointed doorkeeper of the Kirtland Temple. Traveled to Missouri with the Kirtland Camp, 1838. In 1842 settled at Nauvoo, Illinois, where he was appointed counselor to Bishop Jonathan H. Hale and was a 2nd lieutenant in the Nauvoo Legion. Later joined the Reorganized Church. Died at Logan, Harrison County, Iowa. (Nauvoo Ninth Ward High Priests Record, MS., 12; Pearl Wilcox, *Roots of the Reorganized Latter Day Saints in Southern Iowa* [Independence: Pearl Wilcox, 1989], 136.)

Carter, Angeline (1823–1846), born at Benson, Rutland County, Vermont. Daughter of John S. Carter and Elizabeth Kenyon. Died during the Mormon exodus from Nauvoo at Mt. Pisgah, Iowa. (Family Group Records Collection; Nauvoo Restoration Research File.)

Carter, Daniel (1803–1887), farmer; born in Benson, Rutland County, Vermont. Married Clarissa A. Foster, 1829. Converted to Mormonism in 1833. In 1838 he was living in Missouri and was appointed to the Adam-ondi-Ahman high council in Daviess County. After arriving in Utah in 1850 he settled at Bountiful, Davis County, Utah. Appointed selectman of the county, also associate probate judge. (Black, "Membership of the Church," 8:760–63; *History of the Church*, 3:38.)

Carter, Gideon (1798–1838), born at Killingworth, Middlesex County, Connecticut. Married Hilda Burwell. Baptized by Joseph Smith in 1831. Proselyting mission with Sylvester Smith in eastern states and New England, 1832. Member of Kirtland Safety Society and Kirtland high council, 1837. Moved to Far West, Missouri, 1838. Killed in battle at Crooked River, Ray County, Missouri. (Jenson, *Biographical Encyclopedia*, 3:615–16; Cook, *Revelations*, 154.)

Carter, Jared (1801–1849), shoemaker, cordwainer; born at Benson, Rutland County, Vermont. Married Lydia Ames, 1825. Joined the Church and was ordained an elder, 1831. Proselyting in eastern states, New York, and Michigan, 1831–1833. Appointed to the Kirtland high council, 1837, and Far West, Missouri high council, 1838. Member of the committee to oversee construction of the Kirtland Temple. Became disaffected and was disfellowshipped at Nauvoo but promised to return. Died in DeKalb County, Illinois. (Cook, *Revelations*, 73–74; *History of the Church*, 2:277–80, 333; Kirtland, Ohio, High Council Minutes, 19 September 1835; Illinois Mortality Schedule, 1850, Typescript, LDS Church Family History Library.)

Carter, Joanna (1824–1847), born at Benson, Rutland County, Vermont. Living in the Smith home for a time in Missouri and Illinois. Witnessed depredations against Joseph Smith and others in Missouri. Married Lauren Hotchkiss Roundy in Nauvoo, Illinois, 1842. Died at Winter Quarters, Nebraska. (Family Group Records Collection; *History of the Church*, 3:286–88; Black, "Membership of the Church," 9:1–3.)

Carter, Marietta (1820–1840), born at Benson, Rutland County, Vermont. Married Jonathan Harriman Holmes at Kirtland, Ohio, 1837. Died at Nauvoo, Illinois. (Family Group Records Collection; Black, "Membership of the Church," 9:33–34.)

Carter, Nancy (1827–?), born at Benson, Rutland County, Vermont. Living in the Nauvoo 4th ward in the 1840s. (Family Group Records Collection; Black, "Membership of the Church," 9:49.)

Carter, Simeon (1794–1869), farmer; born at Killingworth, Middlesex County, Connecticut. Married Lydia Kenyon, 1818. Converted to Mormonism in Ohio in 1831. Member of the Clay County, Missouri high council, 1834, and Far West, Missouri, high council, 1836. Missionary to England, 1846–1849. Arrived in Salt Lake Valley, 1850. Settled at Brigham City, Box Elder County, Utah, where he died. (Cook, *Revelations*, 74–75; U.S. Census: Box Elder County, Utah, 1860; Esshom *Pioneers and Prominent Men*, 796–97.)

Charles, John F. (1808–?), physician; born in Pennsylvania. Moved to Carthage, Hancock County, Illinois, in 1834 and served in the state legislature, 1840–42. Married Ann Eliza Baldwin, 1834. Practicing medicine in 1850. (*History of Hancock County, Illinois* [Hancock County, 1968], 7, 51, 110, 207; U.S. Census: Hancock County, 1850.)

Chase, Ezra (1796–1873), farmer; born at Colrain, Franklin County, Massachusetts. Married Theresa Wells, 1818. Converted to Mormonism in 1839. Resided in the 3rd ward at Nauvoo, Hancock County, Illinois. Assisted in timber expedition to Wisconsin for Nauvoo building, 1842. During crossing of the plains in 1846–1847 he was a member of the Winter Quarters, Nebraska, municipal council. Arrived in Salt Lake Valley, 1848. Settled at Ogden, Weber County. Moved to Eldorado County, California, in 1849 and San Bernardino, 1853. Returned to Ogden, 1858. Was ordained a patriarch in 1873. Died at Harrisville, Weber County. ("Journal History of the Church, 1842, 1846–49, 1873"; Black, "Membership of the Church," 9:379–82; *Portrait, Genealogical and Biographical Record of the State of Utah* [Chicago: National Historical Record Company, 1902], 152.)

Chase, Nathan (no information)

Clark, Hiram (1795–1853), born at Wells, Rutland County, Vermont. Joined the Church in 1835. Missionary to England, 1839–1841, and 1844–1846. Crossed the plains to Utah in 1849. Served as first president of the Hawaiian Mission, 1850–1851. Unable to cope with situation there, he returned to San Bernardino, where he took his own life. (Jenson, *Biographical Enclyclopedia*, 4:339; Black, "Membership of the Church"; Juanita Brooks, ed., *On the Mormon Frontier: The Diary of Hosea Stout* [Salt Lake City, University of Utah Press, 1964], 506.)

Clark, Josiah (no information)

Clayton, William (1814–1879), born at Penwortham, Lancashire, England. Among the first Mormon converts in England after missionaries arrived in 1837. A year later he became second counselor in the British Mission presidency. Emigrated to America in 1840 and by 1842 was settled in Nauvoo, Illinois. Between 1841 and 1844 served as clerk of the Iowa high council, clerk and recorder of the Nauvoo Temple, secretary to the Prophet Joseph Smith, and treasurer of the city of Nauvoo. One of the official clerks of the pioneer company during the Mormon exodus from Nauvoo to the Salt Lake Valley. In Utah he was treasurer of ZCMI, territorial recorder, auditor of public accounts, and recorder of marks and brands. He died at Salt Lake City. (Jenson, *Biographical Encyclopedia*, 1:717–18; James B. Allen, *Trials of Discipleship: The Story of William Clayton, a Mormon* [Urbana and Chicago: University of Illinois Press, 1987].)

Cleminson, John (1798–?), married Lydia Lightner, 1823. Did clerical work for the Latter-day Saints in Missouri; also served as clerk of the Caldwell County circuit court. Sided with dissenters and testified against Joseph Smith at the Richmond hearing in November 1838. Living in Montrose, Iowa, in 1842, he wrote the Prophet in an attempt to gain reconciliation: "My Character has been torn to pieces and I represented as one of the worst of men. Some of this harsh treatment I have deserved, some I have not." (*History of the Church*, 3:5, 210; John Cleminson to Joseph Smith, May 1842, MS., LDS Church Archives.)

Cleveland, Sarah Marrietta Kingsley (1788–1856), born at Becket, Berkshire County, Massachusetts. Married John Howe in Connecticut in 1807. After his death in Cleveland, Ohio, she married John Cleveland,

1826. Two children born while residing in Cincinnati. Moved to Quincy, Adams County, Illinois, in 1834. Gave lodging to Joseph Smith's family when the Saints were driven from Missouri in 1839. Moved to Plymouth, Hancock County, 1841. Selected as a counselor to Emma Smith when the Female Relief Society was first organized at Nauvoo in 1842. Died at Plymouth. [*History of the Church*, 4:552; Edmund J. Cleveland, *The Genealogy of the Cleveland and Cleaveland Families* [Hartford, Connecticut, 1899], LDS Family History Library; Richard P. Howard, ed., *The Memoirs of President Joseph Smith III [1832–1914]* [Independence: Herald Publishing House, 1979], 1, 416.]

 Coe, Joseph (1774–1854), born at Genoa, Cayuga County, New York. Living in Essex County, New Jersey, in 1830. Proselyting in New York, 1831. Appointed agent to purchase Church property, 1833. Member of the Kirtland high council, 1834–1837. Assisted in purchase of Egyptian mummies for the Church in 1835. Left the Church in 1838. Remained in Kirtland, Ohio, where he died. [Cook, *Revelations*, 86–87; Kirtland, Ohio, Cemetery Records, 26, Microfilm of typescript, LDS Family History Library.]

 Coltrin, Zebedee (1804–1887), born at Ovid, Seneca County, New York. Converted to Mormonism, 1831. Participant in the march of Zion's Camp, 1834. Married Julia Ann Jennings. Appointed one of the presidents of the seventy, 1835. Settled in Nauvoo, Illinois, 1839, but soon after moved to Kirtland, Ohio. Appointed second counselor to Almon Babbitt in the Kirtland Stake, 1841. Crossed the plains with the Mormon pioneer company, 1847. Settled in Spanish Fork, Utah County, 1852; was ordained a patriarch, 1873. Died in Spanish Fork. [Cook, *Revelations*, 75–76.]

 Comer, John B. (1814–?), farmer; born in Ohio. Daviess County, Missouri, deputy sheriff, 1839, 1852. [*The History of Daviess County*, [Kansas City: Birdsall & Dean, 1882], 357.]

 Cook, Phebe Andrews (1766–1850), married Daniel Cook, 1787. Died at Mt. Pleasant, Brant, Ontario, Canada. [*History of Brant County*, 560; International Genealogical Index; Mt. Pleasant Cemetery Records.]

 Coolidge, Joseph Wellington (1814–1871), carpenter, miller, lumber dealer; born at Bangor, Penobscot County, Maine. He was with the Latter-day Saints in Missouri in 1838 and moved with them to Illinois. At Nauvoo he was a member of the Council of Fifty, and after Joseph Smith's death was administrator of his estate. In 1850 he was a miller in Pottawattamie County, Iowa, and ten years later a lumber dealer in San Francisco, California. In 1870 Coolidge had an interview with Joseph F. Smith in Salt Lake City. [Black, "Membership of the Church," 11:569–73; U.S. Census: Pottawattamie County, Iowa, 1850; San Francisco, California, 1860; Newell and Avery, *Mormon Enigma: Emma Hale Smith*, 208, 292.]

Cooper, Harvey John (no information)

Copley, Leman (1781–1862), born in Connecticut. Joined the Latter-day Saints in 1831. Owned 759 acres of land at Thompson, Ohio. When the New York Saints moved to Ohio in 1831 he allowed them to settle on his land but afterward rescinded his agreement. Testified against Joseph Smith at the 1834 Philastus Hurlbut trial and was later disfellowshipped. Reinstated in 1836 but remained in Ohio. Died at Thompson, Ohio. (Geauga County, Ohio, tax lists; Cook, *Revelations*, 67; Violet Warren and Jeannette Grosvenor, "Inscriptions and Interments in Geauga County, Ohio through 1983," p. 591, Typescript.)

Corrill, John (1794–1943), carriage builder; born at Barre, Worcester County, Massachusetts. Living in Harpersville, Ashtabula County, Ohio, when converted to Mormonism in 1830. Moved to Jackson County, Missouri, 1831. Second counselor to Bishop Edward Partridge; presided over a branch of the Church at Independence. A Kirtland, Ohio, blessing said "there are none that surpass him in understanding pertaining to architecture" and that he would "build the house of the Lord in Zion." Directed later stages of construction of the Kirtland Temple. Elected state representative from Caldwell County, Missouri, 1838. Appointed Church historian in 1838 but soon afterward left the Church. Published *A Brief History of the Church of Christ*, 1839. Married Elizabeth Penewell, 1839. Residing at Quincy, Illinois prior to his death. (Cook, *Revelations*, 68–69; Joseph Smith, Sr., Patriarchal Blessing Book, Vol. 1, MS., LDS Church Archives.)

Covey, Almira Mack Scobey (1805–1886), born at Tunbridge, Orange County, Vermont. Cousin of Joseph Smith. Converted to Mormonism in 1830. Married William Scobey in 1831. After Scobey's death in 1833, Almira lived for a time with a Curtis family in Liberty, Clay County, Missouri, before she married Benjamin Covey in Kirtland, Ohio, in 1836. Crossed the plains to the Salt Lake Valley in 1848. Died in Salt Lake City. (Family Group Records Collection; *An Enduring Legacy* [Salt Lake City: Daughters of the Utah Pioneers, 1980], 3:123–24.)

Covey, Benjamin (1792–1868), farmer, shoemaker; born at Frederikstown, Dutchess County, New York. Married Almira Mack, a cousin of Joseph Smith the Prophet, in Kirtland, Ohio, 1836. Incarcerated and later released for alleged crimes against the state of Missouri during the conflict there in 1838. Crossed the plains to the Salt Lake Valley in 1848. Bishop of the Salt Lake Twelfth Ward, 1849–56. Called in 1856 to help settle Carson City, Nevada. A year later returned to Salt Lake City where he was living when he died. (*An Enduring Legacy*, 3:123–24.)

Cowdery, Oliver (1806–1850), teacher, lawyer, newspaper editor; born at Wells, Rutland County, Vermont. Assisted Joseph Smith as a scribe during translation of the Book of Mormon and other clerical work. Witness to early events connected with the foundation of Mormonism.

One of the Three Witnesses to the Book of Mormon, and a participant in the priesthood restoration. Married Elizabeth Ann Whitmer, 1832. Member of the Kirtland high council. Appointed assistant president of the Church in 1834. Left the Church in 1838 but returned ten years later. Practiced law in Ohio and Wisconsin. Died at Richmond, Ray County, Missouri. (Cook, *Revelations*, 14; Jenson, *Biographical Encyclopedia*, 1:246–51; R. L. Anderson, *Investigating the Book of Mormon Witnesses*, 37–65.)

Cowdery, Warren A. (1788–1851), physician, druggist, farmer. Born at Poultney, Rutland County, Vermont. Older brother of Oliver Cowdery. Married Patience Simonds, 1814. Practiced medicine in Vermont and Freedom, New York. Moved to Freedom in 1815; became postmaster, 1824. Converted to Mormonism, 1831. Appointed presiding elder of the Church at Freedom, 1834. Moved to Kirtland, Ohio, in 1836 and was involved in managing the book bindery and printing office. Also editor of the *Messenger and Advocate* and clerk to Joseph Smith. Became disaffected and left the Church in 1838. In 1850 farming at Kirtland, where he died. (Carl C. Curtis, Cowdery Genealogical Material, Typescript, LDS Family History Library; Cook, *Revelations*, 214–15.)

Cowdery, William (1765–1847), born at East Haddam, Middlesex County, Connecticut. Father of Oliver Cowdery. Married Rebecca Fuller about 1787. Father of eight children. Resided at Wells, Vermont, prior to joining Latter-day Saints and moving to Kirtland, Ohio. He died at Kirtland. (Family Group Records Collection; Curtis, Cowdery Genealogy.)

Cowles, Austin (1792–1872), teacher, farmer, wheelwright, minister, merchant; born at Brookfield, Orange County, Vermont. Married Phebe Wilbur in Unadilla, New York, 1813. Methodist Episcopal Church minister prior to joining the Latter-day Saints and moving to Kirtland, Ohio, about 1837. Counselor to William Marks in Nauvoo stake presidency, 1841; member of the high council and supervisor of streets in Nauvoo. Opposed the practice of plural marriage and sided with dissenters against Joseph Smith. Excommunicated in 1844. Lived in Iowa, Ohio, and Illinois prior to moving in 1854 to Pleasanton, Decatur County, Iowa, where he farmed and operated a grist- and sawmill. He died at Pleasanton. (Family Group Records Collection; Calvin D. Cowles, *Genealogy of the Cowles Families in America* [New Haven: Tuttle Morehouse & Taylor, 1929], 1:503–5; *History of the Church*, 4:292, 323, 505; 6:347, 354, 398.)

Crosby, Jonathan (1807–1892), cabinetmaker; born at Wendell, Franklin County, Massachusetts. Converted to Mormonism, 1833. Married Caroline Barnes, 1834. Member of the second quorum of seventy in Kirtland, Ohio, and later became president of the twelfth quorum in Nauvoo. Proselyting in eastern United States, 1838. Resided in Indiana,

1838–1842, before moving to Nauvoo. Proselyting in northern states and Canada, 1842–1843. Worked on Kirtland and Nauvoo temples. Migrated to Utah in 1848. Proselyting mission to the South Pacific, 1850–1852. Died at Beaver, Beaver County, Utah. (Jonathan Crosby Autobiography, MS., Utah Historical Society; Family Group Records Collection.)

Crosier, Harlow (?–1894), married Mary S. Fowler in 1839 in Lake County, Ohio. Died in Du Page County, Illinois. (Lake County, Ohio, Marriage Record, 59, LDS Family History Library; Du Page County, Illinois, Probate Records, 1894.)

Cross, William, manufacturer of "Instantaneous Friction Lights" (matches); native of England. Living in the Nauvoo, Illinois, fourth ward with Alexander Neibaur in 1842. (*Times and Seasons* 3 (15 December 1841): 638.)

Cummings, James (1780–1847), born at Dunstable, Middlesex County, Massachusetts. Between 1806 and 1835 living in Wilton, Franklin County, Maine. Joined the Latter-day Saints, 1837. Died at Winter Quarters, Nebraska, during the Mormon exodus from Nauvoo. (Family Group Records Collection; Black, "Membership of the Church," 12:712–13.)

Cushman, Nathan (1783–?), innkeeper; born in Vermont. Married Polly Weeks in Bennington, Vermont, 1802. Living at Willoughby, Lake County, Ohio, 1840–1858. (U.S. Census: Willoughby, Lake County, Ohio, 1840, 1850; International Genealogical Index; Lake County Court Journal, 1858.)

Cutler, Alpheus (1784–1864), stonemason, builder; born at Plainfield, Cheshire County, New Hampshire. Married Lois Lathrop, 1808. Served in the War of 1812. Joined the Church in New York, 1833. Moved to Kirtland, Ohio, 1834; to Missouri, 1836; and to Illinois, 1839. Appointed to the Nauvoo high council, 1839; the committee to build the Nauvoo temple, 1840; and the Council of Fifty, 1844. Presided over the municipal council at Cutler's Park, Nebraska, during the Mormon exodus to the West. Rejected the leadership of Brigham Young and settled at Silver Creek, Mills County, Iowa. About 1853 moved to Manti, Fremont County, Iowa where he organized "The True Church of Jesus Christ." Died at Manti, Iowa. (Cook, *Revelations*, 255; Richard E. Bennett, "Lamanism, Lymanism, and Cornfields," *Journal of Mormon History* 13 (1986–1987): 45–59.)

Cutler, Louisa Elizabeth (1816–1854), daughter of Alpheus Cutler, was born at Lisle, Broome County, New York. (Family Group Records Collection.)

Daley, Moses (1794–1865), born at Wallkill, Ulster County, New York. Married Almira Barber, 1819. Missionary in Michigan, 1832. Settled at Adam-ondi-Ahman, Caldwell County, Missouri. Participant in the Gallatin election fight in Caldwell County, Missouri, 1838. Crossed plains, 1848. Settled at San Bernardino, California. Died at Riverside, California (Carter, *Our Pioneer Heritage*, 4:433; Black, "Membership," 13:79–82; "Journal History of the Church," 4 June, 6 August 1838.)

Davis, Amos (1813–1872), merchant, landowner, born at Hopkinton, Rockingham County, New Hampshire. In 1836 moved to Commerce, Hancock County, Illinois, where he operated a store and hotel. Married Elvira M. Hibbard, 1837. Appointed postmaster at Commerce, 1839. Converted to Mormonism, 1840. Remained in Nauvoo after the Saints left in 1846. Traveled to California to dig for gold, 1850. Returned east to Michigan, 1853, and Illinois, 1858. Died at Big Mound, Hancock County. (Cook, *Revelations*, 256.)

Davis, Daniel Coon (1804–1850), farmer; born at Petersburg, Rensselaer County, New York. Appointed master of the ferry between Nauvoo, Illinois, and Montrose, Iowa, 1839. Member of the Mormon Battalion in the Mexican War, 1846. Commanding officer of Battalion men in California who re-enlisted for six months. Returned to Utah in 1850 and settled near Farmington, Davis County. Davis County named after him. Died at Fort Kearny, Nebraska, en route to the East. (Jenson, *Biographical Encyclopedia*, 4:741–42.)

Davis, Jacob Cunningham (1815–1883), lawyer, farmer; born in Augusta County, Virginia. Hancock County, Illinois, circuit court clerk, 1842–1843. Served four terms in the Illinois state senate, 1842–1856. Elected to Congress in 1856. Captain of a Warsaw, Hancock County, militia unit, 1844. One of those indicted for the murder of Joseph Smith. Died at Bear Creek, Hancock County. (U.S. Census: Hancock County, Illinois, 1850, 1870, 1880; Hancock County Probate Records; Oaks and Hill, *Carthage Conspiracy*, 55–56, 217; *History of Hancock County, Illinois*, 111, 624.)

Davis, Marvel Chapin (1801–1877), physician, born at Wardsboro, Windham County, Vermont. Married Rebecca Jane Sloan, 1823. Died at Seville, Medina County, Ohio. (Family Group Records Collection; U.S. Census: Medina County, Ohio, 1850.)

Dayton, Hiram (1798–1881), farmer; born at Herkimer, Herkimer County, New York. Married Permelia Bundy, 1820. Living in Parkman, Geauga County, Ohio, in 1830. Joined Latter-day Saints, 1832. Moved to Kirtland, Ohio, 1834; Far West, Missouri, 1838; and Nauvoo, Illinois, 1839. President of twelfth quorum of elders at Nauvoo. Crossed plains to Salt Lake Valley, 1849. Settled at Cedar Fort. Died at American Fork, Utah. (Family Group Records Collection; Black, "Membership of the Church," 13:642–48; Leland M. Dayton and Alta A. Dayton, "Record of the Posterity of Hiram Dayton and Permelia Bundy Dayton," September 1961, pp. 9–17, Typescript, LDS Family History Library.)

Decker, Isaac (1799–1873), farmer, cattle raiser; born at Tycanic, Columbia County, New York. Married Harriet Page Wheeler, 1820. Resided with the Latter-day Saints in Ohio, Missouri, and Illinois. Crossed the plains to Utah in the Brigham Young company of 1847. Two of his daughters, Lucy and Harriet, married Brigham Young. Died in Salt Lake City. (Jenson, *Biographical Encyclopedia*, 3:743; Black, "Membership of the Church," 13:711–15.)

Denton, Solomon Wilbur (1814–?), born at Fitchville, Huron County, Ohio. Participated in the march of Zion's Camp, 1834. Married Fanny M. Stanley in 1835. Proselyting with Don Carlos Smith in New York, 1836. Employed in the Kirtland printing office until he left the Church in 1837. (International Genealogical Index; Robinson, "Items of Personal History," *The Return* 1 [August 1889]: 115–21; Backman, *Profiles*, 21.)

Derby, Erastus H. (1810–1890), tailor; born at Hawley, Franklin County, Massachusetts. Married Ruhamah B. Knowlton in Ohio, 1834. Residing in Hancock County, Illinois, when converted to Mormonism in 1840. In August 1843 Derby was bound over to keep the peace for six months before the Nauvoo mayor's court, at which time he gave up his license as an elder in the Church. Living in Pottowattamie County, Iowa, in 1850. The birthplace of subsequent children indicates he resided in Cook County, Illinois, and Williams County, Ohio, between 1850 and 1860. In 1871 moved to Le Sueur, Le Sueur County, Minnesota, where he died. (*History of the Church*, 5:556; Family Group Records Collection; U.S. Census: Pottawattamie County, Iowa, 1850; Ezra Clark Knowlton, *The Utah Knowltons* [Salt Lake City, 1971], 15–21.)

Doniphan, Alexander William (1808–1887), born in Mason County, Kentucky. Graduate of Augusta College. Opened a law office in Lexington, Missouri, 1830. Moved to Liberty, Clay County, Missouri, 1833, and became a prominent lawyer. Elected to the state legislature, 1836, 1840, 1854. Employed as legal counsel by the Latter-day Saints in Missouri beginning in 1833. During the Mormon difficulties of 1838, he commanded the first brigade of David Atchison's third division of Missouri militia. Later that year he refused to carry out an execution order against Church leaders. Fought in the Mexican War, and later refused a general's commission in both the Union and Confederate armies during the Civil War. Died at Richmond, Missouri. (David C. Roller and Robert W. Twyman, eds., *The Encyclopedia of Southern History* [Baton Rouge: Louisana State University, 1979], 367; *History of the Church*, 1:425; 3:190–91; Gregory Maynard, "Alexander Doniphan: Man of Justice," *BYU Studies* 13 [Summer 1973]: 462–72; also Maynard, "Alexander William Doniphan, the Forgotten Man from Missouri" [M.A. thesis, Brigham Young University, 1973]; Andre Paul

DuChateau, "Missouri Colossus, Alexander William Doniphan, 1808–1887" [Ed.D. diss., Oklahoma State University, 1973].)

Dort, David (1793–1841), miller; born at Surry, Cheshire County, New Hampshire. Moved to Michigan about 1822. Married Joseph Smith's cousin Mary and later her sister Fanny, daughters of Joseph's maternal uncle and aunt, Stephen and Temperance Mack. Converted to Mormonism by Lucy Mack Smith, 1831. Participant in march of Zion's Camp from Michigan, 1834. Member of Kirtland high council, 1837; Far West high council, 1838; and Nauvoo high council, 1839. Left Church and joined Methodists. Died in Nauvoo, Illinois. (Cook, *Revelations*, 256; John and Audrey Cumming, *The Pilgrimage of Temperance Mack* [Mount Pleasant, Michigan: published by authors, 1967], 5, 7, 48–49.)

Douglas, Stephen Arnold (1813–1861), cabinetmaker, lawyer, and politician who became a leader of the Democratic Party. Born at Brandon, Rutland County, Vermont. Moved to Illinois in 1833 and studied law. Elected to the Illinois legislature, 1836. Appointed secretary of state, 1840, and judge of the supreme court, 1841. Elected to the U.S. Congress in 1842 and the U.S. Senate in 1846, serving until his death. Developed the principle of popular sovereignty as a solution to the slavery issue. Candidate for presidential nomination at the Democratic National Conventions of 1852, 1856. In 1860 he received the nomination but lost the election to Abraham Lincoln. Died in Chicago, Illinois. (Newton Bateman and Paul Selby, eds., *Historical Encyclopedia of Illinois* [Chicago: Munsall Publishing Company, 1900], 135–36; *Encyclopedia Britannica*, 15th ed., s.v. "Douglas, Stephen A.")

Draper, William, Jr. (1807–1886), shoemaker, farmer, merchant; born at Richmond, Frontenac District, Ontario, Canada. Married Elizabeth Staker, 1827. Baptized in Canada in 1833. Living in Kirtland, Ohio, 1833–1838. Proselyting in Canada, 1835–1836. Crossed plains to Utah in 1849. Resided successively in Salt Lake City, Draper, Spanish Fork, and Freedom, Sanpete County, where he died. (Family Group Records Collection; "Pioneer Midwives," *Our Pioneer Heritage* 6:486–87; Black, "Membership of the Church," 14:416–21.)

Draper, Zemira (1812–1876), farmer, miller; born at Crambe, Northumberland County, Ontario, Canada. Baptized in 1834. Moved to Kirtland, Ohio, 1835. Married Ellen Bradshaw, 1838. With the Church in Ohio, Missouri, Illinois. Migrated to Utah in 1848; settled in the Salt Lake City tenth ward. Moved to Willow Creek, later renamed Draper, Utah, in 1850. Appointed first counselor in bishopric. In 1862 sent to colonize Rockville, Washington County, Utah, where he died after serving as bishop's counselor and justice of the peace. (Family Group Records Collection; Delbert M. Draper, *The Mormon Drapers* [Salt Lake City:

published by author, 1958], 295–305; Esshom, *Pioneers and Prominent Men*, 848.)

Dunham, Jonathan (1800–1845), born at Paris, Oneida County, New York. Living in Allegany County, New York, in 1830. Proselyting in New York in 1836, and among the Indians there in 1837. Accompanied Kirtland Camp to Missouri, 1838. Expedition among the Indians in Iowa and Missouri in the summer of 1843. Appointed captain of the Nauvoo police, 1843. Named superintendent for construction of Nauvoo Legion arsenal, 1843. Wharf-master at Nauvoo, 1844. Colonel in the Nauvoo Legion; appointed acting major general in June 1844. Among those arrested for destruction of the Nauvoo *Expositor*, 1844. Died while engaged on a mission to the Indians. (International Genealogical Index; U.S. Census: Rushford, Allegany County, New York, 1830; *History of the Church*, 3:92; 5:348, 509, 541ff; 6:149, 229, 847; 7:401, 437; Jonathan Dunham Diary, 1837–1846, MS., LDS Church Archives.)

Eaton, Frazier (1780–?), sexton; born in New Hampshire. Living in Allegany County, New York, both before and after his association with the Latter-day Saints. He evidently lived for a time in Kirtland, Ohio, in the 1830s and in Hancock County, Illinois, in 1840, but by 1850 was back in Rushford. According to George A. Smith, Eaton had donated $700 for the building of the Kirtland Temple, but when he was unable to attend the dedication, after arriving late, he left the Church. (U.S. Census: Allegany County, New York, 1820–1850; New York State Census: Allegany County, 1855; George A. Smith Discourse, 15 November 1864, in *Journal of Discourses*, 11:9.)

Elliott, David (1799–1855), blacksmith; born at Charleston, Montgomery County, New York. Moved to Ithaca, New York. Joined the Latter-day Saints in 1831. Married Mary Cahoon, 1831. Participated in march of Zion's Camp, 1834. Member of the first quorum of seventy. Moved to Missouri with the Kirtland Camp, 1838. Settled at Springfield, Illinois, after departure from Missouri. Died at Salt Lake City. (Backman, *Profiles*, 23, 93, 117, 121; *History of the Church*, 2:203; Family Group Record Collection.)

Emmett, James (1803–1852/3), born in Boone County, Kentucky. Converted to Mormonism in Illinois in 1832. Moved to Clay County, Missouri, 1836. Proselyting in states between Ohio and Missouri, 1835–1837. Disfellowshipped and reinstated, 1837. Appointed to Iowa high council, 1841. Policeman at Nauvoo, 1843. Named to western exploring expedition by Joseph Smith in February 1844. After the death of the Prophet, Emmett led a company west that eventually stopped in what became South Dakota. Most of the company later reunited with the Church. In 1849 Emmett went to California where he died. (Family Group Record Collection; *History of the Church*, 4:352; 6:149; 7:135; Dale Morgan, "Reminiscences of James Holt: A Narrative of the Emmett

Company," *Utah Historical Quarterly* 23 [January, April 1955]: 1–33, 151–79; Gerald E. Jones, "An Early Mormon Settlement in South Dakota," *South Dakota History* 1 [Spring 1971]: 119–31.)

Felshaw, William (1800–1867), contractor and builder. Born at Granville, Washington County, New York. Married Mary Gilbert, 1826. Converted to Mormonism in Boston by Orson Hyde and Samuel H. Smith in 1832. Lived at Hoosick, Rensselaer County, New York, before moving to Kirtland, Ohio, about 1833. Carpenter on Kirtland, Nauvoo, and Salt Lake temples. Migrated to Utah in 1851. Member of Utah territorial legislature, 1854. Traveled to Wyoming to assist in relief of stranded handcart companies in 1856. Died at Fillmore, Utah. (Family Group Records Collection; *History of the Church*, 7:326; Esshom, *Pioneers and Prominent Men*, 868.)

Fielding, Amos (1792–1875), farmer, matchmaker, surveyor; born at Bolton, Lancashire, England. Married Mary Haddock, 1829. After joining the Latter-day Saints, engaged in missionary work and served as Church agent in his native land, 1840–1845. Member of the Council of Fifty in Nauvoo. Migrated to Utah; died in Salt Lake City. (*History of the Church*, 4:149; 7:388; *Deseret News*, 11 August 1875; Early Church Information File.)

Fielding, Joseph (1797–1863), farmer; born in Bedfordshire, England. Emigrated to Ontario, Canada, 1832. Converted to Mormonism by Parley P. Pratt, 1836. Married Hannah Greenwood, 1838. Mission to England, 1837; presided over the British mission, 1838–1840. Returned to Nauvoo, Illinois, 1841. Left Nauvoo in 1846 and arrived in Utah, 1848. Died in Salt Lake City. (Joseph Fielding Diary, 1832–1859, MS. LDS Church Archives; Black, "Membership of the Church," 16:227–33; Jenson, *Biographical Encyclopedia*, 2:762–63.)

Follett, King (1788–1844), born at Winchester, Cheshire County, New Hampshire. Married Louisa Tanner prior to 1816. Living in Cayahoga County, Ohio, when he joined the Latter-day Saints in 1831. Member of second quorum of seventy. During the difficulties in Missouri in 1838, Follett was imprisoned in Richmond and Columbia. He was a Hancock County, Illinois, constable. Killed digging a well at Nauvoo. His funeral sermon became the occasion for the Joseph Smith "King Follett discourse." (Family Group Records Collection; *History of the Church*, 3:335, 401–2; 6:248–49, 302–317; Andrew Jenson, *The Historical Record* [Salt Lake City, 1882–1890], 5:31.)

Ford, Edward R. (1774–?), born in South Carolina. Agent of Missouri Governor Thomas Reynolds sent to Illinois to apprehend Joseph Smith for alleged complicity in the shooting of Missouri ex-governor Boggs in 1842. Living in Boone County, Missouri, in 1850. (U.S. Census, Boone County, Missouri, 1850; Stanley B. Kimball, "Missouri Mormon

Manuscripts: Sources in Selected Societies," *BYU Studies* 14 [Summer 1974]: 477–78.)

Ford, Thomas (1800–1850), lawyer, born at Uniontown, Fayette County, Pennsylvania. Taken by his mother, a widow, to Missouri in 1804, then to Monroe County, Illinois. Judge of the circuit court in northern Illinois, 1835–1837, and for the Galena district, 1839. Elevated to the bench of the state supreme court in 1841 but the following year resigned to accept the Democratic nomination for governor. Served as Illinois governor, 1842–1846. Wrote *History of Illinois from its Commencement as a State in 1818 to 1847*, published in 1854. He died in Peoria. (Newton Bateman, and Paul Selby, eds., *Historical Encyclopedia of Illinois* [Chicago: Munsell Publishing Company, 1900], 168.

Fordham, Elijah (1798–1879), lumber dealer, carpenter. Born in New York City. Married Jane Ann Fisher, 1822. Living in Pontiac, Michigan, 1831–1833. Participant in march of Zion's Camp in 1834. As the only Church member in New York City in 1837, he assisted the missionaries en route to Great Britain. Miraculously healed by Joseph Smith, 1839. Appointed to Iowa high council, 1839. Migrated to Utah in 1850. Died at Wellsville, Cache County, Utah. (Family Group Records Collection; *History of the Church*, 2:183, 494; 4:14; Black, "Membership of the Church," 10:736–42.)

Foster, James (1775–1841), born in Hillsboro County, New Hampshire. Participated in the march of Zion's Camp. Appointed one of the first presidents of the seventy, 1837. One of the leaders of Kirtland Camp, 1838. After the Latter-day Saints left Missouri, he settled in Jacksonville, Morgan County, Illinois, where he died. (Jenson, *Biographical Encyclopedia*, 1:191–92; Cook, *Revelations*, 256.)

Foster, Lucien R. (1806–?), clerk, accountant, bookkeeper photographer; born at New Marlborough, Berkshire County, Massachusetts. Elected president of the branch at New York City, 1841. Proprietor of a daguerreotype shop in Nauvoo. Excommunicated from the Church in New York for apostasy in 1846. Living in Brooklyn, New York, 1870. (*History of the Church*, 4:344; "Journal History of the Church," 13 September 1846; Nauvoo Temple Endowment Register; U.S. Census: Brooklyn, King's County, New York, 1870.)

Foster, Robert D. (1811–1878), physician; born at Braunston, Northampton, England. Converted to Mormonism, 1839. Accompanied Joseph Smith to Washington, D.C., on Missouri redress issue, 1839–40. Served as a regent of the University of Nauvoo, member of the Nauvoo Agricultural and Manufacturing Association, county magistrate of Hancock County, Illinois, and surgeon-in-chief and brevet brigadier-general of the Nauvoo Legion. Joined dissidents against Joseph Smith and was excommunicated in 1844. Assisted in publication of the Nauvoo *Expositor*. Practicing medicine at Canandaigua, Ontario County, New

York, by 1850, and later at Loda, Iroquois County, Illinois, where he died. (Cook, *Revelations*, 257; Iroquois County, Illinois, Register of Deaths, 1878.)

Foster, Solon (1811–1896), farmer; born at Danby, Tompkins County, New York. Joined the Latter-day Saints, 1833. Went to Missouri with Zion's Camp, 1834. Called to first quorum of seventy, 1837. Married Sarah Downing in Nauvoo, 1841. Arrived in Salt Lake Valley, 1850. Called to help colonize St. George, Utah, 1861. Died at Salt Lake City. (Black, "Membership of the Church," 10:917–18.)

Fuller, Amos Botsford (1810–1853), blacksmith; born at Stockholm, St. Lawrence County, New York. Converted to Mormonism in 1836. Migrated to Missouri with Kirtland Camp, 1838. Colonel in the militia of Lee County, Iowa, 1841. Missionary in New England, 1843. Died at Des Moine, Polk County, Iowa. (Black, "Membership of the Church," 17:388–91; Family Group Records Collection.)

Fuller, Elijah (1811–1897), freighter, stockman, farmer, merchant; born at Windham, Greene County, New York. Married Harriet Loomis, 1831. Joined the Latter-day Saints in 1842. Called to go to Las Vegas in 1856. Living in Salt Lake City, Utah, 1850, 1860; Harrisburg, Washington County, Utah, 1863–69, 1884. Died at Leeds, Washington County, Utah. (Black, "Membership of the Church," 17:411–19.)

Fullmer, John Solomon (1807–1883), farmer; born at Huntington, Luzerne County, Pennsylvania. Married Mary Ann Price, 1837. Converted to Mormonism in 1839. Living in Nauvoo, Illinois, 1839–1847. During the exodus of the Mormons from Nauvoo he was one of the trustees appointed to handle Church business and dispose of property for the Saints. Crossed the plains to Utah in 1848. Settled in Davis County. Missionary to England, 1852. Resided at Salt Lake City, Provo, Spanish Fork, and Springville, Utah. Died at Springville. (Family Group Records Collection; Black, "Membership of the Church," 17:515–22.)

Galland, Isaac (1791–1858), merchant, land speculator, doctor; born in Somerset County, Pennsylvania. Married Nancy Harris, 1811. Lived in Ohio and Indiana before moving to Lee County, Iowa, in 1829. Founded the town of Nashville and platted Keokuk. Fought in the Black Hawk War, 1832. Purchased land in the Half-breed Tract in Lee County and sold some 20,000 acres of it to the Latter-day Saints in 1839. Converted and baptized in 1839. Traveled East with Hyrum Smith to collect money for building the Nauvoo House and Temple, 1841. Withdrew from the Church in 1842. Resided in Keokuk, Iowa, 1842–1853; Petaluma, California, 1853–1856, and in 1856 returned to Fort Madison, Iowa, where he died. (Cook, *Revelations*, 258–59; Cook, "Isaac Galland—Mormon Benefactor," *BYU Studies* 19 [Spring 1979]: 261–84.)

Garrett, Henry (1814–?), born at Deerfield, Oneida County, New York.

Gates, Mary (1781–1864), born in the United States and moved to Canada. Married Henry Gates of Burford, 1802. Died at Oakland, Brant, Ontario, Canada. (Family Group Records Collection; Canadian Census: Oakland, Brant, Ontario, 1851; William D. Reid, *The Loyalists in Ontario* (Lambertville, New Jersey: Hunterdon House, 1973), 42–43.)

Gause, Jesse (1784–1836?), born at East Marlborough, Chester County, Pennsylvania. Joined the Society of Friends, 1806. Taught in the Friends' School in Wilmington, Delaware, 1812–1815. Married Martha Johnson in Philadelphia, 1815. After his wife died in 1828 he remarried and joined the United Society of Believers in Christ's Second Appearing ("Shakers"). Moved to the Shaker community at North Union, Cayahoga County, Ohio, in 1831. A short time later he was converted to Mormonism. In March 1832 he was appointed a counselor to Joseph Smith. Traveled to Missouri with Joseph Smith and others in the summer of 1832. After a proselyting mission with Zebedee Coltrin to the Shaker community at North Union in August, he apostatized and was excommunicated. (D. Michael Quinn, "Jesse Gause: Joseph Smith's Little-Known Counselor," *BYU Studies* 23 [Fall 1983]: 487–93.)

Gaylord, John C. (1797–1874), farmer; born in Luzerne County, Pennsylvania. Converted to Mormonism at Niagara, New York, 1835. Appointed a president of the first council of seventy in Kirtland, Ohio, 1837. Excommunicated in 1838 but rejoined the Church two years later in Nauvoo. Married Elvira Edmunds, 1840. Living at Hudson, Walworth County, Wisconsin, in 1850. Joined the Reorganized Church, 1860. Died near Burlington, Wisconsin, where he served as RLDS branch president. (Jenson, *Biographical Encyclopedia*, 1:193; *Times and Seasons* 3 [15 March 1841]: 357; U.S. Census: Hudson, Walworth County, Wisconsin, 1850; *Journal of History*, 7:194.)

Gee, Salmon (1792–1845), born at Lyme, New London County, Connecticut. Married Sarah Watson Crane, 1814. Living in Geauga County, Ohio, when converted to Mormonism in 1832. One of the presidents of the seventy, 1837–1838. Member of the Kirtland high council, 1841–1844. Died at Ambrosia, Lee County, Iowa. (Family Group Records Collection; Jenson, *Biographical Encyclopedia*, 1:192–93.)

Gheen, William Atkins (1798–1845), farmer; born at Downingtown, Chester County, Pennsylvania. Married Esther Ann Pierce, 1823. Soon after his conversion to Mormonism in 1840 he moved to Nauvoo, Illinois, where he purchased a farm and resided until his death. ("Journal History of the Church," 16 July 1845; Black, "Membership of the Church," 18:195.)

547

Gibbs, Elisabeth (no information)

Gibbs, Nancy Miranda (c.1815–1867), born at Benson, Rutland County, Vermont. Married William F. Cahoon at Kirtland, Ohio, 1836. Died in Salt Lake City, Utah. (Black, "Membership of the Church," 18:250–51.)

Gilbert, Algernon Sidney (1789–1834), born at New Haven, Connecticut. Married Elizabeth Van Benthusen, 1823. Merchant at Painesville, Ohio, and later a partner with Newel K. Whitney in the firm Gilbert & Whitney at Kirtland, Ohio. Joined the Latter-day Saints in 1830. Operated a branch of the Gilbert-Whitney store in Independence, Missouri, 1831–33. Among the saints driven from Jackson County, Missouri, 1833. Authored correspondence between Church leaders and Missouri Governor Dunklin during this crisis. Died of cholera during the march of Zion's Camp in 1834. (Cook, *Revelations*, 84; *History of the Church*, 2:118–19.)

Gillett, Truman (1811–?), born at Schyler, Herkimer County, New York. Engaged in missionary work in New York and Iowa, 1840, 1841. With Mormon pioneers crossing Iowa in 1846. (Black, "Membership of the Church," 18:420–21.)

Gould, Dean, son of John Gould, was a non-Mormon member of Zion's Camp in 1834. He was baptized upon his arrival in Missouri. (*History of the Church*, 2:72, 95.)

Gould, John (1808–1851) was born in Ontario, Canada. Baptized in June 1833. Accompanied Joseph Smith to recruit volunteers for Zion's Camp, 1834. Proselyting in New York, 1834–35. Appointed a president in the First Council of Seventy, 1837. Married Abigail Harrington. Died at Cooley's Mill, Pottawatamie County, Iowa. (Cook, *Revelations*, 204; Jenson, *Biographical Encyclopedia*, 1:191.)

Granger, Carlos, (1790–?), born at Suffield, Hartford County, Connecticut. Married Sarah Stiles, 1813. A non-Mormon resident of Nauvoo, Illinois, in the 1840s. Died at Painesville, Ohio. (*Times and Seasons 3* (1 August 1842): 878; James N. Granger, *Launcelot Granger: A Genealogical History* [Hartford: Case, Lockwood & Brainard, 1893], 186.)

Granger, Gilbert (1814–1850), born at Phelps, Ontario County, New York. Son of Oliver Granger. Married Alice Marble in 1838. Went to California in the first days of the gold rush; died at American River. (International Genealogical Index; James N. Granger, *Launcelot Granger*, 402.)

Granger, Oliver (1794–1841), born at Phelps, Ontario County, New York. Married Lydia Dibble, 1818. Sheriff of Ontario County, New York, and colonel in the militia. Converted to Mormonism in the early 1830s. Moved to Kirtland, Ohio, 1833. Proselyting and working on Kirtland Temple, 1833–1836. Appointed to the Kirtland high council, 1837. After moving to Missouri in 1838, he was appointed agent for the Church in Kirtland. After locating at Nauvoo, Illinois, in 1839, he returned as Church agent to Kirtland, where he died. (*History of the Church*, 4:408–9; Cook, *Revelations*, 230.)

Greene, Evan Milbourne (1814–1882), schoolteacher, farmer, stock raiser, merchant; born at Aurelius, Cayuga County, New York. Converted to Mormonism, 1832. Missionary in New England, New York, Ohio, 1833–1835. Married Susan Kent, 1835. Clerk of the elders quorum at Kirtland, Ohio, 1836–1837. Postmaster at Kanesville, Iowa, and recorder and treasurer of Pottawattamie County, 1848–1852. Arrived in Salt Lake City, 1852. Living in Provo, Utah, 4th Ward, 1852–1858. Mayor of Provo, 1852–1856, and postmaster. Member of the Utah territorial legislature. Resided at Grantsville, Tooele County, 1858–1863, Smithfield, Cache County, 1865–1875. Called to colonize Springdale, Washington County, 1873. (Family Group Records Collection; Esshom, *Pioneers and Prominent Men of Utah*, 899; Brooks, *On the Mormon Frontier*, 307; Cook and Backman, *Kirtland Elders Quorum Records*, 85–86; Gordon K. Greene, "Daniel Kent Greene," pp. 1–36, Typescript, BYU Library.)

Greene, John P. (1793–1844), shoemaker. Born in Herkimer County, New York. Married Brigham Young's sister, Rhoda. Living in Mendon, New York, when he joined the Church. Appointed to the Kirtland, Ohio, high council, 1836. Presided over the branch of the Church at New York City, 1839. Elected to the Nauvoo, Illinois, city council, 1841, and became city marshal, 1843. Under his direction as marshal, the Nauvoo *Expositor* was destroyed in June 1844. Among those arrested in the *Expositor* case. Died a short time later at Nauvoo. (Jenson, *Biographical Encyclopedia*, 2:633–36; *History of the Church*, 3:347; 6:124; 7:63, 487ff.)

Grover, Thomas (1807–1886), riverboat captain. Born at Whitehall, Washington County, New York. Married Caroline Whiting, 1828. Converted to Mormonism in 1834. Appointed to Kirtland, Ohio, high council, 1836; Far West, Missouri, high council, 1837; and Nauvoo, Illinois, high council, 1839. Arrived in Salt Lake Valley, 1847; settled at Farmington, Utah. Member of Utah legislature, probate judge of Davis County. Died at Farmington, Davis County, Utah. (Cook, *Revelations*, 259; Jenson, *Biographical Encyclopedia*, 4:137–40.)

Guymon, Thomas (1787–1855), born in Stokes County, North Carolina. Married Sarah Gordon, 1809. Resided in Jackson County, Tennessee, 1816–1823, and Edgar County, Illinois, 1826–1833. Crossed the plains to Utah in 1850 and settled at Springville, Utah County, where he died. (Black, "Membership of the Church," 19:603–6.)

Hancock, Levi Ward (1803–1882), cabinetmaker, born at Springfield, Hampden County, Massachusetts. Joined the Latter-day Saints,

1830. Married Clarissa Reed, 1833. Participant in the march of Zion's Camp, 1834. Appointed a president of the first quorum of seventy, 1835. Moved to Missouri, 1838, and Nauvoo, Illinois, 1839. Member of the Nauvoo Legion. Started West in the exodus of 1846 but joined the Mormon Battalion. Arrived in Salt Lake Valley, 1847. Member of the territorial legislature. Resided at Salt Lake City and Payson and assisted in settlement of Manti and settlements in southern Utah. Was ordained a patriarch in 1872. Died at Washington, Washington County, Utah. (Cook, *Revelations*, 76–77; Jenson, *Biographical Encyclopedia*, 1:188–89.)

Hancock, Solomon (1793–1847), born at Springfield, Hampden County, Massachusetts. Married Alta Adams, 1815. Converted to Mormonism in Ohio in 1830. Moved to Jackson County, Missouri, 1832. Appointed to Missouri high council, 1834. Presided over Yelrome branch in Hancock County, Illinois, 1844. Died in Iowa during exodus from Nauvoo. (Cook, *Revelations*, 77–78.)

Harmer, Elias (1811–1876), born in Chester County, Pennsylvania. Resided at Springville, Utah County, Utah, 1852–1876. (*Deseret News*, 28 July 1876.)

Harris, Emer (1781–1869), carpenter. Born at Cambridge, Washington County, New York. Elder brother of Martin Harris. Married Roxana Peas, 1802. Joined the Latter-day Saints and moved to Kirtland, Ohio, 1831. Proselyting in Susquehanna County, Pennsylvania, with Martin Harris, 1832. Worked on Kirtland and Nauvoo temples. Member of Nauvoo Legion. Migrated to Utah, 1852. Was appointed patriarch, 1853. Presided over high priests at Provo, Utah, 1855. Died at Logan, Cache County, Utah. (Family Group Records Collection; Emer Harris Biographical Sketch, Typescript, BYU Library; Cook, *Revelations*, 154–55; *Deseret Evening News*, 8 December 1869.)

Harris, George Washington (1780–1857), born in Berkshire County, Massachusetts. After the death of his first wife in 1828, he married Lucinda Pendleton Morgan in 1830. In 1834 moved to Terre Haute, Indiana, where he was converted to Mormonism. Moved to Missouri. Appointed to Far West high council, 1838. To Illinois in 1839. Named to the Nauvoo high council, 1839. Elected alderman, 1841. President of Nauvoo Coach and Carriage Manufacturing Association. Started West with the Mormon exodus from Nauvoo, 1846. Bishop at Council Bluffs, Iowa, 1846. Resided at Council Bluffs until his death. (Cook, *Revelations*, 260.)

Harris, Martin (1783–1875), farmer. Born at Easttown, Saratoga County, New York. In 1792 moved to Palmyra, New York, where he became a respected landowner. Assisted Joseph Smith as a scribe during translation of the Book of Mormon; paid printing costs for publication of the book. One of the Three Witnesses to the Book of Mormon. Participant in the march of Zion's Camp to Missouri, 1834. Member of the Kirtland high council. Left the Church in 1837; remained in the East until 1870, when he came to Salt Lake City and was rebaptized. Died at Clarkston, Cache County, Utah. (Cook, *Revelations*, 9; Jenson, *Biographical Encyclopedia*, 1:271–76; Wayne C. Gunnell, "Martin Harris – Witness and Benefactor to the Book of Mormon" [Master's thesis, Brigham Young University, 1955].)

Harris, Preserved (1785–1867), a younger brother of Martin Harris, was born at Palmyra, Wayne County, New York. Married Nancy Warren before 1811. Died at Mentor, Lake County, Ohio. (Family Group Records Collection.)

Haws, Peter (1796–1862), born at Young Township, Leeds County, Ontario, Canada. Converted to Mormonism in Canada. Moved to Illinois, 1839. Appointed to Nauvoo House committee. Member of the Nauvoo Agricultural and Manufacturing Association and the Council of Fifty, and alternate member of the Nauvoo high council. Owned a steam-operated sawmill near Nauvoo. Migrated West with the Saints as far as Council Bluffs, Iowa, 1846. Visited Lyman Wight's colony in Texas in 1848. Excommunicated for apostasy, 1849. Resided successively in Iowa, Nevada, and California, where he died. (Cook, *Revelations*, 260–61.)

Hedlock, Reuben (1801–?), carpenter, builder. Married Susan Wheeler, 1827. Residing at Avon, Livingston County, New York, in 1830. Appointed president of the elders quorum in Kirtland, Ohio, 1837. Moved to Missouri with Kirtland Camp in 1838. Called as a missionary to England in 1840; returned to Nauvoo, Illinois, 1841. Prepared the engravings for the facsimiles in the Book of Abraham, 1842. In 1843 returned to England, where he presided over the mission, 1843–1845. (Early Church Information File; Jenson, *Biographical Encyclopedia*, 4:314; U.S. Census: Avon, Livingston County, New York, 1830; *History of the Church*, 2:526; 4:519, 543.)

Helm, Meredith (1801–1866), physician; born at Williamsport, Maryland. Studied medicine at Baltimore Medical College and practiced medicine in his native town. Married Elizabeth Orendorff, 1824. Moved to Springfield, Sangamon County, Illinois, 1834. Member of the Springfield board of health, 1843. Became the second Grand Master of the Grand Lodge of Illinois freemasonry, 1842. Instrumental in establishment of the Helm and Nye lodges in Nauvoo, 1842. Resigned from masonry in July 1844. Died at Springfield. (*History of the Early Settlers of Sangamon County* [Springfield, 1876], 367–68; Mervin B. Hogan, "Mormon Interfaces with Masonry in Illinois and Iowa Between 1841 and 1844," Typescript.)

Herriman, Henry (1804–1891), shoemaker, farmer; born at Bradford, Essex County, Massachusetts. Married Clarissa Boynton, 1827.

Converted to Mormonism in 1832. Moved to Kirtland, Ohio, in 1834 and participated in the march of Zion's Camp. Appointed a president of the first quorum of seventy, 1838. In Nauvoo he was a captain, and later lieutenant colonel, in the Nauvoo Legion. Migrated to Utah during the Mormon exodus, 1846–1848. One of the founders of Herriman, Utah. Missionary in England, 1857–1858. Colonizing mission to southern Utah, 1862. Later resided at Huntington, Emery County. (Cook, *Revelations*, 261; U.S. Census: Salt Lake City, Utah, 1850, 1860.)

Herritt, John (?-1840), member of the second quorum of seventy in Kirtland. Died while on a proselyting mission to the Fox Islands in Maine. (Black, "Membership of the Church," 22:452.)

Hibbard, Davidson (1786–1852), farmer, cabinetmaker, stonemason; born in New Hampshire. Married Sarah Tilton in Maine in 1816. One of the first settlers of the Commerce/Nauvoo, Hancock County area of Illinois about 1829. Portions of his farm were surveyed and added to Nauvoo City in 1841 and 1842. Co-proprietor of the Davis Hotel at Water and Commerce Streets. Hancock County coroner, 1834–1836. Died at Nauvoo. (Thomas Gregg, *History of Hancock County, Illinois* [Chicago: Chas. C. Chapman & Company, 1880], 221–22; *History of Hancock County, Illinois* [Hancock County, 1968], 126, 441, 624; David E. and Della S. Miller, *Nauvoo: the City of Joseph* [Santa Barbara and Salt Lake City: Peregrine Smith, Inc., 1974], 38.)

Higbee, Chauncey Lawson (1821–1884), legislator, jurist; born at Tate, Clermont County, Ohio, where he was also educated. Living at Nauvoo, Hancock County, Illinois, during his Mormon years. He was accused of immorality at Nauvoo, joined with opponents of Joseph Smith, and was excommunicated. He later continued the study of law and was admitted to the bar in Pittsfield, Pike County. Married Julia M. White, 1854. Elected to the Illinois general assembly, 1854, and in 1858 to the state senate. In 1861, while serving in the senate, he was elected circuit judge and continued as such until his death. Appointed in 1877 a member of the appellate court. President of First National Bank. Died at Pittsfield. (*History of the Church*, 6:407, 464; 7:57, 146; Charles J. Scofield, *History of Hancock County*, [Chicago: Munsell Publishing Company, 1921], 750–51; Melville D. Massie, *Past and Present of Pike County* [Chicago, 1906], 149–50; *Nauvoo Neighbor*, 29 May 1844.)

Higbee, Elias (1795–1843), born at Galloway, Gloucester County, New Jersey. Married Elizabeth Ward, 1818. Baptized, 1832. Among Saints driven from Jackson County, Missouri, 1833. Worked on Kirtland Temple, 1835. Member of Clay County, Missouri, high council, 1836; Far West, Missouri, high council, 1837. Church Recorder, 1838–1843. Member of the Nauvoo Temple Committee. Traveled to Washington, D.C., with Joseph Smith in 1839 to seek redress for Missouri grievances.

Died of cholera in Hancock County, Illinois. (Cook, *Revelations*, 225; Jenson, *Biographical Encyclopedia*, 1:253.)

Higbee, Francis Marion (1820–?), merchant; born at Tate, Clermont County, Ohio. With the Latter-day Saints in Missouri in 1838 and was among those arraigned at the hearing in Richmond, Ray County. Migrated to Nauvoo, Illinois, where he was elected a colonel in the Nauvoo Legion, 1841. Allied with dissenters against Joseph Smith and was excommunicated, 1844. Residing in Hancock County, Illinois, in 1850. Died in New York. (*History of the Church*, 3:209; 4:353; 6:398; 7:57; Family Group Records Collection; U.S. Census: Montebello, Hancock County, Illinois, 1850; *Autobiography of Andrew Jenson* [Salt Lake City: Deseret News Press, 1938], 178.)

Hill, Isaac (1806–1879), blacksmith, brick maker; born near Brighton, Beaver County, Pennsylvania. Married Mary Bell, 1827. Converted to Mormonism, 1833. Participated in march of Zion's Camp to Missouri, 1834. With Latter-day Saints in Missouri and Illinois. Migrated to Utah, 1850. Bishop of Salt Lake City 2nd Ward, 1854–1864. Missionary to Canada, 1857–1858. Moved to Bear Lake, 1864. Died at Fish Haven, Bear Lake County, Idaho. (Family Group Records Collection; *History of the Church*, 2:149; Jenson, *Biographical Encyclopedia*, 4:509; Journal of Isaac Hill, MS., LDS Church Archives.)

Hillman, Mayhew (1793–1839), born at Chilmark, Dukes County, Massachusetts. Living in Washington and Onandaga Counties, New York, 1818–1831. Married Sarah King about 1818. Converted to Mormonism in 1832. Member of the Missouri high council, 1838. Died at Nauvoo, Illinois. (Family Group Records Collection; Black, "Membership of the Church," 23:115.)

Hinkle, George M. (1802–1861), merchant; born in Kentucky. Appointed to the Missouri high council in January 1836 to replace Orson Pratt. During the Missouri conflict in 1838, he commanded the Mormon militia defending Far West, Caldwell County. Under the guise of a truce, he surrendered Church leaders to opposing forces, which resulted in the imprisonment of Joseph Smith and others. Hinkle testified for the state against his former associates at the November 1838 hearing in Richmond, Ray County. Excommunicated in 1839. In later years he practiced medicine, kept a drugstore, and farmed. He died in Iowa. (*History of the Church*, 2:357; 3:188–89, 196–98, 210, 284; Pratt, *Autobiography*, 186; S.J. Hinkle, "A Biographical Sketch of G.M. Hinkle;" *Document Containing the Correspondence*, 125–29.)

Hitchcock, Jesse (1801–c.1846), born in Ash County, North Carolina. Member of the Missouri high council, 1836–1837. Appointed acting scribe for Joseph Smith during illness of Warren Parrish in 1836. Called on mission in Illinois to disabuse public mind over arrest of the Prophet in 1843. Died at Mt. Pisgah, Iowa, while crossing the plains.

(*History of the Church*, 2:482; 5:485; Black, "Membership of the Church," 23:236; Susan W. Easton, "Inscriptions Found on Tombstones and Monuments in Early Latter-day Saint Burial Grounds," p. 11, Typescript, BYU Library.)

Holbrook, Joseph (1806–1885), farmer, carpenter, judge; born at Florence, Oneida County, New York. Converted to Mormonism in Genessee County, New York, 1833. A member of Zion's Camp, 1834. Wounded at the battle at Crooked River in 1838. Commissioned a captain in the Illinois state militia in 1841. Appointed to the Nauvoo, Hancock County, police, 1845. Left Nauvoo with the Latter-day Saints in 1846 and arrived in Salt Lake Valley in 1848. In 1850 moved to Bountiful, Davis County, where he lived until his death. He served as Davis County Judge, was elected to the Utah territorial legislature, and was a bishop's counselor. He built the first schoolhouse in Bountiful. (*Deseret News*, 17 November 1885.)

Hollister, David Sprague (1808–1858), born at Middleburg, Schoharie County, New York. Moved to Newark, Ohio, about 1829. Married Mary Ann Wilson, 1831. In Milwaukee, Wisconsin, 1836–1842. Moved to Quincy, Illinois, 1842. Engaged in steamboat business; captain of a boat that ran between Nauvoo, Illinois, and New Orleans. Member of the Council of Fifty, 1844. (Lafayette W. Case, *The Hollister Family of America* [Chicago, 1886], 421, 611.)

Hollister, John (1792–1839), born at Marbletown, Kingston County, New York. Married Lavina Clearwater, 1817. Living in Caroline, Tompkins County, New York, 1818–1835. Evidently moved to Portage County, Ohio, investigated Mormonism, joined the Church, then moved to Illinois, where he died before 1840. A daughter, Sarah Ann, is listed in the Nauvoo temple records in 1846. (Family Group Records Collection; U.S. Census: Tompkins County, New York, 1830.)

Holman, J. (no information)

Holmes, Erastus (1801–1863), was born in Pennsylvania. Settled at Newberry (later Mulberry), Clermont County, Ohio. After visiting Joseph Smith and expressing interest in the Church in 1835, Holmes apparently did not join the Latter-day Saints. He was postmaster of Mulberry, 1839–1847, and also a merchant in the town. In 1850 he was living in Cincinatti. Died at Milford, Clermont County. (US Census: Clermont County, Ohio, 1830, 1840; Hamilton County, 1850; *History of Clermont County, Ohio* [Philadelphia: Lewis H. Everts, 1880], 465, 469; Whitt, *Clermont County, Ohio, Wills, Estates, and Guardianships, 1800–1851* [New Richmond, Ohio: A.M. Whitt, 1986], 3:144; Daughters of the American Revolution, "Monument Inscriptions Prior to 1900 From Cemeteries in Clermont County, Ohio," Milford I.O.O.F. Cemetery.)

Holmes, Milton (1811–1863), shoemaker; born at Rowley, Essex

County, Massachusetts. Married Aphia Woodman. Living at Napoli, Cattaraugus County, New York, in 1830. Proselyting mission to Canada with Lyman Johnson in February 1834. Participated in the march of Zion's Camp to Missouri, 1834. Member of the second quorum of seventy. Missionary in England, 1840–1841, 1844–1845. Lived remainder of his life in Franklin County, Maine. (*History of the Church*, 2:35; Black, "Membership of the Church," 23:673–74; U.S. Census: Franklin County, Maine, 1850.)

Howe, Harriet, joined the Latter-day Saints in Painesville, Ohio, before 1834. Sister of Eber D. Howe, publisher of the Painesville *Telegraph*. Helped make clothing for workmen, and the veil for the Kirtland Temple. ("Journal History of the Church," 22 October 1867; Journal of Joseph Smith, 30 April 1834.)

Howe, Sophia Hull (1800–1866), born in New York. Wife of Eber D. Howe, Painesville, Lake County, Ohio publisher. Joined the Latter-day Saints before 1834. Donated freely to the Church. Resided in Painesville until her death. (U.S. Census: Painesville, Lake County, Ohio, 1850; Harriet Taylor Upton, *History of the Western Reserve*, 967.)

Hubbard, Elisha C. (no information)

Humphery, Solomon (1775–1834), born at Canton, Hartford County, Connecticut. Married Ursula Andrews. Converted to Mormonism, 1831. Proselyting in eastern states, 1831–1832. Participated in march of Zion's Camp to Missouri, 1834. Died in Clay County, Missouri. (Jenson, *Biographical Encyclopedia*, 4:689–90; Cook, *Revelations*, 78.)

Hunt, Jefferson (1804–1879), farmer, colonizer, scout; born at Edwards, Logan County, Kentucky. Married Celia Mounts, 1823. Converted to Mormonism in 1834. Moved with the saints to Missouri and Illinois. Major in the Nauvoo Legion. Captain in the Mormon Battalion during the Mexican War. Arrived in Salt Lake Valley, 1847. Assisted in the founding of Provo, Utah, 1850, and San Bernardino, California, 1851. Returned to Davis County, Utah, in 1857. Died at Oxford, Bannock County, Idaho. (Jenson, *Biographical Encyclopedia*, 4:747; Black, "Membership of the Church," 24:617–22.)

Hunter, Edward (1793–1883), merchant, farmer; born at Newtown, Delaware County, Pennsylvania. Engaged in mercantile business near Philadelphia, 1816–1822. Served in the cavalry seven years, and three years as Delaware County commissioner. Married Ann Standley, 1830. Converted to Mormonism in 1840. Bishop of Nauvoo 5th Ward, 1844–1846. Migrated to Utah, 1846–1847. Bishop of Salt Lake City 13th Ward, 1849–1854, and presiding bishop of the Church, 1851–1883. Died at Salt Lake City. (*Our Pioneer Heritage* 6:317–26; William G. Hartley, "Edward Hunter: Pioneer Presiding Bishop," in *Supporting Saints: Life Stories of Nineteenth-Century Mormons*, edited by Donald

Q. Cannon and David J. Whittaker [Provo, Utah: Brigham Young University, 1985], 275–304.)

Hunter, Thomas J. (no information)

Huntington, Dimick Baker (1808–1879), shoemaker, constable, Indian interpreter, blacksmith; born at Watertown, Jefferson County, New York. Married Fannie Maria Allen, 1830. Converted to Mormonism, 1835. Constable at Far West, Missouri. Coroner and constable at Nauvoo, Illinois. Among those arrested for destruction of the Nauvoo *Expositor*, 1844. Enlisted with the Mormon Battalion in the Mexican War. Arrived in Salt Lake Valley in 1847. Helped establish settlements in Utah and Sanpete counties. Accompanied Parley Pratt on exploring expedition to southern Utah, 1850. Participated in Indian fights at Battle Creek and Provo; served as interpreter among Great Basin Indians. Died in Salt Lake City. (Orson F. Whitney, *History of Utah* [Salt Lake City, 1904], 4:209–11.)

Hurlbut, Doctor Philastus (1809–1883), United Brethren minister, farmer; born in Chittenden County, Vermont. Attended school in Penn Yan, Yates County, New York. Converted to Mormonism in 1833 but after a few months was excommunicated for immorality. Employed by a Kirtland, Ohio, anti-Mormon committee to collect information disparaging to Joseph Smith and the Church. His findings were published in E. D. Howe's *Mormonism Unvailed* in 1834. Indicted in 1834 for threatening Joseph Smith's life. Married Maria Woodbury, 1834. After residing in Pennsylvania, Ohio, and Michigan, he finally settled in Madison, Sandusky County, Ohio, where he remained until his death. (U.S. Census: Madison, Sandusky County, Ohio, 1850–1880; Statement of Maria Hurlbut, 15 April 1885, MS. Chicago Historical Society.)

Hyde, Heman (1788–1869), farmer; born at Stratford, Orange County, Vermont. Married Polly Wyman Tilton, 1810. Veteran of the War of 1812. Converted to Mormonism in 1834 at Freedom, Cattaraugus County, New York. Moved to Ohio, and accompanied Zion's Camp to Missouri, 1834. Resided with the Saints in Nauvoo, Illinois. In 1846 traveled with the Mormon exodus to Council Bluffs, Iowa, where he served as a member of the high council until he left for the Salt Lake Valley in 1848. Residing in the Salt Lake City 13th Ward at the time of his death. ("Journal History of the Church," 11 June 1869; Black, "Membership of the Church," 24:935–38.)

Hyde, Marinda Nancy Johnson (1815–1886), born at Pomfret, Windsor County, Vermont. Daughter of John Johnson. Moved with her family to Hiram, Ohio, in 1818. Converted to Mormonism in 1832. Married Orson Hyde, 1834. With the Latter-day Saints in Missouri and Illinois. After leaving Nauvoo with the Mormon exodus, she resided at Council Bluffs, Iowa, until 1852, while her husband was engaged in Church business. Continued to Salt Lake Valley in 1852 and settled in the 17th Ward. President of the ward Relief Society there from 1868 until her death. (*Deseret News*, 24 March 1886; *Woman's Exponent*, 1 April 1886; Edward W. Tullidge, *The Women of Mormondom* [New York, 1877], 403–6.)

Hyde, Orson (1805–1878), clerk, school teacher, businessman, lawyer; born at Oxford, New Haven County, Connecticut. Converted by Sidney Rigdon, 1831. Baptized sixty during proselyting mission with Samuel Smith in eastern states, 1832. Appointed clerk to First Presidency, 1833. Participant in Zion's Camp, 1834. Married Marinda Nancy Johnson, 1834. Member of the Council of Twelve, 1835–1878. Sided with dissenters against the Church in 1838 but was readmitted in 1839. Mission to England, 1837–1838, 1846–1847; Palestine, 1841–1842. Member of the Nauvoo city council, 1841. Presided over the Saints at Winter Quarters, Nebraska, 1847–1850, where he also published the *Frontier Guardian*. To Utah in 1852. Appointed associate judge of the supreme court for Utah; member of territorial legislature; president of the senate. He died at Spring City, Sanpete County, Utah. (Cook, *Revelations*, 109–10; Jenson, *Biographical Encyclopedia*, 1:80–82; Marvin S. Hill, "Historical Study of the Life of Orson Hyde, Early Mormon Missionary and Apostle from 1805–1852," [Master's thesis: Brigham Young University, 1955].)

Ivins, Charles (1799–1875), farmer, hotel keeper; born Cream Ridge, Monmouth County, New Jersey. Married Elizabeth Lippencott Shinn, 1823. Family converted to Mormonism following the preaching of Benjamin Winchester and Samuel James, first missionaries to New Jersey. Moved to Nauvoo, Illinois, in 1841 and three years later to Keokuk, Iowa, where he became the proprietor of the Ivins House and an alderman of the town. Joined dissenters against Joseph Smith in 1844 and became bishop of opposition church established by William Law. Excommunicated in May 1844. Associated with those who published the Nauvoo *Expositor*. Reported to have been in the mob that killed Joseph Smith. Died at Keokuk. (U.S. Census: Keokuk, Lee County, Iowa, 1850; *History of the Church*, 6:347, 354, 398; Oakland Cemetery Register, Keokuk, Lee County, Iowa, p. 2, Typescript, LDS Family History Library; Virginia W. Ivins, *Pen Pictures of Early Western Days* [Keokuk?, 1905], 101.)

Ivins, James (1797–1877), brother of Charles Ivins, born at Cream Ridge, Monmouth County, New Jersey. Married Mary Conover. His family was converted to Mormonism in the wake of the preaching of Benjamin Winchester and Samuel James, first missionaries to New Jersey. Resided in the Nauvoo, Illinois 4th Ward. (Family Group Records Collection; Nauvoo, Illinois Census, 1842; Kimball S. Erdman, *Israel Ivins, A Biography* [n.p., 1969], 1–9.)

Jackman, Levi (1797–1876), carpenter. Born at Vershire, Orange

County, Vermont. Married Angeline Myers Brady. Living in Portage County, Ohio, when he joined the Church, 1831. Settled in Jackson County, Missouri, 1832. Appointed to Missouri high council, 1834; Far West high council, 1837; and the Salt Lake City high council, 1848. Returned to Kirtland from Missouri in July 1835 and worked on the temple. Arrived in Salt Lake Valley with Mormon pioneers, 1847. Counselor in Salt Lake City 16th Ward bishopric. Died at Salem, Utah County, Utah. (Jenson, *Biographical Encyclopedia*, 2:769–70; *History of the Church*, 2:124, 524; 7:629; *Deseret Evening News*, 26 July 1876.)

Jackson, Henry, husband of Sarah Jackson. Church member living in Missouri in the 1830s.

Jackson, Sarah (1815–?), born in Kentucky. Living in Kaw Township, Jackson County, Missouri, in 1850. Her first husband, Henry Jackson, had apparently died or they had separated before 1850, as she was living alone at the time. Married James Liptrap in 1853 and resided in Kansas City. (U.S. Census: Kaw, Jackson County, Missouri, 1850; Kansas City, Missouri, 1860.)

Jackson, Truman (c.1801–?), farmer; born in New York. Living at Verona, Oneida County, New York, in 1830–1850. Evidently joined the Latter-day Saints in Ohio but did not follow the Church West. Member of elders quorum in Kirtland, 1836; and seventies quorum, 1837. Married Ann Brown, 1837. (U.S. Census: Oneida County, New York, 1830–1850; *History of the Church*, 2:400; *Messenger and Advocate*, 3:676.)

Jacobs, Henry Bailey (1817–1886), born at Manchester, Niagara County, New York. Converted to Mormonism in 1833. In 1838 he moved to Missouri and served as justice of the peace in Richmond, Ray County. Married Zina Diantha Huntington in Nauvoo, Illinois, 1841. En route to Utah from Nauvoo in 1846, he was called on a proselyting mission to England with his brother-in-law, Oliver B. Huntington. Arriving in Winter Quarters in 1847, both men were excommunicated for bringing plural wives with them but were later rebaptized. Continued on to Utah in 1848. In 1851 he was disfellowshipped and later excommunicated. Moved to California, remaining there until 1880, when he returned to Salt Lake City, where he died. (Family Group Records Collection; Brooks, *On The Mormon Frontier*, 141–42.)

James, Samuel (1814–1876), Bible agent; born in Pennsylvania. After his conversion, appointed to the Kirtland, Ohio, high council, 1836. Married Marian Evans, 1841. Extensive proselyting in eastern states, 1835–1844. He followed Sidney Rigdon after death of Joseph Smith. At a conference in Pittsburgh, Pennsylvania, in April 1845, Rigdon appointed James one of his counselors. Residing in Jefferson County, Ohio, 1850–1870. Died at Steubenville, Jefferson County. (*History of the Church*, 2:366; 5:386; *The History of the Reorganized Church of Jesus*

Christ of Latter Day Saints [Independence, Missouri: Herald House, 1967], 3:8; U.S. Census: Jefferson County, Ohio, 1850, 1860, 1870.)

Jennings, Ebenezer (no information)

Johnson, Ezekiel (1776–1848), farmer, carpenter; born at Uxbridge, Worcester County, Massachusetts. Father of Joseph E. Johnson and Benjamin F. Married Julia Hills, 1801. Living at Pomfret, Chautauqua County, New York, by 1814. Opposed the conversion of his family to Mormonism but moved to Kirtland, Ohio, with them in 1833. Embittered over his family's conversion, he separated from his wife. Died at Nauvoo, Illinois. (Family Group Records Collection; Milas E. Johnson and Rolla V. Johnson, "The Johnson Pioneers of the West," 2:87–94, Typescript, BYU Library.)

Johnson, John (1779–1843), farmer; born at Chesterfield, Cheshire County, New Hampshire. Married Mary Elsa Jacobs, 1800. Settled at Hiram, Ohio in 1818 and joined the Latter-day Saints in 1831. Joseph Smith resided at the Johnson home in Hiram during work on Bible revision. Johnson moved to Kirtland, Ohio, 1832. Member of the Kirtland high council, 1834–1837. Became disaffected and withdrew from the Church, 1838. Died at Kirtland, Ohio. (Cook, *Revelations*, 199; *The Deseret Weekly*, 26 May 1858; Keith Perkins, "A House Divided: The John Johnson Family," *Ensign* 9 [1979]: 54–59.

Johnson, Joseph Ellis (1817–1882), schoolteacher, merchant, farmer, postmaster, editor, horticulturist; born at Pomfret, Chautauqua County, New York. Son of Ezekiel Johnson, brother of Benjamin F. Converted to Mormonism in 1833. Married Harriet Ellen Snider, 1840. To Illinois, 1839. Postmaster and schoolteacher at Ramus, Hancock County, 1840. Left Nauvoo with the Mormon exodus of 1846. Remained in Kanesville, Iowa, eleven years, where he was proprietor of a general store, postmaster, and newspaper editor. Moved on to Salt Lake City, 1860, to St. George, Utah, 1865, and to Arizona in 1882. Died at Tempe, Maricopa County, Arizona. (Milas E. Johnson and Rolla V. Johnson, "The Johnson Pioneers of the West," 2:87–94.)

Johnson, Luke (1807–1861), farmer, teacher, doctor; son of John Johnson. Born at Pomfret, Windsor County, Vermont. Living in Hiram, Ohio, when converted in 1831. Proselyting in Pennsylvania, Virginia, and Kentucky, 1831–1833. Married Susan Poteet, 1833. Accompanied Zion's Camp to Missouri, 1834. Member of Quorum of Twelve, 1835–1837. Left the Church in 1838. Rebaptized in 1846. Arrived in Salt Lake Valley with Mormon pioneers, 1847. Appointed bishop in St. John, Tooele County, Utah. Died at Salt Lake City. (Cook, *Revelations*, 110–11; Jenson, *Biographical Encyclopedia*, 1:85–86.)

Johnson, Lyman Eugene (1811–1856), merchant, lawyer; son of John Johnson. Born at Pomfret, Windsor County, Vermont. Baptized in 1831. Missionary with Orson Pratt to the eastern states, New England,

and Canada, 1832–1833. Married Sarah Lang. One of eight men named in an 1834 revelation to solicit funds and volunteers to assist the Saints driven from Jackson County. Accompanied Zion's Camp, 1834. Member of the Council of Twelve, 1835–1838. Left the Church, 1838. Living in Iowa, 1842. Drowned in the Mississippi River at Prairie du Chien, Wisconsin. (Cook, *Revelations*, 111; Jenson, *Biographical Encyclopedia*, 1:91–92.)

Johnson, Orson (1803/4–1883), innkeeper, farmer; born at Bath, Grafton County, New Hampshire, where he was living in 1830. Converted to Mormonism in 1832. Participated in the march of Zion's Camp, 1834. Member of the Kirtland high council in 1834. Left the Church in 1837. Living at Peoria, Illinois, 1840, 1850; and in 1880 at Altona, Knox County, Illinois, where he died. (*History of the Church*, 2:151; U.S. Census: Peoria County, Illinois, 1840, 1850; Knox County, 1880; "Journal History of the Church," 3 February 1832.)

Johnson, Susan Ellen (1814–1836), born at Pomfret, Chautauqua County, New York. Converted to Mormonism in 1833 and moved to Kirtland, Ohio, with other members of her family. Taught school and did hand work to help build the temple. Died of consumption at Kirtland. (Johnson and Johnson, "The Johnson Pioneers of the West," 2:86.)

Jonas, Abraham (1801–1864), merchant, lawyer; born at Exeter, Devonshire, England. Migrated to America in 1819. Resided in Ohio and then Kentucky, where he served in the state legislature, 1828–1830, 1833. He was grand master of the grand lodge of Kentucky masons, 1833. Moved to Illinois; served in the legislature, and one term as master in chancery. He became the first grand master of Illinois and was instrumental in establishing the Nauvoo Lodge in 1841. Admitted to the Illinois bar in 1844 and practiced law until his death. Served as postmaster of Quincy. A friend of Abraham Lincoln. Chairman of the arrangements committee for the Lincoln-Douglas debate in Quincy. One son served the Union and three others the Confederacy during the Civil War. (Harry Smirnoff, *Jewish Notables in America, 1776–1865* [New York: Greenberg, Publisher, 1956], 348–52; Mervin Hogan, "The Involvement of Freemasonry with Mormonism on the American Midwestern Frontier," Typescript, 1982.)

Jones, Josiah (178?–?), resident of Kirtland, Ohio. Appointed town clerk when Kirtland township was first organized in 1817. Taught school, 1819–1820. (U.S. Census: Kirtland, Geauga, Ohio, 1820, 1830; *History of Geauga and Lake Counties, Ohio* [Philadelphia: Williams Brothers, 1878], 246, 247.)

Kearnes, Hamilton Henry (1817–1893), farmer, blacksmith, wheelwright, millwright; born in Brown County, Ohio. Married Charlotte White, 1840. Resided for a time in Iowa, where his father was a trapper. Emigrated to Utah in 1850 and settled at Springville, Utah

County. Helped build the iron works at Cedar City, Utah. Returned to Springville in 1857, where he served as captain of the police. In 1860 moved to Gunnison, Sanpete County, Utah, where he was appointed bishop. Died at Gunnison. (International Genealogical Index; Emma M. Guymon Kearnes Autobiography, Typescript, LDS Church Archives; Jenson, *Biographical Encyclopedia*, 2:555.)

Keeler, Joseph (1787–1868), born at Ridgefield, Fairfield County, Connecticut. Married Olive Brite, 1811. Joined the Latter-day Saints and lived in Kirtland, Ohio, for a time but evidently left the Church around 1835. Living in Valparaiso, Porter County, Indiana, in 1850. Died in Marshall County, Iowa. (U.S. Census: Centre, Porter, Indiana, 1850; *Counties of Porter and Lake, Indiana* [Chicago: F.A. Battey & Company, Publishers, 1882], 285; James Broughton, comp., *A Genealogy of the Families of John Rockwell, of Stamford, Conn., 1641 and Ralph Keeler of Hartford, Conn., 1639* [New York, 1903], 70.)

Kilbourne, David W. (1803–1876), lawyer, land speculator, railroad executive; born at Marlboro, Hartford County, Connecticut. Married Harriet Rice in Albany, New York, 1827. Became a commission merchant in New York City, but a disastrous fire ruined his business. Moved west in 1836, dividing his time between Peoria, Illinois, and Fort Des Moines, Iowa. Represented the New York Land Company, engaged in the purchase and settlement of land in the Half-breed Tract in Iowa. When Fort Des Moines was abandoned in 1837, he platted the town of Montrose, established a general store, and became postmaster. Moved to Fort Madison, Iowa, 1843. Admitted to the Iowa bar, 1848. Moved to Keokuk, Iowa, in 1852 and became mayor of the town in 1855. Helped found the Des Moines Valley Railroad in 1854 and became the company's financial agent in 1857 and president in 1868. He resigned in 1873 and died in New York City. (U.S. Census: Fort Madison, Lee, Iowa, 1850; *Annals of Iowa* 15 [April 1926]: 310–13; Warren A. Jennings, "Two Iowa Postmasters View Nauvoo: Anti-Mormon Letters to the Governor of Missouri," *BYU Studies* 11 [Spring 1971]: 275–81.)

Kilbourne, Edward (1813–1878), land speculator; born at Marlboro, Hartford County, Connecticut. Brother of David W. Kilbourne. With his brother, opened the first general store in Montrose, Lee County, Iowa, 1839. Living at Keokuk, Iowa, by 1850, where his land holdings were valued at $35,000. Co-founder of the Keokuk Gas-light and Coke Company, 1855. Died at Keokuk. (U.S. Census: Keokuk, Lee, Iowa, 1850; *The History of Lee County, Iowa* [Chicago: Western Historical Company, 1879], 634, 675.)

Kimball, Heber Chase (1801–1868), blacksmith, potter; born at Sheldon, Franklin County, Vermont. Married Vilate Murray, 1822. Converted to Mormonism, 1832, at Mendon, New York. Participant in march of Zion's Camp, 1834. Member of the Council of the Twelve,

1835–1847. Missionary to England, 1837–1838, 1839–1841. Elected to Nauvoo city council, 1841. Arrived in Salt Lake Valley with Mormon pioneers, 1847. Counselor to Brigham Young in the First Presidency, 1847–1868. Died at Salt Lake City. (Cook, *Revelations*, 263–64; Jenson, *Biographical Encyclopedia*, 1:34–37. Stanley B. Kimball, *Heber C. Kimball: Mormon Patriarch and Pioneer* [Urbana, Illinois: University of Illinois Press, 1981].)

Kimball, Hiram S. (1806–1863), merchant; born at West Fairlee, Orange County, Vermont. Cousin of Heber C. Kimball. Residing at Commerce, Hancock County, Illinois, before the arrival of the Latter-day Saints in 1839. Married Sarah Melissa Granger at Kirtland, Ohio, in 1840 but settled at Nauvoo, Illinois, where he was a well-to-do land owner and merchant. Elected alderman at Nauvoo, 1841, and was associate justice of the municipal court. Converted to Mormonism in 1843. Helped defend Nauvoo against mob attack in 1846. Arrived in Salt Lake Valley, 1852. Called to help settle Las Vegas, 1856. Awarded contract to deliver mail between Salt Lake City and Independence, Missouri, 1856, but the contract was canceled before the dispatch of Johnston's Army to Utah in 1857. Called on a mission to the Sandwich Islands in 1863 but was killed when the ship's boiler exploded en route. (Jenson, *Biographical Encyclopedia*, 2:372–73; Jill M. Derr, "The Liberal Shall be Blessed," *Utah Historical Quarterly* 44 [Summer 1976]: 205–22; "Journal History of the Church," 4 October 1841, 1 July 1843, 11 September 1846, 23 October 1856, 24–26 July 1857.)

King, Austin Augustus (1801–1870), governor of Missouri, 1848–1852. Born in Sullivan County, Tennessee. Moved to Missouri in 1830, where he practiced law at Columbia. Elected to the state legislature. In 1837, upon his appointment to a circuit judgeship by Governor Lilburn Boggs, he moved to Richmond, Ray County. Between 1837 and 1848 he served as judge of Missouri's fifth judicial circuit, consisting of the counties of Clinton, Ray, Caldwell, Clay, Platte, and Buchanan. In November 1838 he presided at the preliminary hearing of Joseph Smith and other Mormons at Richmond. Represented Missouri as a Union Democrat in the U.S. Congress, 1862–1864. Had a successful law practice in St. Louis before his death. (*History of Ray County, Missouri*, 259–61; Howard Conard, *Encyclopedia of the History of Missouri* [St. Louis: The Southern History Company, 1901], 3:537; Dumas Malone, *Dictionary of American Biography*, 10:382.)

King, Thomas C. (1810–1854), merchant; born in Virginia. Living in Quincy, Adams County, Illinois, by 1835. Elected Adams County constable, 1835, and coroner, 1836. Served on the Quincy fire department and was junior warden in Bodley Lodge No. 1 of freemasons. Died at Quincy. (U.S. Census: Quincy, Adams, Illinois, 1840, 1850; John C. Reynolds, *History of Masonry in Illinois* [Springfield, 1869], 140, 174;

History of Adams County [Chicago: Murray, Williamson & Phelps, 1879], 420, 422, 476; Adams County, Illinois Probate Records, 1854.)

Kingsbury, Horace (1798–1853), jeweler, silversmith; born in New Hampshire. Married Diantha Stiles, 1826. In 1827 moved to Painesville, Ohio, where he died. Mayor of Painesville, 1848. (U.S. Census: Lake County, Ohio, 1850; Joseph A. Kingsbury, *A Pendulous Edition of Kingsbury Genealogy* [Pittsburgh: Murdoch-Kerr Press, 1901], 230; Benjamin W. Dwight, *History of the Descendants of Elder John Strong* [Albany: Joel Munsell, 1871], 1,039; *History of Geauga and Lake Counties, Ohio* [Philadelphia: Williams Brothers, 1878], 214.)

Kingsbury, Joseph (1812–1898), born at Enfield, Hartford County, Connecticut. Converted to Mormonism in Kirtland, Ohio, 1832. Married Caroline Whitney, daughter of Newell K. Whitney, 1836. Clerk in Newel K. Whitney store at Kirtland. Appointed to the Kirtland high council, 1835, and Iowa high council, 1841. Among Saints expelled from Missouri, 1838. Clerk in Joseph Smith's Nauvoo store. Arrived in Salt Lake Valley, 1847. Bishop of Salt Lake City 2nd Ward, 1851–1852. Appointed superintendent of the Church Tithing Office, 1867. Was ordained a patriarch, 1883. Died at Salt Lake City. (Edward Tullidge, *History of Salt Lake City* [Salt Lake City: Star Printing Company, 1886], 121–23; Whitney, *History of Utah*, 4:114–15; Lyndon W. Cook, *Joseph C. Kingsbury: A Biography* [Provo, Utah: Grandin Book Company, 1985].)

Knight, Joseph, Sr. (1772–1847), born at Oakham, Worcester County, Massachusetts. Married Polly Peck about 1795. Moved to Bainbridge, Chenango County, New York, in 1808 and two years later to Colesville, Broome County, New York, where he resided nineteen years. Owned a farm, gristmill, and carding machines, and, according to his son, "was not rich, yet possessed enough of this world's goods to secure himself and family the necessities and comforts of life." When Joseph Smith obtained the Book of Mormon plates in 1827, Knight was visiting the Smith home in Manchester, New York, and Joseph Smith used Knight's horse and buggy as a means of conveyance on that occasion. Among the first converts to Mormonism, his family formed the nucleus of a small branch of the Church at Colesville. Helped pioneer the Mormon settlement at Independence, Missouri, in 1831. Died at Mt. Pisgah, Iowa, during the Mormon exodus from Illinois. (Journal of Newel Knight, 1, MS., LDS Church Archives; *History of the Church*, 1:47; Cook, *Revelations*, 20–22; Hartley, *"They Are My Friends": A History of the Joseph Knight Family, 1825–1850* [Provo, Utah: Grandin Book Company, 1986], passim.)

Knight, Joseph, Jr. (1808–1866), miller, farmer, wheelwright; youngest son of Joseph Knight, Sr. Born at Halifax, Windham County, Vermont. Family moved to Chenango County, New York, the year he was born. Worked with Joseph Smith on his father's farm in Broome

County, New York. In 1829 transported Joseph and Oliver Cowdery from Harmony, Pennsylvania, to Fayette, New York, where work on the Book of Mormon was completed. Moved to Ohio and on to Missouri in 1831. Married Betsy Covert, 1832. Built the first mill used by the Church in Jackson County, Missouri; also the printing office. Among those driven from Jackson County, 1833. Later lived at Lima, Nauvoo, and Laharpe, Illinois. Bishop at Winter Quarters during Mormon exodus West. Arrived in Utah, 1851. Missionary to Moqui Indians, 1862. Died in Salt Lake City. (Joseph Knight autobiographical sketch, MS., LDS Church Archives; Hartley, *"They Are My Friends": A History of the Joseph Knight Family, 1825–1850*, passim; "Journal History of the Church," 26 October, 16 November 1862; Black, "Membership of the Church," 26:4–8.)

Knight, Lydia Goldthwaite Bailey (1812–1884), born at Sutton, Worcester County, Massachusetts. Married Calvin Bailey in 1828 but was deserted by her husband three years later. Converted to Mormonism by Joseph Smith while proselyting in Canada in 1833. After returning to her parents in New York in 1834 and being derided for her religion, she moved to Kirtland, Ohio, in 1835. While working for Hyrum Smith, she met and married Newel Knight, who was boarding at the Smith home. Moved to Missouri in 1836, and Illinois, 1839. Left Nauvoo with the Mormon exodus in 1846. Because of the death of her husband, she did not arrive in Salt Lake Valley until 1850. Resided successively at Salt Lake City, Provo, Payson, Santa Clara, and St. George, where she died. (Jenson, *Biographical Encyclopedia* 2:775–76; Hartley, *"They Are My Friends"* passim; *Lydia Knight's History* [Salt Lake City: Juvenile Instructor Office, 1883], 12–23.)

Knight, Newel (1800–1847), miller; born at Marlborough, Windham County, Vermont. Living at Colesville, New York, when converted by Joseph Smith. Moved to Ohio, then Missouri in 1831. Among those expelled from Jackson County, Missouri, 1833. Member of Clay County high council, 1834; Far West high council, 1836; and Nauvoo high council, 1839–1845. His first wife, Sally Coburn, died in Missouri in September 1834. Returning to Ohio, he worked on the Kirtland Temple and boarded at the Hyrum Smith home, where he met Lydia Bailey. Died during the Mormon exodus from Nauvoo to the Salt Lake Valley. (Journal of Newel Knight, MS.; Jenson, *Biographical Encyclopedia*, 2:773–75; Cook, *Revelations*, 78–79; Hartley, *"They Are My Friends,"* passim; "Newel Knight's Journal," *Scraps of Biography* [Salt Lake City: Juvenile Instructor Office, 1883], 47–104.)

Knight, Vinson (1804–1842), born at Chester, Washington County, New York. Married Martha McBride, 1826. Owned a farm at Perrysburg, New York, when converted, 1834. Appointed counselor to Bishop Newel K. Whitney in Kirtland, Ohio, 1836. Church land agent,

1839. Appointed bishop of Nauvoo Lower Ward, 1839, and presiding bishop of the Church, 1841. Elected to Nauvoo city council, 1841. Died at Nauvoo. (Cook, *Revelations*, 265.)

Law, William (1809–1892), merchant, miller, farmer; born in Tyrone County, Northern Ireland. Emigrated to Pennsylvania in 1818 and moved to Churchville, Peel County, Ontario, Canada, about 1832. Converted to Mormonism in 1836 by John Taylor. Led a company of Saints to Nauvoo, Illinois, in 1839. Appointed a member of the First Presidency, 1841. Opposition to plural marriage led to his excommunication in 1844. Organized a church in opposition to Joseph Smith and published the *Nauvoo Expositor*. After his defection he lived in Iowa, Illinois, and Pennsylvania before moving to Shullsburg, LaFayette County, Wisconsin, where he died. (Cook, *Revelations*, 265–66; U.S. Census: Delaware, Mercer, Pennsylvania, 1850.)

Law, Wilson (1807–1877), farmer; born in Ireland. Brother of William Law. Elected member of the Nauvoo city council, 1841. Elected brigadier general in the Nauvoo Legion in 1841, and major general the following year. Married Elizabeth Sikes, 1842. Joined dissenters against Joseph Smith and was excommunicated in 1844. Counselor in his brother's opposition church. Living in Delaware, Mercer County, Pennsylvania in 1850. (U.S. Census: Delaware, Mercer, Pennsylvania, 1850; Black, "Membership of the Church," 27:549–50; "Journal History of the Church," 1 February, 6 April 1841; 3 April 1842; 18, 28–30 April 1844;)

Lawrence, Edward, residing in the 1830s in Pickering, Ontario, Canada, where he evidently died.

Lawson, John (1805–1884), farmer, blacksmith; born at Argyle, Washington County, New York. Presided over the branch at Ramus, Hancock County, Illinois, 1841. In Utah he resided for a time at Manti, Sanpete County. Died at New Harmony, Washington County. (Black, "Membership of the Church," 27:574–75.)

Leal, Clark (1805–1845), born at Kortright, Delaware County, New York. Married Jane McClaughry, 1830. Moved to Fountain Green, Hancock County, Illinois in 1837. Died at Fountain Green. (Charles C. McClaughry, *Genealogy of the Mac Claughry Family* [Anamosa, Iowa, 1913], 103–4.)

Lewis, Job, in his fifties, owned a tavern in Westfield, Chautauqua County, New York, in 1833. Wife's name, Margaret. He apparently joined the Church in the early 1830s. Excommunicated for treating the Church with contempt in 1836. (U.S. Census: Chautauqua County, New York, 1830; "Journal History of the Church," 23 May 1836.)

Lewis, Lloyd L., converted to Mormonism in 1835 at Westfield, Chautauqua County, New York, but left the Church later in the year. ("Journal History of the Church," 10 May 1835.)

Lewis, Lorenzo, probably joined the Latter-day Saints at Westfield, Chautauqua County, New York, but left the Church in 1835. ("Journal History of the Church," 28 September 1835.)

Lightner, Adam (1810–1885), cabinetmaker, merchant, hotel keeper; born at Lancaster, Lancaster County, Pennsylvania. Living in Clay County, Missouri, in 1835, when he married Mary Elizabeth Rollins. Opened a store at Far West, Caldwell County, Missouri, 1837. Left Missouri during the Mormon expulsion of 1838–1839. Served a proselyting mission with Amasa Lyman in Tennessee in 1842. Afterward lived in Kentucky, Iowa, Illinois, Wisconsin, Minnesota. Migrated to Utah in 1863 and settled at Minersville, Beaver County, Utah, where he died. (Family Group Records Collection; Mary Elizabeth Rollins Lightner Autobiography, MS., Utah Historical Society.)

Littlefield, Waldo (1797–1879), born at Petersburg, Rensselaer County, New York. Married Mercy Higgins, 1817. Joined Latter-day Saints, 1832. Participant in the march of Zion's Camp, 1834. Resided with the Saints in Missouri and Illinois before crossing the plains to Utah. Died at Cannonville, Garfield County, Utah. (11th Quorum of Seventy, Biographical Record, MS., LDS Church Archives.)

Lott, Cornelius Peter (1798–1850), farmer, sheriff; born in New York City. Married Permelia Darrow, 1823. Living in Pennsylvania, 1824–1836. Manager of Joseph Smith farm near Nauvoo, Illinois, 1842. Commander of Joseph Smith's bodyguard at Nauvoo. Crossed the plains with Mormon pioneers of 1847. Superintendent of the Church farm in Salt Lake Valley for a number of years. Died at Salt Lake City, Utah. (Black, "Membership of the Church," 28:468–72; Esshom, *Pioneers and Prominent Men*, 1,011.)

Loud, Austin (1797–1852), builder, millright; born at Westhampton, Hampshire County, Massachusetts. Married Mehetable Bartlett, 1821. Moved to Kirtland, Ohio, in 1832, where he built a grist and sawmill where lumber for the Mormon temple was sawed. In 1836 moved to Huntsburg, Ohio, where he built a sawmill. Built churches at Montville and Ravenna, Ohio. Died at Huntsburg. (Watson Loud, comp., *Genealogical Record of the Descendants of Caleb Loud, 1st* [Detroit: Winn & Hammond Printers, 1889], 8–9.)

Lowell, Susan (1804–1859), born at Buxton, Cumberland County, Maine. Converted to Mormonism in 1833. Married John F. Boynton in 1836. After leaving Kirtland, Ohio, she resided with her husband at Syracuse, New York, and Saco, Maine. (John F. Boynton and Caroline H. Boynton, *The Boynton Family* [n.p., 1897], 19–20.)

Lutz, Albert (1810–1898), born at Upper Dublin, Montgomery County, Pennsylvania. Resided for a time in Philadelphia. Died at Garden City, Rich County, Utah. (Family Group Records Collection.)

Lyman, Amasa M. (1813–1877), farmer; born at Lyman, Grafton

County, New Hampshire. Joined Latter-day Saints and moved to Kirtland, Ohio, 1832. Participant in march of Zion's Camp, 1834. Married Maria Tanner, 1835. Although arrested with Joseph Smith at Far West, Missouri, in 1838, he was not charged at the Richmond hearing. Appointed an apostle in 1842, a member of the First Presidency the following year, and the Council of Twelve, 1844. Arrived with pioneer company in Salt Lake Valley in 1847. Assisted in colonization of and presided over settlement at San Bernardino, California, 1851–1857. President of European Mission, 1860–1862. Moved to Fillmore, Utah, 1863. Excommunicated in 1870 for teaching false doctrine. Died at Fillmore. (Cook, *Revelations*, 266–67; *Deseret Weekly* 8 (1858): 117–18, 121–22.)

Lyman, Azariah (1777–1857), farmer; born at Westhampton, Hampshire County, Massachusetts. Married Rhoda Rust, 1799. After her death in 1809 he married Sarah Bartlett, 1811. Exchanging his Massachusetts farm for land in the western wilderness, he became a pioneer settler of Geauga County, Ohio, in 1823. Jointly owned a sawmill, grist mill, and seventeen acres of land at Kirtland with Austin Loud. He died at Chester, Geauga County, Ohio. (*History of Geauga and Lake Counties, Ohio* [Philadelphia: Williams Brothers, 1878], 146; U.S. Census: Chester, Geauga, Ohio, 1850.)

Lyman, Richard (1794–1861), born at Lebanon, Grafton County, New Hampshire. Brother-in-law of patriarch John Smith. Married Catharine Lamson, 1815. (Family Group Records Collection, LDS Family History Library.)

Lyon, Aaron (1781–1839), probably born in New York. Died at Bear Creek, Hancock County, Illinois. (*Times and Seasons* 1 [April 1840]: 95.)

Lyon, Windsor Palmer (1809–1849), army physician; born at Orwell, Addison County, Vermont. Married Sylvia Porter Sessions at Far West, Caldwell County, Missouri, in 1838. Officer in the Nauvoo Legion. Converted to Mormonism at Nauvoo, Illinois, in 1846. Died at Iowa City, Iowa. (Black, "Membership of the Church," 28:864–65; Kate B. Carter, ed., *Our Pioneer Heritage*, 10:415.)

Mack, Temperance Bond (1771–1856), born at Gilsum, Cheshire County, New Hampshire. Maternal aunt of Joseph Smith. Mother of 12 children. With her husband, Stephen, pioneered the area of Detroit and Pontiac, Michigan. Husband died in 1826. Crossed the plains with Mormon pioneers and settled in Salt Lake City, where she died. (Archibald F. Bennett, "Solomon Mack and His Family," *Improvement Era* 59 [March 1956]: 154–55, 190–91; [April 1956]: 246; "Journal History of the Church," 24 July 1951, p. 5.)

Markham, Stephen (1800–1878), carpenter, farmer, stock raiser; born at Hartford, Ontario County, New York. Converted to Mormonism,

1837. Colonel in the Nauvoo Legion, 1843. Served as a bodyguard and courier for Joseph Smith. Arrived in Salt Lake Valley with Mormon pioneers in 1847. Located at Palmyra, Utah County, and in 1853 was appointed bishop of the community. Participant in the Walker Indian War. Sent on a colonizing mission to Fort Supply, near Green River, Wyoming, in 1856. Died at Spanish Fork, Utah County, Utah. (Black, "Membership of the Church," 29:351–58; Jenson, *Biographical Encyclopedia*, 3:672; 4:712.)

Marks, Ephraim (c.1824–1842), born in New York. Son of William and Rosanna Marks. Died in Nauvoo, Illinois.

Marks, William (1792–1872), born at Rutland, Rutland County, Vermont. Living in Portage, Allegany County, New York, when he was converted to Mormonism about 1835. In 1837 moved to Kirtland, Ohio, where he published the *Messenger and Advocate* for a time. Appointed to the Kirtland high council and as agent to bishop Newel K. Whitney, 1837. President of Kirtland Stake, 1838, and Nauvoo Stake in 1839. Elected alderman at Nauvoo, 1841. Member of the Council of Fifty, 1844. Left the Church after the death of Joseph Smith. Counselor to James J. Strang, 1847–1850; joined with Charles B. Thompson in organizing a church about 1852, but left Thompson in 1853. Helped found the Reorganized LDS Church in 1860. Appointed counselor to Joseph Smith III in 1863. Died at Plano, Kendall County, Illinois. (Cook, *Revelations*, 230–31.)

Marsh, Thomas B. (1799–1866), born at Acton, Middlesex County, Massachusetts. Married Elizabeth Godkin, 1820. Converted to Mormonism in 1830. Moved to Kirtland, Ohio, in 1831, and Jackson County, Missouri, 1832. Among those expelled from Jackson County in 1833. Member of the Clay County, Missouri, high council, 1834. Named president of the Quorum of Twelve at its inception in 1835. Marsh left the Church in 1838 and remained in Missouri but returned to the Church in Utah in 1857. Settled at Spanish Fork, where he taught school. Died at Ogden, Utah. (Jenson, *Biographical Encyclopedia*, 1:74–76; Cook, *Revelations*, 42–43; *Deseret Weekly* 8 [1858]: 18.)

Marvel, Clarissa, an orphan girl living in Nauvoo, Illinois, in 1842.

Mathews, Anson (1787–?), born at Chatham, Middlesex County, Connecticut. Married Elizabeth Burgess, 1811. Living in McDonough County, Illinois, by 1833. Joined the Latter-day Saints about 1840 and moved to Nauvoo. There is evidence he may have returned to Connecticut after his Nauvoo years. (Black, "Membership of the Church," 29:664–65.)

Matthias, Robert (1788–1841), alias Joshua the Jewish minister. Joiner and merchant; born at Cambridge, Washington County, New York. Resided at Albany in 1830 with his wife and family of five. A religious eccentric who claimed to be God the Father reincarnated in the body of Matthias, the ancient apostle. In 1830 he prophesied the destruction of Albany. Taught that no man who shaved could be a true Christian. Left Albany and his family to embark on a grand apostolic preaching tour through the East and South. Upon his return to New York, he joined with kindred spirits—Elijah Pierson and Benjamin T. Folger. He was described as "one of the most striking figures in the New York of the early Thirties." Committed to the hospital for the insane at Bellevue for a time. Brought to trial in April 1835 at White Plains, New York, on murder charges following the death, in August 1834, of Mr. Pierson after he ate blackberries prepared by Matthias. Matthias was acquitted of the murder charge but confined in jail three months for brutality on a charge of beating his daughter with a whip. Little is known of Matthias after his visit with Joseph Smith at Kirtland, Ohio, in 1835. An 1839 newspaper reported that the people of Little Rock, Arkansas, had seized him, shaved his beard, and threatened him with a closer shave by "Dr. Lynch" if he did not leave town. (Gilbert Seldes, *The Stammering Century* [New York, 1928], 118–31; *Alton Commercial Gazette*, 19 February 1839; Parkin, "Conflict at Kirtland," 244–47; William L. Stone, *Matthias and his Impostures* [New York: Harper & Brothers, 1835]; Scott H. Faulring, "Prophet Meets Prophet: Robert Matthias Visits Joseph Smith," Typescript, Brigham Young University. The trial is reported in the "Trial of Matthias," New York *Evening Post*, 17, 18, 20 April 1835.)

Maughan, Peter (1811–1871), farmer, colonizer; born at Breckinridge, Cumberland County, England. Married Ruth Harrison, 1829. Converted to Mormonism, 1838. Emigrated to America in 1841 and located at Nauvoo, Illinois. Migrated to Utah in 1850. One of the original colonizers of Tooele valley, 1850. County clerk and assessor; also presiding elder at E.T. City. Appointed to establish settlements in Cache Valley, Utah in 1856. Served as president, presiding bishop, probate judge, quartermaster in the territorial militia and as representative to the territorial legislature until his death in Logan, Utah. (Jenson, *Biographical Encyclopedia*, 1:758–59.)

McAllister, Samuel (1774–1865). Living at Mount Pleasant, Ontario, Canada, in the 1830s. Father of Eliza McAllister Nickerson. (Family Group Records Collection.)

McBride, Reuben (1803–1891) was born at Chester, Washington County, New York. Married Mary Ann Anderson, 1833. Baptized in 1834 and participated later that year in the march of Zion's Camp. Resided at Kirtland, Ohio, 1836–1848 to oversee Church interests there after the departure of the main body of the Saints in 1838. Migrated to Utah, 1850. Returned to Kirtland in 1851 and led a remnant of Church members to Utah the next year. Settled at Fillmore, Millard County, Utah, 1852. Member of Millard Stake high council. Missionary in England, 1867. Died at Fillmore. (Jenson, *Biographical Encyclopedia*, 4:690; *Deseret Evening News*, 9 March 1891.)

McBride, James (1793–1839), born at Stillwater, Saratoga County, New York. Brother of Reuben McBride. Converted to Mormonism in 1833 at Villanova, Chautauqua County, New York. Died in Pike County, Illinois. (Flora Belnap, "Pioneer Incidents of Rev. Daniel McBride and Abigail Mead-McBride and their Children of Utah, Michigan and New York," Typescript, BYU Library.)

McBride, Samuel (1789–1874), born at Stillwater, Saratoga County, New York. Brother of Reuben McBride. Served in the War of 1812. Converted to Mormonism in 1833 at Villanova, Chautauqua County, New York. Located with the Saints in Ohio, Missouri, and Illinois. Moved to Iowa in 1841. Arrived in Utah with Mormon pioneers of 1847. Settled at Farmington, Davis County. In 1853 moved to Fillmore, Utah, where he lived until his death. (*Deseret News*, 25 March 1874.)

McCleary, William (1793–?), wagon maker; born at Rupert, Bennington County, Vermont. Married Joseph Smith's older sister, Sophronia, in 1838 after the death of her first husband. Located with the Saints in Ohio, Missouri, and Illinois. Built wagons in Nauvoo in preparation for the Mormon exodus. Died a short time later. (Richard L. Anderson, "What Were Joseph Smith's Sisters Like?" *Ensign* 9 [March 1979]: 42–43; Early Church Information File, LDS Family History Library.)

McFall, Hugh (c.1799–?), carpenter; born in Pennsylvania. Located in Ohio by 1834 and Illinois about 1840. Purchased land north of Nauvoo in 1841. Member of the Nauvoo city council before 1842. In 1844 he was adjutant general of the Nauvoo Legion. Living in Noxubee County, Mississippi, 1847–1860. (U.S. Census: Hancock, Illinois, 1840; No. Twp., Noxubee, Mississippi, 1850.)

McHaney, William L. (1820–?), farmer; born in Virginia. Married Martha Stokes, 1847. Residing in Daviess County, Missouri, 1850. (U.S. Census: Daviess, Missouri, 1850.)

McKown, Marcellus (1806–1881), farmer; born at Tompy, Onandaga County, New York. Living at Farmersville, Cattaraugus County, New York, 1830. At Yelrome, Hancock County, Illinois, in 1845, and Iowa City, Iowa, in 1850. He died in Mills County, Iowa. (U.S. Census: Farmersville, Cattaraugus, New York, 1830; Iowa City, Johnson, Iowa, 1850; *Boston Transcript*, 8 September 1926.)

McLellin, William E. (1806–1883), schoolteacher, born in Smith County, Tennessee. Joined the Church in Missouri, 1831. Excommunicated and reinstated, 1832. Married Emeline Miller, 1832. Member of the Council of Twelve, 1835–1838. Left the Church in Missouri, 1838. Attempted to organize a new church in Kirtland, Ohio, 1847. Published

Ensign of Liberty at Kirtland, Ohio, 1847–1849. Joined Hedrickites, 1869. Died at Independence, Missouri. (Jenson, *Biographical Encyclopedia*, 1:82–83; Cook, *Revelations*, 106–7.)

McWithey, Eliza Ann (1817–?), daughter of Isaac McWithey; born in New York. Married Edwin D. Webb in Kirtland, Ohio, 1835. Living in the Nauvoo, Illinois, 1st Ward, 1842, and in Marquette County, Wisconsin, 1850. Arrived in Utah, 1853. Probably died before 1860, when her husband was living alone at Fillmore, Millard County. (Family Group Records Collection; U.S. Census: Marquette County, Wisconsin, 1850; Millard County, Utah, 1860.)

McWithey, Isaac (c.1778–1851), and family of four were living in Bennington, Genessee County, New York, in 1830, and in Kirtland, Ohio, in 1835. Appointed to Missouri high council, 1836. By 1840 back in Kirtland, where he died. (*History of the Church*, 2:367; U.S. Census: Genessee County, New York, 1830; A. E. Sherman, Lake County, Ohio, Cemetery Inscriptions, p. 29, Typescript, LDS Family History Library.)

Melling, Peter (1785–1844), born in Preston, England. Appointed to preside over several branches of the Church in Lancashire, England, and became the first Church patriarch ordained in England, 1840. Led a company of Saints from England to Nauvoo, Illinois, 1841–1842. Married Sarah Frodsham at Nauvoo, 1842. Died at Nauvoo. (Early Church Information File; International Genealogical Index; *History of the Church*, 4:116, 120; Family Group Records Collection.)

Miles, Daniel Sanborn (1772–1845), born at Sanbornton, Belknap County, New Hampshire. Converted to Mormonism in 1832. Moved to Kirtland, Ohio, in 1836. Ordained a president of the first quorum of seventy, 1837. Located with the saints in Missouri and Illinois. Died at Nauvoo, Illinois. (Jenson, *Biographical Encyclopedia*, 1:192; Cook, *Revelations*, 267.)

Miller, Allen (no information)

Miller, George (1794–1856), farmer, carpenter; born near Stanardville, Orange County, Virginia. Married Mary Catherine Fry about 1826. Lived in Kentucky, Louisiana, and Virginia before moving to McDonough County, Illinois, in the early 1830s. Converted to Mormonism in 1839. Ordained a bishop at Nauvoo in 1840; captain and colonel in the Nauvoo Legion, 1841, and brigadier general in 1842. President of the high priests at Nauvoo, 1841. Headed expedition to Wisconsin to cut wood for Nauvoo construction, 1842–1844. Appointed to the Council of Fifty, 1844. Elected to Nauvoo city council, 1845. Started West with Mormon pioneers in 1846. Rejected Brigham Young's leadership; excommunicated, 1848. Associated with Lyman Wight in Texas and James Strang in Michigan, 1847–1856. Died in Illinois. (Cook, *Revelations*, 268–69; Lyndon W. Cook, " 'A More Virtuous Man

Never Existed on the Footstool of the Great Jehovah': George Miller on Joseph Smith," *BYU Studies* 19 [Spring 1979]: 402–7.)

Miller, Sarah Shersey (1815–1889), born in Rutherford County, North Carolina. Married James Miller in Sangamon County, Illinois, 1831; husband died in Nauvoo in 1840. Resided in the Nauvoo 1st Ward. Died in Washington County, Utah. (Family Group Records Collection; Early Church Information File.)

Miller, William (1814–1875), farmer; born at Avon, Livingston County, New York. Married Phebe Scott, 1834. Converted to Mormonism in Ohio in 1834. Migrated with the Saints to Missouri and Illinois. Crossed the plains to Utah in 1849. Located at Springville, Utah County. An officer in the territorial militia and was elected to the legislature. Served a proselyting mission to Britain, 1856–1857. Appointed president of Utah Stake and bishop of Provo, Utah, 1860. He died at Provo. (Jenson, *Biographical Encyclopedia*, 1:481–85.)

Millet, Artemus (1790–1874), builder, farmer, stone mason; born at Westmoreland, Cheshire County, New Hampshire. Married Ruth Granis, 1815. Converted to Mormonism by Brigham Young, 1833. Resident of Kirtland, Ohio, 1834–1838. Worked on Kirtland and Nauvoo temples. Crossed plains to Utah, 1850. Resided at Manti; president of high council. Died at Scipio, Utah. (Family Group Records Collection; Artemus Millet, Autobiography, MS. LDS Church Archives.)

Millikin, Arthur (1789–1882), clerk, saddler, harness maker; born at Scarboro, Cumberland County, Maine. Married Joseph Smith's youngest sister, Lucy, at Nauvoo, Illinois, 1840. Wounded in the Crooked River battle in Missouri, 1838. Captain in the Nauvoo Legion. He and his wife cared for Joseph Smith's widowed mother for several years. Worked in railroad and mining offices at Colchester, Illinois. (Family Group Records Collection; Richard L. Anderson, "What Were Joseph Smith's Sisters Like.")

Millikin, Nathaniel (1793–1874), farmer; born at Buxton, York County, Maine. A cousin of Arthur Millikin. Married Mary F. Hayes, 1819. Died at Kirtland, Ohio. (Family Group Records Collection; U.S. Census: Lake County, Ohio, 1850, 1870; Black, "Membership of the Church," 31:135–36.)

Mills, Alexander (1801–?), born in Northumberland, England. Married Ann Wood at Nauvoo, Illinois, 1843. Proprietor of a Nauvoo hotel and tavern. (Nauvoo Temple Endowment Register, 1845–46; *History of Hancock County, Illinois* [Hancock County, 1968], 441.)

Minor, James Lawrence (1813–1897), lawyer, farmer; born at Fredericksburg, Virginia. Studied classics and law. Moved to Missouri in 1835 and practiced law. Elected secretary of the state senate in 1838. Secretary of state, 1839–1845. Appointed adjutant-general, 1839, and superintendent of public schools, 1842. Married Sallie C. Goode, 1844.

After her death in 1845, he married L. G. Smith, 1846. Turned to farming in 1845. He also served as curator of the state university, and manager of the state lunatic asylum. (*United States Biographical Dictionary* [New York: U.S. Biographical Publishing Company, 1878], 663–64; Correspondence with W. Avery Minor, Waco, Texas.)

Moore, James (?–1876), boot and saddle maker; early convert to the Church in London, England. (Lynne W. Jorgensen, "The First London Mormons, 1840–1845," [M.A. thesis, Brigham Young University, 1988], 190; *Millennial Star*, 38:176.)

Morey, George (1803–1875), born at Pittsford, Monroe County, New York. Living in Vermillion County, Indiana, in 1830. Married Sylvia Butterfield. Member of the Missouri high council, 1837–1838. Constable at Nauvoo, Illinois, 1841. Left the Church, 1844, and moved to Brown County, Illinois. Settled at Hamilton, Decatur County, Iowa, in 1852; presided over the RLDS Church there. Died at Hamilton. (*History of the Church*, 2:504; *Biographical and Historical Record of Ringgold and Decatur Counties, Iowa* [Chicago: The Lewis Publishing Company, 1887], 682; *History of the Reorganized Church*, 3:238, 252, 276, 339; 4:129.)

Morin, Josiah (179?–?), merchant; born in Bourbon County, Kentucky. Married Harriet Barnet, 1831. One of the pioneer settlers of Millport, Daviess County, Missouri, 1831. Appointed presiding justice of Daviess County upon the resignation of William Morgan in 1837. Elected to the Missouri state senate, 1838. Living at Gallatin, Daviess County, 1840. (Andrew Jenson, "Daviess County, Missouri," *The Historical Record* 1 [January 1888]: 725; *History of Daviess and Gentry Counties Missouri* [Topeka, Indianapolis: Historical Publishing Company, 1922], 66; *The History of Daviess County* [Kansas City: Birdsall & Dean, 1881], 355; U.S. Census, Gallatin, Daviess County, Missouri, 1840.)

Morley, Isaac (1786–1865), farmer, cooper. Born at Montague, Hampshire County, Massachusetts. Married Lucy Gunn, 1812. Settled at Kirtland, Ohio, 1812. Veteran of the War of 1812. One of first converts to Mormonism in Kirtland. Migrating Saints settled on his farm. Appointed counselor to Bishop Edward Partridge in Missouri, 1831. Among those driven from Jackson County, Missouri, 1833. President of the LDS community at Lima, Adams County, Illinois, 1840. Crossed the plains to Utah, 1848. Member of Salt Lake high council, 1849; and Utah Territorial Legislature, 1851–1855. Led initial settlement of Latter-day Saints in Sanpete Valley, Utah, 1849, and presided at Manti, 1849–1853. Died at Fairview, Sanpete County, Utah. (Jenson, *Biographical Encyclopedia*, 1:235–36; Cook, *Revelations*, 79–80; Backman, *Heavens Resound*, 35–36, 70; Richard H. Morley, "The Life and Contributions of Isaac Morley" [M.A. thesis, Brigham Young University, 1965].)

Morton, John (1790–1858), born at Portsmouth, Rockingham

County, New Hampshire. Converted to Mormonism at Mendon, New York, in 1832. Counselor in the elder's quorum at Kirtland, Ohio, 1836, and president, 1838–1840. (Temple Records Index Bureau; Cook and Backman, *Kirtland Elders Quorum Records, 1836–41* [Provo, Utah: Grandin Press, 1985], 95.)

Mulholland, James (1804–1839), born in Ireland. Family migrated to Halton County, Ontario, Canada. Married Sarah Scott. After joining the Latter-day Saints he moved to Missouri. Engaged in clerical work for Joseph Smith, 1838. After the expulsion of the Mormons from Missouri, he was appointed sub-treasurer and clerk for land contracts at Nauvoo, Illinois, 1839. Continued writing for the Church until his death at Nauvoo. (Family Group Records Collection; *History of the Church,* 4:16, 88–89; Black, "Membership of the Church," 31:954; J. H. Pope, *Illustrated Historical Atlas of the County of Halton, Ontario* [Toronto, 1877], 59.)

Murdock, John (1792–1871), farmer; born at Kortright, Delaware County, New York. Married Julia Clapp, 1823. A Campbellite in Ohio when converted to Mormonism in 1830. Wife died following the birth of twins on 30 April 1831. The twins, Joseph and Julia, were adopted by Joseph and Emma Smith. Participant in Zion's Camp, 1834. Appointed to Clay County, Missouri high council, 1834. Bishop of Nauvoo ward, 1842–1844. Arrived with Mormon pioneers in Salt Lake Valley, 1847. Was appointed bishop of Salt Lake City 14th Ward, 1849. Missionary to Australia, 1851–1853. Settled at Lehi, Utah, 1854–1867. Died at Beaver, Beaver County, Utah. (Cook, *Revelations,* 80; Jenson, *Biographical Encyclopedia,* 2:362–64.)

Murdock, Joseph (1783–1844), born at Lebanon, Windham County, Connecticut. Married Sally Stacey, c.1827. Joined the Church about 1840 and moved to Nauvoo, Illinois, 1841. Died in Nauvoo. (Jenson, *Biographical Encyclopedia,* 3:173.)

Myers, Jacob (1782–1867), miller, millwright; born at Pence, Northumberland County, Pennsylvania. Converted to Mormonism in 1834. Moved to Missouri, 1836. Built the mill at the Haun's Mill settlement on Shoal Creek, Caldwell County, Missouri. Wounded during the attack at Haun's Mill, 1838. Presiding elder of the Freedom branch, Adams County, Illinois, in 1842. Appointed bishop to families of Mormon Battalion men, 1846. Built and operated a sawmill and gristmill near Kanesville, Iowa, during the Mormon exodus. Died in Pennsylvania. (U.S. Census: Pottawattamie County, Iowa, 1850; Autobiography of Warren Foote, 1842–1850, Typescript, BYU Library; Black, "Membership of the Church," 32:173–76.)

Nickerson, Eleazer Freeman (1806–1862), merchant; born at Cavendish, Windsor County Vermont. Son of Freeman Nickerson (1779–1847) and Huldah Chapman (1780–1860). Merchant living in Mt. Pleasant, Ontario, Canada, in the early 1830s. Married Eliza McAllister, 1831. (Family Group Records Collection; International Genealogical Index; *Lydia Knight's History*, 13–18.)

Nickerson, Eliza McAllister (1811–1835), born in Canada. Daughter of Samuel McAllister (1774–1865) and Elizabeth (1774–1865). Married Eleazer Freeman Nickerson at Woodhouse, Norfolk, Ontario, Canada, in 1831. (Family Group Records Collection; International Genealogical Index.)

Nickerson, Freeman (1779–1847), seaman; born at South Dennis, Barnstable County Massachusetts. Moved to Vermont and married Huldah Chapman, 1800. Officer in the War of 1812. Joined the Latter-day Saints at Dayton, Cattaraugus County, New York, 1833. Participant in the march of Zion's Camp, 1834. Died in Iowa during the Mormon exodus to Utah. (Family Group Records Collection; *History of the Church*, 1:416; 2:184.)

Nickerson, John (no information)

Nickerson, Moses Chapman (1804–1871), merchant; born at Cavendish, Windsor County, Vermont. Son of Freeman Nickerson (1779–1847) and Huldah Chapman (1780–1860). Merchant living in Mt. Pleasant, Ontario, Canada, in the early 1830s. Selected counselor to John Smith in the Iowa Stake, 1841. (Family Group Records Collection; *History of the Church*, 4:352; *Lydia Knight's History*, 16.)

Nickerson, Richard (1795–1868), farmer; born at South Dennis, Barnstable County, Massachusetts. Brother of Freeman Nickerson (1779–1847). Died at Yarmouth, Barnstable County, Massachusetts. (Family Group Records Collection; U.S. Census: Yarmouth, Barnstable, Massachusetts, 1850; "Index to Deaths in Massachusetts, 1866–1870," Typescript, LDS Family History Library.)

Nickerson, Samuel (1789–1859), mariner; born at South Dennis, Barnstable County, Massachusetts. Brother of Freeman Nickerson (1779–1847). Living in South Dennis, 1850. (Family Group Records Collection; U.S. Census: South Dennis, Barnstable, Massachusetts, 1850.)

Niswanger, William (1796–?), born at Middletown, Frederick County, Maryland. Married Mary Martin. Children born in Pennsylvania, Missouri, Illinois, and Iowa. Living in the Nauvoo, Illinois, 3rd ward in 1842. Elected major in the Nauvoo Legion, 1841. His family living without him in Pottawattamie County, Iowa, in 1850. (*History of the Church*, 4:382; Nauvoo Temple Endowment Register.)

Noble, Joseph Bates (1810–1900), farmer, miller, stockraiser; born at Egremont, Berkshire County, Massachusetts. Joined the Latter-day Saints in New York, 1832. Married Mary Beman, 1834. Participant in the march of Zion's Camp, 1834. Appointed bishop of the 5th ward at Nauvoo, Illinois, and at Winter Quarters. Crossed plains to Utah, 1847.

Counselor to bishop Edward Hunter in the Salt Lake City 13th Ward. Moved to Bountiful, Davis County, Utah, 1862. Member of the Davis stake high council. Died at Bear Lake, Idaho. (Joseph B. Noble Autobiography, MS.; Jenson, *Biographical Encyclopedia*, 4:691; Black, "Membership of the Church" 32:762–71.)

Nourse, E. B. (no information)

Nyman, Margaret, married to Steward M. Agan at Nauvoo, Illinois, 1843. (Black, "Membership of the Church," 32:961.)

Nyman, Matilda (no information)

Olived, John W. (no information)

Olney, Oliver (1796–?), born at Eastford, Windham County, Connecticut; residing at Shalersville, Portage County, Ohio, in 1830. Married Else Johnson, 1820. President of the teachers quorum in Kirtland, 1836–1838. Excommunicated at Nauvoo for claiming to be a prophet, 1842. Published an exposé on polygamy in St. Louis, 1845. Died in Iowa. By 1850 Olney children were living with their maternal grandfather, John Johnson, in Hiram, Portage County, Ohio, indicating Oliver's possible death before that time. (Family Group Records Collection; Olney, *Genealogy of the Descendants of Thomas Olney*, 40; *History of the Church*, 2:371; 4:552; Emma W. B. Hawley, "Cemetery Records of Lake County, Ohio," p. 11, Typescript, LDS Family History Library.)

Orton, Amos R. (1792–1847), born at Tyringham, Berkshire County, Massachusetts. Living in Olean, Cattaraugus County, New York, in 1830. Member of the seventies quorum at Kirtland, Ohio, and worked on the temple. Wife Elizabeth died, 1837. Excommunicated from the Church, 1838. (Edward Orton, *An Account of the Descendants of Thomas Orton* [Columbus, Ohio: Nitschke Brothers Press, 1896], 48–50, 58, 61, 74; U.S. Census: Cattaraugus County, Ohio, 1830; *History of the Church*, 2:206; "Journal History of the Church," 7 January 1838; *Messenger and Advocate*, 3:544.)

Orton, Roger (1799–1851), born in New York. Brother of Amos R. Orton. Married Clarissa Bicknell about 1822. Joined the Church in the early 1830s. Participant in Zion's Camp, 1834. Appointed to the high council at Kirtland, Ohio, 1835. Excommunicated in 1837. In 1850 living in Lee County, Iowa, where he died. (Edward Orton, *An Account of the Descendants of Thomas Orton*, 49–51, 74–76; U.S. Census: Lee County, Iowa, 1850.)

Packard, Noah (1796–1860), farmer, miner; born at Plainfield, Hampshire County, Massachusetts. Married Sophia Bundy, 1820. Living in Parkman, Geauga County, Ohio, when converted to Mormonism, 1832. Proselyting in the eastern states, 1833. Appointed president of Parkman Branch, 1833. Member of the Kirtland high council, 1836–1838. Counselor in the high priest's quorum at Nauvoo, Illinois, 1841–1846. Worked in Wisconsin lead mines, 1846–1850. Crossed plains to

Utah in 1850. Settled at Springville, Utah, 1851. (Jenson, *Biographical Encyclopedia*, 2:684; Cook, *Revelations*, 269–70.)

Page, John Edward (1799–1867), born at Trenton, Oneida County, New York. Joined the Latter-day Saints, 1833. Married Lorain Stevens, 1833. Moved to Kirtland, Ohio, in 1835. Baptized some 600 during proselyting mission to Canada in 1835–1836. Led Canadian converts to Missouri and was appointed to the Council of Twelve in 1838. Moved to Warsaw, Hancock County, Illinois. Failed to accompany Orson Hyde on a mission to the Middle East in 1840. Preaching in eastern states, 1841–1842. To Nauvoo, Illinois, 1842. Presided over the Church in Pittsburgh, Pennsylvania, and published *The Gospel Light* there, 1842–1844. Excommunicated in 1846. Resided in Walworth County, Wisconsin, and DeKalb County, Illinois, where he died. (Cook, *Revelations*, 232–33.)

Palmer, Ambrose (c.1852–1837), manufacturer. Married Susannah Clark. Living in Vernon, Trumbull County, Ohio, 1807–1810. Officer in the War of 1812. Laid out the village of New Portage, Summit County, Ohio, in 1818 and was elected justice of the peace. In New Portage established a glass factory that failed in 1823. After joining the Latter-day Saints in the early 1830s he became presiding elder of the Church at New Portage. Evidently died in Missouri. (W. H. Perrin, ed., *History of Summit County, Ohio* [Chicago, 1881], 587; *History of the Church*, 2:317.)

Parker, John Davis (1799–1891), farmer, wagonwright; born at Saratoga, Saratoga County, New York. Served in the War of 1812. Converted to Mormonism, 1832. Participant in the march of Zion's Camp, 1834; Kirtland Camp, 1838. Proselyting in Louisiana, 1841–1842. Married Almeda Sophia Roundy, 1846 in Nauvoo, Illinois. Crossed the plains to Utah, 1852. Served in the Utah territorial legislature. Died at Kanarra, Iron County, Utah. (Black, "Membership of the Church," 34:778–82; *Deseret News*, 21 March 1891.)

Parrish, Warren (1803–1887), brother-in-law of David Patten; born in New York. Residing at Alexandria, Jefferson County, New York, in 1830. Baptized by Brigham Young, May 1833. Participant in march of Zion's Camp to Missouri, 1834. Married Martha H. Raymond, 1835. Proselyting in Kentucky and Tennessee with Wilford Woodruff, 1835–1836. Member of the first quorum of seventy. Engaged in clerical work for Joseph Smith, 1835–1836. Treasurer of Kirtland Safety Society, 1836. In 1837 he renounced his Church membership and led dissenters against Joseph Smith. Clergyman living at Mendon, Monroe County, New York, in 1850. In 1870 he was insane, residing at Emporia, Lyon County, Kansas, where he died. (*History of the Church*, 2:184, 203, 293, 484–86, 528; Carter, *Our Pioneer Heritage*, 5:333–34; U.S. Census: Jefferson County, New York, 1830; Geauga County, Ohio, 1840; Lyon County,

Kansas, 1870; Lyon County, Kansas, Cemetery Records, p. 104, Typescript, Family History Library.)

Partridge, Edward (1793–1840), hatter; born at Pittsfield, Berkshire County, Massachusetts. Married Lydia Clisbee, 1819. Living in Painesville, Ohio, when converted by Mormon missionaries in 1830. Named first bishop in the Church, 1831. Called to oversee settlement of the Saints in Zion (Jackson County, Missouri), 1831. Victim of mob violence in Jackson County, 1833. Proselyting in the eastern states and New England, 1835. Witnessed the expulsion of the Saints from Missouri in 1838, and was himself jailed. Appointed bishop of the Nauvoo upper ward, 1839. Died at Nauvoo. (Jenson, *Biographical Encyclopedia*, 1:218–22; Cook, *Revelations*, 53–54.)

Patten, David Wyman (1799–1838), farmer. Born in Vermont. Living in Monroe County, Michigan, when he married Phoebe Ann Babcock, 1828. Converted to Mormonism, 1832. Proselyting in eastern states, 1832–1833, and in Tennessee with Warren Parrish, 1834. Member of the Council of Twelve, 1835–1838. Killed in the battle at Crooked River, Ray County, during the Missouri difficulties in October 1838. (Cook, *Revelations*, 226; Jenson, *Biographical Encyclopedia*, 1:76–80; "History of David Patten," *Deseret Weekly* 8 (1858): 18–19.)

Peck, Hezekiah (1782–1850), millwright; brother of Polly Peck, who married Joseph Knight, Sr. Born at Guilford, Windham County, Vermont. Married Martha Long. Living at Bainbridge, Chenango County, New York, in 1830 when converted to Mormonism. Moved to Jackson County, Missouri, 1831. Named counselor to Bishop John Corrill in Missouri, 1833. Counselor in the priest's quorum at Nauvoo, 1841. Bishop of Nauvoo 10th Ward, 1844. Died at Jackson, Andrew County, Missouri. (*Utah Genealogical and Historical Magazine*, 27:78; *History of the Church*, 1:88, 363; 4:312; 7:298; U.S. Census: Chenango County, New York, 1830; Porter, "Origins of the Church," 212; Hartley, *They Are My Friends*, passim.)

Peck, Reed (1814–1894), millwright; born in New York. Son of Hezekiah Peck. Member of the Colesville, New York, branch of the Church. Became disaffected from the Church in Missouri; excommunicated in 1839. Wrote a lengthy account of his Missouri experience. Living in Cortlandville, Cortland County, New York, in 1850. He died at Afton, Chenango County. (Black, "Membership of the Church," 34:327–28; U.S. Census: Cortlandville, Cortland, New York, 1850; Hartley, *"They Are My Friends,"* 67, 130, 136.)

Peixotto, Daniel Levy Maduro (1800–1843), physician, author, linguist. Born at Amsterdam, Holland. Came to New York City in 1807. When Gershom Seixas, father of Joshua Seixas, died while serving as rabbi of the Congregation Shearith Israel, Daniel's father, Moses, succeeded him. Married Rachel M. Seixas, cousin of Joshua Seixas, 1823.

Received his M.D. and M.A. degrees from Columbia College, 1819 and 1825. Pioneer in the field of preventive medicine. Physician at the New York City Dispensary; lectured on abdominal diseases and complaints of females. President of the New York County Medical Society, 1830–1832. Advocate of reform of faulty medical practices. Helped in founding of Academy of Medicine. Member of Washington masonic lodge. Editor of *The New York Medical and Physical Journal*, first quarterly medical journal printed in English language. In 1836 he was called to the presidency of the Willoughby Medical College and moved to Cleveland, Ohio. Later returned to New York, where he died. (Solomon R. Kagan, *Jewish Contributions to Medicine in America* [Boston: Boston Medical Publishing Company, 1889], 10–12; Daniel P. Hays, "Daniel L.M. Peixotto, M.D.," *Publications of the American Jewish Historical Society*, 26 [1918]: 219–30.)

When Joseph Smith met him, Peixotto was Professor of Theory and Practice of Physics and Obstetrics at Willoughby Medical College. (Louis C. Zucker, "Joseph Smith as a Student of Hebrew," *Dialogue* 2 [Summer 1968]: 44; *History of Geauga and Lake Counties, Ohio*, 40.)

Peniston, William Poitras (1808–1850), born in Jessamine County, Kentucky, whence the family moved to Ray County, Missouri in 1831. Married Mary Walls. Among the founders of the town of Mill Port, Daviess County, where the family built a mill, 1832. Daviess County deputy sheriff and sheriff, 1837–1842. Candidate for the Missouri legislature in 1838. Tried to prevent Mormons from voting at the polls in Gallatin, which precipitated a riot. Moved to California in 1849; hotel keeper in Sacramento in 1850, where he died of cholera. (U.S. Census: Sacramento, California, 1850; Rollin J. Britton, "Early Days on the Grand River and the Mormon War," *The Missouri Historical Review* 13 [January 1949]: 112–13; *History of Daviess County, Missouri*, 356–57.)

Penrose, Charles Bingham (1798–1857), lawyer; born at Philadelphia, Pennsylvania. Admitted to the Pennsylvania bar in 1821. Married Valeria Fullerton Biddle, 1824. Elected to the state senate, 1833–1841, serving for a time as speaker. Served as solicitor of the United States treasury, 1841–1845. Practiced law in Pennsylvania until 1856, when he was again elected to the state senate. Died at Harrisburg. (Dumas Malone, ed., *Dictionary of American Biography* [New York: Charles Scribner's Sons, 1936], 14:449–50.)

Perkins, Ute (1761–1844), born in Lincoln County, North Carolina. Revolutionary War veteran. Living at Abbeville, Abbeville County, South Carolina, 1787–1807. In 1826 he became the first permanent settler of Fountain Green, Hancock County, Illinois. Died at Nauvoo, Illinois. (Family Group Records Collection; *History of Hancock County, Illinois*, 129, 301.)

Perkins, William Gant (1801–1886), born at Abbeville, Abbeville County, South Carolina. Family moved to Tennessee in 1805. Married Dicy Ray, 1818. Moved to Hancock County, Illinois, in 1829 where he was converted to Mormonism in 1838. Appointed bishop of Macedonia, Hancock County, 1843. Crossed the plains to Utah in 1848 and became bishop of the Salt Lake City 7th Ward. Sent to help colonize St. George, Utah, in 1861. Was ordained a patriarch in 1870. Died in St. George. (Jenson, *Biographical Encyclopedia*, 2:429–30.)

Perry, William Chadwick (1812–1893), born at Madison, Madison County, New York. Father's family moved to Middlebury, Genesee County, 1815. Converted to Mormonism, 1832. Married Eliza Brown, 1835. Worked on the temple at Kirtland, Ohio. Perry and family of four were among those who migrated to Missouri with the Kirtland Camp in 1838. Member of 2nd quorum of seventy. Alternate high councilman in Nauvoo. (Ivan Perry, *Perry Family History* [Provo, Utah: J. Grant Stevenson, 1966], 1:14–19; *History of the Church*, 3:92.)

Petty, Albert (1795–1869), wagon builder, gunsmith; born in Bourbon County, Kentucky. Married Catherine Petty in Henry County, Tennessee, 1829. Joined the Latter-day Saints in 1835. Resided in Missouri and Illinois. Arrived in Utah with Mormon pioneers in 1848. Helped establish the settlement of Manti, Sanpete County, in 1849. Served as county judge, surveyor, and bishop's counselor, and represented Sanpete County in the territorial legislature. In 1855 he was elected mayor. In 1861 he helped colonize southern Utah by founding the town of Springdale, Washington County, where he died. (Charles B. Petty, *The Albert Petty Family* [Salt Lake City, Deseret News Press, 1954–1955], 160.)

Phelps, William Wines (1792–1872), newspaper editor; born at Hanover, Morris County, New Jersey. Married Sally Waterman, 1815. Converted to Mormonism in New York, 1831. After arriving in Kirtland, Ohio, in 1831, he was appointed to assist in the Church printing office. Editor of *The Evening and the Morning Star* at Independence, Missouri; published Book of Commandments; helped compile 1835 Doctrine and Covenants and first LDS hymnal. Counselor to David Whitmer in the Missouri Church presidency, 1834. Assisted Joseph Smith as a clerk. Left the Church in 1838 but returned in 1840. Came to Utah in 1849. Elected to the territorial legislative assembly, 1851. Died in Salt Lake City. (Jenson, *Biographical Encyclopedia*, 3:692–97; Cook, *Revelations*, 87–88.)

Pierce, Robert (1797–1884), born at Concord, Franklin County, Pennsylvania. Married Hannah Harvey, 1821. Living in Pennsylvania, 1821–1839. Died in Salt Lake City, Utah. (Black, "Membership of the Church," 34:944–47.)

Pitman, James M. (1813–1879), lumberman, builder, real estate broker; born in St. Charles County, Missouri. Moved to Quincy, Illinois, in 1835. Bought interest in a sawmill. Deputy sheriff of Adams County, 1842, and sheriff, 1844–1848. Married Mary McDade, 1845. Served in the Illinois legislature, 1850–1854, and as mayor of Quincy, 1854. Warden of the Illinois state penitentiary and director of the Chicago, Burlington, and Quincy Railroad and the Quincy Gas Works. (*Atlas Map of Adams County* [Davenport, Iowa: Andres, Lyter & Company, 1872], 43; Adams County, Illinois probate records, 1879; Pat H. Redmond, *History of Quincy* [Quincy: Heirg & Russell Printers, 1869], 57–59; *History of Adams County* [Chicago, 1879], 420–21.)

Powers, Stephen W. (1815–?), lawyer; born in Ohio. Living in Keokuk, Lee County, Iowa, in 1850. (U.S. Census: Keokuk, Lee County, Iowa, 1850.)

Pratt, Orson (1811–1881), writer, teacher, surveyor, historian. Born at Hartford, Washington County, New York. Younger brother of Parley Pratt. After joining the Church, he left Kirtland, Ohio, with Lyman Johnson in February 1832 on missionary assignment in the East; returned in February 1833 after traveling four thousand miles, baptizing 104 people, and organizing several branches of the Church. Participant in Zion's Camp, 1834. Member of the Council of Twelve, 1835–1881. Married Sarah Marinda Bates, 1836. Elected to Nauvoo, Illinois, city council, 1843. Entered Salt Lake Valley with Mormon pioneers, 1847. Presided over Church in Great Britain, 1848. Member of Utah Territorial legislature. Appointed Church historian, 1874. Died at Salt Lake City. (*Deseret Weekly*, 9 June 1858; Cook, *Revelations*, 49–51; England, *The Life and Thought of Orson Pratt*.)

Pratt, Parley Parker (1807–1857), farmer, editor, legislator; elder brother of Orson Pratt. Born at Burlington, Otsego County, New York. Married Thankful Halsey, 1827. Participant in Lamanite mission to Missouri, 1830. Traveled to Missouri with Zion's Camp, 1834. Member of the Quroum of Twelve, 1835–1857. Jailed at Richmond and Columbia, Missouri, during difficulties of 1838–1839. Missions to England, 1840–1842, 1846–1847; president of the British Mission, 1841–1842. A prolific writer; edited *The Latter-day Saints' Millennial Star*, 1840. Directed affairs of the Church in New York City, 1844–1845. Returned to Utah, 1847. Led exploration party into southern Utah, 1850. Mission to South America, 1851–1852. Murdered at Van Buren, Crawford County, Arkansas. (Cook, *Revelations*, 46–47; Jenson, *Biographical Encyclopedia*, 1:83–85.)

Pratt, Sarah Marinda Bates (1817–1888), born at Henderson, Jefferson County, New York. Converted to Mormonism by Orson Pratt in 1835. Married Orson Pratt, 1836. Died in Salt Lake City, Utah. (Arthur D. Coleman, "Wives and Daughters of the Pratt Pioneers of Utah," p. 159. typescript; Richard S. Van Wagoner, "Sarah M. Pratt: The Shaping of an Apostate," *Dialogue* 19 [Summer 1986]: 69–99.)

Pratt, William Dickinson (1802–1870), schoolteacher; born at Worcester, Otsego County, New York. Brother of Orson and Parley Pratt. Converted to Mormonism in 1831. Participant in the march of Zion's Camp, 1834. Married Hannah Ward in Kirtland, Ohio, 1837. Migrated to Utah in 1851. Participated in the Utah War and Indian wars. Died at Salt Lake City. (R. Steven Pratt, "The Sons of Jared and Charity Pratt," *Ensign* 9 [October 1979]: 52–57; Esshom, *Pioneers and Prominent Men*, 1,114.)

Prentiss, Lyman (180?–?), living in Brown County, Illinois, in 1840. Attended mass meeting at Warsaw, Hancock County, addressing the issue of the destruction of the Nauvoo *Expositor* in June 1844. Listed among those allegedly involved in the killing of Joseph and Hyrum Smith. (U.S. Census: Brown County, Illinois, 1840; *History of the Church*, 6:466; 7:144.)

Raglan/Raglin, John (1805–?), farmer. Pioneer settler in Caldwell County, Missouri, 1832. (U.S. Census: Daviess County, Missouri, 1850.)

Ralston, James H. (1807–1864), lawyer; born in Bourbon County, Kentucky. Moved to Quincy, Adams County, Illinois, where he practiced law. Fought in the Black Hawk War. Represented his district in the lower house of the state legislature. Served as circuit judge, 1837–1839. Elected to the state senate, 1841. Employed as legal counsel to Joseph Smith in Nauvoo. During the Mexican War he commanded the garrison at the Alamo at San Antonio, Texas. After the war he moved to California, where he served in the first state senate. In 1856 he was an unsuccessful candidate for chief justice of California. Moved to Nevada in 1860. Died near Austin. (David Wilcox, ed., *Quincy and Adams County: History and Representative Men* [Chicago: Lewis Publishing Company, 1919], 144–45; Oaks and Hill, *Carthage Conspiracy*, 92–93.)

Rappleye, Tunis (1807–1883), farmer; born at Ovid, Seneca County, New York. Married Louisa Elizabeth Cutler, 1836. Teamster for Brigham Young during the Mormon exodus from Nauvoo to Salt Lake Valley. Also employed as Brigham Young's head gardener. Missionary in the eastern states. Served in the Utah militia protecting settlements from Indians. Resided many years at Kanosh, Millard County, Utah, where he died. (Jenson, *Biographical Encyclopedia*, 2:791.)

Rathbun, Robert (1799–1856), blacksmith; born in New York. Brother-in-law of George Miller. Baptist minister in Mantua, Portage County, Ohio, in 1830, when the Lamanite missionaries preached at his house. Among the first LDS emigrants to Independence, Missouri. Living at Haun's Mill at the time of the massacre, in which his son was wounded, 1838. Died in Van Buren County, Iowa. (*Saints' Herald* 39 [9 July 1892]: 491–92, 508–09; U.S. Census: Van Buren County, Iowa, 1850; Van Buren County, Iowa Probate Records, 1856.)

Raymond, Martha H. (1804–1875), born in Massachusetts. Married Warren Parrish, 1835. Living in Emporia, Lyon County, Kansas, 1870, where she died. (U.S. Census: Emporia, Lyon County, Kansas, 1870; Lyon County, Kansas, Cemetery Records, p. 104.)

Redfield, David Harvey (1807–1879), farmer, merchant; born at Herkimer, Herkimer County, New York. Joined the Latter-day Saints by 1831. Married Fanny McAtherton, 1837. Traveled from Ohio to Missouri with the Kirtland Camp in 1838. Petitioned Missouri authorities, including Governor Boggs, in behalf of the Mormon people during the difficulties of 1838. One of those charged with riot in the destruction of the Nauvoo *Expositor* in 1844. Crossed the plains to Salt Lake Valley, 1848. By 1854 he was living in Nicolaus, Sutter County, California, where he was county coroner and where he evidently died. (Family Group Records Collection; *History of the Church*, 3:234–35; 6:487ff; Black, "Membership of the Church," 36:235–37; John H. Redfield, *Genealogical History of the Redfield Family* [Albany, New York: Munsell and Rowland, 1860], 144, 242; *History of Sutter County, California* [Oakland, California, 1879], 77; U.S. Census: Sutter County, California, 1860, 1870.)

Redfield, Harlow (1801–1866), farmer; born at Chestnut Hill, Middlesex County, Connecticut. Married Caroline Foster, 1824. Joined the Latter-day Saints, 1831. Appointed to the Kirtland, Ohio, high council in 1837. Living at Pittsfield, Pike County, Illinois, in 1842. Resided at Provo, Utah County, Utah, where he was a member of the first city council. (Family Group Records Collection; *History of the Church* 2:510; 3:287; U.S. Census: Provo, Utah County, Utah, 1850, 1860; J. Marinus Jensen, *Early History of Provo, Utah* [Provo, Utah: Author, 1924], 79.)

Remick, Jacob G. (1798–c.1860), lawyer; born in New Hampshire. Married Hannah Shaw. Iowa land speculator, accused by Joseph Smith of swindling. Living in Keokuk, Lee County, Iowa, in the 1840s and at Galveston, Texas, 1850. Died at Stillwater, Washington County, Minnesota. (U.S. Census: Galveston, Galveston, Texas, 1850; *History of the Church*, 5:334–36; Winifred L. Holman, *Remick Genealogy* [Maine Historical Society, 1933], 130–31.)

Reynolds, Thomas (1796–1844), born in Bracken County, Kentucky. In his twenties moved to Illinois, where he successively held the offices of clerk of the House of Representatives, attorney-general, speaker of the House of Representatives, and chief justice of the Illinois Supreme Court. Moved to Missouri in 1829 and settled at Fayette, Howard County. Represented Howard County in the General Assembly and became speaker of the house. Elected governor in 1840. Four years later he commited suicide. (Floyd C. Shoemaker, *Missouri and Missourians* [Chicago: Lewis Publishing Company, 1943], 422, 425.)

Rhodes, Eric (1798–1843), married Eunice Wright, 1819. Living in Fowler, Trumbull County, Ohio, 1820–1830. By 1840 in Hancock County, Illinois, where he died. (U.S. Census: Fowler, Trumbull County, Ohio, 1820, 1830; International Genealogical Index; Temple Index Bureau, LDS Family History Library.)

Rhodes, Hugh (1800–?), farmer; born at Sackets Harbor, Jefferson County, New York. Residing in Stark County, Illinois, in 1850; Davis County, Utah, 1856. (U.S. Census: Stark County, Illinois, 1850; Utah Territorial Census, 1856.)

Rich, Leonard (1800–1856), farmer; born in New York. Residing at Warsaw, Genesee County, New York, in 1830. One of the presidents of the seventy, 1835–1837. Participant in the march of Zion's Camp to Missouri, 1834. Left the Church and was living in Kirtland, Ohio, after 1845. Wife's name, Keziah. Died at Kirtland. (Family Group Records Collection; *History of the Church*, 2:184, 203; Jenson, *Biographical Encyclopedia*, 1:189–90; Black, "Membership of the Church," 36:582–83; U.S. Census: Genesee County, New York, 1830; Lake County, Ohio, 1850; Kirtland, Ohio, cemetery record, p. 18, Typescript, LDS Family History Library.)

Richards, Levi (1799–1876), teacher, mechanic, physician; born at Hopkinton, Middlesex County, Massachusetts. Brother of Willard Richards. Musician in the Massachusetts militia in 1817. Converted to Mormonism in 1836. Migrated to Missouri. Missionary in England, 1840–1843, 1848–1853. Appointed to the Nauvoo city council and was surgeon-general of the Nauvoo Legion. Personal physician to Joseph Smith. Married Sarah Griffith, 1843. In 1853 settled in Salt Lake City, where he died. Was ordained a patriarch, 1873. (Orson F. Whitney, *History of Utah*, 4:445.)

Richards, Phineas (1788–1874), born at Framingham, Middlesex County, Massachusetts. Brother of Willard Richards. Married Wealthy Dewey, 1818. Appointed county coroner, 1825. Converted to Mormonism in 1837 at Kirtland, Ohio. Served on Church high councils in Kirtland, Nauvoo, Winter Quarters, and Salt Lake City. Appointed to the Nauvoo city council and served as an officer in the Legion. Migrated to Utah in 1848. Member of the territorial legislature and chaplain of the house. Died at Salt Lake City. (J. Grant Stevenson, ed., *Richards Family History* [Provo, Utah, 1977], 8–10.)

Richards, Willard (1804–1854), medical doctor; born at Hopkinton, Middlesex County, Massachusetts. Converted to Mormonism in 1836. Missionary to England, 1837–1841. Married Jennetta Richards in England in 1838. Ordained to the Quorum of Twelve, 1840. Elected to the Nauvoo city council, 1841. Served as temple recorder, recorder of the city council, clerk of the municipal court, Church historian, and private secretary to Joseph Smith. He was with Joseph and Hyrum Smith when they were killed in the jail at Carthage, Illinois, 1844. Accompanied the Mormon pioneers to Utah in 1847. Appointed second counselor to Brigham Young in the Church presidency, 1847. Secretary of Utah territory, postmaster of Salt Lake City, and editor of the *Deseret News*. Died in Salt Lake City. (Jenson, *Biographical Encyclopedia*, 1:53–56.)

Rider, Ezekiel (179?–?), living in Chardon, Geauga County, Ohio, in 1840. Mormon Church member in Kirtland, Ohio. (U.S. Census: Chardon, Geauga County, Ohio, 1840; *History of the Church*, 1:470.)

Rigdon, Elizabeth (1823–1845), born in Pittsburgh, Allegheny County, Pennsylvania. Daughter of Sidney Rigdon. Moved with family to Ohio, Missouri, and Illinois, prior to her death at Pittsburgh. (Arlene Hess, "Collected Materials Relative to Sidney Rigdon," Typescript, BYU Library.)

Rigdon, Nancy (1822–1887), born at Pittsburgh, Allegheny County, Pennsylvania. Daughter of Sidney Rigdon. Living with her family in Ohio, Missouri, and Illinois. Married Robert Ellis, 1846. Died in Pittsburgh. (*Utah Genealogical and Historical Magazine*, 27:161–62; Arlene Hess, "Collected Materials Relative to Sidney Rigdon," Typescript, BYU Library.)

Rigdon, Sidney (1793–1876), tanner, farmer, Campbellite minister; born at St. Clair, Allegheny County, Pennsylvania. Married Phoebe Brook, 1820. Converted by Mormon missionaries at Mentor, Ohio, in November 1830. Scribe for Joseph Smith. Accompanied the Prophet to Upper Canada on proselyting mission and helped keep his diary during the trip, 1833. Counselor in Church presidency, 1833–1844. With Joseph Smith in jail at Liberty, Clay County, Missouri, 1838–1839. Accompanied Joseph to Washington, D.C., to seek redress of Missouri grievances, 1839. Member of Nauvoo city council; postmaster of Nauvoo. Claimed right to lead the Church after death of the Prophet; excommunicated, 1844. Moved to Pittsburgh, where he became the leader of a schismatic group opposed to the pratice of plural marriage, 1844. Moved to Antrim, Franklin County, Pennsylvania, in 1845, and in 1847 to Friendship, Allegany County, New York, where he died. (Cook, *Revelations*, 52–53; Jenson, *Biographical Encyclopedia*, 1:31–34; F. Mark McKiernan, *The Voice of One Crying in the Wilderness: Sidney Rigdon, Religious Reformer, 1793–1876* [Lawrence, Kansas: Coronado Press, 1971]; Daryl Chase, "Sidney Rigdon: Early Mormon," [Ph.D. dissertation, University of Chicago, 1931]; Thomas Gregory, "Sidney Rigdon: Post Nauvoo," *BYU Studies* 21 [Winter 1981]: 51–67.)

Ripley, Alanson (1798–?), surveyor. Born in New York. Participated in the march of Zion's Camp in 1834. Surveyed Adam-ondi-Ahman, Daviess County, Missouri. One of the committee for removing the poor from Missouri in 1839. Bishop in Iowa, 1839–1841. Appointed Nauvoo city surveyor, 1841. Living in Pike County, Illinois, 1850. (*History of* *the Church,* 2:184; 3:252; 4:12, 42, 308, 341; 5:270; U.S. Census: Pike County, Illinois, 1850.)

Robbins, Lewis (1811–1864), blacksmith; born at Stockbridge, Berkshire County, Massachusetts. Converted to Mormonism in New York in 1832. Member of Zion's Camp, 1834. Married Francis Smith, 1837. One of the presidents of the second quorum of seventy. Missionary in England, 1849–1852. Migrated to Utah in 1852. Called to help colonize southern Utah, 1861. Crushed by a rock while helping build the St. George meetinghouse. ("Journal History of the Church," 10 February 1864.)

Robinson, Angeline (1814–1880), schoolteacher; born at Aurelius, Cayuga County, New York. Wife of Ebenezer Robinson. Converted to Mormonism in Kirtland, Ohio, 1835. Died near Pleasanton, Decatur County, Iowa. (*Saints' Herald,* 27 [15 May 1880]: 160.)

Robinson, Ebenezer (1816–1891), printer; born at Floyd, Oneida County, New York. Learned printing trade in Utica, New York, and Ravenna, Ohio. Came to Kirtland, Ohio, in May 1835 and began work in the printing office. Church clerk and recorder and clerk of the Missouri high council, 1838. Publisher, associate editor, and editor of the *Times and Seasons,* 1839–1842. Hancock County justice of the peace, 1842. Left Nauvoo and affiliated with Sidney Rigdon in the East for a time after the death of Joseph Smith. Moved to Iowa and joined the Reorganized Church, 1863. Became a follower of David Whitmer in 1888. Published *The Return,* a publication of Whitmer's Church of Christ, 1889–1891. (Robinson, "Items of Personal History"; Pearl Wilcox, *The Latter Day Saints on the Missouri Frontier* [Independence, Missouri: by author, 1972], 279–80; *History of the Church,* 5:18.)

Robinson, George W. (1814–1878), merchant, clothier, miller, banker; born at Pawlet, Rutland County, Vermont. Married Athalia Rigdon, oldest daughter of Sidney Rigdon, 1837. In September 1837 elected general Church recorder to replace Oliver Cowdery. Sustained as general Church recorder and clerk to the First Presidency at Far West, Missouri, in April 1838. Imprisoned with Joseph Smith and other Church leaders Missouri, 1838. First postmaster at Commerce, later Nauvoo, Illinois, 1839. Helped establish the Nauvoo Agricultural and Manufacturing Association, 1841. Left the Church, 1842. Moved to Friendship, Allegany County, New York, 1847. Founded First National Bank there, 1864. Died at Friendship. (Jenson, *Biographical Encyclopedia,* 1:252–53; *History of the Church,* 6:464; Arlene Hess, "Collected Materials Relative to Sidney Rigdon," Typescript, BYU Library.)

Robison, Chauncey (1805–1891), farmer, accountant, clerk; born in Oneida County, New York. Moved to Hancock County, Illinois, with his parents, 1829. One of the early settlers of Carthage. Land office registrar at Quincy, Adams County. Clerk in a dry-goods store at Carthage, 1837–1839. Postmaster; county recorder, 1839–1847. Married Hannah Hughes, 1841. Secretary of the Hancock masonic lodge, 1843. Probate judge, master in chancery, school commissioner. Driven from Carthage by a mob, 1845. Resided at Nauvoo, 1847–1850 and was mayor of the town, 1849–1850. Owned a farm at Appanoose, Hancock County, 1850. Later moved to Iowa and Kansas. Died at Topeka, Kansas. (Veldron R. Matheson, *The Illustrious Robisons* [private publication, n.d.], 137.)

Rockwell, Orrin Porter (1813–1878), scout, pioneer, frontiersman, lawman, rancher. Born at Belchertown, Hampshire County, Massachusetts. Porter was four years old when the family moved to Manchester, New York, where he befriended Joseph Smith. Among the first converts to Mormonism. Went to Missouri in 1831 and experienced the difficulties there. Married Luana Beebe, 1832. Assisted in Mormon exodus from Missouri, 1839. Accompanied Joseph Smith to Washington, D.C., to seek redress for Missouri wrongs, 1839–1840. Accused, imprisoned, and later acquitted in the 1842 assassination attempt of former Missouri Governor Lilburn Boggs. Scout and hunter for the Mormon pioneers crossing the plains, 1846–1847. Deputy marshal in Utah, 1849–1878. Died at Salt Lake City. (Harold Schindler, *Orrin Porter Rockwell* [Salt Lake City: University of Utah Press, 1966]; Richard L. Dewey, *Porter Rockwell: A Biography* [New York: Paramount Books, 1986]; Nicholas Van Alfen, "The Trusted Messenger," *Our Pioneer Heritage*, 15:375–89; *Utah Genealogical and Historical Magazine*, 26:154–56.)

Rockwood, Albert Perry (1805–1879), born at Holliston, Middlesex County, Massachusetts. Converted to Mormonism in 1837. Located with the saints in Missouri and Nauvoo. Officer in the Nauvoo Legion. Member of the first council of seventy, 1845–1879. Arrived in Salt Lake Valley with Mormon pioneers, 1847. In Utah he was warden of the state penitentiary, a member of the territorial legislature, and a director of the Deseret Agricultural and Manufacturing Society. Died at Salt Lake City. (Jenson, *Biographical Encyclopedia*, 1:194–95.)

Rogers, David White (1787–1881), fur trapper, chair- and cabinetmaker, farmer, lumberman; born at Morristown, Merrimack County, New Hampshire. The family lived in Montreal, Canada, and Chautauqua County, New York, before moving to New York City in 1830. Converted to Mormonism in 1837. Assisted in the location of the Latter-day Saints at Nauvoo. Resided in Montrose, Iowa. Arrived in Utah in 1852. By 1857 living in Provo, Utah County, where he operated a sawmill. Elected one of the directors of the Deseret Agricultural and Manufacturing Society in 1870. Died at Provo. (Black, "Membership of the Church," 37:489–92.)

Rogers, Jacob S. (1814–1914), farmer; born in Kentucky. Residing in Daviess County, Missouri, by 1831. Married Elizabeth Scott, 1834.

Settled on the lower Grand River and operated a ferry at the mouth of Honey Creek. Died in Daviess County. (U.S. Census: Daviess County, Missouri, 1850; Daviess County Probate Records, 1914.)

Rolfe, Samuel Jones (1794–1867), joiner, carpenter; born at Concord, Merrimack County, New Hampshire. Married Elizabeth Hathaway, 1818. Residing in Rumford, Oxford County, Maine, when converted. Moved to Kirtland, Ohio, 1835. Worked on Kirtland and Nauvoo temples. Appointed president of priests quorum in Nauvoo, 1841. Bishop at Winter Quarters, Nebraska, 1846–1847. Arrived in Salt Lake Valley, 1847. Settled in San Bernardino, California, 1851; county treasurer, counselor in stake presidency. (Family Group Records Collection; Cook, *Revelations*, 272–73.)

Root, Henry (1813–1895), banker; born at Clinton, Ontario, Canada. Moved to Missouri about 1837. Through his influence Mormons bought land at DeWitt, Carroll County, Missouri. Left DeWitt with them when they were driven out. Settled at Quincy, Adams County, Illinois. Married Sarah Ann Miller, 1844. Sutler with the American army during the Mexican war. Furnished horses to the government during the Civil War. Prominent banker in Quincy when he died. (*History of Quincy and Adams County* [Chicago and New York: Lewis Publishing Company], 1:276–77.)

Rose, Andrew (1782–1850), born at Morris Plains, Morris County, New Jersey. Living in Canada between 1815 and 1825. Died at South Platte, Lincoln County, Nebraska, while crossing the plains to Utah. (Family Group Records Collection.)

Rose, Joseph (1792–?), born in Orange County, New York. Member of the 2nd quorum of seventy at Kirtland, Ohio. Proselyting in Missouri, Indiana, and Illinois, 1836–1837; and Ohio, 1844. A Joseph Rose living at Union, Fulton County, Illinois, in 1850 could be this man, since he visited Joseph Smith in 1836 with a minister friend from that place. (U.S. Census: Union, Fulton County, Illinois, 1850; *Messenger and Advocate*, 3 [June, July 1837]; 519, 535; *History of the Church*, 3:253; 6:339.)

Roundy, Shadrach (1788–1872), was born at Rockingham, Windham County, Vermont. Married Betsy Quimby, 1814. Family records show him in Spafford, Onondaga County, New York, between 1815 and 1831, and in Willoughby, Ohio, between 1834 and 1838. Converted to Mormonism, 1831. Member of Nauvoo, Illinois bishopric, and Nauvoo Legion, 1841; policeman, 1843. A bodyguard to Joseph Smith. Arrived in Salt Lake Valley, 1847. Member of Salt Lake high council, 1847–1848. Bishop of the Salt Lake City 16th Ward, 1849–1856. Died at Salt Lake City. (Cook, *Revelations*, 273; *History of the Church*, 2:298.)

Rudd, John (1779–?), born in Bennington, Vermont. Married Rosanna Jackson. Family members were among the pioneer settlers of

Springfield, Erie County, Pennsylvania. John Rudd, Sr. (1748–1830) came to Springfield in 1805 from Otsego County, New York, and settled on 350 acres of lake front land. John, Jr., had preceded his father and others of the family to Springfield in 1802 and established a distillery. John, Sr., died in 1830. Three years later some of the family joined the Latter-day Saints. Joseph Smith stayed at the Rudd home traveling to and from the East in 1833. In 1836 the mother, Chloe Hill Rudd, died at Independence, Cuyahoga County, Ohio. At a conference held in Kirtland, Ohio, in August 1834 to investigate charges of misconduct against Joseph Smith during the march of Zion's Camp, John, Jr., signed his name exonerating the Prophet's actions. Beyond this, there appears to be no further reference to him in Church annals. (Benjamin Whitman, *History of Erie County, Pennsylvania* [Chicago: Warner, Beers & Company, 1884], 160–61; 751; *Messenger and Advocate*, 2:382; *Evening and Morning Star*, 2:182.)

Salisbury, Wilkins Jenkins (1809–1856), blacksmith; born at Lebanon, Madison County, New York. Member of the first quorum of the seventy. He married Joseph Smith's sister Katherine at Kirtland, Ohio, 1831; parents of eight children. Participated in the march of Zion's Camp to Missouri, 1834. Expelled from the Church for un-Christian conduct in 1836. Moved with the Church to Missouri and Illinois. Remained at Plymouth, Hancock County, Illinois, where he died. (Mary A. Anderson, *Ancestry and Posterity of Joseph Smith* [Independence: Herald Printing House, 1929], 75; E. Cecil McGavin, *The Family of Joseph Smith* [Salt Lake City: Bookcraft, 1963], 95–108; Richard L. Anderson, "What Were Joseph Smith's Sisters Like?" *Ensign* 9 [March 1979]: 42–44.)

Sanders, John (1801–1844), born in Alston, England, where he kept a grocery and provision store. Married Margaret Bentley. Among the first converts to Mormonism in England. Migrated to America and located at Nauvoo, Illinois, 1841. Died at Nauvoo. (Kate B. Carter, ed., *Our Pioneer Heritage* 18:173–81; *Nauvoo Neighbor* 2 [18 September 1844]: 3.)

Sayers, Edward (1802–1860), gardener, horticulturist; born in England. Married Ruth Vose of Boston at St. Louis in 1841. Resided at Nauvoo, Illinois, before crossing the plains to Utah. Living in Salt Lake City in 1850. (Black, "Membership of the Church," 38:394–95.)

Seixas, Joshua (1802–187?), Hebraist, textbook writer. Lived in New York City. Attracted attention by promising a reading knowledge of Hebrew in six weeks, classes meeting one hour a day. Taught Hebrew in New York, Philadelphia, Washington, at Princeton Theological Seminary, the Seminary at Brunswick, New Jersey, and Andover Theological Seminary. His *A Manual of Hebrew Grammar for the Use of Beginners* was published in 1833. In 1835 he taught at Oberlin College, Ohio.

589

Among his students was Lorenzo Snow, whose sister Eliza had joined the Latter-day Saints and was then living in the Joseph Smith household in Kirtland, Ohio. Joseph possibly first heard of Seixas from this source, or from Daniel Peixotto, whose wife, Rachel, was Seixas's cousin. After completing the course at Oberlin, Seixas was hired for a six-week term of instruction at the Western Reserve College in Hudson, beginning in December and ending 23 January 1836. Three days later he arrived at Kirtland, where he taught Hebrew from 26 January to 29 March 1836. After returning to New York, Seixas founded the first choir of the Spanish and Portuguese Synagogue, where he served many years as instructor of Hebrew. He died in New York. (LeRoi C. Snow, "Who Was Professor Joshua Seixas?" *Improvement Era* 39 [February 1936]: 67–71; Zucker, "Joseph Smith as a Student of Hebrew"; Malcolm H. Stern, *First American Jewish Families* [Cincinnati: American Jewish Archives, 1978], 264; James H. Fairchild, *Oberlin: The Colony and the College, 1833–1883* [Oberlin, Ohio: E.J. Goodrich, 1883], 368–70.)

Sharp, Thomas Coke (1818–1894), lawyer, newspaper editor; born at Mt. Holly, Burlington County, New Jersey. Studied law in Pennsylvania. Located at Warsaw, Hancock County, Illinois, 1840. Married Hannah Wilcox, 1842. Bought and began to publish *The Western World* in 1840; changed the name of the paper to *Warsaw Signal* the following year. Sold the paper in 1842; repurchased it in 1844; resold it in 1846. He was a leading spokesman for the anti-Mormon cause in Hancock County. One of those indicted for the murder of Joseph Smith. Elected justice of the peace, 1851; and first mayor of Warsaw, 1853. Returned to journalism in 1854, when he bought the *Warsaw Express*. Elected county judge, 1864. After expiration of his term, returned to practice of law and edited the *Carthage Gazette*. Died at Carthage, Illinois. (*Portrait and Biographical Record of Hancock, McDonough and Henderson Counties Illinois* [Chicago: Lake City Publishing Company, 1894], 430–33; Oaks and Hill, *Carthage Conspiracy*, 56–58; Annette P. Hampshire, "Thomas Sharp and Anti-Mormon Sentiment in Illinois, 1842–1845," *Journal of the Illinois State Historical Society* 72 [May 1979]: 82–100.)

Sheldon, Crawford Bernon (1799–1869), born at Delhi, Delaware County, New York. Married Joanna C. Trippe, 1820. (Family Group Records Collection.)

Sherman, Lyman Royal (1804–1839), born at Monkton, Addison County, Vermont. Married Delcena Didamia Johnson, 1829. Converted to Mormonism, 1832. Participant in Zion's Camp, 1834. One of the presidents of the seventy, 1835–1837. Appointed to Kirtland high council, 1837. Moved to Far West, Missouri, 1838. Called to apostleship in 1839 but died before he could be notified and ordained. (Cook, *Revelations*, 217; Jenson, *Biographical Encyclopedia*, 1:190.)

Sherwood, Henry Garlie (1785–1862), surveyor; born at Kingsbury, Washington County, New York. Converted to Mormonism, 1832. Moved to Kirtland, Ohio, about 1834. Appointed to the Kirtland high council, 1837; the Nauvoo high council, 1839; and the Salt Lake stake high council, 1849. Elected Nauvoo city marshall in 1841. Commissary general for the Mormon pioneer exodus to Utah, 1847–1848. To San Bernardino, California, in 1852. Appointed surveyor for San Bernardino County in 1853. Returned to Salt Lake City in 1856 and served as agent for the Pony Express. Died at San Bernardino, California. (Cook, *Revelations*, 274.)

Singley, Margaret (1791–?), born at Unity, Allegheny County, Pennsylvania. Married Nicholas Singley. Accompanied Mormon pioneers to Utah in 1847. Living in California in 1850. (Early Church Information File.)

Sloan, James (1792–1886), lawyer, farmer; born in Donaghmore, County Tyrone, North Ireland. Appointed first city recorder of Nauvoo, Illinois, in 1840; general Church clerk and recorder, 1841–1843, and secretary of the Nauvoo Legion. Clerk to patriarch Hyrum Smith, 1841. Missionary to Ireland in 1843. County clerk, Pottawattamie County, Iowa, 1850; elected judge of the Sixth Judicial District, 1851. Migrated to California, where he joined the RLDS Church. Farming in Sacramento, where he died. (Jenson, *Biographical Encyclopedia*, 1:254; U.S. Census: Pottawattamie County, Iowa, 1850; San Joaquin, Sacramento County, California, 1860; *History of the Reorganized Church*, 4:158, 550; Charles H. Babbitt, *Early Days at Council Bluffs* [Washington, D.C., 1916], 95; *Times and Seasons*, 3:585.)

Smith, Agnes Moulton Coolbrith (1811–1876), born at Scarboro, Cumberland County, Maine. Living in Boston when converted to Mormonism, 1833. Married Don Carlos Smith, 1835. After the death of her husband in 1841, she married William Pickett. Moved to St. Louis in 1847 and to California in 1851. Lived in Marysville, Los Angeles, San Bernardino, San Francisco, and Oakland. A daughter of Agnes and Don Carlos, Josephine Donna (Ina Coolbrith), was named Librarian and Laureate of California in 1915. Died at Oakland. (International Genealogical Index; *Utah Genealogical Magazine*, 26:105–6; Josephine D. Rhodehamel and Raymund F. Wood, *Ina Coolbrith: Librarian and Laureate of California* [Provo, Utah: BYU Press, 1973].)

Smith, Alvin (1798–1823), farmer; brother of Joseph Smith. Born at Tunbridge, Orange County, Vermont. After his parents moved to Palmyra, New York, from Vermont, Alvin played a prominent role in the family economy, working hard to pay for and clear land and build a home. Joseph referred to him as "the noblest of my father's family." According to his mother, Alvin died of an overdose of calomel administered by a local physician for a stomach ailment, possibly appendicitis.

(Lucy Smith, *Biographical Sketches*, 87ff; Richard L. Anderson, "The Alvin Smith Story," *Ensign* 17 [August 1987]: 67–69.)

Smith, Amanda Barnes (1809–1886), born at Becket, Berkshire County, Massachusetts. Married Warren Smith in Lorain County, Ohio, in 1826. Converted to Mormonism in 1831. Witnessed the murder of her husband and a son and the severe wounding of another son at the massacre at Haun's Mill in Caldwell County, Missouri, in 1838. Afterward located at Nauvoo, Illinois. Migrated to Utah in 1850. Resided in Salt Lake City until shortly before her death, when she went to live with a daughter at Richmond, Cache County, Utah. (Jenson, *Biographical Encyclopedia*, 2:792–97.)

Smith, Asahel (1773–1848), born at Windham, Rockingham County, New Hampshire. Uncle of Joseph Smith. Served as an officer in the Vermont militia. Married Betsy Shellinger at Royalton, Windsor County, Vermont, 1802. After joining the Latter-day Saints he was appointed to the high council in Kirtland, Ohio, in 1837 and in Iowa in 1839. Was ordained a patriarch in 1844. Died at Iowaville, Wappelo County, Iowa, during the Mormon exodus. (Anderson, *Joseph Smith's New England Heritage*, 102, 109–11, 149; *History of the Church*, 2:510–11; 4:12.)

Smith, Charles H. (1817–?), merchant; born at Potsdam, St. Lawrence County, New York. Married Elizabeth Booth at Nauvoo, Illinois, 1843. Living at Cincinnati, Ohio, in 1850. (U.S. Census, Cincinnati, Hamilton County, Ohio, 1850; Susan Easton Black, "Marriages in the Nauvoo Region, 1839–1845," p. 66.)

Smith, Don Carlos (1816–1841), farmer, printer; born at Norwich, Windsor County, Vermont. Brother of Joseph Smith. Married Agnes M. Coolbrith, 1835. President of the high priests quorum in Kirtland, Ohio, 1836, and in Nauvoo, Illinois, 1841. Managing editor of the *Elder's Journal* in Kirtland in 1837 and of the *Times and Seasons* in Nauvoo, 1839–1841. Member of the Nauvoo city council, 1841. A lieutenant colonel in the Hancock County militia and brigadier general in the Nauvoo Legion, 1841. He died at Nauvoo. (Cook, *Revelations*, 274–75; *History of the Church*, 4:393–94; 398–99; Anderson, "Joseph Smith's Brothers, *Ensign* 9 [September 1979]: 30.)

Smith, Elijah (1776–1855), farmer; born in Connecticut. Uncle to Elizabeth Ann Smith Whitney. Died in Kirtland, Ohio. (U.S. Census: Kirtland, Geauga, Ohio, 1850; Kirtland, Ohio Cemetery Record, p. 21, Typescript.)

Smith, Emma Hale (1804–1879), born at Harmony, Susquehanna County, Pennsylvania. Married Joseph Smith, 1827. Assisted her husband as scribe during early translation work on the Book of Mormon. An 1830 revelation directed her to select hymns for a Church hymnal. With her husband during the movement of the Church from New York to Illinois, 1830–1839. Appointed president of the Female Relief Society at Nauvoo, Illinois, in 1842. Remained in Illinois after the death of her husband in 1844. In 1847 she married Lewis Bidamon. Died at Nauvoo, Illinois. (Cook, *Revelations*, 37; Linda K. Newell and Valeen T. Avery, *Mormon Enigma: Emma Hale Smith* [Garden City, New York: Doubleday and Company, 1984].)

Smith, Frederick Granger Williams (1836–1862), farmer, merchant; born at Kirtland, Geauga County, Ohio. Son of Joseph Smith, the Prophet. Married Annie Maria Jones, 1857. Resided at Nauvoo, Illinois, where he died. (Mary Audentia Smith Anderson, *Ancestry and Posterity of Joseph Smith and Emma Hale* [Independence, Missouri, 1929], 578–79; Newell and Avery, *Mormon Enigma*, 274–75.)

Smith, George Albert (1817–1875), farmer; cousin of Joseph Smith. Born at Potsdam, St. Lawrence County, New York. Baptized, 1832; moved to Kirtland, Ohio, 1833. Participant in march of Zion's Camp, 1834. Appointed to first quorum of seventy, 1835. Member of Council of Twelve, 1839–1875. Mission to England, 1839–1841. Married Bathsheba Bigler, 1841. Member of Nauvoo Legion. Arrived in Salt Lake Valley with Mormon pioneers, 1847. Directed early settlement of southern Utah. Was appointed Church historian, 1854. Member of Utah Territorial Supreme Court, 1855. Counselor to Brigham Young, 1868. (*Deseret Weekly*, 18 August 1858; Cook, *Revelations*, 275–76; Jenson, *Biographical Encyclopedia*, 1:37–42.)

Smith, Hyrum (1800–1844), farmer; born at Tunbridge, Orange County, Vermont. Married Jerusha Barden, 1826. One of the Eight Witnesses to the Book of Mormon. Member of the committee to supervise construction of the temple at Kirtland, Ohio. Participant in the march of Zion's Camp, 1834. Appointed second counselor in First Presidency, 1837. Imprisoned at Liberty, Missouri, with his brother Joseph, 1838–1839. Appointed patriarch and assistant Church president, 1841. Member of Nauvoo city council. Among those charged in the destruction of the Nauvoo *Expositor*, 1844. Killed in the attack upon the jail that also took his brother Joseph's life at Carthage, Illinois. (Cook, *Revelations*, 19–20; Jenson, *Biographical Encyclopedia*, 1:52.)

Smith, John (1781–1854), farmer; born at Derryfield, Rockingham County, New Hampshire. Uncle of Joseph Smith. Baptized, 1832. Member of the Kirtland high council, 1834. Presided over branches or stakes of the Church in Daviess County, Missouri, 1838; Lee County, Iowa, 1839; Ramus, Hancock County, Illinois, 1843; Nauvoo, Illinois, 1844; Salt Lake City, 1847–1848. Accompanied the first Mormon pioneer company to Utah, 1847. Patriarch to the Church, 1849–1854. Died at Salt Lake City. (Jenson, *Biographical Encyclopedia*, 1:182–83; Cook, *Revelations*, 208; Irene M. Bates, "Uncle John Smith, 1781–1854: Patriarchal Bridge," *Dialogue: A Journal of Mormon Thought* 20 [Fall 1987]: 79–89.)

Smith, Joseph (1771–1840), cooper, farmer, schoolteacher, storekeeper; born at Topsfield, Essex County, Massachusetts. Father of Joseph the Prophet. Married Lucy Mack, 1796, in Tunbridge, Vermont. After three crop failures, he moved his family to Palmyra, New York, in 1816. One of the Eight Witnesses to the Book of Mormon. Moved to Kirtland, Ohio, 1831. Was appointed patriarch to the Church, 1833. Member of the Kirtland high council. Appointed assistant counselor to the First Presidency, 1837. Died at Nauvoo, Illinois. (Cook, *Revelations*, 11.)

Smith, Katherine (1813–1900), born at Lebanon, Grafton County, New Hampshire. Sister of Joseph Smith. Married Wilkins Jenkins Salisbury, 1831. Parents of eight children. The family moved to Missouri in 1838, then to Illinois. After the death of her husband in 1856, she remained at Plymouth, Hancock County, Illinois. Although affiliated with the RLDS Church, she maintained contact with relatives and friends in Utah until her death. (*Utah Genealogical and Historical Magazine*, 26:102, 151–52; Anderson, "What were Joseph Smith's Sister's Like?" 42–44.)

Smith, Lucy (1821–1882), youngest sister of Joseph Smith; born at Palmyra, Ontario County, New York. Living with her parents during the migration of the Church from New York to Illinois, 1830–1839. Married Arthur Millikin in 1840; mother of nine children. She and her husband cared for her widowed mother for several years. Joined the RLDS Church in 1873. Died in Illinois. (Anderson, "What were Joseph Smith's Sisters Like?" 42–44.)

Smith, Lucy Mack (1775–1856), daughter of Solomon Mack and Lydia Gates. Mother of Joseph Smith. Married Joseph Smith, Sr., 1796. Family of eight sons and three daughters. Seven of her sons preceded her in death. Led a company of Saints from Palmyra, New York, to Kirtland, Ohio, 1831. With the Latter-day Saints in Ohio, Missouri, and Illinois, 1830–1839. Her *Biographical Sketches of Joseph Smith*, written in 1845, is an important Smith family historical source. After the violent death of her sons Joseph and Hyrum and the departure of the Saints to the West, she remained in Nauvoo, Illinois, until her death. (Jenson, *Biographical Encyclopedia*, 1:690–92.)

Smith, Lyman (c.1817–1837), born at Potsdam, St. Lawrence County, New York. A second cousin of George A. Smith. Participant in the march of Zion's Camp, 1834. Missionary in the eastern states with George A. in 1835. Married Clarissa Lyman, 1835. (Family Group Records Collection; Merlo Pusey, *Builders of the Kingdom* [Provo, Utah: BYU Press, 1981], 19–21; Smith, *History of the Church*, 2:185.)

Smith, Samuel Harrison (1808–1844), farmer; younger brother of Joseph Smith. Born at Tunbridge, Orange County, Vermont. One of the

Eight Witnesses to the Book of Mormon. Proselyting with Orson Hyde in the eastern states, 1832. Hyde said of him, he was "a man slow of speech and unlearned, yet a man of good faith and extreme integrity." Married Mary Bailey, 1834. Member of the Kirtland high council, 1834–1838. Moved to Missouri, 1838. Participated in the battle at Crooked River. Was appointed a bishop at Nauvoo in 1841. Nauvoo city alderman and member of Nauvoo Legion, 1841. Married Levira Clark, 1841. Moved to Plymouth, Illinois, 1842. Died at Nauvoo, Illinois. (Cook, *Revelations*, 34; Jenson, *Biographical Encyclopedia*, 1:278–82; Richard L. Anderson, *Investigating the Book of Mormon Witnesses*, 140–41; and Anderson, "Joseph Smith's Brothers," 30–33.)

Smith, Sophronia (1803–1876), born at Tunbridge, Orange County, Vermont. A sister of Joseph Smith. Married Calvin W. Stoddard at Palmyra, New York, 1828. Mother of two known daughters. After Calvin's death in 1836, Sophronia married William McCleary in 1838. She was numbered with the Saints in Ohio, Missouri, and Illinois but did not follow Brigham Young west. Died in Illinois. (*Utah Genealogical and Historical Magazine*, 26:102, 151; Stoddard Family Bible, in possession of Buddy Youngreen; Richard L. Anderson, "What were Joseph Smith's Sisters Like?" 42–44.)

Smith, Sylvester (c.1805–?), born in Connecticut. Converted to Mormonism, 1831. One of the presidents of seventy, 1835–1837. Missionary to New England with Jared Carter in 1832. Quarrelsome participant in Zion's Camp, 1834. Temporary scribe to Joseph Smith in 1836 during illness of Warren Parrish. Member of the Kirtland high council, 1835–1836. Left the Church in 1837. Living in Kirtland, Ohio, 1840, and Willoughby, 1850. (Jenson, *Biographical Encyclopedia*, 1:191; Cook, *Revelations*, 156; U.S. Census: Lake County, Ohio, 1840, 1950.)

Smith, William (1811–1893), farmer, newspaper editor. Brother of Joseph Smith. Married Caroline Amanda Grant in 1833. Participant in march of Zion's Camp, 1834. Member of the Quorum of Twelve, 1835–1845. Settled at Plymouth, Illinois, 1839. Represented Hancock County in the Illinois State House of Representatives, 1842. Editor of Nauvoo newspaper *The Wasp*, 1842. Was appointed presiding patriarch, 1845. Rebellious and headstrong, he was excommunicated in 1845. Associated with James J. Strang, 1846–1847; joined RLDS Church, 1878. Died at Osterdock, Clay County, Iowa. (Cook, *Revelations*, 276–77; Jenson, *Biographical Encyclopedia*, 1:86–87; Anderson, "Joseph Smith's Brothers," 32–33.)

Snow, Eliza Roxcy (1804–1887), teacher, poet, author, seamstress; born at Becket, Berkshire County, Massachusetts. Sister of Lorenzo Snow. Living at Mantua, Portage County, Ohio, when converted to Mormonism in 1835. When the Relief Society was organized in Nauvoo, Illinois, in 1842 she was appointed secretary. Plural wife of Joseph Smith.

After his death married Brigham Young. Migrated to Utah in 1847. Appointed president of the Relief Society, 1866. President of the board of directors of the Deseret Hospital Association in 1881. Died in Salt Lake City. (Jenson, *Biographical Encyclopedia*, 1:693–97.)

Snow, Erastus (1818–1888), farmer; born at St. Johnsbury, Caledonia County, Vermont. Converted to Mormonism in 1833. Married Artemesia Beman, 1838. Located with the Latter-day Saints in Ohio, Missouri, and Illinois. Engaged in extensive missionary work. Appointed to the Iowa high council, 1839. Member of the Council of Fifty. Accompanied Mormon pioneers to Salt Lake Valley, 1847. Appointed to the Quorum of Twelve, 1849. Established the Scandinavian Mission, 1850; presiding in Copenhagen, 1850–1852. Published and edited the *St. Louis Luminary* in Missouri, 1854. Colonizer in southern Utah; founded St. George, Washington County, 1861. Died in Salt Lake City. (Cook, *Revelations*, 301–2; Jenson, *Biographical Encyclopedia* 1:103–15.)

Snow, Oliver (1775–1845), schoolteacher, farmer; born at Becket, Berkshire County, Massachusetts. Father of Eliza and Lorenzo Snow. Married Rosetta Pettibone. Joined the Latter-day Saints about 1835 and moved to Kirtland, Ohio. Moved to Daviess County, Missouri, 1838, and Hancock County, Illinois, 1840. Died at Walnut Grove, Illinois. (Orrin Harmon, "Historical Facts Appertaining to the Township of Mantua . . . Ohio," MS., Western Reserve Historical Society.)

Snow, Zerubbabel (1809–1888), schoolteacher, merchant, lawyer; elder brother of Erastus Snow. Born at St. Johnsbury, Caledonia County, Vermont. Converted to Mormonism and moved to Ohio, 1832. Commissary of Zion's Camp, 1834. Practiced law in Ohio, 1839–1850. Associate Justice of Utah Territory, 1851–1854. Missionary to Australia, 1856–1858. Probate judge of Iron County, Utah, 1859–1861; and Utah County, 1862–1864. Salt Lake County prosecuting attorney, 1865–1884. (Jenson, *Biographical Encyclopedia*, 4:691; Tullidge, *History of Salt Lake City*, 160–66.)

Snyder, John (1800–1875), mason; born at Pleasant Valley, Brunswick, Nova Scotia. Married Mary Herron, 1822. Converted to Mormonism in Canada in 1836. Missionary to England in 1837. Located in Missouri and Illinois. Appointed on committee to build the Nauvoo House in Nauvoo, Illinois. Member of the Nauvoo Legion. Mission to England, 1842–1843. In 1850 migrated to Utah, where he died. (Cook, *Revelations*, 277–78; Family Group Records Collection.)

Spencer, Orson (1802–1855), born at West Stockbridge, Berkshire County, Massachusetts. Studied law and theology in New York. Converted to Mormonism in 1841. After locating at Nauvoo, Illinois, he served as alderman and in 1845 was elected mayor. Presided over the British mission, 1847–1849. In Utah he was appointed chancellor of

Deseret University and a member of the territorial legislative council. He died in St. Louis after completing a mission to the Cherokee nation. (Jenson, *Biographical Encyclopedia*, 1:337–39.)

Squires, Andrew Jackson (1815–1897), physician; born at Aurora, Portage County, Ohio. Studied medicine at Willoughby Medical College, Willoughby, Ohio, 1840–1841. Married Martha Wilmot, 1850. Began practice of medicine at Mantua in 1864; still practicing in Hiram, Ohio, 1885. Justice of the peace. Served in Ohio state legislature, 1859–1861. (*History of Portage County, Ohio* [Chicago: Warner, Beers and Company, 1885], 750; U.S. Census: Mantua, Portage County, Ohio, 1850; Family Group Records Collection.)

Stanley, Harvey (1811–1862), stonecutter, dairyman; born in New York. Member of the first quorum of seventy. Participant in march of Zion's Camp to Missouri, 1834. Married Lerona Eliza Cahoon, daughter of Reynolds Cahoon, in Kirtland, Ohio, 1836. Lerona died, 1840. Worked on Nauvoo Temple. Living at Keokuk, Lee County, Iowa, 1850. Migrated in the 1850s to Petaluma, Marin County, California, where he died. (U.S. Census: Lee County, Iowa, 1850; Marin County, California, 1860; Marin County, California, Probate Register, 1862; Shurtleff and Cahoon, *Reynolds Cahoon and his Stalwart Sons*, 93–94.)

Stiles, George Philander (1816–1885), lawyer; born at Watertown, Jefferson County, New York. After his conversion to Mormonism he practiced law in Nauvoo, Illinois. Married Sophia Janett Williamson at Nauvoo, 1842. Appointed an alternate Nauvoo city councilor, 1844. United States associate justice for Utah territory, 1854–1857. Excommunicated from the church in 1856. Living at Cardington, Morrow County, Ohio, in 1860. Died at Belton, Bell County, Texas. (Black, "Membership of the Church," 41:773–74; Brooks, *On The Mormon Frontier*, 611; U.S. Census: Cardington, Morrow County, Ohio, 1860; Henry Reed Stiles, *The Stiles Family in America* [Jersey City: Doan & Pilson Printers, 1895], 454.)

Stillman, Dexter (1804–1852), born at Colebrook, Litchfield County, Connecticut. Married Barbara Redfield. With the Latter-day Saints in Ohio, Missouri, and Illinois. Member of the Mormon Battalion in the Mexican War. In Pottawattamie County, Iowa, in 1848. (Black, "Membership of the Church" 41:795–96; International Genealogical Index.)

Stoddard, Calvin (1801–1836), married Joseph Smith's sister Sophronia in Palmyra, New York, 1828. Father of two daughters. Helped build the Kirtland Temple. Died at Kirtland, Ohio. (*Utah Genealogical and Historical Magazine*, 26:102, 151; Stoddard family Bible; *History of the Church*, 2:206; Anderson, "What were Joseph Smith's Sisters Like?")

Strobridge, Richard R. (1816–?), born in New York. Living at Brantford, Brant County, Ontario, Canada, in 1851. Converted to Mormonism and baptized by Joseph Smith at Mt. Pleasant, Ontario, in 1833. (Canadian Census: Brantford, Brant, Ontario, 1851.)

Strong, Elial (c.1810–1834), born at Sullivan, Tioga County, Pennsylvania. One of the first Mormon converts from Tioga County, 1831. One of the missionaries who converted Heber C. Kimball, Brigham Young, and others at Mendon, New York, 1832. He died of cholera in Missouri. ("Journal History of the Church," 31 December 1831; 15 April 1832; Backman, *Profile*, 69.)

Swazey, Ezekiel A. M. (1808–1863), attorney; born in Vermont. Resident of Farmington, Van Buren County, Iowa. Appointed brigadier general of the first division of state militia in 1830. Involved in local politics in Iowa. Died at Farmington from Civil War injuries. (U.S. Census: Farmington, Van Buren County, Iowa, 1850, 1860; *The History of Van Buren County, Iowa* [Chicago: Western Historical Company, 1879], 363, 367–68, 442.

Taylor, James (1783–1870), farmer, carpenter; born at Heversham, Westmoreland, England. Father of LDS Church president John Taylor. Married Agnes Taylor in England, 1805. Government excise officer. Moved to Liverpool in 1819. Emigrated to Toronto, Canada, 1830. Converted to Mormonism in 1836. Resided with the Latter-day Saints at Nauvoo, Illinois. To Utah with Mormon pioneers in 1847. Died at Salt Lake City. (Black, "Membership of the Church," 42:708–11.)

Taylor, John (1808–1887), born at Milnthorpe, Westmoreland County, England. Emigrated to Toronto, Canada, 1829. Married Leonora Cannon, 1833. Converted by Mormon missionaries in 1836. Appointed to the Council of Twelve, 1838. Missionary in England, 1839–1841. Member of the Nauvoo, Illinois, city council, Nauvoo Legion, and editor of the *Times and Seasons* and *Nauvoo Neighbor*. With Joseph Smith when he was killed in Carthage Jail. Mission to England, 1846–1847. Arrived in Salt Lake Valley, 1847. Mission to France, 1850–1852. Editor of *The Mormon* in New York City, 1855–1857. Member of the Utah territorial legislature, 1857–1876. Succeeded Brigham Young as president of the Church, 1880–1887. Died at Kaysville, Davis County, Utah. (Cook, *Revelations*, 234–35.)

Taylor, Jonathan (180?–?), born at Burlington, Hartford County, Connecticut. Residing at Norton, Medina County, Ohio, in 1830. (U.S. Census: Norton, Medina County, Ohio, 1830.)

Thayer, Ezra (1787–1856), bootcutter; born at Randolph, Norfolk County, Massachusetts. Married Polly Wales, 1810. Baptized by Parley Pratt in Ontario County, New York, 1830. Member of the committee to purchase land for settlement at Kirtland, Ohio, 1833. Participant in march of Zion's Camp, 1834. Member of the Council of Fifty in Nauvoo. Returned to place of his birth after death of Joseph Smith. Died in

Randolph, Massachusetts. (Cook, *Revelations*, 47–48; *History of the Church*, 1:335; 2:185; U.S. Census: Randolph, Norfolk County, Massachusetts, 1850; Randolph, Norfolk County, Mass. Death Register, 1856.)

Thomas, David (?–1845), landowner at DeWitt, Carroll County, Missouri, who along with Henry Root solicited Latter-day Saints to settle there in 1838.

Tippets, John Harvey (1810–1890), farmer; born in Rockingham County, New Hampshire. Converted to Mormonism, 1832. Married Abby Jane Smith, 1834. Involved with the Church in Missouri and Illinois. Member of Mormon Battalion, 1846. Accompanied sick detachment to Pueblo, Colorado, then joined the Saints at Winter Quarters. Left pioneer company at Fort Laramie to lead Battalion members and Mississippi Saints to Salt Lake Valley in 1847. Moved to Farmington, Davis County, Utah, 1864. Was ordained patriarch, 1878. Died at Farmington. (Family Group Records Collection; Carter, *Our Pioneer Heritage*, 2:606–7.)

Tippets, Joseph H. (1814–1868), farmer; a cousin of John H. and William Tippets. Born at Lewis, Essex County, New York. Participated in construction of the temple at Kirtland, Ohio. Married Rosella Elvira Perry, 1837. At Quincy, Illinois, in 1840. Crossed plains to Utah, 1848. Resided at Kaysville, Farmington, and Brigham City, where he died. (Family Group Records Collection; Backman, *Profile*, 72, 99; U.S. Census: Adams County, Illinois, 1840.)

Tippets, William (1812–1877), farmer; born at Groton, Hillsboro County, New Hampshire. Joined the Latter-day Saints, 1832. Married Sophia Mead, 1842. Residing at Liberty, Clay County, Missouri, 1844–1850; Salt Lake City, Utah, 1850–1860. Died at Perry, Box Elder County, Utah. (Family Group Records Collection; Lydia Walker Forsgren, *History of Box Elder County* [Box Elder County Daughters of the Utah Pioneers, 1937], 14.)

Turley, Theodore (1800–1872), born at Birmingham, England. Married Frances A. Kimberly, 1821. Emigrated to Canada as a Methodist preacher in 1818. Converted to Mormonism in 1837. Located with the Latter-day Saints in Ohio, Missouri, and Illinois. Missionary in England, 1839–1840. Appointed weigher and sealer in Nauvoo, 1841. Also owned a gun shop. Died at Beaver, Beaver County, Utah. (Theodore Turley Journal, Typescript, BYU Library.)

Turner, James B. (1815–1866), born in Tennessee. County clerk and clerk of the Daviess County, Missouri circuit court, 1837–1838. Member of a joint committee of the Missouri legislature to investigate the Mormon conflict, 1838–1839. Ray County clerk, 1852–1864. Died in Ray County, Missouri. (*History of the Church*, 3:60, 235–38, 246;

U.S. Census: Ray County, Missouri, 1850; Ray County, Missouri, Probate Record, 1866; *The History of Daviess County, Missouri*, 360.)

Vance, John (1794–1882), farmer; born in Cook County, Tennessee. Married Sarah Perkins, 1817. Moved to McDonough County, Illinois. After death of his wife in 1836, married Elizabeth Campbell, 1837. Bishop at Winter Quarters during the Mormon exodus to Utah. Arrived in Salt Lake Valley in 1847. Salt Lake City high councilor, school commissioner, justice of the peace. Counselor in 7th Ward bishopric. Died in Salt Lake City. (Esshom, *Pioneers and Prominent Men of Utah*, 1,222; Black, "Membership of the Church," 44:230– 34.)

Walker, Lorin (1822–1907), born at Peacham, Caledonia County, Vermont. Joseph Smith's nephew. After Lorin's mother died in 1842, leaving ten children, Joseph Smith took the oldest four, including Lorin, into his home. Married Lovina Smith, daughter of Hyrum Smith, 1844. Stayed in Nauvoo, Illinois, after death of Joseph Smith to help his widow Emma. After Emma married Lewis Bidamon in 1847, Lorin and his wife moved to Macedonia, Hancock County, where they lived with Katherine and Sophronia, Joseph Smith's sisters, both widows. Migrated to Utah in 1860 and settled at Farmington, Davis County. Operated a carding mill. After death of his wife in 1876, he moved to Rockland, Idaho, where he died. (Elizabeth Hansen, Biographical Sketch of Lorin Walker, MS.)

Walker, William Holmes (1820–1908), born at Peacham, Caledonia County, Vermont. Brother of Lorin Walker. Converted to Mormonism in 1835. After the death of his mother in 1842, he lived in the home of Joseph Smith at Nauvoo, Illinois. Married Olive Farr, 1843. Started West with Mormon pioneers in 1846 and joined the Mormon Battalion in the Mexican War. Missionary and mission president in South Africa, 1852–1857. Resided in Utah until 1887, when he moved to Idaho. Died at Lewisville, Jefferson County. (*Deseret News*, 13 January 1908; Jenson, *Biographical Encyclopedia*, 1:565.)

Warren, Calvin Averill (1807–1881), lawyer; born at Elizabethtown, Essex County, New York. Before 1832 he worked as a typographer and editor in Vermont and New York. Moved to Hamilton County, Ohio, in 1832, studied law, and began practice at Batavia, Ohio. Married Viola Morris, 1835. Moved to Quincy, Adams County, Illinois, in 1836 and on to Warsaw, Hancock County, where he engaged in the practice of law, brickmaking, land speculation, and merchandising and ran a hotel and livery stable. In 1839 moved back to Quincy, where he was master in chancery for many years and practiced law until his death. (Newton Bateman and Paul Selby, eds., *Historical Encyclopedia of Illinois* [Chicago and New York: Munsell Publishing Company, 1900], 577; *Atlas Map of Adams County* [Davenport, Iowa: Andreas, Lyter, and Company, 1872].)

Warren, Peter (no information)

Wasson, Lorenzo D. (c.1818–1857), born at Amboy, Lee County, Illinois. Son of Emma Smith's sister and brother-in-law, Elizabeth and Benjamin Wasson. Came to Illinois with his parents from Broome County, New York, in 1836. Converted to Mormonism in Illinois in 1842. Married Marietta Crocker, 1843. Appointed to the Council of Fifty, 1844. Died at Amboy. (Black, "Membership of the Church," 44:956–57; *History of the Church*, 4:557; 6:261.)

Waterman, John O. (1797–1876), farmer; born in Orange County, New York. Married Emeline Shepard. Living among the Latter-day Saints in Ohio, 1836. Bought land at Grove, Allegany County, New York, in 1837 and sold it in 1842. Died insane at Moline, Rock Island County, Illinois. (Donald L. Jacobus, *The Waterman Family* [New Haven: E. F. Waterman, 1942], 2:648–49.)

Weaver, Russell (1788–1866), farmer, preacher, physician; born at Shaftsbury, Bennington County, Vermont. Married Lydia Cowell, 1808. In 1809 residing at Cambria, Niagara County, New York, where he died. (Lucius E. Weaver, *History and Genealogy of a Branch of the Weaver Family* [Rochester, New York, 1928], 235–36.)

Webb, Edwin Densmore (1813–?), carpenter; born at Hanover, Chautauqua County, New York. Married Eliza McWithy at Kirtland, Ohio, 1835. One of the seventies in Kirtland, Ohio, 1836. Living in the Nauvoo, Illinois, 1st Ward, 1842, and in Racine, Wisconsin, 1842–1850. Crossed plains to Utah, 1853. Living at Fillmore, Millard County, Utah, 1860, and Sacramento, California, 1870–1880. (Family Group Records Collection; Black, "Membership of the Church," 30:146–47; U.S. Census: Marquette County, Wisconsin, 1850; Millard County, Utah, 1860; Sacramento, California, 1870, 1880.)

Webb, John (1808–1894), wagon maker, farmer; born at Manham, Herkimer County, New York. Married Catharine Wilcox, 1836. Baptized in 1839. Living in Adams County, Illinois, in early 1840s. The federal census lists him in Salt Lake Valley, 1850; Fillmore, Millard County, Utah, 1860; and Petersburgh, Millard County, in 1870. In 1855 he was one of the pioneer settlers of Holden, Millard County. He died at Coyote, Garfield County, Utah. (Family Group Records Collection; *Deseret Evening News*, 12 June 1894; Daughters of the Utah Pioneers, *An Enduring Legacy* [Salt Lake City: Utah Printing Company, 1982], 5:333.)

Wells, Daniel Hanmer (1814–1891), farmer; born at Trenton, Oneida County, New York. Moved to Hancock County, Illinois, in 1834. Married Eliza Robeson, 1835. Residing at Commerce when the Mormons arrived there and sold land to them. An officer in the state militia, constable, justice of the peace, alderman, and municipal court judge while residing at Nauvoo. Baptized in 1846. Migrated to Utah in 1848. Elected general of the Nauvoo Legion, 1849. Second counselor to Brigham Young, 1857–1877; counselor to the Quorum of Twelve, 1877–1891. Mayor of Salt Lake City, 1866–1876. Presided over the European Mission, 1884–1887. President of the Manti Temple, 1888–1891. Died in Salt Lake City. (Jenson, *Biographical Encyclopedia*, 1:62–66; *History of the Church*, 4:154–55.)

Weston, Samuel (188?-1846), carpenter, blacksmith; came to Missouri from Kentucky in 1824. One of the first settlers of the area that later became Independence in Jackson County. Operated a cabinet and blacksmith shop. Elected justice of the county court, 1829. Also served as deputy clerk of the circuit court, ex-officio recorder of deeds, and justice of the peace, 1830–1832. Trustee of the Independence Academy, 1835. Died at Independence. (Pearl Wilcox, *Jackson County Pioneers* [Independence, Missouri, 1975], 123–24, 404, 511.)

Whitcher, Mary (no information)

Whitlock, Harvey Gilman (1809–1874), medical doctor; born in Massachusetts. Married Minerva Abbot, 1830. Converted to Mormonism and moved to Jackson County, Missouri, 1831. Victim of the expulsion from Jackson County, 1833. Excommunicated, 1835; rebaptized, 1836. Withdrew from Church, 1838. Living in Cedar County, Iowa, in 1840. Member of the Grand Council of the Rigdonite Church in 1846. Medical doctor in Salt Lake City, 1850. Resided for a time at Springville, Utah. In 1864 moved to California, where he joined the RLDS Church and served as president of the Pacific Slope. Excommunicated from the RLDS Church, 1868. Died at Bishop Creek, Inyo County, California. (Cook, *Revelations*, 81; Journal of W. W. Blair, MS., RLDS Church Archives, Independence, Missouri; *Saints' Herald* 9 [1 June 1866]: 174.)

Whitmer, David (1805–1888), born near Harrisburg, Dauphin County, Pennsylvania. One of the Three Witnesses to the Book of Mormon. First met Joseph Smith during a business trip to Palmyra, New York, in 1828. Baptized in June 1829. Married Julia Ann Jolly, 1831. Appointed president of the Church in Missouri, 1834. In 1838 left the Church in Missouri and spent the rest of his life there. Operated a livery stable at Richmond, Ray County. Elected mayor of Richmond, 1867–1868. (Cook, *Revelations*, 24–25; Jenson, *Biographical Encyclopedia*, 1:263–71; Anderson, *Investigating the Book of Mormon Witnesses*, 67–92.)

Whitmer, John (1802–1878), farmer, stock raiser. Born in Pennsylvania. Among the first converts to Mormonism. One of the Eight Witnesses to the Book of Mormon. Scribe to Joseph Smith. Appointed Church Historian, 1831. Wrote a history titled "The Book of John Whitmer" covering the years 1831–1838. Married Sarah Jackson, 1833. Appointed counselor to his brother, David, in the Missouri Church presidency, 1834. Editor of the *Messenger and Advocate*, 1835–1836. Left the church in 1838; remained at Far West, Caldwell County, Missouri, where he died. (Cook, *Revelations*, 25–26; Jenson, *Biographical Encyclopedia*, 1:251–52.)

Whitmer, Peter, Jr. (1809–1836), tailor. Born at Fayette, Seneca County, New York. One of the Eight Witnesses to the Book of Mormon. Baptized in June 1830. Participant in the Lamanite mission to Ohio and Missouri, 1830–1831. Married Vashti Higley, 1832. Appointed to the Missouri high council, 1836. Died of tuberculosis in Clay County, Missouri. (Cook, *Revelations*, 26–27; Jenson, *Biographical Encyclopedia*, 1:277.)

Whitney, Elizabeth Ann Smith (1800–1883), born at Derby, New Haven County, Connecticut. Married Newel K. Whitney, 1822. Converted to Mormonism in 1830. Appointed first counselor to Emma Smith when the Relief Society was organized at Nauvoo, Illinois, in 1842 and second counselor in the Relief Society in Utah, 1866–1883. Came to Utah with her family in 1848. Died in Salt Lake City. (Jenson, *Biographical Encyclopedia*, 3:563–64; 4:200.)

Whitney, Sarah Ann (1825–1873), born at Kirtland, Geauga, County, Ohio. Daughter of Elizabeth Ann and Newel K. Whitney. Plural wife of Joseph Smith, 1842. After death of the Prophet, married Heber C. Kimball. Came to Utah in 1848. Died in Salt Lake City. (Kate B. Carter, comp., *Our Pioneer Heritage*, 10:389–90.)

Whitney, Newel Kimball (1795–1850), merchant; born at Marlborough, Windham County, Vermont. Partner with Sidney Gilbert in a mercantile firm at Painesville and, later, Kirtland, Ohio. Married Elizabeth Ann Smith, 1822. Appointed bishop at Kirtland, 1831; Nauvoo Middle Ward, 1839; Salt Lake City 18th Ward, 1849. Traveled with Joseph Smith to Missouri and New York, 1832. Elected alderman at Nauvoo, 1841. Crossed the plains to Utah in 1848. Died at Salt Lake City. (Cook, *Revelations*, 102–3; Jenson, *Biographical Encyclopedia*, 1:222–27.)

Whitney, Samuel (1772–1846), father of Newel K. Whitney, was born at Marlborough, Windham County, Vermont. Married Susanna Kimball, 1792. Joined the Latter-day Saints, November 1835. Died at Kirtland, Ohio. (Poulsen, "The Life and Contributions of Newel K. Whitney," 66; Family Group Records Collection; *Utah Genealogical and Historical Magazine*, 38:64.)

Wiggins, Ebenezer Fairchild (1806–1858), farmer; born at Millersburg, Bourbon County, Kentucky. Owned a farm on the outskirts of Nauvoo, Illinois. Died at Ogden, Weber County, Utah. (Family Group Records Collection.)

Wight, Lyman (1796–1858), farmer; born at Fairfield, Herkimer County, New York. Married Harriet Benton, 1823. Affiliated with the Campbellites in Kirtland, Ohio, when converted to Mormonism in 1830.

Among the Latter-day Saints driven from Jackson County, Missouri, 1833. The revelation that called missionaries to recruit volunteers for Zion's Camp listed Wight and Sidney Rigdon as companions. Member of the Clay County, Missouri, high council, 1834. Imprisoned with Joseph Smith at Liberty, Missouri, 1838–1839. Member of Council of Twelve, 1841–1848. Moved to Texas, 1845. Excommunicated, 1848. Chief justice of Gillespie County, Texas, 1850. Died at Dexter, Medina County, Texas. (Cook, *Revelations*, 82–83; *Doctrine and Covenants* 103:38; Jenson, *Biographical Encyclopedia*, 1:93; U.S. Census: Gillespie County, Texas, 1850.)

Wightman, William (1807–1842), born at German Flats, Herkimer County, New York. Married Dolly Eaton, 1832. Lived for a while in Allegany County, New York, before moving to Illinois. Platted the town of Ramus, Hancock County, in 1840 and served as proprietor and land agent. Officer in the Nauvoo Legion at the time of his death in Nauvoo. (Family Group Records Collection; *The Wasp* (Nauvoo, Illinois), 1 October 1842; Flanders, *Nauvoo*, 138–39.)

Wilcox, Catherine Noramore (1809–1884), was born at Kremina, New York. In 1826 married Eber Wilcox, who died of cholera in Clay County, Missouri, in 1834. Married John Webb, 1836. Lived in Illinois and Missouri. Crossed plains to Utah in 1848. By the 1860 census, Catherine had apparently separated from John Webb. (Family Group Records Collection; U.S. Census: Salt Lake County, 1850; Millard County, 1860.)

Williams, Frederick Granger (1787–1842), physician. Born at Suffield, Hartford County, Connecticut. Married Rebecca Swain, 1815. Converted by Mormon missionaries who came through Kirtland, Ohio, in November 1830. Appointed clerk to Joseph Smith in July 1832. Counselor in the First Presidency, 1833–1837. Participated in march of Zion's Camp, 1834. Disaffected from the Church, 1837; restored to fellowship, 1839. Died at Quincy, Illinois. (Jenson, *Biographical Encyclopedia*, 1:51–52; Cook, *Revelations*, 104–5.)

Williams, John D. (1808–1872), farmer, merchant. Native of Kentucky. Married Eleanor McCosky. Moved to Daviess County, Missouri, in 1841. Served two terms in state legislature, 1850, 1854. Merchant in Old Pattonsburg for many years. Living in Gallatin, 1860. Died in Daviess County. (*History of Daviess County, Missouri*, 363; U.S. Census: Gallatin, Daviess County, Missouri, 1860.)

Williams, William Wheeler (1790–1852), farmer; born at Suffield, Essex County, Massachusetts. Brother of Frederick G. Williams. Married Lavina Dibble, 1814, and, after her death two years later, married Nancy Sherman, 1817. Died at Newburgh, Cuyahoga County, Ohio. (U.S. Census: Newburgh, Cuyahoga, Ohio, 1850; Family Group Records Collection; Cornelia B. Williams and Anna P. Williams, comp., *Descendants of John Williams* [Chicago: privately printed, 1925], 142, 149–50.)

Wilson, Harmon T. (1815–1851), merchant; born in Virginia. One of early settlers of Carthage, Hancock County, Illinois. Elected Hancock County coroner, 1840; served as deputy sheriff. Involved in attempt to arrest Joseph Smith at Dixon, Lee County, Illinois, 1843. Member of the Carthage Greys, Hancock County militia. Married Helen Baldwin Williams, 1846. Proprietor of general stores at Warsaw and Carthage, 1847. Died at Warsaw, Hancock County. (U.S. Census: Hancock County, Illinois, 1850; Thomas Gregg, *History of Hancock County*, 291–95, 688; *Warsaw Signal*, 2 January 1847; Hancock County Probate Records, 1851; *History of the Church*, 5:439–42; 7:143.)

Wilson, Robert (1800–1870), born near Staunton, Augusta County, Virginia. Moved to Franklin, Howard County, Missouri, in 1820. Probate judge of Howard County, 1824–1827. Married Peggy Snoddy, 1825. Clerk of the Randolph circuit and county courts, 1828–1840. Wilson was a brigadier general in the 2nd brigade of John B. Clark's 1st Division of Missouri militia during the Mormon conflict of 1838. Prominent lawyer of central and western Missouri. Represented Randolph County in the Missouri legislature, 1844–1845, and later served two sessions in the state senate representing the district containing Andrew, Holt, and Atchison Counties. Appointed U.S. senator in 1862. Died at Marshall, Missouri. (William Bay, *Reminiscences of the Bench and Bar of Missouri* [St. Louis: F.H. Thomas and Company, 1878], 561–63.)

Witter, Daniel S. (180?–?), owned land at Warsaw, Hancock County, Illinois, as early as 1834. Operated a steam mill there. Engaged in land development scheme to encourage Mormon settlement in the area, 1841–1842. (*History of Hancock County, Illinois* [Hancock County: Board of Supervisors, 1968], 577; U.S. Census: Warsaw, Hancock, Illinois, 1840; Oaks and Hill, *Carthage Conspiracy*, 53–54.)

Wood, Daniel (1800–1892), farmer; born in Duchess County, New York. Family moved to Canada in 1803. Married Mary Snider, 1822. Converted to Mormonism in 1833. Resided with the Latter-day Saints in Ohio, Missouri, and Illinois. Migrated to Utah in 1848. One of the first settlers at Bountiful, Davis County. Died in Bountiful. (Adell H. Fielding, "Sketch of the Life of Daniel Wood," Typescript, 1951, LDS Family History Library.)

Woodruff, Wilford (1807–1898), farmer, miller; born at Farmington, Hartford County, Connecticut. Converted to Mormonism in 1833. Participated in the march of Zion's Camp, 1834. Missionary in the southern states, 1834–1836; New England, 1837–1838; Great Britain, 1839–1841. Married Phoebe Carter, 1837. Ordained an apostle in 1839. Presided over the European Mission, 1844–1846. Returned to Utah in

1850. Member of the Utah territorial legislature. Appointed an assistant Church historian in 1856; president of the Quorum of Twelve, 1880; and president of the Church, 1889–1898. Died at San Francisco, California. (Dean Jessee, "Wilford Woodruff," in *The Presidents of the Church*, edited by Leonard J. Arrington [Salt Lake City: Deseret Book Company, 1986], 116–43; Cook, *Revelations*, 235–36; Thomas G. Alexander, *Things in Heaven and Earth: The Life and Times of Wilford Woodruff, a Mormon Prophet* [Salt Lake City: Signature Books, 1991].)

Woolley, Edwin Dilworth (1807–1881), farmer, merchant; born at West Chester, Chester County, Pennsylvania. Married Mary Wickersham in 1831. Converted to Mormonism in 1837. Moved to Illinois in 1839. Crossed the plains to Utah with Mormon pioneers in 1848. For several years he was Brigham Young's business manager. Member of the Utah territorial legislature. Salt Lake County recorder. Helped organize the Deseret Telegraph company. Bishop of the Salt Lake City 13th ward, 1853–1881. He died in Salt Lake City. (Orson F. Whitney, *History of Utah*, 4:282–85; Leonard Arrington, *From Quaker to Latter-day Saint: Bishop Edwin D. Woolley* [Salt Lake City: Deseret Book Company, 1976].)

Works, Angeline Eliza (1814–1880), born at Aurelius, Cayuga County, New York. A sister to Brigham Young's wife Miriam. Married Ebenezer Robinson in Kirtland, Ohio, 1835. Died at Hamilton, Decatur County, Iowa. (Family Group Records Collection; *Biographical and Historical Record of Ringgold and Decatur Counties, Iowa*, 651–52.)

Yearsley, David Dutton (1808–1849), born at Thornbury, Chester County, Pennsylvania. Married Mary Ann Hoopes, 1830. Converted to Mormonism in 1841. Located at Nauvoo, Illinois. During the Mormon exodus from Nauvoo he was appointed bishop of the 12th Ward at Winter Quarters, Douglas County, Nebraska in 1846. In 1848 he was elected county commissioner of Pottawattamie County, Iowa. Died at Winter Quarters. (Black, "Membership of the Church," 47:981–83; "Journal History of the Church," 24 October 1846; 2 October 1848.)

Young, Brigham (1801–1877), carpenter, painter, glazier. Born at Whitingham, Windham County, Vermont. Married Miriam Works, 1824. Living in Mendon, New York, when he joined the Latter-day Saints in 1832. Moved to Kirtland, Ohio, 1832. With Zion's Camp, 1834. His Kirtland years were divided between missionary work and labor on the temple. Member of the Quorum of Twelve, 1835–1847; succeeded Thomas Marsh as president of the Quorum of Twelve, 1838; Church President, 1848–1877. Directed Mormon evacuation from Missouri, 1838–1839. Mission to England, 1839–1841. Elected to Nauvoo city council, 1841. Directed Mormon migration from Nauvoo to Utah, 1846–1848. Governor of Utah Territory, 1850–1857; Superintendent of Indian Affairs, 1851–1857. Directed colonization of hundreds of communities in western U.S. Died in Salt Lake City. (Jenson, *Biographical Encyclopedia*, 1:8–14; Cook, *Revelations*, 279–81. Leonard J. Arrington, *Brigham Young: American Moses* [New York: Alfred A. Knopf, 1985].)

Young, Joseph (1797–1881), painter, glazier; brother of Brigham Young. Born at Hopkinton, Middlesex County, Massachusetts. Converted to Mormonism in 1832. Married Jane A. Bicknell, 1834. A president of the first quorum of seventy, 1835–1881. Participant in Zion's Camp march to Missouri, 1834; and Kirtland Camp, 1838. Witnessed the Haun's Mill Massacre in Caldwell County, Missouri, 1838. Moved to Nauvoo, Illinois, 1840. Crossed the plains to Utah in 1850. Missionary in England, 1870. Died at Salt Lake City, Utah. (Jenson, *Biographical Encyclopedia*, 1:187–88; Cook, *Revelations*, 281.)

Young, Lorenzo Dow (1807–1895), farmer, nurseryman. Brother of Brigham Young. Born at Smyrna, Chenango County, New York. Married Persis Goodall, 1826. Converted to Mormonism, 1832. During his Ohio years he was a member of Zion's Camp and supervised plastering of the temple at Kirtland, Ohio. Arrived in Utah with Mormon pioneers of 1847. Bishop of Salt Lake City 18th Ward, 1851–1878. Was ordained patriarch, 1877. Died at Salt Lake City. (Family Group Records Collection; Jenson, *Biographical Encyclopedia*, 4:724–25; Whitney, *History of Utah*, 4:53–55.)

Young, Phineas (1799–1879), printer, lawyer, saddler; born at Hopkinton, Middlesex County, Massachusetts. Brother of Brigham Young. Married Clarissa Hamilton, 1818, and, later, Lucy Cowdery. Joined the Church in April 1832 and was en route to Jackson County, Missouri, in 1833 when he received news of the driving of the Saints from that place. Returned to Kirtland, Ohio, and worked in the printing office. Arrived in Utah with the Mormon pioneer company of 1847. Instrumental in the return of Oliver Cowdery to the Church, 1848. Missionary in England and Scotland. Bishop of Salt Lake City 2nd Ward, 1864–1871. Died in Salt Lake City. (*The Deseret Weekly*, 3 February 1858; Jenson, *Biographical Encyclopedia*, 4:511; Carter, *Our Pioneer Heritage*, 2:509.)

Young, Richard Montgomery (1796–1853), born in Kentucky. Studied law and moved to Illinois, where he was admitted to the bar in 1817. Served in the second general assembly of Illinois, 1820–1822, as a representative from Union County. Circuit judge, 1825–1827, 1829–1837. U.S. senator, 1837–1843, when he was commissioned justice of the Illinois Supreme Court. Resigned from the court in 1847 to become commissioner of the General Land Office at Washington, D.C. Died in an insane asylum at Washington, D.C. (Newton Bateman, *Historical Encyclopedia of Illinois, and History of Hancock County* [Chicago: Munsell Publishing Company, 1921], 603–4.)

SELECTED WORKS CITED

Alexander, Thomas G. "The Word of Wisdom: From Principle to Requirement." *Dialogue* 14 (Fall 1981), 78–88.

Allen, James B. and Glen M. Leonard. *Story of the Latter-day Saints.* Salt Lake City: Deseret Book Company, 1976.

Anderson, Karl Ricks. *Joseph Smith's Kirtland.* Salt Lake City: Deseret Book Company, 1989.

Anderson, Richard L. "Atchison's Letters and the Causes of Mormon Expulsion from Missouri." *BYU Studies* 26 (Summer 1986): 14–15.

An Appeal to the American People: Being an Account of the Persecutions of the Church of Latter Day Saints. Cincinnati: Shepard & Stearns, 1840.

Arrington, Leonard J. "An Economic Interpretation of the Word of Wisdom." *BYU Studies* 1 (Winter 1959), 37–49.

———. *Charles C. Rich.* Provo, Utah: BYU Press, 1974.

———. "Oliver Cowdery's Kirtland, Ohio, 'Sketch Book.' " *BYU Studies* 12 (Summer 1972): 410–426.

———, Feramorz Y. Fox, and Dean L. May. *Building the City of God.* Salt Lake City: Deseret Book Company, 1976.

Ashment, Edward H. "The Facsimiles of the Book of Abraham: A Reappraisal." *Sunstone* 4 (December 1979): 33–48.

"Atmospheric Phenomenon." *The Maryland Gazette* (Annapolis, Maryland), 21 November 1833.

Bachman, Danel W. "New Light on an Old Hypothesis: The Ohio Origins of the Revelation on Eternal Marriage." *Journal of Mormon History* 5 (1978): 19–32.

Backman, Milton V., Jr. *The Heavens Resound: A History of the Latter-day Saints in Ohio 1830–1838.* Salt Lake City: Deseret Book, 1983.

Beecher, Maureen Ursenbach. "Eliza R. Snow's Nauvoo Journal." *BYU Studies* 15 (Summer 1975): 391–416.

Bennett, John C. *History of the Saints: An Exposé of Joe Smith and Mormonism.* Boston: Leland & Whiting, 1842.

Bitton, Davis. "The Waning of Mormon Kirtland." *BYU Studies* 12 (Summer 1972): 455–64.

Bode, Carl. *The American Lyceum: Town Meeting of the Mind.* New York: Oxford University Press, 1956.

Brown, Lisle G. "The Sacred Departments for Temple Work in Nauvoo: The

SELECTED WORKS CITED

Assembly Room and the Council Chamber." *BYU Studies* 19 (Spring 1979): 361–74.

Cannon, Donald Q. "Licensing in the Early Church." *BYU Studies* 22 (Winter 1982): 96–105.

Cannon, Donald Q. and Lyndon W. Cook, eds. *Far West Record: Minutes of the Church of Jesus Christ of Latter-day Saints, 1830–1844*. Salt Lake City: Deseret Book Company, 1983.

Cook, Lyndon W. "Isaac Galland – Mormon Benefactor." *BYU Studies* 19 (Spring 1979): 261–84.

———. *Joseph Smith and The Law of Consecration*. Provo, Utah: Grandin Book Company, 1985.

———. *Revelations of the Prophet Joseph Smith*. Provo, Utah: Seventy's Mission Bookstore, 1981.

Corrill, John. *A Brief History of the Church of Jesus Christ of Latter Day Saints*. St. Louis, Missouri, 1839.

Crawley, Peter. "Two Rare Missouri Documents." *BYU Studies* 14 (Summer 1974): 518–527.

——— and Richard L. Anderson. "The Political and Social Realities of Zion's Camp." *BYU Studies* 14 (Summer 1974): 406–20.

Crossby, P. A., ed. *Lovell's Gazetteer of British North America*. Montreal, 1881.

Derr, Jill Mulvay. "Strength in Our Union": The Making of Mormon Sisterhood." In *Sisters in Spirit: Mormon Women in Historical and Cultural Perspective*, eds. Maureen Ursenbach Beecher and Lavina Fielding Anderson, 153–207. Urbana and Chicago: University of Illinois Press, 1987.

———, Janath R. Cannon, and Maureen U. Beecher. *Women of Covenant: The Story of Relief Society*. Salt Lake City: Deseret Book Company, 1992.

Document Containing the Correspondence, Orders, &c. in Relation to the Disturbances with the Mormons; and the Evidence Given before the Hon. Austin A. King. Fayette, Missouri: Boon's Lick Democrat, 1841.

Durham, Reed C., Jr. "The Election Day Battle at Gallatin." *BYU Studies* 13 (Autumn 1972): 36–61.

Ehat, Andrew F. and Lyndon W. Cook. *The Words of Joseph Smith*. Provo, Utah: Religious Studies Center, Brigham Young University, 1980.

England, Breck. *The Life and Thought of Orson Pratt*. Salt Lake City: University of Utah Press, 1985.

Esplin, Ronald K. "Thomas B. Marsh As President of the First Quorum of Twelve, 1835–38." In *Sidney B. Sperry Symposium*. Sandy, Utah: Randall Books, 1984, 167–90.

The Evening and the Morning Star. Independence, Missouri, and Kirtland, Ohio, 1832–34.

"Extract from the Journal of Elder Heber C. Kimball." *Times and Seasons* 6:771ff.

Firmage, Edwin Brown and Richard Collin Mangrum. *Zion in the Courts: A Legal History of the Church of Jesus Christ of Latter-day Saints, 1830–1900*. Urbana and Chicago: University of Illinois Press, 1988.

Flanders, Robert. *Nauvoo: Kingdom on the Mississippi*. Urbana, Illinois: University of Illinois Press, 1965.

Gardner, Hamilton Gardner. "The Nauvoo Legion, 1840–1845 – A Unique Military Organization." *Journal of the Illinois State Historical Society* 54 (Summer 1961): 181–97.

SELECTED WORKS CITED

Gentry, Leland H. "The Danite Band of 1838." *BYU Studies* 14 (Summer 1974): 421–450.

Godfrey, Kenneth W., Audrey M. Godfrey, and Jill Mulvay Derr. *Women's Voices: An Untold History of the Latter-day Saints.* Salt Lake City: Deseret Book Company, 1982.

Gregg, Thomas. *History of Hancock County, Illinois.* Chicago: Charles C. Chapman & Company, 1880.

Hamilton, Marshall. "'Money-Diggersville' — The Brief, Turbulent History of the Mormon Town of Warren." *John Whitmer Historical Association Journal* 9 (1989): 49–58.

———. "Thomas Sharp's Turning Point: Birth of an Anti-Mormon." *Sunstone* 13:5 (October 1989): 16–22.

Hampshire, Annette P. "Thomas Sharp and Anti-Mormon Sentiment in Illinois." *Journal of the Illinois State Historical Society* 72 (May 1979): 82–100.

Hill, Donna. *Joseph Smith: The First Mormon.* New York: Doubleday & Company, 1977.

Hill, Marvin S. "Cultural Crisis in the Mormon Kingdom: A Reconsideration of the Causes of Kirtland Dissent." *Church History* 49 (September 1980): 286–97.

———. *Quest for Refuge: The Mormon Flight From American Pluralism.* Salt Lake City: Signature Books, 1989.

———, C. Keith Rooker, Larry T. Wimmer, "The Kirtland Economy Revisited: A Market Critique of Sectarian Economics." *BYU Studies* 17 (Summer 1977): 391–482.

History of the Church of Jesus Christ of Latter-day Saints, Period I. History of Joseph Smith, the Prophet, by Himself. Edited by Brigham H. Roberts, 7 vols. Salt Lake City: Deseret Press, 1964.

The History of the Reorganized Church of Jesus Christ of Latter Day Saints. 4 vols. Independence, Missouri: Herald House, 1967.

"A History of the Persecution of the Church of Jesus Christ of Latter Day Saints in Missouri." *Times and Seasons* 1, no. 1–12, (December 1839 – October 1840).

Hogan, Mervin B. *The Founding Minutes of Nauvoo Lodge, U.D.* Des Moines, Iowa: Research Lodge Number 2, 1971.

Holzapfel, Richard N. and R. Jeffery Cottle, *Old Mormon Nauvoo, 1839–1846.* Provo, Utah: Grandin Book Company, 1990.

Jackson, Richard H. "The Mormon Village: Genesis and Antecedents of the City of Zion Plan." *BYU Studies* 17 (Winter 1977): 223–40.

———. "Righteousness and Environmental Change: The Mormons and the Environment." In *Essays on the American West, 1973–74,* Charles Redd Monographs in Western History, No. 5, ed. Thomas G. Alexander, 21–42. Provo, Utah: Brigham Young University Press, 1975.

Jennings, Warren. "The Expulsion of the Mormons from Jackson County, Missouri," *Missouri Historical Review* 64 (October 1969): 41–63.

Jenson, Andrew. *Autobiography of Andrew Jenson.* Salt Lake City: Deseret News Press, 1938.

———. *Encyclopedic History of the Church of Jesus Christ of Latter-day Saints.* Salt Lake City, Utah, 1941.

SELECTED WORKS CITED

———. *The Historical Record*. 9 vols. Salt Lake City, 1882–1890.

———. *Latter-day Saint Biographical Encyclopedia*. 4 vols. Salt Lake City: Andrew Jenson History Company and Deseret News, 1901–1936.

Jessee, Dean C. "The Beginning of Mormon Record Keeping." In *The Prophet Joseph: Essays on the Life and Mission of Joseph Smith*, ed. Larry C. Porter and Susan Easton Black, 138–160. Salt Lake City: Deseret Book Company, 1988.

———. "The Original Book of Mormon Manuscript," *BYU Studies* 10 (Spring 1970): 259–78.

———. *The Personal Writings of Joseph Smith*. Salt Lake City: Deseret Book Company, 1984.

———. "Return to Carthage: Writing the History of Joseph Smith's Martyrdom." *Journal of Mormon History* 8 (1981):3–19.

———. "Walls, Grates and Screeking Iron Doors": The Prison Experience of Mormon Leaders in Missouri, 1838–1839." In *New Views of Mormon History: Essays in Honor of Leonard J. Arrington*, ed. Davis Bitton and Maureen U. Beecher, 19–42. Salt Lake City: University of Utah Press, 1987.

———. "The Writing of Joseph Smith's History." *BYU Studies* 11 (Spring 1971): 439–73.

———, and David J. Whittaker. "The Last Months of Mormonism in Missouri: The Albert P. Rockwood Journal." *BYU Studies* 28 (Winter 1988): 5–41.

Journal of Discourses. 26 vols. Liverpool, England: Printed and published by Albert Carrington [and others], 1853–1886.

Kelly, Clyde. *United States Postal Policy*. New York and London: D. Appleton and Company, 1932.

Kimball, James L. "The Nauvoo Charter: A Reinterpretation." *Journal of the Illinois State Historical Society* 64 (Spring 1971): 66–78.

Kimball, Stanley B. *Heber C. Kimball: Mormon Patriarch and Pioneer*. Urbana, Chicago and London: University of Illinois Press, 1981.

———. "New Light on Old Egyptiana: Mormon Mummies 1848–71." *Dialogue* 16 (Winter 1983): 72–90.

Latter Day Saints' Messenger and Advocate. 3 vols. Kirtland, Ohio. October 1834–September 1837.

Launius, Roger D. and F. Mark McKiernan. *Joseph Smith Jr.'s Red Brick Store*. Macomb, Illinois: Western Illinois University, 1985.

London, Lena. "The Militia Fine, 1830–1860." *Military Affairs* 15 (1951): 133–144.

Lydia Knight's History. Salt Lake City: Juvenile Instructor Office, 1883.

Lyon, T. Edgar. "Free Masonry at Nauvoo." *Dialogue* 6 (Spring 1971): 76–78.

Marcombe, Joseph E. "Freemasonry at Nauvoo." *Journal of History* 10:408–439.

Matthews, Robert J. "Adam-ondi-Ahman." *BYU Studies* 13 (Autumn 1972): 27–35.

McCabe, James M. McCabe. "Early Ledgers and Account Books: A Source for Local Vermont History." *Vermont History* 37 (Winter 1969): 5–12.

McKiernan, F. Mark and Roger D. Launius, eds. *An Early Latter Day Saint History: The Book of John Whitmer*. Independence, Missouri: Herald House, 1980.

SELECTED WORKS CITED

McLaws, Monte B. "Attempted Assassination of Missouri's Ex-Governor, Lilburn W. Boggs." *Missouri Historical Review* 60 (October 1965): 50–62.

"Meteoric Phenomenon." *The Oswego Palladium* (Oswego, New York), 27 November 1833.

Miller, David E. and Della S. Miller. *Nauvoo: The City of Joseph*. Santa Barbara and Salt Lake City: Peregrine Smith, Inc., 1974.

Nauvoo Neighbor (Nauvoo, Illinois), 1843–1844.

Newell, Linda King and Valleen Tippetts Avery. *Mormon Enigma: Emma Hale Smith*. Garden City, New York: Doubleday & Company, Inc., 1984.

Nibley, Hugh. *Abraham in Egypt*. Salt Lake City: Deseret Book Company, 1981.

———. "The Facsimiles of the Book of Abraham: A Response by H. W. Nibley to E. H. Ashment." *Sunstone* 4 (December 1979): 49–51.

———. "The Meaning of the Kirtland Egyptian Papers." *BYU Studies* 11 (Summer 1971): 350–399.

———. *The Message of the Joseph Smith Papyri: An Egyptian Endowment*. Salt Lake City: Deseret Book Company, 1975.

Oaks, Dallin H. and Joseph I. Bentley. "Joseph Smith and Legal Process: In the Wake of the Steamboat *Nauvoo*." *BYU Law Review* 2 (1976): 735–82.

———, and Marvin S. Hill. *Carthage Conspiracy*. Urbana, Chicago, London: University of Illinois Press, 1975.

Perrin, William H., ed. *History of Summit County, Ohio*. Chicago, 1881.

Pratt, Parley P., Jr., ed. *Autobiography of Parley Parker Pratt*. Salt Lake City: Deseret Book Company, 1961.

Quinn, D. Michael. "The Practice of Rebaptism at Nauvoo." *BYU Studies* 18 (Winter 1978): 226–32.

Reinders, Robert. "Militia and Public Order in Nineteenth Century America." *Journal of American Studies* 11 (April 1977): 81–101.

Riker, William H. *Soldiers of the States: The Role of the National Guard in American Democracy*. Washington, D.C.: Public Affairs Press, 1957.

Robinson, Ebenezer. "Items of Personal History of the Editor," *The Return*. Davis City, Iowa, 1889–1890.

"Sketch of the Autobiography of George Albert Smith." *Deseret News*, 18 August 1858.

Smith, Joseph. "To the Elders of the Church of Latter Day Saints." *Messenger and Advocate* 1 (September 1835): 179–182; 2 (November 1835): 209–212; 2 (December 1835): 225–230.

Smith, Lucy. *Biographical Sketches of Joseph Smith the Prophet and his Progenitors for many Generations*. Liverpool: Published for Orson Pratt by S. W. Richards, 1853.

Smith, William H. *Smith's Canadian Gazetteer*. Toronto, 1846.

Snow, Eliza R. *Biography and Family Record of Lorenzo Snow*. Salt Lake City, Utah, 1884.

Stevens, Edward W., Jr. "Science, Culture, and Morality: Educating Adults in the Early Nineteenth Century." In *"Schools and The Means of Education Shall Forever Be Encouraged:" A History of Education in the Old Northwest, 1787–1880*, ed. Paul H. Mattingly and Edward W. Stevens, Jr., 69–83. Athens, Ohio: Ohio University Libraries, 1987.

Summerfield, Arthur E. *U.S. Mail: The Story of the United States Postal Service*. New York: Holt, Rinehart and Winston, 1960.

Taylor, John. *A Short Account of the Murders, Roberies, Burnings, Thefts, and Other Outrages Committed by the Mob and Militia of the State of Missouri, upon the Latter Day Saints.* Springfield, Ill., 1839?

"Testimony of Katherine Salisbury." *The True Latter Day Saints' Herald* (Plano, Illinois, and Lamoni, Iowa) 28 (1 June 1881):169.

Times and Seasons (Nauvoo, Illinois). 1839–46.

The Wasp (Nauvoo, Illinois). 1842–43.

Watson, Elden Jay. *Manuscript History of Brigham Young, 1801–1844.* Salt Lake City: 1968.

Whittaker, David J. "The 'Articles of Faith' in Early Mormon Literature and Thought." In *New Views of Mormon History: A Collection of Essays in Honor of Leonard J. Arrington,* ed. Davis Bitton and Maureen U. Beecher, 63–92. Salt Lake City: University of Utah Press, 1987.

———. "The Book of Daniel in Early Mormon Thought." In *By Study and Also by Faith: Essays in Honor of Hugh Nibley,* ed. John M. Lundquist and Stephen D. Ricks, 1:155–201. Salt Lake City: Deseret Book Company, 1990.

Wittorf, John H. "An Historical Investigation of the Ruined 'Altars' at Adam-ondi-Ahman, Missouri." *Newsletter and Proceedings of the Society for Early Historic Archeology* (Brigham Young University) No. 113 (15 April 1969): 1–8.

Unpublished Works

Ames, Ira. Autobiography and Journal. MS., LDS Church Archives, Salt Lake City, Utah.

Atchison, David R., and Alexander W. Doniphan. Letter to Col. Mason, Commanding at Leavenworth, 27 Oct. 1838. MS., National Archives.

Atchison, David R. Letter to Brig. Gen. Jones, Adj. Gen., U.S. Army, 6 November 1838. MS., National Archives.

Bernhisel, John. Letter to Thomas Ford, 14 June 1844. MS., Bernhisel Collection. LDS Church Archives.

Black, Susan Easton. "Membership of the Church of Jesus Christ of Latter-day Saints, 1830–1848." 48 vols. Provo, Utah: Religious Studies Center, Brigham Young University, 1984.

Brooks, Lester and Zebedee Coltrin, Thomas Burdick, and Hiram Winters to the First Presidency and Twelve, 16 November 1841, MS., LDS Church Archives.

Clayton, William. Diary. MS., LDS Church Archives.

Colvin, Don F. "A Historical Study of the Mormon Temple at Nauvoo, Illinois." MA thesis, Brigham Young University, 1962.

Cowdery, Oliver. Diary. MS., LDS Church Archives.

Crosby, Jonathan. "A Biographical Sketch of the Life of Jonathan Crosby written by Himself." MS., Utah Historical Society.

Esplin, Ronald K. "The Emergence of Brigham Young and the Twelve to Mormon Leadership, 1830–1841." Ph.D. diss., Brigham Young University, 1981.

Ford, Edward R. to Thomas Reynolds, 8 September 1842. MS., Missouri Historical Society, St. Louis, Missouri.

Geauga County, Ohio. Common Pleas Court, book M., April 5, 9, 1834; book

P., December 21, 1833; book S., October 26, 1835. Microfilm of MS., LDS Family History Library.

Geauga County, Ohio. Tax Records, 1834. Microfilm of MS., LDS Church Family History Library.

Gentry, Leland H. "A History of the Latter-day Saints in Northern Missouri." Ph.D. diss., Brigham Young University, 1965.

"Grammar and Alphabet of the Egyptian Language." 1 vol., MS. LDS Church Archives.

Hogan, Mervin B. "The Confrontation of Grand Master Abraham Jonas and John Cook Bennett at Nauvoo." Published Typescript.

Hurlbut, Maria S. Statement, 9 September 1883. MS., Chicago Historical Society, Chicago, Illinois.

Jennings, Warren. "Zion is Fled: The Expulsion of the Mormons from Jackson County, Missouri," Ph.D. diss., University of Florida, 1962.

Kimball, Heber C. "Journal and Record of Heber Chase Kimball an Apostle of Jesus Christ of Latter Day Saints." MS., LDS Church Archives.

Kirtland Council Minutes. Kirtland, Ohio. MS. LDS Church Archives.

Knight, Newel. Autobiography and Journal. MS., LDS Church Archives.

Madsen, Gordon. "The Lawrence Estate Revisited: Joseph Smith and Illinois Law Regarding Guardianships." Paper read 21 September 1989 at Nauvoo Symposium, Brigham Young University.

Nauvoo City Council Minutes 1841–1844. Nauvoo, Illinois. MS., LDS Church Archives.

Parkin, Max H. "Conflict at Kirtland: A Study of the Nature and Causes of External and Internal Conflict of the Mormons in Ohio Between 1830 and 1838." M.A. thesis, Brigham Young University, 1966.

———. "History of the Latter-day Saints in Clay County, Missouri, from 1833 to 1837." Ph.D. diss., Brigham Young University, 1976.

Patriarchal Blessings. Book 1, MS. LDS Church Archives.

Peterson, Paul H. "An Historical Analysis of the Word of Wisdom." M.A. thesis, Brigham Young University, 1972.

"A Record of the First Quorum of Elders Belonging to the Church of Christ: in Kirtland Geauga Co. Ohio." MS. RLDS Church Archives.

"A Record of the Organization and Proceedings of The Female Relief Society of Nauvoo," MS., LDS Church Archives.

"A Record of the Transactions of the Twelve Apostles of the Church of Christ." MS. LDS Church Archives.

Rigdon, Sidney. Letter to Colonel Sterling Price, 8 September 1838. MS. draft, LDS Church Archives.

State of Mo. vs. Jos. Smith Jr. et al. Daviess County Circuit Court Papers, MS., State Historical Society of Missouri, Columbia, Missouri.

State of Missouri vs. J. Smith Jr. & L. Wight, MS., Brigham Young University Library.

Stocks, Hugh C. "The Book of Mormon, 1830–1879: A Publishing History." MLA thesis, UCLA, 1979.

SELECTED WORKS CITED

Sweeney, John, Jr., "A History of the Nauvoo Legion in Illinois." Master's thesis, Brigham Young University, 1974.

Woodford, Robert J. "The Historical Development of the Doctrine and Covenants." Ph.D. diss., Brigham Young University, 1974.

Woodruff, Wilford. Diary. MS., LDS Church Archives.

INDEX

Abraham, book of, 45 n. 2; arrangements for printing, 360, 363, 364 n. 3, 366; translating from, 367. *See also* Egyptian artifacts

Adam-ondi-Ahman, Daviess County, Missouri, 244–45; mob attack expected upon, 285–86, 305 n. 1

Adams, George J., 458, 461, 475

Adams, James (judge), 379, 380, 401, 433

Agricultural companies, 274

Aldrich, James, 98

Aldrich, Mark, 342–43, 348

Allred, William (captain), 286

Ames, Ira, 193 n. 1

Andrews, Hazard, 36

Angell, Truman, 98

Angels: protection of, 158, 163–64, 224; seen at temple dedication, 203

Anointing of Church leaders, 156, 159–60, 163

Apostasy: in Kirtland, 216–17 n. 2, 251; Joseph warns against, 220, 238; in Missouri, 249 n. 3; of key brethren, 288 n. 1, 290–91, 298–99

Apostles. *See* Twelve apostles

Arms shipment, interception of, 286

Arrest of Church leaders, 287, 292 n. 3

"Articles and Covenants" of the Church, 94 n. 1

Ashtabula, Ohio, 6

Astronomy, 45, 106, 239, 366

Atchison, David R. (general), 282–83, 285, 292 n. 4, 293–94 n. 2

Atwood, Henry G., 219

Avard, Sampson, 256, 262 n. 2, 288 n. 1; Danite band of, 297 n. 1

Avery, Allen, 44

Babbitt, Almon W., 122, 127, 391; Canadian company of, settles in Missouri, 263, 265 n. 1, 271; transgressions of, 339

Bachelor, Origen, 480

Backenstos, Jacob, 376

Badlam, Alexander, 98

Bagby, Walter, 364

Bailey, Hannah Boutwell, 65 n. 1

Bailey, Joshua, 65 n. 1

Baker, Elizabeth, 138

Baldwin, Caleb, 318 n. 1

Bank, failure of, in Kirtland, 216 n. 2, 218, 223 n. 1

Bankruptcy, Joseph applies for, 377 n. 1, 492, 495, 501–3

Baptism: of converts in Canada, 9–10, 13–14; of Ebenezer Robinson, 52; of John Waterman, 178; of converts in Kirtland, 190–91; of Isaac Galland, 325; vicarious, for dead, 346 n. 2, 373, 457, 471–73; of converts in Nauvoo, 372, 373; for health reasons, 486

Bardslee, Andrew, 20

Barnard, John P., 213, 234

Barnum, Job V., 488

Barton, Reuben, 179 n. 1

Beemer, Philip, 8

from steamboat purchase, 501–2
n. 2

Decker, Isaac, 342

"Declaration of Independence" from
mobs, 248

Dedication of Kirtland Temple, 191–
203; ceremony of, repeated, 207–
8

Denton, Solomon Wilbor, 15, 131

Derby, Erastus, 397, 418; visits
Joseph in hiding, 404, 410–11,
429; blessing pronounced upon,
414–15; travels with Joseph, 450;
travels to East, 455

DeWitt, Carroll County, Missouri,
225 n. 1

Doniphan, Alexander W., 282–83,
292 n. 4, 293–94 n. 2

Doorkeepers of Lord's house, 135,
168, 192, 227

Dort, David, 94, 219

Douglas, Stephen A. (judge), 342,
359, 486, 499, 504 n. 1

Draper, William, Jr., 361

Draper, Zemira, 96–97, 98

Duel, Osmon M., 189 n. 1

Duncan, Chapman, 189 n. 1

Dunham, Jonathan, 404, 417

Dunklin, Daniel, 42 n. 1

Durphy, Elizabeth, 406

Eaton, Frazier, 104

Egyptian artifacts: Joseph translates
from, 45, 87, 88; acquisition of,
45 n. 2; Joseph displays, 53, 85,
92, 101–2, 104, 106, 119, 132,
169; Joshua Seixas examines,
167; arrangements made for
public display of, 176. *See also*
Abraham, book of

Elder's Journal, 238 n. 1

Elders quorum: president called for,
141, 142; anointing of members
of, 163; presidency of, seeks
counsel, 164–65; fails to follow
prescribed order, 170; members
of, are sent out to dispel
falsehoods, 444–47

Elders' school. *See* School of the
prophets

Election-day fight at Gallatin,
Missouri, 268–71

Elias, 210

Elijah, 210

Eliot, David, 56

Elk Creek, Erie County,
Pennsylvania, 6, 22, 27

Ellicottville, Cattaraugus County,
New York, 23

Elliott, David, 5

Emmett, James, 98

Endowment, 77–78; preparations for,
155–56, 161; ceremony of,
introduced in Nauvoo, 380 n. 1

England: first missionary work in,
250 n. 1, 263; mission of Twelve
to, 325; John Snyder's mission to,
343–44, 345–46; proposal to send
agent to, 344–45; converts from,
arrive in Nauvoo, 373

Evening and the Morning Star, 15 n.
1, 21

Extermination order, 287

Far West, Caldwell County,
Missouri, 212–13 n. 3; conference
at, 227–29; revelation concerning,
232–33; apostles to leave from,
on mission, 257; petitioning to
move county seat to, 262, 266;
circuit court convenes in, 263–64

Farmersville, Cattaraugus County,
New York, 23

Felshaw, William, 98

Female Relief Society of Nauvoo. *See*
Relief Society

Fielding, Amos, 383

Fire: in board kiln, 101, 104, 186; in
shoemaker's shop, 101; in
printing office, 221–22 n. 2

First Vision of Joseph Smith, 69, 79

Follett, King, 65

Ford, Edward R., 405, 406 n. 1, 448
n. 3, 503

Ford, Thomas (governor), 498–501,
504–5

INDEX

Priests in Aaronic Priesthood, 141 n. 3

Printing press: established in Kirtland, 14–15; prayer for protection of, 19; burning of, 221–22 n. 2; transferred to Joseph, 358 n. 1; in Nauvoo, 362 n. 1, 496

Questions and answers: on scriptures, 214–15; published in *Elder's Journal*, 239

Quincy, Illinois: prophet and fellow prisoners escape to, 318

Quorums, priesthood: assemble for anointing, 163; blessings sealed upon, 169–71; ordinations to be approved by, 174–75; meet to adopt licensing resolutions, 182–85; seating of, at temple dedication, 192–93

Raglin, John, 284

Ralston, James H. (judge), 403, 405, 430, 437

Ramus, Hancock County, Illinois, 335 n. 2, 340–41

Rappleye, Tunis, 149

Rathbun, Robert, 90

Raymond, Martha H., 94

Records, importance of keeping, 457, 469–71

Redfield, David Harvey, 90

Redfield, Harlow, 219, 243

Relief Society: organization of, 371; Joseph addresses, 374, 378–79, 388, 448 n. 1

Remick, Jacob G., 478–79, 482

Resurrection, erroneous perception of, 74

Rewards placed on brethren's heads, 485

Reynolds, Thomas (governor), 404, 406 n. 1, 485, 503

Rhodes, Eric, 493

Rhodes, Hugh, 374

Rich, Leonard, 100, 120, 220

Richards, Levi, 222

Richards, Phinehas, 219

Richards, Willard, 341, 373, 394–95, 458, 462; is called as apostle, 257; becomes Joseph's secretary, 335, 336; entries in handwriting of, 335; is appointed recorder for temple, 336; prepares city for immigrants, 342; responsibilities of, as recorder, 355 n. 1; turns journal over to William Clayton, 395; falls ill, 490; works on history, 495–96 n. 3; travels to Springfield, 497

Rider, Ezekiel, 28

Rigdon, Elizabeth, 419

Rigdon, Sidney, 135; entries in handwriting of, 6, 7, 9; preaches in Springfield, Pennsylvania, 6; preaches in New York, 7; Joseph's assessment of character of, 12; Joseph's blessing pronounced on, 13; ordained Doctor P. Hurlbut as elder, 20; joins brethren in New York, 25; preaches in Ohio conference, 27, 32; travels to New Portage for conference, 30–32; brethren lay hands on, 31–32, 135; brethren express dissatisfaction with, 43–44 n. 3, 46; preaches in sacrament meetings, 54, 80, 127, 168, 171; speaks out improperly, 67; testifies to Universalian minister, 78; unites with brethren in prayer, 90–91; serves in Kirtland presidency, 132 n. 4; sets apart new high councilors, 134; addresses Twelve, 147; invokes benediction on anointing meetings, 160, 163, 169; discourses in schoolhouse, 168; discusses ordinations, 174; studies Hebrew, 177; delivers funeral sermons, 190, 243; participates in temple dedication, 193–94; moves to Far West, 213 n. 1, 224; is sustained as Joseph's counselor, 217; delivers political addresses, 240, 248, 264; remuneration voted for, 242;

surveys Missouri lands, 243–47; "salt sermon" of, 249 n. 3; is recommended as postmaster, 265–66; is appointed to edit newspaper, 266; addresses Twelve at missionary farewell, 327; is baptized vicariously for parents, 346; joins Masons, 370; Joseph discusses "difficulties" with, 382; renews determination to support Joseph, 419–21; discusses governor's writ, 486; Justin Butterfield's communication with, 500 n. 1

Ripley, Alanson, 243–47, 309, 318 n. 4

Robbins, Lewis, 252, 394

Robinson, Angeline, 361 n. 4

Robinson, Ebenezer, 52, 103, 242 n. 2, 353 n. 1, 356; acts as clerk, 228; transfers printing establishment to Joseph, 358 n. 1; assists in accounting, 360; is commanded to take in Orson Hyde's family, 361; involvement of, with printing business, 362 n. 1

Robinson, George W., 211, 224, 419; acts as clerk, 219, 237; surveys Missouri lands, 243–47; participates in confirmations, 264; is secretary at citizens meetings, 265–66, 272; accompanies Joseph to trial, 283; is appointed Nauvoo postmaster, 492 n. 2; charges against, 496

Robison, Chauncey, 376, 413

Rockwell, Orrin Porter, 383 n. 3, 397–98 n. 2, 439; warrant issued for, 402, 404, 503; rewards offered for capture of, 485

Rockwood, Albert P., 404

Rogers, David W., 458, 461, 475, 482

Rogers, Jacob S., 270

Rolph, Samuel, 98, 142, 396

Root, Henry, 225–26

Rose, Andrew, 14

Rose, Joseph, 132, 321 n. 5

Roundy, Shadrach, 6, 21, 61–62, 99, 234, 367

Rudd, John, 6, 98

Rules and regulations governing house of Lord, 136–38, 139–40, 143 n. 1

Russell, Jonathan, 400 n. 1

Sacrament, administering, in Kirtland Temple, 205, 209

Salisbury, Wilkins Jenkins, 18, 131, 252

"Salt sermon" of Sidney Rigdon, 249 n. 3

Sanders, John, 350

Sayers, Edward, 384, 404, 407, 414 n. 1

School of the prophets, 47, 48 n. 1, 62; dedication of, 65; Joseph attends, 65–66, 74, 78; Hebrew books for, 87

Schweich, George, 226 n. 1

Sealing of blessings, 159–60, 163, 169

Second Comforter, Joseph preaches of, 331

Seixas, Joshua, 129 n. 3, 136, 172; arrives in Kirtland, 162; examines Egyptian records, 167; Joseph preaches to, 168, 177; arranges to visit family, 173, 180; prayer in behalf of, 175–76 n. 2; disputes with brethren, 182; arranging payment for, 186; brings family to Kirtland, 188–89

Seventy, council of, 123, 160, 167; responsibilities of, 206; sustaining of presidents of, 219; new presidents of, 219 n. 1

Sharp, Thomas, 349

Sheldon, Crawford B., 384

Sherman, Lyman, 121–22

Sherwood, Henry G., 336, 386, 417, 494, 497

Silver Creek, Chautauqua County, New York, 22

Singley, Margaret, 252

Sloan, James, 400 n. 4, 413

99; denies charges of treason, 293–94; denies Avard charges, 297; travels to Commerce, Illinois, 309; arrives in Illinois from prison, 318; visits Iowa to purchase land, 318; tells of coming forth of Book of Mormon, 323; declares truth of Book of Mormon, 324; corrects errors in Parley Pratt works, 330; appoints Willard Richards scribe, 336; commences new store, 338, 344, 348–49; instructs scribe to write proclamation, 344; lays cornerstone of Nauvoo House, 346; deposits Book of Mormon manuscript in cornerstone, 347; discovers coal on woodland, 349–50; correcting Book of Mormon for publication, 352–53; debates with mayor, 353, 355–56; interprets dreams, 355; explains scripture to Orson Spencer, 356; instructs Elias Higbee, 362; reads proof of *Times and Seasons*, 364; joins Freemasons, 370; attends masonic lodge, 376, 386; works in garden, 382, 383; receives news of Boggs shooting, 383; publishes denial of involvement in Boggs case, 386; pleads for J. C. Bennett, 387; rides in Masonic procession, 391; sits for drawing of profile, 391; discusses Bennett affair with Rigdon family, 395; hoes potatoes, 397, 400; organizes search for Orson Pratt, 398; publicly reviews Bennett's conduct, 399, 400; learns sword exercise, 401; attends installation of Iowa Masonic lodge, 401; goes into hiding, 403; meets friends on island in river, 403–4; in hiding, 405, 418–19, 443, 449, 468, 487, 488; expresses love, gratitude for family, friends, 414–17, 438–43; exercises in woods, 418; expresses love for Wilson Law, 425; plans move to pine country, 430–32;

determined to prove faithful, 441; calls elders to counteract influence of Bennett, 443–44; addresses the Saints from hiding, 445–47; visited by friends while hiding, 458, 461, 468; sits for painting by D. Rogers, 482; visits sick while ill himself, 490; ploughing at farm, 491; visits with Indians, 491; chopping wood, 497
—Church affairs: ordains Noah Packard, 4; holds conference, three excommunicated, 4; advises elders in work of ministry, 5; proselyting in East and Canada, 6–10; preaches in Lodi, New York, 7; arrives in Canada, 7; ordains E. F. Nickerson, 10; baptizes fourteen, 9–10, 13; prays for means to discharge Church debt, 19; prays for gathering of elect and deliverance of Zion, 19; preaches at Westfield, New York, 21; preaches at Freedom, New York, 24; restores Father Tyler to Church, 29; attends conference at New Portage, 30–32; blesses Cowdery in publishing revelations, 31; blesses Rigdon to lead Church in his absence, 31–32; ordains Cowdery assistant president, 36; covenants to struggle for redemption of Zion, 41–42; meets with and instructs Twelve, 43, 47, 75–78, 124, 146, 188, 323, 325, 345, 353, 357, 362, 364, 374–75, 443–44; works on Egyptian alphabet, 45; baptizes E. Robinson, 52; blesses children, 52, 62; preaches in schoolhouse, 53, 65, 85, 97, 124; attends prayer meeting, 54; defends a brother before high council, 56; baptizes Whitneys, 62; attends patriarchal meeting, 65, 123; regulates errors from Sunday meeting, 67–68; preaches to minister, 78; attends council in Squires case, 88; attends council

for, 416; Joseph escapes to home
of, 449
Whitney, Samuel, 58, 62
Whitney, Sarah Ann, 372
Whitney, Susanna Kimball, 58, 62
Wiggins, Ebenezer, 404, 407
Wight, Lyman, 25, 63, 244–47, 268–
69; receives patriarchal blessing,
123 n. 3; joins stake presidency,
244 n. 3; writ served on, 273 n.
2, 281–82; stands trial, 284;
comments on Avard's
conspiracies, 297 n. 1; escapes
from prison, 318 n. 1; leads
emigrant group from England,
373 n. 3; Joseph visits, 381
Wightman, Charles, 179 n. 1
Wightman, Erastus B., 189 n. 1
Wightman, William, 179 n. 1, 335
n. 2, 336, 340–41
Wilcox, Benjamin, 323 n. 2
Wilcox, Catharine, 138
Wilcox, John R., 341–42 n. 1
Wilkeson, Mr., 8
Williams, Frederick G., 4; Joseph's
confidence in, 12–13; entries in
handwriting of, 13, 20, 21, 28,
46, 120; establishes printing
office, 15 n. 1; unites with
brethren in prayer, 18, 28, 90;
Joseph gives horse to, 29; meets
in council, 32, 36; reports cholera
epidemic, 33–34; delivers Smith
baby, 55; revelation to, about
visiting relatives, 63; studies
Hebrew, 95, 97, 121; preaches in
meeting, 103; addresses Twelve,
147; stitches Hyrum's wounded
arm, 172; sees angel in Kirtland
Temple, 203; is sustained as
Joseph's counselor, 217; returns
to Church after transgressing,
257, 264
Williams, John D., 270
Williams, Joseph Swain, 243
Williams, William W., 30
Wilson, Harmon T., 397
Wilson, Reuben, 26
Wilson, Robert, 238, 240

Witter, Daniel S., 341–43, 348
Wood, brethren provide, for Joseph,
99–100
Wood, Daniel, 360
Woodruff, Wilford, 56 n. 3, 319 n. 1,
341, 482 n. 1; is called as apostle,
257; moves to Montrose, Iowa,
320 n. 2; on Orson Hyde's
penitence, 324 n. 1; blessing of,
prior to mission, 325; gives
missionary farewell address, 327;
on Joseph's remarks about
imprisonment, 327 n. 2; helps
select hymns, 328 n. 1; on
prevailing sickness in Commerce,
328 n. 2; reports on city council
meetings, 359 nn. 1–2; takes
charge of printing establishment,
362 n. 1; birthday celebration of,
364 n. 1; assists in typesetting
book of Abraham, 364 n. 3; on
trial of Gladden Bishop, 369 n. 1;
on establishment of masonic
lodge, 370 n. 3; on Boggs
shooting, 383 n. 4; on cleansing
Church of adulterers, 387 n. 1; on
mission to dispel falsehoods, 447
n. 2
Woolley, Edwin D., 393–94, 413,
455
Word of Wisdom, 230 n. 3
Works, Angeline, 100–101, 102, 103

Yearsley, David D., 389
Young, Brigham, 44, 66; Joseph
shows Egyptian records to, 106;
Joseph sees, in vision, 157–58; is
sustained as apostle, 218; rejects
John F. Boynton as apostle, 218;
arrives in Far West, 222; is
appointed president pro tem in
Missouri, 227; revelations
received for, 231–32, 338–39;
gives missionary farewell address,
327; selects hymns for
publication, 328 n. 1; instructs
building committee, 341; writes
of Orson Pratt's trials, 398 n. 1;

visits Joseph in hiding, 458;
Joseph visits, 493–94, 495
Young, Joseph, 67, 219
Young, Lorenzo, 44, 75
Young, Phineas, 15, 44
Young, Richard M. (judge), 492

Zarahemla, Iowa, 324 n. 2
Zion: persecution of Saints in, 14;
brethren pray for deliverance of,

19; donations for redemption of,
30, 32–33, 208–9; desire to be
seated around table in, 58;
presidency of council in, 132 n. 4;
plans to remove to, 188, 203–4;
Joseph's letter to, 216–20; stakes
of, land surveyed for, 243–47; city
of, plat showing design for, 266–
68 n. 1
Zion's Camp, 21–27, 42–43 n. 3

THE PAPERS OF
JOSEPH SMITH

Volume 2:
Journal, 1832–1842

Designed by Kent Ware

Maps new to this edition by Tom Child

Composed by Patricia J. Parkinson
on the Penta Publishing System
in Trump Mediaeval

Printed by Publishers Press
on Warren Sebago, cream white text stock
(acid free)

Jacket printed by Publishers Press
on Multicolor Corduroy
(acid free)

Bound by Mountain States Bindery
in Roxite A Linen over Eska board
(acid free)
stamped with Kurz metallic
and pigment stamping foils
with
Rainbow Antique
endleaves